RICHARD B. FREEMAN holds the Herbert Ascherman Chair in Economics at Harvard University. He is also director of the Labor Studies Program at the National Bureau of Economic Research and executive programme director for the Programme in Discontinuous Economics at the London School of Economics' Centre for Economic Performance. ROBERT TOPEL is the Isidore Brown and Gladys J. Brown Professor in Urban and Labor Economics at the University of Chicago and a research associate of the National Bureau of Economic Research. BIRGITTA SWEDENBORG is deputy director of SNS, the Center for Business and Policy Studies, Stockholm, Sweden.

The University of Chicago Press, Chicago 60637
The University of Chicago Press, Ltd., London
© 1997 by the National Bureau of Economic Research
All rights reserved. Published 1997
Printed in the United States of America
06 05 04 03 02 01 00 99 98 97   1 2 3 4 5
ISBN: 0-226-26178-6 (cloth)

Library of Congress Cataloging-in-Publication Data

The welfare state in transition: reforming the Swedish model / edited by
    Richard B. Freeman, Robert Topel, and Birgitta Swedenborg.
        p.   cm. — (A National Bureau of Economic Research confer-
    ence report)
    Includes bibliographical references and index.
    ISBN 0-226-26178-6 (cloth : alk. paper)
        1. Sweden—Economic conditions—1945–   —Congresses. I. Free-
    man, Richard B. (Richard Barry), 1943–   . II. Topel, Robert H. III.
    Swedenborg, Birgitta, 1941–   . IV. Series: Conference report (Na-
    tional Bureau of Economic Research)
    HC375.W34 1997
    330.9485'059—dc21   96-50195
                                                                         CIP

⊚ The paper used in this publication meets the minimum requirements of the American National Standard for Information Sciences—Permanence of Paper for Printed Library Materials, ANSI Z39.48-1984.

National Bureau of Economic Research

Officers
Paul W. McCracken, *chairman*
John H. Biggs, *vice chairman*
Martin Feldstein, *president and chief executive officer*
Gerald A. Polansky, *treasurer*

Sam Parker, *director of finance and corporate secretary*
Susan Colligan, *assistant corporate secretary*
Deborah Mankiw, *assistant corporate secretary*

Directors at Large
Peter C. Aldrich
Elizabeth E. Bailey
John H. Biggs
Andrew Brimmer
Carl F. Christ
Don R. Conlan
Kathleen B. Cooper
Jean A. Crockett

George C. Eads
Martin Feldstein
George Hatsopoulos
Karen N. Horn
Lawrence R. Klein
Leo Melamed
Merton H. Miller
Michael H. Moskow

Robert T. Parry
Peter G. Peterson
Richard N. Rosett
Bert Seidman
Kathleen P. Utgoff
Donald S. Wasserman
Marina v. N. Whitman
John O. Wilson

Directors by University Appointment
George Akerlof, *California, Berkeley*
Jagdish Bhagwati, *Columbia*
William C. Brainard, *Yale*
Glen G. Cain, *Wisconsin*
Franklin Fisher, *Massachusetts Institute of Technology*
Saul H. Hymans, *Michigan*
Marjorie B. McElroy, *Duke*

Joel Mokyr, *Northwestern*
Andrew Postlewaite, *Pennsylvania*
Nathan Rosenberg, *Stanford*
Harold T. Shapiro, *Princeton*
Craig Swan, *Minnesota*
David B. Yoffie, *Harvard*
Arnold Zellner, *Chicago*

Directors by Appointment of Other Organizations
Marcel Boyer, *Canadian Economics Association*
Mark Drabenstott, *American Agricultural Economics Association*
William C. Dunkelberg, *National Association of Business Economists*
Richard A. Easterlin, *Economic History Association*
Gail D. Fosler, *The Conference Board*
A. Ronald Gallant, *American Statistical Association*

Robert S. Hamada, *American Finance Association*
Charles Lave, *American Economic Association*
Rudolph A. Oswald, *American Federation of Labor and Congress of Industrial Organizations*
Gerald A. Polansky, *American Institute of Certified Public Accountants*
Josh S. Weston, *Committee for Economic Development*

Directors Emeriti
Moses Abramovitz
George T. Conklin, Jr.
Thomas D. Flynn

Franklin A. Lindsay
Paul W. McCracken
Geoffrey H. Moore
James J. O'Leary

George B. Roberts
Eli Shapiro
William S. Vickrey

Since this volume is a record of conference proceedings, it has been exempted from the rules governing critical review of manuscripts by the Board of Directors of the National Bureau (resolution adopted 8 June 1948, as revised 21 November 1949 and 20 April 1968).

Contents

Acknowledgments

The contributions in this volume are the result of a major research project on the Swedish welfare state organized jointly by the Center for Business and Policy Studies (SNS) in Sweden and the National Bureau of Economic Research (NBER) in the United States.

SNS is a private, nonpartisan, nonprofit organization with the aim of promoting research on economic and social issues of importance to public decision makers and making it readily available to a broad audience. As an organization SNS does not take a stand on policy matters.

The project was initiated by SNS in 1991. SNS turned to the NBER to obtain a qualified outside perspective on the Swedish economy at a time when severe problems were building up in the Swedish economy. Although the project brought together American and Swedish economists as coauthors, the researchers were asked to maintain an American or outside perspective on the issues. The research was finalized in 1994 and presented at a public conference in Sweden in January 1995.

The research for this volume has been made possible by financial support from the following sources: the Jan Wallander and Tom Hedelius Foundation, the Swedish Council for Research in the Humanities and Social Sciences, the Axel and Margret Ax:son Johnson Foundation, the Swedish Council for Social Research, the Marianne and Marcus Wallenberg Foundation, the Marcus and Amalia Wallenberg Foundation, the Wenner-Gren Center Foundation for Scientific Research, the National Bureau of Economic Research, and the Sven and Dagmar Salén Foundation.

Introduction

Richard B. Freeman, Robert Topel, and
Birgitta Swedenborg

This is a study of an economy in transition and in trouble. Not an Eastern or a Central European economy seeking the path to capitalism, but a Western economy once heralded as offering a "third way" of operating a capitalist system. An economy that relies heavily on the state, unions, and employer associations; an economy that equalizes market outcomes with massive welfare state redistributions; and an economy that many regarded as the model welfare state. The troubles that have befallen that economy and the effort to reform its welfare state are well worth understanding.

In the 1950s and 1960s, Sweden's economic performance and effort to gain economic equality for its citizens won worldwide plaudits. Many heralded the "Swedish model" as offering a more rational and humane form of capitalism than more market-driven economies. In the 1970s and 1980s, Swedish economic performance slackened—by how much and why are questions open to debate. In the 1990s, Sweden's economy plunged into crisis. Huge budget deficits created a fiscal crisis in 1993, threatening the funding of welfare state redistributions and benefits. Unemployment, which had for decades been lower than in other developed economies, soared to levels not seen since the 1930s.

Sweden's position as a role model for other countries has been severely, if not irretrievably, tarnished. But rather than turning our backs on the Swedish model and studying more fashionable ones, we believe that there are important insights to be gained from a serious evaluation of the Swedish experience.

Richard B. Freeman holds the Herbert Ascherman Chair in Economics at Harvard University. He is also director of the Labor Studies Program at the National Bureau of Economic Research and executive programme director for the Programme in Discontinuous Economics at the London School of Economics' Centre for Economic Performance. Robert Topel is the Isidore Brown and Gladys J. Brown Professor in Urban and Labor Economics at the University of Chicago and a research associate of the National Bureau of Economic Research. Birgitta Swedenborg is deputy director of SNS, the Center for Business and Policy Studies, Stockholm, Sweden.

These insights should be valuable to other countries as they consider the benefits and costs, the risks and problems, of welfare state solutions to economic and social problems.

How serious are Sweden's economic troubles? Have critics of the welfare state exaggerated those troubles? Are the troubles related to the welfare state? Can Sweden restore its economic health and preserve the successes of its welfare state? What are the limits and excesses of the Swedish welfare state? What can observers in other countries learn from Sweden's experience of having the government play a large role in markets?

These questions motivate this National Bureau of Economic Research (NBER)–Center for Business and Policy Studies (SNS) project. They are not the questions that outsiders to the Swedish scene have previously asked. This is because, until the late 1980s, early 1990s, Sweden seemingly had no greater economic problems than many other Western countries. For example, in 1985–86, American economists associated with the Brookings Institution examined the Swedish economy (Bosworth and Rivlin, 1987). While these economists noted areas in which Sweden, like the United States in the 1980s, consumed beyond its productive means, overall they were impressed by Sweden's living standards and absence of poverty and by how well the economy worked despite high taxes, a huge welfare state, limited wage differentials, and diverse interventions in markets. In 1986, Mancur Olson asked why Sweden did well for so long despite its extensive transfer system. He concluded that part of the answer lay in the competitive traded goods sector and part in high unionization, which internalized potential externalities from special interest negotiations in the labor market (Olson 1990). Other outsiders have given even more positive readings of the Swedish system (Layard 1991; Gibson and Hall 1993).

Swedish economists have been more critical. Many of them have criticized the extent of the welfare state, the inflationary tendencies of centralized collective bargaining, and other features that differentiated Sweden from the normal capitalist economy (Lindbeck 1993; Lundberg 1985; Bergström 1992; SNS Economic Policy Group 1992). The economic crisis of the 1990s made these criticisms more salient. Something went drastically wrong with the Swedish economy—be it the features these analysts stress or something else. In 1992, the Swedish government asked a group of Swedish economists, headed by Assar Lindbeck, to consider the best way to turn the economic situation around (Lindbeck et al. 1994). Many Swedish social scientists contributed background studies for this project, which yielded 113 recommendations for changes in policies.

The NBER-SNS project on Sweden enlisted ten American economists—and an equal number of Swedish economists—to study various aspects of the Swedish economy and welfare state. What is the value of having American economists look at the Swedish economy in 1993–94, so few years after publication of the Brookings study and so shortly after the Lindbeck commission's proposals? What insights might outsiders contribute to understanding Sweden's problems and possible path to recovery?

One thing outsiders bring is their ignorance of the details of the Swedish economy. This has virtues and dangers. Ignorance of details can make it easier to see problems in a broad perspective—the forest instead of the trees—and to question conventional wisdom. A case in point is Swedish thinking on exchange rates. In the fall of 1992, supported by all political parties, union federations, employer groups, bankers, and most economists, the Swedish government committed the nation to defend the krona's fixed exchange rate, almost as a matter of patriotic duty. Impressed by the failure of similar policies elsewhere (e.g., the fall in the British pound, the Italian lira, and the Mexican peso), the historical record of devaluations in Sweden, and the American experience with floating exchange rates, outsiders questioned the rationality of Sweden's commitment. So did currency speculators, who benefited at the expense of Swedish taxpayers when the krona was subsequently devalued again.

Outsiders can also offer an independent assessment of debates within Sweden about the country's economic troubles. For example, some Swedish analysts argue that Sweden has been in substantial relative decline for a long period of time. They are alarmed by Sweden's drop from near the top of international rankings of per capita income (SNS Economic Policy Group 1992; Henrekson, Jonung, and Stymne 1996; Lindbeck 1993). Others claim that these comparisons exaggerate the extent of Sweden's long-term problems and fail to show that these problems were caused by the welfare state (Korpi 1996). In principle, outsiders can offer a more objective view.

There may be a particular virtue in having American economists examine the Swedish scene. In terms of the role of government in economic activity, the United States and Sweden stand at opposite ends of the capitalist spectrum. The United States is the exemplar of unregulated labor markets, highly competitive product markets, and a small welfare state. To the extent that the United States and Sweden have similar economic problems, analyses that blame Sweden's problems on its welfare state or interventions in the economy may be misplaced. To the extent that Sweden moves to a more market-run economy, the American experience can offer some guidance. The poor U.S. record in the area of Sweden's greatest success, reduction of poverty, highlights the distributional problems that Sweden will want to avoid as it reforms the welfare state and gives greater play to market forces throughout its economy. Conversely, the United States and other countries that are confronted with the problem of rising poverty might learn from Sweden's apparent success in this area.

The great risk of an outsider's evaluation is that an outsider will get it all wrong. American economists lack the institutional knowledge of how things work in Sweden that natives gain from daily experience. Living in a society can give insights into social processes that a disinterested scholarly analysis might miss. Moreover, outsiders' analyses can be colored by the analysts' own values. If Americans simply care less about equality than Swedes do—say, for cultural reasons—their analyses may undervalue the virtues of redistributive policies. For these reasons and others, each paper in our project paired the talents of Swedish and American economists.

Did the project succeed in bringing outsiders' insights to bear on Swedish problems? Readers of this volume will make up their own minds, but one indicator of how the project fared can be garnered from the Swedish reaction. In 1995, a summary version of the volume was published in Swedish, and a joint SNS-NBER conference was held in Stockholm to discuss the results. Given the topic and Sweden's economic woes, the volume and conference received considerable attention. Most Swedish commentators took the study as a valuable perspective on the Swedish welfare state, irrespective of whether they agreed or disagreed with specific conclusions. But some took offense. One headline labeled the Americans as "cowboy economists," whose guns shot only blanks at Sweden's wonderful welfare system. Another newspaper likened the American team to a gang of creepy Wall Street financiers, opposed to any form of egalitarian policies. But these were far from the norm. For the most part, commentators reported that the findings (which we describe shortly) developed new arguments or evidence that illuminated Sweden's problems in insightful ways. The project advanced the Swedish debate by doing exactly what we hoped it would do: allowing Swedes to see themselves through outsiders' eyes.

This volume is designed for a broader audience than Swedes. It is meant for policy analysts, economists, and other social scientists in the United States, in the European Union, and elsewhere in the world where people are confronted with questions about welfare states and the role of government in enhancing economic well-being. Why should non-Swedes be interested in Sweden's troubles and its efforts to reform the welfare state? When Sweden was the idealized "third way," some analysts critical of more normal market economies were deeply interested in Sweden's experiences. They saw Sweden as offering a model for other countries to follow. Now that Sweden has run into economic trouble, many of those analysts look elsewhere for a successful alternative to more market-driven economies. Sweden—where's that? Why study a welfare state in trouble? Let's look only at successes. Book my ticket to Frankfurt—no, make that Berlin.

There are lessons from Sweden's economic problems that should be illuminating to those who admired the past successes of the welfare state. By the same token, those who tend to be critical of activist governments and of redistributive policies may learn from Sweden's successes. Sweden's effective elimination of poverty is a unique social achievement that deserves attention. How did Sweden succeed where others had failed? What are the costs of this success, and will reform threaten the basis for Swedish equality? The current economic crisis and the difficulties of reforming the welfare state also deserve attention, particularly from citizens in other European countries with large welfare systems. Sweden's commitment to egalitarian ideals and the welfare state makes it an extreme case among advanced capitalist countries. But we may learn more about the pitfalls facing all countries from an extreme and distinctive case than from modest variants.

Sweden's Economic Troubles

Four issues are involved in judging Sweden's economic problems: (1) how well or poorly the economy performed prior to the 1990s crisis, from, say, the 1950s through 1989; (2) the magnitude and nature of the 1990s crisis; (3) the relation of welfare state institutions to the 1990s crisis; and (4) the consequences of the crisis for Sweden's ability to restore living standards and maintain its egalitarian goals.

The precrisis record has been the subject of controversy. On one side are analysts who stress the drop in Sweden's per capita income in purchasing power parity (PPP) units relative to other OECD countries. These observers also stress the relatively slow growth rate that brought Sweden to its current income level. According to the U.S. Bureau of the Census (1994, table 1370), Sweden's GDP per capita was the third highest of OECD countries in 1970 in purchasing power parity units. By 1990, it had slipped to eighth place, and, with the onset of economic crisis, it fell to seventeenth place in 1993 (U.S. Bureau of the Census 1995, table 1374). On the other side are those who argue that these comparisons exaggerate the country's long-term economic difficulties. They point out that critics' conclusions are sensitive to the countries that are used as bases for comparisons, the years analyzed, and the measure of income utilized. The decline in Sweden's relative position is unarguable, however. In 1970, Sweden's GDP per capita was 8 percent above the OECD average; in 1990, it was 2 percent below and, in 1993, 12 percent below the OECD average.[1]

Cross-country comparisons of living standards and growth rates are always difficult. On the measurement side, data used for cross-country comparisons are imperfect. National income statisticians have problems measuring the output of the public and service sectors, and they do not include household production as a component of income. These problems mar comparisons between countries like Sweden—which has a large public sector and sharply rising female labor force participation—and, say, Germany, which has a smaller public sector and relatively low female labor force participation. Further, exchange rates are inadequate for transforming incomes in one country into those in another in order to compare living standards. These rates fail to reflect differences in costs of living. Using exchange rates, for instance, Switzerland had a

1. Because Mexico is counted with the OECD in 1993 statistics but is not counted as an OECD country in earlier years, the 1993 and earlier comparisons leave Mexico out of the OECD average.

GDP per capita that was 42 percent above that in the United States in 1993. But the costs of nearly all goods and services in Switzerland were markedly above those in the United States at the going exchange rate, with the result that "true" living standards in Switzerland were not higher than those in the United States. Purchasing power parity estimates of the value of currencies provide an alternative way to transform national output into comparable units. Using these estimates, for example, Switzerland's GDP per capita was 5 percent lower than that of the United States in 1993. But estimated PPPs are also imperfect. For some countries, the 1990 OECD purchasing power parity GDP estimates differ from the comparable 1985 estimates in ways that go beyond differences in measured growth of real GDP. Still, income comparisons adjusted for PPP are superior to those based on exchange rates, which fluctuate wildly and remain out of line with living standards for years on end.

On the conceptual side, the extent to which other countries' experiences provide a valid counterfactual for a particular country such as Sweden is debatable. Indeed, some of the argument over Sweden's comparative record concerns which countries constitute the "right" comparison group. Ought that group to include Portugal or Spain or Turkey, or should it be limited to the OECD countries with the highest income per capita? Another conceptual problem relates to the inferences that one can legitimately draw about the effects of policies from broadly based country comparisons. If Sweden does more poorly in growth than countries with smaller welfare states, does this mean that the welfare state has reduced its growth rate? Perhaps, but then how does one square that with the fact that the United States has grown less rapidly than countries with larger welfare states? Many things differ among OECD countries beyond welfare state policies or any other specific economic program or practice. To assess the effects of those or other policies requires more than crude cross-country comparisons. Absent analyses of how specific programs and policies affect economic outcomes in Sweden itself, and simply informed by what other economies do in the same area, we would not be prepared to make any definitive statements about the cause of Swedish economic problems, much less about the possible effects of policy reforms. That is the type of analysis this project seeks to provide.

Problems with cross-country comparisons notwithstanding, such comparisons are still relevant to assessing Sweden's economic situation or that of any other particular country. They set the stage for detailed analyses of policies and programs by delineating what is unique to a particular country, in terms of both economic performance and economic institutions. They give a sense of the range of possible alternatives available to a country and can suggest clues to what may be working well or poorly.

The Pre-1990s Period

Measured against comparable OECD countries, Sweden's pre-1990 economic performance is mixed. Productivity growth, the investment share of

GDP, and some other indicators were comparatively weak over the period during which the welfare state expanded. But the record is not so weak as to make an overwhelming case that the welfare state was a drag on economic growth in the 1970s and 1980s. Here are some indicators:

1. In 1970, Sweden's GDP per capita was 78 percent of that of the United States, which placed it third among OECD countries. By 1989, Sweden's position relative to the United States was essentially unchanged (77 percent), but it had fallen behind Canada and Germany and was approximately tied by France and Japan. By 1993, Sweden had dropped well down in the rankings, being surpassed by France and Japan and such other countries as Austria, Italy, Norway, the United Kingdom, and Australia. The long-term trend after 1970 was that the highest-income countries grew more slowly than did low-income countries in the OECD. This can be illustrated by comparing the incomes of the four richest and four poorest OECD countries over time. In 1970, the ratio of the per capita GDP for the four richest countries to the per capita income of the four poorest was 1.55. This ratio had fallen to 1.27 by 1989. This means that the decline in the position of Sweden relative to the full set of countries through that period reflects a general compression in incomes across countries rather than something unique to Sweden. But the ensuing decline of Sweden to a position far below that of other OECD countries cannot be so explained; the income compression story is one of poorer countries catching up with richer ones, not of richer countries toppling in the per capita income tables.

2. Sweden's GDP per capita in 1989 reflects well on the productivity of the Swedish workforce. Given its lengthy vacations, holidays, generous sick and parental leave programs, and extensive part-time work, Swedish workers put in many fewer hours than American workers. Measured by output per hour worked in 1989, Swedish productivity was approximately 83 percent of American productivity. In addition, in 1989, the average Swedish worker had eleven years of schooling, whereas the average American worker had thirteen—a difference that goes a long way toward explaining the lower productivity per hour.

3. In 1990, Sweden was ranked sixth on the basis of various indicators of competitiveness in the International Institute for Management Development–World Economic Forum's World Competitiveness Report. The only European country that ranked higher was Germany. Measured by use of industrial robots, or information technology, or patents, Sweden rates high among OECD countries. Measured by various indicators of the efficacy of its markets, the country rates a bit above the middle of the pack. In the Competitiveness Report, executives rated Sweden low in the role of the state in the economy.

4. Data on consumption of major household capital items—washing machines, VCRs, telephones, and so on—in nine advanced OECD countries show that Sweden has not been a laggard as use of these goods has proliferated. It ranks high in consumption of some of these modern goods and lower in others, with an average ranking of 4. Given the high public sector share of Swedish

consumption, the position of the country with regard to these private goods confirms that Swedish living standards were among the best in the world at the outset of the 1990s. In part, of course, a high ranking in household capital goods reflects the past high position of Sweden in the OECD rankings of countries by GDP per capita: it takes a long time before changes in income levels show up in changes in consumption of major capital items.

A more negative picture is, however, shown in some other indicators:

5. The rates of growth of labor productivity and total factor productivity in the business sector for 1960–73 and 1973–89 put Sweden in the bottom tier of the growth table in both periods, along with Switzerland, the United States, and the other English-speaking countries (Australia, New Zealand, Canada, the United Kingdom).

6. Swedish outlays on government programs, which were reasonably "normal" until the 1970s, have increased more rapidly than in other OECD countries. Government expenditures averaged 35 percent of GDP in the 1960s. After that, they increased more rapidly than in other OECD countries, reaching an average of 63 percent in the 1980s, much higher than in other OECD countries. The 1990s crisis pushed government expenditures to about 70 percent of GDP.

7. Sweden's record in investment compared to other advanced OECD countries has been modestly below average. The country's capital/labor ratio, corrected for the high price of investment goods in Sweden, has fallen relative to many advanced competitors.

8. Sweden has had a greater rate of price and wage inflation than the United States or most other OECD countries and has consequently devalued its currency at fairly regular intervals. This belies the advantages of centralized or coordinating wage setting in controlling inflation, which analysts once argued was one of the benefits of "neocorporatist" systems such as Sweden's.

In short, from the 1970s through 1990, the Swedish economy showed weaknesses. But most other advanced economies also had problems in the era following the oil price shock, albeit of differing kinds. The United States experienced a 20 percent fall in the real earnings of less-educated young men and a massive rise in inequality. Most European Union countries developed high rates of long-term unemployment. Looking at the pre-1990s crisis data, we appreciate how different analysts, focusing on different contrasts or years or variables, can come down more, or less, harshly on the nation's economic performance. There is no smoking gun in the aggregate data; rather, what we have is a "fuzzy" record of general economic weakness, whose causes are not transparent. But the 1990s downturn in Sweden's economy was so severe as to cast a pall on the country's earlier growth performance and on the more optimistic readings of that performance.

Veering into a Ditch: The 1990s Crisis

From 1990 to 1994, Sweden experienced an extraordinary economic crisis. The contraction of the Swedish economy over this period exceeds the problems of any other developed country (save for Finland, owing in large part to the collapse of the Soviet market):

1. In terms of output, the Swedish economy went into a major tailspin from 1990 through 1993. GDP fell each year, for a cumulative drop of some 5 percent. Industrial production fell by 8 percent, and retail sales dropped by 13 percent. These changes occurred in the absence of a worldwide recession.

2. Gross capital formation fell by nearly one-third, with the largest contraction occurring in residential construction.

3. Employment dropped by over 12 percent, with declines in the number of persons working in the public sector as well as in the private sector. Hours worked in mining and manufacturing fell by 23 percent between 1990 and 1993. The country's exemplary record in controlling unemployment collapsed. In late 1993, aggregate unemployment stood at 9.3 percent; the rate of joblessness (which includes persons on labor board programs for employment training, relief works, youth measures, and so on but not measures for the handicapped) reached over 14 percent. The youth unemployment rate reached 21.4 percent!

4. The central government's financial balance deteriorated sharply, and the deficit/GDP ratio rose to 13 percent in 1993!

The depth of the crisis exceeded the prognostications of the experts. In 1992, SNS analysts (SNS Economic Policy Group 1992, table 1), who were among the most pessimistic, anticipated that GDP would fall by 2.0 percent in 1991 and by 1.5 percent in 1992 and then rise in 1993 by 1.5 percent, for a cumulative drop of about 2.0 percent. They expected unemployment at the end of 1993 to reach 4.5 percent. The OECD economic survey team did no better: a projected cumulated decline in GDP of 0.6 percent, with an unemployment rate of 5.2 percent for 1993.

The ditch into which the Swedish economy fell was a steep one—with some of the characteristics that the economic Cassandras had predicted would be the result of an excessive welfare state.

Diagnosing the Crisis

How one interprets the crisis experience in Sweden is critical to how one assesses the longer-term Swedish economic record. If the crisis was "just" a cyclic problem exacerbated by bad shocks, from which the economy rapidly bounced back, the pre-1990s experience would continue to look like a mixed bag, with some symptoms of economic troubles but nothing definitive to show that the society had truly run aground. If the crisis is a more structural break, the economic woes of Sweden are more serious and better attributed to fundamental economic problems than a severe cyclic downturn.

We find a pure "bad cyclic shocks" reading of the 1990s crisis implausible. We would be shocked (as economists are, sadly, often shocked by future events) if the economy grew sufficiently rapidly to bring GDP to its precrisis levels in short order, much less to raise GDP per capita to the level that it would have been at had economic growth been maintained at the (sluggish) rates of the 1980s. The highest per capita growth rate that Sweden attained in the 1980s was 3.9 percent (1984). It would require two years' growth at that high rate to bring Swedish GDP from its 1993 level to its 1990 level. It would require another four years to bring it to the level that even the modest 2 percent growth rate of the 1980s would have created through the 1990s. In fact, in 1996 Sweden was back to its 1990 level of GDP. Thus, rather than a quick recovery, the economic loss from the 1990s crisis cost the country approximately six years of economic growth. This was a major disaster for the Swedish economy and welfare state.

We identify three (not necessarily exclusive) hypotheses as potential explanations of the disaster. The first is that it was a symptom of long-run economic deficiencies that, for whatever reason, took their toll suddenly in the 1990s, rather than more gradually over time. Lindbeck et al. (1994, 209) refer to this as systems failures: "The most obvious systems failures in the economic sphere are perhaps the high public spending, overly-generous social security, wide marginal tax wedges, low private—including household—saving, detailed regulations and cartelization in various markets, lax anticartel legislation, and an inflation-prone system of wage formation." This explanation posits that underlying structural problems made the Swedish economy susceptible to a major downturn, just as some of the diverse problems of the 1920s presumably made various economies susceptible to the 1930s downturn. To accept this hypothesis, we need both a model and supporting evidence showing that cumulated problems are likely to show up not only in gradual erosion but also in a sharp and sudden drop. It is possible that this is a correct interpretation. But at present we have no such model, and it is no easy task to identify threshold points for crises.

The second explanation is that Swedish policy makers blundered in their policy reforms. Financial market deregulation and tax reform would have improved the functioning of the economy but contributed instead to a real estate boom and bust and a dramatic increase in household savings. The Lindbeck et al. commission refers to "policy mistakes" in its report, blaming some combination of systems failure and policy mistakes for the crisis. Calmfors (1993, 56) comes down more harshly on macroeconomic policy in particular, arguing that a "'softer launching' of non-accommodating policies . . . would have been a much better strategy" than those that were adopted.

The third explanation is that change per se has costs that economic analysts and policy makers typically understate. If Sweden had known no policy blunders—if the government had done exactly what some all-knowing analyst had told it—there still might have been a crisis. Swedish decision makers and institutions had, after all, adapted to a particular economic system, and perhaps any change in the system was bound to create problems. It is plausible that a highly regulated welfare state economy is so tightly connected—a "house of cards"—that changes away from regulations, high benefits, and taxes etc. have greater short-run costs than in a more decentralized economy (Freeman 1995).

On this scenario, reform is costly in the near term, even if it is worthwhile as a long-term investment.

We do not take a position with respect to these (possibly overlapping) explanations. While it is critical for some purposes to assess why the Swedish economy went into a tailspin in the early 1990s and the extent to which the welfare state contributed to this, it is even more important to realize that the crisis has changed the basis for the Swedish welfare state. Sweden today is a much poorer country than it would have been had its growth followed the normal OECD pattern in the 1990s. Swedish real GDP per capita is considerably below what it would have been; the public sector deficit is larger than it would have been and the rate of joblessness higher than under any noncrisis scenario. These facts in themselves carry an important message: they make it nearly impossible for the country to afford its traditional welfare state spending. The Swedish production possibilities frontier has shifted inward, at least for the near term.

A shrunken production possibility frontier raises different issues than the causes of slackened growth. The issue for the 1990s is not only whether to reform the welfare state but also how to bring spending in line with a shrunken budget constraint in the most efficacious way. Those who believe that welfare spending and taxes did not cause Sweden's economic woes face much the same constrained choice as those who believe that they did. Fewer resources mean smaller programs. In this circumstance, it is critical to determine the microeconomic costs and benefits of welfare state policies so that the government cuts in programs are least burdensome and so that socially desirable programs can be made to work more effectively. From this perspective, analyses of the sort undertaken in this NBER-SNS study of the workings of particular aspects of Sweden's economy, of its welfare state programs, and of its interventionist policies in product and labor markets can be particularly cogent in determining directions for policy reform.

Summary of Findings

Foreign economists have been invariably struck by several things about the Swedish economy: by the egalitarian wage and income distribution combined with low unemployment (until the 1990s); by the large public sector and the accompanying high tax burden; by the extent and generosity of income transfer programs; by the regulated and cartelized labor market; and by extensive labor market policies. They have also been struck by the fact that Sweden is a prosperous country with virtually no poverty but with high prices for consumer goods. Finally, they have been struck by the fact that these outcomes are found in a country that is so highly exposed to international competition.

The studies in the NBER-SNS project examined these aspects of the Swedish welfare state and economy by developing new data or analyses or by synthesizing extant knowledge. In this section, we summarize some of the central findings of each study regarding these points. Because our project was not designed to produce a single picture of the Swedish economy, the discerning reader may notice occasional disagreements among chapters in matters of emphasis or interpretation. We regard these internal disagreements as a strength rather than a weakness of the book. Had we all agreed on everything, it would have been a sign that the project leaders had selected the wrong team or had created the wrong intellectual environment for individual analysts to "do their own thing."

The Welfare State

The most important achievement of the Swedish welfare state is that it has succeeded in eliminating poverty. It has done this in part by creating one of the most egalitarian income distributions in the developed world. In the 1980s, the disposable income of households in the highest decile in Sweden was roughly twice as high as that of households in the lowest decile of the distribution. For comparison, top-decile incomes in the United States are about six times greater than those in the bottom decile. As a result, while the United States has a much higher (28 percent) real income per capita, poor Swedes have higher earnings than poor Americans: the incomes of bottom-decile Swedes are 63 percent higher than those of bottom-decile Americans.

Behind the extreme equalization of income in Sweden is a combination of more equal hourly pay, more equal employment (compared to other European countries), more equal distribution of hours of work for those who work (compared to the United States), and, last but not least, strongly equalizing taxes and transfers. In the 1970s and 1980s, the dispersion of factor incomes in Sweden increased. Yet the difference in disposable incomes decreased substantially.

In chapter 1, Anders Björklund and Richard B. Freeman ask how raising the earnings and income of the bottom parts of the income distribution was achieved without creating a massive loss of jobs for the less skilled. The authors refute the argument that the egalitarian outcome can be attributed to an exceptionally homogeneous population: people of Swedish extraction living in the United States exhibit as much inequality as do other Americans, while people of foreign ancestry in Sweden have an income distribution comparable to that of native Swedes. If it is not the Swedes, then it must be the system. One possibility is that the system generates a more equal distribution of years of schooling. This does not seem to be the case: the dispersion of years of schooling in Sweden is actually larger than that in the United States. Another possibility is that, at lower levels of schooling, the quality of education in Sweden is better than in the United States, producing less dispersion in school skills. Spending on education and test scores of students in Sweden are, in fact, less dispersed than in the United States. But the dispersion in test scores in Sweden is no smaller than in European countries that have failed to combine a narrow income distribution with high levels of employment. By itself, a more egalitarian set of school outcomes cannot explain the Swedish success in combining a narrow wage distribution with high employment for so long.

Who is willing to employ low-productivity workers at high wages? One answer has been the public sector. While the public sector has not employed a disproportionate share of low-paid workers, it has employed an increasing share of low-paid workers over time. Another, more speculative answer is that a compressed wage distribution has made able workers (within any given skill group) reduce their working time, which has increased the demand for less-able workers—work sharing of sorts. Who foots the bill? The taxpayers pay for the public sector, but consumers pay for the high wages of less-able workers through higher prices in the nontraded goods sector.

A key question when the public sector has to reduce government spending is the effect of reductions in various programs on the distribution of income. Björklund and Freeman argue that, because Sweden has such a high "social safety net," ongoing and potential reforms are no real threat to the egalitarian income distribution in Sweden, citing child allowances as the one possible exception. Overall, the safety net is so high that reductions in spending are unlikely to cause real poverty or even a substantial rise in income inequality.

Another important aspect of the Swedish welfare state is the public sector. The Swedish welfare state differs from other modern Western economies in that it has greatly enlarged the role of government in the provision of services, especially those that are traditionally produced in the household and family. All employment growth in Sweden since the early 1960s has been in services provided by the local government. And all of that growth has been in the increased employment of women. Underlying this development has been the rapid growth of publicly provided day care for preschool children. Employment in public day care has grown explosively since the mid-1970s to be almost half as large as employment in the education sector. An important reason for this is Swedish family policy. In 1991–92, public expenditures for families with preschool children (parental leave, publicly provided day care, etc.) were almost 3.5 percent of GDP. This comes to about SKr 60,000 ($10,000 at that year's exchange rate) per preschool child.

In chapter 2, Sherwin Rosen raises the question whether this policy has been welfare enhancing. He notes that much of what is produced by Swedish women in the market is services (care of children and the aged) that the family produces in many other countries. These services have economic value in those countries, even though this value is difficult to measure and is not counted in official estimates of GDP. This means that Sweden's economic well-being is overstated because Sweden has made the household sector a part of the money economy.

It is well known that taxes and subsidies distort individual decisions, which reduces overall economic welfare. We also know that tax-induced distortions in one sphere may make other taxes or subsidies optimal for "second-best" reasons. Rosen's analysis of subsidized child care builds on this idea. He shows that there can be an efficiency gain from subsidizing the market work of parents of young children through state-provided child care, which offsets the distortionary effect of high marginal tax rates on the decision to work in the (taxed) market sector. High marginal tax rates imply an implicit subsidy of (nontaxed) work in the home. Even so, it is not necessarily the case that subsidies increase efficiency. They reduce the distortion of the choice between staying at home with one's children and taking a market job. But the subsidy and the higher taxes required to finance it introduce a new distortion, lower prices for the subsidized goods, which produces an excessive consumption of subsidized services and of other services that are produced through (nontaxed) work in the household. Under reasonable assumptions, Rosen shows that subsidies to day care in Sweden imply efficiency losses and that those losses are potentially large. Real living standards could be improved if the subsidies were reduced and households paid for more of these services themselves in the market.

This analysis brings out an often neglected aspect of subsidies that offsets one distortion. They may readily create new and perhaps larger distortions. It is, to varying degrees, applicable to other Swedish welfare state policies. By creating a tax burden that is among the highest in the Western world, Sweden risks large efficiency losses. Successive tax reforms in the 1980s and the reform in 1991 have reduced some of the distortions of economic decisions induced by the old tax system. Yet, as long as government expenditures are as high as 60–70 percent of GDP, distortionary taxes risk large deadweight losses. In many cases, so do the transfer programs the taxes fund. The implication is that tax financing should be used only for programs whose social gains exceed budgetary costs, the deadweight loss from taxes, and the deadweight loss from the transfers.

In chapter 3, Erik Norrman and Charles E. McLure Jr. describe the distortions that the Swedish tax system created and show how these distortions have been reduced by tax reforms. Sweden's tax system prior to "great reform" in 1991 was a hybrid of different principles of taxation. The reforms have moved the tax system closer to an "ideal" income tax system by (i) increasing uniformity and horizontal equity between households, (ii) reducing tax-induced distortions of investment finance and kinds of investment, and (iii) broadening the tax base and lowering formal progressivity. However, it is important to recognize that, even in Sweden, formal progressivity did not correspond to actual progressivity since high-income earners could convert high-taxed labor income to low-taxed capital income through deductions for interest payments. Strikingly, actual progressivity for a high-income earner was unchanged by the reforms.

High progressive taxes can have a redistributive effect. But the redistribution goals of the welfare state have been increasingly realized through transfers to specific groups, where a substantial part is redistribution across an individual's life. The tax system, too, has worked and still works in that way. Much progressivity occurs across age groups rather than across individuals with different lifetime earnings. Both the tax and the transfer systems thereby substitute for saving and insurance that individuals could have arranged privately without the deadweight losses created by taxes.

The authors note that, while the tax reforms (including abolishing double taxation of dividends) have not solved all Sweden's tax-related problems, they have led to vast improvements. They have reduced the disincentives for market work and saving and should lead to a more rational allocation of the nation's capital. The complexity of the system has been reduced. The perceived fairness of the system should improve markedly. Norrman and McLure argue that these changes should be safeguarded—especially since changes in themselves carry costs.

The Labor Market

The "Swedish model" in the labor market has two key elements. The first is centralized wage bargaining. The second is active labor market policies. In the 1970s, this model was widely praised for contributing to Sweden's high living standards, low income inequality, and low unemployment. Two decades of slow economic growth and the 1990s economic crisis with its record high unemployment and enormous government deficit have fueled doubts about the virtues of the Swedish labor market model. Critics argue that Sweden has produced an ossified labor market that has reduced the country's growth prospects.

From the mid-1960s through the 1970s, wage and income inequality fell in Sweden along all observable dimensions (age and education groups, gender, etc.). This decline was larger and more rapid than what would have been generated by market forces alone. In chapter 4, Per-Anders Edin and Robert Topel explore the reasons for the decline in earnings inequality and examine how centralized wage bargaining helped Sweden maintain full employment for so long despite the strong narrowing of wage differentials.

It is important to note that the Swedish Employers' Federation (SAF) was the main initial proponent of centralized bargaining. Coordinated wage setting was seen as a method to prevent costly wage competition between unions. At the same time, coordinated wage setting was a precondition for the strongly egalitarian wage policies that the Swedish Trade Union Association (LO) came to pursue. For ideological reasons, the goal of this policy evolved, in the 1970s, from "equal pay for equal work" to just "equal pay."

Edin and Topel argue that a critical component of the centralized wage settlements was that wages for skilled workers were held down. Employers and unions joined forces to set a wage for skilled workers that was initially lower than their marginal product, creating excess demand for them. The argument is consistent with the constant "shortage of technicians" in Sweden. These wage contracts allowed employers in high-wage sectors to earn higher than normal profits. Excess profits attracted capital, which raised the demand for both skilled and unskilled labor. While there was excess demand for skilled workers, the wages of unskilled workers rose. The result was wage compression and a movement of labor from low- to high-wage sectors of the economy. This was accomplished without creating excess supply of less-skilled labor, which would have shown up as unemployment. The "solidarity" wage policy thus accomplished its objectives in reducing wage differentials and maintaining full employment.

The wage agreements implied a hidden income transfer from high- to low-wage workers. At the same time, the reduced skill differentials meant reduced incentives for workers to acquire skills. In the long run, this implies less investment in human capital. Consistent with this, Edin and Topel show that college enrollment rates fell as the college/high school wage differential was reduced in the 1970s but subsequently rose with the returns to schooling in the 1980s. The authors warn that the imbalance therefore increases over time and increasingly undermines this kind of wage agreement. A complete breakdown of central bargaining would, according to this argument, lead to considerable widening of wage differentials or, if this is not allowed to happen, unemployment for unskilled labor. Both, in fact, occurred in the 1990s.

How do Swedes respond to wage compression, taxes, and transfers? If their economic decisions are not affected very much, perhaps the distortions created by the welfare state and the labor market do not matter very much. A key question is how incentives affect labor supply.

In chapter 5, Thomas Aronsson and James R. Walker show how the welfare state gives a strong incentive for people to participate in the labor market because benefits in most social programs are closely tied to market work. This contributes to high labor force participation in Sweden. But the welfare state also gives incentives to workers to limit hours worked and possibly effort as well. Econometric estimates on Swedish data show that male labor supply is not very responsive to changes in the net wage (after tax and benefits), but they do show responsiveness by women. But Aronsson and Walker criticize these studies for being limited to the number of formal hours of work, which most individuals cannot freely vary. They argue that labor supply can respond along many other dimensions. When you allow for this, there is evidence that the Swedish welfare state has created strong disincentives to work. One example is how Swedes use generous state-provided sickness benefits, which the state has historically funded, giving both the firm and workers an incentive to exploit the system by reporting more sick days than they might under an alternative financing scheme. As a result of this incentive, the healthy Swedish population (which has one of the lowest mortality rates in the world) reported considerably more sick days than workers in other countries for many years. As part of its effort to reform the welfare state, Sweden toughened the rules for sickness benefits in the 1990s, which presumably explains a subsequent sharp drop in sickness leave.

Labor supply can also adjust in a quality dimension. The willingness of individuals to invest in human capital is one such dimension that is affected by economic incentives. As noted, rates of enrollment in higher education in Sweden have varied closely with movements in wage premia to college-trained workers. The internal rate of return to college education declined throughout the 1970s until it was modest around 1980. After that it recovered, but through the mid-1990s it is still significantly below rates in the United States and most other advanced OECD countries. The implication is that Sweden would have had a much better-educated workforce in the 1990s had income differentials not been so compressed in the 1970s.

The other important element of the Swedish model in the labor market has been Sweden's active labor market policies. Many observers have argued that these policies are responsible for Sweden's historically enviable unemployment experience. Total spending on government labor market programs, including unemployment compensation, was close to 3 percent of GDP in Sweden in 1990, with two-thirds going for "active programs." By contrast, the United States spent 0.5 percent of GDP on all labor market programs in the same year. In 1993–94—when unemployment was at a record high in Sweden—spending on all labor market programs rose to nearly 6 percent of GDP, with 2.9 percent of GDP going for the active programs that were supposed to keep unemployment low.

Whatever virtue they might have, active labor market policies did not prevent the dramatic rise in Swedish unemployment after 1990. The analysis of these policies by Anders Forslund and Alan B. Krueger in chapter 6 suggests that the inability of the active programs to arrest the growth of unemployment should not surprise us. They find that employment relief programs, which constitute a sizable share of the active programs, displaced private employment to a considerable extent, at least in the construction sector. In that sector, every public relief worker displaces up to 0.7 regular jobs. Displacement is less clear for health and welfare workers in the public sector. Forslund and Krueger also review micro studies of Swedish training programs that show that the returns on these programs do not readily justify their costs. The rate of return on a training program depends on the effect of training on future earnings and the probability of getting a new job. To motivate the programs, the rate of return generated from higher future earnings should be at least 3 percent. The weighted average of estimated rates of return from extant studies suggests that the payoff is well below 3 percent. In fact, one can question whether the programs have had any effect at all.

International comparisons using 1980s data have shown a negative relation between unemployment and spending on labor market policies. This has given some observers a favorable impression of Sweden's labor market policies. Forslund and Krueger show that the relation does not hold in the 1990s. Indeed, the same analysis for 1993 shows a positive relation: the larger such expenditures, the higher the rate of unemployment! This finding suggests that the earlier cross-country result was not robust and is likely to have been a statistical artifact—a correlation not due to a genuine causal relation.

Although the results are discouraging, they are consistent with American studies of job market programs (which often involve random assignment of people to programs in an experimental design). The U.S. studies show that, at their best, these programs have modest positive effects on the employment and earnings of participants but are no panacea to joblessness (U.S. Department of Labor 1995). The evidence that Swedish labor market programs have, at best, similar marginal returns suggests that the extensive allocation of resources to the programs merits serious reevaluation. Sweden's low precrisis unemployment rate was not the result of labor market policies, and those policies did little to arrest the increase in unemployment during the early 1990s crisis.

Lars Ljungqvist and Thomas J. Sargent explore the unemployment issue from a different direction in chapter 7, which deals with the role of taxes and transfers in unemployment. Their analysis, based on a simulation model, shows how Swedish taxes, in combination with unemployment insurance, affect efficiency and unemployment. They emphasize "search unemployment," the amount of time workers spend searching for a job, and "reservation wages," the lower limit of wage offers that an unemployed worker will accept. The reservation wage increases when unemployment compensation is more generous, which increases search unemployment as well. Many empirical studies show this effect; the longer people are eligible for unemployment compensation, the longer they remain jobless. When unemployment benefits run out, there is invariably a spike in the job-finding rate.

Until the 1990s crisis, Sweden combined generous unemployment compensation with low unemployment, in contrast to the experience of most European countries in the 1980s and 1990s. One reason for this, according to Ljungqvist and Sargent, was the narrow distribution of wages and the progressive tax and benefit system, which reduced the return to searching for a job while unemployed. In a country like the United States, it pays to search more than it does in Sweden because rates of pay vary more across employers. Another reason was that labor market officials could legitimately press the unemployed to take available jobs: after all, the jobs were there.

But the Swedish policy had a cost. Less job search means that individuals are less likely to be employed in their most productive job. The "tax wedge" therefore reduces total output. Note that the narrow wage dispersion in Sweden also reduces search and thus lowers unemployment at the cost of efficiency. The analysis also suggests that the 1990s jump in unemployment in Sweden will not readily be reduced. The reason is both generous unemployment compensation and the fact that it is more difficult to enforce the requirement of job acceptance in a situation with high unemployment. And greater wage inequality raises the equilibrium rate of search unemployment.

Product Markets and Firm Size

Welfare state policies and the institutions in the labor market affect productivity and growth. So does the organization of product markets. It is not clear whether Sweden's product markets are more regulated than markets in other countries or whether its regulatory policies are more distortionary. What is clear, however, is that Sweden has had a more lax attitude toward cartels and other barriers to competition than other countries and that these barriers often endure because of supporting regulations. To Americans schooled in antitrust policy, it is particularly surprising that until recently Sweden allowed cartels among producers and even kept a public record of them. Stefan Fölster and Sam Peltzman make use of this fact in their analysis in chapter 8, where they explore the effect of weak competition and regulations on Swedish prices.

Sweden is a high-price country. In 1990, OECD data show that Sweden had the second highest price level of all OECD countries when GDP per capita is taken into account. The United States had the lowest. After the large depreciation of the krona in 1992, Sweden still had the fifth highest cost level. One reason for this is Sweden's high value added tax. Another reason is the high wages of unskilled labor in the service sector. A third reason is, as Fölster and Peltzman show, lack of competition and regulatory policies.

Even though Fölster and Peltzman restrict their analysis to the traded goods sector, they find evidence that weak competition contributes to high product prices in the Swedish market, with regulations playing a larger role than cartels by themselves. Without the support of regulation, many cartels would not survive. Fölster and Peltzman estimate that interventions in product markets have raised Swedish prices and reduced productivity and growth. These findings suggest that monopoly profits in cartelized industries have been dissipated in higher costs. Although Swedish antitrust policy became more restrictive when the government brought it in line with European Union policy, informal restraints may continue to affect competition. In pursuing a more restrictive antitrust policy, the authors suggest that numerical measures of concentration may be a misleading guide to policy. Firms often grow large because they are more efficient than competitors. Removing institutional obstacles to entry (including imports) and regulatory restraints on competition merits higher priority.

An important but little researched question is how a welfare state like Sweden's affects entrepreneurial activity and the birth of new firms. Some economists have argued that, by providing a high safety net for entrepreneurs who fail, a large welfare state should encourage risky entrepreneurial activity (Sinn 1995). But high and distortionary taxes, high wages, and cost-increasing regulations and cartels will create disincentives for start-up and small firms. In chapter 9, Steven J. Davis and Magnus Henrekson find that Swedish policies have in fact discriminated against new, small, and labor-intensive firms and against family-owned firms as well. High statutory tax rates on corporations (especially prior to tax reform) coupled with deductions for investments translated into low effective taxes for older, capital intensive firms with accumulated profits. The tax system also favored institutional ownership at the expense of family-owned firms. The system of credit rationing prior to the deregulation of the late 1980s was biased in favor of the larger established corporations as well. Centralized wage bargaining, which eliminated the relation between size of firm and pay, and high employment security increased costs for new firms. Finally, the public sector monopoly in many service activities removed private entrepreneurs from a large and growing sector of the economy.

Presumably in part as a result of these policies, Sweden has disproportionately few small firms, and Swedish industry is more dominated by very large firms than the United States. Davis and Henrekson find that the industrial distribution of Swedish employment is tilted away from industries that typically support small firms. Even within manufacturing, Sweden has a larger share of jobs in industries dominated by large firms than the United States. In addition, Sweden has relatively few workers in low-wage industries and more in medium-wage industries. The implication is that Sweden's policy of wage compression has accomplished one of its avowed purposes, eliminating many low-wage jobs, consistent with Edin and Topel's analysis in chapter 4. The costs of such a policy might be low during an era of full employment and rapid economic growth, but, during a period of high unemployment, such policies can be costly. Davis and Henrekson conclude that policies discriminating against smaller, owner-operated enterprises and new entrepreneurs are a potentially sizable drag on the Swedish economy. Some goods and services are likely to be more efficiently produced by small firms, but these firms are "crowded out" of the product market by government services or larger firms. Given the shift in employment from goods-producing to service-producing industries, Swedish policies could be a serious hindrance to the expansion of jobs and recovery from the 1990s crisis.

The International Economy

Sweden is a small open economy, highly dependent on the outside world. In chapter 10, Edward E. Leamer and Per Lundborg describe how the world economic environment affects Sweden and its welfare state. Factors of production, especially financial capital and knowledge capital, are internationally mobile, and manufactured goods are traded internationally. Leamer and Lundborg argue that part of Sweden's laggard growth in recent decades can be explained by the interaction between the welfare state and changes in the global marketplace.

The starting point for Leamer and Lundborg's analysis is that gains from trade accrue especially to countries whose mixes of productive factors are very different from the rest of the world. In the 1950s and 1960s, Sweden was uniquely endowed with both physical and human capital. It experienced large gains from international trade. Subsequently, Sweden had a lower rate of investment in both physical and human capital than other countries, which—according to earlier chapters—can at least be partly attributed to Sweden's redistributive policies. Sweden's mix of factor supplies became less distinct as other countries have caught up in the 1980s. On one side, Sweden was crowded in world markets by countries that are relatively capital rich and thus could compete in products where Sweden used to have a comparative advantage, that is, in capital intensive products. On the other side, Sweden was crowded by poorer countries competing in production that uses relatively large amounts of unskilled labor at wage rates that are unconscionable from a Swedish standpoint.

A lower rate of capital accumulation and increased competition can account for Sweden's slower growth and lost market shares since 1970. Leamer and Lundborg warn that economic liberalization in Asia, South America, and Eastern Europe has meant a dramatic increase in the supply of unskilled workers in the global economy, putting pressure on lower wages for unskilled workers and higher compensation for scarce talents. While Sweden seeks to maintain narrow wage differentials, the international market is dictating increased differentials. They also note that Sweden's strong comparative advantage in forest resource products means that relatively much physical capital is absorbed in the capital intensive forest sector, making the country's endowment in forest resources a mixed blessing: it contributes to national income but necessitates a high rate of investment, which can reduce investment elsewhere to the extent that international capital mobility is imperfect.

Looking into the future, Lundborg and Leamer conclude that, unless Sweden restores its position as a country relatively well endowed with physical capital and skilled workers, Swedish workers will find themselves in direct competition with low-wage, low-skill workers in the international marketplace. If, on the other hand, Sweden is able to resume its position as a relatively capital rich country, it will find that the gains from increased trade will be broadly shared within the country. In order to have high and relatively egalitarian earnings in the future, Sweden must invest in human capital, specialize in human capital intensive tradable goods, and abandon low-skill tradable goods, whose relative price in world markets will be determined by low-wage countries. The dilemma of the Swedish welfare state is that, in order to increase investments in human capital and maintain high incomes and a relatively egalitarian distribution as well as to finance a higher social safety net in the long run, Sweden may have to accept greater income inequality in the short run.

Through a Glass Darkly: Sweden's Welfare State and Its Economy as a Whole

From an outsider's perspective, there are four great puzzles in interpreting Sweden's experience with the welfare state and its supportive economy. The first is how, until the 1990s crisis, Sweden maintained a narrow wage structure with high employment for so long. Why did wage compression fail to create an unemployment problem for low-skill workers, of the type found in many other European countries in the 1980s? If the United States were to double its minimum wage to bring the bottom tier of employees as close to the median as in Sweden (a change far greater than those assessed in studies of any employment effect of the U.S. minimum or proposed by advocates of a higher U.S. minimum), the consequences for employment would surely be serious.

The second puzzle is how, with such a high tax and benefits system, Sweden avoided a supply-side incentive crisis: why did the welfare state–induced gap between market activity and consumption not destroy the work ethic of the ordinary citizen and lock the poor into a welfare trap? With much lower welfare benefits, the United States created a system in which many of the poor are caught in a bind, with such high effective marginal taxes (via loss of benefits) that it barely pays them to work.

Both these puzzles reflect the economist's surprise that the Swedish economy worked as well as it did. Mancur Olson found his answer in Sweden's being a small open economy that had to meet international competition and in the all-encompassing nature of the union movement (Olson 1990). The Swedish debate over just how the economy performed prior to the 1990s crisis offers an alternative perspective, with the claim that the economy was not so successful after all.

The third puzzle, which is especially poignant to Americans who see homelessness and urban blight in virtually all cities, is how Sweden's welfare state conquered poverty. If the Great Society War on Poverty in the United States had succeeded in its lofty goals, opposition to welfare state expenditures in the United States would surely be seriously tempered. But that war failed. The success of Swedish policies seems to have produced a very different debate over welfare spending than that in the United States, with conservative Swedes as well as Social Democrats supporting the basic precepts of the welfare state.

The fourth puzzle, referred to earlier, is why the Swedish economy went "over the brink" in the 1990s. What is it about the welfare state and the Swedish economy that produced a fall in real output at just the time of real reform? The late 1980s, early 1990s changes in the tax system, in wage setting, in the rules for benefits, in the regulation of markets, should have increased economic efficiency. But these reforms did not prevent a major economic downturn.

As noted, our project was not designed to develop a single model or theme to address these "big" puzzles. Some unifying themes, however, emerge from the studies that offer answers.

Sweden as an Interrelated System

The first unifying theme is that many aspects of the Swedish welfare state and economy fit together in a *systemic* way. Low unemployment, high taxes, wage compression, high labor participation with limited hours of work, subsidized day care, etc. reinforce one another in sometimes surprising ways. Using a wide variety of analytic methods, the authors in this volume have stressed the linkages among welfare and economic policies in what we will call the logic of the "welfare state system."

Consider, for example, the relation between wage equalization and employment. The compressed wage structure was associated with effectively constant private sector employment. This made public sector employment growth the necessary engine for full employment. Such growth required in turn high taxation and a reasonably efficient public sector to deliver services that citizens want. The high taxes themselves arguably feed back onto the wage-determining process, making it easier for high-skill workers to accept wage compression: after all, much of a wage increase would be lost in progressive taxes.

The research in this volume also points to several other effects of wage compression on the supply and demand sides of the labor market that buttress employment rather than work against full employment. On the supply side, compression lowers search unemployment: with little wage variation in the economy, people have little incentive to search for the best-paying job. Compression, highly progressive taxes, and welfare benefits work together to reduce the incentive to work long hours and arguably fueled the desire for additional vacation and holiday time.

On the demand side, the limited hours worked by many Swedes may have raised the demand for employees through a form of implicit work sharing. For a period of time, wage compression helped expand high-wage traded goods industries by providing them with less-expensive high-skill workers and buttressed demand for the less skilled in those sectors. In addition, wage compression affects the distribution of industrial employment and the size distribution of establishments. Eliminating low-wage sectors and firms makes it easier to maintain a narrow wage distribution. Compression also affected the price level: if low-skill workers are paid relatively high wages, the goods they produce will be high-priced goods. Even industrial regulation, with legal cartels, has a logic in this analysis, making it easier to maintain the high prices necessary for the high wages.

In short, many of the issues dealt with in this project link together, some in expected ways, others in unexpected ways, to resolve the wage compression–low unemployment puzzle.

As to Sweden's avoidance of welfare poverty traps, the basic answer, stressed in various ways by several researchers, is that most Swedish welfare programs are workfare programs, requiring some labor participation before people receive benefits or as a condition for receiving the benefits. Although not actuarially balanced, most Swedish welfare benefits are sufficiently work related that the term *workfare state* is arguably a more appropriate appellation for Sweden than *welfare state*. High taxation of wages that might otherwise induce people to stay out of the labor market is offset by benefits attached to work. Parents benefit through subsidies for child care. Other workers benefit through generous sick leave and vacation and holiday pay. By making these and other benefits conditional on work, Sweden limits tax-related work disincentives. By conditioning benefits on a limited amount of work rather than making them proportional to hours, moreover, Sweden created "kinked" budget sets that support the low hours or work sharing that characterizes the Swedish employment record.

Taken together, the wage compression, high employment, and work-related welfare system enabled Sweden to make the redistributions necessary for a successful war on poverty. But it did not avoid supply-side disincentives.

With a compressed wage structure, a person with a job is part of normal society. By contrast, in the United States, with highly dispersed wages, many hold jobs that pay so little that they fall into an economic and social underclass. The high rate of employment in Sweden meant that society could pressure people on unemployment insurance to take jobs, which existed. It is difficult to imagine how Sweden could have operated such an extensive welfare system absent the welfare benefit–work linkage. All these factors—along with the magnitude of government redistributive spending—enabled Sweden to conquer poverty while the wealthier United States failed to do so.

In sum, our research portrays Sweden as having a highly interrelated welfare state and economy in which many parts fit together—be they subsidies, taxes, collective bargaining, or wage compression—in ways that maintained high employment and wage compression, helped offset work disincentives from welfare benefits, and ultimately helped eliminate poverty. To say that parts of the Swedish welfare state and economy fit together in a systemic way does not, of course, mean that the fit resulted from some farsighted social engineering. More probably, it is the result of adaptation, as the government, business, consumers, workers, and unions each adjusted their behavior to that of the others. Once certain policies were in place, others followed naturally, until things fit together. To say that Sweden developed a distinct welfare state system also does not mean that all policies or programs were consistent or supportive, much less sustainable.

Viewing Sweden as a system is not, of course, new; virtually all discussions of the Swedish model or the Swedish way have a systemic flavor. But the diverse microeconomic links that make this welfare state and economy so interconnected have not previously been so fully drawn out, nor have so many of the separate links been developed in detail.

The picture of the Swedish welfare state and economy as a tightly connected system that emerges from our study suggests, finally, an interpretation of Sweden's 1990s problems and of the difficulties it may have overcoming them. If Swedish economic and political agents were fully adapted to the advanced welfare state prior to the 1990s, ensuing changes in the economic environment, particularly in the world marketplace, and welfare state reforms would almost by necessity be quite costly, as those agents adjusted to new incentives and market conditions. The analogy is with fitness landscapes in evolutionary theory—a terrain of peaks and valleys, in which creatures (societies) move to new mountain peaks only by descending from an existing peak (Freeman 1995). No single reform or policy can turn around a complex interrelated system in a short time span.

Costs of the Welfare State

The other theme that emerges from our study is that the costs of the Swedish welfare state have been high, both in budgetary expenses and in hidden economic costs due to deadweight or distortionary losses induced by taxes or benefits, and that some programs have not contributed to the society's great success in reducing poverty.

Sweden did not eliminate poverty by "magic." It paid a price, in the form of taxes and the loss of output owing to distortions. In the first instance, Sweden pays for its welfare benefits through taxes or public sector deficits. In the diminished economy of the 1990s, the government share of GDP reached 70 percent in 1993, accompanied by a sufficiently high deficit to produce a rapidly rising public debt/GDP ratio. This is unsustainable by itself. But Sweden also pays indirectly for its welfare benefits through deadweight losses in output as people respond to the incentives created by taxes and benefits. As noted, some taxes and benefits offset one another, keeping distortionary losses low. But other taxes and benefits are not offsetting, and, in a society with high tax rates and benefits, they can produce sizable distortions, even if they induce only modest responses.

The magnitude of the deadweight losses is difficult to assess. Estimates of deadweight losses due to taxes based solely on labor supply responses are as high as 40 percent for the period prior to the tax reforms and lower afterward. Other estimates are lower. But these estimates are limited to only a single dimension of responsiveness (hours worked) and thus may be lower-bound estimates of the labor supply reaction. For instance, they neglect the possible long-term consequences of high taxes and benefits for human capital formation. In a tightly connected system, moreover, partial equilibrium analyses of deadweight losses can be misleading. Much larger estimates have been made in models that seek to bring in additional economic responses, although these models and estimates are best viewed as illustrative: computable general equilibrium models are as much art as science.

The appropriate analytic tool for comparing the benefits of Sweden's welfare state programs and their costs is some form of benefit/cost analysis. For programs that require tax or deficit financing, the excess burden of taxation and the possible adverse effects of deficits on investment and long-term growth imply that the cost of any program exceeds its budget cost. With an estimated excess burden of taxes of 40 percent, for instance, a program is socially justifiable only if its benefits exceed budget costs by 1.40/1.00. In a period of huge public sector deficit, the appropriate benefit/cost ratio would probably be even higher.

The benefit side of programs must be examined by comparing outcomes with and without the programs or at different program levels. If the programs induce distortions in response to benefits or other spending, as they invariably will, the benefits must be reduced by those deadweight losses. Perhaps because it is easy to assume that popular welfare state programs necessarily generate substantial social benefits (why else would they be popular?), or perhaps because economists are more cost conscious than politicians, economic science offers very few estimates of the benefits of social programs. For instance, we have reasonable ideas about the direct and indirect costs of unemployment insurance systems but no real evidence on the value of such insurance to employees. Absent evidence of substantial benefits, one can legitimately question whether even politically sensitive programs could pass the proper benefit/ costs test.

Implications and Lessons

What are the implications of our research for Sweden's efforts to reform its welfare state and reestablish a healthy economy? What can the United States and other countries with less extensive welfare states learn from the Swedish experience?

Implications for Swedish Reforms

Following its 1990s economic crisis, Sweden faces three major problems: lowering the rate of unemployment; reducing the government budget deficit; and attaining a new long-term growth path. It is only by solving these problems that Sweden will be able to achieve a healthy economy and welfare state.

With respect to reducing unemployment, our research has one strong message: active labor market programs, which have cost the society some 3 percent of GDP directly, do not appear to repay such extensive expenditures. Extant studies of programs do not yield the magnitude of returns that would justify such a high level of spending. With respect to "passive programs"—notably unemployment insurance—the general finding is that, the longer the benefits are available, the longer will be spells of unemployment. The social controls that Sweden has used to limit this distortionary response are likely to weaken in a period of extended high unemployment. This suggests that the generous Swedish unemployment insurance system—possibly suitable for a period of low unemployment—may be unsuitable for an era of high joblessness.

Given the state of Sweden's public finances and the high public share of employment, the solution to unemployment must rest with private sector job creation. Increased wage differences for groups with different qualifications can potentially contribute to this, by inducing the less skilled to obtain greater skills and by reducing the cost of low-skilled labor, particularly for private service sector jobs. Sweden offers special subsidies to employ youths. Our analysis suggests that marginal wage subsidies paid out of the public budget have greater costs than their budget value and thus should be compared critically to the alternative of greater wage differentials. By contrast, search unemployment arguments support the long-standing Swedish goal of similar pay for similarly skilled workers in comparable circumstances. This form of pay equalization can reduce unemployment. Equal pay for equal work is a valid principle that is supported by market forces—the law of one price—although there are problems with determining what equal pay means in a world with heterogeneous nonwage working conditions.

Sweden's fiscal deficit in the early 1990s dwarfs the American deficit (and those of virtually all other OECD countries). Reducing the Swedish deficit—fueled by unemployment and reduced GDP—necessitates a contraction of the welfare state. While it would be soothing to report that recovery from the depression would in itself cure the deficit problem, this does not appear to be the case. The scale of cuts in programs or increases in taxes needed to restore fiscal solvency is large. The greater the rate of growth and the faster unemployment can be reduced, the smaller will be the required squeezing of programs or taxpayers. But the costless solution to fiscal woes—"grow the economy"—is even less practical than usual. Sweden's problems will not be solved simply through growth, even if growth reduces unemployment. Contraction of welfare spending is a budget necessity, not a matter of political philosophy.

Our analysis suggests that reductions in spending programs can have a double benefit, cutting both direct budget expenses and indirect deadweight losses. It also suggests that the benefits of some programs (e.g., the active labor market spending) may not justify the magnitude of these expenditures and that the indirect costs of other programs (e.g., subsidised day care) may also call for cutbacks. We also find that reductions in some programs will not seriously affect the income distribution (unemployment insurance) while reductions in others will (child allowances). At the same time, our analysis also suggests the danger of reducing programs or increasing taxes when those programs/taxes offset the distortionary effects of other programs/taxes.

On the growth front, many of our studies stressed the importance of additional human capital formation, through enrollments in universities and presumably through training workers with a given level of education within firms as well, and the need for greater earnings differentials to induce such investments. The tax disincentives that have discouraged the formation of small firms have been reduced and can be further reduced to make it easier to form new businesses. Reduced distortions of taxes on capital should help produce the greater investment that is needed to maintain Sweden on a new steady growth path. Over the long run, Sweden will have to move toward a more human and physical capital intensive society if it wants to maintain high wages and living standards for less-skilled workers. The implicit message in these results is that many features of the Swedish model were not sustainable over the long run.

A Short Postmortem

Since the completion of our project, the Swedish economy has made some progress in getting itself back on track, and policy makers have tried valiantly to restore the government's financial balance. In 1994 and 1995, economic growth picked up, sparked in large part by export industries benefiting from a devalued currency. But the rates of growth are such as to confirm our conclusion that Sweden suffered a permanent loss in its economic well-being. In 1995, Sweden roughly recovered the level of real GDP it had in 1990. The government deficit fell from its extraordinary 13 percent of GDP level in 1993 to below 8 percent in 1995 and is forecast to drop to 2 percent of GDP by 1997. This improvement has been achieved mainly through recovery of revenues as a result of economic growth, increases in taxes, and a general squeezing of programs that has included reductions in replacement rates for various social insurance programs. Despite increased interest payments on a rising public debt, the rate of government expenditures over GDP has fallen.

These developments have moved Sweden "out of the ditch," but, as of this writing, we do not believe that they have gone far enough to bring the economy into a safe zone, where the successes of the welfare state are sufficiently protected from possible adverse economic developments. Unemployment remains high, in double digits when those on labor market programs are included in the jobless total. Sweden appears to have fallen into the European Union position of high and possibly long-duration unemployment, which will make long-term demands on public spending for unemployment insurance or other safety net programs.

Our work suggests that there is still room for a major squeezing of programs before Sweden will risk endangering its conquest of poverty. Low-wage workers are not low wage by U.S. standards. Two-earner families provide an important form of private income insurance. All Swedes receive a significant proportion of their income in the form of social income that is not part of their personal earnings. And, finally, some welfare state programs are either nonredistributive or not particularly effective. Deeper analyses of these programs than we could undertake would provide better evidence on the most effective ways of cutting spending.

The greatest danger to Sweden's welfare state and its elimination of poverty is not sizable cuts in program expenditures to restore fiscal balance but modest cuts that leave the country liable to another economic crisis if Sweden falls into another major recession. The government budget balance in a country with as high a level of public spending as Sweden and significant welfare state committments to its citizens is extremely sensitive to cyclic changes in the economy. Sweden's welfare state may therefore be best served by establishing "clear blue water" between its budget and potential renewed deficits in the next economic downturn. This may in turn require a healthy surplus in government finances in booming times so that Sweden can run moderate deficits in recessions.

Lessons for the United States and Other Countries

The Swedish experience holds lessons for the United States and other countries that have less-extensive welfare states. While Sweden can no longer realistically serve as the "third way" role model that it once did, its success in eliminating poverty still merits attention, and its problems with a large welfare state offer warnings to other countries.

On the positive side, the fact that Sweden succeeded in abolishing poverty through a welfare system that encouraged work and went further than necessary to accomplish that goal offers hope that other countries, such as the United States, can also significantly reduce poverty and can do so without buying into the "third way." At its best, Sweden's welfare system is a workfare system that has avoided creating major poverty traps. Low earners in Sweden gain social benefits by working. The lesson we draw is that welfare and work need not be antithetical. By attaching many benefits to work, welfare can be used to draw people into the job market and into the mainstream of society.

That much of Sweden's welfare state went beyond what was necessary to eliminate poverty is also heartening to outsiders, particularly to Americans, for whom a large welfare state is virtually inconceivable. While our study did not attempt to estimate the magnitude of welfare state benefits or the specific programs necessary to reduce poverty massively, the share of GDP so needed is arguably far below the size of the Swedish welfare state.

Sweden's ongoing welfare state reforms show, further, that it is possible to start reducing a large welfare state (albeit under a financial gun) without destroying the social consensus favoring that state and its successes. The fact that many of the Swedish reforms, such as the tax reforms reviewed in chapter 4, were initiated by Social Democratic proponents of the welfare state and that more conservative Swedes calling for greater reforms have done so with the avowed purpose of preserving the welfare state is in stark contrast to political rhetoric in the United States. The American economists on the NBER-SNS project were continually impressed by the commitment of Swedes of all political persuasions to maintaining the successful elimination of poverty.

Since Sweden did fall into the "ditch," however, it is on the warning side that we draw more lessons—in this case, more for other European countries with large welfare states of their own than for the United States, where policies have gone in a very different direction.

The first warning is that the high level of public spending and taxation in a large welfare state like Sweden may be dysfunctional in the world of low economic growth rates and high joblessness that has characterized OECD Europe since the early 1980s. The danger to which Sweden's experience should alert others is that a severe economic downturn can quickly create massive public sector deficits, constrain policies that might spark a recovery, and force reductions in social safety programs. Generous unemployment insurance and labor market programs may become counterproductive if the economy falls into high unemployment.

The second warning is that the two distinctive aspects of the Swedish labor market—centralized bargaining and an active labor market program—do not appear anywhere near as desirable as their proponents have suggested. Centralized wage bargaining did not guarantee low inflation. And it produced wage compressions that arguably distorted investments in human capital and the industrial composition of employment. The benefits of centralized bargaining may exceed their costs in some situations, but Sweden is far from an exemplar in this respect. As for active labor market programs, our team was surprised that such a widely publicized and expensive set of programs did not seem to have much payoff. It is now clear that unemployment cannot be cured by pouring money into active programs.

The third warning is that one must go beyond the direct costs of welfare state programs to make a rational assessment of their value. One must look at the "true" social costs, including the deadweight losses due to both taxes and benefits. While, in some instances, second-best solutions in which the distortionary incentives of one program are offset by another may be justified, there is danger that this strategy will create other distortions; see the chapter 3 analysis of subsidized child care.

The fourth warning is that economic reforms in a large welfare state are likely to extract a sizable short-run economic cost. No one in Sweden anticipated that the country would veer into an economic ditch as it was reforming its tax system and financial market regulations. There were unintended consequences of Sweden's policy changes, some arguably due to the sequencing of reforms, others due to policy makers' and analysts' lack of foresight. In a complex economy, one cannot be sure on which margins firms, consumers, unions, and government agencies may make adjustments, with feedback for other decision makers.

The Swedish Model and the U.S. Model

Since the end of World War II, many non-Swedish social scientists, often with a leftist bent, have viewed Sweden as some form of social paradise. Swedes were seen as civilized collectivists afflicted by none of the economic problems of the rest of the world.

In the 1980s and 1990s, many non-American social scientists, often with a rightist bent, viewed the United States as some form of neoclassical market paradise. Americans were seen as hard-working individualists with none of the employment woes of the rest of the West. Sweden and the United States were widely viewed as polar opposites in the garden of capitalist economies: the extreme welfare state versus the extreme free market state.

Neither the image of Sweden as the ideal welfare state nor that of the United States as the ideal market economy was or is valid. Both our societies had and have major problems. But both the problems and the ways the two countries have tried to deal with them differ enough to give Americans a unique perspective on the Swedish situation—a perspective that offers both insights and possibly misreadings—as would Swedes presumably have on the American situation. While our study does not undertake this mirror analysis of looking at the United States through Swedish eyes (as Gunnar Myrdal did in the 1940s), we hope that what we found out about Sweden adds to our understanding of how the United States operates, as well.

References

Bergström, V. 1992. *Aspects of the Swedish model and its breakdown.* Stockholm: Trade Union Institute for Economic Research (FIEF).

Bosworth, B., and A. Rivlin, eds. 1987. *The Swedish economy.* Washington, D.C.: Brookings.

Calmfors, L. 1993. Lessons from the macroeconomic experience of Sweden. *European Journal of Political Economy* 9, no. 1 (March): 25–72.

Freeman, Richard B. 1995. The large welfare state as a system. *American Economic Review* 85, no. 2 (May): 16–21.

Freeman, Richard B., Birgitta Swedenborg, and Robert Topel, eds. 1995. *Välfärdsstat i omvandling—Amerikanskt perspektiv på den svenska modellen.* Stockholm: SNS Förlag.

Gibson, K., and P. Hall. 1993. American poverty and social policy: What can be learned from the European experience? Paper presented at the Social Science Research Council's Policy Conference on the Urban Underclass, 10–11 November, Washington, D.C.

Henrekson, M., L. Jonung, and J. Stymne. 1996. Economic growth and the Swedish model. In *Economic growth in Europe since 1945,* ed. N. F. R. Crafts and G. Ronniolo, 240–89. Cambridge: Cambridge University Press.

International Institute for Management Development (IMD) and World Economic Forum. Various years. *World competitiveness report.* Geneva: EMF Foundation.

Korpi, W. 1996. Eurosclerosis and the sclerosis of objectivity: On the role of values among economic policy experts. *Economic Journal* 106, no. 439: 1727–46.

Layard, R. 1991. *Why abandon the Swedish model?* Stockholm: Trade Union Institute for Economic Research (FIEF).

Lindbeck, A. 1993. *The welfare state: The selected essays of Assar Lindbeck.* Vol. 2. London: Edward Elgar.

Lindbeck, A., P. Molander, T. Persson, O. Petersson, A. Sandmo, B. Swedenborg, and N. Thygesen. 1994. *Turning Sweden around.* Cambridge, Mass.: MIT press.

Lundberg, E. 1985. The rise and fall of the Swedish model. *Journal of Economic Literature* 23, no. 1 (March): 1–36.

Myrdal, Gunnar (with the assistance of Richard Sterner and Arnold Rose). 1964. *An American dilemma.* New York: McGraw-Hill.

Olson, M. 1990. How bright are the northern lights. Crafoord Lectures, University of Lund.

Sinn, Hans-Werner. 1995. A theory of the welfare state. CEPR Discussion Paper no. 1278. London: Centre for Economic Policy Research, November.

SNS Economic Policy Group. 1992. Disinflation, integration, and growth. Center for SNS Occasional Paper no. 37, June. Stockholm: SNS.

U.S. Bureau of the Census. 1994. Statistical abstract of the United States, 1994. Washington, D.C.: Government Printing Office.

———. 1995. Statistical abstract of the United States, 1995. Washington, D.C.: Government Printing Office.

U.S. Department of Labor. 1995. *What's working (and what's not), a summary of research on the economic impacts of employment and training programs.* Washington, D.C.: Office of the Chief Economist (January).

1   Generating Equality and Eliminating Poverty, the Swedish Way

Anders Björklund and Richard B. Freeman

Sweden has a remarkably egalitarian distribution of income and low rate of poverty. The living standards of the poor are closer to those of median citizens than in other advanced countries. Until the 1992–93 rise in joblessness, Sweden combined a narrow distribution of earnings and skill differentials with high employment. Wage differentials rose in Sweden when centralized bargaining weakened in the 1980s, and joblessness jumped in 1992, but the country maintained a low rate of poverty and avoided the growth of an underclass and the homelessness that developed in the United States and the United Kingdom. Indeed, so successful has been Sweden's "war on poverty" that the statistical concept of a poverty rate is not part of Swedish public discussion.

What explains Sweden's egalitarian income distribution and success in eliminating poverty? What enabled the country to pay high wages to people in the lower parts of the earnings distribution without generating a mass loss of jobs? How will changes in the welfare state and the 1992–93 economic and financial crisis affect distributional outcomes? Can Sweden maintain its record of generating equality and eliminating poverty into the twenty-first century?

This paper examines these questions. Section 1.1 documents the distributional record of Sweden relative to those of other advanced countries. To deter-

Anders Björklund is professor of economics at the Swedish Institute for Social Research at Stockholm University. He is also a member of the Swedish Economic Council. Richard B. Freeman holds the Herbert Ascherman Chair in Economics at Harvard University. He is also director of the Labor Studies Program at the National Bureau of Economic Research and executive programme director for the Programme in Discontinuous Economics at the London School of Economics' Centre for Economic Performance.

The authors received helpful comments from Sören Blomquist, Robert Erikson, Markus Jäntti, Björn Gustafsson, Robert Lalonde, and seminar participants at Oxford and the Swedish Institute for Social Research. Anders Björklund acknowledges research support from the Bank of Sweden Tercentenary Foundation and the Swedish Council for Research in the Humanities and Social Sciences.

mine whether Sweden's distributional record comes from a homogeneous population or the system of income determination, section 1.2 examines how people of Swedish descent fare in the relatively unregulated American labor market and how people of non-Swedish descent fare in Sweden. Sections 1.3 and 1.4 explore supply-side and demand-side factors that potentially enabled Sweden to combine high employment and a narrow earnings distribution. Section 1.5 considers the potential consequences of market-oriented reforms in the welfare state for Sweden's elimination of poverty.

Although a large proportion of the welfare state budget goes to pensioners, we consider only the nonpensioner population, working-age adults and children. One reason we do this is that most advanced countries have greatly reduced poverty among the elderly and that Swedish outcomes here are therefore not so distinct, although in fact reduction in poverty among the elderly in Sweden exceeds that in most other countries (Coder, Rainwater, and Smeeding 1989; Kangas and Palme 1993). A second reason is that an analysis of how the Swedish welfare state treats pensioners would lead us into complicated issues regarding the effect of state-funded pensions on savings rates, life-cycle allocations of time and income, intergenerational accounting, and so on that would greatly extend our investigation.

We reach six major conclusions:

1. Sweden achieved its egalitarian income distribution and eliminated poverty largely because of its system of earnings and income determination. In support of this conclusion, we note that the narrow income distribution in Sweden cannot be attributed to an exceptionally homogeneous population: the descendants of Swedes in the United States exhibit as much inequality and poverty as do other Americans, while people of foreign ancestry in Sweden have an income distribution comparable to those of Swedish parentage. The narrow income distribution also cannot be attributed to an exceptionally low return to skills due to market forces: Sweden has a less-educated workforce than the United States, which, all else the same, should have yielded high returns to labor skills, contrary to fact. By contrast, changes in earnings inequality in Sweden over time mirror changes in wage-setting policies, and taxes and transfers massively affect the income distribution. While a market-driven system of wage and income determination might not produce as much inequality in Sweden as in the United States, the high level of inequality found among people of Swedish descent in the United States suggests that the increase in inequality would be considerable.

2. Sweden's distinct record of labor outcomes has historically gone beyond compression of earnings differentials. Compared to other advanced European countries, what was unusual, prior to the 1992 recession, was not Sweden's low inequality in earnings but its high rate of employment. Compared to the United States, another high-employment-rate country, Sweden is distinguished by a relatively egalitarian distribution of hours of work among those employed as well as by a compressed wage structure. Indeed, the egalitarian distribution of hours of work—work sharing of sorts—contributes as much to Sweden's

egalitarian earnings distribution as does its compressed distribution of hourly pay. The association of relatively egalitarian distributions of wages and hours of work may be interrelated and necessary components of the traditional Swedish economic system.

3. Tax and transfer policies contribute substantially to Sweden's overall distribution record. Factor income inequality is much greater than earnings inequality because some people are out of the job market, capital income is unequally distributed, and Sweden's income maintenance system gives considerable financial support to those who have worked but are currently not working or not working full-time. In contrast to many social welfare systems, Sweden's is largely a workfare system, with few poverty trap programs: most welfare state programs encourage work. This contrasts with American programs, which face the great difficulty of making work pay more than welfare for those eligible for benefits. In the 1980s, taxes and transfers largely offset trends toward greater inequality in factor incomes.

4. Policies and practices that equalize opportunities appear to be less important in producing Sweden's egalitarian earnings distribution than many observers would like to believe. The dispersion of years of schooling is greater in Sweden than in the United States. On standardized international tests, the distribution of scores for young Swedes is similar to the distribution of scores for young people in other advanced societies, although more compressed than in the United States, an outlier in inequality in this respect. The greater equality of parental incomes in Sweden than in the United States contributes modestly to the overall greater equality of incomes in Sweden. The implication is that policies that tend to equalize opportunities for the young do not explain much of Sweden's exceptional distribution record.

5. Part of Sweden's historic success in maintaining jobs for low-wage workers while raising their wages resulted from policies that directly or indirectly buttress the demand for low-skill workers. One important factor was the expansion of public sector employment. While the public sector does not hire disproportionate numbers of low-skill workers, it greatly increased its share of such workers from 1968 to 1991. Another mode of buttressing demand for low-skill workers has been public subsidization of employment for the 2 percent or so of the population that is counted as disabled. We also note that Sweden pays for or subsidizes indirectly the high wages of less-skilled workers through high prices in nontraded goods and services in the private sector as well as in the public sector. Reforms that reduce those prices should put downward pressure on the wages of low-paid workers. More speculatively, we direct attention to the possible link between the compressed distribution of hours worked and the demand for low-wage labor. In some situations, mandated vacation time, extensive payment for time not worked such as parental leave, and high income taxes that discourage additional work will create demand for additional employment. Reforms that induce some Swedes, say, the more skilled, to work additional hours may reduce demand for labor for others.

6. Changes in the 1980s and early 1990s toward a more market-driven econ-

omy raised inequality modestly but maintained the relative disposable income of low-income families with children. While the 1990s Swedish economic crisis put great strain on government budgets and the welfare system, Sweden's social safety net is so high that ongoing and potential future changes are unlikely to threaten its successful elimination of poverty. The child benefits program, in particular, offers a fruitful tool to offset the effects of increased inequality in factor incomes on children.

1.1 The Swedish Record

> The Welfare State system (is) a major achievement of modern civilization
> . . . (it has) mitigated, or even eliminated destitution among people with extremely low lifetime income.
>
> —Lindbeck (1992: 115, 97)

The basic fact about the Swedish income distribution that makes fans of such disparate social scientists as Assar Lindbeck and Walter Korpi is that income is more narrowly distributed and poverty lower in Sweden than in most other countries. Figure 1.1 documents the low inequality in Sweden using data based on the Luxembourg Income Study (LIS). The figure measures inequality by the ratio of household disposable income adjusted for family size[1] of those in the top decile of the income distribution to those in the bottom decile. Sweden, Finland, and Belgium have the lowest inequality in household incomes.[2] The United States has the highest inequality.

What lies behind Sweden's relatively egalitarian distribution of incomes and correspondingly high living standards for those in the bottom rungs of the distribution? Disposable income per person can be decomposed in various ways to lay bare the anatomy of the income distribution. Wages, hours worked, family composition, taxes, and transfers all affect disposable income. Since labor earnings are the prime source of personal incomes, it is natural to begin with the distribution of wages and hours worked.

1.1.1 Wages and Work

Table 1.1 summarizes the distributions of hourly earnings and annual earnings in Sweden from the Level of Living Survey (Levnadsnivåundersökningarna [LNU]) a panel study of individuals conducted in Sweden[3] in 1968, 1974, 1981, and 1991 in terms of two statistics: the ratio of the earnings of the nineti-

1. The equivalence scale used in this figure is the square root of household size. Alternative adjustments for household size, such as taking incomes per capita, give a similar picture (see Atkinson, Rainwater, and Smeeding 1995, table 4.1).
2. Two important countries missing from these data are Germany and Japan. World Bank data on income distribution (not adjusted for family size or for disposable income) show that Japan has the lowest inequality among advanced countries while Germany is the fifth lowest in inequality (see World Bank 1993, table 10).
3. The first survey was conducted in 1968 when approximately six thousand randomly selected Swedes were interviewed about their level of living and labor market experiences. Later, in 1974,

with wage-setting policies in the period. This was the era of "solidaristic wage policy," when the negotiated pay settlements reduced differentials along virtually all dimensions. By contrast, inequality widened from 1981 to 1991, as wage bargaining became increasingly decentralized. Hibbs (1990) reports a similar pattern for blue-collar LO (the Swedish Trade Union Association) workers: falling inequality from 1970 through the early 1980s, followed by an increase in inequality. The decline in the 90/10 spread from 2.44 to 1.93 in the table is substantial, but what most impresses us is the moderate change in the 10/50 gap in both the 1970s period of decreasing inequality and the 1980s period of increasing inequality. In 1968, before the push for equalization, low-decile Swedish earners had 71 percent of median hourly earnings; in 1981, at the peak of solidaristic wage policies, these workers earned 79 percent of the median; in 1991, with more decentralized wage setting, they had 76 percent of median earnings.

1.1.2   Distribution of Hours Worked

Consider two economies with the same structure of wages. In economy 1, high-wage workers work many hours, while low-wage workers work few hours (possibly owing to substitution effects in labor supply behavior). In economy 2, high- and low-wage workers work the same hours over the year. Inequality of annual earnings in economy 1 will be greater than in economy 2 because the distribution of hours worked is unequal and correlated with hourly wages.[5] These considerations raise the following question: does the distribution of hours worked among Swedes contribute to the country's low level of inequality in annual earnings?

Table 1.2 summarizes data on hours worked in Sweden and in the United States. The top part of the table gives the division of hours worked in the economy by employment status. Row 1 shows that hours worked per adult are moderately less in Sweden than in the United States: a gap of 0.10 ln points. Row 2 shows that, while both countries have high employment/population rates, the Swedish employment rate exceeded the American rate by 0.08 ln points. Hours worked per adult are higher in the United States, not because more Americans than Swedes work over the year, but because those who work put in more hours. The differential in hours worked for workers is a huge 0.19 ln points. One important reason for this differential is that Swedes take at least five to six weeks vacation time (legally, as of 1993, each person has the right to five weeks, plus many public holidays) while Americans take two weeks—a three- to four-week difference that creates a .06–.08-ln-point difference in annual

---

5. We avoid the term *living standards* here because of conceptual issues about how to value nonwork time. In one sense, measured income overstates the advantage of those who work more hours since they have less leisure. If their productivity in nonmarket activities exceeds that of lower-paid workers proportionate to wage differences, the right comparison is the comparison of wages. But, if those who work few hours do so because their opportunities are, for whatever reason, limited, the income comparison may give a better fix on differences in living standards.

Table 1.2   **Comparison of Work Time in Sweden and the United States**

	Sweden	United States	Ln Difference
Aggregate work time (men and women)			
1. Aggregate hours worked/ population	1,231	1,365	−.103
2. Employment/population, 15–64, in 1990	.832	.766	.083
3. Hours worked by workers in 1990	1,480	1,782	−.186

	Sweden			
	Both	Men	U.S. Men	
Distribution of annual hours paid for (hours > 0)				
4. 90th percentile in hours	2,440	2,600	2,912	−.113
5. Median in hours	2,080	2,080	2,080	0
6. 10th percentile in hours	1,010	1,070	960	.108
7. 90/10 spread in hours	2.42	2.43	3.03	−.60
8. 10/50 gap in hours	.49	.51	.46	.05
				Difference
Decomposition of annual earnings inequality				
9. Variance ln annual earnings	.286	.233	1.084	−.851
10. Variance ln hours	.162	.107	.472	−.365
11. Variance ln wage	.082	.091	.481	−.390
12. 2 covariance ln hours and ln wage	.042	.034	.131	−.097

Source: Row 1 is calculated from rows 2 and 3. Row 2 is taken from OECD (1993) and row 3 from OECD (1991). Rows 4–12, for men and women twenty to sixty-four years old, are tabulated from the Level of Living Surveys for Sweden and from the 1990 census for the United States.

Note: The U.S. data on annual earnings inequality are from self-reported data, with considerable potential for error. In rows 4–12, we have eliminated men reporting less than $1.00 per hour or more than $1,000 per hour for the United States as these outliers affect variances but do not noticeably affect the percentiles.

hours worked. Whatever the cause, rows 1–3 show that work hours are distributed more equally among adults in Sweden than in the United States.

The second part of the table gives the distribution of annual hours worked among those with positive hours. The data here are hours paid for rather than hours worked and thus exceed the hours in the first part of the table. Column 1 gives data for men and women in Sweden; columns 2 and 3 contrast men in Sweden with men in the United States. The decile ratios show that hours worked are more equally distributed in Sweden than in the United States. The 90/10 spread in hours is 2.42 for both sexes and 2.43 for men in Sweden, which compares with 3.03 in the United States.

The final part of the table decomposes the variance of ln annual earnings in each country into the part due to the variance in ln hourly pay, the part due to the variance in hours worked, and twice their covariance. The surprising fact that emerges is that the difference in the variance of annual earnings between men in Sweden and men in the United States is due as much to the variance in annual hours as it is to the variance in ln hourly pay. The implication is that there is more to the story of equalization in Sweden than compression of wage differentials: the high proportion employed and the distribution of hours among those working contributed substantially to the relatively egalitarian distribution of earnings.

1.1.3   Household and Disposable Incomes

Relative equalization of labor market incomes is only part of the Swedish income distribution story. The income available to individuals for consumption depends on taxes and transfers, family structure, numbers of earners and children, and the like. Sweden's welfare state tax and transfer policies greatly affect the extent to which inequality in market earnings is transformed into inequality in disposable incomes.

Table 1.3 presents information on the distribution of factor incomes: labor earnings and capital market earnings; and disposable incomes, which depend on taxes and transfers as well, for the nonelderly from 1967 through 1992. We have derived these statistics from data on household incomes and people in households as follows: we calculate incomes per equivalent person using Swedish equivalence scales;[6] allocate the same income to each individual in the family; and then measure inequality among *individuals* of a given type, adults or children.[7] In this way, we give the same weight to every person irrespective of the size of the family: a family with four people, for instance, gives four observations for the income distribution. Some may question the use of equivalence scales in income distribution measurement for adults because the adults choose the number of children, which enters their utility function. This is a valid point for adults but not for children, who do not make these choices. In any case, we have used equivalence scales for both adults and children.

We place greater stress on inequality and relative poverty among children than among adults because the welfare state presumably has a more justifiable role to play in the well-being of children. Some adults will have a low economic standard owing to their choice of hours and effort of work and will reduce hours and effort the greater the welfare benefits. Children, by contrast, create no such moral hazard problem. To the extent that low incomes during childhood adversely affect the formation of human capital, moreover, relative

---

6. In these scales, the first adult is counted as 1.0, the second adult as 0.65, children up to three years as 0.48, children between four and ten as 0.57; and children between eleven and seventeen as 0.65. The scales used in fig. 1.1 above are different, and therefore the numbers are not the same.

7. Our definitions of *factor income* and *disposable income* include realized capital gains but do not capture unrealized gains, e.g., from changing real estate prices. The strongly fluctuating house prices—rising during the 1970s and the second half of the 1980s and falling during 1990–93—are therefore not taken fully into account in our data. We believe that this problem is largely in the upper half of the income distribution and thus are more confident about our relative poverty rate than our measure of overall income inequality.

Table 1.3   **Inequality and Relative Poverty in Household Factor Income (FI) and Disposable Income (DI) per Equivalent Person in Sweden, 1967–91**

	Inequality: 90/10 Ratios				Relative Poverty: 10/50 Ratios			
	Adults (20–64)		Children (0–17)		Adults (20–64)		Children (0–17)	
	FI	DI	FI	DI	FI	DI	FI	DI
1967[a]	5.80	3.19	3.72	2.52	.35	.54	.50	.65
1975	6.87	2.57	4.24	2.21	.27	.59	.43	.67
1978	7.87	2.36	4.03	2.14	.23	.62	.44	.67
1980[a]	8.11	2.65	4.36	2.43	.23	.57	.42	.62
1980	8.19	2.44	4.87	2.27	.22	.60	.37	.65
1981	8.24	2.41	4.47	2.18	.22	.61	.40	.67
1982	8.16	2.44	4.38	2.17	.23	.61	.40	.67
1983	7.82	2.45	4.71	2.09	.23	.61	.37	.68
1984	8.14	2.41	4.49	2.10	.23	.62	.38	.68
1985	8.72	2.44	4.39	2.07	.21	.63	.39	.68
1986	9.24	2.49	4.82	2.08	.21	.62	.36	.68
1987	8.83	2.38	4.78	2.00	.21	.63	.37	.70
1988	9.57	2.39	4.79	2.02	.20	.63	.36	.69
1989	9.46	2.41	5.71	2.10	.20	.63	.32	.68
1990	9.64	2.49	6.15	2.11	.19	.61	.29	.68
1989[b]	9.62	2.53	5.85	2.19	.20	.62	.32	.68
1990[b]	9.44	2.58	6.09	2.16	.20	.60	.30	.67
1991[b]	12.76	2.67	7.47	2.23	.15	.60	.25	.67
1992[b]	18.74	2.68	13.29	2.23	.10	.60	.14	.67

Source: Income Distribution Survey (HINK) data from Statistics Sweden, with the exceptions noted in n. a below.

Note: The definition of income in the Level of Living Surveys differs modestly from that in the HINK data. Statistics Sweden has a broader base for its income after 1991. The second set of figures for 1989 and 1990 is based on the new definition.

[a]From the Level of Living Surveys.

[b]New definition.

poverty among children may have deleterious consequences for national productivity over the long run.

There are four messages to be derived from the table. First, comparing the measures of inequality and relative poverty of factor incomes in table 1.3 with the comparable measures of labor market earnings in table 1.1 above, we see that factor incomes are far more unequally distributed than hourly wage rates or annual earnings. The 90/10 spreads in table 1.3 are on the order of eight or nine to one, roughly double the spreads in annual earnings in table 1.1, while the 10/50 measures of relative poverty are around 0.20, which is about half the 10/50 differentials in annual earnings. There are three reasons for this: the inclusion of people out of the labor market, who have low factor incomes;

the inclusion of capital incomes, which are unequally distributed;[8] and the exclusion of unemployment benefits, early retirement, sick pay, and parental allowances from factor incomes even though these benefits are closely tied to previous work. In the appendix, we show that a measure of income that includes these benefits is more equally distributed than our measure of factor income.

Second, the table shows a huge difference between inequality in disposable incomes per person and in factor incomes. The 90/10 measure of inequality in disposable incomes is about a fourth as great as the comparable measure of inequality in factor incomes. Thus, inequality in disposable income is closer in magnitude to the inequality in hours earnings in table 1.1 than it is to inequality in annual earnings. For instance, in 1990, the 90/10 spread in disposable incomes per person is 2.49, which contrasts to a 4.88 spread in annual earnings and a 2.05 spread in hourly earnings. That Sweden's tax and transfer policies produce a very different distribution of disposable income than factor income is not a new finding. Lindbeck's 1983 study of the Swedish income distribution showed a "much more uneven distribution of factor income than of disposable income," which led him to conclude that "redistributive policies in Sweden must be regarded as quite successful on the basis of egalitarian values" (Lindbeck 1992, 62). Our data confirm this conclusion.

Third, the data show two patterns of change in inequality over time. From 1967 to 1975–78, inequality in disposable incomes falls, despite increases in factor income inequality. This reflects the egalitarian policies of the period, which included high marginal taxes, a large increase in local taxes, and an extension of transfers and publicly provided services in the government budget. Consistent with this, Gustafsson and Uusitalo (1990) show a large increase in the redistributive effects of public transfers over the same period. The second pattern is an upward trend in factor income inequality from the late 1980s through 1991, followed by an even sharper jump in 1992, presumably due to the increase in unemployment.[9] This has, however, only a modest effect on disposable income inequality. Whereas from 1989 to 1992 the 90/10 differential in factor incomes nearly doubled, the 90/10 differential in disposable incomes increased by just 6 percent. Factor income inequality was three times as great in 1991 as in 1967, but disposable income inequality was less! Swedish tax and transfer policies prevented the trend toward increased factor income inequality from widening the distribution of disposable incomes, even in 1992, when unemployment rose substantially.

8. In part, 1991 appears to be an exceptional year because many people changed the timing of their incomes to take advantage of the tax reforms; for further evidence, see Björklund, Palme, and Svensson (1995).

9. But we show in the appendix that inequality of income from work and total income was more stable than inequality of factor incomes in total until 1990. Likely explanations for these diverging trends in the 1980s are rising early retirement and sickness pay. In 1991, inequality of income from work rose substantially.

The fourth result is that tax and transfer policies acted to equalize disposable income between children and reduce the relative poverty among them. The 10/50 ratio in column 8 is nearly constant at about two-thirds the median throughout the period covered in the table—despite rising inequality and relative poverty per person in factor incomes among families with children, as among all families. The major transfer policies here are child allowances and parental leave. During the 1980s, child allowances were raised in real terms and a progressive component introduced, which gives extra amounts for the third and next children. Both the increased amount and greater progressivity of the transfers for larger families have equalizing effects on the distribution of disposable incomes among children. The 1991 increase in child allowances that was part of the tax reform of that year explains why the relative poverty rate of children did not increase from 1990 to 1991 despite the increased relative poverty for people in terms of factor incomes in that period.

For comparison, we estimated income per person in families with children in the United States in 1989, using the Swedish equivalence scales to adjust for family size. The resulting distribution of income per person showed a much wider distribution of income among children than in Sweden. In the United States, the income of children in the bottom decile of the distribution of per person income associated with children was 33 percent of the median of that distribution.[10] Over time, child poverty rates rose from 14.2 percent in 1973 to 19.9 percent in 1990 (U.S. Bureau of the Census 1993, table 718), as earnings differentials widened and Aid to Families with Dependent Children fell in real terms.

These findings are consistent with previous research on the distribution of income among children in Sweden. Analyses based on data from the Luxembourg Income Study show that in the 1980s Sweden was particularly successful in generating equality and reducing poverty among children (Coder, Rainwater, and Smeeding 1989). Jäntti and Danziger (1994) find that Sweden's tax and transfer system eliminated relative poverty (defined as 40 percent of the median income in their study) among children, in contrast to the modest effects of American transfer policies. Poverty among children with single parents is rare in Sweden, both because of high labor force participation among single mothers and because of the transfer system. What is new in table 1.3 is the evidence that Sweden's redistributive system maintained the relative income of these families in the early 1990s, when factor income inequality began to increase.

Should one view the divergence between factor income inequality and dis-

10. In this calculation, we include reported transfers but do not adjust for taxes. Taking account of taxes will have little effect on the difference in income between the tenth decile and the median, but U.S. household surveys typically understate the amount of transfer income relative to administrative records and also understate the amount of capital income. We believe that the 33 percent figure that we calculated is probably lower than the actual figure.

posable income inequality in table 1.3 as a good thing or as a bad thing? On the plus side, the divergence shows the efficacy of Swedish transfer and tax policies in buffering low-income citizens against a market trend toward a decline in their relative economic position—which is what a social welfare scheme focused on relative well-being is supposed to do. On the minus side, by breaking the link from market earnings to disposable income, such a redistributive system adversely affects work incentives, as Lindbeck has stressed in his critical assessment of the welfare state. And as the gap between factor income inequality and disposable income inequality grows, as it did in the late 1980s and early 1990s, the necessary transfers also have to rise, adversely affecting government budgets and increasing deadweight losses from tax or deficit financing.

1.1.4   The Transfer Programs

What are the transfer programs that so greatly affected the distribution of disposable income in Sweden? There are many such programs, each of which merits detailed analysis beyond the scope of our study. We distinguish three types of programs according to their relation to work:

Poverty Trap Programs. These are programs that are antithetical to work in that they go to people who are not working or who earn below a certain amount, require no previous work for eligibility, and are reduced or lost if the person gets a job or increases market earnings. The archetype is a means-tested benefit.

Workfare Programs. These are programs that increase the incentive to work because only people who work can use them but that can have negative effects on hours worked when the person attains eligibility. An example is the subsidized child-care program that is limited to families where parents work at least half-time. Other workfare transfer programs give money to workers who are not working but who had to work previously to be eligible—work injury insurance, sickness cash benefits, and parental leave payment.

Income Effect Programs. These are programs that have an income effect on working by providing money regardless of work activity. An example is the child allowance program, which goes to anyone who fits the criterion regardless of work activity.

Table 1.4 gives expenditures on the major transfer programs classified under these three headings. Medical care is practically free to all citizens and is one of the largest transfer programs, with expenditures (exclusive of pensioners) of 2.6 percent of GNP. It is financed out of general taxes and not counted as part of personal income. While individuals pay for part of dental care through

Table 1.4   The Major Transfer Programs in Sweden for Nonelderly Adults

	Expenditure as Share (%) of GNP (1991)	Relation to Work
General transfers:[a]		
Medical care	2.6	Income effect
Dental care	.4	Income effect
Work-related transfers:[b]		
Sickness cash benefits	2.2	Workfare
Work injury insurance	.8	Workfare
Strongly means-tested transfers:		
For all groups:		
Housing allowance[c]	.4	Poverty trap
Social assistance[d]	.4	Poverty trap
For the disabled:		
Disability pension[b]	1.9	Poverty trap
Sheltered work, wage subsidies and		
rehabilitation[e]	.8	Workfare
For the unemployed:		
Unemployment benefits[b]	1.4	Poverty trap
Temporary jobs, training, wage subsidies,		
employment services[f]	1.3	Workfare
For families with children:		
Day care[g]	1.3	Workfare
Child allowances[b]	1.1	Income effect
Maintenance allowance[h]	.2	Income effect
Parental leave[b]	1.0	Workfare
Temporary parents' cash benefits[b]	.2	Workfare
All listed programs[i]	16.0	
Workfare	7.6	
Income effect	4.3	
Poverty trap	4.1	

[a]Data are taken from the national accounts and from Statens Offentliga Utredningar (SOU) 1993:38. The estimates are constructed from the assumption that the nonelderly consume 40 percent of medical care and that 10 percent is paid by fees. The nonelderly are assumed to consume 80 percent of dental care.

[b]From National Social Insurance Board (1992).

[c]From Boverket (National Board of Housing, Building, and Planning), reported in 1995. Social Insurance Statistics from the National Social Insurance Board.

[d]From Statistics Sweden.

[e]From Samhall and National Labor Market Board, figures for 1 July 1991–30 June 1992.

[f]From National Labor Market Board, figures for 1 July 1991–30 June 1992.

[g]Estimated as the number of children at day-care centers (300,000, according to Statistics Sweden) times SKr 50,000 plus the number of children with subsidized day care in private homes (110,000, according to Statistics Sweden) times SKr 40,000.

[h]From Social Insurance statistics, with the part paid by noncustodial parents excluded.

[i]Sickness cash benefits, work injury insurance, disability pension, training stipends, wages for sheltered jobs and temporary jobs, unemployment benefits, parental leave benefits, and temporary parents' cash benefits are subject to income tax. Thus, gross expenditures overstates the net burden of public budgets.

fees, some dental expenses are subsidized, accounting for an additional 0.4 percent of GNP. The public expenditure on medical care creates an income effect on the labor supply decision.

Sickness cash benefits and work injury insurance are work-related transfers since eligibility requires a previous period of work. Both programs replace a constant fraction of previous earnings up to a limit, which is exceeded by less than 10 percent of all workers. The replacement rate for sickness benefits was 90 percent until it was reduced in early 1991. The replacement rate for the work injury insurance has been similar to that for sickness. Together, the two programs cost 3.0 percent of GNP.

The ultimate safety net is means-tested social assistance. This is a poverty trap program, although the social authorities require that the benefit-recipient actively seek work at the employment office and accept suitable jobs. In 1991, 0.4 percent of GNP was spent on social assistance. Another means-tested transfer, of about equal magnitude, is the housing allowance, which is determined by the income of the family, the wealth, the rent, and the number of children.[11]

We next turn to the programs designed for certain groups. The disability pension amounts to 1.9 percent of GNP. Most disability pensions are given for medical reasons, even though workers above sixty years of age can be granted such for labor market reasons. We describe the program as a poverty trap because disability pensions are purportedly sensitive to regional or cyclic labor market conditions. Still, many persons with disability pensions have such severe medical problems that the work disincentive of the disability pension will have no effect on behavior. Active labor market measures that provide jobs, training, and rehabilitation for the disabled are workfare programs, by our definition. The expenditure on these measures is 0.8 percent of GNP. Around 2 percent of the workforce is employed with some form of subsidy for disability.

The policies for the unemployed consist of "passive" benefits and active measures that provide jobs, training, and employment service. Unemployment benefits have a work disincentive effect, but this is counteracted by temporary jobs and training slots offered to the unemployed at employment offices. A benefit claimant who refuses to accept such jobs (or other jobs) can be denied further unemployment benefits (see Björklund and Holmlund 1991).

Programs for families with children are extensive. They are designed to stimulate work by both parents. The day-care system, which covers the majority of children, is a workfare program that encourages both parents to work since both must work (or study) to qualify for day-care slots. Parents pay a fee for the child, but 80–90 percent of the costs are subsidized. Most local authorities set lower fees for the second and third child of the same family and for single parents. The child allowance (paid to the mother) is, as noted, an income effect program. The parental leave program offers benefits at the level of the

---

11. We ignore the subsidies that cover the costs of the interest payments on housing and the implicit subsidy in the deductibility of interest payments.

sickness benefit for a year for parents who have a work history and much lower support for parents who have not worked before the birth of the child and thus counts as workfare.[12] There is also a temporary parents' cash benefit paid to parents who stay home to care for sick children or for visits to the child's day care or school. This is designed to facilitate parents combining work with parenting. Finally, there is a maintenance allowance paid by the government if the noncustodial parent does not meet his obligations. This program costs the government around 0.2 percent of GNP.

All told, table 1.4 shows that 16 percent of GNP is spent on the listed programs. Nearly half the listed expenditures are workfare programs, a bit over a quarter are for programs that have an income effect on work, and a quarter are for programs that have a poverty trap component. What is impressive is that so much of the Swedish welfare system is work based.

1.1.5   What an Egalitarian Income Distribution Means

How does Sweden's distributional record translate into the economic lives of people? To answer this question, we contrast the living standards of someone in the tenth percentile of the earnings/income distribution in Sweden with a comparable person in the United States. To compare Swedish and American incomes, we use the purchasing power parity statistics of the OECD for 1990 rather than highly volatile exchange rates. In 1990, real gross domestic product per head was 26 percent higher in the United States than in Sweden (OECD 1990, 27), with the result that on average Americans had a higher living standard than Swedes. To estimate how well low-decile Swedish and American men fared, we have calculated the 1991 hourly pay in Swedish kronor of a tenth-percentile Swedish man, and then adjusted this pay for the greater inequality in pay in the United States and for the difference in overall living standards, to see how much tenth-percentile American men would make in krona purchasing power units. The results, shown in figure 1.4a, indicate that, because of the narrower distributions of pretax earnings in Sweden, bottom-decile Swedish workers earned SKr 62.00 per hour in 1991—59 percent more than the SKr 39.00 per hour that a bottom-decile American worker was paid in that year![13] Similarly, we have estimated the 1990 income (adjusted for OECD equivalence scales) of Swedish adults, twenty to sixty-four, and of children, through seventeen years of age, and then adjusted these incomes for the greater inequality in the United States and the higher living standard. Figure 1.4b

---

12. The lower basic amount is offered for three additional months for all parents.

13. Our calculations understate the difference in the earnings or income between low-decile Swedes and Americans because we used mean differences in GDP per head to adjust for differences in living standards but base our decile comparisons on calculations that compare distributions based on medians. Since mean income differences exceed median differences, this implies that we have overstated how much low-income Americans make. Note also that, over time, the advantage of the low-paid Swede has risen. The earnings of low-decile Swedes rose sharply from 1968 through 1981 and moderately thereafter; the real earnings of low-decile Americans have declined since the early 1970s (OECD 1993, table 5.3).

A
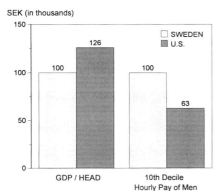

B
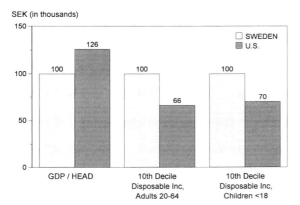

**Fig. 1.4   Comparison of relative hourly earnings (*a*) and disposable incomes (*b*)
of individuals in the tenth percentile compared to GDP per head, United States
and Sweden, 1990–91 (Sweden = 100)**

Sources: GDP per head is taken from OECD (1990, tables 1.3, 3.1).

Hourly pay. Sweden, our calculation from LNU for male workers. United States, estimated from data in OECD (1993) as follows: Table 5.2 shows that the hourly pay of a tenth-percentile American worker was 0.38 of the U.S. median in 1989 whereas the hourly pay of a tenth-percentile Swedish worker was 0.76 of the median in the same year. We multiply the SKr 62.00 by .38/.76 to obtain the earnings that a tenth-percentile American would have if Sweden had the U.S. earnings distribution. Then we multiply this figure by 1.26 to account for the higher overall income per capita in America as shown in the GDP per capita figures.

Disposable income of adults, twenty to sixty-four. Sweden, our calculation from LNU based on the OECD equivalence scales. U.S., estimated from calculations based on the Luxembourg Income Survey done by Markus Jäntti. These calculations show that in 1986 the tenth-percentile adult had disposable income, adjusted for the OECD equivalence scales, that was 0.34 of the median in the United States compared to 0.64 in Sweden. We multiply the SKr 98,700 in Sweden by .34/.64 to obtain the disposable income that a tenth-percentile American adult would have if Sweden had the U.S. income distribution, then multiply by 1.26 to account for the higher overall income in the United States.

Disposable income of children, through age seventeen. Sweden, our calculations from LNU based on the OECD equivalence scales. United States, estimated from calculations based on the Luxembourg Income Survey done by Markus Jäntti. These calculations show that in 1986 the tenth-percentile child had disposable income, adjusted for the OECD equivalence scales, that was 0.33 of the median in the United States compared to 0.59 in Sweden. We multiply the SKr 55,600 in Sweden by .33/.59 to obtain the disposable income that a tenth-percentile American child would have if Sweden had the U.S. income distribution, then multiply by 1.26 to account for the higher overall income in the United States.

Note: Similar results are obtained if we use other estimated income distribution figures. According to Atkinson, Rainwater, and Smeeding (1995, table 4.1), a low-decile person in Sweden had disposable income that was 0.56 of the median in 1987, whereas a low-decile person in the United States had disposable income that was 0.35 of the median.

shows that low-decile adults in Sweden had disposable incomes exceeding those of low-decile adults in the United States by 50 percent and that low-decile children in Sweden had disposable incomes exceeding those of low-decile children in the United States by 42 percent. The greater component of public consumption in Sweden than in the United States and the likelihood that public consumption is more equally distributed than private consumption suggests that even these contrasts understate the difference in living standards of adults and children in the lower part of the Swedish and American income distributions.

The elimination of poverty among people low in the income distribution in Sweden compared to the poverty among people low in the income distribution in the wealthier United States is a major social achievement, per the Lindbeck quote with which we introduced this section.

1.2   System or Swedes?

Comparisons of Sweden and the United States are misleading. Sweden is a small country with a homogeneous population. U.S.-Swedish differences reflect the greater heterogeneity of Americans. Shouldn't Sweden be compared to Minnesota rather than to the United States as a whole?
—A Critic

To deal with this criticism, we have developed a more refined counterfactual to assess the effects of Sweden's supposedly homogeneous population as opposed to its income determination system on distributional outcomes. Our ideal counterfactual experiment would be to move a random sample of Swedes to the United States (and Americans to Sweden) and to contrast the distribution of their incomes after some time with that of peers back home. Such an experiment would eliminate population homogeneity as a cause of differences in distributions and isolate the effect of skill formation, wage setting, taxes, and transfers. The closest we can come to this ideal with existing data is to contrast the income of people of Swedish descent in the United States with that of people in Sweden and the income in Sweden of Swedes with non-Swedish ancestry with that of Swedes with Swedish-born parents.

To identify people of Swedish background in the United States for our test of "system versus Swedes," we used the ancestry question in the 1990 U.S. Census of Population. In 1990, the question was, "What is this person's ancestry or ethnic origin?" The coding allows people to report two ancestry groups (e.g., German-Irish). If people gave *Swedish* and a second group as their ancestry, we categorized them as being of partial Swedish descent; if they gave only *Swedish* as their ancestry, we categorized them as being of full Swedish descent.[14] The 1990 census contains the records of 53,468 men of Swedish ances-

---

14. Another possible analysis would be to compare the distribution of earnings of Swedish immigrants to the United States with that of those who remain in Sweden. Because of the potential selectivity of immigrants, we chose to limit our analysis to people born in the United States with

try. In addition, we extracted a random sample of 98,181 Americans irrespective of ancestry in 1990. On the Swedish side, we have data from the LNU survey of people with Swedish parentage who grew up in Sweden (which eliminates immigrants and the children of immigrants).

Table 1.5 presents the results of our analysis in terms of the 90/10- and 10/50-decile hourly earnings ratios for male workers.[15] Row 1 gives these measures for people of Swedish ancestry raised in Sweden. Rows 2 and 3 show inequality and relative poverty for people of full and mixed Swedish descent in the United States. Finally, row 4 gives figures for all people in the United States. The results are clear: people of Swedish descent living in the United States have an earnings distribution similar to that of other Americans—a distribution utterly unlike that of Swedes in Sweden.[16] By comparing people from the same ancestry, the table isolates the effect of systems of income determination on distributions.[17]

We cannot do the counterfactual of how the descendants of American immigrants fare in Sweden: there are too few such people. We can, however, examine how adults born of all immigrants fare in Sweden. Contrary to the image of homogeneous Sweden, in 1991 in the LNU survey, 15 percent of Swedish residents aged twenty to sixty-four reported that one or two of their parents were not Swedish citizens at birth: roughly three-quarters of these people reported that the language spoken at home was something other than Swedish; and half said it was a non-Nordic language. In the 1970s and 1980s, the fraction of the Swedish population with immigrant background roughly doubled: in 1974, 8.1 percent of Swedes aged twenty to sixty-four had at least one non-Swedish parent, whereas, in 1991, 15.1 percent reported having at least one non-Swedish parent. We tabulated the hourly earnings distribution for all adults twenty to sixty-four who reported that at least one parent was not Swedish at birth (row 5 in table 1.5) and for the subset who reported that the lan-

---

Swedish ancestry. There are too few Swedish immigrants to the United States in recent years to give a reasonable comparison in any case.

15. We performed a similar analysis using the 1980 U.S. census, which coded for only a single ancestry group and obtained results like those in the table. Thus, our findings do not hinge on a particular census year.

16. There are possible selectivity problems for people of Swedish descent in the United States owing to the selectivity of their ancestors, but we doubt that this substantively affects the results. If there is a selectivity problem, it is likely that Swedes in the United States come from a more homogeneous background than Swedes in Sweden. This is because economic analysis suggests that immigrants should be drawn from similar circumstances: the top or bottom of an income distribution rather than randomly. Their descendants might have similar (although presumably much smaller) selectivity.

17. A possible problem with our contrast is that measurement error in incomes may be much larger in the U.S. data than in the Swedish data. The U.S. figures are self-reported, while the Swedish earnings data are from administrative records. But, while this might exaggerate the difference in inequality between the United States and Sweden in general, there is no reason to expect it to affect the comparison of incomes of Americans of Swedish descent with that of other Americans. And it is the absence of any discernible difference between the distributions of those two groups that is the key finding in the table.

Table 1.5   The Distribution of Earnings of Men, Sweden versus the United
                     States, 1989–91

	Earnings of Workers			
	Hourly		Annual	
	90/10	10/50	90/10	10/50
Swedes in Sweden	2.02	.77	2.74	.58
Swedish descent in United States:				
Any Swedish ancestry	5.59	.38	10.4	.20
Only Swedish ancestry	5.05	.41	7.0	.29
United States, total	5.53	.39	10.0	.21
Non-Swedes in Sweden	2.09	.71	4.27	.36
Non-Nordics in Sweden	1.85	.74	4.42	.35

Source: U.S. data are tabulated from public-use census files. We have used all the earnings/income data, including observations for which the census imputed incomes. The Census Bureau made a top-code adjustment in 1990 by giving everyone in a state with income above the top code the median income of top-coded incomes in that state. We experimented with several top codes, but they did not affect our distributions. Swedish data are tabulated from the LNU survey. The number of observations in the Swedish data is limited. There were 1,513 observations for all Swedes in 1989–91, 233 for non-Swedes, and 104 for non-Nordic Swedes. By contrast, we have 53,468 men of Swedish ancestry and a random sample of 98,181 Americans irrespective of ancestry in 1990.

guage spoken at home was neither Swedish nor another Nordic tongue (row 6 in table 1.5). For both groups, the 90/10 and 10/50 ratios of earnings are comparable to those for people with parents born in Sweden.[18] The Swedish system of wage determination produces a dispersion of earnings among those with foreign parentage that is comparable to that of other Swedes, although annual earnings are somewhat more unequally distributed among immigrants than among the native born.

We conclude that the compressed income distribution in Sweden comes, not from some inherent homogeneity of Swedes, but rather from the Swedish system of determining skills and productivity and the wages and income rewards associated with such. This conclusion leads us naturally to the question of what that system actually does to compress incomes and eliminate poverty.

1.3   The Supply Side of the Swedish System

We use a supply-demand framework to examine how Sweden combined low wage inequality and a high employment rate for so many years. Our main con-

18. Despite the fact that people of foreign ancestry earn less than others when a foreign language is spoken at home. We regressed in ln hourly earnings of men on dummy variables for their ancestry in Sweden and obtained the following coefficients and standard errors: for any parent not Swedish at birth, .060 (.037); for parent not Swedish and other Nordic language spoken at home, $-.147$ (.051); for parent not Swedish and non-Nordic language spoken at home, $-.248$ (.047).

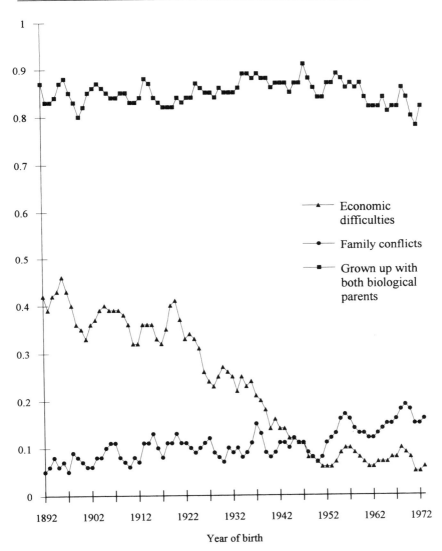

Fig. 1.5   Conditions during childhood by year of birth, 1892–1973
Source: Our own computations from the Level of Living Surveys.

trast is with the high-employment/high-inequality United States, although we occasionally consider low-employment/low-inequality EEC countries as well.

1.3.1   An Egalitarian Skill Distribution?

There are two basic ways in which Swedish practices might produce an egalitarian distribution of skills that supports a compressed wage structure: through egalitarian family incomes, which should act to reduce inequality in human capital formation at home; and through an egalitarian distribution of day-care and public school resources. To see how these factors might affect outcomes, consider a production function that relates the market skills of young people to various background resources:

(1)   skill of young $= f$ (family resources; public resources; genetics; random factors).

Equation (1) represents the transmission and augmentation of skills across generations as a simple reduced form linking resources to outcomes. We use it to examine the likely effects of the distribution of resources in one generation on the distribution of skills in the next. We have already seen that, in terms of disposable income among children, family resources are relatively equally distributed in Sweden. Children living with only one parent also fare reasonably well in terms of income (Jäntti and Danziger 1994), in contrast to the high poverty rates for them in the United States. A skeptic might, however, argue that equalization of disposable income has contributed to the breaking down of the nuclear family, with deleterious consequences for children. We find it difficult to give much credence to this claim, for the basic reason that the Swedish record in family composition is "normal." The percentages of families with children with only a single parent in the early 1980s were as follows: Sweden, 14.2 percent; Great Britain, 13 percent; Belgium and the Netherlands, 12.3 percent; Switzerland, 12 percent; Germany, 11.4 percent; France, 10.2 percent; Ireland, 7.1 percent; and the United States, 26.0 percent (Ermisch 1990). Data from the LIS reported by Danziger and Jäntti (1993) tell a similar story: 14.8 percent of children in Sweden did not live with two parents in the 1980s, compared to 12.5 percent in Canada, 10.5 percent in the Netherlands, and 23 percent in the United States.

Moreover, for Sweden, at least the most important change in family conditions over time has been an improvement in the economic conditions of families with children rather than an increase in single-parent families. This evidence comes from three questions about conditions during childhood in the Level of Living Surveys for different cohorts: whether individuals grew up with both biological parents (until age sixteen); whether their family had "economic difficulties" when they were growing up; and whether their family had "family conflicts." The results, summarized in figure 1.5, show a decline in the proportion brought up with both biological parents, from 85 percent for those born in the late 1890s through the 1960s to around 80 percent afterward; an upward shift in the proportion reporting family conflicts; and, most striking, a drop in the proportion reporting economic difficulties, from around 40 percent for the earliest cohort to less than 10 percent for those born from 1950 to the 1970s. There is evidence, moreover, that these childhood conditions affect adult outcomes: Lundberg (1993) found that adverse outcomes on all three childhood conditions variables have adverse effects on physical and mental health in adulthood, controlling for the social class of the father.

Public resources that are most likely to affect skill formation among the young are also relatively equally distributed in Sweden. The public day-care (or preschool) system (*dagis*) for children from one to seven years old contributes to equal conditions during childhood. This system, run by the local governments, was built up in the 1970s and 1980s. It offers highly subsidized places for children when both parents work (or study) at least part-time. In addition, the social authorities can place children with problems or from families with problems at the centers. Special resources are available for children with physical or social problems. Since the "graduates" of the day-care system have not yet entered the labor force in large numbers, we do not know how the system affects job performance. But two studies based on different (but rather small) data sets have found that children who participate have higher cognitive performance and are more likely to choose the academic track in high school than nonparticipant children with similar parental background (Andersson 1989; Jonsson 1994).

School resources are also relatively equally distributed. Private schools are rare; and public resources are allocated so that, as Swedes say, "the size of the parents' wallet shall not influence the school quality of the child." National tests are given to check that all schools meet certain standards. Special resources are geared toward the least-able pupils. An egalitarian attitude toward allocation of school resources is shared across the political spectrum. It is also embodied in proposed voucher systems designed to allow parents greater choice in schooling. Swedish voucher plans restrict the ways in which parents can "top up" vouchers with private spending.

Has the relatively egalitarian distribution of family or public resources been important in Sweden's attaining egalitarian labor market outcomes? Our answer, derived from crude measures of the distribution of skills and estimates of the effect of family background on labor market outcomes, is, surprisingly, that these are not major factors in Sweden's distributional record.

Consider first the distribution of the simplest indicator of human capital, years of schooling. In an ln earnings equation, the variance of ln earnings depends on the variance of schooling, the variance of returns to schooling, and their covariance. If Swedish wage compression rested primarily on a compression of skills, one might expect an especially small variance in years of schooling. But, in fact, the dispersion of years attained in Sweden is greater than in the United States. Our calculations produce a variance of years attained in Sweden of 12.25 for those aged twenty-five to sixty-four in the LNU survey. The variance of years attained in the United States was 8.96 for men in the same age group.[19]

19. The greater dispersion in years of schooling in Sweden than in the United States is also found in measures of relative variation: the coefficient of variation of years attained in Sweden is 0.33, compared to 0.23 in the United States.

Table 1.6   Test Scores in Science Achievement among Fourteen-Year-Olds in Advanced OECD Countries, 1980s

	Quartile Scores			Scores of Bottom 25%		Ratios of Quartile Scores	
	25% (1)	Median (2)	75% (3)	Mean Score (4)	25% (5)	75%/25% (6)	25%/Median (7)
Sweden	15	19	22	12.2	11	1.47	.79
United States	13	17	20	10.3	9	1.54	.76
Average for others	15	18	22	12.3	10.9	1.47	.81
Australia	15	18	22	12.2	11	1.47	.83
Canada (English-speaking regions only)	15	19	22	12.4	11	1.47	.79
England	13	17	20	10.5	9	1.54	.76
Finland	16	19	22	13.7	13	1.38	.84
Italy	13	16	20	10.4	9	1.54	.81
Japan	17	21	24	13.7	12	1.41	.81
Netherlands	16	19	23	13.1	11	1.44	.84
Norway	15	18	21	12.5	11	1.40	.83

Source: Calculated from IEA (1988, tables 5 and 6).

Notes: "%" refers to the relevant percentile, so, e.g., "75%" means "seventy-fifth percentile." The twenty-fifth percentile of the bottom twenty-fifth percentile is approximately the bottom six percent of students.

Years completed is, to be sure, a crude measure of the resources spent on schooling, much less of human capital formed in that process. In the United States, there is huge variation in the quality of schooling among schools and in achievement scores across (as well as within) schools. In some school districts, some high school graduates may be nearly illiterate. The evidence shows that Sweden has a relatively egalitarian expenditure on nonuniversity schooling. Variation in test scores across Swedish schools is much less than the variation of test scores across American schools or across the schools in many other countries.[20]

But the equalization of school spending and of test scores among schools (as well as the equalization of other public resources and of disposable incomes) has not produced a particularly narrow distribution of achievement scores among Swedish students, according to test scores from the International Association for the Evaluation of Educational Achievement (IEA). Table 1.6 presents IEA statistics on the science achievement of fourteen-year-old stu-

20. Table 7 in IEA (1988) shows that, among developed countries, Sweden, Finland, Japan, and Norway have the lowest variation in achievement scores across schools and the United States, Italy, and the Netherlands the highest. The coefficient of variation in the average score of schools for the United States is .18, which is twice the Swedish coefficient of variation, .09. The ratio of the maximum school score to the minimum school score in the United States is 3.07, compared to a ratio of 1.67 in Sweden.

dents. Columns 1–5 give the quartile scores in Sweden, the United States, and other countries included in the 1988 study. These columns also give the mean score of the bottom quartile and the bottom quartile of the bottom quartile (roughly the lowest 6 percent of students). Columns 6 and 7 give ratios of test scores for the seventy-fifth percentile student to the twenty-fifth percentile student and of the scores for the twenty-fifth percentile to the median. To facilitate comparisons, we give the average of the scores for all advanced OECD countries save Sweden and the United States as well as the scores for each country. The table shows that fourteen-year-old students have a more narrow distribution of science scores in Sweden than in the United States but that the distribution of scores among Swedish students is normal. In each statistic, Sweden has just about the average for all the countries, whereas the United States evinces greater dispersion.

While scores on school achievement tests are far from ideal measures of the dispersion in "economic ability" that presumably contributes to earnings inequality, the distributions in the table lend no support to the notion that, by equalizing opportunities among children, Sweden greatly eased the path of equalizing outcomes in the labor market.

1.3.2   The Role of Family Background

Consider next the possible effect of Sweden's compression of family income differences on the economic outcomes of children, as captured in a simple relation linking sons' earnings (Y) to fathers' earnings (X):

$$(2) \qquad \ln Y = a + b \ln X + u.$$

Taking variances yields a relation between variation in backgrounds and the b coefficient to earnings inequality:

$$(3) \qquad \mathrm{var}(\ln Y) = b^2\, \mathrm{var}\, \ln(X) + \mathrm{var}\, u.$$

The variance of the ln earnings of fathers in Sweden in the LNU ranges from 0.24 to 0.32 over the period 1967–73, for an average of 0.29 (Björklund and Jäntti 1993, table 1). This compares to variances in the U.S. Panel Study of Income Dynamics (PSID) in 1967–71 that range from 0.34 to 0.76, for an average of 0.50 (a much smaller variance than the census-based estimate in table 1.5 for all U.S. men). Given an estimate of b, we can readily calculate how much earnings inequality would rise in Sweden or fall in the United States if Swedes and Americans had the same dispersion of fathers' earnings. To estimate b, we rely on correlations between fathers' and sons' earnings in the two countries from Björklund and Jäntti. They obtain father-son correlations for the United States (based on different years and estimating techniques) that cluster around 0.40, compared to correlations for Sweden of about 0.25 (Björklund and Jäntti 1993, 18). This finding can be interpreted as higher social mobility in Sweden than in the United States.

We combine these estimates in table 1.7 to assess how much the difference

Table 1.7   **Estimates of the Effect of the Variance in Fathers' Earnings on
Sons' Earnings under Swedish and U.S. Intergenerational
Mobility Patterns**

	United States (PSID)	Sweden (LNU)	Difference
Basic data			
1. Posited variance of sons to be explained	.50	.29	.21
2. Variance of ln earnings of fathers	.50	.29	
3. Correlation, fathers' and sons' earnings	.40	.25	
4. Correlation coefficient squared	.16	.06	
5. Contribution of background to variance	.08	.02	.06
6. Residual variance	.42	.27	.15
Predicted variance of ln earnings of son given			
7. Other country's variance of fathers' ln earnings but own-country correlation of fathers' and sons' earnings	.47	.30	
8. Other country's correlation of fathers' and sons' earnings but own-country variance of fathers' ln earnings	.45	.34	
9. Other country's contribution of background, other country's correlation of fathers' and sons' earnings, and other country's variance of fathers' ln earnings	.44	.35	

Source: Calculated from statistics in Björklund and Jäntti (1993).

in variance of fathers' incomes between the United States and Sweden could account for the difference in the variance of sons' incomes. For simplicity (and to obtain as large an estimate of the contribution of background as possible), we assume a stable earnings distribution, with the result that the variance of sons' earnings is the same as that of fathers'. (In fact, the variance of sons' earnings is greater in both Sweden and the United States than of fathers' earnings, potentially reflecting life-cycle factors and trends toward increased earnings inequality.) Row 1 of the table gives the estimated variance of ln earnings: 0.50 in the United States and 0.29 in Sweden. Row 2 gives the variance of earnings of fathers. Row 3 gives the estimated correlation coefficients in the two countries. Row 4 gives the correlation coefficients squared. These figures in turn give us the estimated contribution of the variation in fathers' earnings to sons' earnings in row 5 and, by subtraction, the residual variance in row 6. The difference in residual variances of 0.15 is 71 percent of the difference in initial variances, implying that at most 29 percent of the gap in variances could be due to this background factor.

Rows 7–9 record the variance in earnings that would be found in Sweden or the United States under the counterfactuals that each country had the other's variance in fathers' earnings but its own intergenerational earnings correlation and that each had the other's intergenerational correlation but its own variance in fathers' earnings. These calculations show that giving each group the other's variance in fathers' earnings has a relatively modest effect on the final variance. If Americans had the Swedish dispersion of fathers' earnings, dispersion of earnings would fall to 0.47, .03 points of the 0.21-point gap. If Swedes had the American dispersion of fathers' earnings, the dispersion of earnings would rise to 0.30, a .01 change. Changing to the other country's intergenerational correlation in row 8 has a bigger effect on the final variances of earnings, raising the Swedish variance of the ln earnings of the son by .04 ln points (from .30 to .34). Finally, taking the full effect of the other country's contribution of background in row 9 still leaves unexplained the bulk of the gap in the variance in sons' earnings between the countries. With the contribution of background to inequality in the United States, the variance of ln earnings of sons in Sweden would rise from .29 to .35, far short of the .50 variance of ln earnings in the United States. *At most,* we can attribute 30 percent of the difference in the variance of sons' earnings to differences in the contribution of backgrounds.[21]

The lower father-son earnings correlation in Sweden than in the United States in the table is open to alternative interpretations. A human capital interpretation might be that Sweden's higher provision of social goods and use of day-care facilities for children reduce the contribution of family in the production of children's human capital. Another interpretation would be that the smaller effect of fathers' income on earnings is part of Sweden's compression of wages, which reduces the effects of skill on earnings, including skills obtained from parents. Yet another interpretation would be that Sweden has been more successful in equalizing opportunities.

However one interprets the difference in intergenerational income mobility, table 1.7 shows that equalization of parental earnings produces only limited equalization of outcomes. Equalization of background or opportunities is not sufficient to give the narrow distribution of earnings observed in Sweden. Producing an egalitarian earnings distribution requires direct intervention in the income determination process.

1.4   Demand-Side Contributions

Who demands less-able workers in Sweden at relatively high pay? What programs or policies augment the demand for these workers?

1.4.1   The Public Sector

One widely mentioned possibility is that the public sector operates as an employer of last resort, hiring people who could not obtain comparable-paying

---

21. We explain .06 points of the .21-point difference. The .06 is the difference between rows 1 and 9.

jobs in the private sector. To explore this hypothesis, we tabulated the proportion of workers employed in the public sector from the Level of Living Surveys of 1968, 1974, 1981, and 1991, categorizing level of skill in three ways. First, we use low education, specifically, whether individuals aged forty-five and older at most completed the *folkskola* (which means that they have six or seven years of schooling), as an indicator of low skill.[22] In 1968, roughly one-third of the population of older workers were in this category, but, in 1991, just about 15 percent or so had so little schooling. Thus, the extent to which the group is low-skilled increases over time. Second, we use the quartile distribution of workers by their wages. We use quartiles rather than deciles for reasons of sample size. Third, we use the health status of individuals based on their self-reported mobility from three questions: "Can you walk 100 meters relatively quickly without trouble?" "Can you run 100 meters without much trouble?" and "Can you walk up and down stairs without trouble?" We classify respondents who answer yes to all questions as having normal mobility; those who answer no to one or two questions as having reduced mobility; and those who answer no to all three as having severely limited mobility. Approximately 10–15 percent of the population report some mobility restriction, with the fraction declining over time.

Table 1.8 shows the proportion of workers in these groups working in the public sector. The percentage of less-educated older workers employed in the public sector tends to be below the percentage of all workers in the public sector, especially for men. Men with earnings in the low quartile are also no more likely to be in the public sector than men elsewhere in the earnings distribution in 1991 and less likely to be in the public sector in other years. Women with low-quartile earnings are less likely than other women workers to be in the public sector in all years. As for those with low physical mobility, in 1981 and 1991, individuals with reduced mobility are no more likely to work for the public sector than other workers. Women with severely limited mobility were, however, more likely to be public sector workers in those two years, as are men with severely limited skills in 1991. However, interpreting these figures, note that the employers of the 2 percent or so of the labor force that is handicapped or disabled receive special subsidies; about half are employed in sheltered workshops in a government-run corporation (Samhall) and half at other work sites whose wages the state subsidizes in part. Samhall is part of the public sector, and the figures for those with severely limited mobility may reflect this fact.

That low-skill workers are no more likely to be employed in the public sector in 1991 than other workers does not, however, mean that public sector employment has not buttressed demand for them. The pattern in most countries is

22. For most cohorts born after 1950, at least nine years of schooling was compulsory. Therefore, the group that we identify is an absolutely and relatively low-skilled group over the entire period.

Table 1.8   Percentage of Twenty- to Sixty-four-Year-Old Workers Employed in the Public Sector, by Quartile in the Hourly Earnings Distribution, Low-Skill, and Physical Mobility Status, 1968–91

	1968	1974	1981	1991	Change, 1968–91
			Men		
All	.18	.23	.27	.25	.07
Normal mobility	.20	.23	.27	.25	.05
Reduced mobility	.09	.20	.28	.25	.16
Severely limited mobility	.12	.18	.20	.29	.17
Less educated, 45–64	.13	.19	.20	.19	.06
Low quartile	.10	.18	.24	.29	.19
Middle quartiles	.21	.26	.34	.30	.09
High quartile	.34	.35	.33	.29	−.05
			Women		
All	.39	.48	.57	.58	.19
Normal mobility	.40	.49	.57	.58	.18
Reduced mobility	.33	.38	.55	.55	.22
Severely limited mobility	.35	.53	.64	.74	.39
Less educated, 45–64	.30	.43	.47	.58	.28
Low quartile	.28	.42	.50	.52	.24
Middle quartiles	.45	.55	.65	.66	.21
High quartile	.62	.67	.68	.61	−.01

Source: Tabulated from the Level of Living Surveys. Note that the quartile distributions exclude the self-employed.

for low-skill workers to be underrepresented in the public sector, and finding equal representation is therefore surprising. As the last column in table 1.8 shows, moreover, the proportion of low-skill workers in the public sector increased from 1968 to 1991. We interpret the upward trend and their proportionate representation in Sweden as signs that the public sector has, indeed, been a greater demander of their labor than in other countries.

1.4.2   The Disabled or Handicapped

Handicapped or disabled workers are likely to have lower productivity than other workers, and in many countries these workers are among the poorest. In Sweden, they have relatively normal incomes. Determining how Sweden does this provides an important insight into the Swedish workfare system and clues into the way the Swedish system treats other, less clearly defined, low-productivity groups.

Sweden seeks to get the disabled jobs at wages above their marginal product. As noted, Samhall employs a substantial proportion of these workers; it pays the normal rate for a job and receives half of its budget from the state rather than from the sales of goods. In normal years, about half the budget of the Swedish Labor Market Board is spent on the employment of disabled/handicapped workers. Table 1.9 records the work time of people in Sweden with differing levels of disability, as measured by responses to the questions on mobility in 1981 and 1991. A high proportion of people with reduced or severely limited mobility work, with relatively high contracted hours: only 5 percent or so below the hours worked by persons with normal mobility. This implies that short working hours have not enabled the disabled to get jobs in Sweden. However, in table 1.9, the panel C data on sickness days show that those with reduced or severely limited mobility take many more sickness days than others— three to five times as much among men and two to three times as much among women.

Figures on sick days display the two sides of a welfare state that makes benefits contingent on working. On the one side, the sickness pay program maintains the incomes of those who suffer disabilities. On the other side, the program gives workers disincentive to work once they have a job. Take the disincentive effect first, as economists often do. If we assume that the typical full-time Swedish worker takes five weeks of vacation and two weeks of holiday, he or she would work forty-five weeks a year. The figures for people with normal mobility show that, in 1981, they took an additional three weeks of sickness time, giving forty-two weeks of actual time worked in a year (which

Table 1.9   **Employment Rates, Working Hours, and Sickness Days of Swedish Adults, Twenty to Sixty-four**

	Males		Females	
	1981	1991	1981	1991
A. Percentage at Work at Time of Interview				
Normal mobility	.93	.90	.83	.87
Reduced mobility	.77	.68	.61	.65
Severely limited mobility	.65	.63	.46	.54
B. Annual Contractual Hours Conditional on Work				
Normal mobility	2,040	2,030	1,490	1,680
Reduced mobility	2,030	2,000	1,480	1,660
Severely limited mobility	1,950	2,110	1,460	1,550
C. Annual Sickness Days Conditional on Work				
Normal mobility	13	15	16	22
Reduced mobility	52	81	40	77
Severely limited mobility	75	102	66	105

Source: Level of Living Surveys. Note that the data in panels B and C refer to the previous calendar year.

is consistent with the 1,654 or so hours reported for full-time Swedish workers in OECD [1990, table 1.4]). This is an extraordinarily high rate, as in most countries people have much less sick time; American workers average about a week in workdays lost because of sickness (U.S. Bureau of the Census 1992, table 188). OECD statistics show that 6.1 percent of Swedish work time is lost owing to illness, versus 1.2 percent of U.S. work time (OECD 1991, table 6.3). As there is no reason to believe that Swedes are more sickly than non-Swedes (expected life spans would suggest the opposite, and occupational illness is, if anything, lower in Sweden than in other countries [OECD 1989a, chap. 4]), we interpret this as reflecting economic responsiveness to incentives. Under the prereform Swedish sick-leave system, sick time was paid exclusively by the government, so neither workers nor firms had an incentive to minimize sick time. Indeed, the opposite was probably true in many situations. Just as seasonal employers in the United States and their prospective workers know that part of the job involves several months of unemployment insurance during the off season, Swedish employers may have found that implicitly approving that workers exploit the sick-time system made their workplace more attractive to employees.

To see the redistributive part of Swedish sickness pay policy, assume that the difference in sickness days between workers with reduced or severely limited mobility and those with normal mobility is in fact due to physical problems. Men with limited mobility take roughly nine weeks of sickness leave beyond what men with normal mobility take, working just thirty-three weeks over the year or 21 percent less than men with normal mobility. Does this produce a 21 percent or so difference in annual earnings or a large difference in hourly earnings? To answer this question, we regressed the ln hourly earnings and ln annual earnings of Swedish workers on age, age squared, years of schooling, and dummy variables for mobility status in 1981. We estimate that the hourly earnings of men with reduced mobility were just $-.06$ ln points lower than those of men with normal mobility, with a standard error of .04; similarly, we estimate that the hourly earnings of men with severely limited mobility were just $-.02$, with a standard error of .04. For annual earnings, we found no difference by mobility status: the regression coefficients (standard errors) were .02 (.09) for severely limited mobility and .00 (.07) for those with reduced mobility.

Save for the fact that women work fewer hours on average because they are more likely to work part-time than men, results for women are the same. In 1991, the typical female worker contracted for forty-two weeks of full-time work (= 1,680/40); in 1981, she worked 37.3 weeks (= 1,490/40). Assuming that she took five weeks of vacation time and two weeks of holiday time, she worked 30.3 weeks in 1981. Table 1.9 shows that she also took 3.5 weeks of sickness days; therefore, she worked about twenty-seven weeks full-time over the year. The woman with reduced mobility worked about five weeks less than this (twenty-two weeks), whereas the woman with severely limited mobility worked nearly ten weeks less (seventeen weeks of full-time labor). Thus, those with less than normal mobility worked 19–37 percent less than women with normal mobility. But neither the hourly wages nor the annual earnings of women with mobility limitations were lower than those of women without mobility limitations.

Our results are not peculiar to the LNU survey or our definitions of work disability: Wadensjö (1984, table 14.6) reports similar results in the 1978 Living Conditions Survey. At a cost of excessive use of sickness days by nondisabled workers, Sweden's sickness pay system has kept disabled/handicapped workers close to the median of the annual earnings distribution.

By contrast, consider how workers who are handicapped or disabled fare in the United States. For this purpose, we use the 1990 U.S. Census of Population, which asks workers the following:

> Because of a health condition that has lasted for 6 or more months, does this person have any difficulty—
> a. going outside the home alone, for example, to shop or visit a doctor's office?
> b. taking care of his or her own personal needs, such as bathing, dressing, or getting around inside the home?

In addition, the U.S. census asked:

> Did this person have a physical, mental, or other health condition that lasted for 6 or more months and which—
> a. limits the kind or amount of work this person can do at a job?
> b. prevents this person from working at a job?

To parallel the Swedish mobility questions, we defined disabled workers in three ways. Our first group of disabled workers consists of those who answered yes to any health/physical condition question. Twelve percent of U.S. men aged twenty to sixty-four answered yes at least once. This compares to 11 percent of the Swedish men whom we categorized as having some mobility limitation. Our second group consists of those who answered yes to at least two of these health/physical questions; this is comparable to our definition in the Swedish data of individuals who are severely limited, and in fact 3 percent of U.S. men were in this category, just as 3 percent of Swedish men were in the comparable category. Our third group consists of men who answered yes only once to the three questions; this is comparable to our definition in the Swedish data of persons having reduced mobility.

The U.S. data show that, in the United States, work disability has a massive adverse effect on whether the worker was employed in the survey week.[23] Workers with no disability had an 85 percent employment rate (which compares to the 90 percent rate in Sweden), but those with at least some disability had a 45 percent employment rate (which compares to 68 percent in Sweden).

---

23. Our subsample from the census had 138,531 observations, and therefore all the differences among groups are highly statistically significant.

Only 22 percent of the men who answered yes two or more times to the disability questions worked (which compares to 63 percent in Sweden). To see how the disabled fared in terms of earnings, we regressed the ln hourly earnings and ln annual earnings of American men on age, age squared, years of schooling,[24] and dummy variables for disability status and obtained huge negative coefficients and small standard errors. We estimate that the hourly earnings of men with some disability was $-.16$ (standard error .01) ln points lower than for men with normal mobility and that the annual earnings of men with some disability was $-.49$ (standard error .01) ln points lower than for men with normal mobility.

1.4.3   Earnings Equalization, Relative Prices, Shadow Wages

If low-skill workers are paid more in Sweden than they would be paid in a more market-driven system of wage setting, someone must foot the bill for the higher wages of those workers. In the case of the disabled, it is clear that the rest of society pays by subsidizing their employers or their sickness days. Might something similar be true of other low-skill workers? Does Sweden "pay" for its egalitarian wage policies and full employment through higher prices for the goods produced by the less skilled?

In traded goods, where the price of the commodity is given on world markets, it is presumably not possible to shift the cost of higher wages for the less skilled to consumers. In nontraded goods and services, however, a large share of the increased wages for the less skilled may very well be borne by consumers. If this were the case, we would expect the prices of commodities or services produced by low-wage workers to be relatively higher in Sweden than in the United States, which does not have a compressed wage structure. By contrast, if the compressed wage structure was due solely to a compressed skill distribution, we would not expect to find such a pattern since the cost of an efficiency unit of labor would be no higher in Sweden than in the United States.

We have not explored the relation between relative prices and the share of low-skill labor across sectors and can report only glimmers of evidence on this possible relation. Comparative dollar price levels of final expenditures from the OECD show that Sweden has high relative prices in one nontraded goods sector that hires relatively many low-skill workers—restaurants, cafés, and hotels. The comparative dollar price in Sweden is 1.27 times the price of GDP in purchasing power parity terms, while in the United States it is 0.84 (OECD 1990, table 2.6)—a 51 percent difference in relative prices. In that sector, moreover, labor costs are 73 percent of value added compared to 50 percent in the United States. By contrast, in the finance sector, where workers are relatively skilled, labor's share is 36 percent of value added in the United States,

---

24. The 1990 U.S. Census of Population does not contain a simple years of schooling measure, so we coded the reported highest level of education into a years variable for comparison with the Swedish data.

compared to 31 percent in Sweden (OECD 1989b). To the extent that high collectively bargained wages for low-skill workers are passed on to Swedish consumers in the form of high prices, the consumers are "indirectly" subsidizing those workers.

Finally, and more speculatively, consider the possible effect of the compression of hours worked in Sweden on the demand for less-able workers. Could it be that Sweden has generated demand for less-productive workers by effectively reducing hours worked by more productive substitute workers, creating an implicit system of work sharing? On the supply side, assume that high marginal taxes, the five-week mandated vacation, holiday time, the incentive to call in sick, and parental leave all reduce the hours worked by more able Swedes. This implies that, on the demand side of the market, a firm that would like to hire twenty-six hundred hours from Mr. Able finds that he is willing to work only sixteen hundred hours unless he is paid a substantial premium. If that premium exceeds his value to the firm, the firm will try to get the extra thousand hours from someone else. In effect, the firm faces a shadow cost for an extra hour of a more productive worker far above the hourly wage. What will the firm do? Hire Mr. Less Able to take up the slack. By this argument, Swedish policies that compress wages and provide incentives to work less than the contracted hours have produced massive "work sharing." Raising the shadow price for skilled workers relative to less-skilled workers can, in principle, "undo" the effect of wage compression in reducing demand for the less skilled.

Is there any evidence that creating incentives that limit the hours worked by the more able increases the demand for labor of other workers? What plausibly might happen to the demand for less-able Swedes if, say, the more able worked 30 percent more hours than they currently do (which would give the upper decile of Swedes the same hours worked as in the United States)?

We have not estimated the demand for labor necessary to answer these questions but draw the reader's attention to studies of the trade-off between hours worked and employment, which suggest that, for workers doing similar work, our hypothesis is on the right track. Houpis's (1993) summary of studies of the hours/employment trade-off for the United Kingdom, the United States, Belgium, and Sweden (Pencavel and Holmlund 1988) shows a uniform trade-off with elasticities that range around 0.7. That is, a 10 percent reduction in hours worked is associated with increases in the number employed of about 7 percent.[25] Applied to the entire economy, these estimates suggest that there is a substantial hours/employment trade-off consistent with an "implicit-work-sharing" explanation of part of the puzzle identified in figure 1.3 above: how

25. The analyses of Ehrenberg and Schumann (1982) and others of how demand for labor responds to the premium for overtime (which would reduce hours worked) tell a similar story. They show that, if the United States raised its overtime premium from 1.5 to 2 times the base wage, manufacturing employment would increase by 3 percent.

Sweden managed to combine full employment and a narrow wage distribution.[26]

1.5   Conclusion: Consequences of Reforms and Crisis

This paper has documented the great success of the Swedish welfare state in eliminating poverty and reducing inequality and in combining low dispersion in wages and high employment. Our evidence suggests that much of the success in reducing poverty was due to Sweden's tax and transfer systems and that the combination of high employment and low wage inequality was associated with factors that directly or indirectly twisted labor demand in favor of less-skilled workers. We have also advanced an interpretation of the Swedish experience that highlights the compression of hours worked on the demand for less-skilled workers.

The redistribution and elimination of poverty did not come without cost to Sweden. The huge welfare state that developed in the 1970s and 1980s had both a direct cost in terms of high taxes and indirect costs in the form of excess burdens and disincentives (see Aronsson and Walker, chap. 5 in this volume). As Sweden entered the 1990s, there was widespread opinion among economists that the nation should withdraw from some of its welfare state commitments: the costs of some programs at least seemed to exceed their benefits. The economic crisis and huge budget deficits of the early 1990s also seemed to demand cutbacks in welfare state programs.

How far has Sweden already gone in this "withdrawal from dangerous territory"? What are the consequences for the elimination of poverty? How far can Sweden go in reducing the excesses of the welfare state without seriously threatening the great success of that state in eliminating poverty?

The policy reforms put into place through 1992 do not appear seriously to threaten the country's reduction of poverty. The 1991 tax reform reduced the progressivity of the system but mitigated the effects on lower-income families through higher child allowances and housing allowances. Our table 1.3 showed a sizable rise in inequality (the 90/10 spread) of disposable income from 1990 to 1991 but no increase in relative poverty (the 10/50 spread). The rise in inequality did not continue in 1992 even though factor income inequality became much more unequal owing in large part to increased unemployment.

There have been a substantial number of budget cuts since 1991 that are difficult to describe with a single statistic, and we accordingly discuss only a few, to give the flavor of the ongoing reforms and some of the suggested changes. To help our discussion, we use table 1.10, which gives the distributional profile of three important transfers: sickness benefits, unemployment

26. We also recognize that at some point reductions in hours by at least some of the more able should decrease the demand for the less skilled. Certainly, reductions in the work activity of entrepreneurs or inventors or others whose skills complement those of the less skilled are likely to have adverse effects on the demand for unskilled labor.

Table 1.10   **Disposable Income, Sick Pay, Unemployment Benefits, and Child Allowance (general and progressive part) by Quartile Group in 1990 Distribution of Adjusted Disposable Income (SKr 1,000)**

	Lowest	Second	Third	Fourth
	All 20–64 Years, by Quartile Group			
Mean adjusted DI	48.5	74.1	95.2	139.3
Sick pay	3.6	5.8	7.5	7.9
	(7)	(8)	(8)	(6)
Unemployment benefits	1.1	1.5	1.0	.9
	(2)	(2)	(1)	(1)
Child allowance (general)	2.6	2.2	1.0	.4
	(5)	(3)	(1)	(0)
Child allowance (progressive)	.4	.1	.0	.0
	(1)	(0)	(0)	(0)
	Children 0–17 Years			
Mean adjusted DI	45.7	64.3	77.7	105.8
Sick pay	11.5	11.4	14.5	10.8
	(25)	(18)	(18)	(11)
Unemployment benefits	2.21	2.9	2.2	1.8
	(5)	(5)	(3)	(2)
Child allowance (general)	18.3	15.9	13.0	10.7
	(40)	(25)	(17)	(10)
Child allowance (progressive)	5.8	3.0	1.0	.4
	(13)	(5)	(1)	(0)

Source: Our own tabulations from the Level of Living Surveys.

Note: DI = disposable income. Numbers in parentheses are percentages of DI.

benefits (unemployment insurance plus cash assistance) and child allowances. The table shows the importance of these transfers in the four quartile groups of the distributions of adjusted disposable income for the adults aged twenty to sixty-four and children through age seventeen on whom we have focused. When the share of income attributable to a given transfer is greater for those with low incomes than for those with high incomes, the transfer reduces relative inequality and lowers relative poverty. Conversely, when the share of income from a transfer is smaller for those with lower incomes than for those with higher incomes, the transfer is regressive.

The table shows that, for adults aged twenty to sixty-four, the share of disposable income attributable to sick pay is rather evenly distributed among income classes: the fraction of disposable income for adults is roughly the same in the highest-quartile group as in the lowest-quartile group.[27] This presumably

---

27. The figures in the table exaggerate the amount of sickness benefits relative to disposable income because the benefits are measured gross of taxes when in fact they are taxable.

reflects the widespread use of sickness benefits in Sweden noted earlier. Unemployment benefits constitute a larger proportion of the disposable income of low-income than high-income individuals, but, given the low rate of unemployment in 1990, such benefits are just a minor share of the income of any adult group. The unemployment benefit share of disposable income is likely to be higher for all groups in 1992–94, when unemployment rose sharply, and we would guess that the share would rise more for low-income than high-income individuals, but our data are silent on this point. The most progressive benefits are child allowance benefits, which constitute a much larger proportion of the income of low-quartile than of high-quartile individuals.

The bottom part of the table shows that, for children through age seventeen, all the benefits, including sick pay (for the parents of children), are a considerably higher proportion of disposable income for those from low-income families than for those from higher-income families. Sickness benefits paid to the parents of children in the lowest quartile account for 25 percent of disposable income, compared to 11 percent of disposable income paid to parents whose children are in the highest quartile. Thus, with the exception of sickness benefits for all adults, the transfers in the table are progressive, generally highly so.[28]

How are these benefit systems changing? What are the likely consequences of change for the distribution of incomes?

The sickness benefit system has undergone several changes. In March 1991, the replacement rate for sickness was reduced from 90 to 65 percent for the first three days, left at 90 percent until the ninetieth day, then reduced to 80 percent thereafter. In 1992, employers were required to pay for the first two weeks of sickness benefits, giving them an incentive to monitor the program. In 1993, a waiting period of one day was introduced so that the worker would also lose something by calling in sick. At this writing, there is discussion of further reductions in the replacement rate to 70 percent or to as low as 50 percent. These changes will reduce the earnings of disabled or sick workers but, according to the calculations in table 1.10, are not likely to change inequality or relative poverty. However, they will redistribute income against children in the lower quartile of the distribution unless reductions in benefits disproportionately increase the work time of low-income parents.

In 1993, benefits to unemployed workers were also reduced. The replacement rate dropped from 90 to 80 percent, and a waiting period of one week

---

28. These results can be sensitive to the equivalence scales and to the way the scales treat the costs of having additional children. The Swedish scales do not allow for economies of scale for additional children: the cost of an extra child is the same as the cost of the first child. This raises the possibility that the progressivity of the child allowance is due largely to the equivalence scale. To see if this is the case, we computed a version of table 1.10 with an equivalence scale that allows for economies of scale in children by using a square root of the number of people in the family (see Atkinson, Rainwater, and Smeeding 1995). The child allowance benefits become less progressive with this scale but remain strongly progressive.

was introduced. Similarly, the benefits paid in various training and temporary job programs were also lowered modestly. Some policy makers and analysts favor further reductions in replacement rates to 70 or 60 percent. Read conservatively, the figures in table 1.10 suggest that this will increase inequality but may have little effect on relative poverty since the second quartile receives a similar fraction of disposable income in unemployment benefits as the first. However, we are loathe to make any strong statement on this owing to the massive change in unemployment, which could easily affect the distribution of benefits.

By contrast with sickness pay and unemployment benefits, there have been no reductions in child allowances, although some analysts have proposed such. In 1991, in fact, child allowances were raised to counteract the consequences of the tax reform on children with parents in the lower part of the income distribution. As child allowances are the most progressive transfer in table 1.10, they are an extremely well-targeted benefit, helping children from low-income homes much more than those from high-income homes. Reductions in child allowances, and in particular the discontinuation of the progressive part of the benefit, would raise overall inequality and relative poverty, potentially substantially.[29] Indeed, the low-income profile of this transfer is so distinct that it is an appealing strategy to raise it, in order to counteract the effects of other reductions in welfare state benefits on the well-being of children. This was, indeed, the strategy in the 1991 tax reform.

Another important set of changes has been the imposition of fees for public services. For instance, the fee for child care has been raised substantially. Local governments, which have been forbidden to raise taxes for several years, have been forced to cut expenditures or raise fees. Again, however, our sense is that these changes are more "tinkering" on the edges rather than a major backing away from the welfare state.

A sanguine reading of the ongoing changes is that, while they may lower the Swedish safety net, that net is so high that it will require something akin to a revolution to endanger Sweden's success in eliminating poverty: Mrs. Thatcher cutting the net with a pair of scissors, not the Economics Commission's 113 suggested changes, however one views them. A less sanguine reading of the changes is that over the long run some developments (lower taxes and less statutory vacation time, e.g.) may reduce the twist in labor demand toward the less skilled that tied work, a compressed wage structure, and welfare so closely together in the country. If the 1993 increase in Swedish unemployment marks the beginning of an era of relatively high unemployment, moreover, the welfare state taxes and transfers that have been such an important part of Sweden's way of generating equality and eliminating poverty

29. We note that this result is sensitive to the equivalence scale that we use. While the direction of the effect will be the same with other scales, the magnitude could differ substantively.

could become so costly that the country will respond with further reductions in these programs, with far greater effects on income distribution than those that we have documented in this study.

Appendix

The standard approach to analyzing how taxes and transfers affect incomes compares the distribution of income generated by the "market" with the distribution after taxes and transfers—that is, disposable income. In the text, we use the standard concept of *factor incomes* to reflect market incomes. This concept, however, has some shortcomings that suggest the value of a more detailed picture of how taxes and transfers modify the outcome that the market generates. Accordingly, in this appendix, we examine measures of inequality in various income measures derived from the Income Distribution Surveys (HINK) of Statistics Sweden.

Factor income (*faktorinkomst*) consists of wages and salaries for employed workers and the equivalent salary for self-employed workers. It also includes income from capital and realized capital gains. It excludes sickness and parental allowances in spite of the fact that these benefits are closely tied to previous work. The basic components of income from work are wages and salaries for employed and self-employed individuals (*arbetsinkomst*). This includes the closely work-related sickness and parental leave allowances as well as the "stipends" for retraining unemployed workers. Note that these three transfers are taxable. Total income after deductions for deficits in some sources of income (*sammanräknad nettoinkomst*), finally, consists of total taxable income from all sources of income, like work (including all taxable transfers), income from capital, income from realized capital gains, and income from own estate and own business. It also includes the closely work-related transfers included in retirement pensions that are also related to previous work activity.

Tables 1A.1 and 1A.2 present measures of dispersion for the three income concepts plus disposable income for selected years from 1975 until 1991. We use the same groups as in the text, namely, adults twenty to sixty-four years old (in table 1A.1) and children through age seventeen (in table 1A.2). We also use (as in the main text) the household as the unit of income, the individual as the unit of analysis, and the Swedish equivalence scales.

Factor incomes have the most unequal and erratic pattern. The marked rise in inequality that can be found in factor income is not as dramatic in income from work and total income. This reflects the importance of sickness and parental leave allowances for families in the age groups that we consider. The

Table 1A.1   **Inequality of Various Income Concepts, Adults Twenty to Sixty-four Years**

	Factor Income	Income from Work	Total Income	Disposable Income
		90/10 Ratios		
1975	6.87	6.08	4.21	2.57
	(.842)	(.327)	(.302)	(.212)
1980	8.19	7.22	3.68	2.44
	(.342)	(.327)	(.276)	(.197)
1985	8.72	7.12	3.91	2.44
	(.357)	(.333)	(.276)	(.244)
1988	9.57	7.21	3.80	2.39
	(.358)	(.325)	(.276)	(.203)
1989	9.46	7.17	3.72	2.41
	(.360)	(.322)	(.280)	(.205)
1990	9.64	6.85	3.86	2.49
	(.365)	(.323)	(.290)	(.213)
1989[a]	9.62	7.36	N.D.	2.53
	(.368)	(.324)		(.224)
1990[a]	9.44	6.94	N.D.	2.58
	(.372)	(.325)		(.229)
1991[a]	12.76	8.99	N.D.	2.67
	(.392)	(.345)		(.245)
1992[a]	18.74	15.25	N.D.	2.68
	(.397)	(.366)		(.235)
		10/50 Ratios		
1975	.27	.29	.42	.59
1980	.22	.23	.45	.60
1985	.21	.25	.43	.63
1988	.20	.24	.44	.63
1989	.20	.24	.44	.63
1990	.19	.25	.43	.61
1989[a]	.20	.24	N.D.	.62
1990[a]	.20	.25	N.D.	.60
1991[a]	.15	.20	N.D.	.60
1992[a]	.10	.12	N.D.	.60

Note: Gini coefficients are given in parentheses. N.D. = not defined in same manner after tax reform.

[a]New definition.

detailed tables from the HINK project reveal that these two transfers, which are included in income from work, are higher than income from capital and capital gains, which are included in factor income.

In table 1A.3, we look at income from work in a more detailed way; for men, women, and both sexes individually and for families with the individual as the unit of analysis. In the latter case, equivalence scales are applied. The

Table 1A.2   **Inequality of Various Income Concepts, Children through
                     Seventeen Years**

	Factor Income	Income from Work	Total Income	Disposable Income
		90/10 Ratios		
1975	4.24	3.85	3.65	2.22
	(.301)	(.284)	(.282)	(.181)
1980	4.87	4.36	3.46	2.27
	(.306)	(.288)	(.268)	(.184)
1985	4.39	3.87	3.51	2.07
	(.303)	(.275)	(.268)	(.166)
1988	4.79	3.70	3.41	2.02
	(.308)	(.267)	(.256)	(.164)
1989	5.71	4.17	3.65	2.10
	(.331)	(.277)	(.280)	(.177)
1990	6.15	4.05	3.80	2.11
	(.388)	(.281)	(.285)	(.179)
1989[a]	5.85	4.27	N.D.	2.19
	(.341)	(.280)		(.197)
1990[a]	6.09	4.08	N.D.	2.16
	(.347)	(.282)		(.197)
1991[a]	7.47	4.43	N.D.	2.23
	(.359)	(.291)		(.200)
1992[a]	13.29	5.72	N.D.	2.23
	(.370)	(.321)		(.297)
		10/50 Ratios		
1975	.43	.45	.48	.67
1980	.37	.40	.48	.65
1985	.39	.42	.47	.68
1988	.36	.44	.48	.69
1989	.32	.39	.47	.68
1990	.29	.41	.45	.68
1989[a]	.32	.39	N.D.	.68
1990[a]	.30	.41	N.D.	.67
1991[a]	.25	.38	N.D.	.67
1992[a]	.14	.30	N.D.	.67

Note: Gini coefficients are given in parentheses. N.D. = not defined in same manner after tax
reform.
[a]New definition.

figures reveal an increase in inequality for men irrespective of the measure of
inequality that is used. The opposite pattern is found for women up to 1990.
This development for women reflects the shift from part-time to full-time work
that took place during the 1980s. Even for women there was, however, a marked
increase in inequality from 1990 to 1991. For both sexes together there is also
a downward trend in inequality up to 1990, when there was a marked rise.

Table 1A.3   Inequality of Income from Work with the Individual and the Family as Units of Income, Adults Twenty to Sixty-four Years

	Men	Women	Both Sexes	Family
		Individual		
		90/10 Ratios		
1975	4.98	N.R.	N.R.	6.08
	(.293)	(.494)	(.418)	(.327)
1980	5.83	N.R.	N.R.	7.22
	(.300)	(.411)	(.376)	(.327)
1985	11.62	N.R.	46.97	7.12
	(.327)	(.362)	(.367)	(.333)
1988	10.39	N.R.	20.66	7.21
	(.318)	(.339)	(.349)	(.325)
1989	11.34	128.67	20.71	7.17
	(.317)	(.333)	(.347)	(.322)
1990	10.30	73.50	17.34	6.85
	(.323)	(.331)	(.348)	(.323)
1989[a]	12.04	131.75	N.A.	7.36
	(.322)	(.335)		(.324)
1990[a]	8.13	74.73	77.85	6.94
	(.324)	(.332)	(.350)	(.325)
1991[a]	22.92	61.09	30.72	8.99
	(.353)	(.337)	(.366)	(.345)
		10/50 Ratios		
1975	.33	0	0	.29
1980	.27	0	0	.23
1985	.14	0	.04	.25
1988	.16	0	.08	.24
1989	.14	.01	.08	.24
1990	.16	.02	.10	.25
1989[a]	.14	.01	N.A.	.24
1990[a]	.16	.02	.10	.25
1991[a]	.07	.03	.06	.20

Note: Gini coefficients are given in parentheses. Zeroes are zero because we include people with no income. N.A. = not available. N.R. = not relevant because base is zero.
[a]New definition.

When we use the family as the unit of income and divide the income from work for both spouses by the equivalent number of adults in the family, inequality is remarkably stable from 1975 to 1990. In addition, the 90/10 and 10/50 ratios reveal much more equal distributions for families than for individuals.

Finally, note that tables 1A.1 and 1A.2 show that disposable income is much more equally distributed than total income. Because the main difference between total income and disposable income is taxes and nontaxable transfers, this illustrates the equalizing effects of these parts of the welfare state.

References

Andersson, B.-E. 1989. Effects of public day care: A longitudinal study. *Child Development* 60:857–66.
Atkinson, Anthony, Lee Rainwater, and Timothy Smeeding. 1995. *Income distribution in OECD countries: The evidence from the Luxembourg Income Study (LIS).* Paris: OECD.
Björklund, Anders, and Richard B. Freeman. 1994. Generating equality and eliminating poverty, the Swedish way. Working Paper no. 4945. Cambridge, Mass.: National Bureau of Economic Research.
Björklund, Anders, and Bertil Holmlund. 1991. The economics of unemployment insurance: The case of Sweden. In *Labor market policy and unemployment insurance,* ed. A. Björklund, R. Haveman, R. Hollister, and B. Holmlund. London: Oxford University Press.
Björklund, Anders, and Markus Jäntti. 1993. Intergenerational income mobility in Sweden compared to the United States. Swedish Institute for Social Research Working Paper no. 1993:4. Stockholm: Stockholm University.
Björklund, Anders, Mårten Palme, and Ingemar Svensson. 1995. Tax reforms and income distribution—an assessment using different income concepts. *Swedish Economic Policy Review* 2, no. 2:229–65.
Coder, John, Lee Rainwater, and Timothy Smeeding. 1989. Inequality among children and elderly in ten modern nations: The United States in an international context. *American Economic Review* 79, no. 2:320–24.
Danziger, Sheldon, and Markus Jäntti. 1993. The market economy, the welfare state, and the economic well-being of children: Evidence from four countries. Åbo Akademi University, Finland. Mimeo.
Ehrenberg, Ronald, and Paul Schumann. 1982. *Longer hours or more jobs? An investigation of amending hours legislation to create employment.* Ithaca, N.Y.: New York School of Industrial Relations.
Erikson, Robert, and Rune Åberg. 1987. *Welfare in transition.* Oxford: Clarendon.
Ermisch, John. 1990. Demographic aspects of the growing number of lone parent families. In *Lone parent families—the economic challenge,* OECD. Paris.
Flanagan, Robert. 1987. Efficiency and equality in Swedish labor markets. In *The Swedish economy,* ed. B. Bosworth and A. Rivlin. Washington, D.C.: Brookings.
Freeman, Richard. 1994. How labor fares in advanced countries. In *Working under different rules,* ed. R. Freeman. New York: Russell Sage Foundation.
Gustafsson, Björn, and Hannu Uusitalo. 1990. Income distribution and redistribution during two decades—experiences from Finland and Sweden. In *Generating equality in the welfare state: The Swedish experience,* ed. I. Persson. Oslo: Norwegian University Press.
Hibbs, Douglas. 1990. Wage dispersion and trade union action in Sweden. In *Generating equality in the welfare state: The Swedish experience,* ed. I. Persson. Oslo: Norwegian University Press.
Houpis, George. 1993. The effect of lower hours of work on wages and employment. Discussion Paper no. 131. London: London School of Economics, Centre for Economic Performance.

International Association for the Evaluation of Educational Achievement (IEA). 1988. *Science achievement in seventeen countries: A preliminary report.* Oxford: Pergamon.

Jäntti, Markus, and Sheldon Danziger. 1994. Work, welfare, and child poverty in Sweden and the United States. *Industrial and Labor Relations Review* 48, no. 1 (October): 48–64.

Jonsson, Jan O. 1994. Förskola—en strategi for jämlikhet? In *Sorteringen i skolan,* ed. R. Erikson and J. Jonsson. Stockholm: Carlssons.

Kangas, Olli, and Joakim Palme. 1993. Statism eroded? Labor market benefits and challenges to the Scandinavian welfare states. In *Welfare trends in the Scandinavian countries,* ed. E. J. Hansen, S. Ringen, H. Uusitalo, and R. Erikson. New York: M. E. Sharpe.

Lindbeck, Assar. 1992. *The welfare state: The selected papers of Assar Lindbeck.* Vol. 2. London: Edward Elgar.

Lundberg, Olle. 1993. The impact of childhood living conditions on illness and mortality. *Social Science and Medicine* 36, no. 8:1047–52.

National Labor Market Board. Various years. *Annual report.* Stockholm: National Labor Market Board.

National Social Insurance Board. 1992. *Social insurance statistics facts.* National Social Insurance Board, Stockholm.

OECD. 1989a. *Employment outlook.* Paris.

———. 1989b. *National accounts of OECD countries.* Vol. 1. Paris. (Published annually).

———. 1990. *Purchasing power parities and real expenditures.* Paris.

———. 1991. *Historical statistics, 1960–1989.* Paris.

———. 1993. *Employment outlook.* Paris.

Pencavel, John, and Bertil Holmlund. 1988. The determination of wages, employment, and hours of work in an economy with centralised wage-setting: Sweden, 1950–1983. *Economic Journal* 98:1105–26.

Samhall. Various years. *Annual report.* Stockholm: Samhallsförlag.

U.S. Bureau of the Census. 1992. *Statistical abstract, 1991.* Washington, D.C.: U.S. Government Printing Office.

———. 1993. *Statistical Abstract, 1992.* Washington, D.C.: U.S. Government Printing Office.

Wadensjö, Eskil. 1984. Disability policy in Sweden. In *Public policy toward disabled workers: Cross-national analyses of economic impacts,* ed. R. Haveman, V. Halberstadt, and R. Buckhauser. Ithaca, N.Y.: Cornell University Press.

World Bank. 1993. *World development report 1993.* New York: Oxford University Press.

2   Public Employment, Taxes, and the Welfare State in Sweden

Sherwin Rosen

2.1   The Issues

Public employment accounts for about one-third of employment in Sweden today. Its rapid growth reflects growth in the welfare state. Beginning in the early 1960s, virtually all employment growth in Sweden has been the result of women entering the labor force and working in local government jobs that service the welfare system. Fertility in Sweden is among the highest in Europe, especially considering the high female labor force participation rate.

The rising labor force participation of women and the increasing role of the state in social insurance are worldwide trends in the twentieth century. But in few other countries has the public sector grown so fast or achieved such a large scale relative to the economy as in Sweden and other Scandinavian countries. Public employment and public outlays are from 50 to 100 percent larger than in most developed countries. The standard of living is high in Sweden. However, the causal linkages from the welfare state to economic fortunes are tenuous. Sweden had achieved one of the highest per capita incomes in the world well before the Swedish model was implemented. Perhaps it was the great wealth generated by the Swedish economy that allowed this model to grow and flourish, for, while living standards are still high and generally growing, they have eroded relative to other wealthy nations in the past two or three decades. Economic growth in Sweden has not kept pace with that in Europe

Sherwin Rosen is professor of economics at the University of Chicago and a research associate of the National Bureau of Economic Research.

The author is most indebted to Henry Ohlsson for valuable assistance and support. He is also indebted to Robert Lucas and Nancy Stokey for helpful discussions and to Peter Diamond, Stanley Engerman, Victor Fuchs, Assar Lindbeck, Stephan Lundgren, Derek Neal, Agnar Sandmo, and Birgitta Swedenborg for comments and criticism of an initial draft, although they do not necessarily agree with what remains. He is solely responsible for errors and interpretations.

generally, even excluding the severe macroeconomic slump of the last few years (Lindbeck et al. 1994).

The economics of the welfare state gives cause for concern about these trends. Government expenditures account for more than 60 percent of output in Sweden today, much larger than every other (non-Scandinavian) rich country (see table 2.1). By itself, there is nothing to suggest that the size of government expenditures per se affects either living standards or growth rates one way or another. What is important is that government expenditures must be financed by taxation. All taxes distort economic behavior and blunt the information content of the price system that guides individual behavior. Taxes cause private valuations of taxed goods and services to differ from their true social costs. They introduce potential inefficiencies in an economic system. The size of the public sector has to be considered from both expenditure and tax sides simultaneously to understand this point. Marginal effective tax rates for the average citizen were 70 percent or more a few years ago, and, although they are somewhat smaller today, they remain extremely large relative to other rich countries.[1]

This paper analyzes how the welfare state interacts with the economics of household. The most important finding is that the welfare state encourages extra production of household goods and discourages production of material goods. From the normative view of economic efficiency, too many people provide paid household (family) services for other people, and too few are employed in the production of material goods. From the view of positive economic analysis, this is what explains the growth of local government employment of women and the growth of the welfare state. A rough quantitative assessment of the distorting effects of financing child care suggests that the losses may be substantial. Direct child-care subsidies in Sweden today are approximately SKr 60,000 (about $8,000) per child per year. Unless Swedish women desire to purchase substantially more child-care services than current rules allow, the estimates imply that these subsidies result in large hidden costs—shortfalls of actual from potential output in the overall Swedish economy. These policies accomplish other social goals in Sweden, but their economic efficiency costs must be considered in any thoroughgoing cost-benefit analysis of the welfare state.

The estimated costs cover a broad range, depending on assessments of economic parameters, especially the elasticity of labor supply of women with children. These judgments differ among economists. Nonetheless, the estimates presented below imply that social costs would fall if child-care subsidies were reduced to some extent. These must be weighed against political and other social benefits that are served by these policies. No attempt is made to do so

---

1. In recent years, there has been much excellent discussion of tax wedges in Sweden. For a sketch of the general calculation for Sweden, see Hansson (1984). For analysis of some components of the welfare system, see Lindbeck (1993).

Table 2.1   The Size of the Public Sector, Shares of Total Employment, and GDP, 1990 (%)

	Public Employment	Public Consumption	Public Investment	Public Outlays	Taxes
Canada	6.6	19.8	NA	NA	36.1
United States (1989)	14.4	17.9	1.7	36.3	29.6
Japan	6.0	9.1	5.2	32.0	31.1
France	25.2	18.0	NA	NA	42.6
West Germany	15.1	18.4	2.3	NA	40.3
United Kingdom	19.2	19.9	2.4	41.6	35.5
Sweden	31.7	27.1	3.1	61.6	56.4

Source: OECD national accounts.
Note: N.A. = not available.

here. I hope that this work will stimulate professional thinking and debate on those larger questions.

The role of the household is crucial in any economic analysis of the welfare state in Sweden because that is where most state activities are centered and it is well known that the household sector is a large component of total economic activity in all countries (Quah 1993; Thomas 1992). The government is not involved in public production of ordinary goods and services in Sweden. The production sector largely is in private hands, and most commercial transactions are organized through private markets. Sweden maintains strong private property institutions, free markets in consumer and producer goods, and personal and political freedom, which probably has ensured that resources supplied to the private sector flow to their highest socially valued uses. And, although private business is subject to substantial regulation, it is about on the same scale and magnitude as in other developed market economies. Where Sweden and other Scandinavian states especially differ from modern Western economies is in a greatly enlarged government role in household and family activities. In essence, Sweden has "monetized" the household sector of its economy by substituting publicly for privately produced household services on a grand scale in the past three decades.[2]

The increasing market value of women's time is the primary cause of the growth of both privately and state-provided household services throughout the world. Rising wages and work opportunities for women have increased the cost of staying home to produce household services oneself and have decreased the demand for it. Fertility has declined at the same time that the labor force participation of women has increased in most countries. In addition, technological improvements have made market production more efficient than self-production of many household services. For instance, changing medical tech-

2. Lindbeck (1988) has put it in a more dramatic way, saying that Sweden has "nationalized the family." This view has greatly influenced my thinking.

nology and longer life spans have increased the productivity and demand for formal medical and old-age services. The great value of skilled labor in modern technology requires that the fewer children we have be educated (by others) much more intensively than in the past. But it is exceptional that *all* employment growth in the Swedish economy has been confined to the local public sector, that nearly all of it has been accounted for by women, and that female labor force participation is so large relative to fertility.

In most other countries, a larger share of household activities is provided privately within the informal household sector, often in transactions that never appear in national accounts. In Sweden, a large fraction of women work in the public sector to take care of the children of other women who work in the public sector to care for the parents of the women who are looking after their children. If Swedish women take care of each other's parents in exchange for taking care of each other's children, how much additional real output comes of it? In order for the state to provide services socially that otherwise would be privately produced in the family or in the private sector, many ordinary, inherently personal activities must be reckoned in explicit monetary terms, tax revenues must be raised to finance them, and complex rules and conditions must be imposed to limit undesirable side effects. At the same time that Swedish family policy encourages high fertility and large families, other aspects of the welfare state encourage women to participate in the labor force and shift some of the costs of raising their children to others.

The next section, section 2.2, presents some basic facts about the growth of public employment in Sweden and shows some details of how it has affected the female labor market. Section 2.3 summarizes family policies in Sweden. Section 2.4 sketches the economics of the household and how taxes and subsidies affect behavior, while section 2.5 presents some illustrative calculations of deadweight losses of these policies under various assumptions. Conclusions are found in section 2.6.

Before getting into the details, it is useful to state the main ideas up front. Given that the labor supply activities of women generally are thought to be sensitive to financial considerations and that Sweden has chosen the high-tax road to social welfare, the theory of the second best suggests an efficiency case for subsidizing child care and other complementary costs of the labor force participation of women. Subsidies encourage the market work that income taxes inefficiently discourage. High marginal income tax rates inefficiently subsidize the self-production of household services because the use of one's own time in the household is tax exempt. Women (and men) spend too much time in the self-production of household services that would be more efficiently rendered by buying them in the market. For example, if the marginal tax rate is 50 percent, a woman who could earn SKr 120,000 in the labor market and has to pay SKr 60,000 for child care gets very little net monetary return from the transaction. Many would forgo the market opportunity and stay at home, even though their gross earnings and social contribution to aggregate

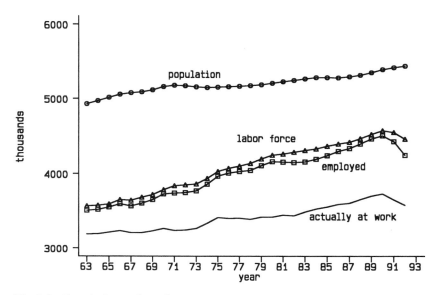

Fig. 2.1   Population and employment

production might exceed social costs. This inefficiently suppresses what otherwise might be an active and viable private market in day care and related services. Subsidizing child care lowers the cost of female labor force participation, eliminates this distortion, and improves social welfare.

But the analysis in section 2.4 shows something more. Such subsidies introduce *other* distortions because they require increased taxes on other goods to
finance them. They decrease the price and excessively increase the social demand for state-provided (i.e., subsidized) household services. Women are encouraged to work too much in the state-subsidized household sector, taking
care of other families' household needs, and not enough in the material goods
sector. There is excessive consumption of child-care-related services. Assessing the efficiency of in-kind work subsidies to women therefore comes
down to balancing one distortion in household production against another in
material goods consumption.

2.2   Trends in Public Sector Wages and Employment

Labor force surveys depict the main developments in the Swedish labor market during the period 1963–92 for people sixteen to sixty-four years of age.[3]
Labor force participation has steadily increased (fig. 2.1) and is now at a very
high level. Population grew at an annual average rate of 0.3 percent, but the

3. The source in most cases is the Swedish Labor Force Surveys, which started in 1963. The
definitions of the surveys were altered somewhat in 1986.

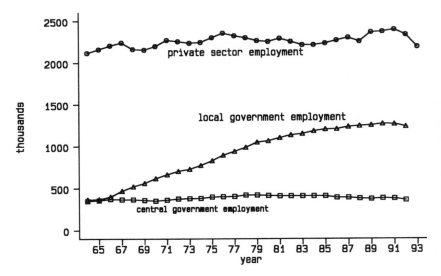

Fig. 2.2   Private and public employment

labor force increased at the rate of 0.8 percent. Employment increased on average by 0.6 percent, while the number of people working increased by only 0.4 percent per year, similar to the rate of growth of the population. Temporary leaves (vacations, sick leave, parental leave, study leave) account for the difference between employment and working.

Figure 2.2 shows that local government jobs account for almost all employment growth in Sweden. They expanded at the rate of 4.4 percent per year. Private sector and central government employment remained essentially flat, growing at only 0.1 percent per year. Local government employment growth is, however, slowing down, averaging 8.3 percent during 1964–72, 4.9 percent during 1972–82, and 0.9 percent during 1982–92.

Figures 2.3 and 2.4 show how the gender composition of employment has changed. Total employment of men was essentially the same in 1992 as in 1963, and the number of men in different sectors also remained constant. Two-thirds of the men have been employed in the private sector. Male central government employment has been very stable, whereas male local government employment has increased slightly. All aggregate employment growth can be attributed to women. Their annual employment growth rate was 1.5 percent, and, by the end of the period, the number of employed women was almost the same as the number of employed men. Female employment in the private sector and in central government has been constant, so almost all employment growth in Sweden is due to the entry of women working in local government jobs.

Employment growth for women was mainly in part-time jobs during the

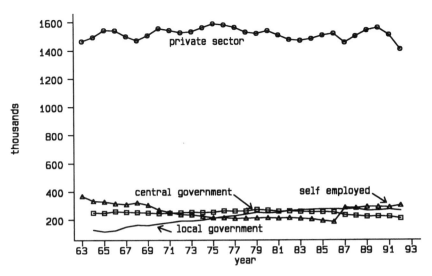

Fig. 2.3   Male employment, by sector

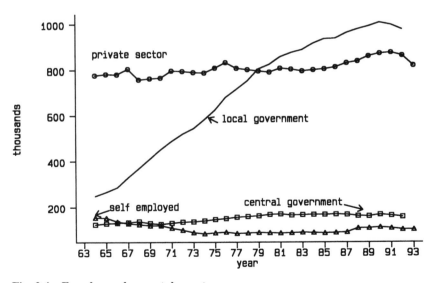

Fig. 2.4   Female employment, by sector

1960s and 1970s. However, during the 1980s, when annual hours worked started to increase, full-time employment grew, and part-time employment remained constant (fig. 2.5). These trends in hours worked are the same for men and women and for the private and public sectors. Note that average hours worked in central government are the same as the overall market average

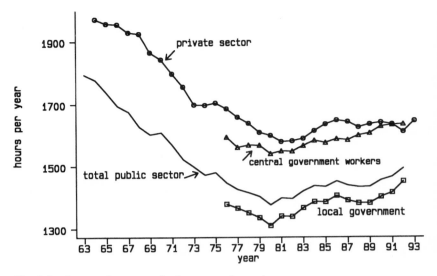

Fig. 2.5   Average hours worked per year, by sector

throughout the period and that average hours worked in local government are substantially smaller than elsewhere. This is one of the reasons why women are more frequently found in local government employment. However, women work fewer hours than men in all sectors. The difference on average is six hundred hours per year (fig. 2.6).

Average hourly wage rates in central and local government have changed substantially relative to the private sector over the period (fig. 2.7).[4] There is a downward trend in relative public sector wages, even though employment increased substantially. The 20 percent public sector wage premium of the mid-1960s was almost extinguished by 1976. The premium increased between 1976 and 1982 and fell during most of the 1980s. Wages of central and local government follow each other closely even though local government employment grew much faster.

Some of these movements can be attributed to changes in the demographic composition of employees in the public and private sectors. Average years of schooling of workers increased in both sectors over the past twenty years. Educational attainment of public sector workers in Sweden is substantially larger than that of private sector workers, but the gap is narrowing. In 1972, public employees averaged 11.04 years of schooling and private sector workers 9.35 years. By 1992, the corresponding numbers were 12.12 and 10.91 years, re-

4. Average hourly wage rates are computed using data on wages and salaries and total hours worked among employees. The sources are the SNEP-W database (1965–69) and unpublished tables (1970–) from Statistics Sweden, both developed for a quarterly econometric model of the Swedish economy at Uppsala University and FIEF (Trade Union Institute for Economic Research).

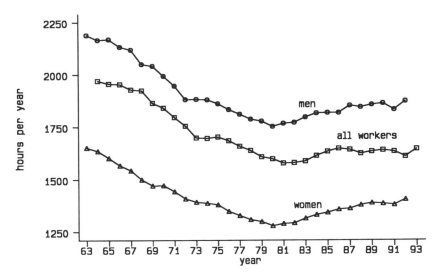

Fig. 2.6 Average annual hours, by gender

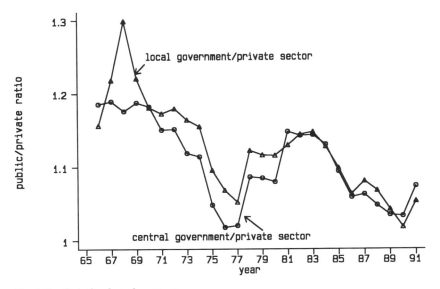

Fig. 2.7 Relative hourly wages

spectively. The initial 18 percent difference in educational attainment fell smoothly and uniformly over the years to 11 percent today.

Narrowing of educational differences explains some of the trend in figure 2.7. Differential hiring rates, the rapid growth of local government employees in the 1970s, and change in relative age structures contribute much to the rest.

New hires tend to be younger workers, who earn less than more-experienced workers. The decreasing average age of workers is closely associated with relative employment expansions and increasing age with relative declines in employment. The average age of central government workers grew slightly over the period, and the average age of private sector employees was unchanged. But, in local government, the average fell during 1966–80, when employment was expanding so rapidly. The average age of local government workers increased thereafter, as employment growth slowed and the day-care sector expanded.

Figure 2.8 shows how the industrial composition of public sector employment changed. During the 1960s and 1970s, employment in medical care and education increased rapidly. Since 1980, employment in education has been constant, and employment growth in medical care slowed down. Publicly provided child care for preschool children at day-care centers was 2 percent of public employment in the mid-1970s but has grown explosively ever since. Presently, employment in public day care is almost half as large as the education sector and a third of the medical care sector. It now accounts for 16 percent of public employment, not including those employed in public after-school-hour care for schoolchildren.

The enormous growth in day-care employment has occurred without any increase in the relative pay of day-care workers. The average monthly pay of preschool teachers is 70 percent as large as that of white-collar manufacturing workers and 90 percent as large as that of blue-collar manufacturing workers. There are no noticeable trends here. The pay of preschool teachers compared

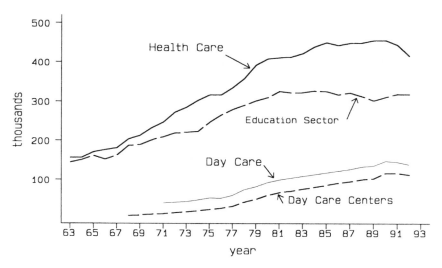

Fig. 2.8   Public employment by industry

with female blue-collar workers in manufacturing has actually decreased. How was it possible to recruit women to the local government sector? If it is not the pay, what has made the benefits exceed the costs in the labor supply calculations of women? There is no doubt that family policy programs in Sweden were crucial to these reallocations.

2.3 Family Policy Programs in Sweden

The increasing price of women's time is the main cause of increasing female labor force participation, in Sweden and elsewhere. However, the apparent concentration of women in local government is pronounced in Sweden, and participation is large relative to fertility. The Swedish welfare state family policies—publicly provided child care, parental leave and parental insurance, child allowances and housing allowances, as well as the design of the income tax—have contributed to this. Sweden experienced a baby boom during the 1980s. In 1989, Sweden had the second highest fertility rate in Europe, next to Ireland.

Personal Income Taxes. Sweden changed its income tax accounting system from families to individuals. In 1966, separate individual income taxation was made optional. It was made individual in 1971, with no exemptions or deductions for dependents. This had a large effect on after-tax wages of "secondary" wage earners in families. For example, for married couples earning the average manufacturing wage, the marginal tax rate on earnings of a half-time working spouse fell from 55 percent in 1970 to 32 percent in 1971. A highly progressive individual income tax system contains strong incentives for spouses to equalize their earning, labor force participation, and hours of work.

Publicly Provided Child Care. The expansion of subsidized, publicly provided child care has decreased the personal costs of labor force participation of Swedish women. Figure 2.9 shows how the number of preschool children and the number of them in publicly provided child care changed.[5] Until recently, virtually all day care was publicly produced. In 1983, 52 percent of preschool children were in publicly provided day care, either at day-care centers, in kindergartens, or in private day-care homes, with "day mothers" employed by the local government. Despite the 1980s baby boom, the share of preschool children in public day care had increased to 57 percent in 1992. Many of the remaining preschool children were with parents on paid parental leave.

The central government used to pay day-care subsidies to local governments, depending on the number of children enrolled. Local governments also subsidize day care. Total public sector expenditure in 1991–92 on day-care subsidies was SKr 26 billion. Since 1975, families on average have paid 10 percent of

---

5. The source is Statistika Meddelanden, Serie S. Gustafsson and Stafford (1994) present an illuminating comparison of publicly provided day-care services across three countries.

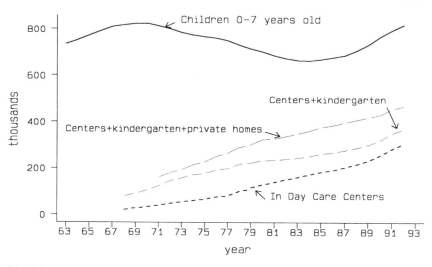

Fig. 2.9   Preschool children and daycare

the cost, while the public sector has paid 90 percent. Of the latter, an increasing proportion was paid by the central government over time (Gustafsson and Stafford 1992). Recently, the system of matching central government grants to local governments has been replaced with lump-sum grants. This has doubled the marginal costs of day care for local governments. The annual per child cost was SKr 62,000, or $7,500–$10,000, using exchange rates of the past few years. These large per child fees reflect the fact that care of small children is extremely labor intensive and that very high-quality care is provided in Sweden. There are four children per server, a much smaller ratio than the student/teacher ratio in elementary schools.

Parental Leave and Parental Cash Benefits. Paid maternity leave was introduced in 1955, when three months were paid. Presently, fifteen months are paid. The system encourages women to establish an earnings history before having children because the parental cash benefit depends on previous earnings. It also encourages women to postpone bearing children if earnings are increasing and to space children more closely. Compensation is at least as large as for the previous child if the next child is born within thirty months. Otherwise, it is lower. The compensation can be obtained until the child is eight years old, so almost all expenditure concerns preschool children. Total expenditure in 1991–92 was SKr 18 billion. The compensation is taxable. Assuming that everyone has the lowest marginal tax rate, the net expenditure for the public sector is SKr 13 billion.

Child Allowances. Beginning in 1948, the central government has paid fixed monthly child allowances to children under sixteen years of age. The allowance was roughly SKr 800 per month or SKr 10,000 per year in 1991–92. Total expenditure was SKr 17 billion. The per child allowance is increased by 50 percent from the third child and on. It is not taxed.

Housing Allowances. Housing allowances are means tested, depending on family income, number of children, and housing costs. For all practical purposes, these are equivalent to a means-tested child allowance. Central government and local government pay 50 percent each. Total expenditure in 1991–92 was SKr 5 billion. The allowance is not taxed.

Summary. An approximate estimate of total public expenditure on programs for preschool children is summarized in table 2.2.[6] Total annual public sector tax expenditure on preschool children was SKr 48 billion, corresponding to SKr 60,000 per preschool child per year ($8,000). In the spring of 1994, the majority in Parliament decided to introduce a child-care allowance. Parents with a child one to three years of age will get SKr 2,000 per month provided that the child is not in publicly provided day care. The allowance will be taxed. Estimated annual expenditure is SKr 3.5 billion.

2.4   Household Welfare Economics

Broadly speaking, the programs described above have two main components. One is payment from general tax revenues for childbirth and parental home care of infants and very young children. The other is subsidized care of preschool children outside the home. These policies were designed to increase the fertility of Swedish women and to tilt the allocation of their time toward market rather than nonmarket uses (Sundstrom and Stafford 1992). Apparently, they have achieved their goals. Some of the economic consequences for the allocation of time are analyzed in this section. Fertility aspects have been more extensively analyzed by others (Aronsson and Walker, chap. 5 in this volume).

The point of departure is a well-known result from the theory of the second best. Subsidizing purchased inputs in household production to reduce the costs of labor force participation improves social efficiency when substantial income tax distortions inefficiently deter market work incentives. What has been missed in the prior discussion is that they also reduce the relative cost of household goods and encourage socially excessive *market* production of household goods at the expense of material goods. Too many people are involved in the household production of other families, and too few are in the production of

6. Child support advances, another program affecting families, are not included. The central government serves as an intermediary between divorced parents. If a parent does not pay child support or the (income-based) support is below a certain threshold, the central government advances basic support. The expenditure on this program was SKr 3 billion in 1991–92.

Table 2.2   **Summary of Direct Expenditure on Child-Care Programs, 1991–92**

Program	Expenditure (SKr billion)	Comments
Day-care subsidies	26	Central and local government
Parental insurance	13	Net of taxes
Housing allowances	2	Excluding housing allowances for schoolchildren
Child allowances	7	Preschool children only
Total	48	

Note: The table does not give the full budget effects because effects on tax revenues are ignored.

nonhousehold goods and services. This second effect does not necessarily mean that household subsidies are inappropriate. Rather, assessing the purely economic consequences of policy requires balancing one distortion against another. These issues are examined in more detail below, using household production theory (Becker 1965; Gronau 1977; Lindbeck 1982) and the economics of the second best (Sandmo 1990).

2.4.1   The Allocation of Time

This section sets the basic model and notation (for complete notation and other details, see the appendix). Consider an economy with two classes of goods: x represents "material" goods and services that are produced in firms and transacted in markets; and z is household goods that are self-produced by combining own time with purchased inputs. Consumer preferences over goods x and z are represented by the utility function $u = u(x, z)$. The material good x is produced by labor services hired in a market (along with capital and other inputs, suppressed here) under constant returns. The self-production function for household goods is $z = f(h, M)$, where h is own time devoted to the household and M is a market good, best interpreted as the hired time of others. Household production is also assumed to exhibit constant returns.

This specification of tastes is restrictive in assigning purely instrumental roles for time used in x and z production. Time spent in direct contact with one's own children, for example, is just treated as an imperfect substitute for purchased inputs and has no utility value in and of itself. This specification biases the case in favor of work-cost subsidies because parental love of children naturally acts to "subsidize" household production; its full implicit price includes the opportunity cost of time *minus* the value of the direct marginal utility of h.

Let t be the amount of time supplied to the labor market, w the market price of time, and p the price of purchased M services. Taking x as numeraire, and normalizing the total amount of time at unity, the time-budget constraint is $t + h = 1$. The financial-budget constraint defining income available for taxation is $wt = x + pM$. Combining these gives $w = x + wh + pM$: *full income*

(w) can be spent to purchase material goods in the market, own time for use in the household, and the market services of household inputs.

The Structure of Demand

It is useful to solve the consumer's problem in two steps.[7] First, fix z, and combine h and M to minimize production costs. Second, given the cost of z, the consumer chooses x and z to maximize $u(x, z)$.

The household rationally charges itself the market opportunity costs of time in assessing the true cost of z. With constant returns and homogeneity, the cost function is

$$(1) \qquad q(w, p) = \min\{wh + pM + \lambda(z - f(h, M))\},$$

where $q(w, p) = \lambda$ is both marginal and average cost of z, increasing in both w and p. Differentiating total cost with respect to w and p gives input demand functions that are separable in output and factor prices: $h = zq_w(w, p)$, and $M = zq_p(w, p)$. The constraint for the second problem is $I = x + q(w, p)z$, where $I = w$ is full income in this case. The consumer chooses x and z to maximize utility. The indirect utility function is defined by

$$(2) \qquad G(w, p) = \max\{u(x, z) + \mu[I - x - q(w, p)z]\},$$

from which ordinary consumer demand functions $x = x(I, q)$ and $z = z(I, q)$ follow.

Taxes and subsidies alter behavior because they affect net wages and prices seen by consumers. The virtue of this roundabout construction lies in decomposing the effects of tax-distorted price changes into two kinds of substitution and income effects, one for production and the other for consumption. Substitute household good demand $z(I, q)$ into the input demands for h and M, and note that I and q depend on w and p from cost minimization. Then repeated application of the scale and substitution decomposition in the derived demands for h and M and the adding-up rule yield the following elasticities (see the appendix):

$$(3) \qquad \eta_{hp} = (1 - \theta)(\sigma_p + \eta_{zq}), \quad \eta_{Mp} = -\theta\sigma_p + (1 - \theta)\eta_{zq},$$
$$\eta_{hw} = -(1 - \theta)\sigma_p + \theta\eta_{zq} + \eta_{zI}, \quad \eta_{Mw} = \theta\sigma_p + \theta\eta_{zq} + \eta_{zI},$$

where η_{ij} is the uncompensated demand elasticity of variable i with respect to j, $\theta = wh/qz$ is the cost share of own time in the production of z, and σ_p is the elasticity of substitution between h and M in $f(h, M) = z$ production. The first and second terms in each of the expressions in (3) represent the direct and indirect effects of factor price changes. The terms in σ_p reflect direct substitu-

---

7. I have chosen to formulate the problem in the traditional way, examining choices and distortions at the intensive margin for the representative household. Bergstrom and Blomquist (in press) outline the approach for studying choices at the extensive margin among heterogeneous agents for this problem.

tion between h and M in z production when relative factor prices change. The terms in η_{zq} reflect indirect changes in factor demand induced by scale effects because factor price changes alter the shadow price of z and change the consumption demand for z relative to x. The third terms in the wage elasticities reflect an additional income effect on the individual demand for z because changes in w change full income.

Production and Supply

Assume that x and M production are linear in their (time) inputs. Write $t = m + \ell$, where m is time supplied to produce good M, and ℓ is time supplied to produce good x. Choose units so that $x = \ell$. Then $M = \alpha m$, where α is a constant reflecting the number of children per day-care mother ($\alpha = 4$ in Sweden). The model should be extended to consider substitution of quality for quantity of purchased services in the household, but that is not pursued here. To a first-order approximation, the total quantity responses in this model can be interpreted as the combined effect of quantity and quality.

Since time spent in M or x production is assumed to be effort equivalent, each must pay the same hourly wage w in a competitive market. The competitive supply price of M is its marginal cost of production, or $p = w/\alpha$, about one-quarter the market wage in Sweden (ignoring the 14 percent share of capital costs in Swedish day care centers [Schwartz and Weinberg 1993]). The marginal product of labor in material goods production is 1.0, and x is the numeraire, so $w = 1$ in a competitive equilibrium. At these prices, the first-order conditions associated with (1) and (2) are feasible, and their solution describes the competitive equilibrium. Think about it as follows. Imagine an economy with a large number (a continuum) of identical households. They all make the same choice of x, z, and h in equilibrium. Aggregate markets for x and M are cleared when the required fraction of workers supply all their market work time to x production and the remainder supply all their market work time to M production.

2.4.2 The Effects of Taxes and Subsidies

The household/market model is now modified to include government expenditure and taxes (Sandmo 1990). Suppose that the government must raise revenue of amount g and that nondistorting poll taxes are not available. In order to isolate the pure efficiency aspects of taxes, g is treated as exogenously determined and redistributed to consumers as lump-sum transfers of x. It must be financed by taxing market income (income taxes), material goods production (VAT or sales taxes), or the value of market inputs in home production (generally a subsidy). With three market goods—labor, material goods, and purchased household services—and the requirement that the government balance its budget, there are only two independent tax instruments: VAT taxes are treated as redundant here.

Let τ be the rate of income tax per unit of market-supplied labor, and let ρ

be the unit tax (if positive) or subsidy (if negative) on M, the purchased input in household production. The government collects revenues from two sources, $\tau(1 - h)$ from income taxation, where $1 - h = t$ is total time supplied to the market sector, and ρM from taxing or subsidizing marketed household inputs. The government budget constraint is

(4) $$g = \tau(1 - h) + \rho M$$

The consumer's budget constraint becomes

(5) $$(w - \tau)(1 - h) = x + (p + \rho)M,$$

from which the social budget constraint follows:

(6) $$w = x + pM + wh + g.$$

In the competitive equilibrium with taxes, w and p remain fixed at $w = 1$ and $p = 1/\alpha$ from the linear cost assumptions.

There are inefficient tax wedges between private and social valuations. An interesting positive question is, Given g, what happens when the subsidy is increased slightly and the income tax simultaneously increased to finance it? If the subsidy is increased, taxes must be raised by just enough to balance the budget after consumers have made all behavioral adjustments to the new situation, satisfying their personal budgets in (5). However, to the first order, all these secondary repercussions cancel out along the social budget in (6). What remains is the condition that socially feasible changes in taxes and subsidies must satisfy the Slutsky-like condition

(7) $$(1 - h)d\tau + Md\rho = 0.$$

In fact, all tax and subsidy variations satisfying equation (7) imply constant utility, with the result that income effects on x and z in consumption are washed out in this experiment (see the appendix).

The behavioral effects of this experiment are found by recomputing the elasticities in (3) under the additional constraint that, when the subsidy changes the price of M, the income tax changes to satisfy (7). For example, the differential dh in the comparative statics now has two terms instead of one:

$$dh = [(\partial h/\partial w)(dw/d\tau)(d\tau/d\rho) + (\partial h/\partial \rho)(\partial p/\partial \rho)]d\rho.$$

Making all the substitutions, repeatedly applying the Slutsky decomposition, exploiting the constant supply price technology, and converting to elasticities ultimately yields

(8) $$\begin{aligned} (d \log M/d \log \rho)_{\text{budget balance}} &= -(1 - \phi)[\theta\sigma_p + (1 - \theta)\sigma_c]/(1 - h), \\ (d \log h/d \log \rho)_{\text{budget balance}} &= (1 - \theta)[(1 - \phi)\sigma_p - \sigma_c]/(1 - h). \end{aligned}$$

Here, $\phi = qz/I$ is the budget share of z in total consumption, and σ_c is the elasticity of substitution between x and z in consumption in $u(x, z)$. Increasing the subsidy on purchased household inputs and financing it by increased income taxation reduces the price of M seen by households and increases demand. Family subsidies encourage households to substitute M for h in household production and to substitute z for x in consumption. Both work in the same direction to increase the derived demand for M. They work in opposite directions on the demand for h: consumption substitution effects increase the demand for own time in the household, but production substitution effects reduce it. The net change in h can go either way, depending on which kind of substitution is greater.

Cost minimization implies that $d \log z = \theta d \log h + (1 - \theta)d \log M$. Substituting from (8) results in

$$(d \log z/d \log \rho)_{\text{budget balance}} = -(1 - \theta)\sigma_c[1 - \phi(1 - \theta)]/(1 - h),$$
$$(9) \ (d \log x/d \log \rho)_{\text{budget balance}} = d \log \ell/d \log \rho)_{\text{budget balance}}$$
$$= -[d \log(m + h)/d \log \rho]_{\text{budget balance}}$$
$$= -[\phi/(1 - \phi)](d \log z/d \log \rho)_{\text{budget balance}}.$$

The first expression in (9) proves that z must increase in this budget-balancing experiment. The second equation indicates how the composition of market output and the allocation of time are altered. Material goods production and the time allocated to it must decrease. *Cross-hauling* is a necessary outcome: *total time* allocated to household production in the economy unambiguously increases. Output of material goods falls.

The change in the composition of household time is slightly more complicated. From (8), the amount of market-purchased household time (m) increases. Because the effects of substitution in production and substitution in consumption work in opposite directions on the derived demand for own household time, h can either rise or fall, but, even if it falls, the amount of hired household time must increase by more. Certainly, subsidies encourage work outside the home. But there is a sense in which all of it is work in someone else's home, not in the material goods sector. Parents work for each other for taxable pay needed to help finance the subsidies that induce them to work for each other in the first place, rather than remain working for themselves, "self-employed," in the tax-sheltered nonmarket household sector. Growth in public employment in the welfare state is a predictable economic consequence of substitution of state-subsidized services for own-provided services.

This experiment has been constructed so that economic welfare remains constant along the way, and the resulting reallocations have no incremental social economic value. Nevertheless, *measured* national income changes. In this economy, real national income at constant prices is $x + pM = wt = 1 - h$, so the sign of the change in NI is the negative of the sign of dh. From (8), measured national income increases or decreases as σ_p is greater or less than σ_c. When $\sigma_c > \sigma_p$, measured national income is actually reduced by family subsidies.

2.4.3 Optimal Taxes and Subsidies

Consider next the "optimal" tax-subsidy scheme, where the government raises the given revenue g at the least social efficiency cost. We seek tax rates τ and ρ that maximize utility subject to the government's budget constraint, that is, that maximize

$$(10) \qquad G(w - \tau, p + \rho) + v[g - (1 - h)\tau - M\rho],$$

where G is the indirect utility function defined in (2) subject now to the constraint in (5), and v is a Lagrange multiplier. It is understood that w and p in (10) are fixed at their general equilibrium supply prices in the economy.[8] First-order conditions are

$$(11) \qquad -G_w - v[(1 - h) - \tau \cdot \partial(1 - h)/\partial w - \rho \cdot \partial M/\partial w] = 0,$$
$$G_p - v[M + \tau \cdot \partial(1 - h)/\partial p + \rho \cdot \partial M/\partial p] = 0.$$

Convert the derivatives in (11) to elasticities, substitute from (3), and solve the two linear equations for τ and ρ. Recalling that μ is the marginal utility of money in the consumer's problem, the result is

$$(12) \qquad \tau = v^{-1}(\mu + v)[\theta\sigma_p + (1 - \theta)\sigma_c]/\theta\phi\sigma_p(\sigma_c - \eta_{zl}),$$
$$\rho = -v^{-1}(\mu + v)(\sigma_p - \sigma_c)/\alpha\phi\sigma_p(\sigma_c - \eta_{zl}).$$

Assume that the M sector is small relative to x and g so that $\tau > 0$ is necessary for government finances. The expression for ρ in (12) shows that the optimal income tax approximately is a weighted average of the inverses of the two substitution elasticities, consistent with standard economic intuition that optimal tax rates are smaller when substitution is greater.

The expression for ρ in (12) is much different than the expression for τ. It depends on the *difference* between the two kinds of substitution effects. If $\sigma_p = \sigma_c$, it is best not to subsidize (or tax) market inputs in household production at all. A subsidy is warranted only when $\sigma_p > \sigma_c$, that is, when the ability to substitute own time for purchased time in household production is greater than the ability to substitute material goods for household goods in consumption. If $\sigma_c > \sigma_p$, hired substitutes for self-production in the home should be taxed extra, to discourage their use, not subsidized and nationalized.

2.4.4 Deadweight Losses

The formulas in (12) above illustrate the main point of this analysis: that the second-best optimality of household subsidies depends on a delicate comparison of substitution effects. Since the child-care sector (M) is a small component of the economy and so many other factors are involved in the setting of

---

8. As usual for this problem, taxes are written in absolute rather than percentage terms. Units can always be chosen to normalize equilibrium prices at unity, and taxes and subsidies therefore have an ad valorem interpretation. On this, see Atkinson and Stiglitz (1980) and Harberger (1971).

taxes and social welfare policy, I present them only to make the analytic point as sharply as possible. Loss of consumer surplus measures (Harberger 1964) is the best available tool for assessing the empirical magnitude of the resulting distortions.

Define the expenditure function $S(w, p; u)$ as the minimum expenditure $x + qz$ necessary to achieve a given level of utility. The compensating variation is found by expanding $S(w, p)$ in Taylor's series up to second order, ignoring remainder terms, and using duality theory to express the first and second derivatives of S as Hicksian demand functions and their derivatives (substitution effects only). Converting to elasticities using the relations in (3) yields

(13) $$\text{deadweight loss} = \{\theta(1 - \theta)\sigma_p[\tau + \rho]^2 \\ + (1 - \phi)\sigma_c[\theta\tau - (1 - \theta)\rho]^2\}qz/2,$$

where τ and ρ are interpreted as percentage rates of tax or subsidy.

Equation (13) captures the efficiency trade-off in a very direct way, depicted in figure 2.10. Differential taxes and subsidies cause distortions in household production. They shrink the production set to the line marked AB. If this was all there was to it, the consumer would choose point A. The production distortion shown in the figure is measured by the term in σ_p in (13). However, taxes and subsidies reduce the implicit price of household production below its (distorted) opportunity cost. This causes consumers to choose B instead of A. The resulting consumption distortion in the figure is measured by the term in σ_c in (13). The total distortion is the sum of these two effects.

Subsidies imply that ρ is negative in (13). If the percentage marginal subsidy

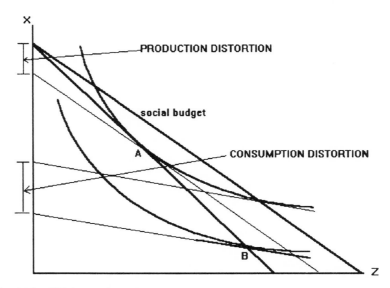

Fig. 2.10   Efficiency distortions

is set equal to the marginal income tax rate, then all welfare distortions in household production are eliminated, and the term in σ_p vanishes, exactly the second-best intuition. However, the subsidy necessarily increases the distortion in the relative allocation of time between material goods and household goods, and the terms multiplying σ_c in (13) become larger. These drawbacks of subsidies have to be weighed against their virtues.

2.5 A Deadweight Loss Calculation for Sweden

Combining income taxes, payroll taxes, and value added taxes, the average marginal income tax wedge in Sweden today is in the 50–65 percent range, down from 65–80 percent a few years ago, but still one of the largest in the democratic world. Taxes of this magnitude cause families to overuse own inputs in household production. Large subsidies to purchased household inputs are necessary to correct these distortions in household production. Since Swedish local governments pay approximately 90 percent of the total costs of day care and home time (leave from work) of mothers with very small children, the average marginal subsidy also must be about 0.9.

It is important to notice that the empirical weight of the terms multiplying σ_p in (13) for Sweden must be much smaller than the weight on σ_c because the share-weighted difference in the absolute values of marginal tax and subsidy rates is much smaller than their sum. The share of own time (θ) in household production involving small children is substantial, even for full-time labor force participants. Whatever it is, the maximum possible value of $\theta(1 - \theta)$ in the first term of (13) is 0.25. Using the large tax and subsidy rates at the upper limits of the ranges in the paragraph above implies $[\tau + \rho]^2 \approx .04$, so $\theta(1 - \theta)[\tau + \rho]^2$ multiplying the term in σ_p is .01 at most. But $[\theta\tau - (1 - \theta)\rho]^2$, the coefficient multiplying σ_c in (13), is 0.065 with these same tax parameters, assuming, conservatively, that $\theta = \frac{1}{2}$. Furthermore, $(1 - \phi)$, the share of material goods in full income, must be substantial, at least 0.75, considering that z is confined to preschool children activities here. The net result is a coefficient on σ_c in (13) of 0.25, at least twenty-five times larger than the coefficient on σ_p. Unless σ_p is extremely large relative to σ_c, the welfare loss calculation for Sweden must be much more sensitive to σ_c than to σ_p.

The division of the model economy into material and household goods sectors does not map onto direct econometric estimates of σ_c and σ_p. However, estimates can be backed out of the formulas in (3) since the elasticity of market labor supply is $\eta_{lw} = \partial \log (1 - h)/\partial \log w = -(h/1 - h)\eta_{hw}$. This and the Slutsky decompositions imply

(14) $[(1 - h)/h]\eta_{lw} = (1 - \theta)\sigma_p + \theta(1 - \phi)\sigma_c - (1 - \theta\phi)\eta_{zl}$.

The wage elasticity of female labor supply η_{lw} in Sweden is in the range [0.1, 0.9] (Blomquist and Hansson-Brusewitz 1990; Gustafsson and Klevmarken 1993; and esp. Aronsson and Walker, chap. 5 in this volume). Economic growth and increasing income everywhere are associated with relative expansion of the material goods sector and relative contraction of the household sector, implying $\eta_{zI} < 1.0$. However, the declining share of the household sector has been affected by technical changes in both sectors, so the true income elasticity probably is greater than what is implied by trends alone. Certainly it is no larger than unity. I use $\eta_{zI} = 1.0$ here. Working mothers with small children spend as much of their time in own household production of child services as in the labor market. Splitting their time fifty-fifty, so that $(1 - h)/h = 1.0$, and using the values for θ ($= \frac{1}{2}$) and ϕ ($= \frac{1}{4}$) above in (14) gives a linear equation restricting σ_c and σ_p for a given value of η_{nw}. The possibilities are shown in table 2.3 in the columns labeled "σ_c." Each of three possible female labor supply elasticities $\frac{1}{3}$, $\frac{2}{3}$, and 1.0 within the empirical range, combined with each of the four alternative values of σ_p, implies an estimate of σ_c. For instance, if $\sigma_p = 1.0$ and the labor supply elasticity is $\frac{1}{3}$, then equation (14) requires $\sigma_c = 1.88$. It requires that $\sigma_c = 3.67$ if $\sigma_p = 1.0$ and the labor supply elasticity η_{nw} is unity.

The columns of table 2.3 headed "DWL" show the estimated deadweight loss in equation (13), expressed as a fraction of qz for marginal tax and subsidy rates of .70 and .90, respectively. State subsidies for child care in Sweden are about SKr 50 billion (see table 2.2 above), so $qz = $ SKr 5,500 per child is a minimum bound on qz per child because it does not include any imputed values for either parental time or material inputs into z production. To illustrate, if the labor supply elasticity is 0.33 and $\sigma_p = 1.0$, the deadweight loss is .46(qz), on the order of SKr 25 billion, or SKr 32,000 (roughly \$4,000) per child. The estimates are sensitive to the assumed decomposition of labor supply elasticity into its σ_c and σ_p components in (14), but almost all of them are positive. Note also that most of these numbers are *large,* on the order of half or more of government child-care-related expenditures. In assessing the plausibility of

Table 2.3　　　　**Deadweight Loss Multipliers for Alternative Substitution Elasticities**

σ_p[a]	$\eta_{nw} = \frac{1}{3}$			$\eta_{nw} = \frac{2}{3}$			$\eta_{nw} = 1$		
	σ_c[b]	DWL[c]	δD[d]	σ_c[b]	DWL[c]	δD[d]	σ_c[b]	DWL[c]	δD[d]
0	3.20	.77	−.90	4.11	.99	−.90	5.00	1.20	−.90
1	1.88	.46	−1.00	2.78	.67	−.98	3.67	.89	−.95
2	.56	.14	−1.60	1.44	.36	−1.15	2.33	.57	−1.07
3	N.A.	N.A.	N.A.	.11	.04	−11.28	1.00	.26	−1.43

Note: N.A. means that the substitution parameter is outside the economically feasible range.
[a]Alternative values of substitution in production.
[b]Implied by eq. (14) for indicated values of σ_p and η_{tw}.
[c]Proportionate deadweight loss from (13) for $\tau = .7$ and $\rho = .9$. These should be applied to a per child base for qz of at least SKr 5,500 (see the text).
[d]$\delta D = (\partial \log DWL / \partial \log \rho)_{\text{budget balance}}$. See the text.

table 2.3, readers might compare them with Hansson's (1984) larger estimates
of deadweight losses for other tax distortions in Sweden.

Table 2.3 reveals two strong regular patterns in the calculated deadweight
losses. First, the estimated loss falls if σ_p is larger and σ_c is smaller, for each
labor supply elasticity. The reason is that the currently large taxes and subsidies
eliminate a small production distortion when σ_p is small and create a large
consumption distortion when σ_c is large. Second, the distortion is larger the
larger the labor supply elasticity because large labor supply elasticities imply
greater substitution elasticities. Only if σ_p is relatively large and female supply
elasticities relatively small are the welfare distortions in table 2.3 of no economic significance.

Of course, substantial portions of the DWL multipliers in table 2.3 can be
attributed to the high marginal income tax rates, not to child-care subsidies per
se. Nonetheless, there is evidence that child-care subsidies are too high in Sweden today. Consider an experiment where the subsidy is reduced a little and
the marginal tax rate is also reduced by the amount required to maintain budget
balance. Expressing the taxes and subsidies as percentages, equation (7) and
the budget constraints imply that

(15) $$d\tau = [(1 - \theta)/(1 - \theta\phi)]d\rho$$

is necessary for government finances.

Totally differentiate equation (13), and substitute (15). Evaluating the re-
sulting equation at $\theta = \frac{1}{2}$, $\phi = \frac{1}{4}$, $\tau = .7$, and $\rho = -.9$, the parameters used
in table 2.3, yields the gradient

(16) $\delta D = (\partial \log \text{DWL}/\partial \log \rho)_{\text{budget balance}} = -0.0571\sigma_p - 0.241\sigma_c.$

Since the two substitution elasticities are positive, equation (16) must be negative. Therefore, if the subsidy is reduced a little (e.g., from $-.9$ to $-.8$, so that
$d\rho$ is positive), the deadweight losses in table 2.3 decrease, and it can be concluded that the current subsidy is too large.

The percentage rate of decline in (16) is calculated for corresponding values
of the substitution parameters in the column labeled "δD" in table 2.3. Remarkably, the estimates cluster around unity for most possible parameter values (except when DWL is itself quite small, where the efficiency gain from
lowering the subsidy is estimated as much larger because the denominator
DWL is itself small). To a first approximation, the estimates in table 2.3
strongly suggest that the deadweight loss is *locally* linearly declining in |ρ|, so
long as budget balance is maintained. For example, a 10 percent reduction in
the subsidy from its current level of $-.90$ to $-.81$ would reduce the deadweight loss, whatever it is, by about 10 percent.

Remember that these derivatives apply in a neighborhood around current
tax and subsidy rates. Were the experiment actually implemented, the gradient
would change because budget shares and elasticities of substitution would
change. It cannot be ascertained theoretically whether the second derivative of

(16) is positive, negative, or zero, nor is there enough empirical evidence to make an educated guess. Hence, caution must be exercised in extrapolating reductions in the subsidy beyond, say, 10 percent or so. Local linearity does not imply that the total elimination of child-care subsidies would remove the deadweight loss of high income taxation in Sweden! Rather, the estimates in table 2.3 imply that the welfare of the average family would improve if the subsidy were reduced because substitution in consumption is heavily distorted under current policy. It is entirely possible that, were we to start from a baseline of no subsidy, an increase in the subsidy would have improved welfare because the household production margin would be so heavily distorted.

A case can be made that the numbers in the upper-right-hand corner are likely the most relevant for Sweden today. First, child-care tax and subsidy distortions largely work on the female labor supply margin, and it is well known that the wage elasticity of females is much larger than that of males. The estimates in the labor economics literature vary depending on whether participation as well as hours of work are included, but a value of η_{hw} pushing toward 1.0 certainly is well within the range of estimates found over the years for women in many countries. The most sophisticated estimates for Sweden examine only a restricted range of variation in panel data and are sensitive to specification. For instance, sick leave policy and switching the tax basis from family to individual accounts are thought to have had a large effect on female labor supply.

Second, there is reason to think that the elasticity of substitution in production, σ_p, might be small at current time allocations in Sweden. The family leave policy implicitly recognizes that hired help is a poor substitute for full parental care when raising very young children. The argument can be extended to older, preschool children by imagining a hierarchy of uses of adult time devoted to children, with parents allocating their own time to "higher-quality" uses and hiring the time of others for "lower-quality" uses.[9] Hired time in Sweden is so large that even more of it would be a very poor substitute for parental time. If this is true, the deadweight losses in table 2.3 are half or more of total spending, or upward of SKr 30,000 ($4,000) per child per year.

2.6 Conclusion

Economic analysis suggests sizable efficiency losses caused by the marginal taxes and subsidies needed to implement the welfare state. Large estimated

---

9. Think of a continuum of child-care activities, distinct in terms of the ratio at which parental time can be substituted by purchased time. Denote this ratio by $r(s)$ for activity s, and choose s so that $r(s)$ is ordered from highest to lowest. If the relative price of purchased time compared to own time is ρ, the household purchased time for all activities for which $r(s) \geq \rho$ and uses own time for those satisfying $r(s) < \rho$. The marginal rate of substitution for own and purchased time is $\rho = r(s^*)$, and σ_p can be shown to depend on the curvature of $r(s)$ in the neighborhood of s^*. For details, see Rosen (1978).

efficiency losses are practically inevitable, given the relatively large empirical estimates of female labor supply responses to wage incentives and the enormous tax burdens in Sweden today.

The applicability of this framework for assessing welfare distortions in Sweden has been questioned on two grounds. One is technical: subsidized child care is not available in unlimited supply to families in Sweden. The other is more philosophical: this analysis respects only individual preferences, whereas many Swedish economists feel strongly that a more adequate basis for public policy must also consider social values. Both points have merit.

First, if the state rations day care, many women do not effectively face the tax-distorted marginal incentives specified in the model. For example, subsidized day care is mainly available to women when they are at work. Rationing imposes a quantity constraint on the choice problem modeled above. If the quantity constraint is not binding, the analysis is unaffected. If it is binding, then the formula in (13) has to be applied to "virtual" subsidy and tax rates— the unrestricted subsidy and tax that would voluntarily induce women to freely choose the rationed quantity. Equation (13) itself is unaffected but must be applied to these virtual or "shadow" rates of tax and subsidy. If Swedish women are not getting all the subsidized child care they desire, the appropriate shadow subsidies relevant for the welfare loss calculation are smaller than the .90 rate used in table 2.3, and the deadweight losses calculated there generally are too large. The importance of this point depends on the extent to which Swedish women truly are rationed in their use of subsidized public child care. This is an empirical question that has not been studied. Some of the relevant economic considerations are as follows.

That subsidized care is tied to jobholding of women in Sweden is not decisive on rationing because it does not tell us how much would be used if it were not tied in that way. After all, child care of the kind in question is largely associated with jobholding of women in all countries, whether or not it is subsidized or provided by the state. The demand price for systematic, day-in and day-out child care falls off sharply during after-work hours and weekends everywhere in the world. Furthermore, most women work many fewer hours than men, both fewer hours per week and fewer weeks per year, both in Sweden (see fig. 2.6 above) and elsewhere. Rations do not bind in these cases unless women are constrained to work fewer hours than they actually do. How many Swedish women are working less because of insufficient day care? Finally, most of the empirical labor supply responses of women occur at the participation decision (whether to work), for which rationing considerations do not apply at all. The whole point of the Swedish system is to encourage, not discourage, work. In my judgment, these factors suggest that the thrust of the conclusions above are not much altered by the possibility of rationing constraints: there is no getting around the staggering marginal taxes and subsidies in the current system and the substantial wage elasticity of female labor supply compared to men. These have to create substantial inefficiencies.

The philosophical and methodological criticism of the basis for public policy is more difficult to answer. After this paper was written, it became apparent that its style and content go against the grain of many strongly held cultural and social values in Sweden. There are serious drawbacks when outsiders, such as myself, analyze a social system in which they have no personal stake or of which they have no intimate cultural knowledge. Any such analysis and criticism must be assessed in that light. But there also are some virtues: outsiders do not carry the same social and political baggage as insiders. They often view things from a different perspective and sometimes stumble into asking politically incorrect questions that never get raised from within. My own baggage is based on my training in an economic calculus that respects individual preferences. Social policies invariably include many additional considerations. For instance, economists have known for almost two hundred years that tariffs and quotas create deadweight losses and economic inefficiency, yet tariffs have persisted in the world economy for all that time. The fact that social and political economic factors affect all economic policies does not eliminate the need to assess the size of the inefficiencies that they create. We must know the full consequences of public policies.

Many economists of my generation feel that it is our professional duty and obligation to point out the possible existence of these distortions, independent of their political or cultural sensitivity. Let the additional political and social values that sustain these policies be considered with full knowledge of their costs. Many Swedish citizens feel strongly that welfare state policies, and what I have termed the *monetization* of the family, are fully warranted for their promoting the economic independence of women and equality between the sexes. Many also feel that government-sponsored day care has extra social value in the raising of children. All these things have value, but the point is that all good things have value. How much are Swedes paying for them? How much are they willing to pay? Evidently, Swedish citizens regard the social value of the welfare state and related egalitarian policies as worth the social costs. Nevertheless, it is worthwhile every now and then to try to assess how large the costs might be.

In many ways, and at least in the aggregate, government-provided household services replace what would have been purchased in other, more decentralized ways without the associated tax burdens. The fundamental manifestations of these costs are tendencies to overconsume subsidized government-provided goods and to engage excessively in personal activities that are beyond the reach of the tax collectors. By reducing the linkages between personal contributions to production and claims on social output, the welfare state encourages people to produce utility in ways that do not have to be shared with others. The real household sector in Sweden is too large on both counts. The monetization of subsidized household services provided through the subsidized state bureaucracy increases the demand for publicly provided services and the size of the public sector but reduces the value of social output and living standards in the overall economy. Total output is smaller than it would have been if household services had been paid for privately and transacted through the market.

Appendix

Notation

h: time spent in household self-production;
m: time spent working in market household sector;
ℓ: time spent working in material goods sector;
$t = m + \ell$: total time spent working in the market sector;
x: market good;
z: good produced in household;
M: purchased inputs in household production;
p: price of M;
w: wage rate;
q: average and marginal cost of z;
I: full income;
θ: cost share of own labor in household production;
$1 - \theta$: cost share of M in household production;
ϕ: budget share of z in consumption;
$1 - \phi$: budget share of x in consumption;
η_{zq}: uncompensated own-price elasticity of demand for z;
η_{zI}: income elasticity of demand for z;
σ_p: elasticity of substitution between h and M in production;
σ_c: elasticity of substitution between x and z in consumption;
g: government revenue;
τ: unit income taxation rate;
ρ: unit tax or subsidy in M.

Elasticities

Equations (1) and (2) imply the following system of equations

$$q = Q(w, p), \quad \text{marginal cost of } z;$$
$$h = H(w, p, z), \quad \text{derived demand for } h;$$
$$M = M(w, p, z), \quad \text{derived demand for } M;$$
$$z = Z(q, I), \quad \text{consumer demand for } z.$$

When w or p changes, optimal factor proportions change. This is the production substitution effect. Factor price changes affect q (and I) and also change optimal consumption. This is the consumption substitution effect.

For example,

$$\frac{\partial h}{\partial w} = H_w + H_z \left(Z_q Q_w + Z_I \frac{\partial I}{\partial w} \right).$$

From the Slutsky decomposition,

$$Z_q = Z_q^s - z Z_I.$$

Constant returns implies $H_z = Q_w = h/z$. Since $I = w$, we have $\partial h / \partial w = 1$. Making all the substitutions,

$$\frac{\partial h}{\partial w} = H_w + (h/z)^2 Z_q^s + (h/z) Z_I (1 - h).$$

Finally, $H_w = -(1 - \theta) \sigma_p h / w$, and $Z_q^s \equiv -(1 - \phi) \sigma_c z / q$, and $\eta_{zI} = Z_I (I/z)$, so that

$$\eta_{hw} = (w/h)(\partial h / \partial w) = -(1 - \theta) \sigma_p - \theta (1 - \phi) \sigma_c + (1 - \theta \phi) \eta_{zI}.$$

Note in text equation (3) that $\eta_{zq} \equiv -(1 - \phi) \sigma_c - \phi \eta_{zI}$. The other formulas in (3) are derived in the same way.

Cross-Hauling

The consumer sees the budget

$$w^*(1 - h) = x + p^* M,$$

where $w^* = w - \tau$, and $p^* = p + \rho$. Differentiating the budget constraint, the demand functions must satisfy

$$(1 - h) - w^* \frac{\partial h}{\partial w^*} - \frac{\partial x}{\partial w^*} - p^* \frac{\partial M}{\partial w^*} = 0,$$

$$M + p^* \frac{\partial M}{\partial p^*} + \frac{\partial x}{\partial p^*} + w^* \frac{\partial h}{\partial w^*} = 0.$$

However, the social budget is

$$wh + x + pM = w - g,$$

where w and p are fixed at their constant supply prices. Totally differentiating the social budget, and noting that $\rho M + \tau(1 - h) = g$,

$$\left(w^* \frac{\partial h}{\partial w^*} + \frac{\partial x}{\partial w^*} + p^* \frac{\partial M}{\partial w^*} \right) \frac{dw^*}{d\tau} d\tau$$

$$+ \left(w^* \frac{\partial h}{\partial p^*} + \frac{\partial x}{\partial p^*} + p^* \frac{\partial M}{\partial p^*} \right) \frac{dp^*}{d\rho} dp = 0.$$

Therefore,

$$(1 - h) d\tau + M d\rho = 0$$

keeps the budget balanced. Equations (8) and (9) in the text follow from the expressions in equation (3) and the condition that $d\tau = -[M/(1 - h)]d\rho$.

Text equation (2) implies

$$du = dG = -\lambda d\tau - \lambda z \left(-\frac{\partial q}{\partial w^*} d\tau + \frac{\partial q}{\partial p^*} dp \right) = -\lambda[(1 - h)d\tau + Md\rho],$$

so $du = 0$ in this experiment.

Separability

It is well known that much of the power of the household production model derives from its separability assumptions. For example, the income elasticities of demand for h and M are identical, and so are the partial elasticities of substitution $\sigma_{Mx} = \sigma_{hx}$. These restrictions are relaxed by using the general utility function $u = u(x, h, M)$ with budget $x + wh + pM = w$. Expanding the associated expenditure function, the deadweight loss formula becomes

$$\phi(1 - \theta)\{1 - \phi)[\sigma_{Mx}\rho^2 + \phi\theta\sigma_{hx}\tau^2] + \phi\theta\sigma_{Mh}(\rho + \tau)^2\}qz/2.$$

Comparison with the expression in the text implies the following restrictions in the text model:

$$\sigma_{hx} = \sigma_{Mx} = \sigma_c,$$
$$\phi\sigma_{hM} = \sigma_p - (1 - \phi)\sigma_c,$$
$$\eta_{zI} = \eta_{MI} = \eta_{hI}.$$

Estimates of own and cross-elasticities of labor supply and child-care demand provide enough information to calculate the more general formula above along the lines indicated in the text and table 2.3. The only such estimates known to me are Ribar (1993) for the United States. Using those numbers and Swedish tax and subsidy rates yields losses that are of the same order as those in table 2.3.

References

Atkinson, Anthony B., and Joseph E. Stigliz. 1980. *Lectures on public economics.* New York: McGraw-Hill.

Becker, Gary. 1965. A theory of the allocation of time. *Economic Journal* 75:493–517.

Bergstrom, Ted, and Soren Blomquist. In press. The political economy of subsidized day care and labor supply. *European Economic Review.*

Blomquist, N. S., and U. Hansson-Brusewitz. 1990. The effect of taxes on male and female labor supply in Sweden. *Journal of Human Resources* 25, no. 3:317–57.

Gronau, Reuben. 1977. Leisure, home production and work. *Journal of Political Economy* 85:1099–1123.

Gustafsson, Bjorn, and N. Anders Klevmarken. 1993. Taxes and transfers in Sweden:

Incentive effects on labour supply. In *Welfare and work incentives: A North European perspective,* ed. A. B. Atkinson and G. V. Mogensen. Oxford: Clarendon.

Gustafsson, Siv, and Frank Stafford. 1992. Child care subsidies and labor supply in Sweden. *Journal of Human Resources* 27:204–30.

———. 1994. Three regimes of child care: The U.S., the Netherlands and Sweden. In *Social protection versus economic flexibility: Is there a tradeoff?* ed. R. Blank. Chicago: University of Chicago Press.

Hansson, Ingemar. 1984. Marginal cost of public transfer, different tax instruments and government expenditures. *Scandinavian Journal of Economics* 86, no. 2:27–71.

Harberger, Arnold C. 1964. The measurement of waste. *American Economic Review* 54 (May): 58–76.

———. 1971. Three basic postulates for applied welfare economics. *Journal of Economic Literature* 9, no. 3:785–97.

Lindbeck, Assar. 1982. Tax effects versus budget effects on labor supply. *Economic Inquiry* 20:473–89.

———. 1988. Consequences of the advanced welfare state. *World Economy* 11 (March): 19–37.

———. 1993. *The welfare state: Selected essays.* Vol. 2. London: Edward Elgar.

Lindbeck, Assar, Per Molander, Torsten Persson, Olof Petersson, Agnar Sandmo, Birgitta Swedenborg, and Niels Thygesen. 1994. *Turning Sweden around.* Cambridge, Mass.: MIT Press.

Quah, Euston. 1993. *Economics and home production.* Aldershot: Avebury.

Ribar, David. 1993. A structural model of child care and the labor supply of married women. Penn State University. Typescript.

Rosen, Sherwin. 1978. Substitution and division of labor. *Economica* 45:235–50.

Sandmo, Agnar. 1990. Tax distortions and household production. *Oxford Economic Papers* 42 (January): 78–90.

Schwartz, Brita, and Susanna Weinberg. 1993. Kommunala kostnadsuariationer—en studie av barnomsorgen, 1990–91 (Cost variations in local governments—a study of public day care, 1990–91). E.F.I. Research Paper. Stockholm School of Economics.

Sundstrom, Marianne, and Frank P. Stafford. 1992. Female labor force participation, fertility and public policy in Sweden. *European Journal of Population* 8:199–225.

Thomas, J. J. 1992. *Informal economic activity.* Ann Arbor: University of Michigan Press.

3   Tax Policy in Sweden

Erik Norrman and Charles E. McLure Jr.

3.1   Introduction

There has recently been a sea change in the philosophy of tax policy in Sweden. Södersten (1991, 16) calls the 1991 reforms "the most far-reaching reform of the nation's tax system for at least 40 years." Neutrality has replaced social and economic engineering and redistribution of income as the key principle guiding tax policy. This revolution in thought is reflected in the tax reforms enacted in 1985, 1991, and 1994. However, proposals to be implemented during the next few years may turn out to increase asymmetries in the system again.

This paper traces the incentives for investment in the Swedish economy created by the tax system. Since taxation of labor income is treated in other chapters of this book, our investigation focuses on the taxation of income from capital and the development of tax policy over the past twenty-five years. The reforms of 1991–94 are examined in detail in order to evaluate their expected effect on resource allocation and the distribution of welfare. The aim is to shed some light on Swedish tax policy and its development.

The theory of optimal taxation seldom gives concrete direction to policy makers. However, one rule of thumb, which is both intuitively appealing and relatively easy to implement, states that taxes should be neutral, unless it is proved that distortive taxes are desirable. *Neutrality* refers in this case to taxes that do not distort the relative prices of different goods or choices of productive factors and methods of finance. This norm suggests that equal tax rates should be applied to all ways of earning capital income (e.g., depreciable assets and

Erik Norrman is associate professor of economics at Lund University and a research associate of Studieförbundet Näringsliv och Samhälle (SNS). Charles E. McLure Jr. is a senior fellow at the Hoover Institution at Stanford University, a research associate of the National Bureau of Economic Research, and economic adviser to the International Tax and Investment Center.

inventories) and to various types of capital income (dividends, interest, etc.). Neutrality is consistent with horizontal equity as well as efficient resource allocation. In this paper, economic neutrality is used as a norm against which to judge the incentives created by the tax system.

Until recently, tax policy has been utilized as an instrument of social and economic engineering in Sweden. In particular, generous incentives were provided for investment, in order to encourage industrialization; it was thought that tax-induced industrial production for export would assist in avoiding balance of payments problems.

Consistent with the egalitarian philosophical underpinnings of the welfare state, highly progressive taxes were levied on the income of individuals. Together with the need to make up the revenue lost through investment incentives, this resulted in extremely high marginal tax rates on the incomes of individuals; in 1980, the top marginal rate was above 85 percent, and 74 percent of full-time employees paid marginal tax rates in excess of 50 percent (Statistiska Meddelanden 1987, table 9.8.2).[1]

These high tax rates had results that should have been anticipated. They discouraged saving and work effort (at least in the market economy—labor increasingly found untaxed outlets, e.g., in the "gray" economy and in self-maintenance of owner-occupied housing). Stuart (1981) estimates that 75 percent of the measured decline in GDP during the 1970s was a result of increasing home activities at the expense of market activities. Hansson (1984) calculates the marginal cost for raising SKr 1.00 by increased average and marginal taxes on labor in order to spend on transfers to be as large as SKr 7.20!

High tax rates also created substantial incentives for illegal tax evasion and for legal tax avoidance—the arrangement of transactions to escape taxes. Perhaps as important, the combination of high rates and structural imperfections created the opportunity for tax avoidance. These behavioral adjustments, which may not easily be reversed, can be particularly unfortunate if they undermine honesty and respect for the state.[2]

Although individual income taxes were very high, corporate income taxes were generally quite low, once investment incentives are taken into account, despite statutory corporate rates in the neighborhood of 60 percent. Moreover, the corporate income tax was quite uneven in its effects. This is best seen by examining marginal effective tax rates (METRs), that is, the tax wedge between the gross returns to investment and the net return to the investor. On balance, considering all sources of funds, methods of finance, assets, and in-

1. The rate referred to includes the income tax system but not the additional wedge from the social security system.

2. Thus, Lindbeck (1993) suggests: "A particularly problematic phenomenon in advanced welfare states is that the incentives to cheat on taxes and benefits are considerable. It becomes expensive to be honest; accordingly, the supply of honesty will gradually fall—even in countries where honesty has originally been relatively pronounced, as in the Nordic countries. There is, therefore, a risk that high-tax welfare states will gradually depreciate the historically inherited 'capital stock' of honesty, and it might be difficult, or at least take a long time, to restore it."

dustries, the METR under the Swedish corporate tax system was only about 2 percent in 1980.[3] Since, considering the effects of both the corporate and the owners' income taxes, the overall METR was 37 percent, it is clear that, while investment in the Swedish corporate sector was heavily subsidized, saving was heavily taxed.

One effect of such a constellation of marginal effective tax rates would have been the creation of incentives for foreigners to own Swedish industry, relative to a system with a more evenhanded treatment of saving and investment, except that the law limited the possibility for foreigners to hold shares in Swedish corporations before 1993. Instead, the incentives led primarily to increased ownership by domestic tax-favored institutions; household ownership fell from 55 percent of the total value of quoted shares to 15 percent during the period 1970–92 (see fig. 3.1). At the same time, domestic institutions (insurance companies, pension funds, etc.) increased their share from 40 to 67 percent. Since the abolition of limitations on foreign holdings of Swedish shares, foreign ownership has risen from 8 percent in 1990 to above 20 percent in 1994.

The heavy subsidization of corporate investment is particularly anomalous since the taxation of returns to investment by foreigners (and low-taxed domestic entities) is one of the reasons commonly offered for the existence of corporate income taxes.

Beginning modestly in 1985, accelerating in 1991, and continuing with the 1994 changes, there has been a marked change in tax policy in Sweden. As in the rest of the world, the emphasis has shifted from redistribution and encouragement of investment to horizontal equity and economic neutrality. Investment incentives have been reduced dramatically. These and other base-broadening reforms have allowed equally dramatic reductions in the marginal tax rates applied to both individual and corporate income while maintaining revenues. Moreover, base broadening has prevented a sharp reduction in progressivity since high-income earners typically have received low-taxed fringe benefits.

Several important additional reforms have been enacted in the taxation of income from capital since 1991. In the beginning of 1992, the tax rate applied to capital gains was reduced from 30 to 25 percent. Beginning in 1994, the statutory corporate tax rate was reduced from 30 to 28 percent, and a deduction for dividends on new shares was abolished.[4] Instead, dividends from publicly held corporations were exempt from tax, and the capital gains rate was reduced once again to 12.5 percent. At the same time, the tax equalization fund system

3. Note, however, that Södersten (1991) estimates a METR of -26 percent at an inflation rate of 10 percent—roughly the rate prevailing at the time. For the difference in methodologies used by Södersten and Norrman, see n. 21 below.

4. The "Annell deduction" allowed the corporation to deduct an amount from the corporate tax base equal to dividends paid out, up to 10 percent of new issued equity capital per year within twenty years from issue date and a maximum of 100 percent of the issued amount. See sec. 3.4 below.

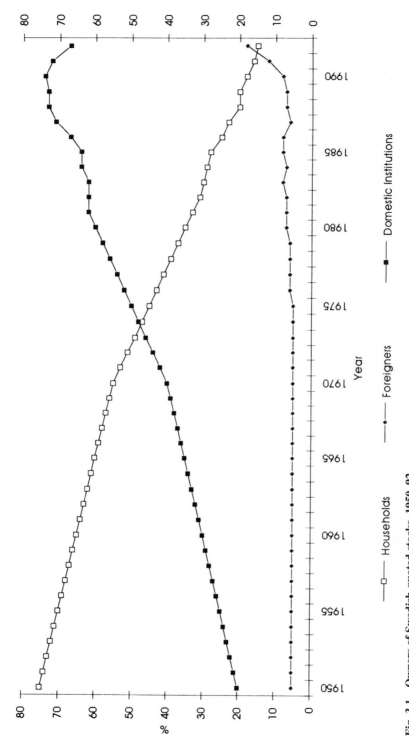

Fig. 3.1 Owners of Swedish quoted stocks, 1950–92
Source: Spånt (1975); and Statistiska Meddelanden (1993).

(*surv*) was replaced by a system allowing tax credits based purely on profits.[5] These reforms had the effect of greatly reducing the discrimination against new issues and retained earnings that survived the 1991 reforms.

Complexity has been one of the hallmarks of Swedish income tax policy. This can be seen in, among other things, the elaborate system of extra investment allowances, the Annell deduction, the investment funds system, and the tax equalization fund. Perhaps equally important is the complexity that results from taxpayers' efforts to avoid, or even evade, high tax rates and the efforts of the fiscal authorities to thwart avoidance and evasion. Such efforts are inevitable if similar types of income are taxed very differently, as taxpayers will attempt to convert high-taxed income to low-taxed income.

The 1991 and subsequent reforms reduced both elements of complexity. They eliminated the Annell deduction and most tax incentives for investment. They reduced the incentives and opportunities for tax avoidance and evasion by lowering tax rates and introducing schedular elements into the system as well as by curtailing investment incentives.

The latter effect is particularly important and thus worthy of note. Arguments for global income taxation assume implicitly that all income will be taxed as it accrues. In such a world, it makes sense to allow deductions for all expenses as they accrue. But asymmetric treatment of income and expenses—as when nominal interest expense is deducted currently but taxation of investment income is deferred—is a recipe for disaster. As taxpayers take advantage of asymmetries to reduce their taxes, simplicity suffers, along with equity and neutrality.

3.1.1 Alternative Models of Tax Policy

Economists commonly espouse two alternative models of tax policy, both of which are (in their pure form) neutral with regard to the allocation of capital.[6] One model is based on the taxation of income, the other on the taxation of consumption. It is common to identify consumption-based taxation with indirect taxes, such as the value added tax and excises. In fact, there is also a form of direct taxation that is tantamount to taxing consumption rather than income.

Historically, direct taxation in Sweden has followed neither of these models closely. Rather, it has contained a mixture of provisions—some of which might be consistent with one or the other model—that, in combination, create complexity and inequity and distort the allocation of capital. Given the importance of this distinction and the disadvantage of adopting a "hybrid" system that

---

5. In the former tax system, 30 percent of the equity capital at the end of the accounting year (i.e., including after-tax profits of the year) formed the basis for additions to untaxed reserves called *surv* (tax equalization fund). In the new scheme, 25 percent of each year's profits may be kept in a fund for a maximum of five years. Taken together, this means that, at an even level of profits over time, 125 percent of the yearly profit may be kept in such funds.

6. For a description of the evolution of thinking about these two models, see McLure and Zodrow (1994).

corresponds fully to neither model, the remainder of this section explains these two forms of direct taxation. The next section presents data on sources of revenue.

The Income Tax Model

The traditional favorite (in theory, if not in practice) is the income tax model. In this model, the objective in the taxation of income from capital is to define the tax base to track economic income as closely as possible. Thus, depreciation allowances should reflect economic depreciation, and there should not be any extra deductions or credits intended to encourage saving or investment.

Inflation erodes the real value of depreciation allowances, the real cost of goods sold from inventories, and the real value of outstanding debt, and it causes the overstatement of capital gains. Ad hoc measures, such as acceleration of depreciation allowances, are sometimes used to offset these effects. But, if the rate of inflation is high enough, explicit adjustment for inflation is required, as explained below.

Some countries employ a "classical" system, in which corporate income and dividends received by shareholders are subject to separate tax regimes, with no attempt to integrate the two, in order to reduce double taxation of distributed earnings. It has generally been agreed that it is impossible to integrate the individual and corporate income taxes completely, for example, by treating corporations like partnerships (in which case, all profits would "flow through" to shareholders, who would pay tax on them, instead of being taxed at the entity level). But many advanced countries provide some sort of relief from double taxation of dividends. The most commonly used means of providing dividend relief is the imputation system, in which the corporate income giving rise to dividends (but not income retained by the corporation) is attributed to shareholders, who are allowed a credit for the part of the corporate tax attributable to such income. An alternative that achieves the same result, at least in principle, is the "split-rate" system, under which corporations pay a lower tax on income that is distributed than on income that is retained. Finally, some countries simply exempt dividends from tax at the shareholder level; unlike the other two alternatives, this does not achieve the goal of taxing distributed corporate equity income at the tax rate of the shareholder if the corporate tax rate and the tax rate of the shareholder are not the same.[7]

---

7. Suppose that a corporation earns 1,000 of income, pays corporate tax of 50 percent, distributes 400 of after-tax income to a taxpayer subject to a marginal tax rate of 60 percent, and retains 100. Under the imputation system, the shareholder would pay personal tax of 480 on grossed-up dividends of 800 (the amount needed to pay dividends of 400, given the corporate tax rate of 50 percent); net of the imputation credit of 400 the shareholder's tax would be 80. Under the split-rate system, the income giving rise to dividends would not be subject to corporate tax; thus, the corporation could distribute 800, on which the shareholder would pay tax of 480, as under the imputation system. Finally, if dividends were exempt from shareholder tax, distributed corporate-source equity income would be subject only to the corporate-level tax of 400, or 50 percent, instead of the shareholder tax of 480, or 60 percent.

In the absence of integration and inflation (or if there is perfect inflation adjustment of the measurement of income), income taxation produces an entity-level effective tax rate on income from equity investment that is equal to the statutory rate.[8] Under the classical system, distributed earnings are then subject to taxation when received by shareholders, producing an aggregate effective tax rate that exceeds both the corporate and the individual statutory rates. The object of dividend relief is to reduce this aggregate tax to the statutory marginal rate of shareholders (in the case of the imputation and split-rate systems) or the corporation (in the case of the exemption of dividends). In the case of income on debt-financed investment, the entity-level tax is zero, but the effective tax rate paid by the debtholder is the statutory rate; thus, the aggregate effective rate of tax is the statutory rate of the debtholder.

These results—an effective corporate tax rate on income from equity-financed investment equal to the statutory rate, a zero corporate effective rate on income from debt-financed investment, and aggregate effective rates on distributed earnings and interest equal to the statutory rate of the recipient—provide a useful benchmark against which to appraise the Swedish tax system. While a pure income tax distorts the choice between saving and consumption, and thus the levels of saving and investment, by taxing future consumption more heavily than present consumption, it does not distort current decisions on the allocation of funds between competing investments.

Inflation generally causes income from capital to be measured inaccurately. This is most easily seen in the case of the sale of a capital asset that was bought for 100 and sold for 300 following a period during which prices have doubled. In the absence of inflation adjustment, tax would be paid on the nominal gain of 200 rather than on the real gain of 100; if prices had quadrupled, tax would again be levied on 200, despite a real loss of 100. Similar reasoning applies to the cost of goods sold from inventory and to depreciation allowances; only explicit adjustment of purchase prices for the increase in the general price level generally avoids mismeasurement of income.[9] Allowance of deductions for the full nominal amount of interest expense and inclusion of nominal interest income in taxable income also cause income to be misstated; accurate measurement of income would recognize that part of nominal interest payments compensate only for the loss of real value resulting from the erosion of principal—and that it may even fail to do that fully, in the case of unexpected inflation. In calculating marginal effective tax rates in a world of inflation, it is necessary to take account of these effects.

---

8. It is difficult to differentiate clearly between corporate and shareholder taxes in the case of the imputation system. The interpretation of aggregate (corporate and individual) tax rates is more straightforward.

9. It is sometimes thought that the use of last-in, first-out (LIFO) accounting for inventories avoids this problem. In fact, the use of LIFO eliminates the effects of shifts in relative prices as well as changes in the general price level.

The Consumption Tax Model

The second competing model for tax policy is the consumption-based direct tax. Under it, immediate deduction (expensing) is allowed for all business purchases, including depreciable assets and additions to inventories. (Thus, there are no depreciation allowances and no deductions for cost of goods sold.) As a result of expensing, the marginal effective entity-level tax rate on income from equity-financed investment is zero.[10] There are two alternative methods of treating debt, at both the entity level and the debtholder level. One is to ignore debt entirely; thus, interest is neither taxable nor deductible. The other is to treat interest as under the income tax but to include proceeds of borrowing in the tax base and allow a deduction for lending and the repayment of debt. These two methods are (under rather stringent circumstances) equivalent in present-value terms to each other and to the exemption of interest income and expense. In short, the marginal effective tax rate on income from business and capital under the consumption-based direct tax is identically zero for both entities and individuals (again, under stringent assumptions). This result is invariant to the rate of inflation (other than that between the time an asset is bought and the time a deduction is taken for it) since inflation does not have the chance to erode the value of expensed purchases and either debt is ignored for tax purposes or the effect of inflation on the real value of debt principal and interest offset each other.

Like the results for the pure income tax, the results for the consumption-based direct tax—zero marginal effective tax rates—provide a useful benchmark for the appraisal of the Swedish tax system. Besides being neutral with regard to the saving-consumption choice (unlike the income tax) as well as the allocation of current investment (like the income tax), the zero METR inherent in the consumption-based direct tax is potentially attractive for a small open economy that is interested in attracting foreign investment.[11]

Problems with "Hybrid" Systems

No country applies either of these models in its pure form. The failure to utilize the consumption tax model can be explained by several factors, including the novelty of the idea, the distributional implications of exempting the

10. One way of seeing this is to think of the government as a partner in all investments. When a taxpayer subject to a 40 percent tax rate makes an investment, that taxpayer must put up only 60 percent of the funds for the investment; the government contributes the rest, in the form of reduced tax receipts. Then the taxpayer receives 60 percent of the return and the government the rest. Since the taxpayer receives 60 percent of the return on 60 percent of the investment, the taxpayer's marginal effective tax rate is zero.

11. The issue is more complicated than this. The zero METR would presumably be attractive to investors from countries that exempt foreign-source income but not necessarily to those from countries that tax the worldwide income of their investors and allow credits for source-country taxes—unless such investors have excess foreign tax credits or defer repatriation of earnings. Also, the fear that the consumption-based direct tax might not be eligible for foreign tax credits has thus far prevented any country from adopting such a tax, except for small businesses.

return from capital, problems of transition, and uncertainty about whether the United States (and perhaps other countries that tax the worldwide income of their taxpayers) would allow credits for taxes paid to source countries using the consumption model. Even so, the tax laws of many countries contain provisions that are consistent with the consumption tax model. These do not, by themselves, constitute a coherent consumption-based tax, and they are inconsistent with the income tax model.

The tax laws of all countries contain provisions that are inconsistent with the income tax model, which commonly forms the conceptual basis for such laws. Among common examples are the acceleration of depreciation allowances and the exemption of certain forms of income. Few countries provide comprehensive inflation adjustment for the measurement of income, except those experiencing high rates of inflation, but many laws include provisions that have been justified as ad hoc responses to inflation; accelerated depreciation is one of these. Such ad hoc provisions are unlikely to compensate adequately for inflation, except at one level of inflation.

Inconsistent treatment of various transactions, including piecemeal adoption of selected features of the consumption tax model (e.g., expensing of depreciable assets while providing income tax treatment of interest expense) and the failure to deal with inflation in a comprehensive manner, creates opportunities for tax planning or "tax arbitrage." Steuerle (1985, 2) provides a description of tax arbitrage and its effects that is worth quoting at length because it describes so well what happened during the 1980s in Sweden as well as in the United States:

> Tax and loan considerations come together in part through tax arbitrage—basically a process whereby taxpayers borrow for the purpose of purchasing [tax-]preferred assets. The difference in the tax treatment of receipts of preferred income, on the one hand, and deductions of interest payments received [*sic*], on the other, has an enormous effect on almost all investment decisions. Tax arbitrage is an important determinant of which investments are made, of who will own particular types of assets, and how large aggregate demand will be for loans. Many loans and tax reductions are provided to persons who play tax arbitrage "games" in which no additional saving or investment is generated in the economy. . . .
>
> All these problems are exacerbated by inflation. A higher inflation rate raises interest rates and usually makes tax arbitrage more profitable per dollar of borrowing and investment. Some investment uses capital unproductively because the value of output made possible by the investment is actually less than the cost of the investment itself.

The overall result of the "Chinese menu" approach to tax policy (some provisions from the income tax column and some from the consumption tax column) is the distortion of economic choices, inequities, the perception that the system is unfair, and complexity, as efforts are made to prevent abuse.

A convenient way to express the distortionary influences of taxation is to calculate marginal effective tax rates (METRs). The METR is the percentage by which taxation reduces the return to capital on an investment that, in the absence of taxation, would be on the borderline between being worthwhile and not being worthwhile. Such calculations consider the effects of inflation, as well as the provisions of tax law, and can be calculated for the corporate and individual income tax separately or for the two combined. METRs can exceed 100 percent, or they can be negative; negative METRs occur when the "after-tax" return to an investment exceeds the before-tax return, implying that the tax system provides a subsidy. If depreciation is accelerated, the marginal effective tax rate on income from equity-financed investment falls below the statutory rate. If the cost of depreciable assets can be deducted in the year of acquisition, the METR on income from equity-financed investments is zero. (The deduction reduces the net cost of the investment by a percentage equal to the statutory tax rate; since taxation reduces the return to the investment by the same fraction, the effect is the same as if there were no taxation.) If interest deductions are allowed for investment that benefits from accelerated depreciation, the METR at the corporate level can be negative. Combining consumption tax treatment of depreciable assets (expensing) with allowance of interest deductions creates large subsidies to debt-financed investments. This is especially true where deductions are allowed for the full amount of interest expense, with no adjustment for inflation.

3.1.2   The Prereform Swedish Model

Direct taxation in Sweden has followed neither the income tax nor the consumption tax model; it was more accurately characterized as a hybrid system. This can be seen by examining structural features of the Swedish income tax.

In 1980, the personal income tax included, in principle, all returns to capital. The sum of capital income and labor income was taxed at graduated rates. Despite the appearance of progressive taxation (at least intended progressivity), the outcome was, in reality, not progressive. Because provisions consistent with the consumption tax model were combined with income tax provisions, there were opportunities for tax arbitrage.

The deviation from the pure income tax model consisted in three main circumstances. First, inflation adjustment depended on type of asset. Second, capital gains were taxed when assets were sold, not when accrued. Third, the return to some assets was tax exempt.

While interest income and interest expense were (and still are) taxed on a nominal basis without inflation adjustment, capital gains on shares were fully taxable only if realized within two years after acquisition; only 40 percent of gains on assets held for more than two years were subject to tax. Moreover, imputed income from owner-occupied houses and any capital gain on real estate were assessed on an inflation-adjusted basis. This, together with the deduction for mortgage interest, provided an attractive opportunity for tax arbitrage—borrowing to invest in owner-occupied housing.

Since capital gains were not taxed on accrual, the effective tax rate on capital gains was lower than the statutory rate. In this situation, the owner of the asset may explicitly postpone taxation of a gain until the asset is sold. This implies an interest-free loan from the government to the taxpayer, compared to the pure income tax situation. One problem, seen from the standpoint of the government, is that the taxpayer may chose to liquidate assets with losses as soon as they accrue while the taxation of capital gains is postponed. In principle, there are two ways to solve this problem. The first one is when capital losses only may be deducted from capital gains. The second one is to admit only a fraction of the loss to be deducted from ordinary income. In 1980, the first principle was used.

Apart from the implicit return to consumer durables, primarily pension capital was tax exempt and therefore treated in accordance with the consumption tax model. Contributions were deductible and therefore exempt from income tax. As a result, the tax on the part of the income that was saved could also be saved with the government as a sleeping partner. When the pension finally was paid out, the government withdrew its investment. Since no taxation took place at the fund level, this implies that the effective rate on pension capital was zero (see also n. 10 above).

The investment incentives that have been available at various times are more consistent with the consumption tax model than the income tax model. In present-value terms, they were in some cases (investment in machinery) more generous than immediate expensing; that is, the present value of the deductions for depreciation allowances including the value of the investment grants exceeded 100 percent of the investment outlays. Combined with the continued existence of full deduction for nominal interest expenses, they resulted in negative METRs.

3.1.3   The 1985 and 1991 Tax Reforms

The development between 1985 and 1991 is best characterized as rate reducing and neutrality increasing. The top marginal income tax rate on labor dropped from 80 percent in 1985 to 51 percent in 1991. The total top marginal effect fell from 88 to 74 percent.[12] Neutrality was increased by base-broadening measures. Most fringe benefits became taxable income valued at market price, and the tax subsidy to interest expenses was reduced from 50 to 30 percent. The system was moved toward the income tax model as the returns to pension capital were taxed at the fund level, first by a special tax in 1987 (*engångsskatten*) and then, from 1991, by a permanent tax. A main principle for the taxation of capital income was introduced in 1991; all returns should be taxed at 30 percent without inflation adjustment. At a rate of inflation of 4 percent and a real rate of interest of 3 percent, this implied a tax rate of 70 percent in real terms.

Still, there were several exceptions from the pure income tax model. As

---

12. This number includes taxation within the social security system, taxes on goods, and marginal effects due to income-dependent housing allowances.

mentioned, inflation was not considered. Also, capital gains were taxed (and still are) on realization, not when accrued. Seventy percent of losses could be deducted from ordinary income instead of from capital gains. Certain types of income were also taxed at a lower rate—primarily capital gains on owner-occupied housing and special tax-favored savings accounts and funds.

The most important part of the reform was, however, the substitution of progressive capital income taxation by proportional taxation. This took place by separating taxation of capital income from that of labor income. The main objective was to achieve a better correspondence between intended and actual taxation of *labor* income by reducing the possibility of affecting the taxation of labor income by interest expenses.

Corporate taxation was also designed in order to increase neutrality. The statutory tax rate was decreased to 30 percent, while possibilities to build up untaxed reserves were reduced substantially. These had earlier been associated with certain types of assets and had therefore strongly affected the investment choice. In 1991, a new possibility based on the own capital of the firm was introduced—the tax equalization reserve. In this way, the importance of the composition of assets in the company for tax reasons was considerably reduced.

In 1994, the right-wing government took a further step toward neutrality in the financial decisions of corporations by abolishing the economic double taxation of corporate profits. In principle, dividends distributed by Swedish corporations became tax exempt, and the tax rate on capital gains was set at 12.5 percent. The system was thereby brought more in line with the pure income tax model. However, the new Social Democratic government has decided to reintroduce double taxation of corporate profits, which will also reintroduce distortions in corporate financial decisions.

3.2   Statistics Describing the Swedish Tax System

3.2.1   Macro Data

Taxation may be characterized in several ways. Here, we begin by describing the total tax burden and continue by analyzing the structure.

Figure 3.2 and table 3.1 illustrate the development of total tax revenue as a percentage of GDP in Sweden, the United States, and the average of the OECD countries from 1955 to the present. Figure 3.10 below shows the situation in 1992 for each OECD country. During the period 1955–91, tax revenues rose in Sweden from 25.5 to 53 percent of GDP, while they increased from 24 to only 39 percent on average in OECD countries. This implies a radically more rapid growth of tax revenues in Sweden than in other developed countries. An expected consequence of this expansion should be rising welfare costs of taxation owing to increasing distortions in the economy.

Table 3.1   Total Tax Revenues as a Percentage of GDP

	1955	1965	1975	1985	1990	1991	1992	1993
Sweden	25.5	35.2	43.6	50.4	56.9	53.2	51.1	50.3
United States	23.6	25.8	29.0	28.7	29.5	29.8	29.4	N.A
OECD:								
Europe	25.1	27.5	34.1	38.8	40.0	40.4	N.A.	N.A.
Unweighted average	24.0	26.7	32.9	37.1	38.6	38.7	N.A.	N.A.

Sources: Revenue statistics of OECD member countries (OECD 1993), except for Sweden in 1993, which is from Konjunkturinstitutet (1994).
Note: N.A. = not available.

An even more striking picture appears when public expenditures as a percentage of GDP are reported (see table 3.2). In 1965, public expenditures were 36.1 percent in Sweden, 27.9 percent in the United States, and 36.2 percent on average in OECD Europe. By 1992, they had increased to 67.3 percent in Sweden but to only 35.4 percent in the United States and 50.7 percent in the OECD. Since expenditures must always be financed and it may be necessary to raise future taxes to repay public debt, this measure is more appropriate than the ratio of taxes to GDP when evaluating the burden of the public sector. The discrepancy between revenues and expenditures also has important generational implications.

Over time, an increasing share of total tax revenues has been derived from consumption taxation. This can be seen most clearly in the relative growth of revenues from indirect taxes.

Since the typical feature of the consumption tax model is that the effective tax rate on capital income is zero, one way of evaluating the extent of income taxation is to look at the total amount of taxes on capital income compared to taxes on labor income. In 1965, taxes on capital income constituted 11 percent of total tax revenues, while, in 1991, they were below 7 percent. However, behind these numbers there are changes toward both models.

The great movement toward consumption taxation is seen in the increasing part of tax revenues raised by social security fees based on labor income. Since returns to capital are not affected by these fees, increasing social security fees implies a move from income taxation to consumption taxation. In 1965, they amounted to 12 percent of total tax revenues but had increased to 32 percent in 1991. Although higher social security fees are accompanied by more social security benefits, it is clear that a large part of the fees may be considered as pure taxes.

Table 3.3 reports the structure of taxation in Sweden, the United States, and OECD Europe for 1965, 1990, and 1991. Figure 3.11 below shows the situation in 1991 for the OECD countries. It is striking that Swedish taxes on personal income were a substantially higher multiple of OECD taxes of the same type in 1965 than in 1990. The relative decline in reliance on the personal

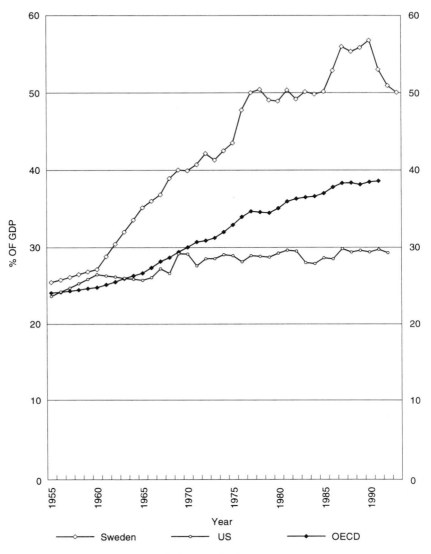

Fig. 3.2   Tax revenues as a percentage of GDP
Source: See table 3.1.

income tax in Sweden has been roughly offset by greater reliance on payroll taxes, especially the expansion of social security contributions. This change implies a shift from progressive taxation to proportional. A possible explanation for this shift may be the relative ease in increasing the tax burden in this way compared to increased income taxation. Other possible interpretations in-

Table 3.2   Total Government Expenditures as a Percentage of GDP

	1965	1975	1985	1990	1991	1992	1993
Sweden	36.1	48.4	63.3	59.1	61.5	67.3	73.6
United States	27.9	33.5	33.2	33.3	34.2	35.4	N.A.
OECD:							
Europe, weighted average[a]	36.2	43.7	49.2	47.8	49.4	50.7	N.A.
Total, weighted average[a]	32.0	36.2	39.5	39.0	40.0	41.2	N.A.

Sources: OECD, *Economic Outlook,* nos. 34 and 53, except for Sweden in 1993, which is from Konjunkturinstitutet (1994).
Note: N.A. = not available.
[a]GDP weights.

Table 3.3   Different Taxes as Percentage of Total Taxation

	1965			1990			1991		
	Sweden	United States	OECD Europe	Sweden	United States	OECD Europe	Sweden	United States	OECD Europe
Personal income	48.7	30.5	25.0	37.9	35.8	27.9	34.0	34.9	28.1
Profits	6.1	15.8	6.4	3.1	7.4	6.8	3.1	7.3	6.4
Goods and services	31.2	21.9	40.1	24.6	16.5	32.0	27.1	16.8	32.1
Social security	12.1	16.4	21.6	30.8	29.5	26.7	31.7	29.8	27.2
Wealth and property	1.8	15.3	6.7	3.5	10.8	4.5	4.1	11.2	4.4
Other taxes						1.4			1.5

Souce: Revenue statistics of OECD member countries (OECD 1993).

clude the demise of redistribution as a prime goal for tax policy and the possibility that taxpayers perceive a strong link between payroll taxes and social security benefits. An important question in this context is the extent to which social security fees are actually seen as taxes or as substitutes for private insurance premiums. If they are seen as akin to insurance premiums that purchase increased benefits, they are not likely to have the adverse incentive effects commonly attributed to high taxes.

Table 3.3 also shows the effects of the tax reform of 1991 on the structure of taxation. The share of revenues stemming from the personal income tax fell sharply, while the share from taxes on goods and services rose. This reflects the elimination of the central government income tax for most income earners, in combination with the broadened tax base of the value added tax.

Another recent development in the Swedish tax structure is the decline in corporate taxes and the rise in taxes on wealth and immovable property. This is probably a consequence of international economic integration. An interesting question in this context is the relation between taxes on the income and consumption of individuals (individual income tax, social security fees, and taxes on consumption), on the one hand, and taxes on profits, wealth, and property,

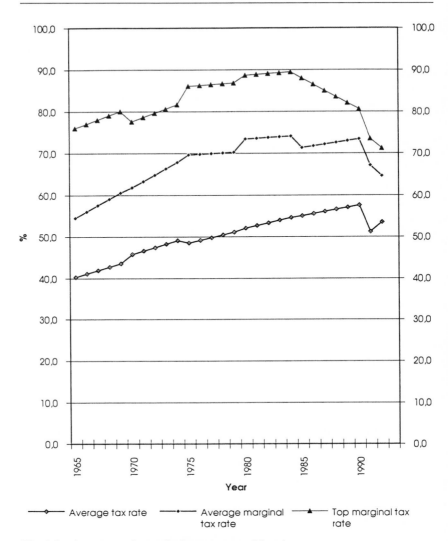

Fig. 3.3   Average and marginal tax rates on labor income
Source: See tables 3.4 and 3.5.

on the other hand. The proportion of the first type of taxes rose from about 87 percent in 1955 to 93 percent in 1991. This does not, however, necessarily imply that the taxation of capital income declined during the period since individual income includes returns to capital and social security contributions may not fully be viewed as taxes, as pointed out above. A more exact analysis of this issue is therefore reported in table 3.4 and shown in figures 3.3 and 3.4.

Taxes on capital income can be defined as taxes that drive a wedge between

Table 3.4   **Average Taxes on Labor and Capital**

	1965	1970	1975	1980	1985	1990	1991	1992
Taxes on labor income:[a]								
As a percentage of GDP	31.4	36.8	41.2	47.7	47.7	53.4	49.0	49.5
As a percentage of labor income	45.1	52.4	57.9	65.2	68.5	71.7	65.8	68.2
Adjusted measure[b]	40.3	45.8	48.5	52.0	55.0	57.6	51.2	53.5
Taxes on capital income:								
Corporate tax, as a percentage of GDP	2.2	1.8	1.9	1.2	1.8	1.8	1.6	.9
Tax on ownership, as a percentage of GDP	1.8	1.6	.7	.1	.8	1.6	2.4	2.6
Total, as a percentage of capital income	19.4	17.7	15.0	8.8	15.2	28.3	33.4	22.0
Total taxes:								
As a percentage of GDP	35.2	40.2	43.6	49.0	50.4	56.9	53.2	52.1
Adjusted measure[b]	35.5	39.8	41.9	45.0	47.2	53.6	48.8	49.1
Labor	.70	.70	.71	.73	.70	.74	.74	.73
Capital	.20	.19	.18	.14	.17	.12	.12	.12
Depreciation	.10	.11	.11	.12	.13	.14	.14	.15

Source: Norrman (1995a).

[a]Taxes on labor income include income taxes on labor, social security fees, and taxes on goods and services.

[b]The adjusted measure is calculated as percentage of labor income and considers to what extent social security benefits and subsidies reduce taxes.

the gross return to capital and the net return to the investor. All other taxes are treated as taxes on labor income. Using this definition, taxes on goods and services are taxes on labor. Taxes on labor have grown in step with the growth of total taxation during the period 1965–92. This is not surprising since labor income constitutes between 78 and 88 percent of total factor incomes net of depreciation during the period and therefore must serve as the major source of tax revenues.

Taxation of labor income has increased from 45.1 to 68.2 percent of such income during this period. A substantial part of this development can be traced to the expansion of the social security system, which includes pension benefits, sickness insurance, work injury insurance, work environment protection, and wage guarantees. The calculation of an alternative measure that considers this fact seems appropriate. Table 3.4 reports an adjusted measure of taxes on labor income. The measure considers the extent to which social security benefits offset the tax component of the contributions. Further, it also includes an assessment of the size of negative consumption taxes, that is, subsidies that reduce the effective tax rate on consumption. A more detailed description of the calculations is found in Norrman (1995a). The adjusted measure discloses both

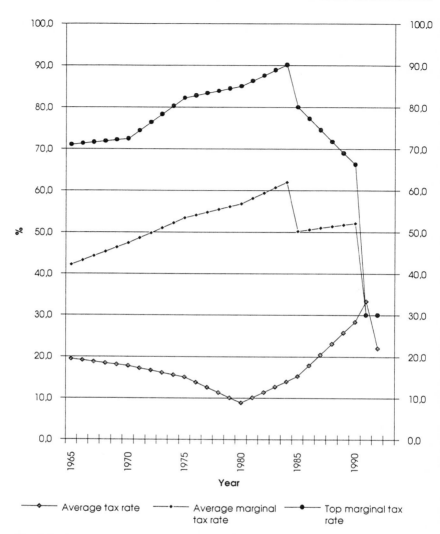

Fig. 3.4 Average and marginal tax rates on capital income
Source: See tables 3.4 and 3.5.

a lower level of taxation of labor income and less rapid growth, from 40.3 to 53.5 percent.

Another way to investigate how taxes influence the situation for households is to look at the importance of transfers in relation to total disposable income. This is obviously closely related to the development of the welfare state. In 1975, labor and capital income constituted 65.8 percent of disposable income for all households and 85.8 percent for households eighteen to sixty-four years

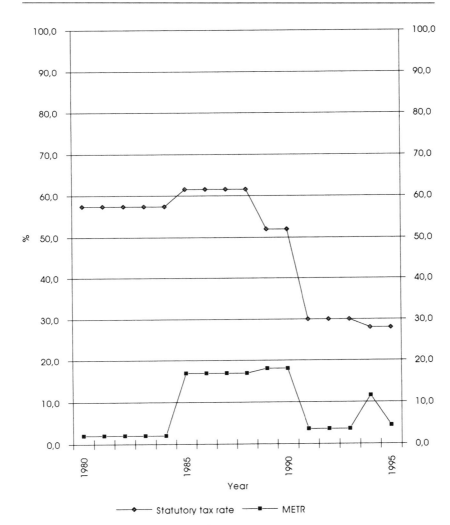

Fig. 3.5   Statutory and marginal effective corporate tax rates on marginal investments
Source: See tables 3.6 and 3.12.

of age. In 1990, the corresponding numbers were 61.3 and 79.4 percent. These numbers reflect the fact that taxable transfers as part of disposable income increased during this period (Jansson and Sandqvist 1993).[13]

When it comes to taxes on capital income, the numbers reported reflect the other side of the same coin; capital income provides only a small tax base. What is more interesting is the fact that capital income appears to be taxed at

13. Taxable transfers are typically income related and substitutes for ordinary income.

a lower rate on average than labor income. A qualification should be made here, however. The tax system has only to a minor extent been constructed to adjust for the effects of inflation. (A lender must, e.g., pay tax on his or her nominal interest income no matter whether the inflation rate is 0 or 10 percent.) Since the national accounts do not consider changes in the real value of capital in calculating income from capital, inflation causes underestimation of the real tax rates on capital income. However, if households respond to inflation by investing in real assets and keeping negative financial holdings, which typically has been the case in Sweden during the 1970s and 1980s, inflation may decrease the tax rate on capital instead of increasing it. A reasonable conclusion is that middle-aged households, who generally keep negative financial assets, have profited from inflation while elderly people have incurred losses on their positive financial holdings.

Taxation of labor displays a steady growth during the period 1965–90, whereas taxation of capital exhibits a U-shaped form over time, with relatively high rates in the beginning of the period, followed by low rates around 1980, and a sharp increase in the 1980s. It is also noticeable that taxes on immovable capital have grown substantially during the latter part of the period. Finally, the reform of 1991 marks a change in the course of tax policy; taxation of labor was decreased considerably, while taxation of capital was increased.

3.2.2   Micro Data

Average tax rates are not as important as marginal tax rates in analyzing the influence of the tax system on the behavior of individuals and corporations. Table 3.5 presents calculations of the average and top marginal tax rates and marginal effective tax rates on labor and capital income during the period 1965–93. The latter numbers include the influence of income-related transfers such as child care.

Figure 3.3 shows an increase in the average marginal tax rates and effective tax rates on labor income from the beginning of the period to the middle, followed by a decline toward the level that was prevailing around 1970. For individuals facing the top marginal effective tax rates, the most important event is the drop in the early 1990s from above 80 percent to nearly 70 percent. Also noticeable is the fact that the average marginal effective tax rates in the middle of the 1980s were higher than the top marginal effective tax rates in the 1990s.

The development of capital income taxation (see fig. 3.4) is similar to that of labor income taxation, except that the drop is still greater at the beginning of the 1990s. Again, the effects of inflation are not included in these numbers.

We add two more numbers of importance in order to assess the incentives of the tax system on portfolio composition. First, the marginal effective tax rates on capital income reported above relate to the taxation of current income, that is, interest payments and dividends. There were no limitations on the deduction of interest expenses until the beginning of the 1980s. Thus, during the 1970s, it became common to deduct interest expense against labor income that

Table 3.5   **Average and Top Marginal Tax Rates on Labor and Capital Income**

	1965	1970	1975	1980	1985	1990	1991	1992	1993
Labor income:									
Average marginal tax rate[a]	42.2	47.4	53.4	56.8	50.2	52.1	39.0	39.0	39.0
Average marginal effective tax rate[a]	54.5	61.8	69.6	73.4	71.3	73.4	67.1	64.6	61.4
Top marginal tax rate	71.0	72.4	82.2	85.0	80.0	66.2	51.2	51.0	51.0
Top marginal effective tax rate	76.0	77.6	86.1	88.7	88.0	80.6	73.5	71.2	70.3
Capital income:									
Average marginal tax rate[b]	42.2	47.4	53.4	56.8	50.2	52.1	30.0	30.0	30.0
Top marginal tax rate[b]	71.0	72.4	82.2	85.0	80.0	66.2	30.0	30.0	30.0
Effective tax rate on capital gains on shares	.0	7.5	8.2	28.7	25.7	23.5	16.6	13.9	13.9
Maximum value of interest deduction	71.0	72.4	82.2	85.0	50.0	40.0	30.0	30.0	30.0

Source: Norrman (1995a).

[a]Average marginal tax rates are calculated as the weighted average over all income groups of their marginal tax rates. Effective rates include social security fees, taxes on goods and services, and housing allowances.

[b]The effective tax rates equal the marginal tax rates.

would otherwise be taxed at high tax rates in response to increasing marginal tax rates.

Second, the effective tax rate on capital gains on shares is calculated assuming an average holding period of ten years. The possibility of deducting interest payments combined with the low tax on capital gains (e.g., from investment in real estate) provided an easy way to convert high-taxed labor income into low-taxed capital income. This possibility seems to be much smaller after the 1991 tax reform. Together with abnormally high real interest rates and the deep recession, this has contributed to the sharp decline of the real estate market.

As was shown in table 3.3 above, corporate taxation fell during the period 1965–91. Figure 3.5 shows the statutory tax rates on corporate profits during the period 1980–95. The tax rate was raised in the mid-1980s owing to the introduction of the profit-sharing tax (which was applied only on profits above a certain level). The purpose of the tax was to finance the so-called wage earners' fund system (Löntagarfonderna). In the mid-1980s, corporate taxation at the local government level was abolished. The numbers in table 3.6, also shown in figure 3.5, are calculated given the profit-sharing tax and the deductibility of the local tax before the change in the tax system.

We return to the tax wedges on different types of investments and their finance in section 3.4 below.

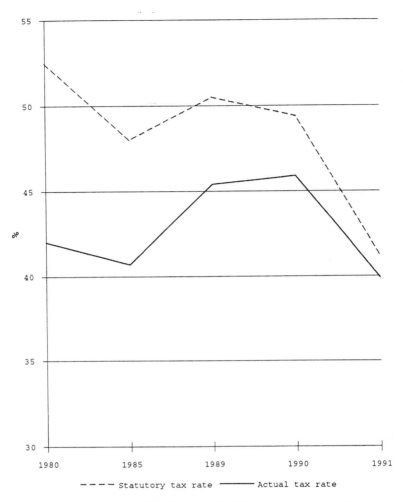

Fig. 3.6 Statutory and actual tax rate on labor earnings—top decile
Source: Malmer, Persson, and Tengblad (1994).

3.3 Distributional Effects of Taxation

3.3.1 Incidence Studies

The data presented in the previous section show that there have been strong incentives for high-income earners to borrow in order to invest in low-taxed assets and to own relatively small amounts of taxable wealth.[14] The ability to use tax planning to avoid progression would also mean less income redistribu-

14. Low taxation could be within either the income tax system or the wealth tax.

Table 3.6   Statutory Corporate Tax Rates

	1965	1970	1975	1980	1985	1990	1991	1992	1993
Including profit-sharing tax	50.3	52.6	55.1	57.4	61.6	52.0	30.0	30.0	30.0
Excluding profit-sharing tax	50.3	52.6	55.1	57.4	52.0	40.0	30.0	30.0	30.0

Sources: Hansson (1983), Statistiska Meddelanden (1992), Statistiska Centralbyrån (1992), and own calculations.

tion than implied by the highly progressive personal income tax schedule. All these expectations were more or less confirmed by several studies during the 1980s (see, e.g., Agell and Edin 1988; Hansson and Norrman 1986; and Jansson 1990). The results of one of these are reported in table 3.7.

Column 1 of table 3.7 shows the distribution of taxes on personal income, as defined by the tax code for 1985. Since lower deciles were paying a lower and higher deciles a higher proportion of income in taxes, compared to the average tax rate, it is obvious that the tax schedule was progressive.[15] However, if taxable deductions for negative capital income are eliminated from the definition of income (the denominator in the calculation), the degree of progression is much lower since interest deductions are claimed disproportionately by those with high incomes.[16] This is confirmed by the fact that the tax rate for people in high deciles was substantially lower if taxes are compared to the assessed income before such deductions, as in column 2. The presence of huge deductions at the top of the income scale dramatically reduced the "effective" progression compared to the statutory one.[17]

In order better to capture the living standard of households, the third column of table 3.7 relates taxes to household income corrected for the effects of inflation on the value of monetary assets, for certain nontaxable transfers, and for the number of household members (consumer units). This computation increases the calculated tax rate for low-income households and decreases it for high-income households.

Further study shows clearly that capital income taxation, especially the asymmetries in the taxation of different returns to capital mentioned above, decreased the progressivity of taxes on labor income. In 1985, the deciles with low income were paying a higher fraction of their capital income in taxes than

15. Another conclusion from the investigation was that progression was reduced when deciles were calculated according to income of households compared to income of individuals. The underlying explanation was that low-income individuals typically are living with someone who earns more than they themselves do, while high-income earners live with people who are paid less.

16. If someone had a labor income of 200,000, paid 50,000 in taxes, and claimed a 75,000 interest deduction, the tax rate in relation to assessed income (125,000) would be 40 percent (50/125), but it would be only 25 percent in relation to the income before the deduction (50/200).

17. This conclusion is obvious since capital income is taxed on a realization basis; i.e., accrued capital gains on funds invested in appreciating assets are not included in the income concept. Further, returns to consumer durables were not included in the tax base. Since high-income earners typically invested borrowed funds in these "low-taxed" assets, the income concept used for taxation did not manage to capture their full income.

Table 3.7   **The Distribution of Tax Burdens, 1985 (taxes as a percentage of income)**

	Basis for Comparison		
Decile	Assessed Income after Deductions (1)	Assessed Income before Deductions (2)	Gross Income[a] per Consumer Units (3)
1	7.6	2.9	19.0
2	12.0	12.2	17.0
3	19.9	17.8	22.4
4	26.3	24.5	25.1
5	29.7	28.2	27.0
6	31.3	29.8	28.9
7	33.6	31.7	32.1
8	35.1	32.3	32.5
9	36.7	33.3	32.7
10	43.6	35.9	38.2
Average	33.6	30.6	30.4

Source: Hansson and Norrman (1986).
[a]Gross income is defined as assessed income corrected for inflationary gains and losses on monetary assets plus nontaxable transfers and a real return to owner-occupied housing.

deciles with high income (see table 3.8). Indeed, high-income households reported negative capital income. This reflected in part the effect of borrowing by higher-income groups, but it may also be interpreted as a consequence of low taxes on securities with high risk. (See also the effective tax rates on capital gains on shares reported in table 3.5 above.) Since retired individuals typically save in low-risk securities and have low incomes, they were the ones who faced the high tax rates on capital income.

The picture has changed with the tax reform of 1991. A study of the effects of the reform shows that the gap between the statutory tax on labor income—a simulated tax—and tax actually levied decreased substantially for individuals in the top decile of the income distribution between 1980 and 1991 (see Malmer, Persson, and Tengblad 1994, chap. 10).[18] In 1980, the simulated tax on labor income was 52 percent, while the actual tax was 42 percent. In 1991, the simulated tax was 41 percent and the levied tax 40 percent. The main explanation is that, while tax rates were being reduced (thus lowering the simulated tax), borrowing has become considerably more expensive compared to the 1980s since the tax subsidy to interest expenses has decreased from over 85 percent in 1980 to only 30 percent in 1991 (preventing a large drop in the actual rate).

The fact that, although marginal tax rates have been cut substantially, the

18. Malmer, Persson, and Tengblad's investigation is based on individuals twenty to sixty-four years of age and on their individual income, but the conclusion that is drawn here would hardly be affected if deciles were formed according to household income.

Table 3.8   Capital Income Taxation, 1985 (capital income taxes as a percentage
                   of income)

	Basis for Comparison	
Decile	Gross Income per Consumer Units	Potential Income per Consumer Units 45–55 Years of Age
1	4.5	8.7
2	3.0	−.5
3	.5	−.8
4	−.4	−.6
5	−2.1	−.1
6	−1.7	−1.8
7	.2	−3.5
8	−.9	−1.0
9	−2.2	−2.5
10	−1.7	−1.7
Average	−.9	−1.2
Gini coefficients:		
Without capital income taxation	20.6	25.5
With capital income taxation	21.7	25.9

Source: Hansson and Norrman (1986).

average tax rate is roughly the same for individuals in decile 10 in 1991 as in 1980 is shown in another way in table 3.9 and illustrated in figure 3.6. Over the whole period, the total simulated individual income tax was decreased by SKr 16 billion; while the simulated tax on labor income was lowered by SKr 33 billion; the difference is an increase in the simulated taxation of returns to capital. Although simulated taxes on labor income were cut by more than SKr 17 billion for decile 10, actual levied taxes decreased only by SKr 3.5 billion. Base broadening prevented the simulated tax reductions from becoming real for high-income individuals. For deciles 1–7, the tax reform had little effect on tax subsidies to income from capital. For them, the changes in simulated and actual tax are quite similar.

Hansson and Norrman (1986) have shown that progression related more to age and to working time than to ability, defined as potential income from a fixed input of time. This is illustrated by table 3.10. Column 1 repeats the average tax rates, by deciles, from table 3.7 above; it suggests substantial progressivity. Column 2 shows the distribution of taxes for households containing at least one individual between forty-five and fifty-five years of age. A major part of the estimated progression disappears, except in the top decile, if age is kept constant.

Column 3 shows the result when differences in working time are also eliminated. The average weekly working time is calculated for each sex (forty-one hours for men, thirty-one for women). The ratio of this number to the actual

Table 3.9   **Changes in Individual Income Taxation on Labor Income (1991 prices) (change in tax [SKr billion])**

	1980–85	1985–89	1989–91	1980–91
All deciles:				
Simulated tax	−3.5	+18.6	−48.4	−33.3
Actual tax	−.1	+21.1	−36.8	−15.8
Decile 10:				
Simulated tax	−7.4	+4.2	−14.2	−17.3
Actual tax	−2.2	+6.8	−8.1	−3.5
Deciles 8–9:				
Simulated tax	−.9	+5.7	−13.6	−8.8
Actual tax	−1.9	+5.1	−9.5	−6.3
Deciles 1–7:				
Simulated tax	+4.7	+8.6	−20.5	−7.1
Actual tax	+4.0	+9.2	−19.2	−6.0

Source: Malmer, Persson, and Tengblad (1994).

working time of each individual in the forty-five- to fifty-five-year-old age group is then multiplied by his or her actual income to calculate "potential income" for a standard work week. In this way, a new income distribution was constructed in which individuals are classified according to potential income.[19] Since taxes are kept constant, they represent a larger fraction of potential income than of actual income for those who work more than average and a smaller fraction for those who work less than average. The result of this adjustment is interesting, indeed, since all progression vanishes.

These observations are sustained by Björklund (1992), who calculates Gini coefficients for two groups of individuals before and after taxes, both on a single-year basis and over seventeen years (which is a proxy for lifetime income). The relative reduction of inequality induced by the tax system—about 20 percent in both cases—is close to the result of column 1 in table 3.10. Björklund's results are reported in table 3.11.

The interpretation of these results is that, up to 1990, the tax system did not redistribute income between individuals with different potential income or ability but leveled the lifetime income for each household. It may be questioned whether this should be a principal objective for taxation since individuals can use capital markets for this purpose. Genuine redistribution was primarily related to differences in working time, which may also be criticized. People who work more hours in the labor market pay a higher share of income in

19. Thus, the income of a woman who works forty hours per week would be multiplied by a factor 0.78. The woman would be classified as belonging to a lower-income decile when all individuals were classified according to their potential income. She would keep a high tax share, while others working less than average time would be pushed upward in the distributions with a low tax share.

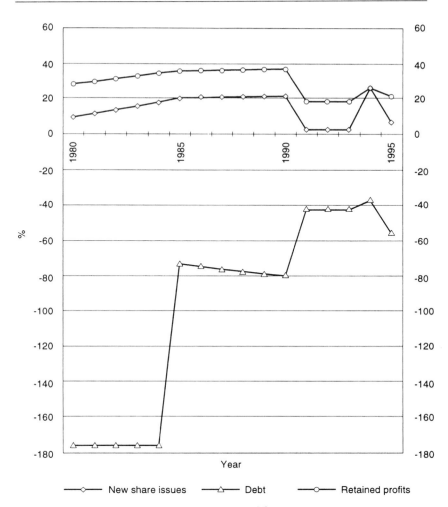

Fig. 3.7   METR on corporate income—type of finance
Source: See table 3.12.

taxes. If taxes are related to potential income, the effect of taxation on the income distribution is negligible or even negative.

Slemrod (1992) contains some results for the United States. He also investigates the income distribution among individuals and calculates the Gini coefficients before taxes as .468 (1972) and .567 (1988). The corresponding numbers after taxes are .445 and .544. These figures indicate a more uneven before-tax distribution of income than in Sweden and a smaller relative reduction in inequality by the tax system, 4 percent (1972) and 5 percent (1988).

Table 3.10   **Taxes as a Percentage of Income in Different Deciles**

		Basis for Comparison	
Decile	Gross Income per Consumer Units	Gross Income per Consumer Units 45–55 Years Old	Potential Income per Consumer Units 45–55 Years Old
1	19.0	31.7	35.9
2	17.0	27.5	27.2
3	22.4	27.1	27.8
4	25.1	31.3	33.4
5	27.0	32.1	29.9
6	28.9	33.4	31.6
7	32.1	33.0	31.2
8	32.5	33.1	33.0
9	32.7	34.1	32.6
10	38.2	40.7	33.1
Average	30.4	33.5	31.7
Gini coefficients:			
Before taxes	25.9	22.7	25.5
After taxes	21.7	19.7	25.9
Relative inequality reduction (%)[a]	16.2	13.2	−1.6

Source: Hansson and Norrman (1986).

[a]This concept measures how much the tax system decreases the Gini coefficients after taxes compared to before taxes.

Table 3.11   **Gini Coefficients, 1974–90 (individuals 18–30 and 31–43 years of age at the beginning of the period)**

	18–30 Years of Age			31–43 Years of Age		
Year	Before Taxes	After Taxes	Percentage Reduction	Before Taxes	After Taxes	Percentage Reduction
1975	.353	.302	14.4	.378	.319	15.6
1980	.280	.239	14.6	.293	.233	20.5
1985	.276	.223	19.2	.280	.217	22.5
1990	.276	.219	20.7	.279	.221	20.8
1974–90[a]	.230	.189	17.8	.269	.215	20.1

Source: Björklund (1992).

[a]Discount rate 3 percent (the result is robust to change in the rate).

3.3.2   Evasion and Attitudes toward the Tax System

Reports about the failure of the tax system have been accompanied by a decreasing faith in the capability of the system. Hence, Myrdal (1978) wrote: "The different deductions that can be made from the income tax base make progressivity illusive and turn us all into a nation of cheaters."[20] Hansson (1980) reports a public survey concerning the black market for labor. Nineteen percent of the respondents admit paying for services illegally. The amount evaded would correspond to only 0.5 percent of national income in 1979. However, Hansson estimates the loss of tax revenues due to evasion to be in the interval of 4–8 percent of national income. His opinion is supported by Tengblad (1994), who estimates the loss at 5 percent of GDP.

The National Tax Board (Riksskatteverket 1993) reports that the attitude of taxpayers toward the tax system has changed substantially during the period 1986–92. Prior to the tax reform of 1991, 65 percent disliked the system, another 24 percent did not have any preference, and only 9 percent thought that it was fairly or pretty good. After the reform, the number who disliked the system fell to 36 percent, the indifferent group increased to 37 percent, and over 25 percent said that they liked it. A noteworthy fact is the concern among Swedish households for tax matters after tax reform; 44 percent reported a substantial interest in these issues and 38 percent a moderate interest in 1992.

3.4   Tax Wedges and Effects on Resource Allocation

3.4.1   Marginal Effective Tax Rates on Capital Income

In 1980, the corporate income tax was extremely nonneutral in its effect on various types of investment and sources of finance. Because of the extra investment allowances (provided at a rate of 20 percent for machinery and 10 percent for buildings) and the investment funds system, equipment benefited from a marginal effective tax rate (METR) of roughly −47 percent (i.e., a subsidy of 47 percent).[21] By comparison, investment in buildings was taxed at a rate of 12 percent, and the METR on investment in inventories was about 25 percent, despite the ability to deduct 60 percent of the purchase price of inventories (Norrman 1995b).[22] (These numbers are reported in table 3.12 and illus-

---

20. "De olika inkomstavdragen m m gör progressiviteten illusorisk och förvandlar oss till ett folk av fifflare."

21. All the calculations reported are based on an assumed inflation rate of 4 percent, unless otherwise noted. In some cases (e.g., investment in buildings and debt financing), the results are quite sensitive to the rate of inflation.

22. The calculations are based on the "fixed r case." Differences between these numbers and numbers presented in Södersten (1991) may be explained by the fact that Södersten's study is based on the "fixed p case." Also, Norrman explicitly considers a risk premium to equity capital. The fixed r case keeps the return after corporate taxes constant (illustrating a case with a fixed world market rate of return), implying for any given saver that all projects yield the same net return but

Table 3.12   Marginal Effective Corporate Tax Rates on Corporate Income
               (real interest rate = 3 percent; inflation = 4 percent; risk premia:
               on loans = 2 percent; on shares = 7 percent)

	1980	1985	1990	1991	1992	1993	1994	1995
Average METR	2.0	17.0	18.1	3.6	3.6	3.6	11.6	4.9
Type of finance:								
Debt	(−176)	−73.4	−79.5	−41.5	−41.5	−41.5	−36.8	−54.9
Retained profits	28.1	35.9	37.4	18.5	18.5	18.5	25.9	21.4
New share issues	9.4	20.3	21.6	2.5	2.5	2.5	26.2	21.8
Type of investment:								
Equipment	−47.4	10.1	11.0	3.8	3.8	3.8	4.7	5.4
Buildings	11.8	18.2	19.2	2.9	2.9	2.9	12.0	−2.0
Inventories	25.4	25.5	27.2	5.9	5.9	5.9	22.7	24.2

Source: Norrman (1995b).

trated in figs. 3.7 and 3.8. Note that they refer only to the effects of the corporate income tax; effects of the taxation of investors are discussed below.)

Whereas, in the aggregate, the corporate METR on investment financed from retained earnings was about 28 percent, investment financed from new share issues was taxed at an effective rate of 9 percent because of the partial deduction of the part of dividends attributable to new issues. Debt-financed investment received a subsidy above 100 percent.[23] The individual income tax more than offset the corporate-level subsidy to debt-financed investment and increased the taxation of new share issues and retained earnings. The unevenness of tax policy produced the appearance, and perhaps the effect, of horizontal inequity.[24] It also stimulated heavy debt financing compared to other countries; debt financing contributed 40 percent of total finance in Sweden, compared to 20 percent in the United States and Great Britain in 1980 (King and Fullerton 1984, table A4).

The 1985 reforms increased the average corporate METR from 2 to 17 percent.[25] Reflecting the elimination of the subsidy to investment in machinery represented by the extra investment allowance, the corporate METR rose from

that the return will differ between different categories of savers. It also means that the pretax returns will differ between projects according to the tax treatment of different types of investments. The fixed *p* case, on the other hand, fixes the return before corporate taxes (assuming arbitrage possibilities between firms concerning investment projects).

23. The high negative tax rate on debt finance depends on the fact that, when the tax rate is calculated, the required rate of return is the denominator. In the case of debt finance, this value is close to zero.

24. Horizontal equity is a question of equal treatment of taxpayers in similar circumstances. To the extent that capital is reallocated to equalize after-tax returns, uneven taxation does not actually create horizontal inequities.

25. The difference in inflation rates in the two years—10 percent in 1980 and 5 percent in 1985—complicates comparison of METRs. Assuming a constant inflation rate makes it possible to isolate the effects of changes in tax policy, but it is not clear which year's inflation rate to use in the comparison.

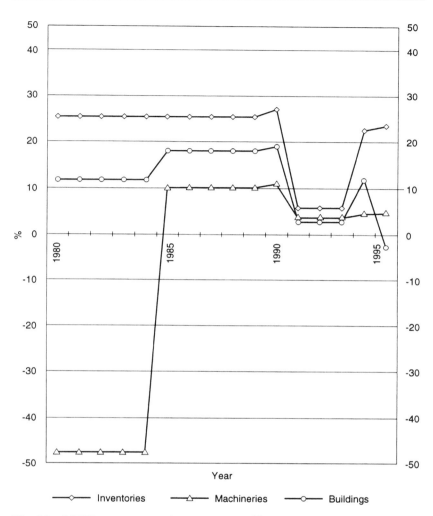

Fig. 3.8   METR on corporate income—type of investment
Source: See table 3.12.

−47 percent in 1980 to +10 percent in 1985. The changes in the METRs on income from investment in buildings and inventories were more modest; the former increased from 12 to 18 percent, and the latter remained unchanged, at 25 percent.

While the 1985 reforms reduced the spread of METRs for investments in various types of assets, the results for different sources of finance and suppliers of funds were not so favorable. Debt-financed investment remained substan-

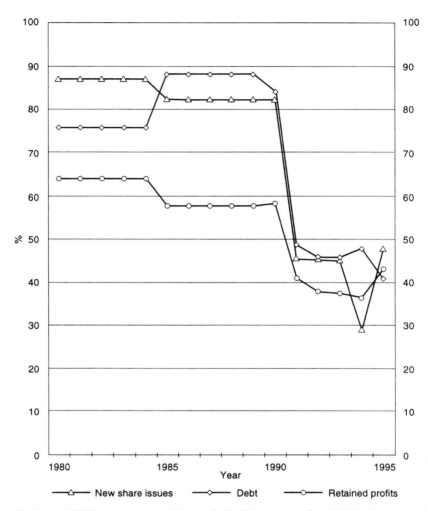

Fig. 3.9   METR on corporate income, including taxes on investors—type of finance
Source: See table 3.13.

tially undertaxed and investments financed from new share issues substantially overtaxed.

The 1991 reforms were more far-reaching. The statutory corporate tax rate was reduced from 52 to 30 percent, the investment funds system was slated for elimination, and the deduction for 50 percent of inventory purchases was eliminated. To provide relief for overtaxation of income from new issues (and a degree of loss offset), a new "tax equalization reserve" was created; in effect, firms could deduct from taxable income up to 30 percent of net increases in equity. This had the effect of reducing the corporate tax rate to 23 percent. Individuals were (and still are) subject to a flat-rate tax of 30 percent on interest, dividends, and capital gains.

As can be seen in table 3.12, the 1991 reform reduced the overall corporate METR, compared to 1985, from 17 to 3.6 percent. Corporate tax policy is markedly more neutral toward investment decisions. Also, financial decisions are less distorted by the tax system, although discrimination against equity finance still exists. Similarly, the tax treatment of various assets remains somewhat uneven. One of the main reasons for nonneutralities is the absence of inflation adjustment of the tax base. As long as the tax system is based on nominal principles, perfect neutrality is not likely to be achieved.[26]

During 1991–93, no changes occurred in the corporate tax system, but, in 1994, the corporate tax rate was lowered to 28 percent, and the tax equalization reserve was replaced by a new profit-based system. These changes are reflected in an increase in the average METR at the corporate level from 3.6 to 11.6 percent. Abolishing the tax equalization reserve has several other effects. Since equity capital no longer constituted the base for tax credits, the effective tax rate on new equity capital increased. At the same time, investments in buildings and inventories were disfavored by this change and the dispersion in METRs with respect to corporate taxation increased.[27] Another change working to increase the dispersion of rates was that in the double taxation of equity capital. This is treated in the next section.

3.4.2 Marginal Effective Tax Rates and Ownership

As noted earlier, the 1994 reform was intended to move the mitigation of economic double taxation of corporate profits from the corporate level to the household level. This change was effectuated by abolishing the Annell deduction and reducing the tax rate on dividends to zero and the rate on capital gains to 12.5 percent. The main reason for this change was harmonization with the tax systems of the EC countries.

Table 3.13 and figure 3.9 compare the METRs for different investors and different forms of finance between 1980 and 1995. Unlike the figures discussed earlier in this section, these calculations consider taxes at both the corporate and the investor levels.

Two major observations should be stressed; the first regards the disfavoring

---

26. This is due to the fact that inflation increases taxation of low risk assets more than that of high-risk assets, at least if the risk premium is not perfectly correlated to inflation (see Norrman 1995b).

27. This occurs because the possibility to get untaxed reserves by using the tax equalization reserve decreased as the investment depreciated. Since machinery depreciates more rapidly than buildings and inventories do not depreciate at all, investments in inventories were favored within the *old system* compared to machinery and buildings in this respect.

Table 3.13   Aggregate Marginal Effective Tax Rates on Corporate Income
                    (real interest rate = 3 percent; inflation = 4 percent; risk premia:
                    on loans = 2 percent; on shares = 7 percent)

	1980	1985	1990	1991	1992	1993	1994	1995
Investor level:								
Debt finance:								
Households	75.7	88.2	84.2	49.1	46.2	46.2	48.0	41.1
Foreign investors	(−176)	−73.4	−79.5	−41.5	−41.5	−41.5	−36.8	−54.9
Pension fund	(−176)	−73.4	−79.5	−16.0	−16.0	−16.0	−19.6	−13.1
Life insurance fund	(−85)	−15.6	−19.7	34.9	22.2	22.2	1.5	20.4
Retained profits:								
Households	64.0	57.9	58.5	41.4	38.0	37.8	36.6	43.3
Foreign investor	28.1	35.9	37.4	18.5	18.5	18.5	25.9	21.4
Pension fund	28.1	35.9	37.4	24.3	24.3	24.3	27.8	30.3
Life insurance fund	33.6	42.0	44.4	39.0	34.8	34.8	29.8	51.4
New share issues:								
Households	86.9	82.3	82.3	45.7	45.4	45.2	29.2	56.2
Foreign investor	29.2	36.8	37.8	22.8	22.8	22.8	40.7	37.2
Pension fund	9.4	20.3	21.6	16.2	16.2	16.2	30.0	38.2
Life insurance fund	29.7	38.6	39.5	43.5	36.6	36.6	33.4	51.4

Source: Norrman (1995b).

of direct finance by domestic households, which may be a basic explanation for the situation depicted in figure 3.1 above. The second is the effect of the 1991–94 reforms mitigating this phenomenon.

In 1985, foreign investors were given a net subsidy of 73 percent, while domestic households, on average, were paying an 88 percent tax in the case of debt finance.[28] The major causes behind the latter number are the overstatement of taxable profits resulting from inflation and the wealth tax. As a result of the reform of capital income taxation in 1991, debt finance by households became more favorable than before, but the first best choice for households was still to buy shares in companies that retained profits, although the difference between debt financing and equity financing became a lot smaller.

An interesting fact is the reversed tax situation between domestic households and other investors in 1994. Before 1994, households were disfavored by the tax system as owners of Swedish shares (although the extremely high tax rates on debt finance still made ownership the best choice for the average household that wanted to invest in corporations). In 1994, the elimination of dividend taxation had a substantial effect on the incentives to own Swedish firms compared to earlier years.

These numbers must, however, be interpreted with great care since the tax situation of foreigners in their home countries is not considered. Another reason for circumspection is the use of average tax rates. There is strong evidence

28. The tax wedge abroad at the investor level is not considered in the calculations, but the Swedish coupon tax on dividends is.

for the existence of clientele effects, that is, comparative advantages in the different forms of finance (Agell and Edin 1988). If these are important, the use of average tax rates may be highly misleading. For example, corporate debt may, in practice, be held by pension funds and households with low marginal tax rates on current capital income (eventually zero), while high-income earners keep corporate shares in order to generate low-taxed capital gains. Such behavior would be consistent with both the incentives disclosed in table 3.13 and our discussion of empirical evidence in section 3.3 above.

It is also noteworthy that different investors may have had different views on the distribution of corporate profits. With the exception of 1994, the average household would prefer retained profits to dividends. At the same time, pension funds should have been more concerned about dividends than capital gains. Foreign investors and life insurance funds were probably more or less indifferent to dividends before 1994 but would now prefer capital gains rather than dividends.

As mentioned, the numbers in table 3.13 are based on averages. In practice, no one actually makes decisions based on average tax rates. This brings about the question of the dispersion in tax rates. The rational behavior of investors is to seek the cheapest way to finance a specific project. In order to illustrate the issue, the variation in the METRs related to table 3.13 is given in table 3.14.

It is clear that the difference in taxation of different investors and investments historically has been very large. At the same time, it is obvious that the dispersion is decreasing, implying fewer tax-induced distortions in the resource allocation after the 1991–94 reforms.

3.4.3   Extending the Portfolio Choice

The analysis above concentrated on financial decisions related to corporate investment. In this section, we focus on household taxation and take a broader view of portfolio choice by comparing additional savings possibilities. Therefore, the investigation is extended to include investments in owner-occupied housing and government bonds.

The approach is to calculate the METRs given that the real rate of return to a risk-free security is 3 percent before taxes. This may be conceived as an assumption of an exogenous world market real rate of interest to Sweden. For owner-occupied housing, the opportunity return is assumed to be an investment in a corporate bond. A risk premium of 2 percent is therefore added to the nominal return to government bonds. Pension funds and life insurance funds are assumed to invest primarily in noncorporate bonds. Like those reported earlier, these calculations are made assuming an inflation rate of 4 percent. Although the METRs of 1985–91 were higher owing to higher inflation rates, this approach is used in order to isolate the importance of the tax rules from the influence of inflation.

Table 3.15 gives the results of these calculations for 1985–95 for an individual with a medium level of income. As before, inflation causes the income

Table 3.14 Percentage Variation in Aggregate Marginal Effective Tax Rates on Corporate Income (real interest rate = 3 percent; inflation = 4 percent; risk premia: on loans = 2 percent; on shares = 7 percent)

	1985		1990		1991		1992		1993		1994		1995	
	Min	Max	Min	Max	Min	Max	Min	Max	Min	Max	Min	Max	Min	Max
Corporate level:														
Type of finance:														
Debt	−79	−47	−86	−48	−51	−11	−51	−11	−51	−11	−45	−10	−75	−11
Retained profits	30	42	5	7	14	20	14	20	14	20	20	33	17	35
New share issues	13	27	2	4	−5	5	−5	5	−5	5	21	33	1	24
Type of investment:														
Machinery	−79	30	−2	5	−51	20	−51	20	−51	20	−45	21	−51	21
Buildings	−78	38	−2	6	−46	19	−46	19	−46	19	−41	27	−75	1
Inventories	−47	42	−2	8	−11	14	−11	14	−11	14	−10	33	−11	35
Investor:														
Households	55	90	55	87	40	60	37	58	37	58	24	58	34	58
Foreign investor	−79	42	−86	44	−51	26	−51	26	−51	26	−45	46	−75	38
Pension fund	−79	42	−86	48	−24	26	−24	26	−24	26	−27	37	−28	43
Life insurance fund	−19	48	−5	69	6	61	−17	39	−17	39	−5	40	10	60

Source: Norrman (1995b).

Table 3.15   **Marginal Effective Tax Rates on Different Types of Capital Income
for Medium Income Earner (real interest rate = 3 percent;
inflation = 4 percent; risk premia: on corporate bonds and owner-
occupied housing on shares = 7 percent)**

Type of Security	1985	1990	1991	1992	1993	1994	1995
Current income:							
Dividends	82.3	82.3	45.7	45.4	45.2	29.2	56.2
Corporate bonds	88.2	84.2	49.0	46.2	46.2	48.0	41.1
Government bonds	126.0	122.7	86.7	85.0	83.3	83.3	83.3
Consumer durables	.0	.0	.0	.0	.0	.0	.0
Interest deductions[a]	−90.0	−72.0	−54.0	−54.0	−54.0	−54.0	−54.0
Noncurrent income:							
Pension claims	.0	.0	21.9	21.9	21.9	21.9	35.0
Life insurance claims	24.5	24.5	53.7	44.8	44.8	46.7	63.0
Capital gains on corporate							
shares (10 years)	57.9	58.5	41.4	38.0	37.8	36.6	43.3
Owner occupied housing:							
15 years ownership, 100							
percent equity financed	128.9	42.3	43.2	42.1	41.0	35.7	35.7

Source: Norrman (1995c).
[a]Rate of interest 9 percent.

from assets fixed in nominal terms to be overstated. Actually, the influence of
inflation more than doubles the value of the METRs compared to the statutory
tax rates in most cases if we use actual inflation rates (see Norrman 1995c). It
should also be noted that, while totally equity-financed owner-occupied housing faced a positive tax rate, the possibility of mortgage financing as well as
the presence of subsidies to newly constructed homes often imply a negative
tax rate on home ownership.

Developments from 1985 to 1995 are extraordinary. If we ignore consumer
durables, the range of METRs has shrunk dramatically, from 0–129 percent to
35–83 percent. Even though the numbers reported in the table must be interpreted with care—the variation in tax position between individuals was considerably greater before 1991 than after, when it comes to capital income taxation—
a firm conclusion must be that the new capital income taxation in 1991 increased neutrality substantially but also that the changes in 1995 will work in
the opposite direction.

In this section, we have pointed out the wide dispersion in the METRs during the last decade. This fact has of course been revealed from time to time by
different investigations, and it is obvious that these observations have exerted
a major influence on the development of the tax system. A fundamental question is to what extent other pressures have been in force when the reforms of
the 1980s and 1990s have been enacted. One of these is international pressure
on tax coordination operating because of the openness of the Swedish
economy.

3.5   International Pressures behind the Reforms

3.5.1   Worldwide Tax Reforms

During the 1980s, a wave of tax reform swept the world.[29] Although details differ, sometimes substantially, from country to country, it is reasonable to say that key common features predominate. In particular, in many countries tax reform combined reductions in statutory tax rates with base broadening, including especially the curtailment of investment incentives. Tax reform in Sweden fits squarely within this worldwide movement toward imposition of income taxes characterized by broader bases and lower rates.

There may be a tendency, especially in the United States, to think that the U.S. Tax Reform Act of 1986 stimulated tax reform elsewhere and that, without the 1986 act, the decade of tax reform would not have occurred. While this view has some legitimacy, it is easily overstated. It is doubtless true that the breathtaking American tax reform captured the attention of the world tax policy community, gave tax reform increased legitimacy, and perhaps acted as a catalyst for action in many countries. But this is hardly enough to explain world tax reform; after all, the world does not follow all the policy initiatives of the United States, even the bold ones.[30] It is also true that some countries reacted defensively to tax reform in the United States, especially the deep reductions in tax rates.[31] Again, this may have been an important contributing factor, but it is probably not enough, by itself, to explain the phenomenon at hand in Sweden.

There are other potential explanations for the unusual phenomenon of worldwide tax reform: common intellectual underpinnings and domestic recognition of the need for tax reform, based on analysis of local conditions. This explanation seems especially important in the case of Sweden. After all, the Swedish debate on tax reform predated the U.S. Tax Reform Act of 1986 and even the proposals for tax reform that the U.S. Treasury Department submitted to President Ronald Reagan in late 1984. Underlying the public debate in Sweden was economic analysis of the effects of the taxation of capital that was every bit as sophisticated as any being done anywhere in the world. Particularly noteworthy is the fact that Sweden was one of the countries included in the

29. On this, see Pechman (1988), Tanzi (1987), OECD (1990), Whalley (1990), and the papers in Boskin and McLure (1990).

30. Moreover, it is important to note that the prior tax reform in the United Kingdom played an important role in convincing American policymakers that the combination of rate reduction and elimination of investment incentives was not unreasonable. See McLure (1992, 102) and, for a discussion that is less generous to Nigel Lawson, chancellor of the Exchequer of the United Kingdom, Dilnot and Kay (1990, 154–55).

31. Canada, with its close economic ties to the United States, is the best example of this. The Canadian tax reform debate, which had been stalled, assumed new urgency when the United States slashed its corporate income tax rates. There was real and justified fear that American firms would organize their affairs to place debt in Canada (to benefit from deductions against high rates) and income in the United States (where it would be taxed at low rates). See Whalley (1990).

influential and pathbreaking NBER study of marginal effective tax rates that helped identify and quantify the distortions caused by uneven taxation (King and Fullerton 1984).

Thus, Södersten (1991, 4) seems correct when he writes, "The U.S. Tax Reform Act of 1986 and its international followers are the obvious sources of inspiration for this reform, but it also has its roots in the . . . reorientation of Swedish tax policy debate that started already in the beginning of the 1980's." Whalley (1990) reaches a similar conclusion. He writes, "These reforms . . . have taken place over a long period of time and clearly predate recent U.S. changes. Reform can be dated to 1981, to the so-called 'wonderful night' agreement between the Centre Party, the Liberals and the Social Democrats." He goes on to note, "The striking feature of these reforms is both the length of the period over which change was underway, and the sweeping nature of the changes now planned for 1991. Much of the reform seems largely independent of U.S. changes" (p. 299).

3.5.2 Response to International Pressures

There is little doubt that Sweden was responding in part to international pressures (not just "following the crowd" or responding to common intellectual developments) when it reformed its tax system. These pressures took several forms.

Tax Rates

If reductions of tax rates in other countries were not matched, Sweden would have been left vulnerable in several respects. First, Sweden would have had difficulty competing with low-rate countries for investment from countries that exempt foreign-source income. Moreover, after the U.S. Tax Reform Act of 1986, many U.S. firms would have viewed the high Swedish rates much like a firm from a country that exempts foreign-source income. This is true because the 1986 act placed many more American firms in an excess credit position; such firms actually pay foreign taxes, instead of automatically crediting them against their U.S. tax liability.

Second, firms operating in both Sweden and low-rate countries would have the incentive and the opportunity to manipulate financial and accounting practices to minimize taxes. They could be expected to borrow in Sweden to take advantage of its higher-value deductions for interest. They might also manipulate transfer prices to shift income to low-tax jurisdictions. Such adjustments could cost the Swedish Fisc large amounts of revenue.

Mitigation of Corporate Double Taxation

Despite having long had the Annell deduction for dividends paid on new issues of stock, Sweden was noticeably out of step, especially in Europe, in its treatment of dividends; it had no generally applicable system of relief for double taxation of dividends. Rather than adopting the imputation system, which is standard throughout Europe, or the split-rate system (which is also used in Germany), Sweden chose the rather unusual technique of exempting dividends from taxation at the shareholder level.[32]

This choice has several clear advantages. It is simpler than the imputation method, which requires the shareholder to include grossed-up dividends in taxable income and then take credit for corporate tax deemed to be withheld against tax on those dividends. The imputation method is commonly chosen over exemption for two reasons: it takes account of the graduated individual income tax on shareholders, and its benefits can easily be withheld from foreigners. (Indeed, it is rather complicated to extend the imputation credit to foreigners; since they have no tax liability in the country where dividends are paid, it is necessary to make refunds to them.) But the first of these advantages does not exist if, as in Sweden, dividends are taxed at a flat rate. The second feature, discrimination against foreign investors, can be interpreted as a disadvantage, rather than an advantage, whether one takes a unilateral (Swedish) or multilateral view of the matter.

EC and Ruding: The Wild Cards

Potential membership in the European Community (EC) added another dimension to the question of foreign influence on Swedish tax policy. In February 1992, a committee of independent experts headed by Onno Ruding of the Netherlands submitted a report on company taxation to the Commission of the EC (Commission of the European Communities 1992 [hereafter referred to as the Ruding Report]). The Ruding committee dealt with several issues that are of relevance to the current discussion. While its recommendations, if adopted, would not pose serious impediments to Swedish membership in the EC, the Ruding Report will almost certainly be considered in any future Swedish debates on corporate tax policy.

To prevent what it calls destructive tax competition, the Ruding Report proposed a minimum corporate tax rate of 30 percent. The Swedish rate of 28 percent adopted in 1994 falls below the proposed floor.

The Ruding Committee did not make any recommendations on the proper relation between corporate and individual income taxes, leaving this matter for later resolution. It is thus difficult to know how Sweden's newly adopted policy of exempting dividends would fare if judged by EC standards.

In one of its less satisfactory conclusions, the Ruding Report condoned the use of investment incentives to encourage investment, provided that they are "nondiscriminatory"; unfortunately, it failed to define *nondiscrimination* in this context. It favored investment credits over rate reductions and incentives built into the measurement of taxable income because they are more cost effective than the former and more transparent than the latter. The committee pro-

---

32. It might be noted that, in its 1986 reform, Colombia adopted this approach because of its simplicity.

posed safeguards on the use of incentives: authorization of the Commission of
the EC, no incentives for financial activities, and "sunset" provisions. Enact-
ment of these recommendations presumably would not have precluded
the elimination of investment incentives, but it might preclude their reinstate-
ment.

3.6 Evaluation

There can be no doubt that the Swedish income tax is vastly better now than
it was in 1980. Statutory rates are much lower, and marginal effective tax rates
fall in a much narrower range. As shown in figures 3.10 and 3.11, the overall
tax burden is still among the highest in the world and is still basically financed
by taxes on labor. The new system is simpler, more neutral, and more equitable
horizontally. And, given the extent to which the previous system provided both
opportunities and incentives for evasion, it is probably not much less progressive when burdens are compared to incomes across income groups.[33]

Before the reforms, revenues from heavy taxes on labor income, including
mandated contributions to social insurance programs, were being used to fill
the gap left by relatively light taxation of income from capital. As other papers
demonstrate, the heavy taxation of labor income has had enormous cost.

The undertaxation of income from capital occurred, despite high marginal
tax rates, because of extremely generous treatment of certain types of investment. The tax treatment of capital was extremely distortionary, as shown by
the range of METRs applicable to various types of assets and to various means
of financing. Moreover, the ability of some taxpayers to convert labor income
to capital income or to offset it with deductions for interest expense under-
mined the revenue potential and fairness of labor taxation. What little progressivity there appeared to be was largely a matter of redistribution across age
groups; within particular age cohorts, there was very little progressivity.

The reforms eliminated many of the anomalous features of the Swedish system, lowered statutory rates, and brought marginal effective tax rates closer
together. In addition to reducing disincentives for market labor, these reforms
should lead to a more rational allocation of the nation's capital. The fairness of
the system, as well as the appearance of fairness, should improve markedly.

Although the two systems reached their 1985 status by somewhat different
routes, the post-1985 reforms of the Swedish and U.S. systems bear some simi-
larities. In both cases, deviations from the income tax model had created complexity, distortions, inequities, and disrespect for the law. In both cases, the

33. In comparing the present market-oriented tax system with its predecessor, which was based
on social engineering and fine-tuning of the economy, one is reminded of the revolution in astron-
omy that resulted when the elegantly simple sun-centered Copernican system replaced the complex earth-centered Ptolemaic system of epicycles. That is high praise—and extreme criticism.
Even if the analogy is overdrawn, the lesson is clear.

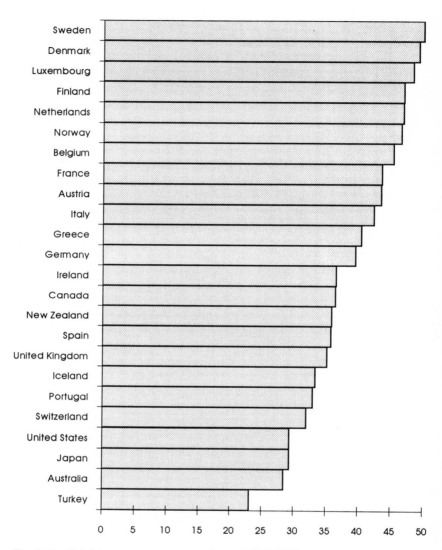

Fig. 3.10   Total tax revenue as percentage of GDP, 1992
Source: Revenue statistics of OECD member countries.

advantages of debt finance, especially in a time of relatively high inflation, had not gone unnoticed. Tax shelters of various types, including owner-occupied housing as well as business deals of questionable economic merit, were undermining the integrity of the system and the productivity of both economies. In both cases, bold initiatives involving a return to the principles underlying the income tax model substantially reduced the problems identified.

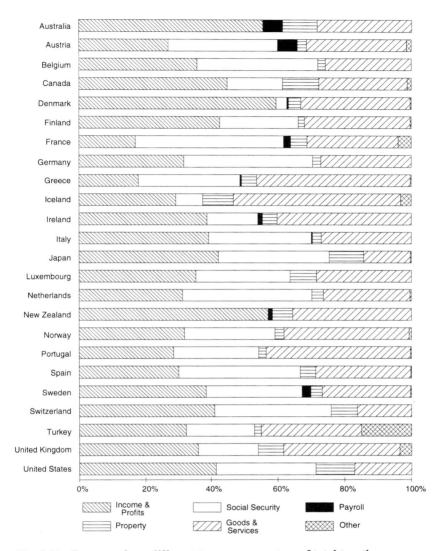

Fig. 3.11   Revenues from different taxes as percentage of total taxation
Source: Revenue statistics of OECD member countries.

However, even though the Swedish tax system has become more equitable and more neutral, taxes in Sweden remain among the highest in the Western world and therefore continue to affect almost every economic decision that households and firms make. This final problem can be addressed successfully only by reducing the overall level of taxation and thus the level of public spending.

References

Agell, Jonas, and Per-Anders Edin. 1988. Marginal taxes and the asset portfolios of Swedish households. Working Paper no. 58. Stockholm: Trade Union Institute for Economic Research.

Björklund, Anders. 1992. *Långsiktiga perspektiv på inkomstfördelningen.* Bilaga 8 till Långtidsutredningen. Stockholm: Allmänna.

Boskin, Michael J., and Charles E. McLure Jr., eds. 1990. *World tax reform: Case studies of developed and developing countries.* San Francisco: ICS Press.

Commission of the European Communities. 1992. *Report of the Committee of Independent Experts on Company Taxation.* Luxembourg.

Dilnot, Andrew W., and J. A. Kay. 1990. Tax reform in the United Kingdom: The recent experience. In *World tax reform: Case studies of developed and developing countries,* ed. Michael J. Boskin and Charles E. McLure Jr. San Francisco: ICS Press.

Hansson, Ingemar. 1980. *Sveriges svarta sektor. Ekonomisk Debatt* 8:595–602.

———. 1983. Totala marginaleffekter i Sverige, 1950–1985. Working Paper no. 1983:87. Department of Economics, Lund University.

———. 1984. Marginal cost of public funds for different tax instruments. *Scandinavian Journal of Economics* 86:114–29.

Hansson, Ingemar, and Erik Norrman. 1986. Fördelningseffekter av inkomstskatt och utgiftsskatt. In *Utgiftsskatt—teknik och effekter,* Statens Offentliga Utredningar 1986:40. Stockholm: Allmänna.

Jansson, Kjell. 1990. *Inkomst- och förmögenhetsfördelningen, 1967–1987.* Bilaga 19 till Långtidsutredningen 1990. Stockholm: Allmänna.

Jansson, Kjell, and Agneta Sandqvist. 1993. *Inkomstfördelningen under 1980-talet.* Bilaga 19 till Långtidsutredningen 1992. Stockholm: Allmänna.

King, M., and Don Fullerton. 1984. *The taxation of income from capital—a comparative study of the United States, the United Kingdom, Sweden and West Germany.* Chicago: University of Chicago Press.

Konjunkturinstitutet. 1994. *Konjunkturläget mars 1994.* Stockholm.

Lindbeck, Assar. 1993. Overshooting, reform and retreat from the welfare state. Seventh Tinbergen Lecture, delivered to the Nederlands Bank, Amsterdam.

Malmer, H., A. Persson, and Å. Tengblad. 1994. *Århundradets skattereform.* Stockholm: Fritzes.

McLure, Charles E., Jr. 1992. The political economy of tax reforms and their implications for interdependence: United States. In *The political economy of tax reform,* ed. Takatoshi Ito and Anne O. Krueger. Chicago: University of Chicago Press.

McLure, Charles E., Jr., and George R. Zodrow. 1994. The study and practice of income tax policy. In *Modern public finance,* ed. John M. Quigley and Eugene Smolensky. Cambridge, Mass.: Harvard University Press.

Myrdal, Gunnar. 1978. Dags för ett bättre skattesystem! *Ekonomisk Debatt* 7:493–506.

Norrman, Erik. 1995a. Average and marginal tax rates on labor and capital income, 1965–1995. Working paper. Department of Economics, Lund University.

———. 1995b. Corporate tax wedges, 1985–1995. Working paper. Department of Economics, Lund University.

———. 1995c. Marginal effective tax rates on different securities in Sweden, 1985–1995. Working paper. Department of Economics, Lund University.

OECD. 1990. *Taxation and international capital flows.* Paris.

———. 1993. *Revenue statistics of OECD member countries, 1965–1992.* Paris.

Pechman, Joseph A. 1988. *World tax reform: A progress report.* Washington, D.C.: Brookings.

Riksskatteverket. 1993. *Inställningen till skatteförvaltningen och kronofogdemyndigheten 1992: En riksomfattande serviceundersökning.* RSV Rapport 1993:5. Stockholm.

Slemrod, Joel. 1992. Taxation and inequality: A time-exposure perspective. Working Paper no. 3999. Cambridge, Mass.: National Bureau of Economic Research.

Södersten, Jan. 1991. The taxation of income from capital in Sweden, 1980–91. Working Paper no. 1991:12. Department of Economics, Uppsala University.

Spånt, Roland. 1975. Förmögenhetsfördelningen i Sverige. Falköping: Prisma.

Statistiska Centralbyrån. 1992. *Skatter, inkomster och avgifter—en statistisk översikt 1992.* Stockholm: Statistics Sweden.

Statistiska Meddelanden. 1987. *Inkomstbeskattningens utveckling sedan 1975.* Be 22 SM 8701. Stockholm. Statistics Sweden.

———. 1992. *National accounts.* N 10 SM 9201. Stockholm: Statistics Sweden.

———. 1993. *Börsaktieägandet 1992.* K 20 SM 9302. Stockholm: Statistics Sweden.

Steuerle, C. Eugene. 1985. *Taxes, loans, and inflation.* Washington, D.C.: Brookings.

Stuart, Charles E. 1981. Swedish tax rates, labor supply and tax revenues. *Journal of Political Economy* 89, no. 51:1020–37.

Tanzi, Vito. 1987. The response of other industrial countries to the U.S. Tax Reform Act. *National Tax Journal* 40, no. 3 (September): 339–55.

Tengblad, Åke. 1994. Beräkning av svart ekonomi och skatteundandragandet i Sverige, 1980–1991. In *Århundradets skattereform,* ed. H. Malmer, A. Persson, and Åke Tengblad. Stockholm: Fritzes.

Whalley, John. 1990. Foreign responses to U.S. tax reform. In *Do taxes matter? The impact of the Tax Reform Act of 1986,* ed. Joel Slemrod. Cambridge, Mass.: MIT Press.

4 Wage Policy and Restructuring: The Swedish Labor Market since 1960

Per-Anders Edin and Robert Topel

When applied to the labor market, the "Swedish model" has two key elements. The first is centralized bargaining. For nearly forty years, the main components of Swedish wages and working conditions were determined in central negotiations between the largest labor organization, LO, and the employers' association, SAF. The other is a set of extensive labor market policies formulated by the government, intended to maintain full employment, encourage investments in human capital, and facilitate labor mobility. In its heyday in the early 1970s, the Swedish model was widely praised for promoting growth while eliminating poverty and avoiding widespread unemployment. By 1980, Sweden had combined one of the world's highest living standards with the lowest level of income inequality in the developed world.

But times have changed. Centralized bargaining was largely abandoned during the 1980s, when key employers and unions defected from the process. Wage inequality and the returns to skill have since risen somewhat, although they remain low by world standards. These changes occurred against a background of slow economic growth, which fueled doubts about the efficiency of Sweden's highly structured labor market, huge public sector, and related welfare state institutions.

Per-Anders Edin is professor of industrial relations in the Department of Economics at Uppsala University in Sweden and an NBER research economist. Robert Topel is the Isidore Brown and Gladys J. Brown Professor in Urban and Labor Economics at the University of Chicago and a research associate of the National Bureau of Economic Research.

Edin's research was financed by the Swedish Council for Research in the Humanities and Social Sciences (HFSR). Topel's research was supported by the National Science Foundation and by the Sarah Scaife Foundation through a grant to the George J. Stigler Center for the Study of the Economy and the State at the University of Chicago Graduate School of Business. Jonas Agell, Anders Björklund, Richard Freeman, Bertil Holmlund, Robert LaLonde, and Johnny Zetterberg made very helpful comments on an earlier draft. The authors made any errors.

The current crisis has only added to those doubts. At this writing, open un-employment is at its highest level since the 1930s, soaring to 18 percent among youths (1993), and real wages have stagnated for over a decade. Critics complain that an ossified labor market is a major contributing factor. They argue that taxes and labor market policies reduce productivity and incentives while Sweden's obsession with equality has discouraged investments in the human capital and skills that drive long-term economic growth (Lindbeck et al. 1993; Henrekson, Jonung, and Stymne 1993).

Our goal in this paper is to understand the allocative effects of labor market institutions and policies in Sweden during the last thirty years. At one level, this involves documenting the "facts" about Swedish labor market institutions and performance, and a large portion of the paper is devoted to this task. How have relative wages evolved in Sweden? How did wage compression affect particular industries? What was the role of the public sector? In the restructuring of the Swedish labor market, who moved from contracting industries, and where did they go? And how did declining returns to skill affect investments in human capital?

Our main findings are as follows:

1. *Centralized Bargaining and Wage Inequality.* Centralized bargaining—which was initiated by employers but later rejected by them—greatly affected wage differentials in Sweden. From the mid-1960s through the 1970s, skill differentials in wages fell along every observable dimension, including age, education, sex, and percentiles of the wage distribution. Our reading of the evidence is that the decline in wage inequality is greater than what would have been generated by market forces alone. There is some evidence that declining returns to skill have reduced investments in human capital and education. Employer attitudes toward centralized bargaining changed in the 1980s, possibly because an artificially compressed wage distribution caused a shortage of skilled workers.

2. *Wage Compression and Employment.* The original advocates of a solidaristic wage policy argued that wage compression would push workers from low- to high-wage sectors and raise overall productivity. Observed labor flows are consistent with this goal. Low-wage industries contracted, and displaced workers were absorbed by growing, high-wage sectors of the labor market. Unlike the experience of other European countries, Sweden's move toward a more compressed wage distribution was not accompanied by rising unemployment.

3. *The Role of Labor Market Policies and the Public Sector.* Sweden maintains an array of government policies designed to maintain full employment. We find that active labor market policies have not had much effect in reducing

unemployment. Further, for men, there is only weak evidence that the rapid expansion of the public sector helped maintain full employment. The story is different for women, however. Virtually all the post-1970 increase in women's employment is accounted for by the growth of public sector jobs. Women's wages have converged toward men's, and female labor force participation has expanded because the public sector hires whatever female labor supply is forthcoming.

4. *The Rising Difference between Individual Productivity and Consumption.* Sweden's redistributive policies go far beyond a compressed wage distribution. Rising payroll taxes, which reached 43 percent in 1989, are used to finance social insurance programs. In the long run, most of this tax is shifted backward onto labor, so real wages have been stagnant or declining in spite of slowly rising productivity. Further, at the margin for skilled workers the payroll tax is a pure wedge. For skilled workers, we estimate that in 1990 the combination of payroll, income, and value added taxes meant that consumable income was only 21 percent of individual productivity.

For students of wage determination, Sweden presents a puzzle. Egalitarian policies that raised the relative wages of the less skilled did not produce widespread unemployment, although these policies did displace large numbers of workers. How was full employment maintained? We close the paper with a new analysis of how wage compression and full employment can occur together. Our analysis shows that a negotiated compression of the wage distribution can *raise* the demand for unskilled labor, with the result that full employment is maintained. But our analysis also predicts that the inefficiencies of centralized bargaining accumulate over time, which may lead to its ultimate demise. Significantly, major industries began to defect from the system in the 1980s, after which negotiations have shifted to the industry and firm levels.

The elimination of extreme poverty in Sweden must be counted as the main achievement of the welfare state. There is no doubt that labor market institutions played a central role in this. Yet egalitarian policies must confront the universal trade-off between equity and efficiency. In the case of Sweden's labor market, it is hard to escape the conclusion that an overriding emphasis on equity carries substantial social costs in terms of misallocated resources and reduced incentives. These costs have probably risen, in part because the inefficiencies of intervening in the labor market tend to accumulate, and also because market forces probably have favored rising income inequality over the past decade. Given the degree of equity that Sweden has achieved, the costs of allowing somewhat more inequality are likely to be small, while the benefits in terms of improved efficiency and welfare may be substantial.

4.1   The Institutional Setting

4.1.1   Collective Bargaining and the Swedish Model

The historical development of centralized bargaining is key to understanding the Swedish labor market.[1] Wages in Sweden are mainly the outcome of collective bargaining, with little or no direct involvement by the government. Union membership figures since 1950 are given in figure 4.1. In stark contrast to the United States, more than 90 percent of Swedish employees belong to labor unions, a figure that has risen from about 75 percent in 1960.[2] Since 1938, there has been more or less formal cooperation in labor relations between the largest labor organization, LO (the Swedish Trade Union Confederation), which represents blue-collar workers, and SAF (the Swedish Employers Federation). LO and SAF were the dominant private parties in the labor market until the 1970s, when unions representing white-collar and professional workers became important.

The unique aspects of the Swedish model evolved after 1950. Before then, the collective-bargaining environment was similar to that in the United States. Industrial unions affiliated with LO negotiated separate agreements with employers, who were affiliated with SAF. Coordination of policies or strategy by the two dominant organizations was limited. Interestingly, SAF was the main proponent of centralized bargaining in the early 1950s, allegedly believing that coordinated wage negotiations would avoid industrial unions' attempts to "leapfrog" each other in wage settlements. Indeed, LO unions were reluctant participants in the first central agreement, which was signed in 1952.

By 1956, however, LO leadership came to view centralized bargaining as a device to achieve a "solidarity" wage policy, which would reduce wage inequality among union members. In its early form, this policy was rooted in ideas of LO economists Gosta Rehn and Rudolf Meidner. They argued that coordinated wage settlements would eliminate pay differences between similarly skilled individuals, thus reducing income inequality, while promoting growth and the restructuring of the economy. One interpretation of this view, which we develop below, is that decentralized collective bargaining produced noncompetitive wage differences among industries. These differences impede the efficient allocation of labor among sectors. Then a coordinated policy of "equal pay for equal work" more closely mimics a competitive wage distribution, with attendant gains in efficiency. On this view, there is no trade-off be-

1. For more detailed descriptions of the institutional setting, see, e.g., Ullenhag (1970), Elvander (1988), and Nilsson (1993).
2. Our estimates of union coverage are ratios of union membership to non-self-employed workers. This makes our estimates larger than those that use the entire labor force as a base. We think the distinction is important, especially in early years, when a large portion of the Swedish workforce worked in agriculture. For an analysis of union growth in Sweden, see D'Agostino (1992).

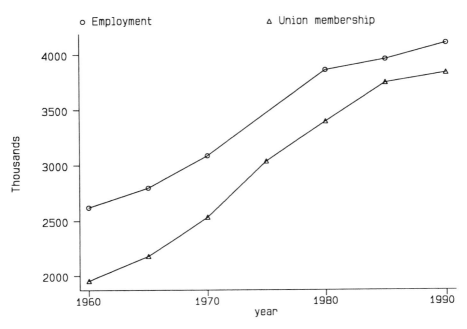

Fig. 4.1   Union membership and total employment, 1960–90
Source: Nilsson (1993).

tween equity and efficiency; instead, they are complements in producing greater social welfare.

Whatever the reasons, egalitarianism became a main ideological force behind LO bargaining policies. Nineteen central frame agreements were concluded between 1956 and 1990, and, at least through the 1970s, they coincided with a vast compression of the blue-collar wage distribution. Wage dispersion between LO and SAF contract areas fell by 66 percent between 1965 and 1972 (Hibbs 1990). From 1970 to 1983, the log wage differential between blue-collar workers in the ninetieth and tenth percentiles was almost halved (see fig. 4.2). Hibbs (1990) argues that LO policy took on an even stronger egalitarian stance around 1969, evolving from a goal of "equal pay for equal work" to just "equal pay." Pay dispersion within firms and across skill groups fell sharply.

LO's dominance of industrial relations has slowly eroded with the secular shift of employment toward white-collar and professional occupations (see fig. 4.3). Unlike in the United States, in Sweden this trend has not reduced overall union coverage because over 80 percent of white-collar workers also belong to unions. Against LO's current membership of 2.2 million, the largest white-collar organization is the Central Organization for Salaried Employees, or TCO, with 1.2 million members, of whom half are women. Workers with uni-

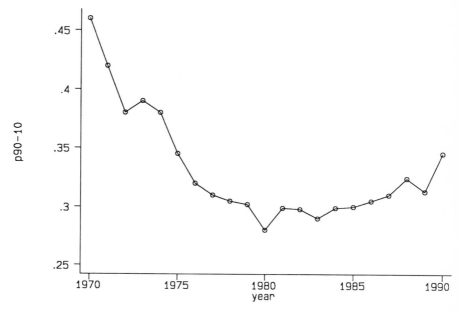

Fig. 4.2   Difference in log wages between the ninetieth and the tenth percentiles, blue-collar workers, 1970–90
Source: Hibbs (1990).

versity degrees are represented by the Swedish Confederation of Professional Associations, SACO, with 330,000 members. Another aspect of the shifting structure of unionism is the rapid increase in the share of union members who work in the public sector (fig. 4.4).

The practical importance of the trends in figs. 4.2 and 4.3 is that an ever larger portion of Swedish wages were determined outside the LO-SAF nexus. In effect, the result was a move back toward the decentralized bargaining of the 1950s. This is one argument for the demise of centralized bargaining in the 1980s: Freeman and Gibbons (1995) argue that LO could no longer deliver coordinated wage restraint, which was the real value of central bargaining. We offer an alternative explanation in section 4.4 below.

A turning point for central bargaining came in 1983. The employers' organization for the engineering industry, Verstadsföreningen—which includes Volvo, Saab, ABB, and other large firms—and the largest industrial union, Metall, went outside the LO/SAF frame and negotiated a separate agreement. Significantly, employers argued that the frame agreements hindered recruiting by underpaying skilled workers. After 1983, the level of bargaining has varied. Central agreements were struck on three occasions during the late 1980s, but a tendency toward more bargaining at industry and company levels seems clear.

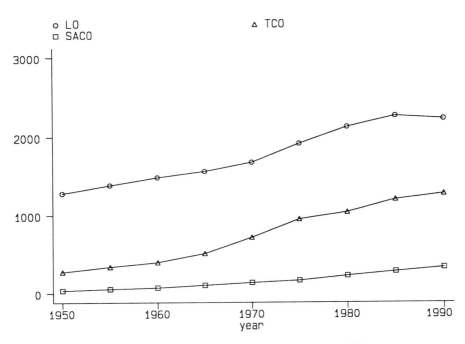

Fig. 4.3   Union membership in LO, TCO, SACO, 1950–90 (1,000s)
Source: Nilsson (1993).

4.2   Labor Market Performance and Policies

4.2.1   Wages, Productivity, and Labor Supply

Figure 4.5 shows the evolution of labor productivity, real wages, and real wage costs since 1960. Wage costs are calculated as wages plus payroll taxes and are deflated by the producer price index, while wages are deflated by the CPI. The series are indexed to 1965, to reflect relative growth rates since that year. The figure shows that productivity roughly doubled, as did wage costs, so labor's share has been roughly constant since 1965. There are substantial short-run deviations, however, reflecting periods of wage inflation and rising payroll taxes.

The 1970s are particularly interesting in this regard. The average payroll tax rose from 18 percent in 1973 to 33 percent in 1976 and 37 percent in 1977! It reached 43.5 percent in 1989. The figure indicates that the incidence of the tax was shifted forward for a while; indeed, real wages were increased in the 1975 bargaining round, in spite of rising taxes and no productivity growth. But demands proved elastic in the longer run, which forced a series of currency devaluations in the late 1970s and early 1980s. These shifted the incidence of the payroll tax back to labor, and real wages fell from 1979 to 1985. By 1990, real

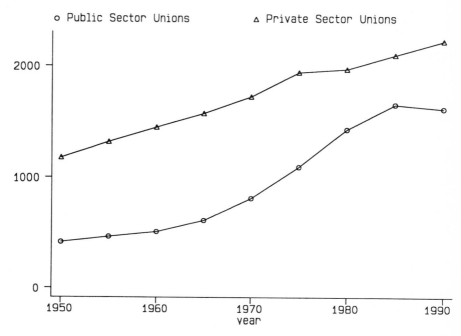

Fig. 4.4   Membership in public and private sector unions, 1950–90 (1,000s)
Source: Nilsson (1993).

wages had returned to their 1979 level, and they have been roughly constant thereafter.

The widening gap between pay and labor cost is not necessarily a tax wedge. Most of the tax finances benefits to individual workers—like sickness insurance and pensions—that are received in proportion to income. But most benefits are also capped, so at the margin for skilled workers the payroll tax is all wedge. For these workers, the combination of payroll, income, and value added taxes meant that consumable income from a marginal dollar earned was only 21 percent of productivity in 1990.[3] For comparison, the corresponding tax wedge in the United States would be about 40 percent.

In spite of high taxes, Swedish labor force participation rates are unusually high (fig. 4.6). By 1990, 85 percent of the population aged sixteen to sixty-four participated in the labor force, and the figures for men (87 percent) and women (82 percent) were trivially different. (During the current recession, these figures have dropped for both sexes.) The figure for women is much higher than in the United States (about 60 percent), which can reflect several factors. One is that social benefits are tied to work, which encourages attach-

3. We assume a payroll tax of 43 percent, a marginal income tax rate of 50 percent, and a value added tax of 25 percent for this calculation.

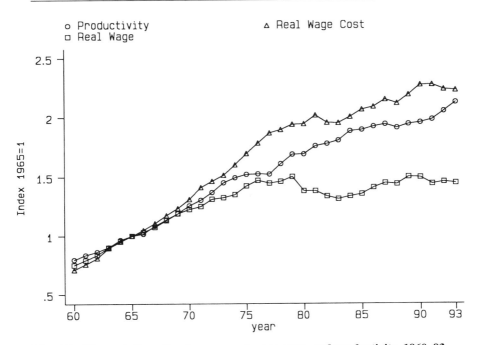

Fig. 4.5   The evolution of real wages, real wage costs, and productivity, 1960–93
Source: NR (National Accounts).

ment to the labor force.[4] Nearly half of women work part-time. Another is that the male-female wage differential is small and declining. As we discuss below, the regression-adjusted differential is slightly over 10 percent, which is far lower than in the United States and other OECD countries.[5]

High labor force participation does not necessarily translate into time worked. As shown by Burtless (1987), although male labor force participation fell by only 5 percent between 1963 and 1984, hours actually worked during the year fell by more than 20 percent.[6] The difference is accounted for by rising absenteeism and declining hours. In Burtless's data, absenteeism accounted for roughly a third of the overall decline in male labor supply, which he attributed to increased generosity of sick leave, vacation, and child-rearing benefits. Thus, in Sweden, the decline of male labor supply is accomplished mainly by

4. For example, parents are eligible for fifteen months of paid parental leave, which encourages women to establish an earnings history before childbearing. Other benefits, like child-care subsidies, require that a woman work but are not tied to earnings. This encourages part-time work.

5. From 1950 to 1960, women's wages averaged about 70 percent of men's. Then LO and SAF agreed to phase out separate wage scales for men and women, and the ratio began to rise. The wage ratio in manufacturing rose monotonically thereafter, reaching about .90 by 1980 (Björklund and Persson-Tanimura 1983).

6. Participation among American men fell by a comparable amount, but their hours fell by only 10 percent.

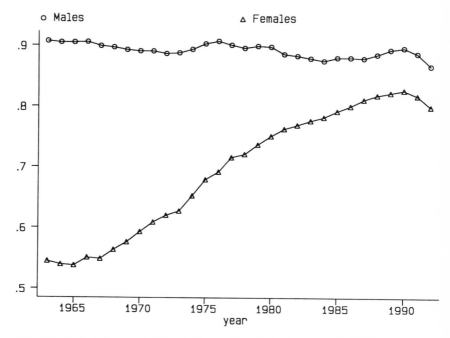

Fig. 4.6   Labor force participation rates of men and women, 1965–90
Source: NR.

reduced work effort among those who participate in the labor market. As shown in figure 4.7, the decline in annual hours worked between 1968 and 1981 was fairly uniform across the wage distribution. Both high- and low-wage men worked less. Exactly the opposite has occurred in the United States, where eligibility for transfer programs is more likely to be contingent on nonparticipation. In the United States, the secular decline in male labor supply is due to permanent labor force withdrawals, not to shortened work weeks or a reduction in weeks worked per year (Juhn, Murphy, and Topel 1991). Further, in the United States, reductions in annual hours and weeks have been concentrated among low-wage workers, who saw their wages fall sharply over this period.[7]

4.2.2   Unemployment and Labor Market Programs

Full employment has been a primary goal of Swedish economic policy and institutions. The outcome of this policy is illustrated in figure 4.8, where we plot the unemployment rate and the labor market program participation rate since 1965. By international standards, the unemployment rate in Sweden is very low. This is true even if we add program participation (training and relief

7. Hours worked among Swedish men have increased slightly (by 6.5 percent) during the 1980s (Rosen, chap. 2 in this volume).

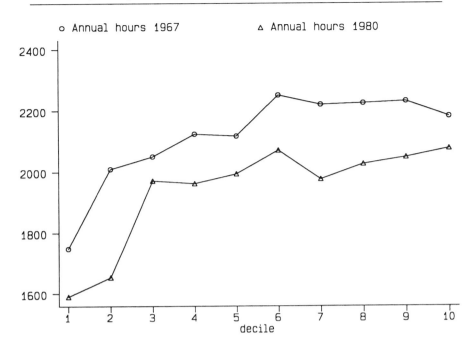

Fig. 4.7 Annual contracted hours by wage decile, 1967 and 1980
Source: LNU (Level of Living Survey).

work) to get a measure of "total" unemployment. In the late 1960s and early 1970s, open unemployment fluctuated around 2 percent. As in the United States, there has been a slight upward trend since that time. In the United States, the secular increase in unemployment is due to both longer and more frequent unemployment spells (Murphy and Topel 1986; Juhn, Murphy, and Topel 1991). In contrast, the secular increase in Swedish unemployment is due entirely to longer spells (Björklund 1993). The difference may be due to the increasing generosity of the Swedish unemployment insurance system, which has liberalized benefit ratios and benefit durations while increasing overall coverage (Björklund and Holmlund 1991; Carling et al. 1996). These changes encouraged longer spells. This is probably not the entire story, however, since the duration of uninsured spells has also increased.

The striking aspect of figure 4.8 is that unemployment stayed so low during the late 1960s and the 1970s, when major changes in the wage structure and sectoral employment occurred. To us, this is the main puzzle. According to the Rehn-Meidner model, full employment should be maintained through active labor market policy, involving among other measures retraining programs and mobility subsidies. While labor market programs have had some effect on measured unemployment, we think that their overall effect on unemployment has been small. We have several reasons for this assessment:

Fig. 4.8   Unemployment and participation in labor market programs as a percentage of the labor force, 1960–93
Source: AKU (Labor Force Surveys); AMS (Labor Market Board).

1. The magnitude of labor market programs is small compared to the major restructuring that took place. Before 1975, the participation rate in retraining programs and relief jobs never exceeded 2 percent. Furthermore, we would think that retraining would be the crucial instrument for moving workers between sectors through upgrading of skills. Relief jobs are more directed at avoiding loss of work habits and skills. The share of training programs in the program participation rate reported in figure 4.8 is roughly half. Thus, the training participation rate is only about 0.5 percent on average between 1965 and 1975.

2. If retraining were an efficient way of transferring labor from low-wage contracting sectors to high-wage expanding sectors, we would expect to see substantial earnings gains for individuals who participate in training programs. According to the survey by Björklund (1991), the evidence on these gains is, at best, mixed. Substantial positive earnings effects have been found in some studies but not in others. We have very limited knowledge about these effects during the late 1960s and early 1970s.

3. Labor market programs are mainly targeted at the unemployed. Consequently, the programs may have acted as a brake on the trend increase in the duration of unemployment, but they would have little effect on rates of entry

into unemployment. In an accounting sense, it is the low inflow rate that makes the Swedish unemployment rate so low (Björklund 1993).

We conclude that labor market programs have only a minor effect on overall unemployment. They do not account for the low levels of Swedish unemployment in the 1960s and 1970s. This interpretation accords with that of Forslund and Krueger (chap. 6 in this volume), who study the effect of relief work programs on regional unemployment.

4.2.3 Inequality and Relative Wages

Changes in relative wages and income inequality are the most interesting and challenging aspect of the Swedish labor market. From the 1960s to the 1980s, every imaginable wage differential declined.[8] The compression of the income and wage distributions was neither small nor gradual. Wage inequality fell in many other countries during the 1970s, but the fall in Sweden was stronger than in most countries. In the most recent decade, there has been a trend toward rising inequality. Here, the increase in Sweden looks modest compared to many other developed countries, especially compared with the United States (Davis 1992).[9] Between 1960 and 1970, the difference in log annual earnings between the ninetieth and the tenth percentiles of the male earnings distribution fell by twenty-five points, from 1.65 to 1.40.[10] Then it fell by another thirty-five points, to 1.05, by 1990. Figures 4.9–4.13 below, along with tables 4.1 and 4.2 below, show the details of this remarkable change.

Using survey data from two comparable sources, figure 4.9 documents changes in the distribution of log hourly wages of Swedish men since 1968.[11] The upper curve shows that, from 1968 to 1984, the 90/10 spread in this distribution fell by twenty-eight log points, from .95 to .68.[12] It is noteworthy that, in 1968, male wage inequality was about the same as in the United States. There, the 90/10 differential in 1970 was about 1.05. But, in the United States, the 90/10 differential in men's wages increased by thirty-five log points, to 1.4, which is about double the corresponding spread in Sweden. This change in

8. The data used here do not reflect nonwage compensation. This may affect our estimates since there is some evidence (LO 1987; Selen and Ståhlberg 1992) that fringe benefits were a substantial part of the compensation package for a large group of workers during the late 1970s and the early 1980s, when marginal tax rates on labor peaked. Unfortunately, there are no good data sources on total nonwage compensation.

9. The trend toward rising inequality was not universal. Inequality also fell in the Netherlands (Freeman and Katz 1994) and in Korea (Kim and Topel 1995). See also OECD (1993).

10. Source: Our calculations from unpublished census data for 1960, 1970, and 1990. The estimates refer to men who worked at least twenty hours in the survey week.

11. The surveys are the Level of Living Survey (LNU), collected by the Institute of Social Research, Stockholm University, and the Household Market and Nonmarket Activities Survey (HUS), collected by the University of Gothenburg. LNU has about thirty-five hundred valid wage observations per year, and HUS has about sixteen hundred. See Erikson and Åberg (1987) and Klevmarken and Olofsson (1993), respectively.

12. In the overall distribution, including females, the 90/10 spread fell by thirty-one log points, from .97 to .66.

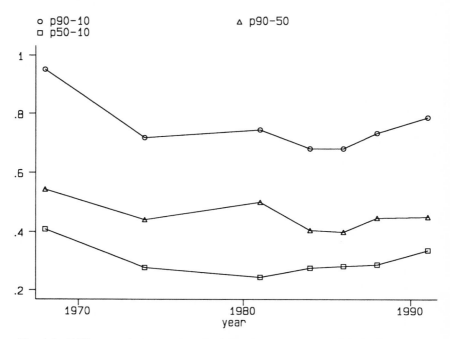

Fig. 4.9 Differences in log wages of Swedish men: ninetieth, fiftieth, and tenth percentiles.
Source: LNU; HUS (Swedish Household Market and Nonmarket Activities Survey).

distributions is even more remarkable when we consider that average living standards were fairly stable in both countries.

The lower two curves in figure 4.9 show that the compression was nearly evenly split between the top and the bottom of the distribution (except for 1981). Both the 90/50 and 50/10 spreads fell by about fourteen log points up to 1984. Then each rose by about five log points from 1984 to 1991. We think it noteworthy that wage inequality increased after 1984, when central bargains between LO and SAF began to unravel.

4.2.4 Male-Female Differentials

Figure 4.10 shows the evolution of the male-female wage gap in Sweden. In 1968, Swedish women earned about 23 percent less than men of comparable age and education. By the 1980s, the gap had narrowed to 11 percent, which is far lower than in any other OECD country (Blau and Kahn 1995). The data also show convergence between the adjusted and the unadjusted wage ratios for women. This is driven by rising relative levels of schooling and experience in the female workforce and, as we will see, by declining returns to these observable dimensions of skill.

Why did the male-female wage gap narrow? There is little doubt that gender differences in human capital—education and experience, for example—have

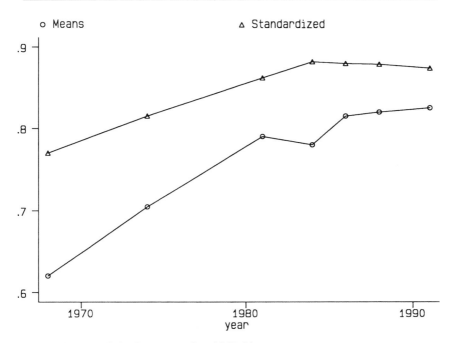

Fig. 4.10   Female/male wage ratios, 1968–91
Source: LNU; HUS.

narrowed over time, as they have in other countries. Reforms in the mid-1960s opened up higher education for women, which produced rapid convergence in educational levels (see Gustafsson and Lantz 1985).[13] But it is difficult to dismiss institutional factors. Before 1960, LO-SAF contracts in the private sector included separate scales for men and women, and the male/female wage ratio in manufacturing had been fairly constant at .70.[14] Then the parties agreed to eliminate the separate scales by 1965, and women's relative wages began to rise. The wage ratio in manufacturing reached .8 in 1970 and .9 by 1980 (Björklund and Persson-Tanimura 1983). This increase in relative prices occurred against a background of public policy that sought to increase female labor supply. Separate taxation of spouses, parental leave, and subsidized child care were all enacted in this period.

These trends suggest that collective bargaining may have forced greater wage convergence for women than would have occurred in an unconstrained market.[15] But, if this is so, what happened to the presumed excess supply of women? Here, the role of the public sector, and its amazing expansion, cannot

13. Edin and Holmlund (1995) show that college enrollment rates for women have exceeded those for men since the mid-1970s, and the gap has been increasing.
14. In the public sector, separate wage scales were eliminated in 1947.
15. Edin (1993) finds that roughly 60 percent of the convergence between 1968 and 1974 is accounted for by the compression of the overall wage distribution.

be denied. Between 1971 and 1984, female employment in Sweden grew by 29 percent, from 1.56 to 2 million. Expansion of the public sector accounted for 96 percent (427,000) of those jobs. As figure 4.11 shows, public sector growth slowed after 1984. This turning point corresponds to the peak of the female/male wage ratio in figure 4.10 above. Thus, the data are consistent with the view that wage convergence is demand driven and market clearing, but the "market" has been made by a burgeoning public sector (see also Edin and Holmlund 1995). In short, the government supported women's wages by hiring them.

4.2.5   Age-Earnings Profiles and the Returns to Job Tenure

The relative wages of new labor force entrants have risen dramatically since 1968. Table 4.1 records the time series of log wage differences for individuals with various amounts of labor market experience, measured relative to peak earners with twenty-one to twenty-five years of experience. We show comparable data for the United States in order to establish a benchmark.

In 1968, new entrants with one to five years of labor market experience had wages that were forty-eight log points lower than peak earners' wages. The comparable estimate for the United States was only thirty-four log points, so

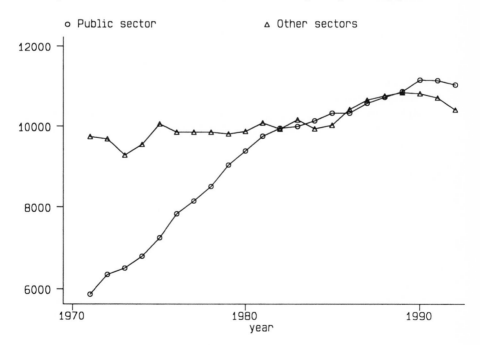

Fig. 4.11   Employment of women in the public and private sectors, 1971–92 (100s)
Source: Labor Force Surveys.

Table 4.1   **Log Wage Differentials of Experience Groups Relative to Peak Earners in the United States and Sweden, 1968–88**

Experience Group	1969	1974	1981	1984	1986	1988
0–5 years:						
United States	−.34	−.44	−.41	−.48	−.49	−.49
Sweden	−.48	−.34	−.31	−.30	−.26	−.21
6–11 years:						
United States	−.14	−.12	−.18	−.19	−.19	−.21
Sweden	−.19	−.10	−.15	−.19	−.14	.17
11–15 years:						
United States	−.04	−.00	−.07	−.05	−.06	−.06
Sweden	−.09	−.05	−.10	−.08	−.06	−.06

Note: Based on regressions including years of schooling and a dummy for gender, using CPS for the United States and LNU-HUS for Sweden.

the experience-wage profile in Sweden was actually steeper than the U.S. profile. Most of the difference was among very recent entrants, however. Over time, relative wages of new entrants in the U.S. fell by fifteen log points, to −.49, which was part of a general trend toward rising skill differences in pay. In Sweden, relative wages of new entrants increased by twenty-seven log points, eliminating more than half the wage differential. By 1988, cross-sectional estimates imply that a new entrant could look forward to only a 20 percent increase in pay over his career.[16]

Evidence on pay profiles within firms also points to flat profiles. Two examples of estimates of the return to job tenure are Edin and Zetterberg (1992) for 1984 and le Grand (1994) for 1991. Both find extremely small effects (see also Björklund and Åkerman 1989). Edin and Zetterberg estimate that ten years of job seniority raises wages by only 3 or 4 percent. Le Grand's estimate is even smaller, less than 2 percent. By comparison, ten years of job seniority yields a return of over 20 percent in American firms (Topel 1991). Tenure profiles in Japanese firms are steeper still.

The effects of flattened experience and tenure profiles on productivity have not been established empirically. But theories abound, and all point toward reduced incentives to invest in human capital and to exert effort (Ben-Porath 1967; Becker 1964; Becker and Stigler 1974; Lazear 1981). For example, if the bargaining process in Sweden forces flat wage profiles within firms, then workers have little incentive to invest in job-specific skills that raise productivity or to strive for advancement and promotion to more responsible positions.[17] Both these effects reduce productivity. It is difficult to argue that American and Japanese firms, which are free to choose whatever wage profile they want,

16. For a discussion of the relative importance of market forces and minimum wages for young workers, see Östros (1994).
17. For an analysis of on-the-job training and wages in Sweden, see Björklund and Regnér (1993).

Table 4.2   **Estimated Effects of an Additional Year of Schooling on Log Wages and College/High School Wage Ratios, Sweden, 1968–91**

	1969	1974	1981	1984	1986	1988	1991
Returns to schooling:							
All workers	.082	.049	.037	.040	.041	.045	.044
0–9 years of experience	.081	.049	.034	.025	.049	.040	.036
College/high school wage:							
Highest degree	1.49	1.48	1.26	1.18	1.25	1.22	1.26
15 vs. 12 years	1.46	1.26	1.14	1.16	1.22	1.18	1.21
16 vs. 12 years	1.82	1.33	1.22	1.22	1.26	1.25	1.29
Males in manufacturing	1.44	1.29	1.19	1.20	1.21	1.30	1.33

Note: Based on LNU and HUS. All regressions include a gender dummy and experience (except the returns to schooling for workers with 0–9 years of experience). Returns to schooling is based on a linear years of schooling variable. The college/high school effect is based on various measures, including highest degree obtained. This measure is not totally comparable over time. Alternatively, we use a specification with dummy variables for individual years of schooling, where we use 15 years and 16 years of schooling for college and 12 years for high school. "Males in manufacturing" refers to mean relative earnings among males in mining, manufacturing, and construction.

would choose steep profiles unless doing so had a substantial effect on productivity. In this sense, Swedish organizations may be hampered by pay compression, unless they are able to provide incentives in other ways.

4.2.6   The Returns to Schooling

As in the United States, the returns to schooling in Sweden fell throughout the 1970s.[18] But Sweden did not experience anything approaching the explosive growth in educational returns that characterized the U.S. labor market in the 1980s. The returns to schooling in Sweden were very low in the early 1980s, and it appears that these low returns have affected human capital investment decisions.

The first panel of table 4.2 records regression estimates of the return to schooling for various years between 1968 and 1991. We report separate estimates for all workers and for those with zero to nine years of experience. The time patterns are fairly similar: starting from a high of over 8 percent per year in 1968, the returns to education fell by more than half by the early 1980s. The sharpest decline occurred between 1968 and 1974, which was the period of the most rapid narrowing in the overall wage distribution (see fig. 4.9 above). Returns increased somewhat after 1984, but they pale next to comparable estimates for the United States. Even at its lowest level in 1979, the effect of an additional year of schooling in the United States never fell below 6 percent, and it peaked at 10 percent in 1987.

18. Here we deal only with the gross wage premium for education. We do not take taxes, stipends, and subsidized loans into account. Including such effects may have nonnegligible effects on the level of returns, but probably not on the basic trends over time. For further discussion, see, e.g., Edin, Fredriksson, and Holmlund (1994).

The second panel shows estimates of the college/high school wage ratio. In 1968, the typical college graduate earned almost 50 percent more than an otherwise comparable high school graduate. That advantage narrowed rapidly, however, falling to just 20 percent in the early 1980s. The rate of return to a year of college was only 4.5 percent. The timing, but not the magnitude, of this decline is roughly coincident with the United States, where the college/high school wage ratio fell from 1.50 in 1968 to 1.35 in 1979. In both countries, the returns to a college education drifted up in the 1980s. By 1991, the wage ratio had reached almost 1.3 in Sweden and a whopping 1.8 in the United States. By this standard, the returns to schooling in Sweden (like in many other countries) remain quite low.

Have low returns affected the incentives to invest in human capital? Enrollment rates suggest that they have.[19] Figure 4.12 simply plots the percentage of Swedish men aged twenty to twenty-four who are enrolled in school against estimates of the current, cross-sectional return to a college education. The correspondence is more than striking. The enrollment rate fell by almost half between 1968 and 1981, while the returns to schooling plummeted. And both recovered slightly in the 1980s.

Why did the returns to schooling fall? There are two obvious explanations. One is that compulsory schooling and the expansion of colleges and universities has increased the number of educated workers. Then factor prices adjust to changes in relative quantities. The very large changes in relative schooling levels, graphed in figure 4.13, suggest that there is some truth to this. The labor force share of compulsory school graduates (up to nine years of schooling) fell by half, to about 30 percent, in only twenty years. At the same time, the share of college graduates doubled. These changes in factor ratios can be expected to reduce the estimated returns to schooling, as has been demonstrated in many countries. Indeed, Edin and Holmlund (1995) make a case that these forces were at work in the Swedish data.

But the decline of returns between 1968 and 1974 appears too large to explain by factor ratios alone.[20] This suggests an institutional explanation grounded in central bargaining and egalitarian wage policies. We believe that the returns to schooling are lower than would occur in an unconstrained market.

4.2.7   Declining Inequality of Contract Wages

In some dimensions, declining wage differences can be partially explained by changing supply and demand factors in the Swedish labor market. For ex-

19. For a more detailed analysis that also considers the rationing of higher education, see Fredriksson (1994).
20. Edin and Holmlund (1995) need estimates of the elasticity of substitution between college and high school labor that are roughly double what is found in the United States. In other words, the elasticity of substitution in Sweden would have to be twice as large as elsewhere in order to explain the decline in the return to schooling with changing factor ratios alone.

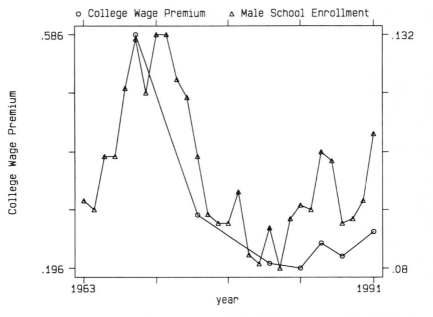

Fig. 4.12   College enrollment rates and the college wage premium, 1963–91
Source: AKU; LNU; HUS.

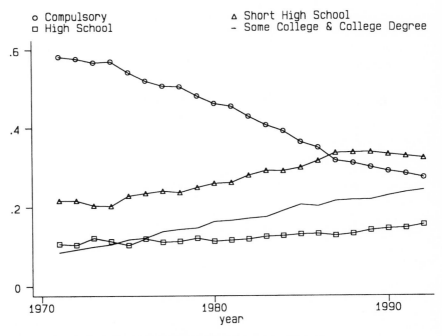

Fig. 4.13   Educational composition of employment, 1971–92
Source: AKU.

ample, declining returns to schooling coincide with a steady increase in the supply of educated workers. Yet, in the unconstrained U.S. market, comparable changes in education yielded much less narrowing of wage differentials. The rapid decline in all wage differentials suggests to us that institutional factors played an important role. The obvious institutional candidate is union wage policy.

We have already mentioned LO's egalitarian goals and "solidarity" wage policy. These goals were operationalized in the 1960s, when negotiated wage increases were given in absolute amounts (*öre*) instead of relative increases (percentage). "Low-wage pots," which were specifically targeted at raising the pay of low-wage workers, were introduced in 1964. Central frame agreements contained both these features until 1983.

Using micro data on blue-collar workers in the LO/SAF contract area, Hibbs (1990) showed that the wage dispersion implied by the central agreements tracks the actual wage dispersion well. Even though this correlation is not a statement about causality, we take it as an indication that union wage policy may have been one of the main reasons for the overall decline in wage inequality. One of the caveats of this interpretation is associated with wage drift, the difference between contracted and actual wage increases, which accounted for 45 percent of overall wage increases over the period, according to Nilsson (1993). As illustrated by Hibbs and Locking (1991), wage drift is more important for high-wage workers in the LO/SAF area. In a decomposition of the 1972–82 mean wage increases by percentile of the wage distribution, they found wage drift to be higher than contracted wage increases for the upper 50 percent of the wage distribution.

4.3   Allocative Effects: Restructuring the Swedish Labor Market

When Rehn and Meidner proposed their model of structural change and solidarity wages, they knew that efforts to raise the pay of low-wage workers would affect employment outcomes. Low-wage industries would be forced to contract, and the workers would have to go elsewhere. Rehn and Meidner thought that they would find work in more productive sectors.

There is abundant evidence that wage compression had allocative effects. For example, low-wage industries like textiles, forestry, and agriculture were concentrated in certain regions. Displacements from those industries called for regional migration as workers sought employment in the expanding regions. Figure 4.14 is consistent with this, showing that regional migration rates were unusually high in the 1960s and early 1970s, when changes in relative wages were largest.

Who moved? Which industries did they leave, and where did they go? In an attempt to answer this, we obtained unpublished tabulations of individual data from the Swedish censuses of 1960, 1970, and 1990. We did not use the 1980

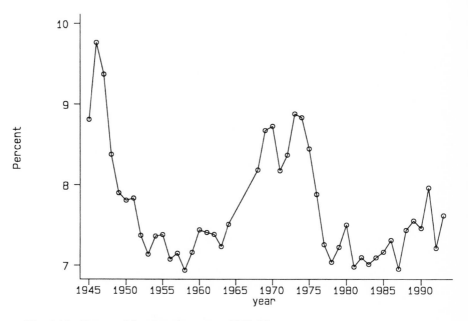

Fig. 4.14   Interparish migration rates, 1945–93
Source: SOS Bef (population statistics, Statistics Sweden).

data because individual earnings were not recorded in that year.[21] The data are organized by two-digit ISIC industry, and they record the number of employees by age, sex, and occupational status (employed vs. self-employed). The data are also stratified to show the number of employees of each type who fall into each of twenty evenly spaced intervals of the overall Swedish earnings distribution for the indicated years. In effect, we know the full earnings distribution for each 2-digit industry in Sweden. The tabulations for 1970 and 1990 are for the total Swedish population, but the 1960 data are a one-thirtieth sample.

If restructuring were consistent with the Rehn-Meidner goals, then it should be the case that low-wage industries contracted and high-wage industries grew.[22] Figures 4.15 and 4.16 show that this was the case in both periods of our data. They plot male employment growth rates for two-digit industries against initial mean earnings in each industry. High-wage industries did have greater growth, apparently absorbing the workers who left low-wage industries. Table 4.3 provides regression estimates of this relation for five-year age

21. We use data on males who are employed and work at least twenty hours per week. The earnings data refer to net taxable income (*sammanräknad inkomst* for 1970 and 1990 and *egen inkomst* for 1960). For 1990, we also have a measure of labor income (*arbetsinkomst*). The results using this measure of income are similar to those presented in the text.
22. For a discussion of wage compression and productive efficiency, see Hibbs and Locking (1996). A critical discussion of the importance of union wage policy is found in Svensson (1996).

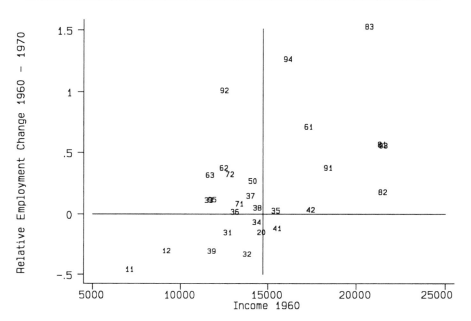

Fig. 4.15   The relation between industry employment growth, 1960–70, and industry income, 1960
Source: Swedish census data.
Note: See the appendix for a list of industry codes.

groups. The effect of mean initial earnings is positive for each group, with somewhat larger effects at younger ages. All age groups migrated toward high-wage industries; expansion was not achieved by simply redirecting the flows of young workers to expanding sectors.

The lack of income data for 1980 is unfortunate since virtually all the compression of the Swedish wage distribution had occurred by then. If employment changes are driven by changing wages, this implies less restructuring of employment after 1980 than before. Census tabulations of industry employment are available for 1980, however, which allowed us to break the 1970–90 employment changes into two parts. The last two columns in table 4.3 show that the relation of employment growth to *1970* initial income was much stronger before 1980 than after.

The identities of the industries shown in figs. 4.15 and 4.16 are of some interest (a complete list of codes is in the appendix). For both periods, the largest proportional reductions in employment occur in agriculture (11), forestry (12), textiles (32), and other manufacturing (39), while public employment in education and health care (93) expands. Similar patterns appear in absolute changes (not shown). The most rapidly expanding sector over the thirty-year period is education and health (93). It is noteworthy that the greatest absolute expansion between 1960 and 1970 was in construction (50), which

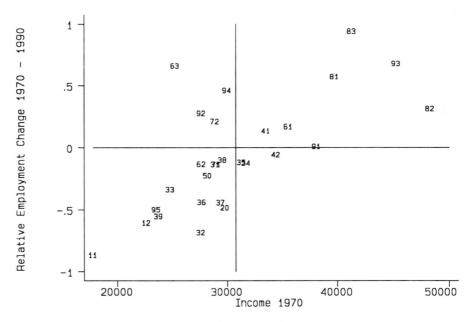

Fig. 4.16   The relation between industry employment growth, 1970–90, and industry income, 1970

Source: Swedish census data.
Note: See the appendix for a list of industry codes.

accords with the migration data shown above. Construction employment fell by about seventy-five thousand between 1970 and 1990, when regional migration slowed.

If wage compression is part of the cause for restructuring, is it not enough that workers are leaving low-wage industries? It has to be the case that wages rose in those industries, which drives the contraction. Figures 4.17 and 4.18 provide evidence that this was the case. They show the relation between industry employment growth and changes in mean industry earnings. On average, shrinking industries had the largest proportional increases in earnings, while expanding industries had the smallest. The relation is especially apparent between 1970 and 1990.[23]

Regression estimates of this relation are shown in table 4.4. We estimate models of the form

$$\ln E_{i,70} - \ln E_{i,60} = a + b(\ln I_{i,70} - \ln I_{i,60}) + e_i,$$

23. There may be two reasons for this. First, the 1960 data are based on a much smaller sample, so sampling error is more important in measuring the 1960–70 changes. Second, Hibbs's (1990) data indicate that the compression of intercontract wage differentials began around 1965. Long-run demands are more elastic, so much of the adjustment to these changes may have occurred after 1970.

Table 4.3   **Relative Employment Change and Income Level**
                       (absolute *t*-values in parentheses)

Age Group	Dependent Variable, Independent Variable			
	$(e_{70} - e_{60})/e_{60}$, Income 1960	$(e_{90} - e_{70})/e_{70}$, Income 1970	$(e_{80} - e_{70})/e_{70}$, Income 1970	$(e_{90} - e_{80})/e_{80}$, Income 1970
All	.064	.046	.025	.018
	(2.67)	(4.86)	(4.12)	(1.34)
21–25	.045	.058		
	(.33)	(1.37)		
26–30	.129	.044		
	(1.70)	(2.43)		
31–35	.048	.047		
	(1.38)	(3.50)		
36–40	.067	.061		
	(3.31)	(5.53)		
41–45	.061	.071		
	(3.17)	(6.08)		
46–50	.052	.051		
	(2.94)	(5.92)		
51–55	.038	.040		
	(2.20)	(6.71)		
56–60	.032	.034		
	(1.62)	(6.99)		
61–65	.004	.028		
	(.15)	(6.55)		

Note: The 1960–70 equation is estimated without ISIC 11, agriculture; the relative employment change for this industry (+50 percent) seems unreasonable. This seems to have to do with the definition of self-employment in agriculture, which decreased dramatically between 1960 and 1970. Using an approximation for the change in agricultural employment, using the 1960 self-employment ratio, yields an estimate of .068 with a *t*-value of 3.18.

where $E_{i,t}$ is employment in industry i, year t, and I is the mean wage (earnings) in the industry. Ignoring capital and other inputs, we can think of b as an "average" of industry-specific labor demand elasticities in response to exogenous changes in the industry wage structure.[24] We treat wages as exogenous in this exercise under the hypothesis that wage compression is the outcome of LO's solidarity wage policy. The same model is estimated for employment changes from 1970 to 1990.

As could be seen from figures 4.15–4.18, the data are much noisier for the 1960–70 changes than they are for 1970–90; the smaller sample in 1960 is one reason for this. The 1960–70 data are even noisier when we break the sample down into age categories, although for prime-aged (thirty-six to fifty-five) workers there is evidence of a negative relation between changes in industry

24. With constant returns to scale, b_i is equal to labor's share in unit cost times the elasticity of demand for industry output. Then let $b_i = b + \beta_i$, where b is the unweighted average of industry labor demand elasticities.

Table 4.4   **Relative Employment Change and Relative Income Change (absolute *t*-values in parentheses)**

| | Dependent Variable, Independent Variable | | | |
| | (e1970 − e1960)/e1960, (i1960 − i1970)/i1960 | | (e1990 − e1970)/e1970, (i1990 − i1970)/e1970 | |
Age group	OLS (1)	IV (2)	OLS (3)	IV (4)
All	−1.158	−3.907	−.448	−.668
	(1.76)	(2.45)	(4.72)	(4.50)
21–25	1.352		−.591	
	(.33)		(1.37)	
26–30	−.730		−.436	
	(.78)		(3.58)	
31–35	.759		−.436	
	(1.31)		(3.28)	
36–40	−.259		−.610	
	(.50)		(4.14)	
41–45	−1.159		−.705	
	(2.64)		(3.69)	
46–50	−.820		−.511	
	(1.38)		(3.67)	
51–55	−.433		−.458	
	(.93)		(5.26)	
56–60	−.092		−.268	
	(.26)		(4.86)	
61–65	.385		−.192	
	(.57)		(4.86)	

Note: The 1960–70 equation is estimated without ISIC 11, agriculture; the relative employment change for this industry (+50 percent) seems unreasonable. This seems to have to do with the definition of self-employment in agriculture, which decreased dramatically between 1960 and 1970. Using an approximation for the change in agricultural employment, using the 1960 self-employment ratio, yields an estimate of −1.314 with a *t*-value of 2.35.

wages and changes in employment. The pattern of change for 1970–90 is much more systematic. There is a negative relation between employment growth and wage changes in every age category. Further, the estimates are nearly uniform across age groups. If we interpret the estimates as reflecting labor demand responses, they imply long-run elasticities of about −.5.

The relation of employment changes to changes in mean wages can be biased if the least-skilled workers are the ones who leave contracting industries. Then selection causes average wages to rise as employment falls. To eliminate the selection effect, we constructed an imputed change in average industry earnings from (i) the number of industry *i* workers in each decile of the income distribution in the base year (say 1960) and (ii) the overall distribution of income in the ending year (say 1970). Then the imputed wage change is caused solely by the change in the overall earnings distribution. Using this variable as

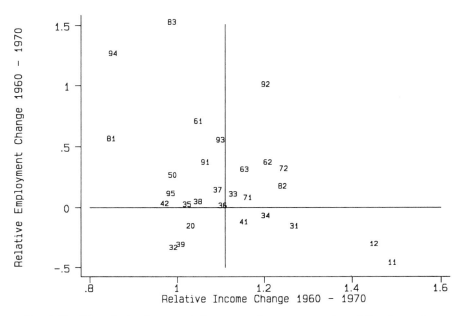

Fig. 4.17   The relation between industry employment growth and the change in industry income, 1960–70
Source: Swedish census data.
Note: See the appendix for a list of industry codes.

an instrument for actual earnings changes in table 4.4 yields stronger results, as shown in columns 2 and 4 of table 4.4. The point estimate for 1960–70 is unreasonably large, although the estimate also has a large standard error. The estimate for 1970–90 ($-.67$) is much more reasonable.

To get an idea of how these relations work in an unconstrained labor market, we once again use the United States as a counterfactual. In table 4.5, we report regression estimates of changes in relative employment on wage changes and initial wage levels for industries in the manufacturing sector in Sweden and the United States.[25] We find that industries with high wage growth had low employment growth in both countries during the 1960s, the Swedish estimate being higher, however. This relation becomes weaker in later periods in both countries. The main difference between the two countries is found in the relation between initial wages and subsequent employment growth. In Sweden, there is a positive and significant coefficient for initial wages for all subperiods, even if the magnitudes become smaller over time. In the United States, we find no evidence of such a relation. Thus, if we use the United States as an indication of how an unregulated market works, high-wage industries grew much more rapidly than in an unconstrained market.

25. We are grateful to Johnny Zetterberg for providing these data.

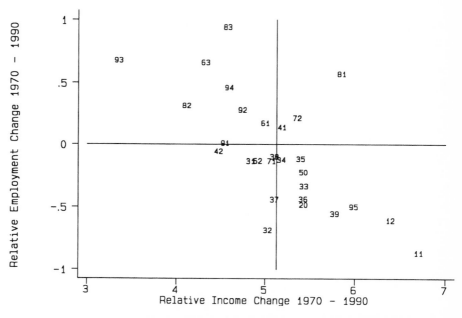

Fig. 4.18   The relation between industry employment growth and the change in industry income, 1970–90

Source: Swedish census data.

Note: See the appendix for a list of industry codes.

The uniform adjustment pattern across age groups in the 1970–90 data implies that restructuring was not accomplished by merely redirecting the flow of young workers. Prime-aged men had to leave some industries and go elsewhere. Further evidence on this is presented in tables 4.6 and 4.7. Table 4.6 repeats the regression exercise for within-cohort employment changes. Again focusing on the 1970–90 data, the estimates show significant restructuring within cohorts in response to changes in average industry earnings. Notice that the estimated elasticities are about half as large as those for fixed age groups. This is implied if part of the employment adjustment is achieved by changing the distribution of the inflow of youth.

Table 4.7 extends the cohort analysis, showing the cross-industry distributions of employment for various birth cohorts in 1960, 1970, and 1990. The table leaves no doubt that workers left some industries and entered others. For example, consider the cohort born in 1935–39, who were twenty-one to twenty-six years old in 1960. Workers in this cohort left agriculture and manufacturing, both of which contracted in the aggregate, and entered public administration and the service industry, which nearly doubled in share. Almost all the overall and within-cohort expansion of the latter industry is due to the growth of employment in the public sector. The growth of this sector was not

Table 4.5   **Relative Employment Change in Manufacturing: Sweden and the United States (absolute *t*-values in parentheses)**

Years	Sweden	United States
	Dependent Variable, $(e_{t+1} - e_t)/e_t$; Independent Variable, $(w_{t+1} - w_t)/w_t$	
1963–70	−2.820	−1.728
	(3.479)	(2.79)
1970–75	−.282	−.098
	(.78)	(.43)
1975–80	.186	−.744
	(.34)	(3.51)
1980–85	1.039	.489
	(1.76)	(1.50)
	Dependent Variable, $(e_{t+1} - e_t)/e_t$; Independent Variable, w_t	
1963–70	.165	.039
	(2.48)	(.64)
1970–75	.051	.0001
	(2.69)	(.00)
1975–80	.037	−.007
	(3.61)	(.31)
1980–85	.015	.0005
	(2.23)	(.04)

Note: The employment data refer to annual hours worked within each three-digit ISIC industry within manufacturing (twenty-eight industries).

accomplished merely by hiring ever-larger proportions of new entrants. Rather, every cohort gravitated toward the public sector, and in roughly equal proportions.

Does this mean that public employment is the sponge that soaked up the excess supply of low-wage workers? The evidence points in this direction, but this may not be the only factor at work. Other industries also grew, and some might have declined by more if wage compression had not occurred. For example, most observers would agree that fabricated metals is the type of "high-wage" industry that the Rehn-Meidner program and associated public policies were meant to expand. This industry accounted for 16.5 percent of male employment in 1970 and exactly the same proportion in 1990. But the comparable industry in the United States accounted for 16 percent of employment in 1970 and only 8 percent in 1990, a relative decline of 50 percent. With the United States as a counterfactual, fabricated metals "grew" as a source of employment.

We close this section with evidence on changes in the relative skill composition of some key industries. We index *relative skill* by each person's position in the overall wage distribution for each year: 1960, 1970, and 1990. Six indus-

Table 4.6   Cohort Relative Employment Change and Relative Income Change (absolute t-values in parentheses)

Age 1960	Dependent Variable, $(e_{70} - e_{60})/e_{60}$; Independent Variable, $(i_{60} - i_{70})/i_{60}$	Age 1970	Dependent Variable, $(e_{90} - e_{70})/e_{70}$; Independent Variable, $(i_{90} - i_{70})/i_{70}$
11–15	...	21–25	.126
			(.97)
16–21	...	26–30	−.071
			(.68)
21–25	.945	31–35	−.229
	(3.09)		(2.68)
26–30	−.020	36–40	−.287
	(.04)		(4.65)
31–35	.831	41–45	−.173
	(2.06)		(4.36)
36–40	−.155	46–50	−.046
	(.37)		(1.38)
41–45	−.732	51–55	...
	(2.18)		
46–50	−.677	56–60	...
	(2.03)		
51–55	−.805	61–65	...
	(2.42)		

Note: The 1960–70 equation is estimated without ISIC 11, agriculture.

tries are shown in figures 4.19–24. The figures show a slight increase in skills in low-wage agriculture, especially from 1970 to 1990, as we would expect from a compression of the wage distribution. At the other extreme, relative skills declined in fabricated metals and machinery, where the share of workers in the first and second quintiles grew steadily over time. Similar declines in relative skill levels appear in the growing public sector. In public administration, the decline is gradual, but, in education and health, there is an abrupt decline. From a distribution that was heavily concentrated in the top quintile in 1970, the 1990 distribution of income roughly matches the distribution for the overall population.

4.4   Driving Forces in the Swedish Labor Market

What factors have driven the performance of the Swedish labor market? Writing in the 1940s, Rehn and Meidner offered a radical agenda for managing the wage distribution and transforming employment in Sweden. While vague on details, they backed up their policy prescriptions with bold predictions (even for economists) of what the outcomes would be. They thought that egalitarian wage policies, implemented through central bargaining, would push la-

Table 4.7   **Industry Distribution of Employment by Birth Cohort and Year: Males**

	Birth Cohort								
Year	1895–99	1905–9	1915–19	1925–29	1935–39	1945–49	1955–59	1965–69	Total
	Agriculture, Forestry, and Fishing (ISIC 1)								
1960	13.5	9.9	8.2	8.9	10.0				10.4
1970		5.4	12.6	10.0	6.6	5.4			10.2
1990				2.9	2.1	1.6	2.1	2.1	2.0
	Mining (ISIC 2)								
1960	1.2	1.2	1.2	1.3	1.5				1.2
1970		.9	.8	.9	.9	.9			.9
1990				.2	.7	.5	.4	.4	.5
	Manufacturing (ISIC 3)								
1960	43.6	39.8	40.9	39.3	43.7				41.5
1970		35.7	34.0	33.7	34.6	37.2			34.9
1990				32.3	31.8	28.1	29.4	34.3	30.7
	Thereof Textiles (ISIC 32)								
1960	3.7	3.2	3.0	2.5	2.2				2.9
1970		2.5	1.8	1.5	1.2	1.2			1.6
1990				1.0	.6	.5	.4	.5	.5
	And Fabricated Metal Products (ISIC 38)								
1960	14.1	15.3	19.3	19.6	20.6				18.6
1970		13.1	15.4	16.1	17.5	19.5			16.5
1990				16.4	16.6	15.1	16.2	19.2	16.5
	Electricity, Gas, and Water (ISIC 4)								
1960	2.0	1.2	1.8	1.5	.8				1.5
1970		1.0	1.5	1.2	1.0	.8			1.1
1990				1.9	2.6	1.7	1.4	.7	1.4
	Construction (ISIC 5)								
1960	14.8	18.1	14.9	12.6	12.9				14.1
1970		14.2	14.1	13.5	15.4	18.3			15.0
1990				10.2	11.5	12.2	11.7	16.1	12.9
	Trade (ISIC 6)								
1960	6.7	6.4	7.3	9.4	9.8				8.7
1970		10.0	9.7	11.3	11.5	12.0			11.1
1990				12.3	11.2	11.5	13.4	17.0	12.3

(continued)

Table 4.7   (continued)

| | Birth Cohort | | | | | | | |
Year	1895–99	1905–9	1915–19	1925–29	1935–39	1945–49	1955–59	1965–69	Total
				Communication (ISIC 7)					
1960	5.0	8.5	11.5	11.2	9.8				9.8
1970		5.0	10.5	10.1	9.4	9.9			9.3
1990				7.0	9.5	10.3	11.2	8.9	9.7
				FIRE (ISIC 8)					
1960	3.6	2.2	2.6	3.0	1.3				2.6
1970		3.7	3.7	4.4	1.8	4.7			4.5
1990				9.1	9.1	10.3	9.6	7.2	9.0
				Public Administration and Other Services (ISIC 9)					
1960	9.2	11.2	11.4	12.4	8.5				10.2
1970		11.7	12.8	14.9	15.1	10.8			13.0
1990				23.8	21.6	25.3	20.0	12.5	19.7
				Thereof Public Sector (ISIC 31, 33)					
1960	7.3	9.4	10.1	11.1	7.0				8.9
1970		9.2	10.8	12.6	12.9	8.6			11.8
1990				20.9	18.9	19.8	16.8	9.8	16.7

bor into more productive uses and promote economic growth. By raising labor costs in low-wage sectors, they argued, low-wage employers would be driven out of business. Labor would then flow to high-wage sectors, which are more productive. To them, equity and efficiency were complements in the development process.

Even with fifty years of hindsight, it is hard to quibble with the broad outlines of what Rehn and Meidner predicted. From 1960 to the early 1970s, LO's egalitarian strategy compressed wage differentials along virtually every observable dimension. Industry and regional differences were the first to fall, which reduced employment in low-wage industries and forced migration from the north. Labor market programs were implemented to deal with the displacements, as Rehn and Meidner had advocated, but the remarkable thing to us is that they seem to have played such a minor role. The sum of open unemployment and participation in labor market programs remained low throughout the process, while average wages and productivity grew rapidly. At this level, even Rehn and Meidner must have been surprised.

While the story after 1970 is less sanguine, these facts present an important puzzle. How was full employment maintained in the face of interventions that sharply raised the relative price of low-wage workers? It does no good to argue that labor demands were inelastic—low-wage industries contracted as their labor costs rose. Instead, the demand for these workers was apparently rising

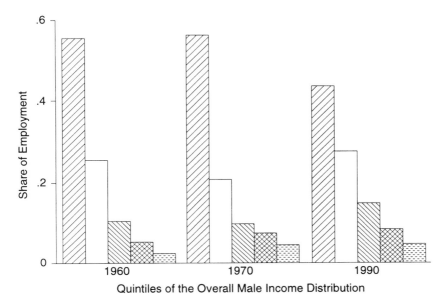

Fig. 4.19   Male income distribution in selected industries, 1960, 1970, 1990: agriculture

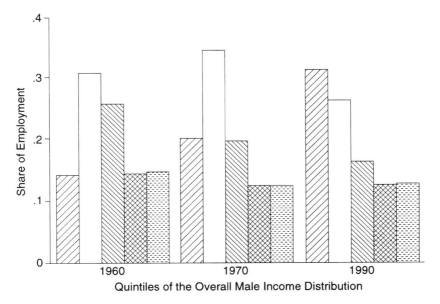

Fig. 4.20   Male income distribution in selected industries, 1960, 1970, 1990: textile

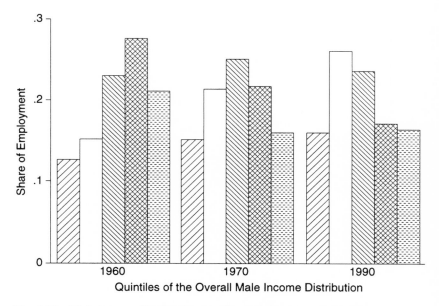

Fig. 4.21   Male income distribution in selected industries, 1960, 1970, 1990: machinery

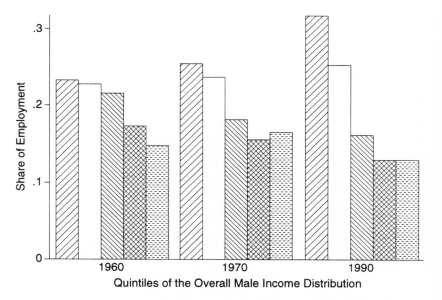

Fig. 4.22   Male income distribution in selected industries, 1960, 1970, 1990: retail trade

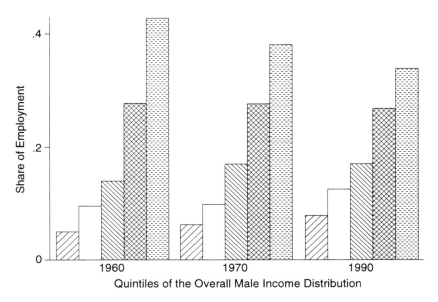

Fig. 4.23   Male income distribution in selected industries, 1960, 1970, 1990: public administration

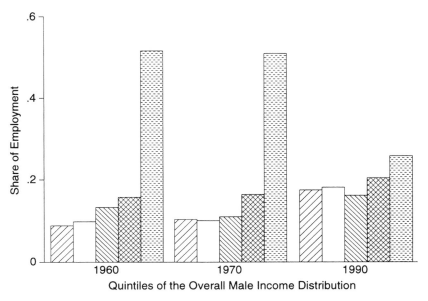

Fig. 4.24   Male income distribution in selected industries, 1960, 1970, 1990: education and health care

in other sectors. What drove the increase in demand? Several theories are possible, and all may contain a grain of truth.

The most obvious explanation is the growth of the public sector, which accelerated after 1970. The government may have supported the price of low-wage workers by simply hiring them, soaking up the excess of supply over private demand. As we indicated above, this is broadly consistent with the facts for women, for whom the public sector accounts for virtually all increased employment and labor force participation. But only 15 percent of men held public sector jobs in 1990, up five points from 1970. Men and women must be good substitutes in low-wage occupations if the public sector is to have an important effect on male earnings. At least for men, we do not think that expansion of the public sector is the whole story (see also Edin and Holmlund 1994).

Another explanation is that negotiated wage settlements simply tracked market equilibrium outcomes. With regard to skill groups, this implies either (i) rising relative demand for products produced by less-skilled workers or (ii) declining relative supplies of the less skilled. Edin and Holmlund (1995) find little evidence in favor of implication (i), but changes in relative shares of workers with different levels of education do favor implication (ii). Their evidence that returns to schooling move with relative supplies of education groups (see figs. 4.11 and 4.12 above) suggests that at least some of the move toward wage equality was "swimming with the tide."

It seems obvious that wage inequality would have declined even without a solidarity wage policy on the part of LO. The reduction in the market share of low-skill workers, driven by increased schooling levels, was huge. This would reduce inequality directly by reducing the share of the low-wage workers and also indirectly by changing relative prices, as Edin and Holmlund show. But it also seems obvious that inequality fell by more, and more quickly, than can be explained by market forces alone. Hibbs's (1990) estimate that wage differences between contract areas fell by more than half in a period of six years (1966–72) is too large to explain as an outcome of slowly changing factor proportions. The similarly large and rapid contraction of within-firm and between-occupation differentials, which continued through the 1970s, also appears to indicate "overshooting" of what would have occurred in a competitive market.

Thus, the overall compression of wages in Sweden must exaggerate the effect of central bargaining and LO policies. Some of it would have occurred anyway. But, in our view, LO also achieved its egalitarian goals. Wage differentials and inequality fell by more than can be explained by market forces alone.

These conclusions mean that central bargaining did constrain the Swedish wage structure. Yet there is little evidence of excess supply. There are at least three theories that are consistent with these facts. Each relies on expanding labor demand, driven by declining wages in high-wage industries, to soak up displaced workers. A common theme is that the LO-SAF bargains delivered cheap labor to high-wage employers in SAF. LO and SAF were more clever than simply to impose a wage floor and watch unemployment rise. We outline the models in turn.

4.4.1 Model 1: Decentralized Bargaining and Industry Rents

Sweden was already heavily unionized in 1950, with about 75 percent of the non-self-employed workforce belonging to labor unions. Bargaining took place at the company and industry level, and there were significant interunion wage differences. It was in this environment that SAF—the employers federation—pushed for central bargaining. Most explanations of this fact point to SAF's fears of "leapfrogging" in wage negotiations with separate unions. We think that it is equally plausible that high-wage employers—who allegedly dominated SAF—recognized their gains from compressing the interindustry wage distribution. They counted on LO to deliver cheap labor and expand the "modern" sector of the labor market.[26]

In this model, the costs of a solidarity wage policy are small. Indeed, central bargaining and the compression of interindustry wage differences may be efficient. High wages in some sectors can reflect unions' success in extracting rents in bilateral negotiations, with the result that equally productive workers are paid differently across sectors. In traditional models of monopoly unionism, the resulting distribution of workers will be inefficient, and high-wage sectors of the labor market will be "too small."

Central bargaining can internalize these costs in the same way that it internalizes tendencies toward wage inflation (Olson 1982). With near-universal union coverage, a central bargain can more closely replicate a Walrasian wage distribution. Wage levels in high-wage industries will fall and their demand for labor expand. Low-wage sectors contract, but there is full employment during restructuring because underlying market forces are pulling workers toward expanding industries. Labor market programs would therefore play a minor role. In its broad outline, these movements are consistent with the industrial restructuring of the 1960s and early 1970s, when between-contract wage differences were greatly reduced (Hibbs 1990; Holmlund and Zetterberg 1991).

4.4.2 Model 2: Equalizing Wage Differences

The "rationale" just given posits voluntary and efficient mobility from low- to high-wage sectors. But some discussions of the process, and of Rehn and Meidner's proposals, emphasize involuntary mobility. Wage differences between sectors were "too large," in the sense of being inconsistent with egalitarian ideals, but not large enough to induce workers to move. Then the point of raising wages in low-wage sectors was to force people to seek work at a higher wage.

This scenario can make sense if some wage differentials reflect differences

---

26. Moene and Wallerstein (1993) contains similar ideas in a political model of winners and losers from central bargaining.

in amenities across sectors rather than differences in skills. Imagine two sectors, one high wage (H) and the other low (L). Jobs in the two sectors offer amenities a_H and a_L. In equilibrium, the marginal worker's welfare is equalized across sectors, so $u(w_L, a_L) = u(w_H, a_H)$ and $w_H > w_L$ if $a_H < a_L$. Now suppose that an egalitarian wage policy sets a wage floor above w_L. Higher wages force some workers to leave sector L, which contracts, raising labor supply and reducing relative wages in sector H. The equilibrium outcome entails contraction of the low-wage sector, migration from L to H, full employment, and declining wage inequality. Mobility is involuntary in the sense that workers who move are worse off than before, as are all workers in sector H, who now work for a lower wage. Intramarginal workers in L gain—their wage is higher—as do owners of capital in H.

This model is consistent with key features of the Swedish restructuring. Induced migration from the low-wage north to the high-wage south was part of the Rehn-Meidner program for economic growth. Nilsson (1993) and Henrekson, Jonung, and Stymne (1993) report growing resentment against these "moving van" policies by the early 1970s, resulting in a policy shift that favored the maintenance of full employment within regions over forced restructuring. Unlike the previous model, the outcome is inefficient, although income redistribution benefits some low-wage workers and all high-wage employers.[27]

4.4.3   Model 3: Compressed Skill Differentials

The models just presented make opposite assumptions about the initial wage distribution that is compressed by central bargaining. Under the rents hypothesis, the initial distribution was inefficient because of differences in bargaining power across sectors. Wage compression was Pareto improving. With equalizing differences, wage differences represent efficient compensation for amenities. Wage compression reduced welfare. We believe that both have application to the Swedish experience, but even their combination is not the complete story. It is difficult to argue that the compression of wage differences across industries eliminated only union rents or that intersectoral differences in pay reflected only amenities.[28] And neither model applies to the large compressions of pay that occurred within firms or between occupations and educational groups. These changes reduced the relative price of skill.

Other factors were at work. In thinking about what they were, we believe that it is relevant that SAF, not LO, was the initiator of central bargaining in

---

27. A related growth model is discussed in Agell and Lommerud (1993). In their analysis, the expanding high-wage sector creates growth externalities along the lines of Lucas (1988) or Romer (1986). Then a case can be made that forced restructuring enhances growth as a form of "industrial policy." Welfare is lower today, but it may be higher in the future.

28. In the United States, where only 12 percent of the private sector workforce is unionized, interindustry wage dispersion is much larger than in Sweden. These differences do not reflect union rents. This is another case where using the United States as a benchmark suggests that the wage distribution is constrained relative to competitive outcomes.

the 1950s and tended to support the process for the next thirty years. The dominant faction in SAF saw that it had something to gain. But, in 1983, it was Verstadsföreningen and Metall—the largest private-bargaining pair in Sweden—that first abandoned central bargaining. They claimed that skilled workers were underpaid in the central frame agreements. For the employers in Verstadsföreningen, the costs of compressed skill differentials had come to outweigh the benefits, whatever those might be, so they left the coalition. Central bargaining began to crumble, and skill differentials in pay began to rise.

These points suggest that a reduced price of skilled labor was an important element of central bargaining, which kept SAF involved in the short run but which eventually led to the demise of frame agreements. On this interpretation, frame agreements did not just raise the compensation of low-wage workers; they also reduced the absolute wage of skilled workers. We build a simple two-sector, three-factor model to illustrate the forces at work.[29]

We assume three factors of production: unskilled labor (U), skilled labor (S), and capital (K). Factor prices are W_u, W_s, and r. Skilled and unskilled labor are inelastically supplied in the short run, while capital is in perfectly elastic supply on the world market. Both types of labor have rising supply price in the long run.

Sector 1, the low-skill sector, is U intensive. Think of it as retail trade. We take this to the extreme and assume that sector 1 output depends only on employment of unskilled labor: $y_1 = F(U_1)$. Sector 2 is skill and capital intensive; think of it as manufacturing. Output is $Y_2 = G(U_2, S, K)$, which embodies the simplifying assumption that all skilled labor is employed in sector 2. We assume that the price of sector 2 output is $p(Y_2)$ with $p'(\cdot) < 0$, and we normalize the price in sector 1 to unity. Then competitive equilibrium implies

(1)
$$F_u(U_1) = W_u,$$

(2a)
$$pG_u(U_2, S, K) = W_u,$$

(2b)
$$pG_s(U_2, S, K) = W_s,$$

(2c)
$$pG_k(U_2, S, K) = r,$$

(3)
$$U_1 + U_2 = U.$$

Now assume that a central bargain caps the wage of skilled workers at $W <$ W_s. Sector 2 employers earn rents because the contract effectively cartelizes the market for skilled labor. At the old allocation of resources, (2b) no longer holds as an equilibrium condition. Skill has a positive shadow price, as in figure 4.25, because there is excess demand.

How is a new equilibrium attained? In the short run, rents accrue to the owners of capital in sector 2, so we expect capital to enter the industry. This means that (2c) no longer holds; instead, it is replaced by the condition that capital flows to sector 2 until there are zero profits:

---

29. For a related model, see Flam (1987).

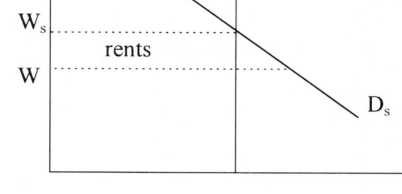

Fig. 4.25   Positive shadow price of skilled labor

(4) $$pG(U_2, S, K) - W_u U_2 - WS - rK = 0.$$

Sector 2 becomes inefficiently large and capital intensive.

Displacement of (1), (2), and (4) yields the allocative effects of a price ceiling on skilled labor. These are

(5) $$dk/dW_s \propto -S < 0,$$

(6) $$dU_1/dW_s = -dU_2/dW_s \propto -S(pG_{uk} + G_u G_k p'),$$

(7) $$dW_u/dW_s \propto -S(pG_{uk} + G_u G_k p').$$

Equation (5) indicates that the wage cap ($dW_s < 0$) attracts capital to sector 2 and that the effect is proportional to the utilization of skilled labor in that sector.[30] In turn, rising capital intensity increases the demand for unskilled labor in sector 2 so long as capital and labor are sufficiently strong gross comple-

---

30. The model assumes that capital is in perfectly elastic supply, although this is inessential. With a closed capital market, investment is the outcome of domestic saving, which implies rising supply price. The model then implies that saving and investment increase with a wage cap, so that capital grows over time to a new long-run equilibrium, while intertemporal consumption decisions are distorted.

ments ($G_{uk} > 0$).[31] Unskilled labor migrates from sector 1 to sector 2, which is what occurred. This change in demand is also the condition for the unskilled wage to rise in (3), further reducing wage inequality. Notice that the market for unskilled labor always clears—there is no induced unemployment in the model because the egalitarian policy actually increased the demand for unskilled labor. The market that does not clear is for skilled labor, where there is excess demand.

This point takes on added relevance in the long run, when the assumption of inelastic supplies of skill groups is less appropriate. Lindbeck et al. (1993), Henrekson, Jonung, and Stymne (1993), and others have argued that the distortionary effects of egalitarian policies are large because participants will eventually adjust to changed incentives. Lindbeck is especially forceful on this, pointing out that long-run distortions are likely to be much more serious because patterns of behavior adjust slowly.

Our model has this flavor and produces additional implications. With endogenous investment in human capital, the long-run supply of skilled workers will depend on the skill premium, $W_s - W_u$. A higher wage premium encourages investment and raises overall productivity. Wage compression causes the relative supply of skilled labor to fall over time, much as we found for the returns to schooling in table 4.2 above. By raising the marginal product of skilled labor, a declining share of skilled labor increases the wedge between the social value of skill and its price. The welfare costs of wage compression cumulate because incentives to invest in skill are distorted. Inefficiencies are small in the short run, when stocks of skill are fairly fixed, but they loom large in the long run, when the supply of skill is elastic.

This fact is consistent with the ultimate unraveling of centralized bargaining. As the shadow price of skill rises, the gains to defecting from the central agreement also rise. Firms that hire skilled labor are tempted to compete to get it, and the skilled unions they deal with also have more to gain from defection. This is our interpretation of why Verstadsföreningen and Metall eventually dropped out of the central frame. In the short run, central bargaining effectively cartelized the market for skilled workers and artificially increased the demand for unskilled ones. Skill-intensive firms gained. But the cost of maintaining narrow skill differentials rises through time because human capital investments are discouraged. As skilled labor becomes more scarce, the gains from cooperation are eventually swamped by the benefits of defection, which spells the demise of central bargaining.

To provide some empirical information on this hypothesis, we report a measure of the relative scarcity of skilled workers in figure 4.26. Our admittedly imperfect measure of scarcity is obtained from survey data on firms. We use the proportion of firms that report difficulties in recruiting skilled workers rela-

---

31. Complementarity is sufficient if Sweden is a price taker on world markets for sector 2 output, so $p'(Y_2) = 0$.

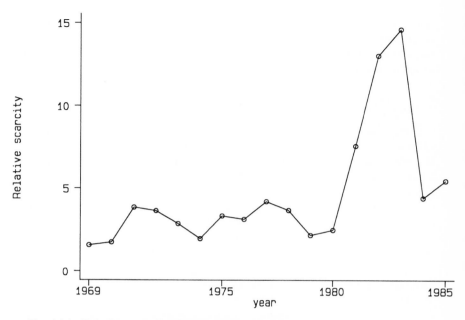

Fig. 4.26   Relative scarcity of skilled blue-collar labor
Source: KI (National Institute of Economic Research).

tive to the proportion of firms that report difficulties in recruiting other (un-skilled) workers.[32] This measure shows a dramatic increase in the relative scar-city of skilled workers in the early 1980s. This picture seems consistent with the hypothesis that excess demand for skilled labor contributed to the break-down of centralized bargaining. The question, however, is to what extent this excess supply was due to a reduced supply of skills. It seems reasonable that compressed skill differentials should produce a trend decline in the supply of skills. Our measure of scarcity does not show a strong trend prior to 1980. Together with the very sharp increase in the early 1980s, it seems that other factors than a gradual decline in the supply of skills were also at work.

In this model, a complete breakdown of central bargaining spells the col-lapse of the market for unskilled workers (and of investment). In fact, if mar-kets are allowed to clear, there will be even more wage inequality than would have occurred without egalitarian policies. The reason is that long-run factor ratios adjusted to the egalitarian wage structure, so the ratio of unskilled to skilled workers is artificially high. If unions try to stem the tide and keep the unskilled wage high, the result will be unemployment.

We do not believe that the end of central bargaining caused a reversion to market wages; skill premiums and inequality have widened, but not dramati-

32. We are grateful to Bertil Holmlund for making us aware of, and providing, these data.

cally. But it is true that the burden of the current crisis has fallen more heavily on fewer workers than in any earlier contraction, with unemployment rates not seen since the 1930s. In our model, this is a consequence of the end of wage compression.

4.5 Conclusions

Our reading of the evidence is that Swedish labor market institutions matter. Centralized bargaining, which was first initiated by employers but later rejected by them, played an important role in compressing wage differences. Compared to market outcomes, egalitarian wage policies reduced pay differences along virtually every dimension of skill, to different degrees. This was an important component, perhaps the important component, of Sweden's sharp decline in income inequality.

Our evidence indicates that pay compression had important effects in shifting the allocation of labor across sectors. Low-wage industries were forced to contract, as one would expect from an increase in the pay of low-wage workers. The puzzle is that wage compression did not generate high unemployment: Swedish unemployment rates were unusually low during the period of declining inequality. We find that public policies had little role in maintaining low unemployment. Expansion of the public sector helped bolster demand for low-wage workers, especially for women. Yet it appears that the relative private demand for less-skilled labor was rising. The labor market cleared at negotiated wage levels.

Despite evident market clearing for unskilled labor, we do not believe that wage bargains simply tracked what would have occurred in an unconstrained market. Wage compression occurred much too quickly for that. Instead, negotiated wage bargains may have bolstered the demand for less-skilled workers while delivering "cheap" skilled labor to large employers. This policy achieves redistribution at low cost in the short run, but distorted incentives can cause large inefficiencies in the long run.

Appendix
Industry Codes

The following is a list of ISIC industry codes used in the analysis of 1960, 1970, and 1990 census data. A limited number of industries were excluded owing to difficulties in linking the 1960 industry code to the ISIC code used in 1970 and 1990.

11   Farming, hunting
12   Forestry

13   Fishing
20   Mining and quarrying
31   Manufacture of food, beverages, and tobacco
32   Textile, wearing apparel, and leather industries
33   Manufacture of wood and wood products, including furniture
34   Manufacture of paper and paper products, printing and publishing
35   Manufacture of chemicals, petroleum, coal, rubber, and plastic products
36   Manufacture of nonmetallic mineral products, except products of petroleum and coal
37   Basic metal industries
38   Manufacture of fabricated metal products, machinery, and equipment
39   Other manufacturing industries
41   Electricity, gas, and heating services
42   Water services
50   Construction
61   Wholesale trade
62   Retail trade
63   Restaurants and hotels
71   Transport and storage
72   Communication
81   Banking and financial services
82   Insurance
83   Real estate
91   Public administration, defense, police and fire departments
92   Sanitary services
93   Education, research, health care
94   Recreational and cultural services
95   Domestic services

References

Agell, J., and K.-E. Lommerud. 1993. Egalitarianism and Growth. *Scandinavian Journal of Economics* 95:559–79.
Becker, G. 1964. *Human capital: A theoretical and empirical analysis, with special reference to education.* New York: National Bureau of Economic Research.
Becker, G., and G. Stigler. 1974. Law Enforcement, Malfeasance, and Compensation of Enforcers. *Journal of Legal Studies* 3:1–18.
Ben-Porath, Y. 1967. The production of human capital and the life cycle of earnings. *Journal of Political Economy* 75:352–65.
Björklund, A. 1991. Evaluation of labour market policy in Sweden. In *Evaluating labour market and social programmes.* Paris: OECD.

————. 1993. Unemployment in Sweden. Swedish Institute for Social Research, Stockholm University. Mimeo.

Björklund, A., and J. Åkerman. 1989. Piece-rates, on-the-job training and the wage-tenure profile. Working Paper no. 246. Stockholm: Industrial Institute for Economic and Social Research.

Björklund, A., and B. Holmlund. 1991. The economics of unemployment—the case of Sweden. In *FIEF studies in labour markets and economic policy*, ed. A. Björklund et al. Oxford: Oxford University Press.

Björklund, A., and I. Persson-Tanimura. 1983. Youth employment in Sweden. In *Youth at work: An international survey*, ed. B. Reubens. Totowa, N.J.: Rowman & Allenheld.

Björklund, A., and H. Regnér. 1993. Humankapital-teorin och utbildning på arbetsplats-erna (Human capital theory and training in the workplace). In *Sveriges arbets-platser—Organisation, personalutveckling, styrning*, ed. C. le Grand, R. Szulkin, and M. Tåhlin. Stockholm: SNS Förlag.

Blau, F., and L. Kahn. 1995. The gender gap: Some international evidence. In *Differences and changes in wage structures*, ed. R. Freeman and L. Katz. Chicago: University of Chicago Press.

Burtless, G. 1987. Taxes, transfers, and Swedish labor supply. In *The Swedish economy*, ed. B. Bosworth and A. Rivlin. Washington, D.C.: Brookings.

Carling, K., P.-A. Edin, A. Harkman, and B. Holmlund. 1996. Unemployment duration, unemployment benefits, and labor market programs in Sweden. *Journal of Public Economics* 59:313–34.

D'Agostino, H. 1992. *Why do workers join unions: A comparison of Sweden and OECD countries.* Dissertation Series no. 22. Swedish Institute for Social Research, Stockholm University.

Davis, S. 1992. International change and the wage structure. *NBER Macroeconomics Annual,* 239–92.

Edin, P.-A. 1993. Swimming with the tide: Solidarity wage policy and the gender-earnings gap. Uppsala University. Mimeo.

Edin, P.-A., P. Frederiksson, and B. Holmlund. 1994. Utbildningnivoch utbildningsav-kastning is Sverige (The level of education and the return to education in Sweden. Studier av svensk utbildning, Ekonomiska Rådets årsbok 1993. Stockholm: Konjun-kturinstitutet.

Edin, P.-A., and B. Holmlund. 1994. *Arbetslösheten och arbetsmarknadens funktions-sätt* (Unemployment and the functioning of the labor market). Bilaga 8 till LU94. Stockholm: Fritzes.

————. 1995. The Swedish wage structure: The rise and fall of solidarity wage policy? In *Differences and changes in wage structures*, ed. R. Freeman and L. Katz. Chicago: University of Chicago Press.

Edin, P.-A., and J. Zetterberg. 1992. Interindustry wage differentials: Evidence from Sweden and a comparison with the United States. *American Economic Review* 82:1341–49.

Elvander, N. 1988. *Den svenska modellen: Löneförhandlingar och inkomstpolitik, 1982–1986* (The Swedish model: Wage negotiations and incomes policy, 1982–1986). Stockholm: Allmänna.

Erikson, R., and R. Åberg. 1987. *Welfare in transition.* Oxford: Clarendon.

Flam, H. 1987. Equal pay for unequal work. *Scandinavian Journal of Economics* 89:435–50.

Fredriksson, P. 1994. The demand for higher education in Sweden: Theory and evidence. Working Paper no. 1994:14. Department of Economics, Uppsala University.

Freeman, R., and R. Gibbons. 1995. Getting together and breaking apart: The decline of centralized bargaining. In *Differences and changes in wage structures,* ed. R. Freeman and L. Katz. Chicago: University of Chicago Press.

Freeman, R., and L. Katz. 1994. Rising wage inequality: The United States vs. other advanced countries. In *Working under different rules,* ed. R. Freeman. New York: Russel Sage.

Gustafsson, S., and P. Lantz. 1985. *Arbete och löner* (Work and wages). Stockholm: Almqvist & Wicksell.

Henrekson, M., L. Jonung, and J. Stymne. 1993. Economic Growth and the Swedish Model. Working Paper no. 118. Stockholm: Trade Union Institute for Economic Research.

Hibbs, D. 1990. Wage compression under solidarity bargaining in Sweden. Research Report no. 30. Stockholm: Trade Union Institute for Economic Research (FIEF).

Hibbs, D., and H. Locking. 1991. Wage compression, wage drift, and wage inflation in Sweden. Working Paper no. 87. Stockholm: Trade Union Institute for Economic Research (FIEF).

———. 1996. Wage dispersion and productive efficiency: Evidence for Sweden. In *Essays on Swedish wage formation,* ed. H. Locking. Department of Economics, University of Gothenburg.

Holmlund, B., and J. Zetterberg. 1991. Insider effects in wage determination: Evidence from five countries. *European Economic Review* 35:1009–34.

Juhn, C., K. Murphy, and R. Topel. 1991. Why has the natural rate of unemployment increased over time? *Brookings Papers on Economic Activity,* no. 2:75–142.

Kim, D. I., and R. Topel. 1995. Labor markets and economic growth: Lessons from Korea's industrialization, 1970–1990. In *Differences and changes in wage structures,* ed. R. Freeman and L. Katz. Chicago: University of Chicago Press.

Klevmarken, A., and P. Olofsson. 1993. *Household market and nonmarket activities: Procedures and Codes, 1984–1991.* Stockholm: Industrial Institute for Economic and Social Research.

Lazear, E., 1981. Agency, earnings profiles, productivity, and hours restrictions. *American Economic Review* 71:606–20.

le Grand, C. 1994. Löneskillnaderna i Sverige: Förändring och nuvarande struktur (Wage differentials in Sweden: Change and present structure). In *Vardagens villkor,* ed. J. Fritzell and O. Lundberg. Stockholm: Brombergs.

Lindbeck, A., P. Molander, T. Persson, O. Peterson, A. Sandmo, B. Swedenborg, and N. Thygesen. 1993. Options for economic and political reform in Sweden. *Economic Policy* 17:219–63.

LO. 1987. *Kartläggning av de sociala villkoren* (A mapping of social terms). Stockholm.

Lucas, R. 1988. On the mechanics of economic development. *Journal of Monetary Economics* 22:3–22.

Moene, K. O., and M. Wallerstein. 1993. Egalitarian wage policies. University of Oslo. Mimeo.

Murphy, K. M., and R. Topel. 1986. Unemployment, risk and earnings: Theory and evidence from a model of equalizing wage differentials. In *Unemployment and the structure of labor markets,* ed. J. Leonard and K. Lang. London: Basil Blackwell.

Nilsson, C. 1993. The Swedish model: Labour market institutions and contracts. In *Labour market contracts and institutions,* ed. J. Hartog and J. Theeuwes. Amsterdam: Elsevier Science.

OECD. 1993. *Employment outlook.* Paris.

Olson, M. 1982. *The rise and decline of nations.* New Haven, Conn.: Yale University Press.

Östros, T. 1994. Do minimum wages matter? The case of Swedish mining and manufacturing. Working Paper no. 1994:17. Department of Economics, Uppsala University.

Romer, P. 1986. Increasing returns and long-run growth. *Journal of Political Economy* 94:1002–37.

Selen, J., and A.-C. Ståhlberg. 1992. Non-wage benefits in Sweden. Institute for Social Research, Stockholm University. Mimeo.

Svensson, L. 1996. Har lönepolitiken spelat en självständig roll i den samhällsekonomiska utvecklingen? En kommentar till Hibbs och Locking (Has union wage policy played an independent part in the economy? A comment on Hibbs and Locking). *Ekonomisk Debatt* 24: 139–43.

Topel, R. 1991. Specific capital, mobility, and wages: Wages rise with job seniority. *Journal of Political Economy* 99:145–76.

Ullenhag, J. 1970. *Den solidariska lönepolitiken i Sverige: Debatt och verklighet* (Solidarity wage policy in Sweden: Debate and reality). Stockholm: Norstedts.

5   The Effects of Sweden's Welfare State on Labor Supply Incentives

Thomas Aronsson and James R. Walker

Sweden's extensive social insurance programs that care for Swedes "from cradle to grave" necessitate a tax burden that is among the highest in the world. This paper contributes to the discussion by summarizing the incentive effects of the principal tax and transfer programs that affect the Swedish labor supply. We adopt a broad definition of *labor supply* to cover a wide array of potential incentive effects. First, we describe the institutional details of how Sweden's cash transfer programs and tax system affect incentives and for whom. Second, we review the voluminous labor supply literature and recent empirical evidence obtained from Swedish data to measure the most important behavioral effects and to assess probable consequences of legislative reforms.

5.1   Dimensions of Labor Supply

It is common to think of labor supply as a homogeneous quantity, such as the number of hours worked or the number of people employed. Yet one important insight to be gleaned from the labor supply research conducted over the last three decades has been the recognition of the many distinct dimensions of labor supply. We consider three dimensions: (1) participation (whether an individual works); (2) the number of hours supplied in a period; and (3) quality or skill of the worker (also called *human capital,* where the worker's skill is to

Thomas Aronsson is associate professor of economics at the University of Umeå, Sweden. James R. Walker is professor of economics at the University of Wisconsin and a faculty research fellow of the National Bureau of Economic Research.

The authors gratefully acknowledge research support from the National Institutes of Health and Child Development Projects HD-19226 and HD-28685. They thank Roger Axelsson, Anders Björklund, Soren Blomquist, Richard Blundell, Karl Löfgren, J. Karl Scholz, and Jörn Stage for helpful comments and suggestions on earlier drafts.

some extent a choice variable). We also make the distinction between short- and long-run measures of labor supply.[1]

5.2   Theory of Labor Supply Response

We begin with a description of the individual's choice of hours of work in a static framework, which will be referred to as the *canonical model*. Its simple structure is useful for discussing the basic effects of taxes and transfer programs on labor force participation and hours of work.

5.2.1   The Canonical Model

We represent the individual's preferences over consumption goods and leisure by the utility function $u = u(c, L)$, where c is a composite consumption good, $L = T - h$ is leisure, T is total time available (i.e., the time endowment), and h is hours of work. The utility function is assumed to be increasing and strictly quasi concave in its arguments. The budget constraint is written

$$(1) \qquad\qquad wh + y - \Gamma + B = c,$$

where w is the hourly gross wage rate, y is nonlabor income, Γ is the total tax payment, and B is a transfer payment received by the individual. To illustrate the outcome of utility maximization subject to equation (1), let us start by assuming that $B = 0$ (i.e., that the individual receives no transfer payment) and that the income tax is proportional in the sense that $\Gamma = \tau wh$, where τ is the marginal tax rate.

In figure 5.1, consumption of goods is measured along the vertical axis, while leisure and hours of work are measured along the horizontal axis, where we make use of the fact that $h = T - L$. The budget constraint is represented by the line E-E with slope $-w(1 - \tau)$ and intercept y. I_0, I_1 and I_2 are indifference curves; that is, each such curve represents combinations of c and L such that the utility is constant along the curve. The farther away from the origin an indifference curve is located, the higher the utility level corresponding to the curve. To reach the highest possible utility level without violating the budget constraint, the individual will choose the combination of goods and leisure consumption where an indifference curve becomes tangent to the budget constraint. This occurs at point A in the figure, where we also find that h_0 represents the optimal hours of work. A key insight provided by the theory of consumer choice is that the response in the hours of work to a change in the budget constraint can be decomposed into a substitution effect and an income effect. This is important in order to understand how to interpret the influence of economic policy such as taxes and transfer payments on hours of work. To illus-

---

1. The "longest" long run would consider the effect of taxes and transfer programs on the size and age composition of the population. The effects of Sweden's public policies on fertility and immigration are active topics of public discussion. For a discussion of the literature, see Walker (1995) and Gustafsson and Klevmarken (1993).

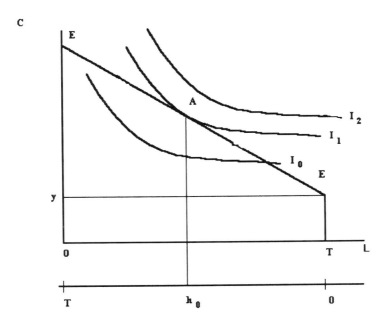

Fig. 5.1 **Labor-leisure choice**

trate, suppose that the marginal tax rate increases from τ to τ', and consider figure 5.2.

Prior to the change in the marginal tax rate, figure 5.2 coincides with figure 5.1, meaning that the initial optimal hours of work are h_0. An increase in the marginal tax rate will change the slope of the budget constraint, and the new budget constraint is represented by the line $E\text{-}E'$ with slope $-w(1 - \tau')$. The new solution is given by the point D, where the optimal hours of work are h_1. To decompose the movement from h_0 to h_1 into a substitution effect and an income effect, suppose that following the policy change individuals were compensated with a lump-sum subsidy for the utility loss from increased marginal taxation. This would shift the new budget constraint ($E\text{-}E'$) outward to $E''\text{-}E''$, which is tangent to the old indifference curve at point F. The movement from A to D can now be decomposed into a substitution effect, $A\text{-}F$, and an income effect, $F\text{-}D$. The substitution effect of increased marginal taxation (a decrease in the marginal wage rate) is always nonpositive, which has to do with the fact that increased marginal taxation makes leisure cheaper relative to consumption goods. On the other hand, if leisure is a normal good (i.e., if leisure is positively related to real income), the income effect will increase the hours of work. Since most empirical studies of the labor supply have found that leisure is a normal good, the qualitative response in the hours of work from increased marginal taxation depends on whether the substitution effect dominates the income effect. The distinction between the substitution effect and the income effect is

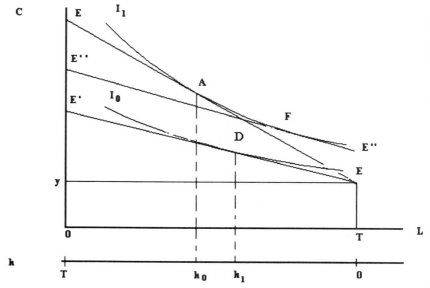

Fig. 5.2   **Proportional income tax**

important for two reasons. First, following an increase in the marginal wage, economic theory requires that the substitution effect (i.e., the compensated wage effect) be nonnegative. The latter is usually referred to as the Slutsky condition. Second, the social loss of taxation is related to the substitution effect (but not to the income effect). The latter implies, for example, that lump-sum taxes, which do not affect the slope of the budget constraint, cause no social loss because there is no substitution effect involved. We will return to this issue in the next subsection, where the welfare effects of taxes and transfer programs are discussed.

There is one special case where a change in the after-tax wage has an unambiguous effect on labor supply. For individuals not participating in the labor market (i.e., those consuming full leisure and consumption y of market goods), if it has any effect at all, an increase in the wage can only increase labor supply. An increase in the market wage will then induce some nonparticipants to enter the labor market since for nonparticipants an increase in the market wage has only a substitution effect.

Let us now complicate the analysis by assuming that taxes are progressive, but, for the time being, we will continue to assume that $B = 0$. In a progressive tax system, the marginal tax rate is positively related to income, although it is usually constant within given income intervals. To simplify the analysis, suppose that only labor income is taxed and that the marginal tax rate, $\tau(wh)$, is determined according to the tax schedule $\tau(wh) = 0$ if $wh < X_1$, $\tau(wh) = \tau_1$ if $X_1 \leq wh < X_2$, and $\tau(wh) = \tau_2$ if $wh \geq X_2$, where $\tau_2 > \tau_1$, while X_1 and X_2 are

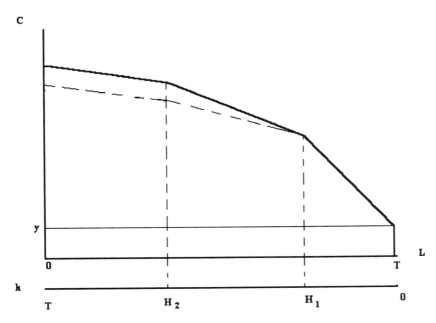

Fig. 5.3   Kinked and piecewise linear budget set

lower and upper limits of the second tax bracket measured in terms of income. This means that the budget constraint will contain three segments, as illustrated in figure 5.3.

In figure 5.3, H_1 and H_2 are the limits of the tax brackets expressed in terms of hours of work; that is, $H_1 = X_1/w$, and $H_2 = X_2/w$. The budget constraint is represented by the heavily drawn kinked line. By starting at the point on the budget constraint where $h = 0$ and then moving leftward along the budget constraint, we see that the marginal wage, $w[1 - \tau(wh)]$ is reduced each time the individual enters a new tax bracket. Since both substitution and income effects are involved, it is generally not possible to predict the influence of piecewise linear taxation on the labor supply. However, some predictions can be made, as illustrated by the following example (borrowed from Blomquist 1989). Suppose that the marginal tax rate on the second segment, that is, for $h \in (H_1, H_2)$, is increased while it remains constant at the other segments. This means that for $h > H_1$ the budget constraint is now replaced by the dotted line in figure 5.3. To be specific, we see that the first segment of the budget constraint is the same as prior to the change. The second segment has a smaller slope than previously because of the increase in the marginal tax rate τ_1. Finally, the third segment is subject only to a parallel shift inward because individuals on the third segment now pay more taxes on the part of their income that falls short of X_2SKr. What predictions are possible? If the initial hours of work are located on the first segment, the tax reform will have no effect on behavior since the first segment of the budget constraint is not affected by the reform. If the preform hours of work are located on the second segment, it is not possible to give a qualitative prediction because there is both a substitution effect and an income effect involved when the slope of the budget constraint is altered. Finally, if the preform hours of work are located on the third segment, there is only an income effect involved. The reason is that, although the consumption possibility is reduced when taxes are increased, the marginal tax rate remains constant. In this case, if leisure is a normal good, the hours of work will increase.

What are the conclusions from this example? If we decrease the marginal tax rates corresponding to low-income tax brackets, a low-income individual would increase his or her labor supply if the substitution effect dominates the income effect. However, given that the marginal tax rates corresponding to high levels of income remain unaltered, an individual with high income would be subject only to an income effect, meaning that he or she would decrease hours of work if leisure is a normal good. Similarly, if we decrease the marginal tax rates corresponding only to high levels of income, high-income individuals may either increase or decrease their labor supply, depending on whether the substitution effect dominates the income effect, while the behavior of individuals with low income would not be affected by the latter reform.

Income-dependent transfer programs introduce nonlinearities in the budget constraint in a way similar to progressive taxes. To see this, suppose that the transfer B in equation (1) decreases when income increases. This means that, if an individual has a sufficiently low level of income to qualify for the benefit, his or her effective marginal tax rate will be $\tau(wh) + B'$, where B' is the marginal reduction of benefits when income increases. As income continues to increase, the benefit will continue to decrease and will eventually be zero. When that happens, the effective marginal tax rate becomes equal to the marginal income tax rate, $\tau(wh)$. An important effect of income-dependent transfer programs is that they may introduce nonconvexities in the budget set in the sense that the effective marginal tax rate decreases when income increases. When this occurs, we can no longer rule out the existence of multiple solutions to the utility-maximization problem. As in the convex case, the concepts of substitution and income effects are still useful in analyzing labor market intervention. However, elasticities and other local measures of comparative statics are less meaningful here because a small change in the budget constraint may cause a large change in behavior.

5.2.2   Welfare

By introducing taxes and transfers, the government creates a wedge between the price a consumer pays and the price a producer receives. These wedges create distortions for the allocation of goods and services (see also Norrman

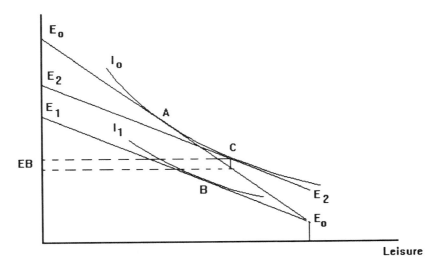

Fig. 5.4   Excess burden based on the compensated variation

and McLure, chap. 3 in this volume; and Rosen, chap. 2 in this volume). Distortions are commonly measured by the excess burden (or deadweight loss), which is the cost of a tax system beyond the revenue it collects. As explained by King (1987) and Auerbach (1985), measures of the excess burden suffer from an index number problem of whether post- or preform prices are used as a basis. Blomquist (1983) and Hausman (1981) advocate Diamond and McFadden's measure of the excess burden, which equals the compensating variation less the tax that would be collected at the compensated optimum. Blundell et al. (1988) and Aronsson (1993) define the excess burden as the equivalent variation less the tax collected at the individual's optimum position. The compensating variation uses the posttax prices as a reference case and measures the income compensation required by the individual to reach the same utility level as in the absence of the tax. The equivalent variation uses the (hypothetical) optimum in the absence of the tax as a reference case and measures the income reduction that is equivalent to the tax in terms of utility reduction.

These welfare measures are illustrated in figures 5.4 and 5.5. E_0-E_0 is the pretax budget constraint, and E_0-E_1 is the posttax budget constraint. Point A is the optimum in the absence of taxes, while point B is the optimum in the presence of the tax. In figure 5.4, the individual is compensated for the tax so as to restore the pretax utility level. The excess burden is then computed as the compensation required to achieve this (called the *compensating variation*) less the tax payment made at the compensated optimum (point C). In figure 5.5, we reduce the individual's income in the pretax state so that the income reduc-

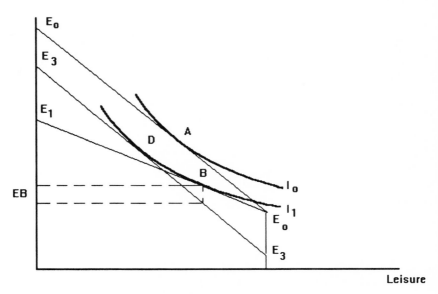

Fig. 5.5   Excess burden based on the equivalent variation

tion (called the *equivalent variation*) is equivalent to the tax payment in terms of the loss of utility. The excess burden is then computed as the equivalent variation less the actual tax payment, that is, the tax payment at point *B*.

The primary difficulty of using these welfare measures is moving from the individual to the society. If we admit differences in tastes or even in the distribution of income across individuals, any aggregate measure of the excess burden will depend on the distribution of income unless the utility function corresponds to the "Gorman polar form."[2] The problem is partly mitigated, although not eliminated, by looking at welfare changes within different interest (or target) groups of consumers. If individuals are identical within a group, then within-group comparisons across alternative reforms are well defined. Comparison of gains and losses across groups, however, requires some subjective notion of equity. Rather than pushing measures of the excess burden this far, it can serve a descriptive role as a scalar measure to summarize the gains and losses of tax reform. It places alternative reforms on a common footing and permits simple description of the distributional effects of a change in the tax or transfer system.[3]

The excess burden of a single tax increases with the curvature of the indifference curve (as measured by the substitution effect) and increases with the

---

2. The Gorman polar form requires that the expenditure function be written as $e(p, u) = a(p) + ub(p)$, for price vector p and utility u. The functions $a(p)$ and $b(p)$ must be linearly homogeneous and concave. (See Deaton and Muellbauer 1980, 144–45.)

3. For an insightful discussion, see King (1987).

square of the tax rate.[4] Even with a low compensated wage elasticity of labor supply, a high marginal tax rate can yield a large excess burden. Similarly, even at low marginal tax rates, a high compensated substitution effect may produce a large excess burden.

5.2.3   Restrictions and Extensions

The canonical model focuses on only two dimensions of labor supply, participation and hours of work, and even then it is highly stylized. Among the most restrictive assumptions are its static nature (individuals make one choice), its assumption of perfect certainty (workers have complete information on all jobs and on the economy), its simple characterization of jobs and particularly the absence of consideration for the demand side of the market (the wage is a sufficient statistic to describe a job, and workers have complete freedom to vary their hours of work), and its emphasis on atomistic behavior (workers make consumption and labor supply decisions in isolation from others, including family members). Tied to the static nature, with no opportunity to invest in skills (or education), the canonical model is silent on quality dimensions of labor supply. Each of these deficiencies have received attention in the literature, although not usually in connection with the tax and transfer system.[5]

Family Issues

The simplest extension of the canonical model to incorporate family decision making endows the household with preferences defined over the consumption and leisure of each member of the household, for example, $U(c_1, c_2, L_1, L_2)$. Each individual in the household has a time constraint and can work in the labor market at an exogenously determined wage (although, of course, not necessarily the same wage). The key insight is that, since family members jointly determine their labor supply, the labor supply function for an individual in the household depends on the wage rates of all people in the household.[6]

Dynamic Models

In order to construct a simple life-cycle model, suppose that individuals maximize an intertemporally separable utility function:

---

4. The effects of the tax are compared to the no-tax equilibrium because, by the theory of the second best, in the presence of an initial distortion introducing an additional distortion may or may not decrease welfare (it may attenuate or exacerbate the preexisting situation). Also, with more than one good, we have to consider compensated cross-price effects (the off-diagonal terms of the Slutsky matrix), which may be positive or negative. However, most applications are partial equilibrium in nature and do not model the other distortions or demand for other commodities. Thus, in most applications, the intuition presented in the text will hold.

5. Several surveys of labor supply cover these topics in detail and need not be repeated here (see Pencavel 1986; and Killingsworth and Heckman 1986).

6. Empirical models of household labor supply as well as results from the estimation of such models can be found in Ashenfelter and Heckman (1974), Hausman and Ruud (1984), Kapteyn, Kooreman, and van Soest (1990), and Aronsson (1993).

(2)
$$U_0 = \sum_{t=0}^{T} u(c_t,h_t)(1 + \rho)^{-t},$$

where c_t and h_t represent consumption and hours of work in period t, and ρ is the rate of time preference. The dynamic budget constraint may be written as

(3)
$$A_t = (1 + r)A_{t-1} + w_th_t - \Gamma(w_th_t + rA_{t-1}) - c_t,$$

where A_t is the asset at the end of period t, r is the interest rate, w_t is the hourly gross wage rate in period t, and $\Gamma(w_th_t + rA_{t-1})$ is the tax payment in period t. How can we make this model empirically manageable if we do not have information on the path of future wage rates? Following Blomquist (1985) and Blundell and Walker (1986), we note that together A_t and A_{t-1} form a set of sufficient statistics for information about future periods. This means that, if we condition on the asset positions at the beginning and end of period t, it is possible to rewrite the budget constraint in such a way that it becomes similar to that of the canonical model:

(4)
$$w_th_t + \mu_t - \Gamma(w_th_t + rA_{t-1}) = c_t,$$

where $\mu_t = rA_{t-1} - S_t$, and $S_t = A_t - A_{t-1}$. Hence, μ_t is a measure of nonlabor income that is consistent with intertemporal optimization since it includes not only capital income as in static models but also saving. If the form of the utility function does not change over time, we can derive a life-cycle-consistent within-period labor supply function by maximizing $u(c_t, h_t)$ subject to equation (4).[7]

Just as in the household model of labor supply, where the labor supply function of each individual in the household depends on the wage rates of all people in the household, in dynamic models of labor supply, labor force participation and hours of work depend on current and expected future wages and nonlabor income flows. The dependence on expected future wages and incomes implies that an anticipated future increase in a social insurance benefit or income tax rate may induce a labor supply response in the current period. Many of Sweden's social insurance benefits are work conditioned (i.e., benefits depend on past labor supply; the public pension system is a leading example) and may induce complicated, dynamic labor supply responses as individuals attempt to become entitled to a higher-benefit stream.

Human Capital Accumulation

Models of human capital accumulation incorporate the possibility of spending time in education as part of the utility-maximization problem (see, e.g.,

---

7. Instead of conditioning on asset positions, Heckman and MaCurdy (1980) and MaCurdy (1981) condition on the marginal utility of wealth and derive what are often referred to as λ-constant labor supply functions. However, the marginal utility of wealth will be a sufficient statistic for information about future periods only if the budget constraint is intertemporally separable, a condition that nonlinear taxation of capital income (which was the case in Sweden prior to the tax reform) violates.

Blinder and Weiss 1976; and Heckman 1976). An individual is assumed to allocate his or her time endowment between leisure, market work, and investments, where the latter is defined as time spent in education. Time spent in education accumulates human capital (knowledge or skill), which, in turn, tends to increase the market wage rate. Hence, the incentive to spend time in education has to do with the assumption that the market wage rate is positively related to the stock of human capital. In a similar way, the opportunity cost is the forgone earnings during periods of investment.

Taxes and transfer programs affect the incentives to spend time in education. This means that, in addition to distorting the life-cycle path of hours of work, taxes and transfer programs will also have an effect on the quality of the labor supply. In appendix A, we illustrate within a simple model of occupational choice how taxes and transfer programs affect the incentives to invest in human capital (see also Edin and Topel, chap. 4 in this volume).

Other Behavioral Effects

Another important insight is that, as marginal tax rates increase, workers have an incentive to seek nontaxable forms of compensation. If it is cost effective for firms to use nontaxed sources of compensation, they will do so. Among other mechanisms, workers may receive compensation in the form of improved fringe benefits or increased on-the-job consumption. The wage is only one form of compensation, and, as marginal tax rates increase, it becomes more costly. Some responses may occur in quantity dimensions; however, with a large number of dimensions to the employment relation, the necessary equilibrating adjustments in any one dimension may be small and empirically difficult to detect. This implies that the structure of compensation is not independent of the tax system.

Just as individuals have an incentive to minimize their tax liability by accepting nontaxed forms of compensation, they also have an incentive to lie to the tax authorities and underreport their taxable income. Tax evasion can be modeled as a form of occupational choice—in one job, within the covered sector, reporting rules imposed on the employer make it impossible for the employee to hide income from the tax authorities; in the other job, within the "uncovered" sector (or, more colorfully, the "underground" sector), it is possible to hide (or shelter) income.[8] Modern tax collection systems make nearly all employee jobs within the covered sector subject to withholding or other collection mechanisms. Self-employment is the prototypical example of a job in the "uncovered" sector. With a change in terminology, the analytic framework of the occupational choice model can be used to investigate this issue (see Cowell 1990).

Given Sweden's overall high level of taxation and benefits, the theory we

---

8. It is interesting to note that many European countries adopted value added taxes (VAT) because taxpayers did not voluntarily comply with income taxes.

have reviewed suggests possibly large behavioral responses that affect the quantity and quality of the labor supplied to the market. The theory makes it clear that the responses depend on the details of how programs affect budget sets. We turn next to the detailed transfer and tax system.

5.3   Sweden's Transfer Programs

Historians of Sweden's welfare state recognize three epochs in its development. Phase 1 (1890–1930) established national social assistance and social insurance programs. Programs in this phase are comprehensive in coverage but offer meager benefits. Phase 2 (1930–60) established the basic safety net of welfare programs to guarantee an adequate standard of living for all—the aged, the sick, the disabled, the unemployed, low-income families with children—without the stigma of the old poor law. Phase 3 (1960–90) raised the income-replacement ratios to 80–90 percent of market income for those temporarily forced out of gainful employment, led the state to assume large-scale obligations for the care of the elderly and children that previously had been provided within the family, and generalized social services previously available only in large urban areas to small towns and rural areas through massive municipal consolidation (Einhorn and Logue 1989). Hence, most programs date from the turn of the century, and, while their structure has remained unchanged since the first half of the century, the rapid expansion of costly entitlement programs is a relatively new phenomenon. Reforms since 1990 suggest that Sweden has entered a new epoch, phase 4 (1990–), an attempt to scale back the expansive entitlement programs.

Next, we review the major entitlement programs expected to affect labor supply decisions. Table 5.1 summarizes the structure, expenditure, and recent changes in the largest programs.

5.3.1   Pensions

There are two national pension systems developed in Sweden to provide old-age, disability, and survivorship benefits. The basic pension began in 1948 and provides flat-rate payments to all pensioners.[9] The unusual feature of the basic pension is its universality—it is a right of citizenship—no work or contribution requirements exist. The second pension, called the National Supplementary Pension or ATP, was introduced in 1960, began full payouts in 1969, and provides earnings-related payments.

Benefits from the two public pension systems are related by a measure called *the basic amount*. Introduced in 1957, and indexed against inflation, the basic amount is thought to correspond to a yearly income for which a basic pension should be sufficient (Agell 1979). It has also become an index basis for other social benefits.

---

9. Its predecessor began in 1913, was means tested, and guaranteed a minimum standard for everyone (Hansson-Brusewitz 1992, app. C).

Table 5.1   **Primary Social Insurance Programs**

Program	Main Form of Benefit in 1989	Expenditure in 1989 (SKr million)	Changes during the 1990s
Pension system:			
Old age (basic and ATP)	Flat rate payments to all pensioners. Benefits are indexed for inflation and payable at age 65.		
	Earnings related (ATP) replace 65% of pensionable income during the best 15 years of employment.	97,346[a]	
Partial	Available to individuals aged 60–65 with 10 or more years of employment after age 45. Workers replace 65% of forgone earnings from reduced hours of work. Workers retain right to draw a full pension at official retirement age.	1,523	In July 1994, minimum eligibility age increased to 61, and replacement rate reduced to 55% of forgone earnings. Workers may reduce hours of work by at most 10 hours per week.
Disability	Covers individuals aged 16–65 with reduced capacity to work. Has same structure of basic and supplementary pensions as old-age system. Supplementary benefits based on potential earnings (if not disabled).	22,060	
Health insurance	Public health and hospitals. Sickness cash benefits replace 90% of earnings. Benefits start on the first day of illness.	84,143	Several reforms during the 1990s reduced the replacement rate and increased the waiting period for coverage. By 1993, no benefits paid for the first day of illness; for the second and third days, 65% of normal earnings replaced. Maximum replacement rate is 80% on fourth day of illness. In 1996, the replacement rate was set to 75% from the second day.
		55,611	Instituted "sickness wage" paid directly by the employer. Replaces public sickness benefits for first two weeks of illness.

(*continued*)

Table 5.1   (continued)

Program	Main Form of Benefit in 1989	Expenditure in 1989 (SKr million)	Changes during the 1990s
Unemployment insurance	Replaces 90% of earnings.	6,225	July 1993 replacement rates decreased to 80%, and benefit period begins on the sixth day of unemployment. New (more stringent) eligibility rules in July 1994.
Family and children:			
Child allowances	Paid monthly to child's guardian until child becomes age 16. Annual base allowance equaled SKr 9,000. Supplementary allowance for third and higher-order births.	10,494	Supplementary allowances for higher-order births reduced by approximately half and were finally abolished in the mid-1990s. Basic allowance reduced.
Parental benefits	At childbirth, parents share 450 days of benefits, 360 of which replace 90% of the earnings, and earnings for the remaining 90 days replaced at the guaranteed rate of SKr 60.00 per day.	12,145	In July 1994, eliminated the 90 days paid at the guaranteed rate. Reinstated in January 1995. The replacement rate was reduced to 75% in 1996.
Child care	Parents pay approximately 10% of publicly provided child-center care.	22,313	

Source: Expenditure estimates from *Statistisk Årsbok 1992* (Stockholm: Statistics Sweden), table 365.
[a]Includes SKr 4,356 million as special housing allowance for the aged. Pension expenditures equal December expenditures multiplied by twelve; all other expenditures are annual values.

The basic pension benefit is a fixed multiple of the basic amount. Since 1968, single individuals receive 95 percent of the basic amount, and married couples, both of retirement age, receive 155 percent of the basic amount. Prior to 1968, these payout proportions were 5.5 percentage points lower for singles and 10.2 percentage points lower for married couples.

The earnings-related ATP covers all individuals over age sixteen with earnings above the basic amount for at least three years since 1960. ATP benefits accrue on pensionable income, defined as all employment-related income (e.g., wages, salary, sickness benefits, parental benefits) between 1 and 7.5 times the basic amount. Entitlement to a full supplementary pension requires thirty years of work. Full supplementary pension benefits are reduced by one-thirtieth for each year of pensionable income less than thirty. A full ATP pension replaces 60 percent of the pensionable income earned during the worker's best fifteen years (since 1960).[10]

In addition to the public old-age pension, there are also certain contractual pensions. These contractual pensions are not part of the legislation; rather, they are determined by agreement between the parties in the labor market. The benefits are paid out according to centralized negotiated agreements. There are in principle four such contractual pension systems: (1) pensions to national government employees; (2) pensions to local government employees; (3) pensions to white-collar workers in private employment; and (4) pensions to blue-collar workers in private employment. The contractual pensions are not coordinated with the public old-age pensions but supplement the public pensions.

Since 1963, Swedish workers have had the right to draw basic pension benefits starting at age sixty-three or wait until age seventy. Until July 1976, the official retirement age to receive full benefits was age sixty-seven. Workers retiring before the official age receive benefits for the entire retirement period reduced by 0.6 percent per month for each month of early retirement. Workers postponing benefits also receive benefits for the retirement period higher by 0.6 percent per month. A major reform in 1976 gave workers additional flexibility. The pension reform in 1976 reduced the official age of retirement for full benefits to age sixty-five. The penalty for early retirement was reduced to 0.5 percent per month. (The reward for postponing retirement was unaffected.) Most important, the 1976 reform introduced the partial pension system. Individuals age sixty to sixty-five with earnings of at least one basic amount for ten or more years after age forty-five are eligible to receive a partial pension. Workers accepting a partial pension retain eligibility for full pension benefits at the official retirement age. To receive a partial pension, the individual must reduce hours of work by at least five hours per week and must work between seventeen and thirty-four hours following the reduction. The partial pension replaces a fraction of the earnings lost by the work reduction. From July 1976 until January 1981, 65 percent of the forgone earnings were replaced. From January 1981 until June 1987, the replacement rate was reduced to 50 percent. In July 1987, the replacement rate was returned to 65 percent. Recent legislation tightened the requirements and reduced the benefits of the partial pension. As of 1 July 1994, the minimum entitlement age increased from sixty to sixty-one, and workers are allowed to reduce their hours of work by no more than

10. In 1969, a general supplement to the basic pension was implemented for low earners, essentially the recently retired who were not fully vested in the earnings-related ATP pension. The basic pension supplement was tied to the basic amount at 3 percent with a graduated rate of increase of 3 percentage points for every year of work after 1969 until 1976, when the graduated rate increases to 4 percentage points per year of work until 1981, when the maximum supplement of 45 percent is reached. The basic pension supplement is reduced krona for krona by the amount of ATP benefits received.

ten hours per week. Importantly, the replacement rate of forgone earnings was reduced to 55 percent.

Since its inception, the public pension system has included a disability pension for individuals with reduced work capacity due to illness or injury. Individuals aged sixteen to sixty-five are eligible to receive a disability pension if their work capacity has been reduced by at least 50 percent.[11] (Individuals with partial disabilities may receive partial disability pensions of either half or three-quarters of the full pension.) The disability pension is structured in the same way as the public old-age pension and contains a basic and supplementary pension. To calculate the supplementary part of the disability pension, pension points are assigned on the earnings assumed had the individual been able to work (e.g., "assumed pension points"). The assumed pensions points are constant over time and are calculated either as (1) the average pension points obtained in the best two of four previous years of pensionable income or (2) the average of the pension points obtained during the better half of the earnings history.

Since 1960, regulations governing eligibility for disability pensions have changed several times. In June 1970, in addition to medical conditions, special consideration was to be given to labor market conditions of the older (age sixty-three and above) insured individuals. The premise is that "older workers are not to be forced to change location or occupation" (Wadensjö 1985, 5). By July 1972, it became possible to grant a disability pension to an individual age sixty-three or older solely for labor market conditions. Since July 1976, the age limit for both medical and labor market reasons was lowered to sixty. Also, since July 1977, consideration of disability should be independent of the causes of reduced working capacity. The "no-fault" disability pensions gave wider latitude to alcoholism, drug addition, and "sociopathy" as approved diagnoses (Wadensjö 1985, 7).

The pension funds have never been actuarial programs. Prior to 1975, employee contributions and central and local government contributions from general revenue financed the national basic pension scheme. Employee contributions for the basic pensions were levied at a flat rate of 5 percent on their taxable income (maximum contribution SKr 1,500). The supplementary pension plan (ATP) never required direct employee contributions; instead, contributions were paid through a payroll tax on the employer's tax bill. In 1975, employee contributions for the basic pension were abolished and their share offset by an increase in the payroll tax levied on employers.

5.3.2   Health Insurance and Health Services

In the mid-nineteenth century, voluntary sickness benefit societies arose to provide their members health care and income loss protection during a time of

---

11. Individuals with long-term illnesses of one to two years usually receive disability pensions automatically.

illness. The extent of program coverage as well as cash benefits provided by the voluntary societies were idiosyncratic. Labor unions began lobbying for national health insurance in the early 1920s. Overcoming strong resistance by the medical profession, national health insurance was enacted in 1955. In 1963, the system was integrated into the national insurance system that includes pensions and work injury insurance.

Although many changes have been made to the generosity of benefits, the basic structure of the program remains unchanged since its inception in 1955. The program has two components. First, like most other social insurance programs in Sweden, there is a universal component, and all individuals are eligible to receive the guaranteed benefit. Second, there is a supplemental benefit tied to the individual's employment history to protect earnings against loss during illness. Major increases in benefit levels occurred in 1963, 1967, and 1974. Benefits were not indexed for inflation at this time, and the increases in 1963 and 1967 increased the guaranteed benefit in real terms and maintained the after-tax replacement rate of the supplemental benefits at approximately 80 percent. From their introduction until the 1967 reform, benefits started on the fourth day (three days of coinsurance) of the illness and were, in principle, of unlimited duration. A physician's certificate was needed after the eighth day. In 1967, the waiting period decreased to one day.

The 1974 reform of the health system integrated all health services and made all cash benefits taxable and pensionable income. The minimum replacement ratio was 64 percent from the second day and rose to replace 90 percent of earnings.[12] A 1987 reform eliminated the one-day waiting period, as sickness insurance cash benefits replaced 90 percent of earnings from the first day of illness and no "free days" were deducted. Benefits were reduced in March 1991 and replaced 65 percent of normal income for the first three days of illness, 80 percent from the fourth to the ninetieth day of illness, and 90 percent thereafter. A reform in April 1993 made an additional reduction of benefits. There was no benefit for the first day of sickness. For the second and third days, the replacement ratio was 65 percent of gross earnings. For the fourth day of sickness, the replacement ratio was 80 percent. Since 1996, the replacement rate is 75 percent from the second day of illness. Individuals who have been on sick leave for more than one year receive 70 percent of their income. Since 1992, employed individuals are entitled to a sickness wage paid directly by the employer. The sickness wage replaces health insurance benefits in the first fourteen days of illness.

---

12. The statutory replacement rate was 90 percent of earnings. The daily replacement rate equals 90 percent of normal twelve-month earnings divided by 365. For the first week of sickness, only normal working days are covered, and benefits are not paid for normal days off (known as the "free-day" rule). No more than two free days can be deducted. If the sickness period lasts more than a week, no days off will be deducted either during the first week or during subsequent weeks of illness.

5.3.3   Child-Rearing Benefits

Sweden has an extensive system of family benefits that may affect time allocation within the household and to the marketplace. We briefly describe the programs below.

Child Allowances

Each child in Sweden receives a general allowance until the age of sixteen. This allowance is tax free and is paid monthly to the child's guardian. These child allowances are in lieu of income tax deductions as in the United States.[13] From August 1948 until July 1983, allowances were roughly indexed to inflation and were the same for each birth. In 1993, the annual basic child allowance was SKr 9,000. In January 1983, a supplement to the basic child allowance was introduced for third and higher-order births. By 1989, the supplemental allowance was 50 percent for the third child, 190 percent for the fourth, 240 percent for the fifth, and 160 percent for the sixth and subsequent children. In 1991, and again in 1994, the supplemental allowances have been reduced for birth orders 4 and above. After the reform in 1994, the supplemental allowance was 100 percent for the fourth and subsequent children. The supplemental allowance was abolished and the basic allowance reduced in 1996.

Maternity and Parental Benefits

Sweden has been at the forefront in legislating child-related benefits. In 1955, maternity benefits were made universal as part of the coverage provided by national health insurance. Prior to this time, childbirth benefits were provided by membership in voluntary recognized insurance societies. Means-tested benefits were available since 1938 to women who were not members of the insurance societies. The passage of national health insurance abolished the maternity benefits provided by the insurance societies. The maternity benefit system followed the usual program structure with a universal minimum benefit guarantee and an earnings-related supplemental component to replace earnings in the event of childbirth. The maximum duration of the benefits was 180 days. The compulsory maternity benefit was repealed in 1974 and replaced by the parental benefit program. In 1974, either parent (but not both simultaneously) could receive benefits in connection with childbirth. Several program revisions increased the generosity of childbirth benefits. In 1993, the couple shared 360 days with the replacement rate of 90 percent of gross earnings up to seven and a half times the basic amount and another 90 days at the guaranteed rate of

---

13. There are some differences between European countries regarding how support to families with dependent children is organized. These differences are primarily (*a*) whether child allowances are income dependent and (*b*) whether tax deductions are related to family composition. For example, in the German system, child allowances are income dependent, and there is also a special deduction called *the child tax allowance,* which depends on the number of children (see Zimmermann 1993).

SKr 60.00 per day.[14] The replacement rate was reduced to 80 percent in 1994 and to 75 percent in 1996. The benefits can be used anytime until the child's eighth birthday.

Expansion of child-care facilities was regarded in Sweden as the most important family policy issue of the 1970s. Even after substantial expenditures, by the early 1980s sizable "excess demand" for child day-care services remained. Continued expansion of the public child-care sector during the 1980s eliminated most of the excess demand, especially in large urban regions such as Stockholm, Gothenburg, and Malmö. Child-care programs are a municipal responsibility. These programs are financed primarily through local tax revenues and parental fees. Most communities have fees that vary according to the income of the parents. Until recently, parental fees typically covered a small fraction (about 10 percent) of the operating costs (Gustafsson and Stafford 1992). Parental fees have increased lately.

5.3.4   Housing Policy

Sweden formulated a national housing policy in 1948 when it established the National Swedish Housing Board as the central housing authority. An underlying principle of the housing policy was to provide the entire population with healthy, spacious, and functionally equipped housing of good quality at reasonable prices.

A major government policy instrument for one-family owner-occupied dwellings has been interest deductibility of mortgage interest payments. Another major government instrument in housing policy has been in home financing. The central government has provided low-interest and subsidized long-term loans for housing construction.

A third policy instrument is housing allowances available to the elderly and to families, especially low-income families with children. Both types of housing allowances are administered by the communities within rules prescribed by the central government. The legislation on housing allowances for families with children is complicated by frequent changes in benefit levels and income restrictions. However, with one exception, the structure of the program has remained constant. Prior to 1958, housing allowances were restricted to families with two or more children under the age of sixteen. In 1958, housing allowances were extended to families with only one child (under age sixteen). The age limit on children was increased to seventeen in 1972. Housing allowances were extended to childless families and individuals in 1974.

During the period 1948–68, the central government administered housing allowances, although payments varied slightly within region.[15] The number of

---

14. In July 1994, the ninety days at the (low) guaranteed rate were abolished. From 1995, one month of the parental leave is reserved for the father (and cannot be transferred to the mother).

15. Housing allowances increased with the number of children up to and including the sixth child. The additional benefits per child are equal to the difference in benefits for families with two vs. three children.

families receiving housing allowances peaked in the late 1970s. During the 1980s, income ceilings were not increased for inflation, and the number of families eligible to receive benefits declined. Benefit levels were improved in the late 1980s and restored some of the loss suffered in the 1980s.

A major transformation of housing allowances occurred in 1969. In addition to state (central) government allowances, a state-community housing allowance system began in 1969. The state-subsidized municipal housing allowance covers 80 percent of the monthly housing (rental) cost within prescribed limits. A second change in 1969 revised the application of the income restrictions. From 1969, housing benefits were reduced by a fraction of income in excess of the income limit qualifying for a standard allowance. The percentage applied to reduce benefits increased with income. These limits have also changed several times. The implicit marginal tax rates vary by the number of children in the household and whether it is a single-parent household.

Housing allowances are paid from local income tax revenue. The central government also provides financing for the housing allowances and supplies the state loans and interest subsidies out of general tax revenues.

5.3.5 Unemployment Insurance

Unemployment insurance is administered by recognized unemployment insurance societies, which historically have been operated by trade unions. Society membership was voluntary until 1974, when membership by trade union members became compulsory. Unions continued their responsibility with little change after 1974 when payroll taxes on employers were introduced to help fund unemployment benefits.

To be eligible for unemployment insurance, a society member must register with the local employment office and be fit, able, and willing to work. The individual must also have been a member of the society (and making contributions) for the previous twelve months and during this period have been employed seventy-five or more hours per month for at least five months or sixty-five hours per month for ten months. Benefits are taxable and, prior to 1 July 1993, replaced 90 percent of gross earnings up to a maximum SKr of 598 per day. From 1 July 1993, the replacement rate declined to 80 percent of gross earnings, and, since 1 September 1993, the benefit period begins as of the sixth day of unemployment. The replacement rate was reduced to 75 percent in 1996. Prime-age workers may receive uninterrupted cash payments for a maximum of 300 days (five days per week). Members fifty-five to sixty-four years old are entitled to receive benefits for up to 450 days.[16]

---

16. It is interesting to make comparisons with other European countries regarding the generosity of the unemployment insurance benefit. In Denmark, the official replacement rate is 90 percent, but this rate is supplemented with a rather low benefit maximum (which gives an average degree of compensation of about 65 percent). The Danish system has no waiting period for unemployment insurance benefits, and the duration of the benefit period is 2.5 years (Pedersen 1993). In Germany,

Individuals who are not members of a recognized unemployment society are also eligible for unemployment cash benefits, although under less-favorable conditions than those of the societies. These benefits fall within the "labor market cash assistance" program. The program is administered by the National Insurance Board, and one-third is financed out of general tax revenues and two-thirds from employers' fees. The state eligibility requirements for public unemployment benefits are the same as those of the societies. However, *employment* is defined liberally, and claimants therefore need have no work record to receive benefits (Wilson 1979, 82). The cash assistance program is extended to new labor market entrants and other nonmembers of the recognized unemployment insurance societies.

5.3.6   Educational System and Policy

The Swedish educational system has undergone a continuing series of reforms since the 1950s. Since the early 1960s, the system has had four major components, compulsory primary school, voluntary secondary school, university and other forms of higher education (*högskola*), and an extensive adult education system. All individuals receive nine years of primary education (ages seven to sixteen). Also, children are entitled to at least one year of preschool before starting (the preschools are part of the public child-care programs and do not belong to the regular school system). Secondary school offers schooling tracks of two, three, or four years' duration and also a large number of specialized courses of varying length. The latter may follow compulsory school or a previously completed line of secondary school. Secondary schools offer both academic programs of study in preparation for university entrance and vocational studies for a broad range of technical fields. A major reform of the vocational education system is currently under way. The reform will standardize vocational education in Sweden. Vocational lines of study will be made more uniform, and the reforms are designed to confer wider and deeper knowledge compared with the previous system of vocational education.

The higher education system was unified through a major reform in 1977. The reform created a single, coherent system for all types of postsecondary education, decentralized decision making, and broadened admissions policies. There are thirty-five higher education institutions (mostly colleges) in Sweden, all (save one) central government agencies. Their employees are national civil servants, and their students pay no tuition. A fundamental principle of Swedish higher education is that all students who need help to finance their studies should receive assistance from the central government for this purpose. The aid takes the form of student grants and loans, generally called *study assistance*. The grants are means-tested but consider only the candidate's income

---

unemployed persons receive unemployment insurance benefits equal to 68 percent of their previous earnings. After one year, this system is replaced with what is called *unemployment assistance,* with (in principle) unlimited duration, where the replacement rate is 58 percent (Zimmermann 1993).

and resources and disregard the financial resources of the student's partner and/ or parents. Study assistance is roughly indexed for inflation and consists of a taxable nonrepayable grant (usually 30 percent) plus a larger repayable loan. The interest rate on the repayable loan portion is quite low, half the state deposit rate. Repayment schedules for the loan are income related, with a general rule of 4 percent of annual income. The rate of interest is fixed annually by the government, and the interest payments are not tax deductible.

5.4   The Tax System

To pay for this extensive system of benefits, by the late 1980s Sweden had the highest tax burden among OECD countries. The most important direct taxes are the national and local income taxes. The most important indirect taxes are the value added tax and the social security payroll tax on employers. In this section, we describe the development and the administration of these various tax schemes.[17]

5.4.1   Indirect Taxes

A sales tax of 4.17 percent was reintroduced in Sweden in 1960 (it had been abolished in 1948). The base of the sales tax included most consumption items, even basic items such as food. The sales tax was increased several times during the 1960s and by the end of the decade equaled 11.1 percent. In 1969, the sales tax was superseded by an 11.1 percent value added tax. Sweden's general policy has been to increase the value added tax to offset revenue losses from reductions in the national income tax rates (1971 and 1991). Consequently, as is evident from figure 5.6, except for a few temporary reductions, the value added tax increased steadily. Since the fall of 1992, the value added tax is 25 percent, with a few exceptions. The value added tax on food was reduced to 12 percent in 1996.

As a general rule, social security contributions have been formally levied on the employer in the form of payroll taxes. Prior to 1975, employees paid 5 percent of their taxable income for the basic pension and a compulsory health insurance fee that depended on income and region. However, in 1993, a minor employee contribution was reintroduced in the form of a health insurance fee. As of 1 January 1994, employees are also required to pay an unemployment insurance fee. Social security contributions by employers cover approximately 40 percent of the cost of social insurance programs (pensions and health insurance programs). The remaining 60 percent is paid from general revenues of the national and local governments. With the exception of the National Supplementary Pension charge that is levied only on incomes within 7.5 times the basic amount, and unlike social security taxes in the United States, social security contributions are levied without an earnings limit.

---

17. For more information, see Norrman and McLure (chap. 3 in this volume).

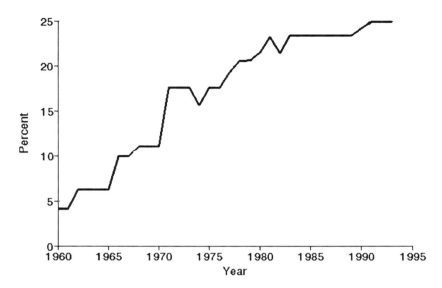

Fig. 5.6   The value added tax

Figure 5.7 shows the pattern of Swedish payroll tax rates over time as a percentage of gross wage rates. The remarkable increase in tax rates reflects the increasing generosity of Sweden's social insurance programs. Only the economic slowdown of the late 1970s broke the sequence of steady rate increases. Subsequently, rate increases were confined to three years, 1983, 1987, and 1991. Concerned about its competitive position in international markets, Sweden made substantial reductions in the payroll tax in 1992 and 1993 and returned rates to their late 1970s level.

5.4.2   Income Tax

Sweden has an integrated and complex income tax system. Individuals pay both a local and a national income tax. Each resident with income above a minimum level must file an income tax return.[18] The national government determines the tax base for both national and local income taxes, but each locality (communities and counties) has the authority to set its own rate. Generally, the same rules governing exemptions and deductions apply, and individuals file only one return for both local and national taxes. Local income taxes are proportional, while the national income tax is progressive. Tax schedules change nearly every year, and, since 1960, two major tax reforms have occurred. The first, in 1971, defined the individual as the unit of taxation and established one national tax schedule independent of marital status and household composi-

18. In addition to individuals actually living in Sweden, residents include any Swede with strong links to Sweden. A Swedish citizen can be taxed in Sweden for five years after departure unless he or she can show that a strong link to Sweden does not exist (Andersson 1986, 3).

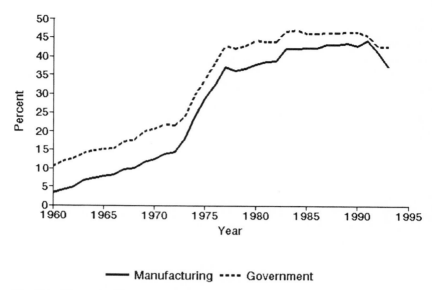

Fig. 5.7   **The payroll tax**

tion. The second reform, in 1991, simplified the national tax schedule and established more uniform taxation for different sources of income. To appreciate the radical nature of the 1991 reform, and because most empirical studies of taxes and labor supply analyze data from the old regime, we discuss the rules of the pre-1991 tax system.

Swedish tax law recognized six sources of income: agriculture, business, employment, housing, capital, and casual economic activities (capital gains). All receipts were classified into one of these six classes. Each class had its own set of deductions that could be applied only against income within the class. However, a loss in one class could be deducted from income in other classes to reduce the total taxable income. Only a few sources of income were tax exempt—housing allowances, child allowances, and maintenance allowances from a former partner are the primary examples. Since 1974, pension benefits, sickness insurance payments, and unemployment cash benefits are taxable. All labor income is taxable, including an imputed value of nonmonetary benefits (e.g., a company automobile). What made the Swedish tax system so complex is that each person's income was divided between two income categories: A (earned) and B (capital). The 1971 tax reform required that individuals be taxed separately on their A incomes. Couples living together were taxed jointly on their pooled capital income.

Until the 1991 reform, the imputed income from owner-occupied housing was taxable. The tax on owner-occupied housing was progressive, ranging from 2 to 6 percent of the assessed value. However, rules governing the deductibility of mortgage interest were generous and frequently produced a loss from housing income.

Even before the restrictions on deductions in the 1991 tax reform, the availability of deductions and tax credits in Sweden was much more limited than in the United States. As a rule, deductions are allowed only for expenses necessary for obtaining the income. Various tax credits gave some tax relief to target populations (e.g., the poor, the elderly, and single-headed households with dependent children); however, as a general rule, since 1971 Sweden has had no special tax rules or deductions based on household composition.

Sweden enacted a radical change in the tax system to take effect as of 1 January 1991. With the goal of making the system more neutral, and to treat different kinds of income more equally, the reform broadened the tax base and sharply reduced tax rates. Now, every attempt is made to tax *all* types of compensation (monetary and nonmonetary) for labor and capital on an equal basis and at market value. Some previously exempted fringe benefits are now taxed, and fringe benefits that were previously taxed (e.g., the use of a company automobile) are now taxed at a higher rate. The 1991 tax reform implies that individuals with income under SKr 170,000 pay only the local tax (which remains proportional at around 30 percent), while individuals with higher incomes also pay a 20 percent national income tax. The distinction between A and B income and the joint household taxation of B income had been gradually eliminated during the 1980s. The reform eliminated the income tax on the flow of housing services and instituted a separate proportional tax of 30 percent on capital income (including capital gains). The 1991 tax reform also severely restricted deductions to offset income.

Income tax rates in Sweden are high. Figure 5.8 presents the time-series profile of average local tax rates. The decentralization and expansion of local government services are evident from the rapidly rising local tax rates during the 1960s and 1970s. Figure 5.9 represents the relation between posttax and pretax income for calendar years 1980, 1989, and 1991. The steep progressivity of the Swedish national tax system before the 1991 reform is evident from figure 5.9. In 1980, the marginal tax rates of the national income tax schedule ranged from 0 to 58 percent. Average tax rates of 50 percent were not unusual; local and national tax schedules combined to produce marginal tax rates of over 70 percent. Indeed, tax limitation rules were enacted in 1980 to limit the maximum marginal tax rate at 85 percent. During the 1980s, a series of reforms reduced the number of income brackets and national tax rates. For example, whereas the 1980 national tax schedule had eighteen income brackets, the 1991 tax schedule has only two.

5.5   Effects of Taxes and Transfers on Swedish Work Effort

We review the budget set in 1981 and 1991 for three representative types of individuals to gain an appreciation of the effect of Sweden's changing tax and

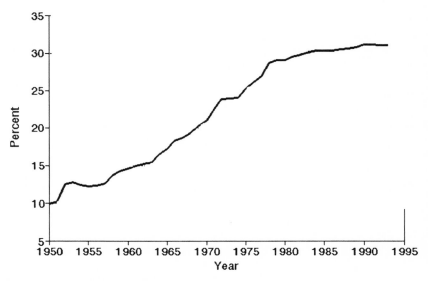

Fig. 5.8   The local tax, 1950–93

social policies on individual work incentives. We then combine knowledge from formal econometric analyses of taxes and labor supply with recent descriptive evidence on time-series trends and cross-sectional patterns to complete our evaluation of taxes and labor supply incentives.

5.5.1   Budget Sets

As Becker (1962) forcefully argued, most of our predictions on individual behavior come from changes in the budget set. It is, therefore, the natural device to summarize the structure of programs and taxes facing Swedish households. To focus our discussion, we compare budget sets from 1981 and 1991 for three types of individuals. We chose 1981 to represent the pre-1991 tax system characterized by its complicated mix of income-dependent programs and fine-grained national tax schedule. The last year is the important "low-marginal" tax system reflecting the 1991 reform. While many of the budget sets and implicit marginal tax rates exhibit stark changes from 1981 to 1991, it is important to recall that a decade of piecewise reforms separate these systems; comparisons between these systems overstate the short-run change faced by any household.

For each of the representative individual types, we present two sets of figures: (1) after-tax household income as a function of annual hours of work and (2) the implicit marginal tax rate (the sum of the value added tax, the marginal income tax from the national and local tax schedules, and the reduction of income-dependent benefits, e.g., housing benefits), also as a function of annual hours of work. Using the estimates reported in Andersson (1989) and Anders-

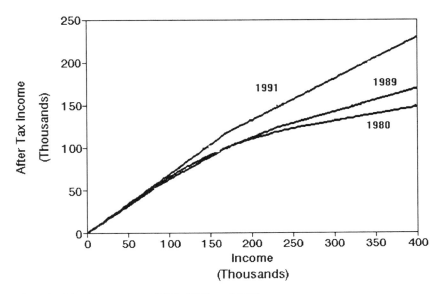

Fig. 5.9   **Total income tax, 1980, 1989, and 1991**

son and Gustafsson (1992), we incorporate deductions for work-related expenses and union dues. The schedules include standard deductions and, in 1981, the rules for tax reductions and tax limitation.[19] We include the VAT under the assumption that consumer prices increase by the full amount of an increase in the VAT.[20] Because of Sweden's penchant for substituting consumption taxes for income taxes, it is necessary to include the VAT in order accurately to measure the marginal tax rate facing consumers. There are other social programs and fees that will affect the budget set and implicit marginal tax rates for (small) subsets of the population.[21] One important simplification is that households are assumed to have no capital income. Implicit marginal tax rates calculated under this assumption are a lower bound (at given hours of work and earned income) for individuals with a large positive capital income.

19. For other representations of the budget set, see Andersson (1989), Andersson and Gustafsson (1992), and Andersson and Klevmarken (1993).

20. The VAT changed by only 1.5 percentage points between 1981 and 1991, and our estimates of implicit marginal tax rates are not sensitive to the assumed incidence of the VAT. Results in Ballard, Scholz, and Shoven (1987) suggest that a more important issue is the number and type of exemptions to VAT.

21. For example, households with children in public day-care centers pay fees according to their household income. How these situations affect the budget set and implicit marginal tax rate can be found in Gustafsson and Klevmarken (1993). Gustafsson and Klevmarken exclude the VAT and report the implicit marginal tax rate by household income. We include the VAT and report the budget sets and the implicit marginal tax rates by hours of work for a given household member to isolate the incentive effects on labor supply.

Because of the joint taxation of capital income in 1981, capital income affects the 1981 more than the 1991 calculations. Another simplification is the neglect of the incentive effects created by the social insurance system (e.g., sickness benefits, pension benefits)—a consequence of the atemporal nature of these budget sets. However, even in a dynamic framework, these incentive effects would be difficult to measure.[22]

To eliminate the effects of the wage growth between 1981 and 1991 (real female wages grew at an annual growth of 1.5 percent, while real male wages grew 1.3 percent annually between 1981 and 1991), real wages are fixed at their 1991 value. That is, wages in 1991 equal the gender-specific manufacturing wage, while wages in 1981 equal the appropriate 1991 value deflated by the consumer price index. (Because of the wage growth between 1981 and 1991, these wages are higher than the actual 1981 manufacturing wages.) The manufacturing wage is slightly higher than the median wage in the population, but, given the tight distribution of Swedish wages, it is nevertheless representative of the average wage.

Single Male

The three panels of figure 5.10 report the budget set for a single male with no children for a low-wage worker (half the manufacturing wage), an average wage worker (wage equal to the manufacturing wage), and a high-wage worker (twice the manufacturing wage). The panels of figure 5.11 report the corresponding implicit marginal tax rate. Half to twice the manufacturing wage covers all but the highest-wage workers in Sweden. Female wages are 90 percent of male wages, so comparable figures for single women will therefore be quite similar to those presented in figures 5.10 and 5.11.

Several general patterns appear in figures 5.10 and 5.11 that hold for the other representative households. The greatest gains from the 1991 tax reform accrue to high-wage individuals as they benefit from the substantial reduction in marginal tax rates. Low-wage individuals with low labor market attachment (below 750 hours) experience little change in opportunity (fig. 5.10a). The many tax brackets are clearly evident by the large number of jumps of the marginal implicit tax function. Jumps in the marginal implicit tax function at low hours of work are the result of the tax bracket and reductions of the income-dependent housing allowances. These generate a nonconvex budget set for some hours of work, as does the increased general deduction on mid-level incomes in 1991. (A nonconvex budget set appears for hours between fifteen and seventeen hundred for low-wage workers in 1981.) The shape of the implicit marginal tax level is similar across wage levels. The basic difference is that it is compressed over fewer hours of work at higher wage levels as the

22. If the social insurance programs were actuarially fair and the present value of taxes paid over the life cycle equaled the present value of benefits received, then the social insurance system would be neutral.

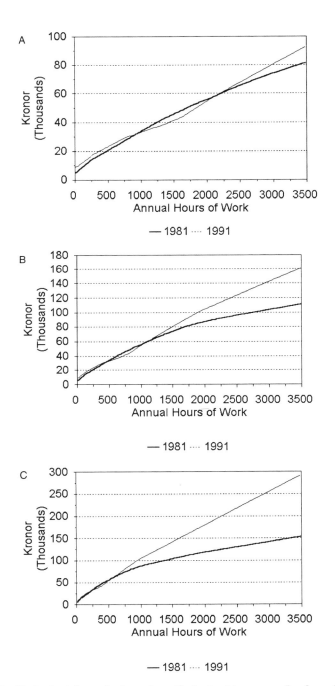

Fig. 5.10   Budget set for a single male. *a*, Budget set low wage (bs_2.wpg). *b*, Budget set mean wage (bs_0.wpg). *c*, Budget set high wage (bs_1.wpg).

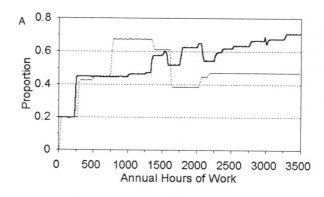

— 1981 ···· 1991

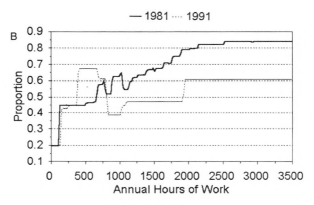

— 1981 ···· 1991

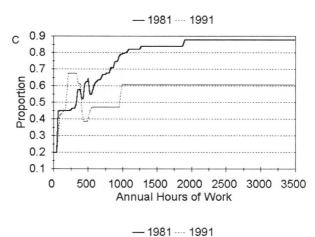

— 1981 ···· 1991

Fig. 5.11   Implicit marginal tax rate for a single male. *a,* Implicit marginal tax rate low wage (mtr_2.wpg). *b,* Implicit marginal tax mean wage (mtr_0.wpg). *c,* Implicit marginal tax high wage (mtr_1.wpg).

income guarantees of the benefit programs and the tax brackets are reached with fewer hours of work. That is, low-wage individuals face the same pattern of marginal tax rate changes with jump points, in terms of annual hours, spaced farther apart. Another key feature is that implicit marginal tax rates are lower for most hours of work for all wage groups in 1991 compared to 1981. Only low-wage earners working less than full-time in 1981 face a lower implicit tax on their work effort in 1981 than in 1991. Even then, the higher implicit marginal tax rate is due to the recovery of the more generous housing allowances in 1991; direct tax rates are lower in 1991 than in 1981.

Married Man

Figures 5.12 and 5.13 present the budget set and implicit marginal tax rates for a married man earning the manufacturing wage with no children and a wife with varying levels of labor market earnings. In both figures, panel *a* assumes that the wife does not work; panel *b* assumes that the wife works part-time (one thousand hours) at a low-wage job (half the manufacturing wage); panel *c* assumes that the wife works part-time at the manufacturing wage; panel *d* assumes that she works full-time at the manufacturing wage; and panel *e* assumes that she works full-time in a high-wage job (twice the manufacturing wage).

The large gain from the 1991 tax reform for high-wage individuals is apparent in all panels of figure 5.12. Men married to wives with no or low earnings face nearly the same budget set in 1991 as in 1981 for low hours of work (say fewer than one thousand hours). For hours of work chosen by most males (fifteen hundred to two thousand), the tax reform of 1991 substantially increases their consumption set. A household with both adults working full-time at an average wage will experience roughly a 20 percent increase in after-tax and after-program income. Gains are smaller for households with lower levels of labor market earnings.

Figure 5.13 presents implicit marginal tax rates corresponding to the budget sets in figure 5.12. Because the individual, not the household, is the basic tax unit of the Swedish tax system, a married man's marginal tax rate is independent of the household structure. Housing allowances depend on household income, so his implicit marginal tax rate is dependent on his partner's labor market activity. The effect of interdependence is concentrated in low annual hours of work for the male, and the range of affected hours increases as spouse's earnings decrease. For example, once the spouse works full-time at the manufacturing wage or at a higher wage rate, the household is no longer eligible to receive housing allowances, and the male's implicit marginal tax schedule is independent of his wife's earnings. Indeed, across all alternative earning levels for the wife, males working 1,250 hours face the same implicit marginal tax schedule appropriate for that year. For men working more than 1,250 hours, the 1991 tax reform reduced their implicit marginal tax rates by as much as 20–25 percent.

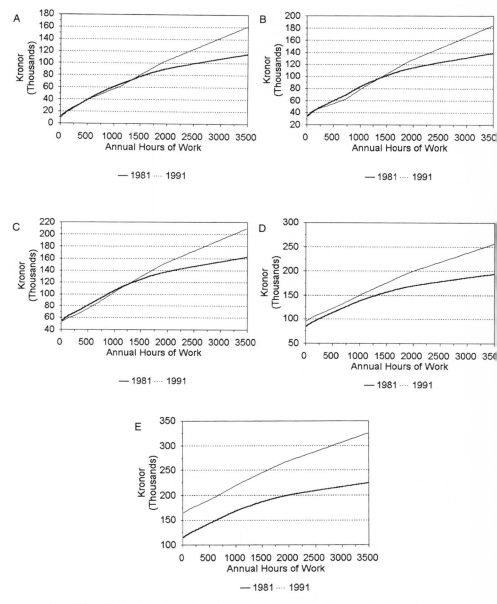

Fig. 5.12   Budget set for a married man. *a*, Budget set nonworking wife
(bs_11.wpg). *b*, Budget set wife works part-time at low wage (bs_9.wpg). *c*,
Budget set wife works part-time at mean wage (bs_7.wpg). *d*, Budget set wife
works full-time at mean wage (bs_6.wpg). *e*, Budget set wife works full-time at
high wage (bs_10.wpg).

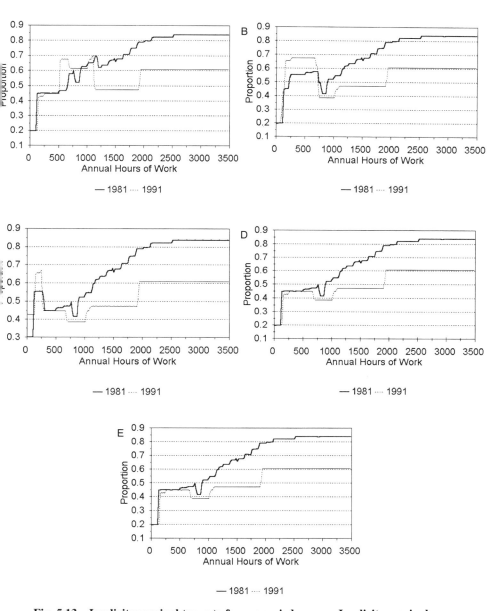

Fig. 5.13   Implicit marginal tax rate for a married man. *a,* Implicit marginal
tax rate nonworking wife (mtr_11.wpg). *b,* Implicit marginal tax rate wife works
part-time at low wage (mtr_9.wpg). *c,* Implicit marginal tax rate wife works part-
time at mean wage (mtr_7.wpg). *d,* Implicit marginal tax rate wife works full-
time at mean wage (mtr_6.wpg). *e,* Implicit marginal tax rate wife works
full-time at high wage (mtr_10.wpg).

Woman with Two School-Age Children

Figures 5.14 and 5.15 present the budget set and implicit marginal tax rates for a woman earning the manufacturing wage and living in a household with two school-aged children. In panel *a,* the woman is assumed to be single, while, in the remaining panels, she has a partner assumed to be working full-time. In panel *b,* the partner works in a low-wage job; in panel *c,* the partner works in an average-wage position; and, in panel *d,* the partner works in a high-wage job. With (school-aged) children present, the budget sets in figure 5.14 incorporate the (nontaxed) child allowances, measured in 1991 kronor; these amount of SKr 11,314 in 1981 and SKr 18,000 in 1991 and account for a large part of the improvement of the budget set for the single-parent household (panel *a*).

Nonconvexities in the budget sets are also apparent, although many are outside the usual levels of annual hours of work. For unmarried women, one nonconvex portion occurs between twenty-three hundred and three thousand hours in 1981. However, nonconvexities resulting from the additional general deduction affect households at low hours of work, for example, in the neighborhood of five to eight hundred hours. Finally, as for previous households, the largest gains accrue to households with the largest labor market income.

Figure 5.15 presents implicit marginal tax rates corresponding to the budget sets in figure 5.14. Somewhat surprisingly, only for women married to the average wage earner is there a significant range of hours of work for which the implicit marginal tax rate is higher in 1991 than in 1981. Even then, this range is confined to a region of low hours of work (two to eight hundred hours). In this range, each hour of work by the woman reduces the household's housing allowance. The loss of housing allowances is partially offset by the additional general deduction, which is exhausted at 1,250 hours of work. From 1,250 hours, the implicit marginal tax rate equals the marginal tax rate. For all other groups, and for all other hours of work, implicit marginal tax rates are lower in 1991 than in 1981.

5.5.2   Trends in Participation and Hours of Work

Since 1980, labor force participation rates by young men and women have been similar, in terms of both level and time-series pattern (see app. B). The recent economic problems have been particularly marked for the youngest age group; their participation rates have dropped by approximately 20 percent (11 percentage points) in the last three years. For the other two age groups, gender differences in participation rates have narrowed, yet the time-series profiles are quite different across gender. Among prime-age workers (aged twenty-five to fifty-four), female labor force participation rates rose sharply, increasing 35 percentage points in twenty-five years. Since 1985, labor force participation rates for both men and women of this age group have generally exceeded 90 percent. While female participation rates rose rapidly, labor force participation

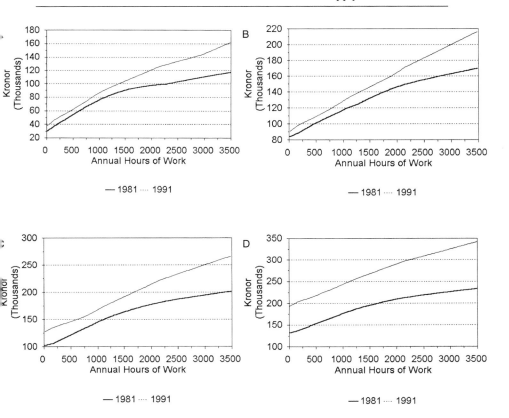

Fig. 5.14   Budget set for a woman with two children. *a,* **Budget set single woman (bs_12.wpg).** *b,* **Budget set husband works full-time at low wage (bs_13.wpg).** *c,* **Budget set husband works full-time at mean wage (bs_14.wpg).** *d,* **Budget set husband works full-time at high wage (bs_15.wpg).**

rates for prime-age males remained within a narrow band around 95 percent. For the oldest age group of workers (aged fifty-five to sixty-four), male participation rates have steadily fallen from the mid-1960s, and female rates have steadily increased. By 1992, men near retirement have labor force participation rates only 5 percentage points greater than comparably aged women (72 vs. 67 percent).

Time-series patterns in average weekly hours of work exhibit a similar U shape. Weekly hours of work declined from the early 1960s until the early 1980s; then weekly hours increase during the 1980s and level off or slightly decline in the 1990s. Increases in hours of work during the 1980s were stronger for women than for men and for prime-age workers than for older workers. While the time-series profiles are similar, women consistently work six to eight

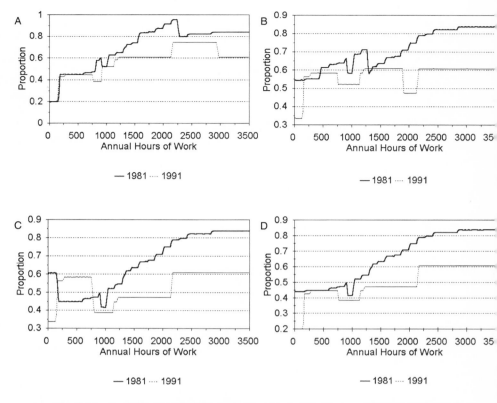

Fig. 5.15   Implicit marginal tax rate for a woman with two children. *a,* Implicit marginal tax rate single woman (mtr_12.wpg). *b,* Implicit marginal tax rate husband works full-time at low wage (mtr_13.wpg). *c,* Implicit marginal tax rate husband works full-time at mean wage (mtr_14.wpg). *d,* Implicit marginal tax rate husband works full-time at high wage (mtr_15.wpg).

fewer hours per week than do men. Only among the youngest age group has the gender gap in hours increased, and even for this group the increase is modest and has been stable since the mid-1970s.

The large number of legislative changes to Sweden's social insurance programs and tax system during the last thirty years makes it nearly impossible to use aggregate time-series data to identify the behavioral responses to any single policy. Even if the policy environment were stable, the irregularities of the budget set confronting Swedish consumers vitiates any attempt to glean behavioral responses from the aggregate time-series data. Consequently, we do not attempt to do so and make only one broad observation. The large increase in female wages generated by the "solidarity" wage policy initiated in the early 1960s, the adoption of the individual as the unit of taxation (which lowered the marginal tax rate facing Swedish women), and the increasing marginal tax rates that occurred during most of this period and gave strong incentives to equalize taxable income among household members all contributed to the impressive increase in labor force participation by Swedish women. Obtaining more precise estimates of the effect of the Swedish welfare state on labor supply requires a review of the microeconometric evidence.

5.5.3 Econometric Evidence

In this section, we review the empirical labor supply literature to assess the incentive effects of Sweden's tax and cash benefits on labor supply. Several recent surveys address similar issues.[23] We concentrate on studies of Swedish behavior and augment this literature only as needed. We review the empirical literature on taxes and labor supply first and then discuss estimates of the welfare costs.

Labor Supply Elasticities

The canonical model presented in section 5.2 has been the workhorse in estimating labor supply elasticities. To a greater or lesser extent, researchers have invoked its structure in an attempt to recover the holy trinity of labor supply studies—the uncompensated wage elasticity, the income elasticity, and the compensated wage elasticity. The canonical model's simple theoretical structure does not translate into a simple econometric model. Even more surprising, the consensus model of labor supply does not lead to consensus estimates of the labor supply elasticities. The range of labor supply elasticities is large, especially considering the amount of resources devoted to the task. The lack of consensus has led to a proliferation of studies, each making one or two extensions to the canonical model of participation and hours of work. To labor supply analysts, the question seems to be how to tweak the canonical model to improve its fit. To most outside observers, the question frequently is, "Why did you expect the canonical model to fit in the first place?" Yet, as we now discuss, knowledge about labor supply behavior has accumulated.

Studies of male labor supply are most prevalent because the high participation rates of males permit simpler econometric procedures. Table 5.2 presents estimates of the labor supply elasticities for men from recent studies using Swedish data. All the papers represented therein explicitly consider Sweden's tax and benefit system. The studies differ in their specification of the budget constraint facing the male worker—as either convex or nonconvex and as smooth or "kinked," the latter usually characterized by piecewise linear segments. The studies also make different assumptions about the source of distur-

---

23. Pencavel (1986) reviews studies of male labor supply, while Killingsworth and Heckman (1986) survey the literature on female labor supply. Both are wide-ranging surveys that discuss taxes and labor supply as one (small) portion of their papers. Killingsworth (1983) offers a comprehensive review of both literatures. Hausman (1985) concentrates on the public finance aspects of labor supply. Atkinson (1987) reviews the incentive effects of social insurance programs.

Table 5.2   **Male Labor Supply Elasticities, Swedish Data**

Study	Description	Uncompensated	Income	Compensated
		Elasticities		
Blomquist (1983)	LNU 1973, married men aged 25–55, linear l.s.	.08	−.04	.11
Blomquist and Hansson-Brusewitz (1990)	LNU 1980, married men aged 35–55:			
	Linear l.s., convex b.c.	.081	.002	.082
	Linear l.s., nonconvex b.c.	.076	−.008	.079
	Linear l.s., nonconvex b.c., random preferences	.127	−.013	.133
	Quadratic l.s., convex b.c.	.12	−.008	.123
Aronsson and Karlsson (1993)	LNU 1980, married men aged 25–55:			
	Quantity-constrained linear l.s., convex b.c.	.086	−.021	.109
	Nonlinear l.s.	.111	−.009	.115
Flood and MaCurdy (1992)	HUS 1984, married men aged 25–55:			
	L.s. convex	.16	−.10	.24
	IV, linear l.s., wage, nonlabor income exogenous	.107	−.079	.169
	IV, linear l.s., wage, nonlabor income endogenous	−.244	.028	−.266

Note: LNU = Level of Living Survey; HUS = Swedish Household Market and Nonmarket Activities Survey; l.s. = labor supply; b.c. = budget constraint; IV = instrumental variables.

bances (e.g., are hours of work measured with error? are consumer preferences fixed or allowed to have unobserved differences across members of the population [random preferences]?). For all these important econometric differences, with the exception of the last row of the table, all the uncompensated wage elasticities are positive but small. For this dimension, an increase in the wage generates a small but positive increase in hours of work. The range of the uncompensated wage elasticities is similar to Hausman's (1985) summary of estimates obtained from studies incorporating explicit controls of the U.S. tax and benefit system and is higher than Pencavel's (1986) estimated range of from −.17 to 0, with a mean of −.12, from his comprehensive review of labor supply studies. In part, the positive uncompensated wage effect may be due to the restriction to prime-age males aged twenty-five to fifty-five by the studies reported in table 5.2. It is unlikely to be due to the reliance on linear labor supply functions and its monotonic effect of wages on labor supply. Two studies permitting more flexible functional forms also report positive uncompensated wage effects. The estimated income elasticities also show a narrow range and a small effect. Unlike studies of U.S. and British data, the estimated income elasticities are quite small and precisely estimated. Increased nonlabor

Table 5.3   **Female Labor Supply Elasticities**

		Elasticities		
Study	Description	Uncompensated	Income	Compensated
Blomquist and Hansson-Brusewitz (1990)	1980 LNU, married women aged 25–55, linear l.s., convex b.c. (FIML)	.790	−.243	.863
	Linear l.s., random preferences	.773	−.061	.794
	Linear l.s., convex b.c., two-step estimator	.386	−.030	.395
Aronsson (1991)	1980 LNU, married women aged 25–55, nonlinear l.s. with minimum hours constraint	.93	−.04	1.07
Hausman and Ruud (1984)	Married women aged 21–65, 1975 PSID, U.S., linear l.s.	.76	−.36	1.12
Mroz (1987)	Married women aged 30–60, 1975 PSID, U.S., instrumental variables	.215	−.030	.239
Blundell and Walker (1982)	Prime-age British women, FES 1974, linear l.s., convex b.c.	.43	−.22	.65
Blundell, Duncan, and Meghir (1993)	Prime-age British married women, FES 1979–89, nonlinear l.s. two-step estimator	.232	−.374	.380

Note: The first three studies use Swedish data, the studies by Blundell and his coauthors analyze British data, and the last two studies use U.S. data. Also, l.s. = labor supply; b.c. = budget constraint; FIML = full information maximum likelihood.

income has a negative but small effect on hours worked. The small uncompensated wage elasticity and small negative income elasticity yield a positive, although again small, compensated wage effect of around .10, near Pencavel's point estimate of the compensated wage effect of .12. The main implication from the estimates in table 5.2 is that men's hours of work are not very responsive to changes in wages and nonlabor income. The estimates show that moderate changes in the marginal tax rate will not induce a large labor supply response by men. However, for nonconvex sections of the budget, small wage changes may induce large changes in hours of work.

Table 5.3 reports estimates of female labor supply elasticities. Even from these two studies using Swedish data and explicitly incorporating taxes, the range of estimates of female labor supply elasticities is larger than for men. Uncompensated wage elasticities are positive and several times larger than for males. The greater responsiveness of women's labor supply to changes in wages is repeatedly found in nearly all empirical analyses. Given the large increase in female labor force participation rates in Sweden and elsewhere, it would be surprising to estimate negative uncompensated wage elasticities for women.

Reviewing the income elasticities reported in table 5.3, estimated income elasticities are small, while the compensated wage elasticities are large, near 0.8, several times larger than the comparable value for males.

The middle two entries in table 5.3 are commonly cited studies using U.S. data. These studies are included in the table to exhibit the wide range of estimated elasticities in the literature. Notice that, from just two studies using comparable procedures and comparable data, the uncompensated elasticity varies by a factor of more than two, the income elasticity by a factor of ten, and the compensated elasticity by a factor of four.

The paper by Blundell, Duncan, and Meghir (1993) reports labor supply elasticities for married women in Britain. The British study also incorporates explicit controls for taxes and benefits using a more robust estimation procedure of the labor supply function. Including this additional study increases the range of estimates for uncompensated wage effect but adds little to the range of the income elasticity or the compensated elasticity. From these estimates, it is clear that women's labor supply behavior is more responsive than men's to changes in wages and incomes, although the range of estimates remains uncomfortably large.

Welfare Effects of Taxes and Benefits

Estimates of the excess burden are commonly used to measure the welfare costs of taxes and benefits. Table 5.4 reports several estimates obtained from Swedish data. The first three studies in the table consider only the effect of income taxes—that is, they replace only the income tax with a lump-sum tax while leaving other taxes in place. The estimates measure the excess burden as a percentage of the income tax revenue. As expected under Sweden's progressive tax system, the loss increases as one moves up the income distribution. Also, as expected in the light of recent reforms, the welfare costs of the income tax appear to have decreased considerably during the last decade.[24] As a comparison, we also include the results reported by Hausman (1981), which are based on data for the United States from 1975 and refer to the excess burden of the federal tax in a model of male labor supply. Notice that Hausman's estimate of the excess burden for the United States is smaller than most of excess burdens reported in table 5.4, reflecting Sweden's high marginal tax rates.

The results suggest that the excess burden in the prereform system may have been considerable.[25] Considering the magnitude of indirect taxes in Sweden,

24. The qualitative conclusion of a large reduction in the excess burden from the 1991 income tax reform is also supported by the results in a recent paper by Aarberge, Dagsvik, and Strom (1993).

25. The large excess burdens reported by Aronsson and Palme (1994) are similar to those reported by Hansson (1984). Hansson applies a general equilibrium model to data from 1979 and computes the marginal cost of public funds, which measures the change in the excess burden from additional tax revenues and depends on how these additional tax revenues are spent. Hansson reports some huge excess burdens (214–620 percent) from the taxation of labor. With an assumed elasticity of substitution between labor and capital of 0.79–0.96 and a postulated savings function,

Table 5.4   **Estimates of the Deadweight Loss of the Swedish Tax System**

Study	Group	Tax	Deadweight Loss as a Percentage of Tax Revenue
Blomquist (1983)	Low-wage males aged 25–55	Progressive tax	4
	Middle-wage males aged 25–55	Progressive tax	14
	High-wage males aged 25–55	Progressive tax	28
Blomquist and Hansson-Brusewitz (1990)	Married males aged 25–55	Progressive tax	16
	Married women aged 25–55	Progressive tax	26
Aronsson (1993)	Married couple with median income	1980 income tax	30
		1989 income tax	23
		1991 income tax	8
	Married couple with above-median income	1980 income tax	33
		1989 income tax	28
		1991 income tax	11
	Married couple with below-median income	1980 income tax	27
		1989 income tax	16
		1991 income tax	5
Hausman (1981)	Prime-age males in the U.S.	1975 income tax	22
Aronsson and Palme (1994)	Married couple aged 25–55	1980 tax and benefit system	45
		1989 tax and benefit system	40
		1991 tax and benefit system	32

an obvious weakness of these studies is their narrow focus on the excess burden of income taxes. Aronsson and Palme (1994) incorporate the VAT and examine the labor supply and welfare effects of the sequence of tax and benefit reforms in Sweden during the last decade. The bottom portion of table 5.4 reports their estimates of the excess burden (defined as a percentage of the net tax payment, where the latter is measured as the sum of payments of income taxes and value added tax less transfer payments received). When indirect taxes are incorporated, their results indicate that much higher excess burdens occur. The relative

---

nearly all the inefficiency of the taxation of labor in Hansson's estimates operates through the capital market. When the capital stock is assumed fixed (so there is no substitution between labor and capital), as in the partial equilibrium framework of the labor supply studies, Hansson's measure of the excess burden declines (to a first approximation) to 16 percent. Hansson's paper cautions against the narrow focus of the labor supply studies and an overemphasis on excess burden *levels*. Rather, relative comparisons (within a given parametric model) of the excess burden of alternative reforms are informative, not the absolute level of any excess burden. Thus, the microeconometric estimates of the excess burden from the labor supply studies give important insights into the distributional consequences of tax reforms.

ranking of estimated excess burdens across population groups and across tax reforms is similar to the earlier studies. They also find, in agreement with the regressive nature of consumption taxes, that the distribution of disposable income is more unequal in the 1991 regime than in the 1980 and 1989 regimes.

Summary

Although there remain serious econometric issues (see app. C) in the existing labor supply studies, we believe that this work reveals some important insights, which deserve to be summarized. First, the labor supply behavior of women appears to be more sensitive to changes in marginal wage rates and virtual nonlabor income than that of men. Second, the labor supply response (as measured by hours of work) to tax reform is likely to be relatively moderate, primarily because of the inelastic labor supply functions. For example, Aronsson and Palme (1994) predict that the average labor supply increase among prime-aged individuals following the 1991 tax and benefit reform is about one hundred hours per year for men and even smaller for women (by comparing the predicted behavior under the 1989 tax and benefit system with the predicted behavior under the 1991 system). Third, the welfare loss associated with the prereform tax system may have been considerable. Hence, even in the light of small labor supply elasticities, the high marginal income tax rates produce a large excess burden. The tax and benefit reform of 1991 appears have led to a large reduction of these welfare losses.

5.5.4   Evidence on the Effect of Sickness Benefits and Pensions

We consider next the effect of programs commonly perceived to have induced strong disincentives to work—the sickness insurance cash benefit and the pension system.

The Sickness Insurance System

Figure 5.16 presents the unemployment rate for individuals aged sixteen to sixty-four and the number of days per employee of sickness benefits paid (the left-hand vertical axis) from the initiation of the national insurance system in 1955 until 1991. The vertical lines at 1963, 1967, 1974, and 1987 denote the major reforms of the system. Several striking features appear in figure 5.16. Notice first that, as early as 1955, the mean number of sick days is nearly twelve days per insured worker. By the end of the sample period, per capita usage of benefits more than doubled, reaching a peak of twenty-five days in 1988. Even the initial usage is high, and it is important to realize that other reasons for excused (and usually compensated) work absences are not included in the sickness cash benefit. (Permanent and temporary disabilities fall within the pension system, while other common sources of job absences such as pregnancy, childbirth, and temporary child-care benefits are in the child-care system and have a separate accounting.) Even by international standards, Sweden's

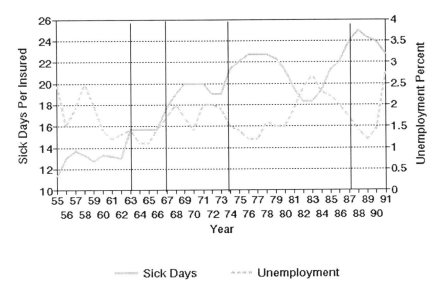

Fig. 5.16   Sickness benefit days

use of sickness benefits is high. Henrekson, Lantto, and Persson (1992) report that only Denmark's use of sickness benefits is close to Sweden's.[26]

Taken at face value, the increased usage of sickness cash benefits implies increased morbidity within the Swedish population, a conclusion at odds with its fine public health record. However, the timing of increased usage coincides with program reforms improving the generosity of the system. Noticeable increases in usage occurred in 1963, 1967, 1974, and 1987. The most persuasive evidence that increased usage of cash benefits does not reflect the health status of the population comes from a comparison with usage rates over the business cycle. Until the three-day coinsurance period was removed in 1967, there was no relation between sickness days and the cycle. However, since 1967, usage of sickness cash benefits has been strongly procyclic (the simple correlation between unemployment and sickness days is −0.7). It appears that sickness benefits are used to smooth hours of work. When demand for labor is high (unemployment is low), sick days increase; when demand for labor is low and unemployment is relatively high, the use of sick days is low. This is exactly the pattern that would emerge if workers use sickness benefits to intertemporally smooth their consumption stream.

Additional evidence on the disincentive effects of sickness cash benefits

---

26. International comparisons are always difficult; however, from the information reported in Henrekson, Lantto, and Persson (1992), sickness insurance systems in Denmark and Sweden appear to be among the most generous.

comes from a cross-sectional study by Björklund (1991). Björklund analyzes the determinants of paid days of sickness benefits. He separates usage for a twelve-month period into two categories: accumulated days of sickness benefits from all short spells and accumulated days of sickness benefits from all long spells. Short spells are seven or fewer days, absences for which no medical certificate is required, while all longer absences are classified as long spells. He regresses these variables on characteristics of the worker and the job. Björklund finds that, for both long and short spells, workers on jobs requiring monotonous work make greater use of sickness benefits. Also, usage of sickness benefits differs significantly by age. Young workers take more days of sickness benefits in short absences, while older workers are more likely to take their sickness benefits in long spells. These age patterns follow morbidity patterns and suggest that young people's usage of sickness benefits is less related to medical need than to work preferences.

In order to reduce these apparent work disincentives, the sickness cash benefit system was subject to reforms in both 1991 and 1993. As was explained in subsection 5.4.2 above, these reforms were designed primarily to reduce the generosity of benefits corresponding to shorter spells of illness. The influence of the 1991 reform is discussed in a recent paper by Johansson and Palme (1993). Using panel data for the period 1981–84, Johansson and Palme estimate a model of worker absenteeism where the decision to be absent from work is closely related to (or part of) the labor supply decision. As the influence of the sickness benefit is taken into account in the estimation, the estimated model provides a natural framework for the simulation of reforms. The simulation conducted by the authors is to compare the predicted and observed behavior in 1990 and 1991. As the experiment turned out, the average number of sick days was predicted to fall by 4.45 percent (an underprediction of the actual reduction, which was 6.25 percent). About 79 percent of the predicted change in sick days can be attributed to the 1991 reform of the sickness benefit system, while the rest can be attributed to the change in the unemployment rate (which was higher in 1991 than it was in 1990). A natural conclusion is, therefore, that recent reforms of the sickness benefit system appear to have reduced work disincentives.

The Effect of Publicly Provided Pensions on Labor Supply

The labor force participation of men nearing retirement age (fifty-five to sixty-four) declined from 90 to 75 percent during the thirty years spanned by the AKU (Arbetskraftsundersokningen) surveys. This large decline in labor force attachment is frequently attributed to the increased generosity of the public pension system. The vast (and growing) literature on the labor supply incentives of old-age security programs implies that this reasoning is far too simple. In his encyclopedic review of the literature, Atkinson (1987) describes a depressingly wide range of findings regarding the incentive effects on labor supply. Although no study has found that increased social security benefits lead to a large increase in labor supply, studies are evenly divided between finding moderate to large negative effects and no or negligible positive effects. While informative on the algebraic sign of the effect, the literature again provides little guidance on magnitudes.

The inherent complexity of the retirement problem contributes to the conflicting findings in the literature. The retirement decision is fundamentally an intertemporal decision and requires a dynamic model. Also, modeling the retirement decision highlights the many different dimensions of labor supply. The most frequently analyzed dimension is the dichotomous participation decision—whether to continue working or to retire. Yet programs such as the partial pension that subsidize reductions in hours of work before full departure from the labor market encourage the analysis of hours worked in addition to the participation decision. The work-conditioned benefit schemes of the supplementary pension system (ATP) generate entitlement effects that may induce workers to increase their labor supply in the periods prior to retirement. Thus, total hours of work over the life cycle may increase. Indeed, Hansson-Brusewitz (1992) finds a positive effect on total labor supply from the partial pension system and the earnings replacement rates of the supplementary old-age pension.

Several studies exist of the effect of disability pensions on labor supply incentives. Evidence of disincentive effects emerges more frequently than in the retirement literature, but again the range of estimated effects is depressingly large (Atkinson 1987). Consideration of Sweden's situation suggests a negative effect on participation. Administered exactly like the old-age pension, cash benefits for a disability pension rise as benefits for the basic and supplemental pensions rise. The major revision in the disability program was the incorporation of nonhealth considerations in awarding disability pensions to those near retirement. Direct evidence is not available, but several time-series trends suggest a negative incentive effect on labor force participation. First, the number of new disability pensions has risen seven times faster than the population eligible to receive a disability pension. From 1971 to 1988, the population aged eighteen to sixty-four increased 6 percent. The number of new disability pensions over the same period increased 42 percent. Roughly 15 percent of new awards are temporary disability pensions, a share that has been stable over time, which means that the fraction of the population on disability pensions increased dramatically during the last twenty years. Adding to the public burden, the age composition of disability pensions has slightly shifted to younger ages. In 1971, 44 percent of the new disability pensions were awarded to individuals sixty to sixty-four years old. In 1988 (the last year of data), that fraction had declined to 38 percent. Moreover, an increased willingness to award labor market disabilities to older workers is apparent from the data. In 1977, 3.6 percent of all new pensions were due to labor market disabilities. In the mid-1980s, as the number of new disability pensions increased, a remarkable 20 percent of all disability pensions were for labor market reasons (recall that, since 1972, older workers may receive a disability pension rather than be forced to change location or occupation). By the late 1980s, the share of labor market pensions had declined to 10–11 percent. Among those receiving a labor market pension, the age composition of recipients of labor market pensions has tended toward younger workers among the sixty to sixty-four age group. The insurance board is more willing to extend labor market disability pensions and is more willing to award them to younger workers.

The extension of disability pensions to labor market conditions does not explain all the rise in disability pensions. That is, even without the labor market conditions provision, the share of the population covered by a disability pension increased during the last twenty years. Sweden's fine public health record means that the increased prevalence of disability pensions is *not* due to a less-healthy work environment. The rapid rise in disability pensions and its burden on society warrants a review of its effects on labor supply.

5.5.5 Education and the Investment in Human Capital: The Supply of Skilled Labor

In this section, we review the evidence on the incentive effects on the quality composition of the workforce. Uncovering effects of the tax and benefit system on quality or skill is difficult because it is harder to identify changes in compositions than changes in magnitudes. Moreover, the large number of compensation mechanisms implies that incentive effects can be spread across many monetary and nonmonetary forms. In the same vein, adjustments made through the underground economy will also not be observed. Hence, empirical evidence on this dimension is less systematic and more qualitative than the evidence on quantity dimensions of labor supply. Rather than consider changes in the occupational distribution (which can be due to technological advances, i.e., demand-side influences), we concentrate on the willingness of individuals to invest in human capital.[27]

We first review the trends in educational attainment. Since 1960, the Swedish labor force has become more skilled as better-educated young members joined the workforce. From 1960 to 1986, the share of the labor force with twelve or more years of schooling rose from 5 percent to approximately 30 percent.[28] The growth appears to have peaked in the mid-1980s as the share of the workforce with college degrees has remained constant.

Such economywide measures as the educational attainment of the workforce respond at the slow rate of demographic change; to move the aggregate measure requires that new entrants have much higher educational attainments than retiring older members. A review of enrollment rates offers another perspective on educational process. Enrollment rates peaked in the late 1960s, declined during the 1970s, and then increased steadily during the 1980s. Until the early

---

27. For a complementary review of this literature, see Edin and Topel (chap. 4 in this volume).
28. A review of other education levels (e.g., postsecondary schooling) yields similar patterns.

1970s, men were more likely to remain in school during their early twenties than were women. Since then, women are more likely to remain in school. The rates also exhibit a strong cyclic pattern, rising during the 1977–78 recession and again during the stagnant years of the early 1980s; they fall slightly in the mid-1980s and then rise again strongly during the recent economic slowdown. Indeed, Edin and Holmlund (1993) document that the relative supply of skilled workers closely corresponds to movements in the wage premia to college-trained workers. However, while this is evidence of the validity of a neoclassical model of the labor market, it is hard to discern direct supply effects.

Most interesting from our point of view is an analysis of the return to education incorporating the effects of the tax and transfer system. With both subsidies and taxes, no theoretical predictions were forthcoming on the incentives to invest in education (see app. A). Estimates by Edin and Holmlund (1993) show that the progressive tax system (and probably wage solidarity) had the effect of depressing the return to education. According to their estimates, in 1968 the internal rate of return to higher education for a male worker was 11.9 percent. By 1974, the rate had fallen to 3.6, and it fell again to a minuscule 0.5 percent in 1981! Hence, it is not surprising that the share of college graduates in the workforce remained constant since the mid-1980s. Since its trough in 1981, the internal rate of return increased slowly during the 1980s. By 1991, the estimated return was still below its 1968 level but above its 1974 value. Including the loans and subsidies, the estimated return for 1991 about doubled, and it appears that educational subsidies have a larger effect than does the income tax system.

While no strong evidence appears on educational attainment decision, weak evidence suggests that the tax and transfer system (*a*) distorted the incentives and (*b*) may have reduced the incentive to receive education. Other factors did not remain constant during the period (e.g., macroeconomic conditions and government training programs, although the latter is probably not relevant for this group), making it impossible to make strong statements on this issue.

5.5.6   Tax Avoidance, Tax Evasion, and the Underground Economy

The high marginal tax rates (statutory and implicit) make honesty expensive in Sweden. Did Swedes continue to comply with the legislated tax burdens as marginal rates increased dramatically during the 1970s and early 1980s? Or did Swedes begin to free ride and reduce their burden by underreporting their taxable income? No convincing evidence exists to answer this important question. The little evidence that exists does not suggest rampant tax evasion or other fraudulent behavior. Studies of taxpayers from the United States reveal high rates of compliance (although at marginal tax rates far below Sweden's). A few surveys attempt to gauge individual perceptions of the fairness of the Swedish tax system (Vogel 1974; Wärneryd and Walerud 1982). These studies show only a slight increase in the perceived unfairness of the tax system. Public opinion polls report that support for Sweden's social insurance programs is high and that strong sentiments continue against inflating deductions or under-reporting taxable income. The continued broadening of the definition of tax-able income suggests that public decision makers are not unaware of these issues.

While there is little evidence of tax evasion, there is evidence of tax avoid-ance. Feldstein (1993) notes, for example, that there is substantial sensitivity of deductions for mortgage interest and charitable contributions to marginal tax rates. This redirection of expenditures in response to the high marginal tax rates creates additional deadweight losses that are conceptually different from the conventional measures of excess burden. Changes in the marginal tax rate can induce changes in labor supply and may also induce changes in the struc-ture of taxable income. The occupational choice model implies that high mar-ginal tax rates encourage individuals and firms to structure employee compen-sation in untaxed or effectively low-tax forms. Examples of nontaxed compensation include first-class travel, use of a corporate automobile, and in-house sports facilities. Forms of compensation that are taxed at effectively low rates include deferred compensation plans, life insurance, and stock options. High-income and wealthy individuals also have the income flow from assets, capital income, to supplement labor market earnings. Difference in income tax rates on earned and capital income create additional incentives to structure asset portfolios to minimize tax liability (holding constant risk exposure of a portfolio). Preferential tax treatment of capital gains provides an additional incentive to time the realization of capital gains to the individual's advantage.

A review of the effects of taxation on the incentives to save and the portfolio effects is beyond the scope of this review.[29] The magnitude of these effects, and particularly the sensitivity of taxable income to changes in marginal tax rates, is unresolved. Feldstein (1993) finds that elasticity of taxable income with respect to a change in marginal tax rates is at least one and may be higher. Yet neither Scholz (1993) nor Slemrod (1992), analyzing the last major tax reform in the United States (the Tax Reform Act of 1986), find evidence of portfolio effects. Using a different approach and different data, Triest (1992) finds some support for the endogeneity of deductions. That a central aspect of the 1991 income tax reform in Sweden was to simplify and unify the treatment of capital income suggests that these are nontrivial issues.

It is easy to miss the provocative implications that these studies have for the analysis of taxes and labor supply. One way to organize these findings is to distinguish between the effect of taxes on real dimensions (e.g., labor supply, savings, and portfolio risk exposure) and the effect of taxes on the recognition and reporting of income. Feldstein (1993), Slemrod (1992), and Scholz (1993) suggest that taxes affect reported taxable income but have little direct effect on behavior generating that income. The minimal behavior effect of taxes esti-

29. For a fine review, see, however, Sandmo (1985).

mated in the labor supply literature and summarized in the preceding sections is consistent with this interpretation.

Moreover, the responsiveness of reported taxable income to a change in the structure of taxes has important policy implications. Knowledge of the responsiveness is absolutely central for predicting the expected revenue gain (or loss) from a change in the structure of taxes. As Feldstein (1993) points out, because there is so much flexibility in the recognition of income, naive predictions of revenue gains from an increase in tax rates that do not recognize these opportunities may overstate actual revenue gains. Forecasting errors is one cost, but a far larger cost is that tax avoidance activities require real resources. Tax planners, tax accountants, and tax lawyers engaged in tax avoidance all represent a reallocation of resources and an inefficiency that is in addition to the excess burden calculations presented earlier.

The responsiveness of labor supply, savings, and financial portfolio composition are all outcomes of complicated, multidimensional choice processes. It is not surprising that they show little responsiveness to taxes in the short run because tax consequences are only one of many aspects of the decision. In terms of labor supply, most individuals cannot offer an indivisible unit of labor supply as posited in the canonical labor-leisure model. Rather, changes in hours occur through entry and exit decisions or, as the evidence from Björklund (1991) suggests, through adjustments made via days of sickness benefits.[30]

5.6 Summary

The income tax and every social insurance program affect the budget sets of consumers and consequently their incentive to work. The influence of taxes and transfer programs on labor force participation and hours of work has been the subject of extensive research during the last twenty years. Answers are elusive, and measuring the labor supply effects, the efficiency costs, and the distributional consequences of these government interventions remains an active and challenging area of economic and policy research.

From the extensive research, several observations emerge for the Swedish context. We take labor force participation first. Because benefit levels are closely related to earnings, the structure of social insurance benefits gives strong incentives for all individuals (men and women) to participate in the

---

30. Studies by Feldstein (1993) and others imply that the real limitation of the existing labor supply studies is their reliance on a two-good (static) model. Triest's (1992) results on the endogeneity of deductions imply that a three-good model is required to capture the differences between deductible and nondeductible consumption expenditures. The three-good model would be an important first step toward capturing some of the responsiveness found by Feldstein (1993) and others. Since housing expenditures are a significant expenditure for most households, and because housing has been and is heavily subsidized through the deductibility of mortgage interest, a natural first investigation along these lines would be to analyze the joint determination of labor supply, housing, and nonhousing consumption.

labor market. Moreover, individual taxation and high marginal tax rates provide strong incentives to equalize labor earnings between household partners. Econometric studies applying the canonical model to Swedish data confirm that female labor supply is more elastic than male, with most of the response at the extensive margin of labor for participation and not via hours of work (among those already working).

The response in the hours of work to tax and benefit reforms among those who are already participating appears to be of less importance. Although estimation procedures vary considerably across studies, a common finding of the econometric studies of male labor supply behavior is that the estimated compensated wage elasticity is small. However, even in the presence of low compensated labor supply elasticities, the high marginal tax rates of the 1970s and 1980s produced large welfare costs.

Our broad perspective on labor supply recognizes that hours of work is only one dimension of labor supply and that sole concentration on it will miss responses in other dimensions. As observed hours of work is the outcome of both supply and demand factors, hours of work may exhibit little responsiveness to changes in taxes because demand-side factors (e.g., coordination activities) may impose quantity restrictions on the structure of the work week that will limit the flexibility of workers to change their hours of work in the short run. Indeed, Björklund's evidence of the strong cyclic use of sickness benefits reveals that work disincentives are present and cautions against the belief that high marginal tax rates or subsidies have weak labor supply effects because few have been recovered from labor supply functions estimated from hours of work data. Similarly, Edin and Holmlund's finding that the share of students is sensitive to the return to higher education provides initial evidence that the quality dimensions (e.g., skill) of labor supply are also important.

These studies suggest that responses to changes in tax and program incentives occur in labor supply dimensions that are hard to measure and that consequently have received less attention in the economics literature. High marginal tax rates give consumers strong incentives to change the structure of compensation away from monetary sources, to work in the underground economy, and to misreport taxable income. Almost by definition, the latter two responses defy measurement. The large number of potential dimensions over which to define compensation (both in terms of fringe benefits and in terms of the timing of compensation) also serves to severely complicate the measurement problem. Moreover, the intertemporal nature of many of these decisions implies that there may be a long lag between policy change and behavioral response. The complexity of the measurement issue means that clear, conclusive evidence on the disincentive effects in these dimensions does not exist.[31] The challenge

---

31. Other authors have noted the wide range of labor supply elasticities and the resulting lack of consensus about the magnitude of disincentive effects (Atkinson 1993; Gustafsson and Klevmarken 1993). Perhaps not surprising, most of the controversy centers on the magnitude of more

for future research is to determine the magnitude of behavioral responses in these dimensions.

To guide the policy discussion, we speculate on the relative magnitudes and the expected effect of recent policy reforms.

5.7 Expected Future Changes

The 1991 income tax reform lowered marginal tax rates and broadened the tax base. Motivated by concern over the disincentive effects created by high marginal tax rates, it is the last of a sequence of reforms intended to simplify and unify the tax system. The best available evidence suggests that the 1991 reform led to a considerable reduction in the excess burden, especially for high-wage workers. The small labor supply elasticities estimated in several recent studies using Swedish data imply little response in labor force participation or hours of work. The broadening of the tax base and the more uniform treatment of capital income remove incentives to avoid taxation by searching for other forms of compensation. Even without direct labor supply effects, these latter reforms should tighten the connection between realized and taxable income.

As a response to the recent financial crisis, several changes have been initiated to reduce the work disincentives of the social insurance programs. A one-day waiting period has been introduced into the sickness insurance system, and benefit levels have been reduced in both the unemployment insurance and the sickness insurance systems. The increased use of deductibles (the one-day waiting period) and coinsurance (reduced compensation of earnings) will ameliorate the disincentive effects of these programs. Moreover, having employers bear some of the program costs for the first fourteen days of absence should further lessen the abuses of the sickness insurance system.

Several proposals will extend these and other reforms into other social insurance programs (e.g., Lindbeck 1993; Lindbeck et al. 1993, 1994). Increased use of coinsurance and deductibles is strongly advocated. Equally persuasive is the suggestion that the actuarial nature of insurance be introduced into health and pension systems. On the firm side, these reforms would introduce differentiated insurance fees for disability insurance to reflect the frequency of injury. For consumers, the suggestion is that both the sickness insurance and the pension systems become actuarially based programs whereby the expected present value of benefits equals the expected present value of lifetime fees (Lindbeck

---

subjective and speculative effects. Those most concerned about the disincentive effects stress the important but hard-to-measure dimensions of labor supply, including intertemporal aspects and general equilibrium effects, and sometimes including broad-ranging considerations of the effect on family structure and the loss of personal freedom (e.g., Lindbeck 1993). Others more concerned about equity restrict attention to a few dimensions of choice and recognize the positive incentive effects (e.g., risk sharing, consumption smoothing, work incentives of the employment conditioned benefits) and the need to balance efficiency and equity trade-offs (e.g., Atkinson 1993).

et al. 1994, 37–38). Development of an actuarially based social insurance system will require removing those components of the social insurance system that do not provide risk insurance (e.g., parental benefits and child-care benefits) but are more properly seen as transfer programs for particular subpopulations. Incorporation of these latter programs as a separate item in the government budget will initiate an important, and long awaited, distinction between insurance and transfers (Lindbeck et al. 1994, 38).

Development of an actuarial system is required for the long-term viability of the social insurance systems. Maintaining pay-as-you-go social insurance programs makes the system vulnerable to changes in macroeconomic conditions such as the economic downturn of 1991–93, which has resulted in a substantial redistribution of income to the elderly (Lindbeck et al. 1994, 28) or secular demographic trends. The aging of the Swedish population and its implications for intergenerational transfer payments are widely recognized (Johnson 1993) and loom just beyond the horizon. Although the consequences of the demographic shift will not appear until well into the next century, equity considerations and the importance of the long-term contractual nature of public pensions require immediate, although gradual, reform.[32]

The reforms discussed above can be accomplished within the basic structure of the current welfare state—that is, the basic structure of the welfare state will remain roughly the same as prior to these reforms. The long evolution of the Swedish welfare state makes it too strong to admit radical reforms in the short run. Democratic systems reflect the will of the people, and it is fair to say that Swedes have (at least approximately) the tax system and social insurance programs they desire. Public opinion polls reveal substantial agreement with the basic structure of the welfare state (Huber and Stephens 1993). It is reasonable to believe that the Swedish welfare state will retain its Nordic flavor and will not approach the relatively laissez-faire structure of the United States. However, although very large changes are unlikely (at least in the short run), it is important not to underestimate the problem of a large budget deficit, as well as other economic problems, facing Sweden as a small open economy. Seen in this light, a gradual process of reform may reshape entitlement programs in the years ahead. Recent reforms have reduced the disparities between individual and social benefits, but income tax rates in Sweden are still high and generate continual pressures on the Swedish welfare state.

---

32. The Swedish Parliament is well aware of these issues. In April 1994, it adopted a set of principles for the reform of the public pension system. Making the system more actuarially based is among the set of principles adopted.

Appendix A
Occupational Choice in the Presence of Taxes and Transfers

We first explore the equilibrium in the absence of taxes and transfers. Workers may supply one unit of labor to either of two occupations. Occupation 0 requires no education, while occupation 1 requires s (exogenous and fixed) years of school. Once employed, individuals work in the chosen occupation forever. Ex ante, individuals are otherwise identical but differ in their tastes for schooling. Those with the lowest values of ξ have the least distaste for school. Let $\Psi(\xi)$ represent the monetary value of the psychic costs of schooling for a type-ξ individual. The cost function is such that $\Psi(0) = 0$, $\Psi' > 0$, $\Psi'' > 0$.[33] The distribution of ξ in the population has density $f(\xi)$.

To focus on supply decisions, demand for each occupation is infinitely elastic at earnings E_j in occupation j, $j = 0, 1$. Hence, workers face an exogenously determined and constant earnings differential of $\Delta = E_1 - E_0$. Workers entering occupation 0 can do so immediately (time 0), with a real interest rate r, and have net wealth equal to $W_0 = E_0/r$. Workers entering occupation 1 defer their earnings stream for the length of schooling. A type ξ's gross wealth from entering occupation 1 is $W_1 = (E_1/r)e^{-rs}$ and net wealth is $W_1 - \Psi(\xi)$.

An individual will acquire an education and enter the skilled occupation if it yields the highest net wealth,

(A1)
$$W_1 - \Psi(\xi) - W_0 \geq 0,$$

or

$$K \geq \Psi(\xi);$$

where

$$K = \frac{\Delta}{r} + \frac{E_1}{r}(e^{-rs} - 1).$$

The inequality condition in (A1) holds as an equality for the individual indifferent between the two occupations. That individual has index $\xi^* = \Psi^{-1}(K)$. Individuals with lower values of ξ attend school and enter the skilled occupation. With a (fixed) population of size N, supply to the skilled occupation is

(A2)
$$N^s = N \int_0^{\xi^*} f(z)dz = N \int_0^{\Psi^{-1}(K)} f(z)dz.$$

---

33. While it is important for educational policy, it is not important for this application whether Ψ measures preferences or opportunities.

Now introduce a progressive income tax. Earnings in the low-education occupation are untaxed, while those in the high-education occupation are taxed at rate τ. Entry into the skilled occupation is determined by modifying the decision rule in equation (A1) as

$$
\begin{aligned}
\text{(A3)} \qquad (1-\tau)W_1 - \Psi(\xi) - W_0 &\geq 0, \\
K - \tau W_1 &\geq \Psi(\xi).
\end{aligned}
$$

The progressive tax system reduces the value of entering the skilled occupation, and the number supplied to the occupation declines. By reducing the earnings differential between occupations, the tax system reduces the incentive for some individuals to acquire the skills to enter occupation 1. Notice that, unlike incentives that change hours or labor force participation, incentives here change the composition of the labor force, not necessarily the size.[34]

Progressive taxes reduce investment in human capital. It is easy to see that transfer programs that subsidize education or reduce its psychic cost to consumers will lead to increased investments in human capital and to an increased supply of skilled workers. Whether the net effect of the modern welfare state creates positive or negative incentives for investing in human capital is context specific and depends on the system of benefits and taxes.

Reinterpret ξ as the reciprocal of ability and Ψ as direct educational expenses so that high-ability individuals have low values of ξ and low costs of acquiring the skills to enter occupation 1. Full deductibility of educational costs offsets, but does not eliminate, the reduced supply to the skilled occupation.[35] The reduced supply to occupation 1 means that the average ability increases in both occupations. In a richer specification of the labor market, with more attention paid to the demand side, we should expect to see some response by firms to the higher ability levels in each occupation, perhaps by changing the wage rate or one or more conditions of employment. Hence, the assumption of an exogenous constant wage is artificial and restrictive; the tax system can have important effects on the demand for labor. Knowledge of both supply and demand effects is required to fully evaluate a tax reform.

---

34. If earnings in the first occupation were also taxed, say at rate $\tau_0 < \tau$, and we assume that consumers have nonlabor income, then some individuals will choose not to work, and labor force participation will decline. There will still be a compositional effect and, depending on the relative magnitudes of the tax rates, the fraction of the labor force employed in the unskilled sector may increase. Heckman (1976) shows that the deductibility of interest payments increases human capital investments with a proportional tax system.

35. The decision rule is $K - \tau W_1 \geq (1 - \tau)\Psi(\xi)$.

Appendix B
Tax Rates and Labor Supply Measures

Table 5B.1   **Components of the Payroll Tax for Manufacturing Workers and Total Payroll Tax in Manufacturing and the Civil Service, 1960–93**

	Manufacturing					
Year	ATP Pension	Health	Add for Law Enforcement	Determined during Bargaining	Total	Total Civil Servants
1960	1.9	1.1	.4	.0	3.4	10.50
1961	2.7	1.1	.4	.0	4.2	11.80
1962	3.4	1.1	.4	.0	4.9	12.70
1963	4.1	1.5	.4	.6	6.6	14.20
1964	4.9	1.5	.4	.6	7.4	14.90
1965	5.4	1.5	.4	.5	7.8	15.10
1966	5.8	1.5	.4	.5	8.2	15.50
1967	6.2	2.6	.4	.5	9.7	17.20
1968	6.6	2.6	.4	.5	10.1	17.80
1969	7.1	2.6	1.4	.6	11.7	19.90
1970	7.6	2.9	1.4	.6	12.5	20.70
1971	7.8	3.1	2.4	.6	13.9	21.80
1972	8.0	3.1	2.35	1.0	14.45	21.70
1973	8.0	3.2	4.35	2.55	18.1	24.10
1974	8.0	3.8	8.05	4.25	24.1	29.70
1975	8.3	7.0	8.95	4.47	28.72	33.70
1976	8.6	8.0	11.66	4.4	32.66	38.70
1977	9.2	8.0	14.88	5.0	37.08	42.80
1978	9.1	9.6	12.37	5.1	36.17	42.10
1979	8.9	10.6	11.78	5.4	36.68	42.80
1980	9.2	10.6	12.65	5.36	37.81	44.30
1981	9.4	10.5	13.11	5.51	38.52	44.00
1982	9.4	10.5	13.16	5.66	38.72	43.90
1983	9.6	9.5	17.16	5.78	42.04	46.60
1984	10.0	9.5	16.66	5.9	42.06	47.00
1985	10.0	9.5	16.96	5.86	42.32	46.20
1986	10.0	9.3	17.15	5.86	42.31	46.20
1987	10.2	9.3	17.58	6.1	43.18	46.30
1988	10.6	10.1	16.37	6.1	43.17	46.30
1989	11.0	10.1	16.37	6.0	43.47	46.40
1990	13.0	10.1	15.87	3.9	42.87	46.57
1991	13.0	10.1	14.93	6.3	44.33	45.63
1992	13.0	7.8	14.03	6.18	41.01	42.48
1993	13.0	8.3	9.73	6.18	37.18	42.48

Table 5B.2   Average Local Tax Rate and Value Added Tax, 1960–93

Year	Average Local Tax Rate	Value Added Tax Rate	Year	Average Local Tax Rate	Value Added Tax Rate
1960	14.63	4.20	1977	26.85	19.38
1961	15.00	4.20	1978	28.71	20.63
1962	15.24	6.30	1979	29.02	20.63
1963	15.46	6.30	1980	29.09	21.58
1964	16.5	6.30	1981	29.55	23.3
1965	17.25	6.30	1982	29.74	21.51
1966	18.29	10.00	1983	30.14	23.46
1967	18.71	10.00	1984	30.30	23.46
1968	19.34	11.10	1985	30.37	23.46
1969	20.24	11.10	1986	30.34	23.46
1970	21.00	11.10	1987	30.44	23.46
1971	22.54	17.65	1988	30.56	23.46
1972	23.79	17.65	1989	30.80	23.46
1973	23.94	17.65	1990	31.16	24.23
1974	24.03	15.66	1991	31.15	25.00
1975	25.23	17.65	1992	31.04	25.00
1976	26.15	17.65	1993	31.04	25.00

Source: The average annual local tax rates are from Lodin (n.d.).
Note: The VAT is reported as a percentage of the pretax price.

Table 5B.3   Labor Force Participation Rates by Gender and Age, 1963–92

Year	Males 16–24	Males 25–54	Males 55–64	Females 16–24	Females 25–54	Females 55–64
1963	71.9	96.3	89.6	62.3	56.4	39.9
1964	71.8	96.3	88.5	62.4	55.5	40.1
1965	71.7	96.1	88.3	60.5	56.0	39.2
1966	70.3	96.3	88.4	60.2	57.4	42.2
1967	68.0	95.6	89.2	57.6	57.7	43.5
1968	68.4	95.1	89.0	59.7	59.8	42.9
1969	68.2	95.0	86.6	58.8	61.5	44.3
1970	67.0	94.8	85.4	59.4	64.2	44.5
1971	66.9	94.7	84.7	60.1	66.5	44.7
1972	67.1	94.2	83.5	60.8	67.8	45.5
1973	67.9	94.3	82.7	60.1	69.8	46.3
1974	70.5	94.5	82.0	63.5	71.4	47.6
1975	72.4	95.2	82.0	66.1	74.2	49.6
1976	72.9	95.7	81.3	67.7	75.6	50.2
1977	71.9	95.5	79.7	68.0	77.5	51.7
1978	70.8	95.3	79.1	68.1	79.3	53.3
1979	71.8	95.3	79.2	69.7	81.1	54.5
1980	71.5	95.4	78.7	70.1	82.9	55.3
1981	67.9	94.9	78.4	67.8	84.8	57.5
1982	67.0	94.9	77.7	66.4	85.8	58.9
1983	65.7	95.0	77.1	65.1	87.0	59.7
1984	64.6	94.9	76.2	64.8	88.1	59.6
1985	65.7	95.2	76.0	66.4	88.9	59.9

Table 5B.3   (continued)

Year	Males			Females		
	16–24	25–54	55–64	16–24	25–54	55–64
1986	65.2	95.3	75.5	65.6	89.8	61.4
1987	66.1	94.7	74.9	66.6	90.4	64.1
1988	67.9	94.7	74.9	67.8	90.8	64.7
1989	69.4	95.1	74.8	69.0	91.0	64.3
1990	68.9	95.1	75.5	67.7	91.3	66.3
1991	65.3	94.6	75.5	64.4	90.5	66.9
1992	58.6	93.6	73.6	58.4	89.5	65.9

Source: AKU surveys.
Note: Since 1987, the method used by the AKU to measure unemployment and hence labor force participation changed slightly.

Table 5B.4   **Hours of Work per Week by Age and Gender, 1963–92**

Year	Males			Females		
	16–24	25–54	55–64	16–24	25–54	55–64
1963	43.6	47.1	46.0	40.7	34.0	34.6
1964	43.7	46.4	45.2	40.7	33.9	33.6
1965	43.8	46.5	45.7	40.4	33.3	33.0
1966	43.3	46.1	45.8	39.5	32.6	31.9
1967	42.6	45.6	44.6	38.9	32.6	32.0
1968	41.6	44.7	43.9	37.9	32.0	31.9
1969	41.5	44.8	43.6	36.8	32.0	32.1
1970	40.8	44.6	43.8	36.9	31.9	31.2
1971	40.2	43.8	43.6	36.4	31.7	31.1
1972	38.2	42.4	42.1	35.3	31.0	30.6
1973	38.0	42.1	41.9	35.1	31.1	30.0
1974	38.0	42.1	41.8	36.0	31.1	30.0
1975	38.0	41.8	41.6	34.4	31.2	30.0
1976	38.1	41.8	41.1	34.0	30.9	29.9
1977	37.6	41.4	40.4	33.5	30.7	29.5
1978	37.3	41.3	39.9	33.3	30.7	29.0
1979	37.3	41.2	39.7	33.0	30.8	29.2
1980	37.2	41.2	39.2	33.0	30.8	29.4
1981	37.0	41.0	39.1	32.7	30.9	29.1
1982	37.1	41.1	39.1	32.6	31.3	29.2
1983	36.8	41.2	39.6	32.4	31.5	29.5
1984	37.1	41.6	39.5	32.1	31.9	29.9
1985	37.2	41.6	39.8	32.4	32.3	30.5
1986	37.0	41.6	39.6	32.4	32.5	30.8
1987	37.7	42.4	40.4	32.7	33.2	30.6
1988	37.6	42.5	39.9	33.1	33.6	31.0
1989	37.5	42.7	39.9	33.3	34.0	31.4
1990	37.5	42.6	40.0	33.1	34.3	31.6
1991	37.2	42.2	39.5	32.7	34.1	31.5
1992	36.7	42.3	38.9	32.2	34.1	31.4

Source: AKU surveys.

Appendix C
Econometric Issues Surrounding Recent Estimates of Labor Supply

In an area so dominated by econometric issues, it is difficult to avoid these issues in our discussion of the literature. Indeed, understanding these issues should also help understand the wide range of elasticities shown in tables 5.2 and 5.3 above.

Until the mid-1970s, the literature either neglected taxes and transfer programs in the estimation of the labor supply function or tried to incorporate it using relatively simple methods. For example, a common approach was to linearize the budget constraint around the observed hours of work—a method that, in the presence of steeply progressive tax schedules, fails to recognize the endogeneity of the marginal wage rate (a review of this literature can be found in, e.g., Heckman and MaCurdy [1981]). The more recent literature, which represents the budget set as a series of piecewise linear segments, arose as a procedure for incorporating the endogeneity of the marginal wage rate in estimation. In principle, such an approach can be used to represent any budget constraint and can therefore be used to handle complexities such as nonlinearities and nonconvexities (e.g., poverty traps, kinks, and flats) during the estimation. The generality is more illusionary than real, however, because numerical problems effectively prohibit all but simple assumptions of the source of stochastic disturbances (Heckman and MaCurdy 1981).

Several criticisms can be directed at the taxes and labor supply literature. First, until recently, labor supply analysts have put their main effort into locating the "kinks" in the consumer's budget set (see the special issue of the *Journal of Human Resources,* vol. 20, no. 3 [1990]). Because of the aforementioned computational limitations, the focus on nonlinearities and "kinks" in the choice set has, to a large extent, restricted the representation of consumer preferences to the individual, static (and often linear) labor supply model, while richer behavioral specifications went unexplored. Consequently, the labor supply research became more focused on the (one-period) trade-off between consumption and leisure, as other important dimensions of the labor supply were, to a large extent, neglected. For example, the assumption of exogenous gross wage rates neglects the possibility that labor supply is part of a decision involving human capital accumulation. A third line of criticism recognizes that structural econometric models impose restrictions on the labor supply parameters. Below, we briefly review some of this criticism and discuss its importance for the reliability of the results presented in previous subsections.

Papers such as MaCurdy, Green, and Paarsch (1990) and Blundell, Duncan, and Meghir (1993) show that there is a relation between integrability conditions (i.e., the Slutsky condition) and the model's statistical coherence (the latter is needed to ensure meaningful probability statements). Satisfaction of the Slutsky condition is necessary for the estimated labor supply model to fulfill the axioms of choice. The welfare analysis of tax reform presented above is valid only if the Slutsky condition is fulfilled. In the case of labor supply models under piecewise linear budget constraints—once the problem is made stochastic by the introduction of unobserved heterogeneity—there is a strong link between integrability conditions and coherency. More precisely, statistical coherency requires that the model fulfill the Slutsky condition. As a consequence, the estimated model is not a suitable framework for testing hypotheses related to the axioms of choice. The latter is a particular problem for the linear labor supply model since coherency in this case may require a forward-sloping labor supply curve everywhere, but the discussion easily generalizes to nonlinear labor supply functions as well. Therefore, one of the more recent topics in the labor supply research has been to develop estimation methods that eliminate or at least weaken the link between coherency and integrability conditions (see, e.g., Blundell, Duncan, and Meghir 1993). There have also been attempts to weaken the link between local coherency conditions and the global properties of the model by using more flexible specifications of consumer preferences.

It is also important to examine to what extent the common choice of linear labor supply functions has affected the conclusions concerning the labor supply responses to wages, nonlabor income, and the tax system. For example, Blundell, Duncan, and Meghir (1993) find evidence of backward-bending labor supply curves for part of the sample of British women using a more flexible model. However, for Sweden, the choice of a linear labor supply function appears to be less restrictive. While Blomquist and Hansson-Brusewitz (1990) found evidence in favor of the quadratic labor supply function for men, their counterfactual policy simulations of these specifications yield similar predictions. In a nonlinear labor supply model accounting for quantity constraints, Aronsson and Karlsson (1993) found no evidence of a backward-bending labor supply curve for men. Moreover, their study also found that the behavioral differences between a linear and a nonlinear model are small. For women, we are, as expected, less conclusive about the restrictiveness of commonly used functional forms because of the wide dispersion of the results. However, Aronsson (1991) estimates a nonlinear labor supply function for women, accounting for both taxes and quantity constraints, and found no evidence in favor of a backward-bending labor supply curve.

Another line of criticism questions the assumption that the gross wage rate and nonlabor income are exogenous (Flood and MaCurdy 1992). Flood and MaCurdy (1992) present estimates for several specifications of male labor supply functions under different estimation methods and exogeneity assumptions. When they fit a linear labor supply function assuming a convex budget set and that wages and nonlabor income are exogenous, Flood and MaCurdy (1992) estimate a negative income elasticity, a small positive uncompensated wage elasticity, and a small positive compensated wage elasticity (the first column of Flood and MaCurdy estimates in table 5.2 above). They recover qualitatively the same labor supply elasticities when they change the estimation method from a maximum-likelihood estimator to an instrumental variables estimator while maintaining all other assumptions of the previous specifications (row 2 of the Flood and MaCurdy estimates in table 5.2). However, when the gross wage and nonlabor income are considered endogenous (row 3 of the Flood and MaCurdy estimates in table 5.2), their instrumental variables estimator yields a positive income elasticity, a large (in absolute value) negative uncompensated wage elasticity, and a negative compensated wage elasticity. Hence, relaxing the assumed exogeneity of wages and nonlabor income leads to a violation of the Slutsky equation (i.e., the negative compensated wage elasticity). Flood and MaCurdy conclude that their instrumental variables results give strong support for considering richer specifications of labor supply behavior—life-cycle and household models of labor supply. However, in apparent neglect of the same evidence, the authors conclude that their instrumental variables results treating gross wages and nonlabor income as endogenous are most likely to be correct. Unfortunately, Flood and MaCurdy do not elaborate or support this conclusion.[36] Moreover, to generalize from their specification requires evidences that the convex budget set procedures work well in the presence of nonconvex budget sets. The latter is a problem, especially when the nonconvexities appear near the observed hours of work, which may be the case for low-income earners according to the budget sets described in section 5.6.1 above.

References

Aarberge, R., J. K. Dagsvik, and S. Strom. 1993. The Swedish tax reform: Labor supply, income distribution and excess burden. University of Oslo. Typescript.

Agell, A. 1979. Social security and family law in Sweden. In *Social security and family law*, ed. Alec Samuels. London: United Kingdom Comparative Law Series.

Andersson, I. A.-K. 1989. Familjebeskattning, konsumtion, och arbetsutbud: En ekonometrisk analys av löne- och inkomstelasticiteter samt policysimuleringar för svenska Hushåll. Ph.D. diss., Gothenburg University.

36. As is usual when reviewing instrumental variables estimates, one can argue with the choice of instruments that are assumed always to be exogenous. For Flood and MaCurdy (1992), these variables are husband's and wife's educational attainment, interaction between the husband's education and his age and age squared, and several demographic variables, including the number of children younger than seven years old in the household, the number of people in the household, whether the household owns or rents its home, an age dummy (for younger than fifty-five years old), and an urban residence dummy. All these can be considered endogenous from the perspective of the wider class of behavioral models that they support. Without additional evidence, it is not clear whether the endogeneity problems operate through the wage and nonlabor income variables or through the maintained set of "exogenous" variables.

Andersson, I. A.-K., and B. Gustafsson. 1992. Modeling poverty traps and marginal effects in Sweden. Gothenburg University. Typescript.

Andersson, I. A.-K., and N. A. Klevmarken. 1993. What does the budget set tell us about labor supply? Paper presented at the conference Fiscal Incentives and Labor Supply in the Nordic Countries, 1–2 April 1993, Uppsala.

Andersson, K. 1986. The Swedish tax system. University of Lund. Typescript.

Aronsson, T. 1991. Nonlinear taxation and minimum hours constraints in a model of women's labor supply. Economic Studies no. 256. University of Umeå.

———. 1993. Labour supply and tax reform in the neoclassical model of household behavior. University of Umeå. Typescript.

Aronsson, T., and N. Karlsson. 1993. Taxes and quantity constraints in a model of male labour supply in Sweden. Economic Studies no. 302. University of Umeå.

Aronsson, T., and M. Palme. 1994. A decade of tax and benefit reforms in Sweden—effects on labour supply, welfare and inequality. Economic Studies no. 351. University of Umeå.

Ashenfelter, O., and J. Heckman. 1974. The estimation of income and substitution effects in a model of family labor supply. *Econometrica* 42:73–85.

Atkinson, A. B. 1987. Social insurance. In *The handbook of public economics,* vol. 2, ed. A. Auerbach and M. Feldstein. New York: North-Holland.

———. 1993. Conclusions. In *Welfare and work incentives: A North European perspective,* ed. A. B. Atkinson and G. V. Mogensen. New York: Clarendon.

Auerbach, A. 1985. The theory of excess burden and optimal taxation. In *The handbook of public economics,* vol. 1, ed. A. Auerbach and M. Feldstein. New York: North-Holland.

Ballard, C., J. K. Scholz, and J. Shoven. 1987. The value-added tax: A general equilibrium look at its efficiency and incidence. In *The effects of taxation on capital accumulation,* ed. M. Feldstein. Chicago: University of Chicago Press.

Becker, G. S. 1962. Irrational behavior and economic theory. *Journal of Political Economy* 70:1–13.

Björklund, A. 1991. Vem får sjukpenning? En empirick analys av sjukfrånvarons bestamningsfaktorer. Expertrapport nr 4 till Produktivitet Delegationen. Stockholm.

Blinder, A., and Y. Weiss. 1976. Human capital and labor supply: A synthesis. *Journal of Political Economy* 84:449–72.

Blomquist, N. S. 1983. The effect of income taxation on the labor supply of married men in Sweden. *Journal of Public Economics* 22:169–97.

———. 1985. Labor supply in a two-period model: The effect of a nonlinear progressive income tax. *Review of Economic Studies* 52:515–24.

———. 1989. Beskattningens effekter på arbetsutbudet (The impact of taxation on labor supply). Del 4, bilaga 7i Statens Offentliga Utredningar (SOU) 1989:33 angående reformerad inkomstbeskattning. Stockholm.

Blomquist, N. S., and U. Hansson-Brusewitz. 1990. The effect of taxes on male and female labor supply in Sweden. *Journal of Human Resources* 25:317–57.

Blundell, R., A. Duncan, and C. Meghir. 1993. Tax policy reform and the robust estimation of labour supply responses. University College London. Typescript.

Blundell, R., C. Meghir, E. Symons, and I. Walker. 1988. Labor supply specification and the evaluation of tax reforms. *Journal of Public Economics* 36:23–52.

Blundell, R., and I. Walker. 1982. Modeling the joint determination of household labor supplies and commodity demands. *Economic Journal* 92:351–64.

———. 1986. A life-cycle consistent empirical model of family labour supply using cross-section data. *Review of Economic Studies* 53:539–58.

Cowell, F. A. 1990. *Cheating the government: The economics of Evasion.* Cambridge, Mass.: MIT Press.

Deaton, A., and J. Muellbauer. 1980. *Economics and consumer behavior.* New York: Cambridge University Press.

Edin, P.-A., and B. Holmlund. 1993. The Swedish wage structure: The rise and fall of solidarity wage policy? Working Paper no. 4257. Cambridge, Mass.: National Bureau of Economic Research.

Einhorn, E. S., and J. Logue. 1989. *Modern welfare states: Politics and policies in Social Democratic Scandinavia.* New York: Praeger.

Feldstein, M. 1993. The effect of marginal tax rates on taxable income: A panel study of the 1986 Tax Reform Act. Harvard University. Typescript.

Flood, L., and T. MaCurdy. 1992. Work disincentive effects of taxes: An empirical analysis of Swedish men. University of Gothenburg. Typescript.

Gustafsson, B., and A. Klevmarken. 1993. Taxes and transfers in Sweden: Incentive effects on labor supply. In *Welfare and work incentives: A North European perspective,* ed. A. B. Atkinson and G. V. Mogensen. New York: Clarendon.

Gustafsson, S., and F. Stafford. 1992. Child care subsidies and labor supply in Sweden. *Journal of Human Resources* 27:204–30.

Hansson, I. 1984. Marginal cost of public funds for different tax instruments and government expenditures. *Scandinavian Journal of Economics* 86:115–30.

Hansson-Brusewitz, U. 1992. Labor supply of elderly men: Do taxes and pension systems matter? Ph.D. diss., Uppsala University.

Hausman, J. 1981. Labor supply. In *How taxes affect economic behavior,* ed. Henry J. Aaron and Joseph A. Pechman. Washington, D.C.: Brookings.

———. 1985. Labor supply and taxes. In *The handbook of public economics,* vol. 1, ed. Alan Auerbach and Martin Feldstein. New York: North-Holland.

Hausman, J., and P. Ruud. 1984. Family labor supply with taxes. *American Economic Review: Papers and Proceedings* 74:242–48.

Heckman, J. 1976. A life cycle model of earnings, learning, and consumption. *Journal of Political Economy* 84 (August): S11–S44.

Heckman, J., and T. MaCurdy. 1980. A life cycle model of female labor supply. *Review of Economic Studies* 47:47–74.

———. 1981. New methods for estimating labor supply functions: A survey. *Research in Labor Economics* 4:65–102.

Henrekson, M., K. Lantto, and M. Persson. 1992. *Bruk och missbruk av sjukförsäkringen.* Stockholm: SNS Förlag.

Huber, E., and J. D. Stephens. 1993. The Swedish welfare state at the crossroads. In *Current Sweden.* Stockholm: Swedish Institute.

Johansson, P., and M. Palme. 1993. The effect of economic incentives on worker absenteeism: An empirical study using Swedish micro data. Department of Economics, University of Umeå.

Johnson, P. 1993. Aging and European economic demography. In *Labor markets in an aging europe,* ed. P. Johnson and K. F. Zimmermann. Cambridge: Cambridge University Press.

Kapteyn, A., P. Kooreman, and A. van Soest. 1990. *Quantity constraints and concavity in a flexible household labor supply model. Review of Economics and Statistics* 72:55–62.

Killingsworth, M. 1983. *Labor supply.* Cambridge: Cambridge University Press.

Killingsworth, M., and J. Heckman. 1986. Female labor supply: A survey. In *Handbook of labor economics,* vol. 1, ed. O. Ashenfelter and R. Layard. New York: North-Holland.

King, M. 1987. Empirical analysis of tax reforms. In *Advances in econometrics,* vol. 2, ed. T. Bewley. Cambridge: Cambridge University Press.

Lindbeck, A. 1993. Overshooting, reform and retreat of the welfare state. The Seventh

Tinbergen Lecture, delivered 1 October 1993, at the de Nederlandsche Bank, Amsterdam.

Lindbeck, A., P. Molander, T. Persson, O. Petersson, A. Sandmo, B. Swedenborg, and N. Thygesen. 1993. Options for economic and political reform in Sweden. *Economic Policy* 17:220–63.

———. 1994. *Turning Sweden around.* Cambridge, Mass.: MIT Press.

Lindbeck, A., T. Persson, and A. Sandmo. In press. Options for economic and political reform in Sweden. *Economic Policy.*

Lodin, S.-O. N.d. The Swedish tax system and the Swedish tax reform of 1991. Stockholm: Federation of Swedish Industries. Typescript.

MaCurdy, T. 1981. An empirical model of labor supply in a life cycle setting. *Journal of Political Economy* 89:1059–85.

MaCurdy, T., D. Green, and H. Paarsch. 1990. Assessing empirical approaches for analyzing taxes and labor supply. *Journal of Human Resources* 25:415–89.

Mroz, T. 1987. The sensitivity of an empirical model of married women's hours of work to economic and statistical assumptions. *Econometrica* 55:765–800.

Pedersen, P. 1993. The welfare state and taxation in Denmark. In *Welfare and work incentives: A north European perspective,* ed. A. B. Atkinson and G. V. Mogensen. New York: Clarendon.

Pencavel, J. 1986. Labor supply of men: A survey. In *Handbook of labor economics,* vol. 1, ed. O. Ashenfelter and R. Layard. New York: North-Holland.

Sandmo, A. 1985. The effects of taxation on savings and risk taking. In *The handbook of public economics,* vol. 1, ed. A. Auerbach and M. Feldstein. New York: North-Holland.

Scholz, J. K. 1993. Tax progressivity and household portfolios: Descriptive evidence from the Surveys of Consumer Finances. Paper prepared for the Office of Tax Policy Research Conference on Tax Progressivity, 11–12 September 1992, Ann Arbor, Mich.

Slemrod, J. 1992. On the high-income Laffer curve. Paper prepared for the Office of Tax Policy Research Conference on Tax Progressivity, 11–12 September 1992, Ann Arbor, Mich.

Triest, R. 1992. The effect of income taxation on labor supply when deductions are endogenous. *Review of Economics and Statistics* 74:91–99.

Vogel, J. 1974. Taxation and public opinion in Sweden: An interpretation of recent survey data. *National Tax Journal* 28:499–513.

Wadensjö, E. 1985. Disability pensioning of older workers in Sweden: A comparison of studies based on time-series and cross-section data. Working Paper no. 15/1985. Institute for Social Research, University of Stockholm.

Walker, J. R. 1995. The effect of public policies on recent fertility behavior in Sweden. *Journal of Population Economics* 8:223–51.

Wärneryd, K.-E., and B. Walerud. 1982. Taxes and economic behavior: Some interview data on tax evasion in Sweden. *Journal of Economic Psychology* 2:187–211.

Wilson, D. 1979. *The welfare state in Sweden.* London: Heinemann.

Zimmermann, K. 1993. Labour responses to taxes and benefits in Germany. In *Welfare and work incentives: A North European perspective,* ed. A. B. Atkinson and G. V. Mogensen. New York: Clarendon.

6   An Evaluation of the Swedish Active Labor Market Policy: New and Received Wisdom

Anders Forslund and Alan B. Krueger

A visitor to Sweden is struck by the breadth and generosity of the labor market programs designed to limit the adverse effects of unemployment and expand employment. These programs include extensive job training, public sector relief work, recruitment subsidies, youth programs, mobility bonuses, and unemployment benefits. About 3 percent of GNP was spent on government labor market programs in Sweden in 1990, compared to 2 percent in Germany and less than 0.5 percent in the United States. Several prominent observers have argued that the active Swedish labor market policies are responsible for the enviable unemployment experience of Sweden in the 1970s and 1980s. Layard, Nickell, and Jackman (1991, 473) go so far as to recommend that Sweden's "active labor market" programs serve as a model for other countries.

Figure 6.1 illustrates the Swedish unemployment rate semiannually over the past twenty-five years. In the 1970s, Sweden managed to maintain a low unemployment rate in the face of adverse oil price shocks that caused high unemployment and severe recessions in other industrialized countries. The unemployment rate in Sweden also remained low in the 1980s, while it trended upward in other European countries. But a dramatic increase in the unemployment rate can be seen beginning in 1991. In July 1993, the U.S. Bureau of Labor Statistics calculated that the unemployment rate in Sweden reached 9.5 percent, on a comparable basis to the U.S. unemployment concept. The U.S. rate at the same time was 6.8 percent. For the first time in our lifetimes, the

y are grateful to Anders Björklund, Per-Anders Edin, Richard Freeman, Bertil Holmlund, Lawrence Katz, Birgitta Swedenborg, Bob Topel, and two reviewers for helpful comments. Naturally, the authors are responsible for any errors.

267

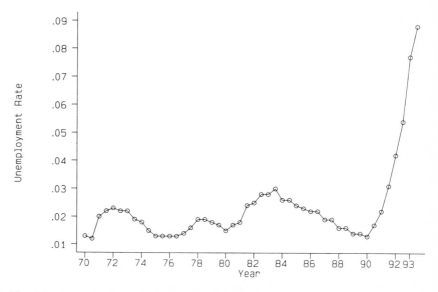

Fig. 6.1   Swedish unemployment rate, by half year, 1970–93

unemployment rate is higher in Sweden than in the United States! The dramatic increase in unemployment in Sweden over the last two years casts doubt on the ability of the active labor market policies to blunt unemployment. At the same time, Sweden's history of low unemployment in the 1980s suggests that its labor market programs are not responsible for the 1991–93 downturn because the programs were substantially as generous in the 1980s as in the early 1990s.

The expense of the Swedish labor market programs may be justifiable if they produce benefits that exceed their costs. But the programs are a very expensive luxury if unemployment is high and if the programs are not effective at reducing unemployment or raising workers' skills. Given the rising level of unemployment and other changes in the Swedish economy, an assessment of the effectiveness of the active labor market programs is especially timely.

As the pattern in figure 6.1 suggests, macroeconomic indicators can give a possibly misleading indication of the efficacy of Sweden's labor market policies. In this paper, we first review microeconometric evidence on two major active labor market programs in Sweden: public relief work and job training. One concern with public relief work is that such programs may displace other workers. We provide new evidence on "fiscal substitution" between public relief workers and other workers using county-level data. Specifically, we find evidence that public relief workers tend to displace private construction workers, which potentially limits the usefulness of public relief workers in reducing unemployment. The evidence is less clear on whether relief workers displace social welfare workers, which is another major sector in which relief workers are dispatched.

We also review previous evidence on the effect of job-training programs on wages and reemployment probabilities. Owing to the small samples used in past studies, we find it very difficult to draw precise conclusions about the payoff to job-training programs. In sum, our view of the microeconometric evidence is that one should remain agnostic about the effectiveness of job-training and public relief programs in fighting unemployment.

We then attempt to reconcile the macroeconomic and international evidence—which has been cited by many as support for the effectiveness of Sweden's active labor market programs—with the microeconometric evidence. We first provide evidence on the stability of the Beveridge curve in the 1980s across counties in Sweden. One possible explanation for the stable Beveridge curve is that rapid expansion of public sector employment has absorbed unemployed workers. We test this hypothesis with county-level data and find little support for it. Second, we evaluate and update the cross-country unemployment rate analysis that Layard, Nickell, and Jackman (1991) and others have performed. Using 1993 unemployment rate data, we find that greater spending on active labor market programs has a statistically insignificant and positive effect on unemployment. This finding is in sharp contrast with estimates for the 1980s. We also discuss several statistical limitations of the cross-country approach.

Finally, we present evidence on the reaction of employment and unemployment to regional shocks in Sweden. Specifically, we compare our findings on regional evolutions in Sweden to comparable results for the United States based on Blanchard and Katz (1992) and for the rest of Europe based on De-cressin and Fatas (1993). These results suggest that Sweden's response to shocks is not particularly different from other countries', implying that Sweden's extensive labor market programs have not had a marked effect on regional labor market adjustments.

In our judgment, the evidence provides little support for the view that Sweden's past success in maintaining low unemployment stemmed primarily from its active labor market policies. On the other hand, the extensive labor market programs in Sweden are most likely not the cause of Sweden's current economic crisis. But our analysis of the evolution of unemployment suggests that there is a real danger that the current high level of unemployment will persist for some time in the future. We conclude by considering policies that might help improve the active labor market programs in the current economic climate.

6.1 Overview of Programs

By way of background, it should be noted that, within the central blue-collar trade union (LO) in the early 1950s, the question of how to combine full employment and price stability was discussed.[1] These discussions led to the formulation of a program subsequently adopted by the Social Democratic government, based on a few cornerstones, one of which was active labor market policies. First, LO would pursue a so-called solidaristic wage policy. In its original form, this policy aimed at "equal pay for equal work," irrespective of the productivity levels of individual firms. Later, the policy principle (still under the same name) changed to one of unconditional wage equalization, or "equal pay for unequal work." Second, a strict stance of stabilization policies (primarily fiscal policy) was advocated in order to keep inflation low. One intended result of these two principles was shut downs of low-productivity firms and layoffs. This motivated the third cornerstone of the program, "active labor market policies," which were given the role of transferring laid-off workers to expanding high-productivity firms.

Two points about the origin of the programs are worth noting. First, labor market policies are not considered a substitute for stabilization policies. Second, labor market policies entail the so-called work principle—the aim of the programs is to accomplish a smooth and rapid transfer of laid-off workers to new employment rather than to provide welfare for the unemployed (i.e., "workfare" rather than welfare). Starting in the 1950s, a system of manpower policy emerged based on active labor market policies. The present system can be described in terms of the following main ingredients: unemployment insurance, measures to create employment, mobility-enhancing measures, and measures targeted at the handicapped.

6.1.1 Unemployment Insurance

Unemployment compensation is provided in two forms: First, there are a number of so-called certified unemployment insurance (UI) funds, run by the trade unions at the industry level, but to a large extent tax financed. In 1990, the coverage was slightly less than 80 percent of the labor force. Second, in addition to the UI system administered by the trade unions, since 1974 there has also been a supplementary compensation system (*kontant arbetsmarknadsstöd,* KAS), mainly designed for new entrants in the labor market, who usually are not members of any UI fund. UI fund members are entitled to compensation for 300 days (450 days for workers over age fifty-five), whereas cash benefit assistance runs for 150 days (300 days for those over age fifty-five, 450 days for those over age sixty). Daily compensation in the UI fund system is, within limits, fixed by the government regulating minimum and maximum levels at 80 percent (90 percent before 5 July 1993) of the recipient's normal income prior to unemployment. The level of compensation in cash benefit assistance is significantly lower than the average paid by the certified UI funds (in 1990, SKr 174 vs. SKr 402 per day). Carling et al. (1996) find that the duration of

---

1. For excellent overviews of the labor market programs, see Björklund (1990), Calmfors (1993), Flanagan (1987), and Stafford (1981).

unemployment spells for those on KAS benefits is only slightly shorter than for those on UI benefits, in spite of the large benefit differential.

A special feature of the UI fund system is that fund coverage roughly coincides with wage-bargaining units, as the funds are run by trade unions at the industry level. But the state grants to the UI funds are designed so that the marginal cost of extra unemployment among a fund's members is zero.[2]

A number of criteria, many of which are common to the UI funds and KAS, have to be met in order for a person to be entitled to unemployment compensation. The two most important conditions are that recipients actively search for a job at a public employment office and that an offer of "suitable" work must be accepted. Refusal to accept a job offer might lead to expulsion from compensation. To receive compensation from a UI fund, a "membership condition" and a "work condition" have to be met: the claimant must have paid membership fees to the UI fund for at least twelve months and must have been working for at least seventy-five days distributed over at least four months during the twelve months preceding the current unemployment spell. Participation in relief work as well as in labor market retraining programs counts as work in this respect.

Workers who do not meet the membership condition are entitled to KAS benefits if they meet either a work requirement of roughly the same type as for UI fund compensation or an "education condition." The education condition is met if individuals have finished at least one year of school in excess of the nine compulsory years and searched for a job at a public employment office for at least ninety days.

As the duration of compensation is limited in principle, the system also creates incentives to find a job before compensation runs out.[3] This aspect has been stressed by Layard, Nickell, and Jackman (1991) as a key factor behind the high observed Swedish real wage sensitivity to changes in unemployment. This, in turn, is a potential explanation for Sweden's favorable unemployment experiences during the 1980s. It is important to note, however, that the system has recently changed. Since the late 1980s, participation in labor market programs qualifies for new periods of unemployment compensation, so in practice there is no limit on the amount of time a jobless person can spend outside the regular labor market by switching between training and unemployment compensation.[4] There is some indirect evidence suggesting that this is the case: Axelsson and Löfgren (1992), studying the effects of retraining programs on income, found a significant positive effect on those who finished training pro-

---

2. Changes in the UI system initiated in 1994 make membership compulsory and add funds administered by the state.

3. When unemployment compensation runs out, individuals are eligible for social security, which offers significantly less generous compensation.

4. The change in the system pertains to training programs; relief work has always been considered "work."

grams in 1981, whereas Regnér (1993) finds significant negative income effects for 1989 and 1990 program participants. A possible explanation for this difference is that, in the latter period, training qualified for unemployment compensation, so the negative income effect therefore reflects negative selection of program participants. Unfortunately, there is a lack of direct evidence (e.g., in the form of event histories) on the extent of a "circular flow" between unemployment and programs.

6.1.2 Measures to Create Employment

The principal measure to create employment has for a long time been public relief work. The primary stated aim is to counteract temporary downturns in labor demand, but relief jobs have also been targeted for groups with permanently high unemployment risks. Unemployed UI fund members who run out of unemployment compensation are in principle granted the right to a relief job. To qualify for a relief job, one must be registered as an unemployed job applicant at a public employment office for a minimum number of days (about a week). The duration of relief jobs is normally capped at six months, and payment is according to collective agreement in the regular labor market. Relief workers are obliged to accept suitable job offers and can be expelled from relief jobs on refusal. Relief work can be arranged by central or local governments or (rarely) by the private sector. The typical relief job has traditionally been in building and road construction, but the emphasis has gradually changed to jobs in health and welfare. From the "workfare" point of view, relief work offers a "work test": if the employment office fails to find a suitable job for the applicant, it can test his or her willingness to work by offering a relief job.

Recruitment subsidies, introduced in 1984, aim at facilitating employment for the long-term unemployed and at creating permanent jobs in the local public sector for the long-term or partially unemployed. Subsidies normally amount to at most 60 percent of the total wage cost and can be given for a maximum of 6 months.

Beginning in 1984, a variety of special "youth measures" have been used, and their use has intensified recently. The most recent form (introduced in July 1992) is called *youth practice* and is targeted at youths between eighteen and twenty-four years of age. Participants receive compensation roughly equal to unemployment benefits, and employers receive free labor. In addition to keeping participants out of unemployment, youth practice offers a work test of the same kind as relief work. The combination of youth practice and a deep recession is believed to have weakened significantly the incentives to hire youths.

Finally, since January 1993, the unemployed can prolong their period of unemployment compensation by taking part in so-called labor market developments. These last for at most six months, and the participant receives income equivalent to unemployment compensation benefits. The employer, normally organizations, associations, or the public sector, gets free labor. To prevent crowding out, participants are supposed to perform duties that would otherwise not have been performed. As the number of participants has increased rapidly, this last condition might prove to pose problems: either participants do what they are supposed to do, in which case large numbers of people perform superfluous tasks, or, alternatively, crowding out will prove to be an important issue.

6.1.3 Mobility-Enhancing Measures

The traditional mobility-enhancing measure is the employment service administration. The Swedish employment service is not limited to just a brokerage function—another important function is to administer both unemployment insurance and selection to labor market programs. A distinguishing feature of the Swedish setup regarding job brokerage is that the public employment service has had a legal monopoly position. Since the late 1970s, there has also been compulsory notification of vacancies through the public employment service.[5]

Another mobility enhancing measure is "mobility grants/starting allowances." These grants are intended to facilitate geographic mobility by making moving an economically feasible alternative to unemployment in the home region. To qualify, one must be an unemployed person looking for a job in another region through the public unemployment service. Other, more strict criteria, such as belonging to certain "scarce" professions, have also been applicable from time to time.

Last, but not least, among the mobility-enhancing measures is labor market retraining. The official aims are to help the unemployed or those facing unemployment risks get a job, help those with little education or obsolete education attain a stronger position in the labor market, and help firms find workers with adequate education. Labor market retraining comes in many different forms and is produced by a plethora of educational institutions on requisition by county-level authorities under the National Labor Market Board. Retraining eligibility is conditional on being unemployed or facing the risk of unemployment and job search through public employment service. Compensation under retraining programs is roughly equivalent to unemployment compensation.

6.1.4 Measures Targeted for the Disabled

There are four basic measures targeted at the disabled: employment in community enterprises, public sheltered work, wage-subsidized employment, and vocational rehabilitation. A common feature of these measures is that their goal is to provide work for those who, owing to various disabilities, have difficulty obtaining employment in the regular labor market.

---

5. One side benefit of the employment service's monopoly is that Swedish vacancy data are likely to be of high quality.

Table 6.1   Comparison of Labor Market Policies in Sweden, the United States, and Germany

Labor Market Policy	Sweden		United States, 1990	Germany, 1990
	1982	1990		
Average unemployment compensation per recipient[a]	10,843	17,655	2,111	12,782
Average training costs per recipient[b]	9,214	6,568	2,035	N.A.
Trainees as a proportion of labor force[c]	.0085	.0094	.0103	.0102
Trainees as a proportion of unemployed[c]	.32	.62	.19	.16
Public relief workers as a proportion of unemployed	.39	.12	.00	.04
Proportion of GNP devoted to labor market policies[d]	.039	.028	.004	.021

Sources: Unemployment benefit data for United States are from 1991 Green Book, p. 466. Training data for the United States are from 1991 Green Book, pp. 1454–56, and pertain to JTPA IIA, and JTPA IIB, and Job Corps programs. Swedish data are from *Statistisk Arsbok 1992* and *OECD Economic Surveys*. German data are from Statistisches Bundesamt (1993) and *Zahlen zur Wirtschaftlichtlichen Entwicklung der Bundersrepublik Deutschland 1992,* Institut der Deutschen Wirtschaft.

Note: All monetary figures (rows 1 and 2) are in 1990 U.S. dollars. Swedish kronor were converted to dollars using the exchange rate and were converted from 1982 to 1990 dollars with the CPI-U. N.A. = not available.

[a]Only certified UI fund benefits are included for Sweden.

[b]Net training costs are reported for Sweden (i.e., average unemployment benefits have been subtracted off). For the United States, training programs include the Job Training Partnership Act (JTPA) and the Job Corps.

[c]Only trainees who receive government compensation are included for Germany.

[d]Policies included in U.S. figure are job training, summer youth employment, unemployment benefits, and employment services. Policies included in Sweden figure include job training, relief worker, youth measures, unemployment benefits, and handicapped programs. Policies included for Germany include unemployment benefits, retraining, employment services, preretirement benefits, subsidized employment programs, compensation for short-time workers, compensation of construction workers during inclement weather, and administrative costs.

6.1.5   Quantitative Description

Table 6.1 summarizes the magnitude of key labor market programs in Sweden, the United States, and Germany in various years. It is clear that Sweden spends much more on training and unemployment benefits per recipient than the United States. Sweden's unemployment benefits are particularly generous by comparison to the United States.[6] Since workers who are in training programs also qualify for unemployment benefits, the total amount spent on work-

6. Sweden reduced its replacement ratio by 10 percentage points in 1993, but benefits are still well above the U.S. level.

ers undergoing training is roughly of the same order of magnitude as the cost of tuition, room, and board for a year at Harvard![7]

Readers may be surprised to see, however, that 1 percent of the labor force is enrolled in public training programs in the United States, which is slightly *higher* than the comparable figure for Sweden or Germany. This fact casts some doubt on the relative importance of "disguised unemployment" in labor market programs in Sweden. Even if one counted all Sweden's workers who are on training or public relief programs as unemployed, the unemployment rate in the 1980s would have increased only by roughly 1 percentage point. Thus, disguised unemployment cannot account for much of Sweden's historically low unemployment rate.

Although the proportion of the labor force receiving training is about the same, a much higher proportion of the unemployed undergo training in a given year in Sweden than in the United States. In 1990, government training participants represented 62 percent of the number of unemployed workers. Moreover, a sizable proportion of the unemployed are also placed in public relief jobs in Sweden, a program for which there is no current analog in the United States. Sweden devotes about 3 percent of GNP to labor market programs, which exceeds the amount spent in Germany (2.1 percent) and the United States (0.4 percent). The increase in unemployment in Sweden in the past two years can be expected to cause a substantial increase in expenditures on labor market programs relative to GNP.

The changing importance of some of the main Swedish labor market programs is illustrated in figure 6.2. The figure presents the proportion of the labor force that is directly involved in retraining, relief work, youth programs, or recruitment subsidies. A number of features stand out. First, relief work shows a clear countercyclic pattern. Second, the incidence of relief work has trended steadily downward in the 1980s. Third, labor market retraining has not had the same cyclic variability as relief work, again except for the past few years. Fourth, the incidence of retraining gradually trended upward in the 1980s. As a result of these contrasting trends, the relative importance of retraining has grown in the 1980s and 1990s, while the relative importance of public relief work has declined. Sixth, there has been a dramatic increase in the prevalence of youth measures in recent years. Finally, the incidence of retraining measures declined in 1993. This decline was partly a result of budgetary cutbacks and partly a result of greater participation in "labor market ventures."

6.2 Theoretical Framework

The Swedish labor market programs are diverse and extensive. It is important to consider each program in this overall context. For example, one must

---

7. As Richard Freeman has pointed out to us, this is also roughly equivalent to the cost of a year in a high-security prison in the United States.

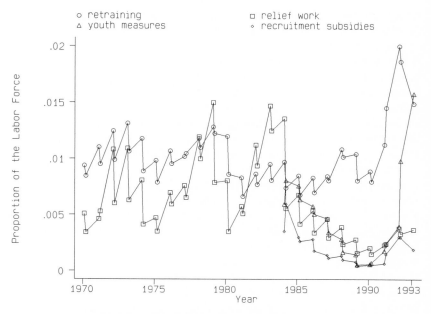

Fig. 6.2   Participation in labor market programs as a fraction of the labor force, 1970:1–1993:2 (semiannually)

recognize that solidarity wage policy is likely to set a floor on wages; workers whose productivity levels fall below this floor will find it difficult to obtain employment (see Edin and Topel, chap. 4 in this volume). Thus, the benefit of raising worker productivity through government training, say, is greater given the preexisting wage rigidity. Similarly, wage subsidies to employers of low-wage employees will relax the constraint imposed by the solidarity policy and thus could increase employment and enhance efficiency.

Moreover, the social cost of unemployment (or low productivity) is especially high in Sweden because unemployed workers qualify for generous transfer benefits, retraining, and public relief work. The high income tax also raises the social cost of unemployment or low productivity because tax revenue is forgone, which requires even higher tax rates (which in turn probably cause further labor supply distortions). And the fact that income taxes are progressive reduces the incentive to invest in human capital and search for better-paying jobs. The adverse effects of these distortions could be reduced by effective government intervention to encourage training, mobility, and employment.[8]

If one takes the network of government programs as given, then the proper

8. Notice, however, that government intervention does not necessarily have to involve government-provided training. For example, the government could provide vouchers to individuals for private training, or it could lower tuition costs through grants or loans.

theoretical framework is to start from a situation with preexisting distortions. As is well known, in this second-best setting, government intervention could improve economic efficiency. In this framework, the benefits of successful labor market programs in Sweden are potentially greater than in the United States, which may explain why the Swedish labor market programs are more extensive. But, if the external environment changes (if there is, e.g., a reduction in marginal tax rates or unemployment benefits—as has been the case in Sweden), then this theoretical framework suggests that the social benefit of active labor market programs may be reduced.

One must also consider possible indirect effects of labor market programs on wage and employment outcomes. Theoretical bargaining models predict that labor market programs will exert upward pressure on wages. Aggregate time-series studies provide some empirical support for this prediction (Calmfors and Forslund 1991; Calmfors 1993; and Calmfors and Lang 1995), although Edin, Holmlund, and Östros's (1993) county-level analysis finds that labor market programs do not put upward pressure on wage bargains. It is thus possible that labor market programs cause higher wages and depress employment.

The total social costs and benefits of labor market programs must be compared to determine their optimal level. Rational design of policy would take into account the efficacy of labor market programs. If, on the margin, a krona spent on retraining has a higher reward than a krona spent on public relief work, then the retraining program should receive a larger share of the available resources. Such cost-benefit comparisons are especially important given the rising expense of labor market programs and the rising government budget deficit. Next, we present an evaluation of the effectiveness of retraining programs and public relief works, drawing on the past literature and some new analysis.

6.3   Displacement Effects of Public Relief Workers

There was a large shift away from public relief work and toward job training in the 1980s. Nevertheless, over 10 percent of unemployed workers were placed on public relief jobs in 1990, and there is some discussion of expanding public relief in response to the current economic crisis. One potential drawback of public relief work is that public relief workers may displace private sector workers. There is an extensive literature on this topic in the United States, beginning with Johnson and Tomola (1977). The theoretical argument is straightforward: if the public sector provides relief workers to a local government agency or private sector firm, the local government or private firm will hire fewer workers than it otherwise would have hired.

Johnson and Tomola conclude that public sector employment programs used in the United States in 1966–75 tended to displace other workers, on net creating few additional jobs after six quarters. This conclusion is not without con-

troversy. Borus and Hamermesh (1978) argued that Johnson and Tomola's estimates are sensitive to their Almon lag specification and nonrobust because of
strong multicollinearity in their aggregate time-series data. Adams, Cook, and
Maurice (1983) estimate displacement effects using a panel data set of annual
observations on cities in 1970–79. They find that public sector employment
grants had a significant negative effect on payrolls in 1978 and 1979 but not in
1977. In 1978, for example, seventy-seven cents of every dollar in public sector
employment grants were reflected in higher city payrolls. Adams, Cook, and
Maurice attribute the finding of less of a displacement after 1977 to a redesign
of the program, which tightened eligibility and required specific projects.

There has been only one previous study of the displacement effects of public
relief workers in Sweden. That study, by Gramlich and Ysander (1981), analyzes fourteen annual time-series observations from 1964 to 1977. The authors
focus on the two largest categories of public relief expenditures and employment: health and welfare workers and road construction workers. They estimate aggregate time-series models, similar to Johnson and Tomola. Gramlich
and Ysander find evidence of considerable displacement in road construction
but not in the health and welfare sector.

We investigate the displacement effects of public relief workers using annual
data for twenty-four counties in Sweden over the period 1976–91 for all construction workers and over the period 1982–90 for health and welfare workers.[9]
Specifically, we estimate employment equations of the form

(1) $E_{it} = \beta_0 + \beta_1 PRW_{it-1} + \beta_2 W_{it} + \beta_3 X_{it} + \mu_i + \tau_t + \varepsilon_{it},$

where E_{it} is employment in county i in year t, PRW_{it-1} is the total number of
public relief workers in county i in year $t - 1$, W_{it} is the log of the average real
wage in county i in year t, and X_{it} is a vector of cyclic demand measures, such
as the unemployment rate and vacancy rate. We also include unrestricted
county fixed effects (μ_i) and unrestricted year effects (τ_t). Equation (1) is estimated separately for construction workers and for health and welfare workers.
Relief workers should not be counted among the workers included in the dependent variable. Thus, fiscal substitution (i.e., displacement) will imply a negative coefficient on PRW, and complete fiscal substitution will imply a coefficient of -1.0. We have also experimented with specifications using various
lags of public relief workers and with subsets of the covariates.

Results for construction workers are presented in table 6.2. Each specification shows a negative and statistically significant coefficient on public relief
workers, implying substantial displacement. Column 6, which includes the
largest set of covariates, indicates that 0.69 fewer private construction workers
are employed for every additional public relief worker hired. The lowest estimate of displacement that we find is -0.36, in specifications where we omit
the year effects.

---

9. The health and welfare workers series is shorter because of comparability problems with the
county-level data in earlier years.

Table 6.2   **Displacement Effects of Public Relief Workers (dependent variable: number of private construction workers)**

	Model					
Variable	(1)	(2)	(3)	(4)	(5)	(6)
Relief workers	−.65	−.59	−.36	−.59	−.36	−.69
($t-1$)	(.11)	(.17)	(.11)	(.18)	(.13)	(.19)
County dummies	Yes	Yes	Yes	Yes	Yes	Yes
Year dummies	No	Yes	No	Yes	No	Yes
Log wage	. . .	. . .	1.65	−12.38	1.65	−11.88
($\times$ 1,000)			(.22)	(6.62)	(.22)	(6.27)
Vacancy rate	. . .	. . .	64.77	95.28	66.78	94.27
($\times$ 1,000)			(28.31)	(50.36)	(37.89)	(49.83)
Unemployment rate	. . .	. . .	. . .	. . .	.97	44.64
($\times$ 1,000)					(12.18)	(23.24)
R^2	.98	.98	.98	.98	.98	.98
Sample size	384	384	360	360	360	360

Note: Standard errors are in parentheses. Equations also include intercept terms. Mean of dependent variable is 9,385. Observations in cols. 1–2 are for 1976–91; observations in cols. 3–6 are for 1976–90. There are twenty-four counties in the sample each year.

The results for health and welfare workers, reported in table 6.3, are much less clear. The estimated displacement effect for health and welfare workers is not stable when different sets of covariates are included—it bounces from −2.26 to +0.91. Moreover, the standard errors are quite large, and the estimated effect is statistically insignificant in column 6, which includes the full set of covariates. Unfortunately, it is difficult to draw much of a conclusion about the extent of displacement for this group of workers.

One potential problem with our estimates of displacement is that causality may run in the reverse direction. A prolonged downturn in the economy may stimulate the use of relief workers, thus generating a negative correlation between (lagged) relief workers and nonrelief employment. We include cyclical demand measures (unemployment and vacancy rates) in the regressions to control for this possibility. Nevertheless, in a highly cyclical industry like construction, reverse causality may still be a concern. To explore this issue further, we also estimated vector autoregressions for employment and relief workers in each sector. These estimates are reported in table 6.4. The results indicate that lagged relief workers and lagged employment have a statistically significant effect in the employment equations but that lagged employment does not have a statistically significant effect in the relief worker equations. This finding suggests that causality does not run from employment to relief workers, but, with our relatively short time period, it is hard to draw firm conclusions from the vector autoregressions.

Table 6.3   **Displacement Effects of Public Relief Workers (dependent variable: number of health and welfare workers)**

Variable	Model					
	(1)	(2)	(3)	(4)	(5)	(6)
Relief workers	−2.26	−1.09	.91	−.46	.58	−.56
($t - 1$)	(.39)	(.59)	(.40)	(.62)	(.43)	(.63)
County dummies	Yes	Yes	Yes	Yes	Yes	Yes
Year dummies	No	Yes	No	Yes	No	Yes
Log wage	...	...	12.61	48.76	17.45	53.15
(× 1,000)			(2.02)	(26.55)	(3.09)	(27.00)
Vacancy rate	...	...	343.95	375.34	374.06	365.43
(× 1,000)			(146.90)	(198.88)	(146.39)	(199.17)
Unemployment rate	...	...	...	...	123.91	72.04
(× 1,000)					(60.21)	(73.81)
R^2	.98	.99	.99	.99	.99	.99
Sample size	240	240	216	216	216	216

Note: Standard errors are in parentheses. Equations also include intercept terms. Mean of dependent variable is 33,140. Observations in cols. 1–2 are for 1982–91; observations in cols. 3–6 are for 1982–90. There are twenty-four counties in the sample each year.

As a final check on the plausibility of our estimates, we estimated a vector autoregression for the durable manufacturing sector, an industry that is *not* directly affected by public relief workers. Since the durable manufacturing sector is highly cyclic, this industry provides a test of whether our previous results of the construction industry are spuriously reflecting cyclical patterns. The p value for a joint test of three lags of the public relief variable in the employment equation for durable manufacturing workers is .11 ($F = 2.03$). The corresponding test for construction workers has a p value of .0000 ($F = 9.07$). These results suggest that the effect of relief workers on construction employment is not just spuriously reflecting the business cycle.

To summarize, we find evidence of substantial displacement in the construction sector but not in the health and welfare sector. This conclusion is very much like Gramlich and Ysander's, even though we analyze data for a more recent time period, exploit county-level data, and use different estimation methods.

6.4   Job Training

In view of the large amount of resources devoted to job retraining in Sweden, one would expect to find a vast microeconometric literature on the effectiveness of training programs. This is not the case. There have been only about

Table 6.4   **Vector Autoregressions for Employment and Relief Worker, by Sector**

Variable	Construction		Health and Welfare	
	Employment	Relief Workers	Employment	Relief Workers
Relief workers $(t - 1)$	−.68	1.12	.020	.79
	(.15)	(.06)	(.654)	(.05)
Relief workers $(t - 2)$	.37	−.71	−.38	−.21
	(.20)	(.08)	(.85)	(.07)
Relief workers $(t - 3)$	−.35	.37	−.72	.04
	(.16)	(.06)	(.60)	(.05)
Employment $(t - 1)$	.79	−.02	.58	−.007
	(.06)	(.02)	(.08)	(.007)
Employment $(t - 2)$	−.15	.01	−.13	−.009
	(.08)	(.03)	(.09)	(.008)
Employment $(t - 3)$	−.19	.02	.13	−.005
	(.07)	(.03)	(.07)	(.006)
F statistic for relief workers[a]	9.07	137.68	2.31	150.02
	[.00]	[.00]	[.08]	[.00]
F statistic for employment[b]	146.19	.64	28.16	.54
	[.00]	[.59]	[.00]	[.65]
Sample size	288	288	168	168

Note: Equations also include county dummies, year dummies, log average wage, vacancy rate, and unemployment rate. Standard errors are given in parentheses.

[a]p value for lagged relief workers is in brackets.

[b]p value for lagged employment is in brackets.

a half dozen studies of the effect of job training on earnings with Swedish data. These studies use a variety of econometric models and data sets, and some studies use several estimation techniques. In Sweden, as in the United States, there is considerable uncertainty regarding the proper estimation method and specification for estimating the "treatment effect" of job training. But, in Sweden, problems of imprecise estimates are at least as important as model specification. In summarizing the literature, we report fixed effects estimates when multiple estimates were available.[10]

Figure 6.3 summarizes the past literature on the effect of job training on earnings. The figure shows the estimated payoff to training as a proportion of earnings, with a bound of plus or minus two standard errors around the estimate. As a benchmark for these estimates, one should bear in mind that, if job training raises participants' annual earnings by 3 percent for twenty years, then the present value of the payoff to the training roughly equals its costs.[11] Thus, one should hope that studies have enough precision to detect payoffs on the

10. For a thoughtful summary of this literature, see Björklund (1990).

11. In making this calculation, we assume that the typical participant earns $15,000 per year, that job training increases annual earnings permanently by 3 percent, and that the individual works

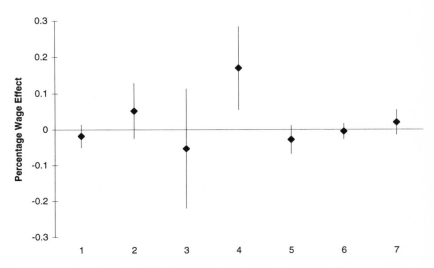

Fig. 6.3   Returns to retraining programs in Sweden—selected estimates with plus/minus 2 standard error band
Note: Studies: 1, Edin (1989); 2, Björklund (1989); 3, Ackum (1991); 4, Axelsson and Löfgren (1992); 5, Regnér (1993); 6, Inverse-variance weighted average; 7, Arithmetic average.

order of 3 percent. Unfortunately, there is a wide range of estimates, and each of the estimates has a large standard error. Two of the estimates are significantly below .03, and one is significantly above .03.

To improve the precision of the estimates, we calculated the weighted average of the estimates, using as weights the inverse sampling variance of the estimate. (We also calculated the standard error of the weighted-average estimate.) This is reported as study 6 in figure 6.3. The weighted-average payoff is slightly negative (-0.8 percent) but not statistically different from zero (SE = 1.2 percent). One could, however, reject the null hypothesis of a payoff on the order of 3 percent using the weighted average of the estimates. On the other hand, the arithmetic average of the estimated effects in the studies is positive, but it is not statistically different from zero or from 3 percent.

These studies show that there is not enough support to reject the null hypothesis that training has no effect on participants' subsequent earnings. If we use the weighted average of the estimates, we would reject the null hypothesis that the payoff is on the order of 3 percent, which is roughly the break-even level for the training programs.

Individually, the studies of earnings lack sufficient power to reach a convincing conclusion on this critical issue. A high priority for researchers in Sweden

for twenty years. If we apply a real interest rate of 3 percent to future earnings, the present value of the payoff to training is $6,695, which exceeds the average cost of $6,568 in 1990. This calculation ignores the time costs of participants while they undergo training.

should be the construction of data sets that permit precise estimates of the effect of job-training programs. The following calculation indicates approximately how large a sample is required to draw reasonably precise inferences.[12] Suppose a standard error of about 1 percent is desired. If we take Regnér's (1993) sample and estimates as representative, we would need a sample of roughly forty-one thousand observations to achieve a standard error of .01, compared to the actual sample of five thousand observations. We feel that Björklund's (1990, 12) recommendation is worth repeating: "More attention must be paid to these—less glamorous—issues of data quality in order to get estimates of reasonable precision." In the light of Heckman and Smith's (1993) finding that JTPA (Job Training Partnership Act) experimental and nonexperimental evaluations yield similar results when the comparison sample for nonexperimental sample is carefully selected, we feel that this suggestion is particularly prescient.

There is an even smaller set of studies to review that examine the effect of training on subsequent employment probabilities. A careful study by Björklund (1989) finds that retraining programs raise the probability that participants are subsequently employed by 4.4–5.5 percent if a linear control function is estimated and by 2–8 percent if a fixed-effects model is estimated, depending on the period. Only the 8 percent estimate is significantly different from zero, however. Duration models estimated by Korpi (1992) indicate that longer experience in labor market programs is associated with greater employment stability for youths in Stockholm and that youths who found jobs directly after participating in manpower programs tended to stay on the job longer.

Until sufficient data are available to make precise estimates for Sweden, we believe that estimates for the United States could prove informative for Sweden. The U.S. literature consistently finds that job-training programs have their largest percentage payoff for women. Men tend to have smaller payoffs, and the available estimates for youths suggest that training has little effect on their subsequent labor market outcomes (see LaLonde 1992). Although selection into training programs and the content of programs in Sweden are likely to be quite different, the American estimates may provide a rough indication of the likely returns in Sweden. In the absence of compelling evidence to the contrary, we suspect that a similar qualitative pattern will hold in Sweden. Moreover, the small payoff to training based on the weighted-average study in figure 6.3 is consistent with the modest payoffs found in the American literature. All this suggests to us that one should not expect heroic returns from job-training programs. The benefits may justify the costs (especially in Sweden because of preexisting distortions noted earlier), but the returns are likely to be in the neighborhood of 3 percent higher income per year.

---

12. Another issue to consider is the proper statistical methods and specifications to estimate the payoff to job training.

6.5 Beveridge Curve

The stability of the unemployment-vacancy relation, or Beveridge curve, is one of the features of the Swedish labor market that many observers have pointed to. One possible explanation for the stable Beveridge curve in Sweden is that active labor market policies have improved the matching of workers to vacancies. But there are alternative explanations as well. First, the public relief jobs and training programs may mask unemployed workers. Second, public sector employment has grown rapidly in Sweden, with the percentage of Swedish workers directly employed by the government increased from 20 percent in 1965 to 38.2 percent in 1985. The increase in public sector employment is even more dramatic for women, rising from 29.5 percent in 1965 to 54.8 percent in 1985. Government employment may have soaked up workers who otherwise would be unemployed, preventing an outward shift in the Beveridge curve.[13] We explore these alternative explanations for the stable Beveridge curve.

We consider two sources of unemployment data: labor force survey data and register data. Figure 6.4a documents the stability of the Beveridge curve using biannual unemployment data from the labor force survey. Figure 6.4b contains the corresponding plot using register data. The unemployed counted in the register data consist of people looking for work and immediately available to take a job. In both figure 6.4a and 6.4b, the vacancy rate is measured by the number of vacancies listed in the register divided by the labor force.

The unemployment–vacancy rate relation is fairly stable over time when the unemployment rate is derived from the labor force survey. The register data, by contrast, indicate that the unemployment-vacancy relation shifted in somewhat between 1990 and 1992 (see fig. 6.4b). Both these patterns present a sharp contrast with most other industrialized countries, which experienced a shift out of the unemployment-vacancy locus in the 1970s and 1980s. We utilize the register data in our county-level analysis because the relatively small sample size in the labor force survey would induce considerable sampling variability in county-level estimates. Our goal then is to explain why the Beveridge curve has shifted in for Sweden.

Table 6.5 presents estimates of the Beveridge curve using county-level data for Sweden for 1981–91. In the first four columns, the unemployment rate derived from the registers is the dependent variable. Columns 5 and 6 contain estimates that use a broader measure of the unemployment rate as the dependent variable; the broader measure also counts workers on public relief jobs, training programs, and youth programs as among the unemployed. Results with either dependent variable cast some doubt on the importance of public sector employment for the stability of the Beveridge curve in Sweden.

The regression reported in column 1 reveals a negatively sloped relation

13. This explanation is hypothesized by, e.g., Lindbeck (1990) and OECD (1992).

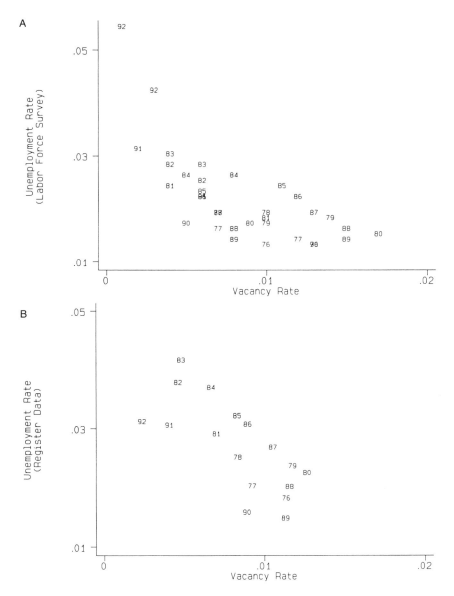

Fig. 6.4 **Beveridge curve. *a*, Survey data. *b*, Register data.**

Table 6.5   Exploration of Stability of Beveridge Curve in Sweden, County-Level Data, 1981–91

	Dependent Variable					
	Unemployment Rate				UR + Programs	
Variable	(1)	(2)	(3)	(4)	(5)	(6)
Vacancy rate	−2.34	−1.70	−1.83	−1.76	−2.07	−2.22
	(.19)	(.16)	(.18)	(.16)	(.25)	(.25)
Year (÷ 100)	. . .	−.16	. . .	−.19	−.22	−.31
		(.01)		(.02)	(.02)	(.03)
Proportion public	. . .	. . .	−.13	.052	. . .	.123
sector			(.02)	(.025)		(.039)
23 county dummies	Yes	Yes	Yes	Yes	Yes	Yes
R^2	.69	.80	.74	.81	.80	.81
Sample size	264	264	264	264	264	264

Note: Regressions also include constants. Proportion public sector is the proportion of the labor force employed in the public sector. Vacancy rate is the number of registered vacancies relative to the labor force. Unemployment rate is the unemployment rate derived from the registers. "UR + Programs" is (unemployed + relief workers + number on training programs + number on youth programs)/labor force. Standard errors are given in parentheses.

between the unemployment rate and the vacancy rate. Notice that the coefficient on the linear time trend reported in column 2 indicates that the county-level Beveridge curve has shifted in, as expected from figure 6.4*b* above. In the model in column 3, we substitute a variable measuring the proportion of workers in the county who are employed in the public sector for the time trend. The estimates in column 3 are consistent with the view that public sector employment has absorbed unemployed workers, as the public sector share has a negative and statistically significant effect on the county unemployment rate. However, once we add a linear year trend to the model in column 4, the public sector employment variable changes sign. Moreover, the year trend is hardly affected by the inclusion of the public sector employment variable. In columns 4 and 5, we use the broader definition of the unemployment rate. These results also indicate that the Beveridge curve has shifted in and that the proportion of workers employed in the public sector has a positive effect on unemployment when a linear time trend is included.

From the estimates in table 6.5, one may be tempted to conclude that a growing public sector absorbed many unemployed workers, only that the growth in public sector employment was roughly constant, making it difficult to distinguish from a linear time trend. In other words, including both public sector employment and the time trend causes a multicollinearity problem. Although this interpretation is possibly correct, the time path of public sector employment differed across counties, enabling us to estimate the model with both variables in columns 4 and 6. Importantly, the standard error of the estimate for the proportion in the public sector increases only slightly once the time trend is added to the model, suggesting that multicollinearity is not a serious problem.

We are also aware that a valid criticism of the regressions in table 6.5 is that public sector employment is possibly an endogenous variable. Nevertheless, we consider these results suggestive that growing public sector employment does not account for the inward shift of the Swedish Beveridge curve. In addition, when we use a broader measure of unemployment—one that includes program participation as well as open unemployment—we still find that the Beveridge curve has shifted in. Thus, we have no satisfactory explanation for the time trend in the Beveridge curve in Sweden.

Although the reasons for Sweden's unemployment-vacancy relation are unclear, we should stress that a stable or inward shift of the Beveridge curve is not necessarily a virtue if the unemployment rate has increased. If the Beveridge curve had shifted out, at least there would be substantial job vacancies at the prevailing high unemployment rate, and the issue would be matching people to jobs. But, in Sweden's current economic environment, the level of vacancies is low, and the level of unemployment is high. Unless we were confident of steps that would move the Swedish labor market down along a stable Beveridge curve, this is not a desirable situation.

6.6   International Evidence on Active Labor Market Programs

Our main approach in this paper has been to try to measure the effect that specific labor market programs (such as public relief work) have on key outcome variables (such as construction worker employment). For the programs and outcome measures that we have been able to study, this analysis provides little support for the view that Sweden's labor market policies have greatly enhanced the operation of the labor market. Most of the favorable impression of active labor market policies, however, is due to a different approach—cross-country analyses. In these studies, an aggregate measure of a country's labor market performance (usually the unemployment rate) is related to institutional characteristics of the country, such as variables measuring the extent of its active labor market programs and other economic variables (e.g., Bean, Layard, and Nickell 1986; and Layard, Nickell, and Jackman 1991). The international evidence has generally found that countries with greater spending on active labor market policies tend to have lower unemployment. In this section, we review, update, and evaluate the international evidence on the effectiveness of labor market programs.

In their influential book, Layard, Nickell, and Jackman (1991, chap. 1) present a cross-country regression of the average unemployment rate for 1983–88 on a variable measuring active labor market programs and several other variables. Their sample consists of twenty OECD countries. Active labor market programs are measured by expenditures on these programs per unemployed person relative to GDP per capita in 1987. Their regression coefficients (t-ratios in parentheses) are reported below:

unemployment rate (%) = 0.24 (0.1)
+ 0.92 (2.9) benefit duration (years)
+ 0.17 (7.1) replacement ratio (%)
− 0.13 (2.3) active labor market spending (%)
+ 2.45 (2.4) coverage of collective bargaining (1–3)
− 1.42 (2.0) union coordination (1–3)
− 4.28 (2.9) employer coordination (1–3)
− 0.35 (2.8) change in inflation (% points),
R^2−adj. = 0.91,   SE = 1.41, N = 20.

The statistically significant point estimate on the active labor market variable implies that the derivative of the unemployment rate with respect to the share of the labor force in programs equals −1.5, so the reduction in open unemployment therefore exceeds the direct effect of lifting people out of unemployment by means of active labor market policies (see Calmfors 1994, n. 18).

In related work, Zetterberg (1993) pools time-series data for nineteen OECD countries for the period 1985–91 and regresses unemployment on the ratio of expenditures on active labor market measures relative to total expenditures on labor market policies. Consistent with Layard, Nickell, and Jackman, he finds that, as the share of expenditures on labor market policies increases, the national unemployment rate declines.

We think that there are two major weaknesses with the cross-country analyses that limit their usefulness in evaluating active labor market programs. The first problem arises because the source of variability in the countries' labor market policies is unclear. In this situation, one would like to control for a great many variables that might influence the unemployment rate and national labor market policy. However, with only twenty observations, the number of variables that one can hold constant is greatly restricted.

A related issue is that cause and effect in the cross-country regressions are very difficult to ascertain. If a nation is in a prolonged downturn, it may be difficult to deny generous unemployment insurance benefits to unemployed workers. In this scenario, high unemployment causes high UI replacement rates and long benefit durations, not vice versa. A possible approach to solving this simultaneity bias problem would be to instrument for the labor market variables, but valid instrumental variables are difficult to find for this problem.

A similar concern arises with the active labor market variables. As Grubb (1993) and OECD (1993) point out, spending on active labor market measures tends to rise less than in proportion with unemployment in most OECD countries. As spending on unemployment benefits typically varies approximately in proportion to unemployment, this has induced a negative correlation between unemployment and spending on active labor market measures per unemployed worker and between unemployment and the share of total labor market program expenses devoted to active labor market programs.[14]

Our second, and perhaps more important, concern is that the cross-country evidence on the active labor market programs is not very stable over time. The cross-country evidence has been conducted mainly using data for the 1980s, when the unemployment rate in Sweden and other countries with extensive active labor market programs was relatively low. The situation has changed quite dramatically in the early 1990s. To probe the stability of the international evidence, we have conducted a cross-country analysis of the 1993 unemployment rate that is similar in spirit to the work of Layard, Nickell, and Jackman (1991) and Zetterberg (1993).

Specifically, we regress the unemployment rate in 1993 on two measures of active labor market programs, the change in inflation and the same institutional variables used by Layard, Nickell, and Jackman (1991). For comparison, we present corresponding estimates for the years 1983–88, the period analyzed by Layard, Nickell, and Jackman. We measure the importance of active labor market programs in two ways. First, we calculate the fraction of GDP spent on active labor market programs. Second, we use Zetterberg's (1993) variable, which equals the share of expenditures on active labor market measures relative to total expenditure on labor market programs. Both these measures have problems. Most obviously, active labor market expenditures relative to GDP may rise when unemployment rises because more people become eligible for programs—the simultaneity problem we noted previously. The simultaneity bias is likely to impart the opposite bias for the share of expenditures on active labor market programs relative to total expenditures on labor market programs. But bear in mind that our main interest here is in examining whether the effect of the active labor market variables has changed between the 1980s and 1993, not whether the estimates are biased at any one time.[15]

Table 6.6 summarizes the main regression results.[16] The table indicates a striking change in the coefficients for the active labor market variables. In the period 1983–88, both active labor market variables have a negative association with unemployment, whereas they both have a positive association in 1993. The *t*-ratio for a test of the difference between the estimates for the active labor variable in columns 3 and 4 is 1.89. It is also worth noting that the union coverage and union coordination variables have changed signs and become statistically insignificant in 1993. On the other hand, the duration and generos-

14. This point is demonstrated in OECD (1993, annex 2.A), which shows that the significant effect of active labor market programs found by Layard, Nickell, and Jackman vanishes when spending on active labor market programs is instead related to the total wage bill.

15. The correlation between Layard, Nickell, and Jackman's active labor market variable (expenditures on active labor market programs per unemployed worker relative to GDP per capita in 1982) and ours (the fraction of GDP devoted to active labor market programs ca. 1993) is .82.

16. Because the sample size is small, in each model we use the largest available sample. This leads to different samples of countries in different years. However, our results are qualitatively similar when we restrict the samples to a common set of countries.

Table 6.6   **Models for Cross-Country Differences in Unemployment, 1983–88 and 1993 (dependent variable: unemployment rate [%])**

	Year			
Independent Variable	1983–88	1993	1983–88	1993
ALM spending relative	−.42	1.73	. . .	. . .
to GDP	(1.18)	(1.42)		
ALM spending relative	. . .	. . .	−8.78	10.19
to all labor market			(3.19)	(9.49)
programs				
Union coverage (1–3)	2.68	−.79	3.00	1.48
	(1.38)	(2.12)	(1.05)	(1.59)
Union coordination (1–3)	−1.98	1.16	−2.01	1.48
	(.84)	(1.57)	(.66)	(1.59)
Employer coordination	−4.42	−5.15	−3.76	−6.31
(1–3)	(.77)	(1.22)	(.64)	(1.44)
Unemployment insurance	.15	.25	.14	.32
replacement ratio	(.03)	(.07)	(.02)	(.07)
Unemployment insurance	.96	1.68	.60	1.60
duration (years)	(.36)	(.60)	(.36)	(.72)
Change in inflation	−.39	−1.04	−.41	−.99
	(.15)	(.89)	(.13)	(.84)
Sample size	20	19	20	17
R^2-adj.	.85	.63	.91	.75
SE	1.79	2.96	1.41	2.51

Note: Standard errors are in parentheses. The ALM (active labor market) spending relative to GDP and ALM spending relative to all labor market program variables pertain to 1987 in cols. 1 and 3 and available years between 1991 and 1993 in cols. 2 and 4 (*source:* OECD 1993). The change in inflation variable is for 1983–87 in cols. 1 and 3 and 1992–93 in cols. 2 and 4 (*source: OECD Main Economic Indicators*). All other explanatory variables are from Layard, Nickell, and Jackman (1991).

ity of unemployment insurance benefits continue to have a positive association with the unemployment rate, and an increase in the inflation rate continues to have a negative (albeit statistically insignificant) effect on the national unemployment rate in 1993.

One could argue that 1993 is an aberration—that the international evidence in other years suggests that active labor market programs have reduced unemployment. But, together with the statistical issues that we raised previously, we think that the results of the updated cross-country regressions challenge the favorable impression of active labor market programs that several observers have drawn from international comparisons.

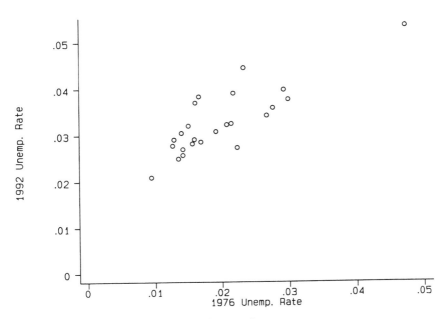

Fig. 6.5   Persistence of county-level unemployment

6.7   Comparison of Regional Evolutions

Finally, we examine the responsiveness of employment and unemployment to regional shocks in Sweden. This analysis is motivated by two issues. First, if Sweden's labor market policies are unusually successful, we would expect economic shocks to have less persistent effects in Sweden than in other countries. Second, Sweden's past record of adjustment to economic shocks may tell us something about how the labor market will react to the current economic downturn.

Specifically, we investigate the evolution of employment and unemployment using pooled time-series and cross-sectional data for the twenty-four counties in Sweden. As a first look, figure 6.5 presents a plot of the unemployment rate in 1992 against the unemployment rate in 1976 using data on each of the twenty-four counties in Sweden. There is considerable persistence in the level of unemployment across regions in Sweden. This is similar to the pattern found for regions in France, Germany, Spain, and the United Kingdom by Decressin and Fatas (1993) but quite different from the pattern for states in the United States found by Blanchard and Katz (1992). Figure 6.6 shows a plot of each county's percentage growth in employment between 1983 and 1991 against its growth between 1976 and 1983. There appears to be little persistence in employment growth rates across counties in Sweden. Again, the pattern for Sweden more closely resembles the European pattern found by Decressin and Fatas than the U.S. pattern found by Blanchard and Katz.

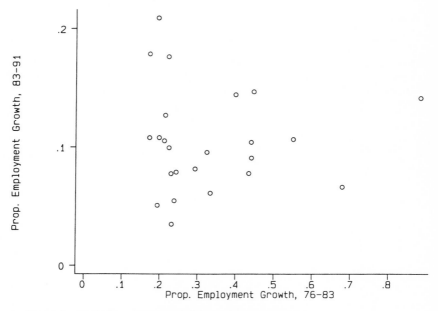

Fig. 6.6   Evolution of county-level employment growth

Following Blanchard and Katz (1992), we define $\Delta\eta_{it}$ as the change between year t and $t - 1$ in the logarithm of employment in county i minus the change in the logarithm of employment in Sweden nationwide between year t and $t - 1$. We estimate the same univariate process for employment as Blanchard and Katz:

$$(2) \qquad \Delta\eta_{it} = \alpha_i + \beta(L)\Delta\eta_{it-1} + \varepsilon_{it},$$

where we allow four lags in $\Delta\eta_{it-1}$, α_i represents a county fixed effect, and ε_{it} is an idiosyncratic error term.[17]

Results are presented in table 6.7, and the implied impulse response function is shown graphically in figure 6.7. For comparison, we also report Blanchard and Katz's estimates for the fifty U.S. states. Regional shocks to relative employment have lasting effects in Sweden; they are 86 percent of their original size after twenty years. In the United States, regional employment shocks also have permanent effects, but they tend to be amplified over time. Interestingly, Decressin and Fatas (1993) find that the Swedish pattern is more typical of other European countries.[18] The United States would thus seem to be the outlier here, not Sweden.

17. A Dickey-Fuller test did not reveal a unit root in the Swedish county-level employment series. Nevertheless, we estimate the same specifications as Blanchard and Katz for comparability.

18. Decressin and Fatas's results are not directly comparable to our estimates and to Blanchard and Katz's because they deviate regional employment from country-specific coefficients times

Table 6.7   **Univariate Models of Relative Employment and Unemployment across Regions**

Coefficient on Lagged Dependent Variable	United States		Sweden	
	Δ Log Employment (1)	Unemployment Rate (2)	Δ Log Employment (3)	Unemployment Rate (4)
One lag	.492	.899	−.103	1.020
	(.023)	(.032)	(.039)	(.051)
Two lags	−.099	−.159	−.028	−.289
	(.025)	(.033)	(.038)	(.052)
Three lags	.010	. . .	−.026	. . .
	(.024)		(.024)	
Four lags	−.054	. . .	−.003	. . .
	(.022)		(.022)	
σ_ε	.017	.083	.018	.002
Sample period	1952–90	1972–90	1981–91	1978–92
	Implied Impulse Responses			
Year 1	1.00	1.00	1.00	1.00
Year 2	1.49	.90	.90	1.02
Year 3	1.63	.65	.88	.75
Year 4	1.67	.44	.86	.47
Year 5	1.62	.29	.86	.26
Year 10	1.52	.04	.86	.00
Year 20	1.53	.01	.86	.00

Note: Models include state dummies (United States) or county dummies (Sweden). Columns 1 and 2 are from Blanchard and Katz (1992). Change in log employment and unemployment rate are measured relative to national levels. Standard errors are given in parentheses.

Next, we examine the evolution of relative unemployment rates. Specifically, we follow Blanchard and Katz and estimate

$$(3) \qquad \mu_{it} = \alpha_i + \beta_1 \mu_{it-1} + \beta_2 \mu_{it-2} + \varepsilon_{it},$$

where μ_{it} is the unemployment rate in county i in year t minus the aggregate unemployment rate in Sweden in year t, α_i is a county effect, and μ_{it-1} and μ_{it-2} are one- and two-year lags of the relative unemployment rate.

As shown in table 6.7 (cols. 3 and 4) and figure 6.8, the relative unemployment rate series in both Sweden and the United States displays less persistence than the relative employment growth series. Half the effect of an innovation in a county's relative unemployment rate is predicted to dissipate three years after

aggregate European employment. But their country coefficients are close to one, and they report similar results for the United States as Blanchard and Katz when they apply their procedure to U.S. data.

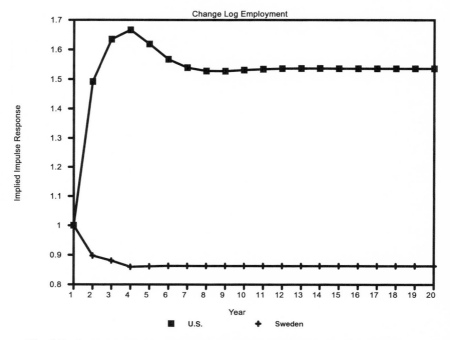

Fig. 6.7   Impulse response function, Sweden and United States: Change log employment

the initial shock. Ten years after a shock, the innovation is predicted to have completely dissipated.

The implied impulse response functions for the unemployment rate are quite similar in Sweden and the United States, and Decressin and Fatas find a similar pattern for regional data in several European countries. Our finding of similar regional evolutions in the relative unemployment rate series in Sweden, the United States, and Europe suggests that active labor market programs in Sweden have not had a marked effect on unemployment adjustment in regional labor markets in Sweden.

6.8   Conclusions

We conclude by considering what our review of the literature and our original analysis imply for the current problems facing the Swedish labor market. We also consider possible lessons from Sweden's experiences for labor market policy in the United States and elsewhere.

One important question that we can partially address is whether the recent dramatic increase in unemployment in Sweden is likely to have a persistent effect. We can base our estimate on the estimated unemployment rate equation in table 6.7 above if we make two strong assumptions: (1) the regional shocks that identify the autoregressive models in table 6.7 have similar effects as the

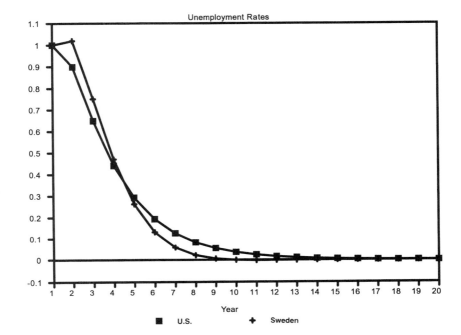

Fig. 6.8   Impulse response function, Sweden and United States: Unemployment rates

shocks causing the current depression in the Swedish labor market; and (2) the 7 percentage point increase in the unemployment rate in Sweden between 1990 and 1993 is the entire innovation to the unemployment rate series. If these assumptions are valid, the coefficients in table 6.7 imply that the Swedish unemployment rate will gradually decline but will still be at historically high levels for at least the next few years, and probably longer.

Our analysis also suggests that the active labor market programs are not as effective at combatting unemployment or enhancing workers' skills as some observers believe. How might certain policy changes affect the labor market programs, especially in the current high-unemployment environment? The answer to this question is particularly important if the high rate of unemployment persists in the future. Indeed, relatively generous unemployment benefits (compared to the United States) is a reason why one might expect the high rate of unemployment to persist.

First, Sweden's UI fund benefits are very generous by U.S. standards and are available for a long duration. Benefits last for three hundred days, which is more than twice the maximum duration of unemployment benefits in the United States. Furthermore, the maximum duration of unemployment benefits in Sweden may be effectively longer given the possibility of requalifying for benefits after working on public relief jobs or undergoing retraining. The extent to which individuals rotate between receiving unemployment benefits and participating in labor market programs should be investigated. If this appears to be a widespread phenomenon, one possible response would be to limit the total duration that individuals may receive unemployment benefits in a specified window of time.

A second possible response is an expanded set of programs to encourage entrepreneurial activity by unemployed workers. Experimental evidence and experience in the United States suggests that a minority of unemployed workers are interested in self-employment and that government assistance can help increase the number of unemployed who start their own businesses. For example, the state of Washington has had favorable results from providing unemployment benefits in a lump sum to those who are interested in obtaining seed capital to start their own business (U.S. Department of Labor 1992). In addition, training in business activities and other support services may prove useful. The social reward to pursuing this kind of a policy is likely to be greater in Sweden, where high marginal tax rates discourage entrepreneurial ventures. Another possible issue to study is that, to encourage more entrepreneurial activities, the government might allow some "tax and regulation havens" in which start-up businesses are exempted from tax and regulatory requirements for a specified period of time. Although only a small minority of the unemployed could possibly become successful entrepreneurs, this is a margin in which employment could possibly be expanded, especially in a downturn.

Third, our review of studies of training lead us to the same conclusion reached by Robert Flanagan (1987): "There is disappointingly little evidence that these expenditures have improved the productivity of the Swedish work force." Although the handful of studies on the effect of training employ state-of-the-art statistical methods, the data have proved insufficient for deriving precise estimates of the payoff to training. Aggregating over several studies, we conclude that the payoff is modest, at best. The U.S. evidence supports a similar conclusion. Furthermore, the immediate benefit of job training when the labor market is weak is likely to be smaller than when the labor market is strong. An important question is whether some training expenditures could be more profitably redirected, perhaps toward programs that would stimulate aggregate demand. From a research standpoint, it would be useful if any policy changes could be implemented in such a way as to facilitate evaluation of the effect of the policies. Specifically, this may include selection of individuals for certain policies on the basis of an arbitrary criterion (e.g., birthday falls after certain date) and administrative monitoring of nonparticipants and program exhaustees for data-collection purposes and subsequent analysis. Finally, our results and those of Gramlich and Ysander (1981) suggest that, in the past, public relief workers have displaced other workers, on net creating few new jobs in the construction sector. It is possible that displacement effects could be limited by requiring local governments to propose new projects in order to qualify for relief workers. If public relief work assumes a greater role in the current downturn, this issue would be worthy of further study.

What does our analysis imply for the United States? The United States seems to be moving in the opposite direction of Sweden, having in 1992 elected a president with a platform of "putting people first" by improving the skills of the workforce. In addition, unemployment benefits have recently been extended in the United States in some regions, whereas the level of benefits was recently cut in Sweden. It is possible that both countries are moving in the "optimal" direction since the active labor market programs in the United States are much smaller than those in Sweden. The optimal level of labor market programs may lie somewhere in between the two countries. Nevertheless, Sweden's experience that active labor market programs alone are not capable of fending off high levels of unemployment should be instructive to the United States and other countries. Countries should not expect supernormal returns from government labor market programs. Policy makers in Eastern European countries who look to Sweden as a model for labor market institutions would be well advised to keep this lesson in mind.

References

Ackum, Susanne. 1991. Youth unemployment, labor market programs and subsequent earnings. *Scandinavian Journal of Economics* 93:351–543.

Adams, C., R. Cook, and A. Maurice. 1983. A pooled time-series analysis of the job creation impact of public service employment grants to large cities. *Journal of Human Resources* 18 (Spring): 283–94.

Axelsson, R., and K. G. Löfgren. 1992. Arbetsmarknadsutbildningens privat-och Samhällsekonomiska effekter. Rapport 25. Stockholm: Delegationen för Arbetsmarknadspolitisk.

Bean, Charles, Richard Layard, and Steven Nickell. 1986. The rise in unemployment: A multi-country study. *Economica* 53, no. 2:S1–S22.

Björklund, Anders. 1989. Evaluation of training programs—experiences and suggestions for future research. Discussion Paper no. 89-13. Wissenchaftszentrum Berlin.

———. 1990. Evaluation of training programs. *Finnish Economic Papers* 3 (Spring): 3–13.

Blanchard, Olivier, and Lawrence Katz. 1992. Regional evolutions. *Brookings Papers on Economic Activity*, no. 1:1–75.

Borus, Michael, and Daniel Hamermesh. 1978. Estimating fiscal substitution by public service employment programs. *Journal of Human Resources* 13 (Fall): 561–65.

Calmfors, Lars. 1993. Lessons from the macroeconomic experience of Sweden. *European Journal of Political Economy* 9(1): 25–72.

———. 1994. Active labor market policy and unemployment—a framework for analysis of crucial design features. *OECD Economic Studies*, no. 22:7–47.

Calmfors, Lars, and Anders Forslund. 1991. Real-wage determination and labor market policies: The Swedish experience. *Economic Journal* 101 (September): 1130–48.

Calmfors, Lars, and Harald Lang. 1995. Macroeconomic effects of active labor market programs—basic theory. *Economic Journal* 105:601–19..

Carling, Kenneth, Per-Anders Edin, Anders Harkman, and Bertil Holmlund. 1996. Unemployment duration, unemployment benefits, and labor market programs in Sweden. *Journal of Public Economics* 59:313–34.

298 Anders Forslund and Alan B. Krueger

Decressin, Jörg, and Antonio Fatas. 1993. Regional labor market dynamics in Europe and implications for EMU. Washington, D.C.: IMF. Typescript.
Edin, Per-Anders. 1989. *Individual consequences of plant closures.* Studia Oeconomica Upsaliensia, vol. 15. Uppsala, Sweden: Uppsala University.
Edin, Per-Anders, Bertil Holmlund, and Thomas Östros. 1993. Wage behavior and labor market programs in Sweden: Evidence from micro data. Working Paper no. 1993:1. Uppsala University, December.
Flanagan, Robert. 1987. Efficiency and equality in the Swedish labor markets. In *The Swedish economy,* ed. B. Bosworth and A. Rivlin. Washington, D.C.: Brookings.
Gramlich, Edward, and Bengt-Christer Ysander. 1981. Relief work and grant displacement in Sweden. In *Studies in labor market behavior,* ed. G. Eliasson, B. Holmlund, and F. Stafford. Stockholm: Industrial Institute for Economic and Social Research.
Grubb, David. 1993. Some indirect effects of active labor market policies in OECD countries. Paris: OECD. Typescript.
Heckman, James, and Jeffrey Smith. 1993. Presentation on JTPA [Job Training Partnership Act] evaluation project. Cambridge, Mass.: National Bureau of Economic Research, October.
Johnson, George, and James Tomola. 1977. The fiscal substitution effects of alternative approaches to public service employment. *Journal of Human Resources* 12 (Winter): 3–26.
Korpi, Tomas. 1992. Employment stability following unemployment and manpower programs. Stockholm Research Reports in Demography no. 72. Stockholm University, December.
LaLonde, Robert. 1992. The earnings impact of U.S. employment and training programs. University of Chicago, December. Typescript.
Layard, Richard, Stephen Nickell, and Richard Jackman. 1991. *Unemployment: Macroeconomic performance and the labor market.* Oxford: Oxford University Press.
Lindbeck, Assar. 1990. The Swedish experience. Seminar Paper no. 482. Stockholm: Institute for International Economic Studies.
OECD. 1992. *OECD economic surveys: Sweden 1991/1992.* Paris.
———. 1993. *Unemployment outlook.* Paris.
Regnér, H. 1993. Choosing among alternative nonexperimental methods for estimating the impact of training: New Swedish evidence. Meddelende 8:1993. Swedish Institute for Social Research, Stockholm University.
Stafford, Frank. 1981. Unemployment and labor market policy in Sweden and the United States. In *Studies in labor market behavior,* ed. G. Eliasson, B. Holmlund, and F. Stafford.
Statistisches Bundesamt. 1993. *Statistisches Jahrbuch 1993, die Bundesrepublik Deutschland.* Stuttgart: Metzler-Poeschel.
Statistisk Arsbok 1992. 1991. Stockholm: Statistics Sweden.
U.S. Department of Labor. Employment and Training Administration. 1992. The Washington reemployment bonus experiment: Final report. Unemployment Insurance Occasional Paper no. 92-6. Washington, D.C.
U.S. House of Representatives. Committee on Ways and Means. 1991. *1991 Green Book.* Washington, D.C.: U.S. Government Printing Office.
Zahlen zur Wirtschaftlichlichen Entwicklung der Bundersrepubllik Deutschland 1992. 1992. Berlin: Institut der Deutschen Wirtschaft.
Zetterberg, Johnny. 1993. Arbetsloshet, arbetsmarknadspolitik och loneforhandlingssysytem. In *Politik mot Arbetsloshet,* Betankande av Delegationen för Arbetsmarknadspolitisk, Statens Offentliga Utredningar 1993:43. Stockholm.

7   Taxes and Subsidies in Swedish Unemployment

Lars Ljungqvist and Thomas J. Sargent

Figure 7.1 reproduces a version of the first chart in *Turning Sweden Around* (Lindbeck et al. 1994). It shows two striking features of unemployment in Sweden in the years after 1960. Until 1992, unemployment in Sweden remained persistently lower than in the average OECD country. After 1992, it jumped to share with other OECD countries a high recession level. This situation prompted Assar Lindbeck and his coauthors to write: "During the 1970's and 1980's, long-term unemployment became a serious social problem in most Western European countries. There is now an obvious risk that Sweden will go the same way. Although Sweden's total unemployment, including people in various labor market programs, has recently reached European levels, long-term unemployment has not yet emerged. It should be an overriding task of economic policy to prevent creating a large group of permanently unemployed citizens—without giving up the ambition of low inflation, an efficient use of economic resources, and satisfactory economic growth" (p. 6).

Our work for the SNS-NBER project has aimed to help understand those two striking features of figure 7.1 and to offer insights about government policies that promote or retard labor market efficiency and flexibility. We focused on three sets of forces that can influence the level and average duration of unemployment: (1) unemployment compensation programs, (2) income tax schedules, and (3) administrative procedures to prevent unemployed workers from abusing the unemployment compensation system. These forces moved in Sweden over the last thirty years in ways that help account for changes in the level and structure of unemployment.

Lars Ljungqvist is professor of economics at the Stockholm School of Economics and a senior economist at the Federal Reserve Bank of Chicago. Thomas J. Sargent is professor of economics at the University of Chicago, senior fellow at the Hoover Institution, Stanford University, and a research associate of the National Bureau of Economic Research.

The views expressed here are the authors' and not necessarily those of the Federal Reserve System.

299

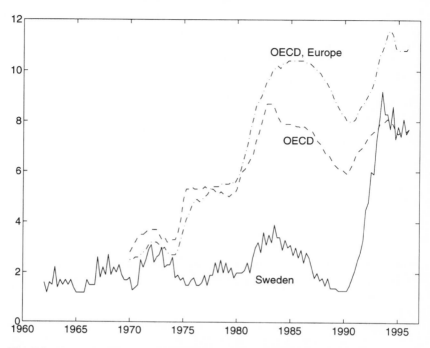

Fig. 7.1   The unemployment rate in Sweden and the OECD average unemployment rate

High and progressive tax systems tend to reduce the level of unemployment, but at a potential cost in terms of decreasing the efficiency of the labor market.[1] Between the 1960s and the 1980s, tax wedges in Sweden increased dramatically, a movement that by itself should have helped keep the unemployment rate low (see fig. 7.2). Between the 1960s and the 1980s, unemployment compensation became more generous (see fig. 7.3), which tended to increase the unemployment rate in Sweden. However, at least until very recently, in order to combat the adverse unemployment effects of generous unemployment compensation, Sweden supplemented its unemployment compensation system with a mechanism to monitor and coax unemployed workers into taking "acceptable jobs." The observed unemployment rate balances these forces.

7.1   Summary of Findings

We interpret the persistently low Swedish unemployment rate from the 1960s through the 1980s as emerging from movements in our three counter-

1. Pissarides (1983) was the first to emphasize the effects of higher tax rates in reducing the unemployment rate in a search model of unemployment. Mortensen (1986), Stigler (1961), and McCall (1970) are key references on search models and their application to labor markets.

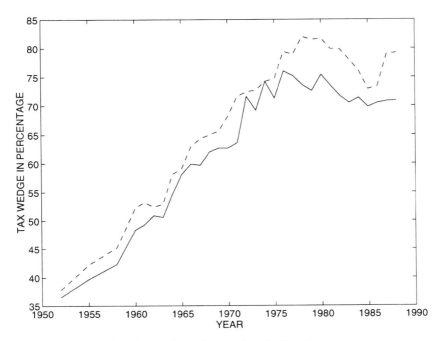

Fig. 7.2   Time-series observations of tax wedges in Sweden
Source: Gustafsson and Klevmarken (1993).
Note: The solid line is the tax wedge for blue-collar workers. The dashed line is the tax wedge for white-collar workers.

vailing forces. In their effects on the unemployment rate, increases in tax wedges and progressivity tended to offset the increased generosity of unemployment insurance benefits. The monitoring program that supplemented the unemployment compensation system to safeguard it from abuse also helps us account for why unemployment in Sweden was as low in the 1980s as it was in the 1960s. We interpret the rise in unemployment after 1992 in terms of a relaxation of that program in response to adverse macroeconomic shocks. In the absence of a resuscitation of that program, and unless unemployment benefit levels are reduced, Sweden is in danger of inviting persistently high levels of unemployment like those borne by other European countries in recent years.

7.2   Two Views of Unemployment

We analyze the juxtaposition of the forces described above with a quantitative model that incorporates aspects of two views about unemployment. One view, that too high an unemployment rate represents waste and inefficiency, was stated by Alan Blinder (1987, 33) when he called unemployment the "biggest inefficiency of them all." The other view, that unemployed workers are not

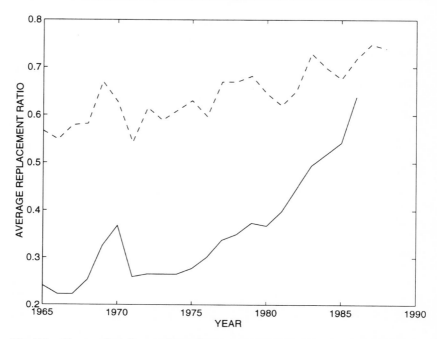

Fig. 7.3   Time-series observations of average replacement ratios in Sweden
Source: Björklund and Holmlund (1991).
Note: The solid line is the average replacement ratio for all unemployed workers. The dashed line is the average replacement among insured male blue-collar workers.

just wasting time but are investing in useful information, was stated by George Stigler (1962, 104), who wrote: "From the social viewpoint, the return from investment in information consists in a more efficient allocation of the labor force: the better informed the labor market, the closer each worker's (marginal) product is to its maximum at any given time." We need a quantitative model to evaluate whether the unemployment rate is too high (resources are being wasted in idleness) or too low (resources are being committed with too little information about alternative and superior uses).

7.3   Overview of a Model

Our analysis is based on a computer model of a labor market that we designed to imitate salient features of the Swedish labor market.[2] It is a version of the search model that Stigler recommended for labor markets. Search models cast an unemployed worker as facing uncertainty about the wages that he can earn from different jobs and about the prospects that he will be offered a

---

2. The technical details of the model are described in Ljungqvist and Sargent (1995a, 1995b).

job. Our model represents the labor market as consisting of a large number of workers, each of whom either does or does not have a job. We model each job situation as evolving over time in ways that often lead to "promotions" but sometimes cause workers to be fired or to quit their jobs. In particular, at the beginning of each period, a worker is exposed to a small probability that his job is destroyed, in which case he enters the ranks of unemployed workers whether he likes it or not. Also, at the beginning of each period that a job continues, there is a small chance that the nature of the job will change. It may be upgraded or downgraded. Job reclassifications confront workers with the choice of staying with a reclassified job or quitting and searching for a new job. Thus, job destructions and rejected reclassifications are the immediate sources of unemployment.

To find a job, an unemployed worker must search for one. Searching requires that the worker expend some effort or other resources. The potential reward for searching is finding a job offer. A job offer has some of the features of a financial option: it promises a particular stated pretax real wage so long as the job is not terminated or is not reclassified. When the worker accepts a job, he is accepting the bundle of possible reclassifications and terminations associated with it. Job offers—which we summarize by initial wage offers—are from a probability distribution. This distribution helps determine the prospective gains from further searching. The unemployed worker cares about the dispersion of after-tax wages, which is affected by the tax system.

An unemployed worker who has received an offer to work at a particular wage balances the gains and losses from accepting the current offer. The gain is the after-tax wage that the worker will receive this period, plus the value to him of starting next period with this job in hand. The loss comprises any unemployment benefits he would have qualified for and the prospective return from searching one more period and perhaps drawing a better job offer next period. The worker does best to accept the first offer that he receives that exceeds a reservation wage. An unemployed person increases the likelihood that he will leave unemployment by lowering his reservation wage. The value of the reservation wage depends first on the level of unemployment benefits. In general, increases in the generosity of unemployment benefits cause the worker to increase his reservation wage and to increase the expected duration of his unemployment. The value of the reservation wage also depends on the after-tax distribution of wages that the worker faces. A decrease in the dispersion of the after-tax wage distribution diminishes the rewards to search and thereby causes the worker to decrease his reservation wage and to decrease the average duration of his unemployment.

Employed workers whose jobs have just been reclassified also set a reservation wage for staying on the job. They face a choice similar to that of unemployed workers who have just received a new offer: they can accept the new offer or else quit and enter unemployment. However, quitters are not eligible for unemployment compensation during the subsequent spell of unemployment. This means that potential quitters face a different potential gain from entering unemployment than do workers who qualify for unemployment compensation and that they choose a different reservation wage.

Unemployed workers' reservation wage policies determine a rate of transition from the states of (involuntary and voluntary) unemployment to employment.[3] Employed workers' reservation wages and the process for reclassifying jobs determine a rate of transition from employment to (voluntary) unemployment. We also specify an exogenous rate at which existing jobs are extinguished, triggering an (involuntary) move to unemployment. These three transition rates determine flows into and out of unemployment and enable us to calculate the unemployment rate that emerges from the experience of a large number of workers. Any force that alters workers' reservation wages will in general alter the implied unemployment rate.

The rule for administering unemployment benefits is one determinant of the reservation wage and therefore the unemployment rate. We use a one-parameter rule designed to capture in a simple way the spirit of the institution described by Björklund (1996, 177). "In order to receive unemployment compensation, the worker must be registered as a job seeker at the public employment office, and an offer of 'suitable' work must be accepted. If a 'suitable' offer is turned down, benefits can be denied for 4 weeks; further denials may occur if offers are repeatedly turned down. Manpower training programs may in some cases be regarded as 'suitable' work, and the same holds for temporary jobs (relief work) provided by the Labour Market Board. The disqualification rules also apply to workers who are dismissed for failure to perform their jobs and those who quit into unemployment." We embody a version of this institution by specifying a "suitable wage" level, w_g, any offer above which must be accepted if an unemployed worker is to remain eligible for unemployment compensation. By lowering the parameter w_g, we tighten the rule.

An important macroeconomic element of our model is a feedback loop from the level of general government expenditures and expenditures on unemployment benefits to the tax rates borne by workers. This makes the tax rates in our model "endogenous," meaning that, because they depend partly on the level of unemployment (which they in turn influence), they must be determined simultaneously with the unemployment rate.

The model captures Stigler's notion of unemployment as being, at least in part, a valuable social activity of information gathering, perhaps even one worth subsidizing. By waiting, unemployed workers are speculating that a more worthwhile job might come along. Inefficiencies can arise either because

3. Our model distinguishes between two classes of unemployed workers, depending on whether they qualify for unemployment compensation. Involuntarily unemployed workers are those whose previous jobs were exogenously terminated. Voluntarily unemployed workers are those who quit their previous job after a reclassification plus those who have been disqualified from receiving unemployment compensation. In our simulations, we keep track of the numbers of both categories of unemployed workers because we have to compute the national bill for unemployment compensation.

workers wait too long (the unemployment rate is too high, tending to make output lower than it could otherwise be) or because they wait for too short a time (the unemployment rate is too low, making output lower than it could be because workers are mismatched and work at lower-productivity jobs than they might hold).

To judge whether an observed unemployment rate is too low or too high, we have to unravel the factors that create it. That is what our quantitative model is for.

7.4 Numerical Experiments

We used a computer to design experiments to tell us how different hypothetical settings of government policy variables would affect the level and structure of unemployment. Below, we summarize the results of three sets of experiments that focus on variations in (a) the progressivity of the tax system, (b) the level of unemployment compensation, and (c) the vigor with which the program to suppress abuses of the unemployment compensation system is enforced.

7.4.1 Effect of Taxes on Unemployment and Output

Figures 7.4 and 7.5 report the effects of unemployment of variations in a parameter I_τ that measures the progressivity of the tax system. If a worker receives a pretax wage of w, he pays taxes in the amount $\tau w + .5\tau \times \max(w - I_\tau, 0)$, where τ is the base marginal tax rate, and I_τ is a wage level at which the marginal tax rate jumps up by 50 percent. In the range reported in figure 7.4, increases in I_τ correspond to decreasing the progressivity of the tax system.[4] Figure 7.4 shows how increases in progressivity of the tax system cause the unemployment rate to decrease. Both voluntary and involuntary components of unemployment decrease with increases in progressivity.

These reductions in unemployment result from workers' responses to the narrowing of the after-tax wage distribution caused by an increase in progressivity. A reduction in the dispersion of after-tax wages lowers the potential rewards to further search, prompting workers to lower their reservations wages and on average to accept offers sooner. This causes the unemployment rate to fall. However, there is a social cost associated with this reduction in unemployment, alluded to by Stigler in the passage quoted above. This cost is captured in figure 7.5, which shows the locus of unemployment-output pairs traced out as we vary the progressivity of the taxes, holding other parameters constant.[5] Increases in progressivity decrease both unemployment and output. This happens because workers are accepting jobs at which their marginal products are

4. This is because we have calibrated the mean of the distribution of new wage offers to .5. As I_τ increases above .5, a larger and larger fraction of workers do not pay the higher marginal tax rate on any part of their incomes and in effect just face a flat-rate tax of τ.
5. The adjusted GNP in fig. 7.5 refers to the economy's output net of utility costs of search.

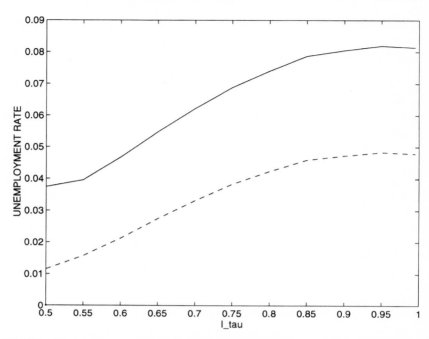

Fig. 7.4   How unemployment rates vary as functions of the progressivity of the tax system, as measured (inversely) by I_τ

Note: The tax system becomes *less* progressive as I_τ increases. The solid line is total unemployment; the dashed line is voluntary unemployment.

farther and farther from their "maximum" (in Stigler's terms) as the tax system is made more and more progressive.

In the next section, we describe how variations in unemployment compensation can be used to offset the covariation of unemployment and output depicted in figure 7.5.

7.4.2   Effects of Unemployment Compensation

Figures 7.6 and 7.7 show effects of increasing the level of unemployment compensation on unemployment and output. Increasing unemployment compensation drives up the total unemployment rate, even though it has a minor tendency to reduce the level of voluntary unemployment. (The reason that the voluntary unemployment rate goes down with an increase in unemployment benefits is that voluntarily unemployed workers do not receive benefits, but the tax rates of employed workers must go up to pay for the higher benefit levels. This diminishes the reward to workers to leave their jobs following reclassifications.) Figure 7.7 shows how increasing unemployment compensation causes output to decline as it drives unemployment upward.

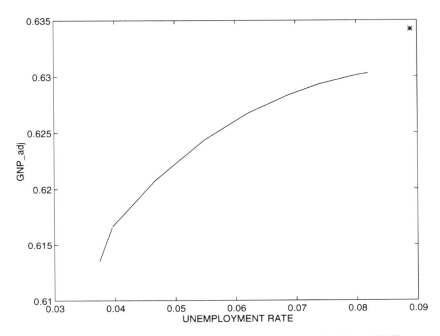

Fig. 7.5   Relation between the total unemployment rate and adjusted GNP when varying I_τ as in fig. 7.4

Note: The efficient unemployment, adjusted GNP pair is denoted by an asterisk (*).

7.4.3   Effects of Monitoring the Unemployed

Figure 7.8 shows how the unemployment rate varies with a parameter w_g designed to capture the way that the government administers unemployment compensation. If wage offers exceeding w_g are tendered and refused, it triggers termination of unemployment benefits during the current spell of unemployment. Thus, w_g parameterizes the unemployment compensation branch of the worker's "option" in a particular way. We have calibrated things so that $w_g = .55$ represents quite a stringent policy and $w_g \geq .7$ represents a very lax policy. Figure 7.8 shows how effective this policy is in reducing unemployment, even in the face of very generous unemployment compensation payments.

We have "calibrated" the various parameters underlying figure 7.8 to match some key features of the Swedish labor market. In particular, we have set parameters governing taxes and unemployment compensation to approximate their levels in Sweden in the 1980s.[6] At those levels of parameters, we find that setting a "tough" (i.e., low) value for the administrative parameter w_g is im-

---

6. Figure 7.8 holds I_τ fixed at .50, which corresponds to a very progressive tax system, and the unemployment compensation is set at a very generous level of .55.

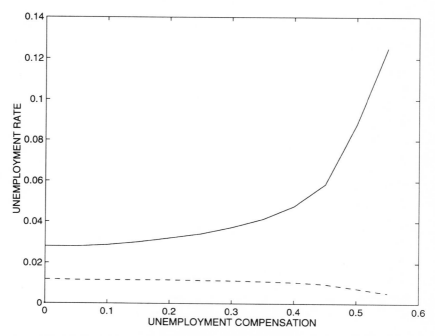

Fig. 7.6   Unemployment rates as functions of unemployment compensation
Note: The solid line is total unemployment; the dashed line is voluntary unemployment ($I_\tau = .50$).

portant in holding down the level of unemployment. To match a comprehensive level of unemployment of around .056 (this level counts people in various training programs as unemployed and is more comprehensive than the concept reported in fig. 7.1 above), we find that we have to set w_g at a value of about .55.

The dotted line in figure 7.8 shows the level of unemployment that would be efficient, in the sense that it maximizes the average rate of output. This rate (being the comprehensive measure) is about .089 and exceeds by about .03 the .056 rate of unemployment observed from the 1960s until the 1980s. Our model imputes the excess of the efficient rate of unemployment over the average rate of .056 observed to the particular Swedish constellation of income tax rates and structures, the unemployment compensation rate, and the rules in place for administering unemployment compensation.

To explore the effect of the administrative rules, figure 7.9 depicts the locus of unemployment, GNP pairs that would be associated with alternative levels of our administrative parameter w_g. Notice how far below the efficient point, depicted by an asterisk in figure 7.9, this locus lies. In figure 7.9, tightening (i.e., lowering) the administrative parameter w_g drives unemployment down and production up.

Figure 7.8 asserts that the monitoring program supplementing unemploy-

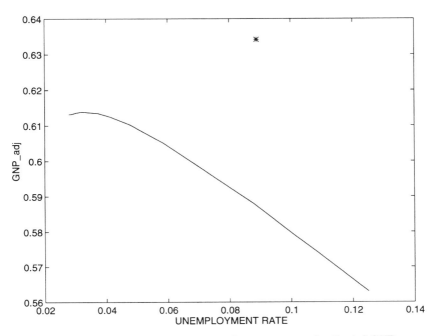

Fig. 7.7   Relation between the total unemployment rate and adjusted GNP when varying unemployment compensation, as in fig. 7.6 ($I_\tau = .50$)

Note: The efficient unemployment rate, adjusted GNP pair is denoted by an asterisk (*).

ment compensation was an important ingredient in delivering low unemployment and that relaxing enforcement of that program could show up in much higher unemployment rates if other government policies were not adjusted. This "nightmare" is depicted in figure 7.10, where we posit a dashed line that depicts a "policy response" function that makes the seriousness of enforcement depend inversely on the aggregate unemployment rate. At low unemployment rates, a tough enforcement policy (low w_g) is easier to sustain than at high unemployment rates, which imparts a positive slope to our policy response line. This policy response function generates the occurrence of "multiple equilibria": in addition to the type of low unemployment, strict enforcement pair discussed above, there is another lax enforcement, high unemployment equilibrium. The value of the unemployment rate at the high-unemployment equilibrium matches up well with the .13 comprehensive unemployment observed in Sweden during 1993.

The story embodied in figure 7.10 is capable of reconciling our explanation of the low unemployment rates observed in the 1980s with the much higher unemployment rate observed after 1992. This occurrence is to be interpreted in terms of a jump from the low unemployment rate to the high unemployment

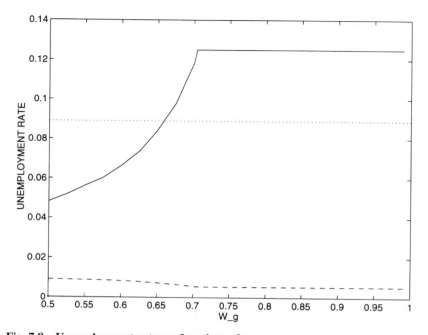

Fig. 7.8   Unemployment rates as functions of w_g

Note: The solid line is total unemployment; the dashed line is voluntary unemployment. ($I_\tau = .50$, and unemployment compensation is set at .55.) The laissez-faire unemployment rate is indicated by the dotted line.

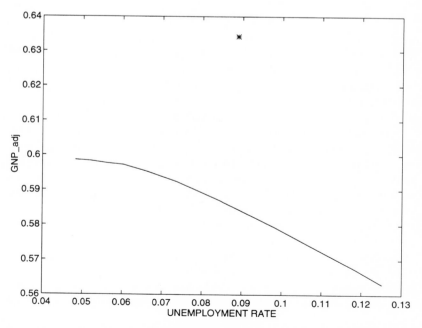

Fig. 7.9   Relation between the total unemployment rate and adjusted GNP when varying w_g, as in fig. 7.8 ($I_\tau = .50$, and unemployment compensation is set at .55$_g$)

Note: Lower unemployment rates are associated with lower levels of w_g. The efficient unemployment rate, adjusted GNP pair is denoted by an asterisk (*).

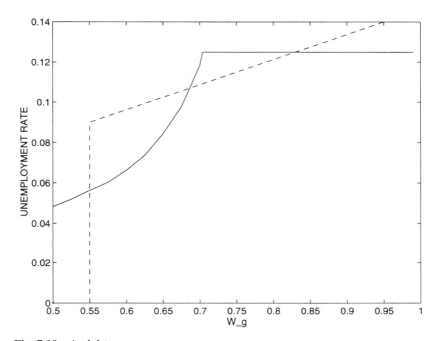

Fig. 7.10   A nightmare

Note: The dashed line is an example of a policy relation between the unemployment rate and w_g. The solid line is the equilibrium relation between the unemployment rate and w_g as earlier shown in fig. 7.9. ($I_\tau = .50$, and unemployment compensation is set at .55.)

equilibrium, a jump occasioned by macroeconomics shocks outside our model.[7]

7.5   Other Aspects of the Computer Model

Our model has other features that we trace out in Ljungqvist and Sargent (1995a).

1. We are able to calibrate separate 1960s and 1980s versions of the model, the first having less-progressive taxes and lower unemployment benefit levels, the second having more-progressive taxes and higher benefit levels. These calibrations give realistic sets of tax wedges and replacement ratios for the two periods at the same unemployment rates for both periods. These calibrations are the foundation for our explanation of how offsetting forces accounted for the persistently low unemployment rate from the 1960s through the 1980s.

2. Our calibrations imply that, despite the stability of the unemployment rate from the 1960s to the 1980s, its structure should have changed. In particu-

---

7. We certainly do not regard the increase in unemployment after 1992 as the response to a *spontaneous* weakening of the rules for qualifying for unemployment compensation.

lar, our model implies that the new constellation of tax wedges and benefit levels that emerged in the 1980s should have led to a substantial increase in the average duration of unemployment as well as to a reduction of flows into and out of unemployment. Such changes in the structure of unemployment in Sweden have been observed between the 1960s and the 1980s.

7.6   Relationship to Other Chapters

In constructing our model, we have taken to heart and incorporated key conclusions of Edin and Topel and of Forslund and Krueger (chaps. 4 and 6 in this volume, respectively), namely, that labor market programs have had at most a minor effect on the overall unemployment rate in Sweden. Our model embodies a stark version of their finding, by assigning no role to public expenditures on retraining and relief jobs.[8] In our model, a government program does suppress unemployment, but, instead of retraining and relief jobs, it is the administrative apparatus for restraining abuse of unemployment compensation, alluded to in the above quotation from Anders Björklund.

While we have not mentioned unions and central bargaining, any wage compression attributable to those institutions would serve to reinforce the mechanism that we have adduced to explain the low Swedish unemployment of the 1980s. In our search model, anything that compresses the after-tax wage distribution—be it a progressive income tax or pretax wages compressed through centralized bargaining—will tend to lower the unemployment rate by diminishing the rewards to search.

7.7   Implications for Sweden

A given level of the unemployment rate can be attained in various ways, from diverse packages of public policies and external circumstances. To interpret or judge the social desirability of a given unemployment rate requires understanding the particular package of policies and circumstances that produced it. We require a way to probe the composition of unemployment and to evaluate whether spells of unemployment and employment are too long or too short from the standpoint of the efficiency of matching workers to suitably productive tasks. Our research has studied how aspects of public policy influence workers' incentives to modify those aspects of their behavior that determine flows into and out of employment.

We attribute the persistently low Swedish unemployment rate from the 1960s to the 1980s to a triumvirate of forces—high and progressive taxes, generous unemployment benefits, and administrative procedures to prevent abuse of unemployment compensation—that excludes Swedish government

---

8. A very minor macroeconomic role surfaces in their effects on equilibrium tax rates through the government budget constraint.

expenditures on labor market policies such as relief jobs and retraining. We are able to account for the level of the Swedish unemployment rate in the 1960s and 1980s while ignoring those expenditures. In our view, the administrative procedures' successful containment of "abuse" of unemployment compensation coalesced with lower job mobility emerging from higher income tax wedges to sustain a low unemployment rate. But the unemployment rate was suppressed by accepting the cost of a less-efficient labor market, symptomized by increased duration of unemployment.

Our analysis asserts that the changes in the structure of unemployment between the 1960s and the 1980s signified increasing labor market distortions. The increase in the average duration of unemployment spells and the lower flow of workers into unemployment can be explained by the increased progressivity of the tax system and more generous unemployment compensation of the 1980s. A less efficient labor market harmed the performance of the Swedish economy during the last fifteen years. Lindbeck et al. (1994) describe the slowdown in productivity growth that has sent Sweden from third to fourteenth place among OECD countries in terms of per capita GDP.

Our analysis raises apprehensions about Sweden's ability to cope with its present high unemployment rate. If, as seems likely, the administrative procedure for monitoring unemployment compensation—the system's dike—breaks down at high unemployment rates, then our analysis predicts persistently high unemployment rates. In the absence of effective administrative controls, our analysis suggests that the way to diminish such structural unemployment is to lower unemployment compensation benefits.

References

Björklund, Anders. 1996. Unemployment in Sweden. In *Unemployment in Nordic countries,* ed. Anders Björklund and Tor Eriksson. Amsterdam: North-Holland.

Björklund, Anders, and Bertil Holmlund. 1991. The economics of unemployment insurance: The case of Sweden. In *Labour market policy and unemployment insurance,* ed. Anders Björklund, Robert Haveman, Robinson Hollister, and Bertil Holmlund. Oxford: Clarendon.

Blinder, Alan S. 1987. *Hard heads and soft hearts.* Reading, Mass.: Addison-Wesley.

Gustafsson, Björn, and N. Anders Klevmarken. 1993. Taxes and transfers in Sweden: Incentive effects on labour supply. In *Welfare and work incentives: A North European perspective,* ed. A. B. Atkinson and Gunnar Viby Mogensen. Oxford: Clarendon.

Lindbeck, Assar, Per Molander, Torsten Persson, Olof Peterson, Agnar Sandmo, Birgitta Swedenborg, and Niels Thygesen. 1994. *Turning Sweden around.* Cambridge, Mass.: MIT Press.

Ljungqvist, Lars, and Thomas J. Sargent. 1995a. The Swedish unemployment experience. *European Economic Review* 39:1043–70.

———. 1995b. Welfare states and unemployment. *Economic Theory* 6:143–60.

McCall, John J. 1970. Economics of information and job search. *Quarterly Journal of Economics* 84:113–26.

Mortensen, Dale T. 1986. Job search and labor market analysis. In *Handbook of labor economics,* ed. Orley Ashenfelter and Richard Layard. Amsterdam: North-Holland.

Pissarides, Christopher A. 1983. Efficiency aspects of the financing of unemployment insurance and other government expenditure. *Review of Economic Studies* 50:57–69.

Stigler, George J. 1961. The economics of information. *Journal of Political Economy* 69:213–25.

———. 1962. Information in the labor market. *Journal of Political Economy* 70, no. 5, pt. 2 (October): 94–105.

8   The Social Costs of Regulation and Lack of Competition in Sweden: A Summary

Stefan Fölster and Sam Peltzman

8.1   Introduction

Sweden is a "high-price" country. This seems evident to the casual visitor, and it is confirmed by more systematic evidence. For example, table 8.1 shows that, even after the 20 percent depreciation of the krona in 1992, Swedish consumer prices remain higher than in most developed countries. Moreover, available data indicate that Sweden's high-price status goes back at least to the late 1960s (Lipsey and Swedenborg 1993), a period encompassing considerable exchange rate fluctuations. These high prices cannot be entirely explained by Sweden's income level (see fig. 8.1) or by its high indirect taxes (Lipsey and Swedenborg 1993). In this paper, we will try to assess the contribution of Swedish competition and regulatory policy to these high prices.

To an outsider, especially an American conditioned by that country's antitrust laws, Swedish policy on competition has been remarkably lax. Until June 1993, cartel agreements were legal in Sweden. While they could not be enforced in the courts, firms were free to enter into essentially the whole range of agreements—price fixing, sharing of markets, allocation of retail outlets among manufacturers, etc.—that are per se violations subject to criminal penalties under American law. Only resale price maintenance agreements and joint tendering on public contracts were prohibited. Cartel agreements had to be publicly registered on request from the SPK (Swedish National Price and Cartel Board). In principle, agreements could be struck down if found to be against the public interest. However, the (1946) legislation establishing the cartel register put few sanctions at the government's disposal, and, in spite of successive strengthening of the government's powers (1953, 1956, 1982), cartel

Stefan Fölster is assistant professor at the Industrial Institute for Economic and Social Research, Stockholm. Sam Peltzman is the Sears Roebuck Professor of Economics and Financial Services at the Graduate School of Business, University of Chicago.

Table 8.1   **Relative Consumer Prices at Current Exchange Rates, Index Sweden = 100**

Countries	October 1992	May 1993	September 1993
Japan	91	128	145
Switzerland	94	112	127
Norway	95	109	117
Denmark	91	108	112
Iceland	91	105	109
Germany (W)	76	91	101
Sweden	100	100	100
Austria	74	89	99
Finland	79	88	92
Netherlands	70	83	92
Belgium	71	85	91
France	71	85	91
Canada	59	71	79
United States	55	74	79
Spain	61	69	76
Ireland	65	71	75
England	57	68	75
Italy	61	70	74
Australia	55	68	71
New Zealand	47	60	67
Greece	54	65	67
Portugal	50	58	60

agreements were largely unrestrained until 1993. In 1992, there were 1,250 agreements in the cartel register. As of 1989, about 15 percent of total sales of goods and services in Sweden were found to be affected by horizontal cartel agreements (SPK 1992). Of these sales, around 55 percent were affected by price-fixing agreements, 15 percent by market-sharing agreements, 15 percent by combined price-fixing and market-sharing agreements, and the remainder by other forms of horizontal cartel agreements.[1]

In principle, these cartel agreements are constrained by exposure to international competition. However, as shown in table 8.2, a considerable share of Swedish output does not face import competition. In this sense, the outsider's view of Sweden as the quintessential "small, open economy" is exaggerated. Table 8.2 also shows that a considerable share of Swedish output is sheltered from competition by regulation, cartel restrictions, or subsidies.

In 1993, Sweden's law on competition was changed to bring it in line with EC rules. The overriding objective is to widen the applicability of the per se

1. The SPK and another authority, the competition commissioner (SKA, established in 1982), also investigated restrictive business practices. In principle, the SKA could prosecute practices that injured competition in a market court. In practice, however, most cases were settled by negotiation; 1 or 2 percent were referred to the market court.

Relative price level (OECD=100)

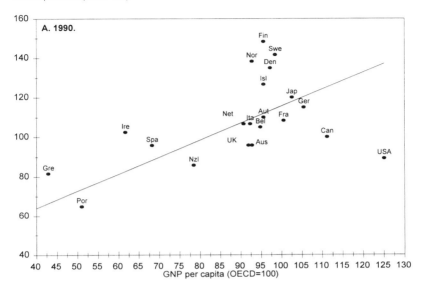

Relative price level (OECD=100)

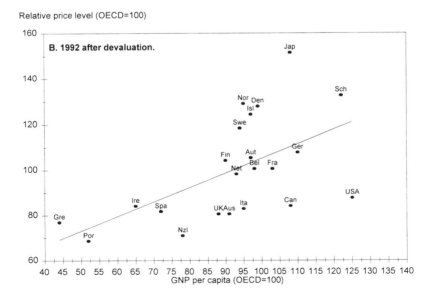

Fig. 8.1   Real incomes and relative market prices. *a*, **1990.** *b*, **1992 after devaluation.**

Table 8.2   **Three Measures of the Swedish Economy's Exposure to Competition**

Measure of Exposure to Competition	Share of Total (%)
Import competition:	
1. Import penetration in private production	15.1
2. Share of private production with import penetration greater than 16 percent	16
Output subsidies:	
3. Share of production affected by government subsidies:	
Private production	17
Private and public production	36
4. Share of consumption affected by restrictions on competition:	
Private consumption	62–79
Private and public consumption	75–84

Source: Measures 1 and 2 come from Flam, Horn, and Lundgren (1993). Measures 3 and 4 come from Andersson et al. (1993).

Note: Measures 1 and 2 refer to the year 1989. Measures 2 and 4 are based on import penetration per industry branch. Measures 3 and 4 refer to the year 1991.

rule. Most notably, horizontal price-fixing and market-sharing agreements are now illegal regardless of whether they can be proved to have harmful effects.[2] The only ground for exemption is increased competition. For example, an agreement between smaller firms can be accepted if it is shown to strengthen competitive pressures on larger firms. By conforming its rules to those in the EC, Sweden joins a European trend toward more reliance on the per se rules that are common in U.S. law. Prior law in the European Community as well as Sweden permitted action against restrictive practices only if they could be proved to be against the public interest.

Economists rarely get the opportunity to study the actual effects of cartels. Sweden's relaxed pre-1993 institutions, in which cartels were a matter of public record (the cartel register was abolished in the 1993 law), provide such an opportunity, and we take advantage of it. The results we obtain may, however, be of more than purely academic or historical interest. At this writing, no one can be sure how Sweden's new law will work in practice. In particular, if past formal arrangements among rivals are replaced by similar informal understandings, some of the effects we uncover may endure.

8.1.1   Government Regulation

Much concern has been expressed, most recently by the Lindbeck Commission (Lindbeck et al. 1994, chap. 3), that government regulation of markets in Sweden contributes to high prices by reducing competition. In this respect, the Lindbeck Commission reflects a growing wariness among economists about the potential anticompetitive effects of regulation that emerged from the so-

2. Fines for violation of the law have also been increased considerably (at most 10 percent of annual sales).

called economic theory of regulation.[3] More specifically, the report evinces concern that Sweden's regulatory institutions may be especially restrictive. It cites food and housing (together accounting for half of private consumption) as prime examples. In the food sector, government intervention begins with raw material prices, which are set considerably above world market prices. In this respect, Sweden does not differ from the European Community, but the implied subsidies are higher. The high input prices then engendered various tariff and regulatory barriers (e.g., product standards, minimum prices) to protect processors against import competition. Finally, entry at the retail level was subject to municipal zoning regulation, which was often used to protect the two biggest chains. It is perhaps unsurprising that this "vertically integrated" regulatory structure parallels the important participation of farmers' cooperatives at all three levels.

In housing, regulation originated with public subsidies intended to overcome shortages induced by rent control. The government specified the features of buildings that qualified for the subsidies. As with food, the housing regulation bred a web of political interests, including builders and their suppliers, that influenced the subsequent evolution of the regulation. Design standards, product registration laws, licensing requirements, etc. tended to keep foreign contractors and suppliers out and to retard domestic entry as well (OECD 1992, 82–83).

Food and housing may be extreme cases, but they exemplify a tendency toward regulatory intervention that many Swedes believe goes well beyond the ostensible public purpose (assuring the supply of food or housing) in the direction of reducing competition and raising costs. This belief, combined with Sweden's move to harmonize its regulatory system with EEC rules, has produced counterpressures. During recent years, a number of areas have been deregulated. For example, the restrictions on entry of food stores have been eased, and a large number of low-price supermarkets have opened. The European Economic Space (EES) treaty is likely to add to the pressure for less regulation. A basic principle within the EES is that any product that is legal in one member country can be freely imported into another (Cassis de Dijon principle). While exceptions to the principle may be granted for a variety of reasons,[4] the EEC court has so far granted exceptions sparingly. Accordingly, the sort of protection that has been granted to the Swedish food and building industry may be reduced.

As with Swedish competition law, it is too early to tell how the legal changes in the regulatory sphere will work out in practice. In this paper, we examine the effect of a selected and undoubtedly poorly measured set of Swedish regu-

---

3. The original development of the economic theory is due to Stigler (1971). A summary of subsequent work may be found in Peltzman (1989).

4. These include safety, protection of life, public order, protection of national treasures, protection of industrial or commercial ownership, effective tax control, good trading practices, public resource savings, consumer protection, protection of culture, environment, and work environment.

latory policies on prices and productivity. We find that they have, at the same time, promoted cartelization and have had more profound price and productivity effects than cartelization. Therefore, the speed with which Swedish prices will converge toward those in the European Economic Community depends in part on how quickly Swedish regulatory practice accommodates to the pressure for deregulation.

8.1.2   Industrial Concentration

The success of large multinational firms is one of the hallmarks of Swedish economic development. In areas like automobiles and trucks, telephone equipment, domestic appliances, electrical machinery, metal fabrication, and industrial machinery, Swedish firms are well-known and substantial players all over the world. Per unit of GDP, Sweden has twice as many corporations among the five hundred largest in the world as Japan and four times as many as the United States. These large Swedish multinationals convey the impression that Sweden is a land of big businesses. Because much of the production and sales of these multinationals takes place abroad, this impression is perhaps exaggerated. But it is not altogether misleading. At least in the industrial sector, the available data suggest that Swedish production is relatively concentrated. For example, in a cross-country comparison of twelve industries (Scherer et al. 1975), the average four-firm concentration ratio in Sweden (.834) was the highest among the six countries studied.[5] In only nine of the seventy-two cases studied did the concentration ratio reach 1.0, but six of these were Swedish. So Swedish industries seem characterized by unusually few firms as well as high concentration.[6]

The database used in this paper, which we describe more fully later, gives concentration data at the product level. Concentration data at this fine level of disaggregation are scant, so international comparison is impossible. However, our data leave little doubt that Swedish product markets are highly concentrated by any reasonable standard. For the eighty-three broadly representative products in our sample, the average Herfindahl index (the sum of squared shares) for annual Swedish production from 1976 through 1990 was .50. This is the equivalent of just two equal sized producers per product. The actual number of producers per product in our sample averages 2.5 and never exceeds 5.

---

5. Canada was second (.708). The other countries studied included the United States, the United Kingdom, France, and Germany. In part, higher concentration ratios for Sweden may of course reflect a small-country effect.

6. There is also extensive conglomeration of ownership and control. In 1985, the five biggest final owners held some 44 percent of the total voting rights in companies with more than five hundred employees, while the ten biggest had more than half (SOU 1990). In addition, these final owners tend to hold shares through intermediaries, such as investment companies, which in turn are linked through joint ownership. Fourteen such "empires" dominate the corporate sector, with three major ones alone controlling companies that account for some two-thirds of employment, sales, and total assets of the 270 largest corporations in Sweden.

High concentration tends to evoke concern about the vigor of competition. This concern is reflected in antitrust laws like those in the European Community that Sweden has adopted. Mergers, which were essentially unrestricted in Sweden before, will now come under greater legal scrutiny. However, it is far from clear on purely a priori grounds whether Sweden's high concentration has been a source of competitive strength or weakness. To some degree, achieving economies of scale requires higher concentration in smaller countries. More generally, high concentration can reflect differential efficiency, which results in lower rather than higher prices (Demsetz 1973). For example, if one or two producers discover lower marginal cost production methods, their output and market share will rise, and the extra output will tend to lower prices. A highly restrictive merger policy could end up penalizing efficiency if it slows the spread of low-cost production methods. Indeed, some of the results in this paper lend weight to this possibility.

While Swedish concentration remains high, it has been declining recently. In our sample, the average Herfindahl index declined from .563 in 1976 to .483 by 1984 and remained at this level thereafter. This decline has roughly the same effect on average concentration as would adding one average-sized firm to every third or fourth product market. In fact, however, new entry played no role in this decline of concentration. It was driven entirely by a sharp decline in the average market share of the largest firm from .64 in 1976 to .52 in 1990. As indicated above, this development does not necessarily signal an increase in competition. It could reflect waning productivity advantages of the largest firms.

Perhaps as interesting as the decline in concentration is the fact that it has been accomplished without any net new entry. Davis and Henrekson (chap. 9 in this volume) argue that Swedish tax policy has been biased in favor of large, capital intensive, widely held firms. This bias may have been motivated by the fact that income in small firms is difficult to separate from the owner's personal income. Therefore, small firms' income was taxed progressively in accordance with the welfare state's ambition to equalize incomes. Whatever the motivation, this tax bias may have discouraged new entry of small, privately held firms and thereby removed potential competitive constraints on the established firms.

8.1.3 Public Procurement

Public procurement accounts for about 20 percent of GNP. Forty percent of that is procurement by the central government, while the remainder is accounted for by municipalities and counties. In addition, many services are produced publicly that could be bought from private producers. In recent years, municipalities have begun to expose their technical and even social services to competition, and in some cases they have also turned to private producers. Table 8.3 summarizes the results of a recent study (Fölster 1993) that shows that substantial quality-adjusted cost savings were achieved in municipal and

Table 8.3   Quality-Adjusted Cost Reductions after Privatization in Municipal Services

	Privatized	Exposed to Competition	Decentralized	Control Group
Municipal costs	−7.9	−9.1	−4.2	−3.6
Cost effectiveness	−12.3	−9.8	−4.2	−3.6

Source: Fölster (1993).

Note: Cost effectiveness is the change in quality-adjusted municipal costs plus the entrepreneur's profit.

county services by procurement from private producers and from exposing public services to competition.

Rules concerning public procurement are sharpened considerably by a new law that will go into effect simultaneously with the EES treaty. The new law requires publication of calls for tenders in the entire EES area for large procurements. In addition, uniform rules are introduced for the conduct of procurement. A law requiring mandatory competitive tendering is being discussed but has not yet been enacted.

8.1.4   Motivation of the Study

This study tries to estimate the effect of Swedish cartels, regulation, and market structure on prices in Sweden and on costs and productivity. For reasons detailed in the next section, our estimates are biased downward. Accordingly, we view our results as indicating which of Sweden's unusual set of institutions have had important effects rather than the precise magnitude of these effects.

Since the pioneering work of Bain (1951), many cross-sectional econometric studies have focused on the relation between industry concentration, profits, and, sometimes, productivity.[7] These studies generally attempt to test the structure-conduct-performance paradigm. Concentration is considered the main dimension of structure and the main determinant of performance: attempts to exercise market power are likely to be more successful in industries that are highly concentrated. The main conclusion of this literature is that concentration has some effect on profitability, but not a substantial effect.[8]

This type of study, which was more common a decade ago, has been criticized mainly because it became increasingly clear that concentration was a poor measure of monopoly power. Also, the interpretation of results was increasingly thrown into doubt. A number of studies implied that the relation

7. Geroski (1982), e.g., estimates a simultaneous equation model with multifactor productivity and the concentration ratio as the dependent variables.
8. For a summary, see Schmalensee (1989).

between concentration and profits primarily reflected the fact that larger firms earn higher profits and that innovative, rapidly growing firms earn temporary rents to innovation. That is, high profitability could reflect either high prices or low costs.

Many recent studies of the relation between concentration and profitability have also integrated foreign trade into the analysis. Examples are Pugel (1978), Marvel (1980), and Chou (1986). A number of recent Swedish studies also follow these methods. Olsson (1991), for example, regresses dependent variables such as productivity growth and price increase at the industry level over independent variables such as concentration, export share, import share, and the occurrence of regulation. Erixon (1991) presents similar regressions both at the industry and at the company level. Stålhammar (1991) conducts a more sophisticated analysis following a method that has been applied by a number of other authors as well. Stålhammer calculates a parameter of implicit collusion for various manufacturing industries. The parameter is based on a model by Cowling and Waterson (1976) and is a function of the industry's price-cost margin and price elasticity and the firm's market share. The parameter for implicit collusion is then regressed over concentration as well as import and export shares. Stålhammar (1992) integrates both foreign trade and wage determination into the analysis.

The study reported here is based on considerably more detailed data than previous work, and it utilizes new sources of information on collusion and relative prices.

8.2 Empirical Analysis

This study uses data from a sample of Swedish manufactured products. All price data are at the wholesale level. For our purposes, this sample is a source of both strength and weakness. The data are unusually rich: we have output, price, cost, employment, etc. for every firm[9] producing a product. As far as we know, this is the first study that compares Swedish to foreign prices at the wholesale level; all the others focus on retail prices. Our data have a time-series dimension often lacking in similar studies. All these are strengths. The major weakness stems from our focus on manufacturing, where departures from competition are heavily constrained by foreign competition. The important departures from competition in Sweden probably lie elsewhere, in nontradeables like services, housing, and retailing. Accordingly, our results for manufacturing should understate the importance of restraints on competition for the whole economy. Put differently, if we do find effects of cartels, regulation, etc. in this generally competitive sector—and we do—it would suggest that similar restraints in other sectors have larger effects.

---

9. Except for some very small producers (fewer than ten employees) in a few cases.

8.2.1   Product Markets

Most empirical work uses the industry as the unit of observation. Many industries, however, contain a variety of distinct product markets, some of which are highly concentrated and oligopolistic, while others display intense competition. This is especially true of technology-oriented industries such as SNI 3852 (computers and office machines) or SNI 3831 (electrical industrial machinery). Some studies have already shown that using more detailed data significantly changes basic results. Kwoka and Ravenscraft (1986), for example, use "line-of-business" data and report, in contrast to previous studies, that higher concentration is correlated with lower profits.[10] Here, the level of disaggregation is even lower. A unit of observation in our study is a specified product (the seven-digit level in the United States SIC).

Product markets were selected from the list of products used to calculate the producer price index. This is in itself a representative list of products produced in Sweden or imported into Sweden. From this list, forty-eight products were selected specifically because their cartel registration status had been changed during the period 1976–90. An additional eighty-five products were randomly selected. After discarding those products that did not meet all data availability requirements, eighty-three products were left in the sample, of which thirty-four had experienced at least one change in their cartel registration status. The sample is therefore not a random sample of Swedish industry, containing as it does some bias toward product markets with cartel registration. However, the bias, if any, is slight: in 1989, 20 percent of our sample's total sales is covered by cartel agreements, as compared to SKA's estimate of 15 percent for horizontal cartels in the whole Swedish economy in that year. The sample also provides a reasonable cross section with observations from most industries. Table 8.4 shows the share of sales in each industry accounted for by our sample.

For every product in the sample, we have annual data on each Swedish producer's sales, costs, and assets, (employment, etc., for the period 1976–90). These data were provided to us by the Industrial Institute for Economic and Social Research.[11]

8.2.2   Prices

The counterfactual that we want to address is, What would Swedish prices be in the absence of various impediments to competition? The way in which we actually pursue this inquiry is to focus on the Swedish/EEC price ratio for

---

10. A *line of business* denotes a firm's operations in one of the industries in which it is active.

11. The data were assembled from two surveys conducted at the Industrial Institute for Economic and Social Research, the annual "Planning Survey" conducted by the Federation of Swedish Industry, as well as companies' annual reports. Some of the data (costs, assets) are at the firm or division, rather than product, level. However, product sales average around 80 percent of firm or division sales in our sample.

Table 8.4   **Sample Characteristics by Industry, 1976–90**

Products Group	U.S. SIC/SNI[a]	Number of Products	Average Sales per Product (million kronor)	Sample's Share of Industry's Output
1. Food	20/1, 31	10	2,011	.17
2. Apparel and leather	23, 31/ 32	4	416	.14
3. Wood and paper	24, 26/ 33, 34	8	2,415	.15
4. Packaging	30, 32, 34/35, 36, 37	3	1,563	.21
5. Industrial chemicals	28/35	7	734	.15
6. Drugs and cosmetics	28/35	3	593	.13
7. Petroleum products	29/36	4	294	.07
8. Rubber	30/36	2	519	.13
9. Stone, clay, and glass	32/36	8	324	.34
10. Fabricated metal	34/381	10	403	.07
11. Industrial machinery	35/382	7	639	.08
12. Electrical equipment and electronics	36/383	9	1,075	.12
13. Transport equipment	37/384	7	2,200	.15
14. Miscellaneous		3	878	.09
Total		85	1,314	.09

[a]Generally, two-digit level.

the same good. We ask if this ratio is higher than average when Swedish producers have cartel agreements, when Swedish regulation is unusually severe, etc. Implicitly, then, we are using the EEC prices as a "competitive" benchmark. This has considerable advantages over using accounting costs for the competitive benchmark. For example, we can avoid problems raised by the lack of correspondence between accounting and economic concepts of costs, by the aforementioned difficulty of distinguishing monopoly rents from efficiency rents, etc. In addition, the Swedish products in our sample actually do compete with EEC producers for sales to EEC customers. In this sense, there is a factual basis for treating the EEC price as a competitive benchmark. But there are also problems raised by use of this benchmark. All our measures of cartelization and regulation pertain exclusively to Sweden. Ideally, we would like similar measures for the European Economic Community. Without them, our estimates of the effects of departures from competition in Sweden are likely to be understated. For example, if a product is cartelized in both Sweden and the European Economic Community, prices in both areas could be raised without affecting the Sweden/EEC price ratio. We would then conclude erroneously that the Swedish cartel was ineffective. This sort of possibility deserves to be taken especially seriously when applied to regulation. We know that some heavily regulated areas in Sweden (food, environmentally sensitive products) tend also be regulated in the European Economic Community. Accordingly, we will probably underestimate the effect of Swedish regulation.

Our focus on products actually exported from Sweden also imparts a downward bias to our estimates. Such a sample necessarily excludes the worst examples of inefficiency, namely, products with costs so high they cannot be competitive in export markets. Outsiders, who tend to view Sweden as a small open economy, might rule out the possibility that such great inefficiency could survive in tradable goods. However, according to Flam, Horn, and Lundgren (1993), it is not uncommon for Swedish product markets to be segmented from international competition. In such markets, the effect of reduced competition is likely to be larger than in our sample.

Our measure of Swedish producer prices relative to EEC prices for the same product uses data from both areas. The Swedish data come primarily from comparisons of export prices to prices from the home market. This information is collected by SCB (Statistics Sweden) in order to calculate changes in the producer price index.[12] A problem with these data is that the composition of countries to which Swedish firms export changes over time and differs between industries. Building material firms, for example, export much to Norway, which is an equally protected market with high prices; they export little to Central Europe, where prices generally are much lower.

To avoid this problem, a measure of export prices was calculated that corrects for the destination of exports. The basis for this correction is a producer price comparison (by Eurostat) in 1985 among European countries. Using country producer price indices backward and forward from 1985 yields a matrix of price relations among EEC countries for our sample period 1976–90. Export prices for exports from the Swedish companies to EEC countries were then related to the EEC average using the matrix described above.

More precisely, let the export price in year y be $X_{y,c,d}$ for export from country c to destination d. The home market price is $P_{y,c}$ in country c. Using the producer price comparison among EEC countries in 1985 allows calculation of the average (GDP-weighted) EEC price E_{1985}. Using national product price indices, an index (I) could then be calculated of each country's price for a product relative to the EEC average:

---

12. These SCB data are not available for all product groups, in part because the price information is not released in cases where individual firms can be identified. We have therefore also relied on data on domestic and export producer prices, which can also be calculated from foreign trade statistics that are divided into narrow product groups following the so-called harmonized system. For each product group, the quantity produced, the quantity exported, the quantity imported, and the sales values in nominal prices for each of these categories is published. A potential problem with this database is that, within a product group, the products that are exported may differ from those that are sold in the home market. For the product group "computer software," this is obviously an important problem. The large majority of product groups are, however, so narrowly defined that this should not be a major problem for a statistical analysis as long as the measurement error is not systematic. In some cases, we have also relied on firms' own estimates or on measurements conducted by the National Competition Board. For those product groups where we have two or three price measures, t-tests reveal no significant difference.

$I_{y,c} = P_{y,c}/E_y$ for $y = 1976 \ldots 1990$ (years of our time series),
$c = 1 \ldots 12$ (EEC countries).

To illustrate, assume the following for 1985: (1) Swedish (S) widgets exported to Germany (G) sell for DM 104 ($x_{85, S, G} = 104$). (2) The closest comparable German-produced widget, which is the item used in the EEC price comparisons, sells for DM 100 ($P_{85, G} = 100$), or 4 percent less than the Swedish import. (3) The EEC price comparison shows that the German widget price is 8 percent above the EEC average price ($I_{85, G} = 1.08$). So the average EEC-produced widget would sell for DM 92.00 (DM 100/1.08).

Our procedure results in:

$$XE_{85} = X_{85, S, G}/I_{85, G} = 104/1.08 = 96.$$

This amounts to assuming that the 4 percent premium for the Swedish widgets sold in Germany is a quality premium and then adding this quality premium to the EEC average price of DM 92 to arrive at an estimate of what Swedish widgets would sell for in the European Economic Community. If we have exports to several EEC countries simultaneously, then XE is calculated as a weighted average of the separate export prices. For goods that have exports some years and no exports other years, product price indices are used to fill in the gaps.

Finally, we calculate our measure of "Swedish prices relative to EEC prices," as $P_{y, S}/XE_y$. In our example, if the Swedish widgets sold for the equivalent of DM 120 in Sweden, we would get[13]

$$P_{85, s}/XE_{85} = 120/96 = 1.25.$$

Table 8.5 shows this measure for the fourteen product groups. All prices leading to the measure shown in table 8.5 exclude VAT, so differences in relative prices cannot be explained by higher Swedish indirect taxes. There appears to be a pervasive tendency for Swedish industrial goods prices to exceed those of comparable goods in the European Economic Community. No product category, indeed, not one of the eighty-three sample products, has sold at lower average prices in Sweden than the European Economic Community over a fifteen-year sample period. However, the Swedish price premium, which averages 13.6 percent in our sample, is smaller—on the order of half—than typically found in consumer markets. This suggests that Swedish retail margins are also higher than those in the European Economic Community. In fact, there is evidence that competitive pressures in retailing are weak in Sweden.

In order to check the validity of our price comparisons, we collected two alternative price comparisons for a subsample of products. For nineteen products, firms were asked to quote prices in Sweden and the average price for the European Economic Community. For fifteen products, price comparisons were

---

13. Conceptually, this 25 percent Swedish premium stems from two sources: (1) the 15.4 (120/104) percent premium of the Swedish price over the German price for the same widget compounded by (2) the 8 percent premium of German widget prices over the EEC average.

Table 8.5   Swedish Prices Relative to EEC Prices, 1976–90 (average, EEC = 100)

Products Group	Swedish Relative Prices	Standard Deviation
1. Food	118.3	5.9
2. Apparel and leather	120.3	15.4
3. Wood and paper	119.9	19.0
4. Packaging	109.2	1.9
5. Industrial chemicals	120.5	12.3
6. Drugs and cosmetics	110.6	8.1
7. Petroleum products	113.4	5.6
8. Rubber	115.3	7.4
9. Stone, clay, and glass	107.0	3.9
10. Fabricated metal	109.2	5.5
11. Industrial machinery	110.7	3.5
12. Electrical electronics	111.8	6.3
13. Transport equipment	113.3	3.8
14. Miscellaneous	108.2	1.4
Total sample	113.6	10.1
Minimum	101.5	
Maximum	169.3	

available that had been prepared by the Swedish Competition Authority and by Eurostat. Neither of the alternative price comparisons differed significantly from our relative price measure as described above.[14]

8.2.3 Cartels and Regulation

Our data on cartels come from the Swedish cartel register. This uniquely Swedish institution, abolished in 1993, provided a public record of cartel agreements. This record is incomplete because some agreements may not have been registered. (And some agreements may have remained on the register after their substantive termination.) Nevertheless, the cartel register gives us a rare opportunity for empirical analysis of the effects of cartels across a variety of products. Moreover, although formal cartels are now illegal, cartel practices may persist. So our empirical analysis is of more than historical interest.

Our measure of the intensity of regulation is even "noisier" than our cartel data. It comes from a classification of product groups by the Swedish Competition Authority (SKA) according to the "significance" of various forms of regulation. We used the classification to assign dummies for significant regulation of (1) the *environmental* damage from manufacture of the product, (2) the *price* of the product, and (3) *technical standards* imposed on domestic sales of the product. The last category comprises goods that must meet peculiarly Swedish specifications of product or design. These could be a nontariff barrier

---

14. Chi squares of 1.95 (comparing firms' estimates with relative prices) and 1.57 (comparing price comparisons by independent institutions with our measure) were calculated with eighteen and fourteen degrees of freedom.

Table 8.6   **Cartel Frequency and Type**

	Product Years		% of Product Years			
Products Group	Total	With Cartel Agreement	Any Agreement (2)/(1)	Vertical Agreement Only	Horizontal Agreement Only	Both Types
1. Food	150	113	75.3	10.7	4.7	60.0
2. Apparel and leather	60	20	33.3	33.3	0	0
3. Wood and paper	120	50	41.7	15.0	10.0	16.7
4. Packaging	45	23	51.1	28.9	0	22.2
5. Industrial chemicals	105	43	41.0	21.9	0	19.0
6. Drugs and cosmetics	45	9	20.0	6.7	0	13.3
7. Petroleum products	60	6	10.0	0	10.0	0
8. Rubber products	30	0	0	0	0	0
9. Stone, clay, and glass	120	19	15.8	0	15.8	0
10. Fabricated metal	150	0	0	0	0	0
11. Industrial machinery	105	18	17.1	0	0	17.1
12. Electrical electronics	135	14	10.4	0	10.4	0
13. Transport equipment	75	15	20.0	0	20.0	0
14. Miscellaneous	45	36	80.0	0	53.3	26.7
Total	1,245	366	29.4	7.5	7.8	14.1

to imports, as when Swedish construction specifications effectively precluded some imported building materials. The standards could also restrict domestic entry if domestic firms have different compliance costs.

Tables 8.6 and 8.7 summarize the frequency of cartels and regulation across product groups in our sample. Since we have fifteen annual observations for each product, we use the "product year" to measure frequency; there are 1,245 product years (83 products × 15 years) in our sample.

Table 8.6 reveals that 366 product years, or 29.4 percent of the sample, are covered by some type of cartel agreement. The data in the cartel register allow us to distinguish horizontal (primarily price-fixing and market-sharing) from vertical (mainly exclusive-dealing) agreements. About half the agreements (14.1 percent of product years) are both vertical and horizontal, with the remainder roughly equally divided between the two types.[15] Of the horizontal agreements (detail not shown), the majority involve price fixing.[16]

15. We include "other" types under vertical, although these can have horizontal dimensions; these other agreements constitute eighteen of ninety-seven product years classified as vertical.

16. Ninety percent of the horizontal agreements have price-fixing provisions; 42 percent contain market-sharing arrangements.

Table 8.7   **Frequency of Regulation**

Products Group	% of Product Years			
	Any Regulation	Environmental	Price	Technical Standards
1. Food	100.0	8.7	70.0	100.0
2. Apparel and leather	0	. . .	. . .	. . .
3. Wood and paper	100.0	100.0	0	12.5
4. Packaging	33.3	0	0	33.3
5. Industrial chemicals	100.0	100.0	0	0
6. Drugs and cosmetics	0	. . .	. . .	. . .
7. Petroleum products	100.0	100.0	0	25.0
8. Rubber products	0	. . .	. . .	. . .
9. Stone, clay, and glass	0	. . .	. . .	. . .
10. Fabricated metal	0	. . .	. . .	. . .
11. Industrial machinery	0	. . .	. . .	. . .
12. Electrical electronic	0	. . .	. . .	. . .
13. Transport equipment	60.0	0	. . .	60.0
14. Miscellaneous	33.3	33.3	0	0
Total	410	25.1	8.4	19.3

A notable aspect of the table is the substantial concentration of cartels by industry. Here, the food industry deserves special mention. It accounts for slightly more than one-tenth of the sample but around one-third of all the cartel activity. This high incidence of cartelization may be rooted in the previously discussed Swedish agricultural policy, which has simultaneously pushed the prices of the industry's raw agricultural inputs above even those in the European Community and led Sweden to protect the processors against import competition. This relaxed threat of foreign entry may have encouraged domestic cartelization. Two other industry groups (wood/paper and chemicals) together account for another one-quarter of the cartel activity. In these cases, other forms of domestic regulation may be providing entry barriers conducive to cartelization.

Table 8.7 elaborates on this last point by summarizing the industrial distribution of the three types of regulation as classified by the SKA. In our sample, price regulation occurs exclusively in the food sector, and it is invariably combined with tariffs and quotas against processed food imports from the European Economic Community.[17] Thus, the price regulation category here reflects another aspect of Swedish agricultural policy. The other forms of regulation are also concentrated in a few industries: the forest products, chemical, and petroleum refining industries are subject to significant environmental regulation in Sweden, as in most developed countries. In technical standards, once more the food industry stands out; it accounts for nearly two-thirds of the sample products subject to significant technical standards.

17. This is the only product category in our sample with tariffs or quotas against EEC imports.

The tendency of cartels to form in regulated industries can be summarized by the following regressions estimated across the eighty-three sample products:

(1)   HORIZ = .089 + .207·ENV + .558·PRICE + .147·TECH,
                        (3.2)   (4.5)   (1.7)
(2)   VERT = .117 + .104·ENV + .644·PRICE + .111·TECH.
                       (1.4)   (4.5)   (1.0)

The dependent variables are the share of a product's sample observations under the indicated type of cartel, and the right-hand side variables are dummies for the indicated type of regulation. We place t-ratios below coefficients, and the intercepts give the cartel frequency for products with no significant regulation. The regressions show that the presence of regulation is associated with cartel frequencies, which are, depending on the type of regulation, anywhere from two or three to around seven times the cartel frequency in unregulated markets.

Our main interest is in how this panoply of cartelization and regulation has affected Swedish economic performance. By *performance* we mean mainly prices but also the level of costs and productivity growth. Our initial exploration of these issues heeds Schmalensee's (1989, 957) advice "that the primary objective of cross-section studies (in industrial organization) must be to describe the main patterns in the data set employed as clearly and completely as possible." Thus, we begin with the main regularities in the data without claiming that they represent the reduced form of an explicit model.

8.2.4   Cartels and Regulation: Prices

Table 8.8 provides the most basic and durable such description. It shows results of regressions of Swedish relative prices (see table 8.5 above) on various cartel and regulation dummies.[18] It tells a fairly straightforward story:

1. Taken as a group, products under horizontal cartels have prices around 3 percent higher than the sample average (col. 1). This estimate does not rest heavily on conditions peculiar to the food industry (col. 2).

2. However, regulation rather than cartels seems to be the primary source of these high relative prices (col. 3). Holding constant the effect of regulation, horizontal cartels have no higher prices than the sample average.

3. The price premia associated with regulation are substantial—enough to roughly double (price regulation) or raise by half (environmental regulation) the typical Swedish price premium of 13.6 percent for affected goods.[19] These

18. The regressions also include a set of year dummies, the results of which are not reported in the table.

19. The size of the coefficients, which are estimates of these extra premia, deserves more emphasis than the t-ratios. The reported (OLS) t-ratios are exaggerated because of the persistence over time of cartels and regulation. This means that we do not really have 1,245 independent observations. Regressions that suppressed all the time variation in prices by using fifteen-year averages of the data across the eighty-three products yielded t-ratios around half those shown in the table.

Table 8.8   **Regression of Swedish Relative Prices on Cartel and Regulation Variables, 1976–90**

Independent Variables	(1)		(2)		(3)	
	Coef.	$\lvert t \rvert$	Coef.	$\lvert t \rvert$	Coef.	$\lvert t \rvert$
A. Cartel agreement:						
1. Vertical	−.1	.1	−.8	.8	−2.5	2.5
2. Horizontal	3.4	3.4	2.2	2.2	.1	.1
B. Food industry			4.4	3.8	−2.0	.9
C. Regulation:						
1. Environmental					7.0	9.1
2. Price					12.8	6.0
3. Technical standards					.8	.7
D. Year dummies:[a]	Yes		Yes		Yes	
$\bar{R}^2$	.09		.10		.18	
SEE	11.9		11.8		11.3	

Note: All regressions are based on 1,245 observations: 83 products × 15 years of data. Cartel/regulation variables = +1 if indicated type of cartel or regulation is in force in the year, 0 otherwise.
[a]All regressions include fourteen dummies, each = +1 for observations in years 1976 . . . 1990, coefficients not shown.

results suggest that Swedish environmental regulation is more costly than EC environmental regulation. They also reveal price regulation as the primary source of Sweden's unusually high food prices: note that food products not covered by this regulation (row B, col. 3) actually have slightly below-average price premia. However, technical standards have no marginal effects on prices in this sample.

4. Vertical restraints have theoretically ambiguous competitive effects. The frequent conjunction of vertical restrictions with horizontal cartels in our sample might arouse skepticism that vertical restrictions enhance competition in Sweden. But our results (col. 3, row A.1) are more consistent with that view than the contrary.

5. Because our measure of regulation is concentrated in a few industries, the price-increasing effects do not account for a substantial part of the overall Swedish price premium vis-à-vis the European Community. If the effect of the regulation is removed, the regression in column 3 implies that the average price premium would shrink from 13.6 to 11.3 percent. This result should be taken as a call for further work rather than as definitive estimate. If our rather crude measures of regulation can account for nearly 20 percent of the overall price premium, perhaps a more refined analysis will expand on this estimate.[20]

20. The sort of refinement permitted by our data proved unavailing. We investigated the interaction between regulation and cartels (e.g., do cartels have different effects in regulated industries than in unregulated industries?) without uncovering a consistent pattern. We also looked unsuccessfully for different effects from price-fixing and market-sharing agreements. Again, it is premature to conclude that such subtleties are absent. Rather, they may be hidden by the small number of products in our sample that fit the relevant subcategories.

Table 8.9   **Market Structure, Regulation, Cartels, and Prices, 1976–90**

Independent Variables	(1)		(2)		(3)	
	Coef.	|t|	Coef.	|t|	Coef.	|t|
A. Cartel agreement:						
1. Vertical	−2.3	2.3	−2.0	2.0	−2.0	2.1
2. Horizontal	0	0	−.8	.8	−.8	.8
B. Regulation:						
1. Environmental	7.1	9.3	6.8	8.9	6.6	8.7
2. Price	11.6	7.2	12.3	7.6	12.3	7.6
3. Technical standards	.2	.2	−.8	.8	−.9	.8
C. Market structure:						
1. Herfindahl index	1.19	1.4	−9.3	2.9	−9.1	2.9
2. Number of firms			−2.9	3.9	−2.8	3.9
D. Average wage (000 1990 krona)					.06	2.3
E. Year dummies:[a]	Yes		Yes		Yes	
$\bar{R}^2$	.18		.19		.19	
SEE	11.3		11.2		11.2	

Our database has enough firm-specific data to enable us to add some conventional market structure measures to the regression. Since Bain (1951), well over a hundred studies have investigated the relations between market structure measures (usually concentration) and measures of market performance (usually of profitability used as a proxy for the price marginal cost ratio). Because we have a direct measure of price performance across a variety of products, we need not rely exclusively on indirect measures like profit ratios. However, we lack EC market structure measures that should in principle be included.

The results are summarized in table 8.9. Standing alone (col. 1), concentration as measured by the Herfindahl index (the sum of the firms' squared market shares) has a weak positive effect on prices, as in most of the post-Bain literature. However, this result is decisively reversed when the number of firms is added to the regression (col. 2). The negative coefficient on concentration is consistent with the differential efficiency interpretation, whereby efficient firms raise their output (and market share) and prices decline. For example, suppose one of three initially equal size firms doubles its market share. According to column 2, row C.1, the resulting increase in the Herfindahl index $(.167)^{21}$ would be associated with a price reduction of about 1½ percent. That price reduction implies that the market share gained by the now dominant firm was accompanied by a net increase in output, which presumably results from this firm's lowered marginal costs.

At the same time, the regression suggests an important role for entry. Hold-

---

21. The difference between $3(1/3)^2$ and $(2/3)^2 + 2(1/6)^2$.

ing concentration constant, each additional firm is associated (col. 2, row C.2) with about 3 percent lower prices. This is a potentially significant magnitude in the Swedish context, where most goods have few producers. The regression suggests that with, say, two more producers per product roughly half the Swedish price premium could be eliminated. Entry in most of our product markets is not limited by explicit legal barriers. Therefore, actually achieving an increased number of firms would require more import competition or a change in policies that discriminate against new firms. More stringent policy on mergers could prevent decreases in the number of firms, but our results on the benefits of concentration suggest some caution. Finally, the caveat about structural interpretation of the regressions deserves special emphasis here. Causation running from lower prices, via widened markets, to more firms cannot be ruled out.

Column 3 of table 8.9 adds the industry average wage. The positive coefficient is reasonable but economically unimportant. The main reason for this is that wage differences across Swedish manufacturing industries are vanishingly small. The fifteen-year average of the real (1990 krona) wage across the eighty-three products in our sample is SKr 275,000, while the standard deviation is only SKr 5,000, or less than 2 percent of the mean. Thus, the regression implies that even a four-standard-deviation move in the average wage would not affect prices by much more than 1 percent.

All the previous results on cartels and regulation remain essentially unaltered when the market structure and wage variables are added to the regression.

8.2.5 Time-Series Analysis

By exploiting the time-series dimension of our data, we gain a check on the rather negative findings on the effects of cartels that emerged from the cross-sectional analysis. Our sample has forty changes in cartel agreements. There are about as many (twenty-one) cartel formations (new agreements, added provisions) as terminations (nineteen). The time pattern of these changes is striking. Eighteen of the formations and eleven of the terminations, or over 70 percent of all the changes, occur in 1979–83. This period saw considerable macroeconomic changes, such as an oil price "shock" and a major devaluation of the krona. Our turnover data suggest that the need for price realignments in this period stimulated new cartels but also put pressure on existing agreements.[22]

In the next set of tables, we examines price *changes* that occurred around thirty-eight of these cartel changes.[23] We also examine output changes around cartel changes. Output provides a measure of cartel effects that is, in principle,

---

22. A few of the terminations in 1982–83 may have been stimulated by a 1982 change in antitrust law that increased the government's power to terminate cartels proved to have harmful effects. But this law cannot have been a powerful deterrent given the high rate of cartel formation in the period.
23. Two occur in the terminal years of our sample.

Table 8.10   **Price Changes and Cartel Changes**

	Type of Cartel Change						
	Formation				Termination			
	Horizontal		Vertical		Horizontal		Vertical	
Price Variable and Interval[a]	% Δ	|t|	% Δ	|t|	% Δ	|t|	% Δ	|t|
A. Swedish relative price:								
1. Year of change (0)	.9	1.2	.0	.0	1.0	1.3	−3.5	3.4
2. Year after (+1)	−1.0	1.3	.9	1.3	−.6	.8	1.7	1.6
3. Year before (−1)	−1.3	1.7	.9	1.2	−.2	.2	.8	.8
4. 0 to +1	−.1	.1	1.2	1.2	.4	.3	−1.8	1.2
5. −1 to 0	−.5	1.1	.9	1.0	.9	1.1	−2.4	1.5
6. −1 to 1	−1.5	1.1	2.1	1.7	.3	.2	−.5	.3
B. Swedish domestic price:								
1. 0	.0	.0	.5	1.7	.2	.6	−.4	.9
2. +1	.2	.6	.3	1.1	.2	.7	−.2	.3
3. −1	−.4	1.2	.3	.8	.3	.9	.1	.2
4. 0, +1	.2	.4	.9	2.0	.4	.9	−.6	.9
5. −1, 0	−.4	.8	.8	1.8	.6	1.0	−.4	.5
6. −1, 1	−.2	.3	1.2	2.1	.8	1.3	−.5	.9

Note: Based on regressions with change in log of price as dependent variable. Independent variables include up to three cartel change dummies, year dummies, and, for the Swedish price change, the current and two lagged values of the changes in the log of the EEC price index for the good. Sample sizes vary from 913 to 1,162 depending on the lag structure.

[a]Each row indicates a different assumed lag structure. For example, in row 1, it is assumed that all effects occur in year of cartel change; in row 6, the effects are assumed to begin a year before and end a year after the change.

complementary to price effects (if price rises, output should decline). However, if prices are more poorly measured than output, or if product demands are sufficiently elastic, output may provide the more sensitive measure of cartel effects. Indeed, the time-series analysis supports this view. It essentially corroborates our previous negative findings on the price effects of cartels while revealing some substantial output effects.

Table 8.10 shows results for two measures of price change. They are extracted from regressions of the price change on various sets of dummies for change in cartel agreements plus controls. Because cartels can form or break up before this appears in the cartel register, we include dummies for the year preceding the change. Dummies for the year following a cartel change allow for any lagged effects of the change. Panel A shows the change in the Swedish relative (to EEC) price net of year effects. Panel B shows the change in the numerator of this price ratio—the Swedish domestic price—after controlling for current and two lagged changes in the denominator (the EEC price) and year effects. There is some evidence of price increases around formation of vertical cartels and of price decreases around their dissolution. But the overwhelming pattern in the table is of small price changes, typically 1 percent or less and typically indistinguishable from zero. The one exception covers dissolution of vertical agreements, and here the change seems temporary and is sensitive to the way price is measured.

Table 8.11 uses nonparametric tests to hedge against the possibility that these negative results are due to a few atypical price changes or to price indexes that understate price changes. Here, we simply count signs of residuals from regressions of the price changes on controls. We want to see if positive residuals usually accompany new cartel agreements and negative residuals accompany cartel terminations. These sign counts are compared to counts in the whole sample and in a control group consisting of products in the same industry group with no change in cartel status. The results are perhaps a bit sharper than those in table 8.10 above. The main tendency is for prices to tick up when cartels are formed and down when they dissolve. But statistical significance is often lacking. The relatively small sample sizes limit the power of our tests and more refined analysis of, for example, the interaction of cartel changes with regulation.[24] Nevertheless, they add to the impression that Sweden's tolerance of cartel agreements was not a major source of its historically high prices.[25]

The evidence on output is much less equivocal: output fell substantially when cartels were formed and rose when they were dissolved. This is shown in tables 8.12 and 8.13, which are the analogs for output to tables 8.10 and 8.11 above. Table 8.12 shows that, depending on the time span and type of agreement, output fell anywhere from 6 to 13 percent when a cartel was formed and rose a comparable amount when a horizontal cartel was terminated.[26] (The apparently weaker results for vertical cartel terminations should be discounted because they are based on only one "pure" case.)[27] Table 8.13 shows that these results are not due to a few outliers. In over 90 percent of the cases, cartel formation is accompanied by abnormally low output growth and cartel termination by abnormally high growth in the year of the change. There is no similarly strong pattern for the year preceding and the year following cartel changes.

Half the cartel formations involve products subject to stringent environmen-

24. We did attempt to divide each sample into subsamples of products subject to some form of regulation and those not so subject. The consistent pattern was that prices of the regulated products rose and fell *less* frequently than other goods when cartels formed or dissolved. But this difference was insignificant.

25. The tests in tables 8.5 and 8.6 above were repeated—with essentially identical results—on (1) a sample consisting only of products that had undergone cartel switches in the period 1976–90 and (2) price change variables measured as deviations from the 1976–90 mean change for the product.

26. Essentially identical results were obtained from a sample including only those products with change in cartel status. So, e.g., for these products, output growth was 6 percent below trend in the year in which a horizontal cartel formed.

27. In eight other cases, vertical and horizontal agreements are terminated simultaneously.

Table 8.11 **Frequency of Positive Residuals for Price Changes around Cartel Changes**

Price Variable, Type of Change (number of cases)	Frequency Positive Residuals	Control Group Frequency	Difference	$\lvert t \rvert$
A. Swedish relative price:				
I. Cartel formation:				
1. Horizontal (10):				
a) Year of change	.80+	.42	.38	2.2
b) Year before	.70	.68	.02	.2
c) Year after	.40	.56	−.16	1.1
2. Vertical (13):				
a) Year of change	.62	.47	.14	.9
b) Year before	.75+	.61	.14	1.1
c) Year after	.69	.62	.07	.4
II. Cartel termination:				
1. Horizontal (17):				
a) Year of change	.41	.51	−.10	.8
b) Year before	.65	.53	.12	.8
c) Year after	.50	.59	−.09	.6
2. Vertical (9):				
a) Year of change	.00−	.53	−.53	5.2
b) Year before	.78	.54	.24	1.3
c) Year after	.75	.59	.16	1.0
B. Swedish price:				
I. Cartel formation:				
1. Horizontal (10):				
a) Year of change	.80	.51	.29	1.60
b) Year before	.56	.75	−.19	1.12
c) Year after	.70	.68	+.02	.11
2. Vertical (12):				
a) Year of change	.83+	.56	.27	2.19
b) Year before	.64	.61	.03	.16
c) Year after	.75	.68	.07	.46
II. Cartel termination:				
1. Horizontal (16):				
a) Year of change	.44	.73	−.29	2.39
b) Year before	.86+	.77	.08	1.04
c) Year after	.60	.69	−.09	.66
2. Vertical (9):				
a) Year of change	.22−	.73	−.51	3.40
b) Year before	.89+	.76	.13	1.20
c) Year after	.63	.57	.06	.43

Note: Numbers in parentheses are number of cases. Cartel with both horizontal and vertical provisions (three formations, eight terminations) is counted twice. Cases used in computations vary because of different underlying lag structures of the two regressions used to generate residuals and because 1975 and 1991 data are unavailable. + (−) = significantly (5 percent) greater (smaller) than overall sample frequency. Control group is products in same industry group with no change in cartel status in the relevant period.

Table 8.12 **Output Changes and Cartel Changes**

	Type of Cartel Change							
	Formation				Termination			
	Horizontal		Vertical		Horizontal		Vertical	
Interval	% Δ	| *t* |	% Δ	| *t* |	% Δ	| *t* |	% Δ	| *t* |
1. Year of change (0)	−5.8	2.7	−10.5	5.7	+6.7	3.3	+2.5	.9
2. Year after (+1)	−3.0	1.4	+3.8	2.0	−.4	.2	−.4	.1
3. Year before (−1)	−4.1	1.9	1.0	.5	−.2	.1	−1.3	.4
4. 0 to +1	−8.8	2.9	−7.1	2.7	+6.2	2.1	+1.9	.5
5. −1 to 0	−10.0	3.3	−9.7	3.6	+6.5	2.2	+1.4	.3
6. −1 to 1	−13.3	3.5	−6.4	1.9	+6.2	1.7	+1.3	.3

Note: See the note to table 8.10 above. This table is based on regressions with the change in log of output, year *t* minus the average annual change, 1976–90 as the dependent variable, and year dummies as independent variables. Sample size varies from 996 to 1,162 depending on the log structure.

tal regulation. In the year of a cartel formation, output of these goods fell much more (17 percent for horizontal and 20 percent for vertical cartel formations) than for other goods. These differences, which are statistically significant, may imply that the usual threat to cartel stability from potential output expansion is weakened by environmental restrictions. Actual output expansion when cartels terminated proved to be no different for goods subject to environmental regulation (one-third of terminations) than for others.

There is an obvious tension between the results on price changes and those on output changes that we cannot resolve here. Taken literally, the results seem inconsistent with rational cartel behavior, which employs output restriction only if this raises prices. Alternatively, our results might suggest that our price measure is not accurately reflecting transaction prices or nonprice attributes (quality, delivery time, etc.) of products. However, tests for changes in two measures of profit margin around cartel changes yielded the same negative results as for prices.[28] This lack of response of profit margins to cartel changes implies that measurement problems alone do not account for our odd results on prices.

8.2.6 Cartels Regulation and the Efficiency of Production

Standard theory does not have much to say about the effect of cartelization or regulation on the efficiency of production. Nevertheless, at least since Adam Smith contended that "monopoly . . . is a great enemy to good management," economists have suspected a connection between competition and production

28. The two measures, described more fully in the next section, are profits before capital costs/sales and value added per employee. All else the same, these would increase if prices rose or lower-quality goods were sold at unchanged prices.

Table 8.13   **Frequency of Positive Residuals, Output Changes around Cartel Changes**

Type of Change (number of cases)	Frequency Positive Residuals	Control Group Frequency	Difference	$\lvert t \rvert$
I. Cartel formation:				
1. Horizontal (10):				
a) Year of change	.20−	.62	−.42	2.2
b) Year before	.20−	.45	−.25	1.9
c) Year after	.70	.38	.32	1.5
2. Vertical (13):				
a) Year of change	.00−	.65	−.65	13.5
b) Year before	.31	.48	−.18	1.2
c) Year after	.69	.49	.21	1.5
II. Cartel termination:				
1. Horizontal (17):				
a) Year of change	.94+	.46	+.48	4.4
b) Year before	.41	.52	−.11	.8
c) Year after	.63	.57	+.05	.4
2. Vertical (9):				
a) Year of change	1.00+	.38	+.62	9.2
b) Year before	.44	.48	−.04	.2
c) Year after	.50	.67	−.17	1.0

Note: See the notes to tables 8.11 and 8.12 above.

efficiency. Our data allow us to investigate this connection for Sweden and thereby to shed light on the question of whether lack of competition in Sweden has contributed to the perceived high-cost structure of its manufacturing sector. We begin with regressions describing the connection between measures of static efficiency and productivity growth, on the one hand, and cartelization and regulation, on the other.

8.2.7   Static Efficiency

We use two measures related to static efficiency: gross profits as a percentage of sales (the "price-cost margin") and value added per worker.[29] All else the same (including prices), more efficient use of resources would raise both measures. The two measures differ in their treatment of labor rents. These reduce profitability but not value added.[30] So labor rents show up as an inefficiency in the profit-based measure but not in value added per worker. Our choice of measures is dictated in part by lack of data on raw material prices. This precludes investigation of efficiency in the use of raw materials. Finally, our efficiency measures are for the aggregate of the firms or divisions producing a product, while the competition measures are product specific. Recall,

29. Gross profits are before depreciation and capital costs, and value added is just gross profits plus employment costs.

30. Any rents to outside suppliers would reduce both profits and value added.

Table 8.14   **Profits/Sales, Value Added per Worker, Competition and Regulation**

	Profits/Sales $\times 10^2$				Value Added/Worker (SKr 000)			
	(1)		(2)		(3)		(4)	
Independent Variables	Coef.	$|t|$	Coef.	$|t|$	Coef.	$|t|$	Coef.	$|t|$
A. Cartels:								
1. Vertical	$-.2$	.3	$-.0$	.0	-21	1.5	-15	1.1
2. Horizontal	1.3	1.3	1.7	1.7	29	2.1	30	2.1
B. Regulation:								
1. Environmental	3.8	5.2	3.8	5.3	46	4.3	44	4.1
2. Price	7.5	4.9	7.4	4.8	77	3.4	81	3.6
3. Technical standards	.4	.4	.7	.7	22	1.5	19	1.3
C. Capital intensity:								
1. Capital/sales	7.3	3.5	7.4	3.5				
2. Capital/worker (SKr 000)					.22	19.4	.22	19.3
D. Market structure:								
1. Herfindahl index			9.0	2.9			68	1.5
2. Number of firms			1.1	1.5			-4	0.4
E. Year dummies:	Yes		Yes		Yes		Yes	
$\bar{R}^2$	.20		.21		.39		.40	
SEE	10.8		10.8		158.0		156.9	

however, that these products account for around 80 percent of firm or division sales in our sample.

Table 8.14 summarizes the relation between both measures and competition/regulation. (The regressions include capital intensity variables as controls.) The results here need to be interpreted in the light of the previously discussed price effects summarized in tables 8.8 and 8.9 above because either higher prices or greater efficiency can raise profits or value added. Specifically, if b_{π_i} or b_{v_i} denotes a coefficient of interest in the profit or value added regression, respectively, of table 8.14, and if b_{p_i} is the coefficient of the same variable in the earlier price regression, the following approximations[31] obtain:

$$(3) \qquad \frac{\% \, \Delta \text{ cost/unit}}{\Delta i} = \frac{b_{p_i}}{\text{price}} - b_{\pi_i}\left(\frac{\text{sales}}{\text{costs}}\right),$$

31. These follow from the relations

$$\frac{\text{profits}}{\text{sales}} = \frac{\text{price} - \text{unit cost}}{\text{price}},$$

$$\frac{\text{value added}}{\text{worker}} = (\text{price} - \text{purchases per unit})\left(\frac{\text{output}}{\text{worker}}\right).$$

We assume that "purchases per unit" is a parameter.

Table 8.15   **Estimated Effect of Competition and Regulation on Unit Costs and Output per Worker**

Variables	Effect of Unit Change on: Cost/Output (%)	|t|	Effect of Unit Change on: Output/Worker (%)	|t|
A. Cartels:				
1. Vertical	−1.8	1.5	+1.6	.5
2. Horizontal	−2.8	1.9	+4.0	1.1
B. Regulation:				
1. Environmental	+1.3	1.2	−6.8	2.5
2. Price	1.8	.8	−12.1	2.1
3. Technical standards	−1.9	1.3	5.5	1.5
C. Market structure:				
1. Herfindahl index	−19.2	4.0	34.3	3.0
2. Number of firms	−3.9	3.5	5.8	2.3

Note: Based on coefficients from col. 2 of table 8.9 and cols. 2 and 4 of table 8.14. For formula combining these coefficients, see the text. Estimates are taken at sample means of all relevant variables.

$$(4) \quad \frac{\% \, \Delta \text{ output per worker}}{\Delta i} = \frac{b_{v_i}}{\text{value added/worker}} - \frac{b_{p_i}}{(\text{price}) \, (\text{value added/sales})}.$$

We can then estimate the effect of a change in competition or regulation (Δi) on efficiency by appropriately combining the two coefficients. The results of this exercise are shown in table 8.15, which uses the price regression in column 2 of table 8.9 above and the regressions in columns 3 and 4 of table 8.14 above to generate estimates of the effect of competition and regulation on static efficiency at the sample means of the relevant variables. To illustrate how these estimates were arrived at, we can work through a specific case. Table 8.15 says that Swedish environmental regulation has reduced output per worker by 6.8 percent.[32] This is the net result of effects on price (table 8.9) and on value added (table 8.14). It is computed as follows. According to column 2 of table 8.9, environmental regulation raises Swedish relative prices by 6.8 points, or 6 percent of the mean value (113.6) of the Swedish relative price index. By itself, a 6 percent price increase would raise sales by 6 percent. Because value added is only about 40 percent of sales, a 6 percent sales increase would be amplified

32. The associated \|t\| of 2.5 (and all other *t*-ratios in the table) is subject to two offsetting biases: (1) the aforementioned (n. 18) upward bias stemming from overstatement of the true degrees of freedom and (2) a downward bias resulting from the assumed independence of the coefficients b_{p_i} and b_{v_i} or b_{π_i} when they are likely to be positively correlated.

into a 15 percent (6/.4) rise of value added, which would translate into an extra SKr 78,000 per worker (in 1990 prices, given a mean value added per worker of around SKr 520,000). However, column 4, row B.1 of table 8.14 tells us that only SKr 44,000, or 56 percent of the potential increase in value added, is attained. Table 8.15 attributes this shortfall of SKr 34,000 to a decline in output per worker. In short, the actual increase in value added (about 8 percent) is the result of the 15 percent potential increase from higher prices and the partly offsetting roughly 7 percent reduction in output per worker.

The results in table 8.15 suggest that cartels are not associated with a loss of production efficiency. In fact, if anything, cartelized industries were more efficient. Environmental regulation and price regulation, however, do seem to be associated with nontrivial productivity losses. The former is expected because expenses for environmental protection do not produce measurable output. The large (12.1 percent) productivity loss for price-regulated goods implies that the minimum prices shelter considerably inefficiency. And the correspondingly modest unit cost effect (1.8 percent) suggests that suppliers and workers are sharing the costs of this inefficiency with firms and consumers.

The results for the market structure measures imply an important connection between competition and efficiency, but one that needs to be interpreted carefully. At the margin, an extra firm is associated with 6 percent increased output per worker. But the results for the Herfindahl measure of concentration imply that attempts to maintain the number of firms by a vigorous anticoncentration policy would be mistaken. Consistent with the previously articulated differential efficiency story, the more concentrated industries tend to be the more efficient. The large numbers in row C.1 of table 8.15 need to be discounted because they refer to an unrealistic shift from atomistic competition to monopoly. A more realistically modest change in the Herfindahl index, say .2,[33] would still suggest a considerable productivity gain (around 7 percent higher output per worker) from expansion of efficient leading firms. Similarly, the results imply that the decline in Swedish concentration over the sample period is associated with reduced output per worker and higher unit costs. The average decline in the Herfindahl index has been .08. The results in table 8.15 translate this into a 1½ percent reduction of output per worker. Recall that all the reduced average concentration has come from the largest firm's loss of market share. So the differential efficiency story would link the reduced efficiency to a steady weakening of the largest firms' productivity advantages. If there is a policy implication in these results, it would be to eliminate any barriers to new entrants while allowing market forces to determine how concentrated markets become.

---

33. Approximately the result when one of three previously equal sized firms doubles its market share.

8.2.8   Productivity Growth

For each product in our sample, we estimated the average annual growth in productivity for 1976–90 under two measures: a "Solow residual" estimate of total factor productivity (TFP) growth and the more traditional growth of output per worker. The TFP growth estimate is

output growth $-$ α(labor input growth) $-$ $(1 - \alpha)$(capital input growth),

where α is labor's share of output. This is an estimate of the growth of output per unit of input.[34] We are limited to a two-input production function by the aforementioned lack of data on material inputs, and we also recall that our output measure is at the firm rather than the product level. We estimated α as (wage costs/value added) over the fifteen-year period for each product.[35] It is of particular importance to note that our output series is obtained by deflating sales by a product price index. Total employment and an estimate of the real value of fixed assets constitute our input measures. For our sample, TFP growth averages 1.62 percent per year, while labor productivity grows at 2.46 percent per year. These are broadly typical of manufacturing in Europe and North America over the period 1976–90.

The relation between TFP growth and competition and regulation is spelled out in table 8.16. The first two regressions show that cartelized and regulated industries have experienced generally subpar productivity growth. These negative effects are not always precisely estimated, but they tend to be numerically large. For example, regression (2) implies essentially zero TFP growth for products subject to horizontal cartels. This regression also implies, somewhat in contrast to the results for the level of productivity, that higher concentration and more firms are associated with lower TFP growth. This is similar to Salinger's (1990) finding that concentrated industries in the United States experienced a reversal of previously favorable cost trends in roughly the same period.

The third regression in table 8.16 adds an industry-group EEC price trend variable. This is meant as a control for industry-specific factors, hopefully unrelated to Swedish competitive and regulatory conditions, which affect productivity in all countries. For example, productivity in electronics has generally been well above average, and this is reflected in generally declining relative prices for electronics products both in Sweden and the European Economic Community. Since we lack direct estimates of industry sector TFP growth outside Sweden, we use the EEC price trend as a proxy. The addition of this variable essentially wipes out every previous result and dramatically boosts the

---

34. It is based on the assumption of factor neutral technical progress and Cobb-Douglas technology.

35. An alternative in which the share of capital was obtained by multiplying the samplewide fifteen-year rate of return by the capital stock yielded essentially identical conclusions.

Table 8.16   **Total Factor Productivity Growth, 1976–90**

Independent Variables	(1) Coef.	$\lvert t \rvert$	(2) Coef.	$\lvert t \rvert$	(3) Coef.	$\lvert t \rvert$
A. Cartels:						
1. Horizontal	−1.22	1.7	−1.56	2.1	−.04	.2
2. Vertical	+.46	.7	.47	.7	.11	.6
B. Regulation:						
1. Environmental	−.47	1.1	−.53	1.3	+.19	1.6
2. Price	−.41	.5	−.15	.2	−.20	.8
3. Technical standards	−.74	1.3	−.96	1.7	+.01	.4
C. Market structure:						
1. Herfindahl index			−3.30	1.7	−.25	.4
2. Number of firms			−.77	1.7	−.10	.8
D. Median industry price change in EEC, 1976–90					−.98	30.4
$\bar{R}^2$	.10		.11		.93	
SEE	1.54		1.53		.42	

Note: Sample = 83 products. Dependent variable is annual percentage growth of total factor productivity between 1976–77 and 1989–90. For definition of total factor productivity, see the text. Cartel, regulation, and market structure measures are 1976–90 averages of annual values. EEC industry price change is the median value for the industry group of the annual rate of change of EEC product price indexes for 1976–77 to 1989–90.

regression's fit. The coefficient of this variable is around –1, which might suggest that it is a perfect proxy for industrywide TFP trends.[36]

There is, however, need for caution in taking this result at face value. Recall that output growth is estimated as the difference between the growth of sales and of product prices. Any measurement error in industry price trends common to Sweden and the European Economic Community will be translated into an opposite-signed error in estimated TFP growth. For example, if electronics price indexes generally understate quality improvement, TFP growth in electronics will be correspondingly understated. The coefficient of –1 on the EEC price variable would also be consistent with the (probably unrealistic) extreme case in which the common measurement error accounted for all the variance in price trends across products. Correlation of this error with the cartel and regulatory variables could then bias their coefficients in the third regression.[37]

Table 8.17 repeats the exercise in table 8.16 using a labor productivity measure. Growth of capital per worker is added as a control. The results of interest are nearly identical. So any conclusions seem insensitive to the way productivity growth is measured.

36. If TFP growth is translated point for point into lower price growth.
37. Electronics and fabricated metals have the best measured price performance in both the European Economic Community and Sweden, and they show relatively little cartel and regulatory activity.

Table 8.17   **Growth Rate of Output per Worker, 1976–90**

	(1)		(2)		(3)	
Independent Variables	Coef.	$\lvert t \rvert$	Coef.	$\lvert t \rvert$	Coef.	$\lvert t \rvert$
A. Cartels:						
1. Horizontal	−1.17	1.6	−1.48	2.0	−.02	.1
2. Vertical	+.39	.6	.41	.6	.05	.5
B. Regulation:						
1. Environmental	−.51	1.2	−.56	1.4	.15	1.9
2. Price	−.25	.3	−.01	.0	−.05	.3
3. Technical standards	−.78	1.4	−.98	1.8	+.02	.2
C. Market structure:						
1. Herfindahl index			−2.99	1.5	−.05	.1
2. Number of firms			−.72	1.6	−.90	.05
D. Growth rate of capital per worker	.91	3.8	.86	3.6	.90	20.2
E. Median industry price change, EEC					−.97	45.8
$\bar{R}^2$		.18		.19		.97
SEE		1.49		1.48		.27

Our conclusions about dynamic efficiency have to be tentative. What is clear is that the cartelized and regulated sectors in Sweden generally have been substantial laggards in TFP growth. This tendency is especially pronounced for horizontal cartels and for environmental and technical standards regulation. What remains unclear is the precise role of Swedish cartels and Swedish regulation in bringing this result about. Among the possibilities that we must acknowledge are that (1) the pressure to cartelize an industry and provide regulatory barriers to entry is greater where productivity growth is low and (2) barriers to competition similar to those in Sweden operate in the European Economic Community for similar products and hinder productivity growth there to roughly the same extent as in Sweden. The one reasonably clear conclusion from our data is that cartelization and regulation have not enhanced productivity growth in Swedish manufacturing.[38]

8.2.9   Simultaneous Equations

In the previous analysis, determination of firms' productivity growth and market prices were analyzed separately. For several reasons, there may be important linkages between the two. A productivity increase tends to lower the

---

38. We can also say that any effects of cartelization take some time to show up. For the sample of products with changes in cartel status, we regressed the difference between annual and long-run TFP growth on cartel and year dummies. A similar regression was estimated for labor productivity growth. The coefficients of the cartel dummies were small and insignificant in both regressions. This means that productivity growth for the same product does not noticeably lag behind its long-run trend in the years just following a cartel agreement.

Table 8.18   **Simultaneous Estimation of Relative Prices and TFP Growth**

Independent Variables	Relative Price		TFP Growth	
	Coef.	t	Coef.	t
A. Cartels:				
1. Vertical	−.046	1.2	−.0001	0
2. Horizontal	.015	.3	.0001	0
B. Regulation:				
1. Environmental	.06	2.5	.04	2.0
2. Price	.12	2.2		
3. Technical standards	−.001	0	.004	.2
C. Median industry price change in EEC, 1976–90			−.98	28.1
D. Dependent variables:				
1. Relative price	−.03	.6	−.21	.8
2. TFP growth				
$\bar{R}^2$	.11		.93	
SEE	.09		.057	

profit-maximizing price, even for a firm with monopoly power. Holding constant the level of cartelization and regulation, one would therefore expect firms with faster productivity growth to charge lower prices.

The price that a firm charges may in turn affect productivity growth. Monopoly power should be reflected in the price levels, even after controlling for our measures of cartelization and regulation, since these probably contain a considerable measurement error. To the extent that monopoly power affects productivity growth, one would therefore expect a relation between the price level and productivity growth.

In order to test these linkages, the simplest approach is to estimate a simultaneous equation model following the structure of the productivity growth equations reported in the previous section. In the first system in table 8.18, TFP growth and relative (to EEC) prices are the dependent variables in a cross-sectional estimation over the eighty-three product markets. Relative prices and "level" variables are averages over the period 1976–90.

As in any simultaneous system, a key question is how well the equations are identified. In this estimation, the EEC price trend variable is a natural choice as a variable to identify the productivity growth equation. For the relative price equation, we use the price regulation dummy as an identifying variable. This assumes that price and quantity regulation affect productivity growth via price changes.

The results in table 8.18 broadly confirm the single-equation results reported above. Environmental regulation affects both productivity and prices. The independent linkage between relative prices and TFP growth appears small. One could argue that productivity growth should affect the relative price change rather than the relative price level. Substituting relative price change for relative price levels yields similar conclusions, however, and is therefore not reported here.

Instead, a more careful modeling of how prices affect productivity seems to bear fruit. The most frequently stated argument is that high prices may imply high profits. High profits in turn reduce employees' efforts and therefore depress productivity growth. The link between prices and profits, however, may be quite weak. Therefore, one may get stronger results by explicitly modeling the effects of prices on the profit rate and the effects of the profit rate on productivity growth.

We replace the simple productivity growth variable with a new variable, "relative productivity growth," which shows productivity growth relative to that in EEC countries. This is calculated as

$$\text{relative productivity growth} = (1 + \text{TFP growth})/$$
$$(1 - \text{median industry price change in EEC}).$$

This achieves essentially the same as was done in previous regressions by introducing EEC price change as an independent variable. However, it ensures that productivity growth is also corrected by EEC price change in the profit equation.

Since productivity growth also affects profits, we model this as a system with three simultaneous equations with the dependent variables being the profit rate, relative productivity growth, and relative prices. The profit equation contains relative productivity and relative prices as explanatory variables, and the wage rate is used to identify the equation. The relative productivity equation contains profits and the cartel and regulatory variables. It is identified by the cartel and regulatory variables since we let the relative price enter recursively only into the profits equation. Thus, the relative price is a function only of the cartel and regulatory variables. This is motivated because theoretically relative prices should affect relative productivity only through profits, not directly.

The results are shown in table 8.19. They indicate that relative productivity growth has a significantly positive effect on the profit rate. The profit rate, on the other hand, has a significantly negative effect on productivity growth. Environmental regulation and price and quantity regulation raise relative prices and thus feed through to the profit rate and relative productivity growth.

These results indicate that monopoly power may indeed have a significantly negative effect on productivity growth via the profit rate. However, our measures of monopoly power in the form of the cartelization variables may contain too much measurement error to pick up much of a direct link from cartelization to productivity growth.

Finally, a common argument is that high profits lead to high wage demands. Therefore, wages should be treated as an endogenous variable. We have estimated such models also, but the results remain broadly the same. This is not

Table 8.19   **Simultaneous Estimation of the Profit Rate, Relative TFP Growth, and Relative Prices**

Independent Variables	Profit Rate Coef.	t	Relative TFP Growth Coef.	t	Relative Prices Coef.	t
A. Cartels:						
1. Vertical			−.012	.6	−.04	1.1
2. Horizontal			.006	.23	.03	.7
B. Regulation:						
1. Environmental			.009	.6	.07	2.2
2. Price			−.032	.99	.115	2.1
3. Technical standards			.008	.5	−.0005	.01
C. Wage level	−.004	.2				
D. Dependent variables:						
1. Profit rate			.39	2.5		
2. Relative TFP growth	1.85	3.3			−.13	.3
3. Relative price	.34	1.75				
$\bar{R}^2$	.13		.15		.11	
SEE	.2		.09		.09	

surprising since wage levels in Sweden have primarily been determined at more central levels than the firm. For that reason, they do not differ much between firms.

8.3   Summary and Conclusions

The broad conclusion to which our results point is that Sweden's tolerance of cartels and its regulatory policy have negatively affected the performance of Swedish manufacturing. We have found evidence of such negative effects on prices, output, productivity, and productivity growth. These effects are summarized in table 8.20. It can be seen at a glance that virtually all the effects that we have been able to detect are negative and that they are often substantial. As between the effects of cartels and regulation, the latter are the more substantial.

The effects that we have been able to measure are probably understated. In essence, we have measured these effects as differences between a "treatment" group and a "control" group of products. To estimate the effects of the treatment (cartels, regulation) properly, we would need a control group entirely free of treatment effects. However, this is not what we have. The control group includes products with no *publicly registered* cartel agreements. But it includes products with undisclosed cartels. The control group include products without unusually severe regulation of three *specific* types. But it includes products subject, in varying degrees, to some of these and to other kinds of regulation that may have effects on competition. Accordingly, we are able to estimate only

Table 8.20   Summary of Effects of Cartels and Regulation

Institution (main affected sectors)	Prices	Output	Productivity Output/Worker	TFP Growth (per year)
Cartels (food, wood/paper, packaging, chemicals)	−2% in vertical agreements	−6% to −13% after agreement, +6% after agreement is terminated	No	−1.6% for horizontal agreements
Regulation:				
1. Environmental (wood/paper, chemicals, petroleum)	+6%	. . .	−7%	−.5%
2. Price (food)	+11%	. . .	−12%	No
3. Technical standards (food, packaging, transport equipment)	No	. . .	No	−1%
Relevant averages from sample	+13.6% Sweden v. EEC	5.6% standard deviation of yearly output change	SKr 520,000 value added per worker	+1.6%/ year TFP growth

Note: "No" = no effect found. . . . = data unavailable.

differences between more and less cartelization and regulation rather than the full effects of these treatments. Also, recall that there is a further downward bias in our estimates of price effects stemming from our inability to control for effects of policies within the European Economic Community that are similar to those in Sweden. Specifically, the estimated price effects of environmental and price regulation (+6 percent) and +11 percent) are the (extra) premiums over similar products sold in EEC markets. But those products (e.g., chemicals and food) are also heavily regulated in the European Economic Community. So our estimates imply that Swedish regulations has historically been more stringent than EEC regulation. They do not, however, reveal the full price effects of the regulation.

Finally, recall that we analyzed prices of tradables that Sweden exports. Thus, the Swedish producers in our sample have survived the rigors of international competition. By focusing on this relatively efficient and competitive sector, we have missed the worst examples of inefficiency and high prices induced by regulation or lack of competition in Sweden. The fact that we found any significant price and efficiency effects in this sample suggests larger, more widespread effects in the more sheltered areas of the economy.

Because of the preceding caveats, our results should be regarded as suggestive rather than as precise estimates of the negative effects of cartelization and regulation. It seems safe to conclude that these effects are hardly trivial. They have, if anything, grown worse over time given the reduced productivity growth that we have found in the regulated and cartelized sectors of Swedish manufacturing.

Sweden's prospective entry into the European Community has begun to force changes in the institutions that governed the period we have studied. Because of this, our results give grounds for optimism about the likely evolution of Swedish manufacturing. The adoption of EC antitrust standards will presumably narrow the scope for cartels in Sweden. Our results imply that a less heavily cartelized Swedish manufacturing sector will be more efficient, both statically and dynamically. Inevitably, integration into the European Community will bring pressure for a convergence of regulatory institutions. This will lead to a corresponding convergence of costs, which, our results imply, will improve Sweden's relative position. Indeed, there is evidence that some of this has already occurred. We broke the period 1976–90 into halves and estimated separate price effects of regulation in each half. For both price and environmental regulation, the effect on Swedish prices was greater in the first half (1976–82) of this period than in the second. In the case of environmental regulation, the extra Swedish price premium narrows significantly from 10 percent in 1976–82 to around 3 percent subsequently. A smaller and less statistically reliable[39] narrowing occurred for goods subject to price regulation, from a 15 percent to a 10 percent extra price premium. Pressures for further narrowing of these Swedish price premiums can only grow as Sweden integrates into the European Community. These pressures will be uneven because the degree of regulation and cartelization has varied across Swedish industries. The food sector, in particular, stands out among those Swedish industries that will be most substantially affected by the convergence of Swedish and EC policies. Much of this industry has been cartelized, subjected to minimum price regulation, and protected from entry by products not meeting Swedish technical standards. If these practices are eliminated, our data suggest that Swedish food prices will decline by around 10 percent in real terms at the wholesale level and that output per worker will grow a like amount. At the same time, the industry is likely to reverse its distinctly subpar record of productivity growth.

Swedish manufacturing is highly concentrated, and this can raise concerns about the vigor of competition. Our results, however, suggest that such concerns are overstated. Indeed, we find that the most concentrated Swedish industries tend to have significantly lower domestic prices and a substantial, although narrowing, advantage in output per worker over less concentrated industries. We interpret this to mean that, where regulatory barriers to entry are absent, high concentration in Sweden reflects cost advantages of large firms. The proviso here is potentially important because we find lower prices and higher productivity where there are more firms. These twin results suggest the need for distinguishing between concentration and the number of firms in evaluating Swedish market structure. In particular, it would not be surprising

---

39. The relevant *t*-ratio is 1.9 vs. 5.1 for the environmental case.

if Swedish production becomes more concentrated as its markets become more accessible to EEC producers. This would occur if less-efficient domestic production is replaced by imports. In this case, as long as the number of sellers is not reduced, our results imply favorable price and productivity effects flowing from the increased concentration. The implications for competition policy seem fairly straightforward. It is our layman's impression that EEC policy toward mergers is generally less restrictive than that of the United States. Were it otherwise, Sweden might be ill served by legal restraints on the mergers and exits that will accompany the realignment of its manufacturing capacity when it joins the European Economic Community. Removal of institutional obstacles to entry and regulatory restraints on competition would appear to merit more attention than restraints on concentration.

References

Andersson, T., P. Braunerhjelm, B. Carlsson, G. Eliasson, S. Fölster, L. Jagrén, E. Kasa-maki, and K. Sjöholm. 1993. *Den långa vägen.* Stockholm: Industrial Institute for Economic and Social Research (IUI).

Bain, J. 1951. Relation of profit rate to industry concentration: American manufacturing, 1936–1940. *Quarterly Journal of Economics* 65:293–324.

Chou, T. C. 1986. Concentration, profitability and trade in a simultaneous equation analysis: The case of Taiwan. *Journal of Industrial Economics* 34:429–43.

Cowling, K., and M. Waterson. 1976. Price-cost margins and market structure. *Economica* 43:267–74.

Demsetz, H. 1973. Industry structure, market rivalry, and public policy. *Journal of Law and Economics* 16, no. 1 (April): 1–10.

Erixon, L. 1991. Omvandlingstryck och produktivitet. In *Konkurrens, regleringar och produktivitet, Expertrapport nr 7 till Produktivitetsdelegationen.* Stockholm: Produktivitetsdelegationen.

Flam, H., H. Horn and S. Lundgrens. 1993. EES-avtalet, ny lagstiftning och Konkurrensen i Sverige. Expert report no. 8 to the Government Commission on Economic Policy. Stockholm.

Fölster, S. 1993. *Sveriges Systemskifte i fara?* Stockholm: Industrial Institute for Economic and Social Research (IUI).

Geroski, P. 1982. Simultaneous equation models of the structure performance paradigm. *European Economic Review*:359–67.

Kwoka, J. E., and D. J. Ravenscraft. 1986. Cooperation v. rivalry: Price-cost margins by line of business. *Economica* 53:351–63.

Lindbeck, A., P. Molander, T. Persson, O. Peterson, A. Sandmo, B. Swedenborg, and N. Thygesen. 1994. *Turning Sweden around.* Cambridge, Mass.: MIT Press.

Lipsey, R., and B. Swedenborg. 1993. The high cost of eating: Agricultural protection and international differences in food prices. Working Paper no. 4555. Cambridge, Mass.: National Bureau of Economic Research.

Marvel, H. P. 1980. Foreign trade and domestic competition. *Economic Inquiry* 18:103–22.

OECD. 1992. *Economic Surveys: Sweden.* Paris.

Olsson, H. 1991. Konkurrensförhållandenas betydelse för produktiviteten. In *Konkur-*

rens, regleringar och produktivitet, Expertrapport nr 7 till Produktivitetsdelegationen. Stockholm: Produktivitetsdelegationen.

Peltzman, S. 1989. The economic theory of regulation after a decade of deregulation. *Brookings Papers on Economic Activity: Microeconomics,* 1–41.

Pugel, T. A. 1978. *International market linkages and US manufacturing: Prices, profits and patterns.* Cambridge, Mass.: Ballinger.

Salinger, Michael. 1990. The concentration margins relationship reconsidered. *Brookings Papers on Economic Activity: Microeconomics,* 287–335.

Scherer, F. M., A. Beckenstein, E. Kaufer, R. D. Murphy, and F. Bougeon-Maassen. 1975. *The economics of multi-plant operation: An international comparisons study.* Cambridge, Mass.: Harvard University Press.

Schmalensee, R. 1989. Inter-industry studies of structure and performance. In *The handbook of industrial organization,* vol. 2, ed. R. Schmalensee and R. Willig. Amsterdam: North-Holland.

SOU (Statens Offentliga Utredningar). 1990. Demokrati och makt i Sverige, 1990:44. Stockholm: SOU.

SPK (Statens Pris och Konkurrensverk). 1992. Horisontell Prissamverkan och marknadsdelning, SPKs rapportserie, 1992:3. Stockholm: SPK.

Stålhammar, Nils-Olov. 1991. Domestic market power and foreign trade: The case of Sweden. *International Journal of Industrial Organization* 9:407–24.

———. 1992. Concentration, prices and profitability in the Swedish manufacturing industry. In *Internationalization, market power and consumer welfare,* ed. Y. Bourdet. London: Routledge.

Stigler, G. 1971. The theory of economic regulation. *Bell Journal of Economics and Management Science* 2 (Spring): 3–21.

9   Industrial Policy, Employer Size, and Economic Performance in Sweden

Steven J. Davis and Magnus Henrekson

Sweden has experienced slow economic growth during the past quarter century compared to its historical record and compared to the average performance of other OECD countries. From 1970 to 1992, Swedish output per capita grew at only 60 percent of the OECD average, and Sweden's relative PPP-adjusted income per capita fell from third to seventeenth among OECD countries. This dismal post-1970 growth performance stands out in especially sharp relief when set against Sweden's remarkable record of economic growth during the previous one hundred years. From 1870 to 1970, Swedish output per manhour rose seventeen fold, the highest growth rate among sixteen OECD countries for which comparable data are available (Maddison 1982).[1]

While output growth has been slow in recent decades, a casual inspection of the data suggests that—until recently—Sweden's relative employment performance looked attractive: unemployment rates were very low, labor force participation rates rose secularly, and private sector employment grew strongly in the late 1980s. But the 1991–93 economic crisis triggered unprecedented job losses, and employment contracted by approximately 15 percent in three years. In fact, a closer scrutiny of the data points to long-term problems in Swedish employment performance. We return to this matter below. Here, we

Steven J. Davis is professor at the University of Chicago Graduate School of Business and a research associate of the National Bureau of Economic Research. Magnus Henrekson is associate professor at the Industrial Institute for Economic and Social Research (IUI) in Stockholm.

The authors thank Eugenia Kazamaki Ottersten, Per Skedinger, Birgitta Swedenborg, and the participants at seminars at IUI and the University of Chicago for useful comments and suggestions. Needless to say, the usual caveats apply. Henrekson gratefully acknowledges financial support from Jan Wallanders och Tom Hedelius stiftelse för samhällsvetenskaplig forskning. Davis gratefully acknowledges financial support from the National Science Foundation.

1. Henrekson, Jonung, and Stymne (1996) provide a detailed discussion of Sweden's record of economic growth.

353

simply highlight one of our most important observations: from 1950 to 1992, all net job creation in Sweden took place in the public sector.

Slow output and productivity growth during the past quarter century, forty-odd years of stagnation in private sector employment, and a profound economic contraction during the early 1990s—these are some unpleasant facts, and they cry out for an explanation of what went wrong. We consider one set of factors that may constitute an important part of the answer. In particular, we consider whether tax policy and other important features of Swedish economic policies and institutions hampered economic growth and efficiency by distorting the industrial, employer size, and employer age structure of employment and output.[2] Distorting policies and institutions are ones that encourage the misallocation or inefficient use of capital and labor. Such distortions include an inefficient allocation of physical capital between industries, inefficient organizational forms for carrying out economic activities, and an inefficient allocation of work time within the market sector or between the market and home sectors.

It will be helpful to set out the main elements of our thesis briefly:

1. Several aspects of Swedish tax policy disfavor smaller, younger, and less capital intensive firms. Tax policy also discourages entrepreneurship and family ownership in favor of institutional forms of ownership. As a consequence, tax policy retards entry by new firms, distorts the size structure of employment within industries, and distorts the industrial distribution of employment and output.

2. Other important aspects of the Swedish system—including credit market policy, employment security laws, and a system of centralized wage bargaining that compressed wage differentials—also disfavored smaller, younger, and less capital intensive firms and distorted the industrial distribution of employment.

3. These policy-induced distortions in business ownership patterns and in the distribution of employment and output by industry and by employer size and age hamper the efficient allocation of resources, reduce productivity, and retard economic growth.

4. The adverse growth and efficiency effects of these policy-induced distortions have been exacerbated by exogenous changes in the economic environment related to the widespread shift from goods-producing to service-producing industries and the downsizing of production units in many goods-producing industries.

The weight and nature of our evidence differ greatly among the elements of our thesis, and we note at the outset that the available evidence is incomplete on key points. Our aim here is to build a plausible case for our thesis, recognizing that the evidence is largely suggestive. For this reason, we regard our research as an exploratory investigation rather than an exhaustive study of distor-

---

2. Myhrman (1994) is an attempt to explain the (relative) rise and decline of the Swedish economy as a result of institutions and policies.

tions in the structure of Swedish employment and their adverse economic consequences.

To set the stage for our analysis more fully, we review several noteworthy aspects of the postwar Swedish employment record in section 9.1. The subsequent two sections describe how tax policy and other key features of the Swedish system disfavor younger, smaller, and less capital intensive employers and distort the industrial distribution of employment.

Next, in section 9.4, we offer several reasons why unfavorable policy treatment of younger, smaller, and less capital intensive employers undermines productivity and growth. Reflecting a paucity of evidence in the literature, we can say little about the magnitude of these productivity and growth effects. Instead, section 9.5 develops evidence of significant employment distortions by relating U.S.-Swedish differences in the industrial distribution of employment to a variety of industry characteristics such as capital intensity, the distribution of workers by establishment and firm size, the structure of wages, and the pace at which jobs are reallocated among establishments within an industry.

The pattern of U.S.-Swedish differences in the industrial distribution of employment conforms well to the implications of our thesis, and a plausible reading of the evidence attributes many of U.S.-Swedish differences in the industrial distribution of employment to distortions associated with the tax, regulatory, and wage-setting policies and institutions described in sections 9.2 and 9.3. After developing this evidence, we review some international trends in the industrial and size distribution of employment. These trends are indicative of exogenous changes in the economic environment that probably exacerbate the adverse economic consequences of the employment distortions induced by Swedish policies and institutions. We conclude in section 9.7 with a few remarks about the policy implications of our findings.

9.1 Noteworthy Aspects of the Postwar Swedish Employment Record

Figure 9.1 shows the secular increase in Sweden's employment rate, which rose from slightly above 70 percent of the working-age population in the early 1950s to a peak of 84 percent in 1990. Remarkably, more than 100 percent of this development is accounted for by increased employment among women. From 1970 to 1990, the female employment rate increased by 22 percentage points, whereas the male rate declined by 1.5 percentage points.[3] As of 1992, the male employment rate exceeded the female rate by only 2.2 percentage points, in striking contrast to the gap of 27.6 percentage points in 1970.

The rise in the ratio of female-to-male employment is a ubiquitous phenomenon among OECD economies in recent decades. In part, this development reflects common and pronounced changes in the structure of labor de-

3. According to Silenstam (1960), the female participation rate was 44.8 percent in 1950. By 1970 and 1990, it had increased to 58.3 and 80.3 percent, respectively.

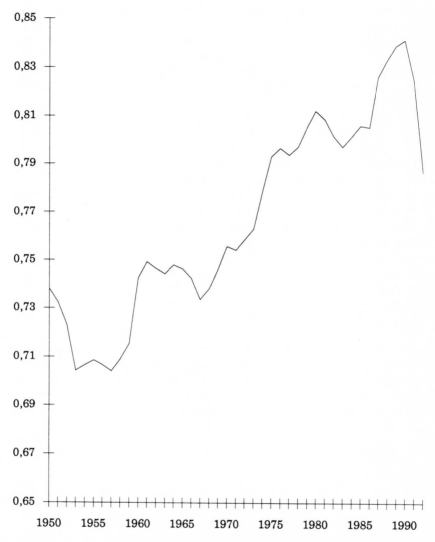

Fig. 9.1   Total employment as a share of population aged sixteen to sixty-four, 1950–92

Source: Statistics Sweden.

Note: Public employment is defined as average number of employees in local and central government, including social security funds.

mand, as evidenced by the widespread shift in employment from goods-producing to service-producing sectors and the relatively rapid growth of public sector employment in many countries, two trends that increase the relative demand for women workers.[4] But, as emphasized in Rosen's (chap. 2 in this volume) analysis, major components of Swedish economic and social policy have accentuated shifts in the structure of labor demand and contributed strongly toward the rise in female employment and participation rates. Indeed, Rosen reports that almost all Swedish employment growth between 1963 and 1992 is accounted for by the growth of female employment in the local public sector.

Public sector employment growth is in fact a central feature of Swedish economic policy in recent decades. As figure 9.2 shows, the public sector accounts for all Sweden's net employment growth after 1950. Between 1950 and 1992, public sector employment grew by 1.1 million, whereas private sector employment actually shrank by roughly 200,000 jobs.[5] Even at the peak of the most recent employment boom in 1990, private sector employment exceeded the 1950 level by only 40,000 jobs, despite an increase of 820,000 persons in the working-age population (sixteen to sixty-four years). Private sector jobs as a fraction of the working-age population fell from 67 percent in 1950 to 53 percent in 1992. Seen in this perspective, the employment performance of the private sector in Sweden is weak indeed, and the employment expansion during the long boom in the second half of the 1980s appears far less impressive.

Another noteworthy trend—also partly driven by rising public sector employment—is the secular decline in Sweden's rate of self-employment.[6] Figure 9.3 shows that self-employment fell from 19 percent of total employment in 1950 to only 7 percent in 1991. Virtually all this decline occurred between the late 1950s and the early 1980s. The continual, albeit slower, decline throughout the 1970s is chiefly explained by a drop in agricultural employment. In recent years, the self-employment rate has stabilized at a low level relative to Sweden's historical experience and relative to the contemporaneous situation in other countries. Indeed, a recent OECD study reports that, since the early 1970s, Sweden has exhibited the lowest ratio of nonagricultural self-employment to civilian employment among all OECD countries (see table 9.1.)[7]

---

4. In this respect, we note that women account for 72 percent of Swedish public sector employment in 1991, as compared to only 34 percent of private sector employment.

5. Lindh (1994) argues that the employment figures used here overestimate the employment level for the 1950s. Using Lindh's estimate of the employment level in the 1950s as a point of departure, the private sector employment contraction would be roughly 100,000 less. However, this does not change any of the conclusions. Furthermore, it may be noted that private sector employment fell by an additional 169,000 in 1993.

6. Sweden's growth in public sector employment contributed to the decline in self-employment both by drawing workers into a sector with no scope for self-employment and by publicly providing services such as child care and medical care with potentially high self-employment rates in a system of provision by the private sector.

7. Strangely enough, that OECD study finds an increase in the Swedish self-employment rate of 67 percent between 1986 and 1990. However, a corresponding increase cannot be detected in

Another recent study finds that Sweden has a lower self-employment rate in 1992 than a dozen member countries of the European Community (EC) for which data are available; the Swedish self-employment rate is less than half the EC average (see the last column of table 9.1).

A low self-employment rate is but one aspect of broader differences between the structure of employment in Sweden and other countries. For example, large firms account for a disproportionately high fraction of employment in Sweden. Table 9.2 illustrates this point by drawing on a recent Statens Offentliga Utredningar (SOU) study that compares the distribution of employment by firm size among several European countries. In 1986, firms with at least five hundred employees account for 60.4 percent of total employment in Sweden, as compared to only 30.4 percent in the European Community as a whole. Even in the much larger economies of Germany, France, and the United Kingdom, the largest firm size class accounts for less than 40 percent of employment. At the other end of the size distribution, firms with fewer than ten employees account for only 9.5 percent of employment in Sweden, less than half the employment share of very small firms in the European Community.[8]

Table 9.3 presents complementary evidence on the relatively small role of small firms in Sweden. Among sixteen European countries, Sweden shows the largest value for mean enterprise size in 1990. Average enterprise size is thirteen in Sweden, more than twice the corresponding average value for the sixteen European countries.[9]

The interpretation of these cross-country comparisons of average firm size and the employment distribution by firm size is clouded by ambiguities in the economic concept of a firm, by differences among countries in the legal definition of a firm, and by differences in measurement procedures. But there seems little doubt that Sweden's reputation as a land of big business is well founded. If anything, the figures in tables 9.2 and 9.3 fail to fully convey

---

fig. 9.3, which casts serious doubt on this figure. Between 1986 and 1987, there is an increase of 109,000, or 63 percent, in the number of self-employed in the OECD data for Sweden. Apparently, some mistake has been made in the data-collection process, possibly that the self-employed in the agricultural sector are accidentally included after 1986. According to the 1995 annual report put out by the European Observatory for SMEs (Zoetermeer, 1995), Swedish self-employment (including agriculture) amounted to 6.8 percent of the labor force in 1990.

8. Table 9.2 probably overstates the relative importance of large firms in Sweden because the public sector accounts for such a large fraction of Swedish employment. With few exceptions, public sector employees are categorized as working in very large firms. However, even if we restrict attention to the construction, extraction, and manufacturing sectors (for which public employment is very small), the share of Swedish employment accounted for by large firms (five hundred or more employees) is still unusually high. There is only one exception among the set of countries included in table 9.2: For NACE 2-4 (extraction and manufacturing), the United Kingdom share in the five hundred or more category is 0.9 percentage points higher than in Sweden. This fact may reflect the inclusion of British coal mines, which were still operating in 1986.

9. Although not directly addressing the question whether most jobs are created in large and old firms, it may be noted that Davidsson, Lindmark, and Olofsson (1994) found that, of the 207,903 jobs that were created net in the period 1985–89 in the private sector, only 16 percent were created in firms consisting of only one establishment. Note that 1985–89 is the only reasonably sustained post-war period when there is any employment growth in the private sector.

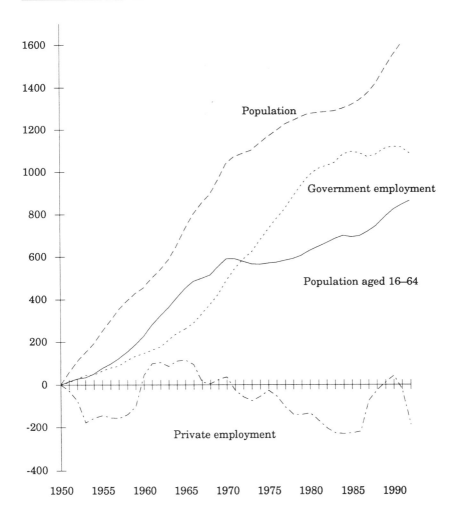

Fig. 9.2   Cumulative change of private employment, government employment, and population in Sweden, 1950–92 (thousands)
Source: Statistics Sweden.

the extent of concentrated ownership and control in Sweden. In this regard, Fölster and Peltzman (chap. 8 in this volume) note that, in 1985, "the five biggest final owners held some 44 percent of the total voting rights in companies with more than five hundred employees, while the ten biggest had more than half." In addition, they write that "these final owners tend to hold shares through intermediaries, such as investment companies, which in turn are linked through joint ownership. Fourteen such 'empires' dominate the corporate sector, with three major ones alone controlling companies that account for some

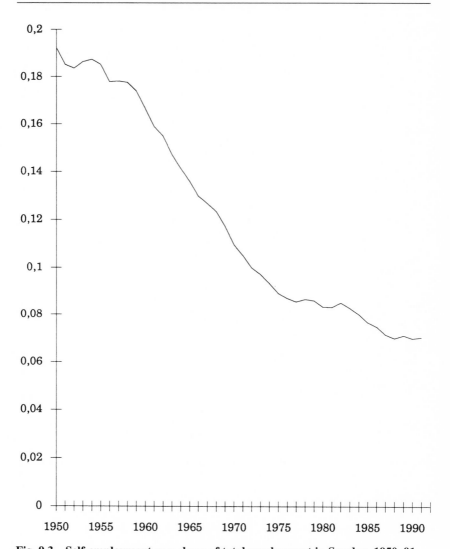

Fig. 9.3   Self-employment as a share of total employment in Sweden, 1950–91

Source: Statistics Sweden, national accounts.

Note: Owing to the inclusion of the agricultural sector, the level of self-employment is consistently higher than in table 9.3.

two-thirds of employment, sales, and total assets of the 270 largest corporations in Sweden." Coupled with the figures in tables 9.2 and 9.3, these remarks highlight the dominant economic role of large corporate organizations in Sweden.

Finally, while available data are limited, there is evidence to suggest that

Table 9.1 **Nonagricultural Self-Employment as a Proportion of Civilian Employment in OECD Countries, 1973, 1979, 1986, and 1990, and Self-Employment Including Agriculture as a Share of the Labor Force in the Twelve EC Countries and Sweden, 1992 (%)**

Country	1973	1979	1986	1990	1992
Australia[a]	9.5	12.4	12.7	12.4	...
Austria	11.7	8.9	6.1	6.4	...
Belgium	11.2	11.2	12.6	12.9	14.1
Canada[a]	6.2	6.7	7.2	7.4	...
Denmark	9.3	9.2	7.0	7.2	8.0
Finland	6.4	6.1	6.8	8.8	...
France	11.4[a]	10.6[a]	10.5[a]	10.3[a]	11.2
Germany	9.1	8.2	7.6	7.7	8.1
Greece	N.A.	32.0	27.5	27.2[b]	32.6
Ireland	10.1	10.4	11.3	13.3	19.0
Italy	23.1	18.9	21.6	22.3	23.2
Japan[a]	14.1	14.0	12.7	11.5	...
Luxembourg	11.1	9.4	8.4	7.1	8.9
Netherlands	N.A.	8.8[a]	8.2[a]	7.8[a]	9.6
New Zealand[a]	N.A.	9.5	13.3	14.6	...
Norway[a]	7.8	6.6	6.5	6.1	...
Portugal	12.7	12.1	16.9	18.5	22.9
Spain	16.3	15.7	17.9	17.1	17.4
Sweden	4.8	4.5	4.2	7.0	6.8
Turkey	N.A.	N.A.	N.A.	27.6	...
United Kingdom	7.3[a]	6.6[a]	10.0[a]	11.6[a]	11.3
United States[a]	6.7	7.1	7.4	7.6	...
EU-12	...	...	...	...	13.8

Sources: OECD *Employment Outlook,* July 1992, 158 for 1973, 1979, 1986 and 1990. European Observatory for SMEs, Third Annual Report 1995 (Zoetermeer, 1995), for 1992.

Note: N.A. = not available.

[a]Excluding owner-managers of incorporated businesses (in the U.K. data this category is partly included).
[b]1989.

Sweden experiences low rates of new firm formation. Drawing on the recent study by Braunerhjelm and Carlsson (1993), figure 9.4 displays annual entry rates from 1920 to 1991 of new manufacturing firms with more than one employee. The figure shows that rates of new firm formation in the Swedish manufacturing sector became quite low by the 1950s. The entry rate fell to 1.5 percent in the 1970s, and the average entry rate was even lower in the 1980s and early 1990s.[10]

To summarize, Sweden has undergone an extended period of stagnation in

10. On the other hand, using data from the late 1980s, Lundström et al. (1993) find that the rate of new firm formation in Sweden is at a level comparable to that of several other European countries. However, we do not know how sensitive this finding would be to the exclusion of new firms with no employees.

Table 9.2   The Distribution of Employment according to Firm Size in Selected European Countries, 1986

	Number of Employees			
	1–9	10–99	100–499	500–
Sweden	9.5	17.3	12.6	60.6
European Community	20.9		48.7[a]	30.4
Germany	18.2	27.3	18.7	35.8
France	15.1	28.6	16.7	39.6
United Kingdom	23.2	23.9	22.9	30.0
Netherlands	14.0	27.7	17.1	41.3
Denmark	16.8	42.4	23.2	17.6

Source: SOU (1992, 308).
Note: Firms with no employees and firms in the primary sector are excluded. The public sector is included.
[a]10–499.

Table 9.3   Average Enterprise Size in Sixteen European Countries in 1990

Country	Size	Country	Size
Belgium	6	Austria	12
Denmark	9	Finland	12
France	7	Norway	10
Germany[a]	9	Sweden	13
Greece	3		
Ireland	8	EFTA-4	12
Italy	4		
Luxembourg	10		
Netherlands	10		
Portugal	5		
Spain	4		
United Kingdom	8		
EU-12	6	Europe-16	6

Source: The European Observatory for SMEs, Third Annual Report 1995 (Zoetermeer, 1995).
Note: Concerns nonprimary private enterprises.
[a]Only western Germany.

private sector employment during the past four decades. Since 1950 all net job creation occurred in the public sector. The strong secular growth in public sector employment during recent decades probably generated much of the impetus behind other important employment trends in recent decades, including the absolute and relative rise of female employment and the decline in the Swedish self-employment rate. In comparisons among OECD countries, Sweden stands out as having the highest ratio of public sector to total employment, the lowest rate of self-employment, a dominant role for larger firms, and highly

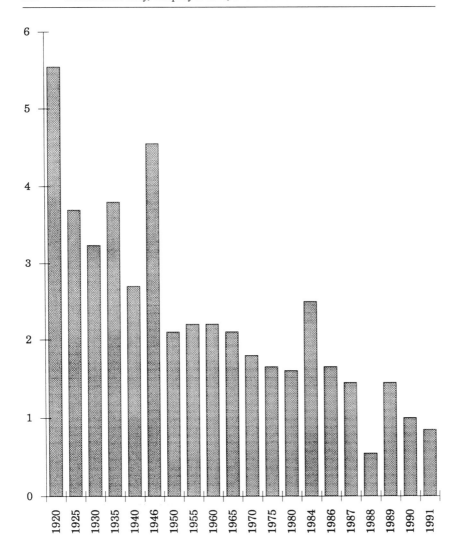

Fig. 9.4   Newly started manufacturing firms relative to the total number of manufacturing firms, 1920–91 (percentage)
Source: Braunerhjelm and Carlsson (1993).
Note: Only firms with more than one employee are included.

concentrated ownership and control of private sector enterprises. The available evidence also points to low entry rates of new Swedish firms in recent decades. In section 9.5 below, we develop new evidence of distortions in the industrial structure of Swedish employment related to capital intensity, establishment size, the wage structure, and other factors.

9.2   Tax Policy and the Structure of Employment

This section outlines several features of the pre-1990 Swedish tax system that disfavored younger, smaller, and less capital intensive firms and that discouraged entrepreneurship and family ownership in favor of institutional forms of ownership. International comparisons indicate that these tax-induced distortions were more severe in Sweden than in other countries.

Several important distortions stem from high statutory rates of corporate income taxation coupled with other policies that led to much lower effective tax rates. Figure 9.5 shows that the statutory corporate income tax rate was very high throughout the period until 1990. The level was consistently in the 50–62 percent interval, until it was almost halved from roughly 55 to 30 percent in the 1991 tax reform. But these high statutory rates tell only part of the story. Until the late 1950s, the difference was slight between statutory and effective tax rates, but, beginning in 1958, a large gap between the two emerged, and this gap widened considerably over time. These observations lead us to a discussion of the main sources of the discrepancy between statutory and effective tax rates and to some remarks about the implications for the structure of employment.

The low effective corporate income tax rates resulted from the introduction of tax-reducing depreciation rules, inventory valuation rules, other more ad hoc tax reductions,[11] and the so-called investment fund system. Bergström (1982) and Södersten (1984, 1983) describe the rules in detail, but what is crucial here is that these low effective tax rates reflect behavioral responses by firms to the rules in place. The rules that enabled firms to attain effective tax rates well below the statutory rates had powerful effects on the allocation of capital and other resources.

Two of the most important types of rules involve liberal provisions for accelerated depreciation and the Swedish investment fund system. Since the 1950s, Swedish firms have been able to switch freely between two options for depreciating the acquisition cost of machinery and equipment for tax purposes. One option is to depreciate at a rate of 30 percent per annum on a declining balance basis. The second option is five-year straight-line depreciation of the historical acquisition cost. For a single investment, it is profitable to calculate depreciation under the first option in years 1 and 2 and to switch to the second option in the third and subsequent years. But, for a growing firm with many young vintages of capital, it is more profitable to use the 30 percent rule. These generous depreciation allowances provide ample opportunities for fast-growing firms that are, at the same time, capital intensive in machinery and equipment to reduce their tax load. Similar tax-avoidance opportunities are less available

---

11. Typically, these ad hoc rules implied that firms were allowed a total depreciation of more than 100 percent of the investment cost.

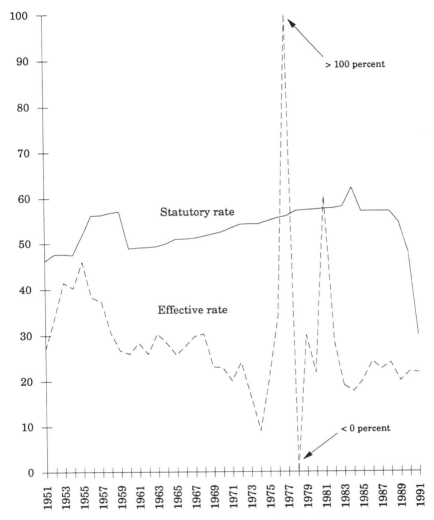

Fig. 9.5   Statutory and effective corporate tax rates in Swedish industry, 1954–91 (percentage)

Source: Jan Södersten.

Note: The statutory tax rate includes the profit-sharing tax, which was part of the wage-earner fund system, effective in 1984–90. In 1977, the effective tax rate exceeded 100 percent, which was due to the fact that aggregate profits were negative, while firms that despite losses wanted to pay dividends had to show book profits.

for stagnant firms and for firms that are capital intensive in other dimensions such as human capital, structures, financial capital, and intangible capital.

The claim that the depreciation rules have benefited fast-growing firms is also subject to an important qualification: because of other impediments to growth at the early stages of the life cycle of a firm, newly formed firms may find it difficult to exploit tax avoidance provisions. A fast-growing firm benefits from certain features of the tax system, but there is no mechanism inducing a firm to become fast growing.

The investment fund (IF) system gained in importance after 1955, and it was effective until the end of 1990. The purpose of the system was to induce firms to change the timing of investments from booms to recessions. The details of the system have varied somewhat over time, but typically a firm was allowed each year to deduct up to 50 percent of taxable profits by transfering that amount to its IF. However, 50 percent (roughly) of the total allocation had to be deposited in a non-interest-bearing account at the central bank.[12] The other half could be used for any purpose. Thus, as long as the statutory corporate tax rate exceeded 50 percent, which it did from 1955 to 1990, it was always profitable to make maximum allocations to the IF system, even if the funds were never used for investments.

In addition, firms were often granted an additional 10 percent allowance against current profits on funds drawn from their IF for investment purposes. For example, a firm with profits of 100 and an allocation of 50 to its IF in year $t - 1$ would be eligible to draw 25 for investment purposes in year t. If it did so, it would receive an additional deduction of 2.5 against profits in year t. Investments financed by an IF were considered to be fully written off for tax purposes. Since IF financing of investments was also possible for buildings, which enabled immediate tax writeoffs of structures instead of the usual twenty-eight- to thirty-six-year straight-line depreciation, a tax-minimizing firm would use its IF for investments in buildings rather than machinery.

These features of the Swedish corporate tax system had a number of implications. The most crucial one is summarized by Bergström (1982, 20) as follows: "The system has a built-in conservative mechanism giving lower capital costs and greater financing possibilities for firms which have, historically, been performing well." But, as shown in the early studies by Little (1962) and Cragg and Malkiel (1968), growth in the past is not a good predictor of growth in the future. Moreover, the system does not necessarily favor firms with a high level or growth rate of total factor productivity. Firms that are stagnating in terms of investment requirements and employment growth may nevertheless have higher than average productivity levels or even higher than average productivity growth rates. Baily, Haltiwanger, and Hulten (1996), for example, find that,

---

12. The release of IF funds on deposit with the central bank required explicit government decisions. Over time, releases became more and more frequent. Beginning in the latter half of the 1970s, this change enabled firms to use IFs continuously during a ten-year period (Södersten 1993).

among U.S. manufacturing plants experiencing positive productivity growth during the 1980s, a large fraction experienced employment declines.

Through discretionary releases of funds on deposit with the central bank, the IF component of the corporate tax system also encourages firms to make investments in recessions, which is probably more attractive for older firms in mature industries that face a comparatively predictable future. Firms or sectors that, during recessions, confronted greater uncertainty about the returns to sunk investments were less able to take advantage of the cyclic investment incentives offered by the IF system.

As a distinct consideration, high statutory tax rates strongly favor debt financing over equity financing of investments. To the extent that debt financing is less costly and more readily available for larger, more established firms, high statutory tax rates coupled with tax-deductible interest payments work to the disadvantage of smaller firms and potential entrants. Debt financing is also more easily available to firms with ready forms of collateral. Hence, firms and sectors that more intensively use physical capital reap greater benefits from tax code provisions that favor debt financing. In practice, this aspect of the tax system favors the capital intensive manufacturing industries relative to other industries.[13] In hindsight, it is not obvious that it was a growth-promoting strategy to favor manufacturing relative to other industries since manufacturing has declined in relative importance in virtually all industrialized countries subsequent to the mid-1960s.

To sum up the discussion thus far, several features of the Swedish corporate tax system distort the structure of employment and output because their usefulness as tax avoidance mechanisms differs greatly across industries and types of firms. On the whole, the tax system favors large, well-established, capital intensive firms.[14]

To provide a sense of the magnitude of the distortions introduced by the Swedish tax system, table 9.4 presents effective marginal tax rates for different combinations of owners and sources of finance. Three categories of owners and sources of finance are identified, and the effective marginal tax rate is calculated assuming a real pretax rate of return of 10 percent. A negative number means that the real rate of return is greater after tax than before tax.

The table highlights several important aspects of the Swedish tax system. First, debt financing consistently receives the most favorable tax treatment and new share issues the least favorable treatment. Second, the taxation of households as owners is much higher than for other categories, and their rate of

---

13. Södersten (1984) shows that, during the 1960s, the effective marginal tax rate on manufacturing was considerably lowered relative to that of other industry and commerce.

14. The wage earners' funds instituted in 1984 meant, among other things, the introduction of a "profit-sharing tax" (PST) that was operated parallel to the regular corporate tax system. The PST rate was 20 percent, but on a base that differed substantially from the regular corporate tax base. In effect, this resulted in fairly small overall PST payments. But how the introduction of the PST influenced firm behavior and whether it had differential effects on expanding and contracting firms or on firms of different sizes are unknown. The PST was abolished in the 1991 tax reform.

Table 9.4   **Effective Marginal Tax Rates for Different Combinations of Owners and Sources of Finance, 1960, 1970, 1980, 1985, and 1991 (real pretax rate of return 10 percent at actual inflation rates)**

	Debt	New Share Issues	Retained Earnings
1960:			
Households	27.2	92.7	48.2
Tax-exempt institutions	−32.2	31.4	31.2
Insurance companies	−21.7	41.6	34.0
1970:			
Households	51.3	122.1	57.1
Tax-exempt institutions	−64.8	15.9	32.7
Insurance companies	−45.1	42.4	41.2
1980:			
Households	58.2	136.6	51.9
Tax-exempt institutions	−83.4	−11.6	11.2
Insurance companies	−54.9	38.4	28.7
1985:			
Households	46.6	112.1	64.0
Tax-exempt institutions	−46.8	6.8	28.7
Insurance companies	−26.5	32.2	36.3
1991:			
Households	31.7	61.8	54.2
Tax-exempt institutions	−9.4	4.0	18.7
Insurance companies	14.4	33.3	31.6

Source: Jan Södersten.

Note: All calculations are based on the actual asset composition in manufacturing. The following inflation rates were used: 1960: 3 percent; 1970: 7 percent; 1980: 9.4 percent; 1985: 5 percent; 1991: 5 percent. The calculations conform to the general framework developed by King and Fullerton (1984). The average holding period is assumed to be ten years.

taxation increased during the 1960s and 1970s, whereas the reverse took place for insurance companies and tax-exempt institutions. From some point in the 1960s until the 1991 tax reform, more than 100 percent of the real rate of return was taxed away for a household buying a newly issued share. Third, tax-exempt institutions benefit from a large tax advantage relative to the other two categories of owners, and this advantage increased strongly during the 1960s and 1970s. It is particularly noteworthy that tax-exempt institutions have a substantial relative tax advantage throughout when investing in newly issued shares. Fourth, insurance companies are always in an intermediate position in terms of tax burden.[15]

The calculations for households in table 9.4 are based on an average house-

15. The figures in table 9.4 show that, in 1980, a real rate of return of 10 percent before tax for a tax-exempt institution investing in a debt instrument became 18.3 percent after tax, whereas for a household investing in a newly issued share 10 percent before tax became -3.7 percent after tax.

Table 9.5   **The Effective Rate of Corporate Taxation for Firms of Different Size and Ownership, 1984–87**

Employment	1984	1985	1986	1987
Family-owned firms:				
0–19	20	24	27	30
20–49	16	24	24	27
50–199	16	20	22	26
200–	19	14	19	17
Other firms	14	19	18	21

Source: Familjeföretagens skatteberedning (1989).

hold, but for a household owning a successful small or medium-sized firm the tax rate was often higher. The main reason was the combined effect of wealth and income taxation. Until 1993, the wealth tax was levied on 30 percent of the net worth of a family-owned company, incorporated or not. In the mid-1980s, the maximum wealth tax rate was 3 percent (for all household wealth exceeding SKr 1.8 million). But, since the wealth tax was not deductible at the company level, funds required to pay the wealth tax were first hit by the income tax and the mandatory payroll tax.[16]

Gandemo and Lundström (1991) provide evidence consistent with the view that this feature of the tax system altered business ownership patterns in Sweden. In their study of manufacturing firms with 100–499 employees, they found that "family-owned firms decreased from 38 percent in 1978 to 26 percent in 1986. Most were acquired by other Swedish firms. Apart from owner retirement, firms were sold to secure financial resources for continued development, and because of the high wealth tax in Sweden" (p. 72). Another piece of evidence consistent with this view is developed in Norrman and McLure (chap. 3 in this volume), who show that direct household ownership of publicly listed stock went from 75 percent in 1950 to 16 percent in 1992.

These remarks and the entries in table 9.4 make clear the extraordinary extent to which the Swedish tax system favored institutional ownership and discouraged direct household ownership of firms. The structure of taxation summarized in table 9.4 encouraged the strong postwar trend toward an increased share of institutionalized ownership of firms and the increased importance of debt financing. The preferential tax treatment of debt over equity and of institutions over individual ownership benefited larger, publicly traded, and more established firms.

As direct evidence on this point, table 9.5 reports effective rates of corporate taxation for family-owned and other corporations during the period 1984–87.

---

16. In practice, the wealth tax was not—or only to a limited degree—paid on boats, artwork, condominiums, etc. This was a further factor that decreased the relative attractiveness of investment in the owner-managed and small business sectors.

Table 9.6   **The Estimated Tax Wedge at 5 percent Real Interest Rate and 1985 Inflation Rate for Business Capital (percentage points)**

	Machinery	Buildings	Total Business Capital
United States:			
Old	−5.26	−2.41	−3.25
New	−2.32	−.68	−1.16
Japan	−1.67	−.81	−1.08
Germany	−2.37	−2.40	−2.38
France	−3.45	−3.29	−3.35
United Kingdom:			
Old	−5.55	−3.21	−4.58
New	−3.03	−1.67	−2.46
Italy	−3.85	−3.95	−3.91
Canada:			
Old	−3.61	−2.22	−2.77
New	−1.53	−1.28	−1.38
Australia	−7.98	−2.31	−4.78
Belgium	−6.95	−4.39	−5.51
Netherlands	−4.52	−2.17	−3.20
Spain	−6.21	−4.64	−5.32
Sweden	−9.11	−5.09	−7.05

Source: Fukao and Hanazaki (1987).

Smaller family-owned firms typically show a higher effective rate of corporate taxation than larger firms, and family-owned firms show a higher rate than other firms.

Major reasons for this result are that other firms had a larger proportion of profits in forms that were taxed at reduced rates (capital gains, dividends from subsidiaries), and they also had greater opportunities to take advantage of loss deductions. Also, large corporations (consisting of many legal entities) are able to lower the overall rate of taxation by transferring profits from high-profit to low-profit units within the group. This observation implies that a large corporation can more easily take initial losses in new activities than an individually owned firm (Familjeföretagens skatteberedning 1988, 1989).

How do these distortions in the Swedish tax system compare to other countries? In order partially to address this question, table 9.6 reports corporate tax wedges for investments in machinery, buildings, and total business capital (an aggregate of machinery and buildings) in several OECD countries as of 1985.[17] According to the table, the tax wedges are invariably negative, which means that after-tax rates of return exceed pretax rates of return. Among all listed

17. The tax wedge equals the difference in percentage points between the before-tax and the after-tax real cost of capital. Because of major changes in their corporate tax codes around 1985, the table reports wedge values for both old and new tax systems in the United States, Canada, and the United Kingdom.

Table 9.7   **Actual Effective Rates for Four Countries in 1980 (at 10 percent real pretax rate of return and actual inflation rates)**

	United Kingdom	Sweden	Germany	United States
Households	42.0	105.1	71.2	57.5
Tax-exempt institutions	−44.6	−51.8	6.3	−21.5
Insurance companies	−6.7	35.6	48.1	37.2

Source: King and Fullerton (1984).

Note: The figures in the table constitute the averages for each category, given its specific investment pattern in the respective countries.

Table 9.8   **The Estimated Tax Wedge at 5 Percent Real Interest Rate and 1985 Inflation Rate for Housing Investment by a Household in 1985 (percentage points)**

	Borrowing Case	Asset Drawdown Case
United States:		
Old	−5.26	−2.41
New	−2.32	−.68
Japan	−1.67	−.81
Germany	−2.37	−2.40
France	−3.45	−3.29
United Kingdom	−5.55	−3.21
Canada	−3.61	−2.22
Australia	−7.98	−2.31
Sweden	−9.11	−5.09

Source: Fukao and Hanazaki (1987).

countries, Sweden exhibits the largest negative wedges and, hence, the largest corporate tax bias toward capital intensive firms and industries.

For a smaller set of countries, table 9.7 reports effective total tax rates (capturing both corporate and personal income taxes) by ownership category. Here, we see that Sweden was the only country where more than 100 percent of the real return was taxed away in 1980 for households making corporate investments. This high figure comes about even though it may be presumed that, within each country, owners choose an asset distribution that is reasonably optimal relative to the tax system they face. Note that Sweden also exhibits the most favorable treatment of tax-exempt institutions.

While strongly discouraging direct household ownership of businesses, the Swedish tax system has generously subsidized investment in the housing stock. On this point, table 9.8 reports the estimated tax wedge for housing investment in 1985 at a 5 percent real interest rate for eight countries. The table shows that housing investment received preferential tax treatment in all countries, but more so in Sweden. Investment in the housing stock was especially favored in the asset drawdown case, in which the housing investment is financed by the liquidation of other assets. Given the generous tax subsidies for investment in the housing stock and the truly punitive treatment of direct business ownership by households, it is surprising that Swedish households undertake any direct business investments.

Finally, high marginal tax rates on personal income—another outstanding and extreme feature of the pre-1990 Swedish tax system—also discourage employment in smaller and less capital intensive firms and thereby distort the industrial distribution of output and employment. As a generalization, economic activities that are highly substitutable between market and home production sectors (cooking, laundering, landscaping, home repairs, etc.) offer greater than average scope for self-employment, employment in small firms, start-ups, and family-owned businesses. Thus, in addition to the distortions described above, high marginal income tax rates alone work against a vibrant entrepreneurial and small-firm sector.

In summary, we have identified several features of the pre-1990 Swedish tax system that strongly disfavored less capital intensive firms, smaller firms, entry by new firms, and individual or family ownership of businesses. Many of these features are present in other tax systems as well, but international comparisons indicate that tax wedges are larger—often much larger—in Sweden. The magnitude of the tax wedges points to the Swedish tax system as a major source of distortions in the industrial distribution of employment and in the structure of employment within industries.

9.3   Other Policies and Institutions That Disfavor Younger and Smaller Employers

These features of the tax structure were not the only aspects of the Swedish system that disfavored smaller and younger employers. We now briefly describe four other aspects of economic policy and institutional arrangements that disfavored smaller, younger, and less capital intensive firms: credit market regulation, the mandatory national pension system, employment security laws, and a centralized wage-setting institution associated with highly compressed relative wages.

Throughout the postwar period until the late 1980s, the Swedish credit market was highly regulated. Inspired, among other things, by Gunnar Myrdal's 1944 paper on "high taxes and low interest rates," Swedish credit market policy was for a long time aimed at low interest rates for favored sectors of the economy. In a situation of full employment, rapid economic growth, and a long-lasting boom in construction, the government felt compelled to extend credit market regulations in several steps. These developments continued until the early 1980s, when a rapid process of deregulation began. The process was

Table 9.9   **Net Saving as a Percentage of GDP, Annual Averages 1950–92**

	1950–59	1960–69	1970–79	1980–92
Total	11.9	14.7	11.5	4.3
Household	4.5	3.6	2.1	.9
Corporate	4.0	2.6	3.0	3.7
Consolidated government	3.4	8.4	6.4	−.4

Source: National accounts.

completed in 1989, when the remaining foreign exchange controls were lifted.[18]

Lending to the construction and government sectors received priority over other sectors until the mid-1980s. Typically, the government imposed a ceiling on lending increases to other sectors by banks and other financial intermediaries. At the same time, interest rate ceilings were imposed in these other sectors, which led to a great deal of credit rationing. This set of regulations clearly favors credit access by larger, older, better-established firms and by capital intensive firms with ready sources of collateral. Human capital and knowledge, on the other hand, are of less value as collateral. Data presented in Ashgarian (1993) regarding the financing structure of different firms give some indication that knowledge- and human capital-intensive firms have lower debt/equity ratios.

The development of Swedish net saving is indicated in table 9.9. Net saving rose between the 1950s and the 1960s and thereafter declined sharply. For our purposes, the most noteworthy feature is the extremely important role of the government sector for net saving in the 1960s and 70s. Close to two-thirds of net saving took place there, and a large part of these funds had to be channeled to the private sector. But, as long as the government shunned ownership of industry, this pattern of national saving presupposed lending on a massive scale to the private sector.

In particular, saving in the social insurance system increased from zero in 1959 to 4.7 percent of GDP in 1972. This saving took place within the mandatory national pension scheme, the ATP (Allmän Tilläggs pension) system, which was introduced in 1959.[19] It accumulated large surpluses for a long time, with the result that in the early 1970s the AP fund system accounted for 35 percent of the total supply of credit. The AP (Allmänna Pensionsfondend) fund lent to industry primarily through intermediate credit institutions. At the end of 1976, it accounted for 69 percent of the long-term liabilities of these institutions (Pontusson 1992). This fund has been (and still is) subject to politically

18. For an overview of regulations, see Jonung (1993).
19. Originally, there were actually three funds; later, two more funds that invest in the stock market were added.

determined rules concerning the composition of its portfolio, and priority has been given to the housing sector and the government sector. Generally, only one-third or less of the financial assets in the AP fund have been invested outside the government, construction, and real-estate sectors. A very small fraction of AP-fund lending has been directly to firms.[20]

In order to channel all the public saving back to the private sector, it was logical, and perhaps even necessary, to favor debt over equity financing to a great extent. However, it appears that the negative side effects of this policy, which have been stressed here, were largely ignored at the time. In any case, the national pension system reinforced the distorted pattern of credit allocation in the Swedish economy.

The Swedish Employment Security Act (Lagen om Anställningskydd or LAS) provides employees with extensive protection against unfair dismissal. Notably, Sweden is the only country where the order of dismissal is laid down in law (Kazamaki Ottersten 1994) and where the probationary period before automatic tenure is a mere six months—very short by international comparison.[21] Furthermore, it seems that, in most countries other than Sweden, unfair dismissal regulations are not extended to small firms (Commission of the European Communities 1993).[22]

Under the LAS, the only legal grounds for worker dismissal are gross misconduct and redundancies. Moreover, the LAS stipulates the "last in, first out" principle in case of dismissals caused by redundancy. The principle also applies to situations where a firm expands employment following an employment contraction. A worker laid off because of redundancy is guaranteed to get the job back if the firm fills the position within one year from dismissal.[23] This principle may be overruled through special agreements between the local labor union and the employer. To our knowledge, there is no study quantifying the importance of this possibility. In general, there is scant evidence available on the application of the last in, first out principle in different countries, but Rasmussen (1993) argues that it is followed more strictly in Sweden than in the other Nordic countries.

20. For example, in 1980, 7 percent of total assets constituted direct lending to firms. This lending was mainly so-called lending back (återlån) based on the rule that employers were allowed to borrow up to half the amount they had paid in to the fund during the previous year. The potential for using this credit channel was therefore proportional to the wage bill of the firm. This type of lending was abolished in 1987. It should also be noted that banks acted as intermediaries and determined credit conditions under the lending-back system. Thus, in practice, this type of lending constituted cheap refinancing for the banks rather than a direct source of funds for firms.
21. In many instances, the probationary period has been shortened even further through collective agreements, and, in several industries, the trade union can veto temporary employment and the use of probationary periods. Storrie (1994) finds that the probationary period is less than six months for about one-third of the blue-collar workers in the private sector (the LO-SAF area).
22. Given how large the employment security issue looms in the public debate, we were surprised to learn that no good cross-country survey of collective agreements and legislation and their de facto application seems to be available.
23. There is anecdotal evidence that firms delayed employment expansion in the manufacturing sector after the 1992 devaluation in order not to be restricted by this rule.

In a survey study, Agell and Lundborg (1993) finds that the LAS leads to increased recruitment costs and to a lower propensity to expand employment in an economic upturn.[24] Holmlund (1978) evaluates econometrically whether the introduction of the LAS in 1974 had any effect on hiring frequency. He found that hiring frequency was lowered, ceteris paribus, by 5–10 percent as a result of the introduction of the LAS. Holmlund (1986) also found some evidence of a reduction in new recruitments resulting from an increased wariness on the part of firms.

Several international studies have examined the effect of labor security legislation on unemployment and employment variations across countries (for a survey, see OECD [1993]). The results are ambiguous, although it may be noted that there appears to be a significant positive relation between the labor security laws and long-term unemployment. We also note here that employment security legislation is on average stricter in Europe than in North America and Japan (Bertola 1990).

None of these studies shed light on the issue of whether strict employment security provisions are more harmful for smaller employers. Nevertheless, there are good reasons to think that the LAS imposes greater costs on smaller businesses. One reason involves the gains from efficiently matching heterogeneous workers to a variety of tasks and positions. As an employer learns about a workers's abilities over time, or as those abilities evolve with the accumulation of experience, the optimal assignment of the worker to various tasks is likely to change. The scope for task reassignment within the firm is likely to rise with firm size. In an unfettered labor market, optimal task reassignment often involves mobility between firms, and such mobility is more likely when the initial employment relation involves a small business. Thus, any inefficiencies induced by the LAS in the assignment of workers to tasks are likely to be more severe and more costly for smaller firms. Furthermore, the law of large numbers in combination with risk aversion leads to the same conclusion and for an obvious reason: one bad recruitment is proportionately more costly to bear for a small firm.

The only direct evidence we know of on this matter is an interview study by Kazamaki Ottersten (1994). She found that the LAS is mostly a restriction for medium-sized firms. Large firms have typically either found ways to circumvent the rules, or learned to live with them, or made special agreements with the trade union that remove the costly effects. In small firms, it is often the case that the importance of firm survival is perceived so tangibly by all employees and the trade union alike that, at least in times of hardship, it is fairly easy to agree on measures that do not strictly adhere to LAS stipulations. Nevertheless, many companies report that the LAS restricts them in detrimental ways,

---

24. Kazamaki (1991, chap. 3) presents theoretical evidence that the introduction of labor security legislation of the LAS type results in stricter quality requirements of applicants and increased recruitment costs.

leading to increased wariness in recruitment. Such firms cite the rigid order of dismissal and the increased cost caused by the employment protection. In addition, it has to be emphasized that, if the LAS has impeded the formation of new firms and not just the growth of existing firms, this aspect cannot be uncovered in an interview study (selection bias).

Other evidence is also consistent with the view that the employment security provisions fall more heavily on smaller firms and some other classes of firms. In the United States, both the rate at which workers separate from jobs and the rate at which employers destroy job positions decline with the size, age, and capital intensity of the employer (Brown and Medoff 1989; Davis, Haltiwanger, and Schuh 1996). These patterns in worker separation and job destruction rates suggest that any costs imposed by a regulation similar to the LAS are likely to fall more heavily on younger, smaller, and less capital intensive employers and to distort the distribution of employment toward industries characterized by more stable establishment-level employment and longer job tenures.

Finally, Swedish labor organizations successfully pursued egalitarian wage policies from the mid-1960s until the breakdown of centralized wage bargaining in 1983 (Hibbs 1990; Edin and Holmlund 1995). The strength of Swedish labor organizations and the centralized nature of the wage-setting institutions appear to have facilitated a remarkable compression of the wage structure during this period, judging by cross-country comparisons of wage inequality trends (Davis 1992). To the extent that Swedish wage-setting developments drove wages up in the lower tiers of the distribution relative to outcomes under other institutional arrangements, they reinforced the concentration of Swedish economic activity in larger, older, and more capital intensive employers. This inference follows from the ample evidence that wages rise with the age, capital intensity, and—especially—the size of the employer (e.g., Brown and Medoff 1989; and Davis and Haltiwanger 1991).

Indeed, in the 1950s, the LO economists Gösta Rehn and Rudolf Meidner advocated a solidaristic wage policy and centralized wage setting, in part, to promote a restructuring of the economy. Rehn and Meidner "knew that efforts to raise the pay of low-wage workers would affect employment outcomes. Low-wage industries would be forced to contract, and the workers would have to go elsewhere" (Edin and Topel, chap. 4 in this volume). Edin and Topel provide evidence that this restructuring occurred after 1960. High-wage industries did have greater growth in Sweden than in the United States, absorbing the workers who left low-wage industries. The contraction of low-wage industries seems to have been fueled by increased relative wages in those industries. Hence, there is good reason to believe that the solidaristic wage policy reinforced the concentration of economic activity to large and more capital intensive firms since these firms, relatively speaking, benefit from a high average wage in combination with a compressed wage distribution.

In summary, we have identified several features of the Swedish institutional setup during most of the postwar period that, in addition to the tax system, contributed to an excessive concentration of economic activity in large, old, and capital intensive firms. Credit market regulation, the national pension system, employment security laws, and the successful pursuit of a compressed wage structure all played a role in this regard.

9.4   Adverse Consequences of Policies That Disfavor Younger and Smaller Employers

The two preceding sections identify several aspects of the Swedish model that favored institutional forms of business ownership and that disfavored younger, smaller, and less capital intensive businesses. This section considers whether and how these aspects of the Swedish model impair productivity and welfare and retard economic growth. We do not quantify the various effects that we discuss or adduce any hard empirical evidence. Our more modest ambition is simply to advance several points in favor of the proposition that the policies and institutions described in sections 9.2 and 9.3 lower productivity and welfare and reduce the potential for economic growth.

To start with a basic point, certain goods and services are more efficiently produced by smaller, owner-operated enterprises. This proposition is difficult to deny, for, in looking across countries, we see systematic industry-level patterns in ownership and in the size distribution of employment. Restaurants, specialty retail outlets, and many personal services tend to be organized into smaller, owner-operated firms and production units. In contrast, the manufacture of durable goods is typically organized into larger establishments and larger firms with considerable separation of ownership and control. The ubiquity of these employer size and ownership patterns across countries with widely varying levels of economic development and often quite different regulatory environments indicates that they reflect strong and pervasive cost-saving motives.

It follows that policies and institutions that penalize direct business ownership and smaller organizational units carry adverse economic consequences. Such policies and institutions harm productivity by distorting business enterprises away from the most efficient organizational forms. They harm consumer welfare by raising the cost of goods and services that are most efficiently produced by the disfavored organizational forms. And they retard growth by limiting the economy's capacity and incentives to respond to changes in the economic environment, some of which will call for a redirection of resources toward disfavored organizational forms.

What are the cost-saving motives that underlie the efficiency advantages of smaller organizational forms in some sectors? Articulating a full and precise list of motives is beyond the scope of our discussion, but a few observations help convey the larger point. For instance, smallness facilitates concentrated ownership. In turn, concentrated ownership mitigates adverse selection and moral hazard problems that undermine efficient allocation and utilization of assets. Hence, policies that hamper the organization of economic activity into smaller enterprises exacerbate incentive and informational problems, thereby undermining productivity and welfare. Morck, Shleifer, and Vishny (1988), for example, provide empirical evidence that concentrated ownership mitigates agency problems.

Policies that disfavor labor-intensive sectors and techniques of production also cause productivity and welfare losses. Since certain goods and services are more efficiently produced by labor-intensive techniques, policies that disfavor such techniques will harm welfare and productivity for reasons parallel to the ones identified above in the context of business size and ownership patterns.

Thus far, our discussion stresses static efficiency and welfare losses induced by policies that disfavor direct business ownership, smaller organizational forms, and less capital intensive production techniques, but several observations point to potentially large dynamic efficiency and welfare losses as well. For example, the successful development of markets for certain new products may require a form of flexibility that is best provided by smaller, newer companies. The history of the market for personal computers seems to fit this hypothesis. IBM started with a huge lead in this market but over the course of a few years experienced a rapid erosion of market share and profitability. IBM's dismal performance in the market for personal computers and workstations seems linked to a reluctance to substitute away from its (at one time) hugely profitable mainframe computer business. Obviously, new firms that entered the personal computer business had no such reluctance to encourage the substitution away from mainframe computers. As an example of another, distinct effect, the small business sector may provide a low-cost mechanism for identifying and developing managerial and entrepreneurial talent. Since fewer assets are at stake, managerial blunders or simple ineptitude are less costly when they occur in smaller firms.

Two closely related hypotheses involve ease of entry by new firms rather than smallness per se. First, it is seldom obvious ex ante exactly which variation of a new technology, a new marketing or distribution tool, or a new organizational form is most efficient. Consequently, the most efficient innovation process may entail "planting a thousand seeds" to see which ones develop successfully. When market participation is effectively limited to only a handful of large firms, inadequate variety and experimentation may occur, slowing the growth process. Second, ease of entry facilitates competition; in turn, entrants are frequently small, especially in younger, less-mature markets. While economists lack convincing formal models of the phenomenon, many believe that competition facilitates innovation and productivity growth, and entry is often an important aspect of competition.

Returning to the matter of enterprise size, largeness hampers the external market for corporate control, especially in economies that lack financial institutions and regulatory structures that facilitate corporate takeovers or reorganizations of poorly performing companies. The market for corporate control is one tool for aligning the interests of shareholders and managers and overcoming agency problems (Jensen 1993). Government policies that undermine the market for corporate control, directly or indirectly, are likely to lead to more severe agency problems, especially when other mechanisms for aligning the interests of managers and shareholders are absent or relatively ineffective.[25]

Finally, throughout the OECD economies, recent decades witnessed a shift in employment away from goods-producing to service-producing industries. Since smaller and less capital intensive businesses play a relatively more important role in service-producing industries, the Swedish system impeded this transformation and probably slowed the growth of private sector output and employment.

The preceding discussion only scratches the surface of a broad and complicated set of issues, but it suggests how various aspects of the Swedish model may have reduced productivity and welfare by distorting the structure of employment and the organization of market activity. Our discussion of potential dynamic efficiency losses associated with Swedish policies and institutions suggests that their adverse consequences may have cumulated over time. Our discussion also suggests how the consequences might be more severe in periods that require intensive restructuring of the economy.

9.5   Evidence of Distortions in the Swedish Industrial Distribution of Employment

We now relate U.S.-Swedish differences in the industrial distribution of employment to measures of employer size, capital intensity, the wage level, and other industry characteristics. Our interpretation of the evidence rests on the premise that the U.S. industrial distribution reflects a much more neutral set of economic policies and institutions. For this reason, we take the U.S. industrial distribution as a benchmark against which to evaluate the extent of distortions in the Swedish distribution.

Of course, not all U.S.-Swedish differences in the industrial distribution of employment arise from the distortionary policies and institutions that we highlight. Natural comparative advantage undoubtedly plays an important role as well (see Leamer and Lundborg, chap. 10 in this volume). But the U.S. industrial distribution can serve as a suitable benchmark for identifying and quantifying systematic distortions in the Swedish distribution, even though factor endowments and other determinants of the industrial distribution differ between the two countries. The key issue is whether omitted determinants of U.S.-Swedish differences are correlated with the variables we consider. To gauge whether an omitted variables problem underlies our regression results,

25. Perhaps because of compressed compensation structures and high marginal tax rates, direct forms of incentive pay may be relatively ineffective in Sweden in aligning the interests of managers and shareholders. Hence, government policies that favor the organization of economic activity into large firms might create more severe agency problems in Sweden than in other countries.

we consider the effect of omitting from our regressions certain industries in which Sweden or the United States plausibly has a pronounced comparative advantage. We also group our data in such a way as to minimize the effect of U.S.-Swedish differences in the extractive industries (mining, forestry, fishing), where natural comparative advantage is likely to play the largest role.

Table 9.10 highlights U.S.-Swedish differences by listing industries with large absolute values of the log of the ratio of industry share of U.S. employment to industry share of Swedish employment. The listed industries are ordered by ascending values of this ratio, as reported in the rightmost column. Inspection of the table yields four impressions:

1. Relative to the United States, Swedish employment is concentrated in basic manufacturing industries that are typically dominated by larger firms and production units.

2. Sweden exhibits a much larger share of employment in health, education, and social services. In large part, this difference reflects public provision of and other subsidies for child care, elderly care, and related social services in Sweden.

3. Except for items in the health, education, and social services category, the United States has a larger employment share in most service sectors.

4. The industries with relatively large U.S. employment shares appear to be drawn disproportionately from the extremes of the human capital and wage distributions: (i) personal and household services, retail trade, textiles and apparel, and restaurants and hotels rely heavily on low-skill labor and pay relatively low wages (at least in the United States); (ii) business services, instruments, aircraft and missiles, and financial institutions rely heavily on high-skill labor and pay relatively high wages.

This last pattern fits nicely with the view that Sweden has a more compressed skill distribution and more compressed skill prices than most other OECD countries, especially the United States. More generally, the impressionistic evidence garnered from table 9.10 points to distortions in the Swedish industrial distribution along the lines predicted by our characterization of tax policy and other aspects of the Swedish system.

We turn now to a more detailed investigation of U.S.-Swedish differences in the industrial distribution of employment. Two considerations prompt us to consider the manufacturing and nonmanufacturing sectors separately in our investigation. First, industry-level data are available in more disaggregated form for the manufacturing sector. Second, we have at our disposal a much richer set of covariates for manufacturing industries.

With one exception, we carry out our analysis at the most disaggregated level allowed by our data, bearing in mind the requirement to match U.S. and Swedish industries and to construct industry-level covariates for the regression analysis. The exception involves the extractive industries. Employment shares in these industries are largely determined by natural resource endowments and are probably not closely related to the factors emphasized in our earlier discus-

Table 9.10   **Differences in the Industrial Distribution of Employment, Sweden[a] and the United States,[b] Selected Industries**

	% of Employment			
	Sweden		United States,	Log Ratio,[c]
	1987	1992	1987–88	1987–88
Industry:[d]				
Motor vehicles	2.6	2.2	1.1	−.89
Fabricated metals	3.0	2.6	1.3	−.85
Primary metals	1.4	1.0	.6	−.79
Wood and paper products	3.6	3.2	1.8	−.71
Ships and rail equip.	.4	.3	.2	−.63
Machinery and equip.	5.7	4.6	3.3	−.55
Health, education, social services,				
and community org.[e]	30.8	33.0	19.8	−.44
Food and drink	2.0	1.9	1.4	−.34
Transportation and public utilities	9.4	9.4	6.8	−.33
Construction	5.9	6.3	4.7	−.23
Personal and household services[f]	1.0	1.0	1.4	.34
Real estate and business services	5.2	6.4	8.5	.49
Insurance	1.1	1.1	1.9	.55
Retail trade	6.6	6.5	12.0	.60
Financial institutions	1.6	1.7	3.0	.62
Textiles and apparel	1.0	.5	1.8	.65
Instruments	.4	.4	.9	.94
Aircraft and missiles	.2	.2	.8	1.09
Restaurants and hotels	1.9	1.9	7.1	1.34

[a]The Swedish employment data are tabulated by Statistics Sweden and cover all economic sectors.

[b]The U.S. industry-level data are from the 1988 County Business Patterns data (nonmanufacturing) and the 1987 Longitudinal Research Data Base (manufacturing). Together, these two data sets cover the population of taxpaying private business establishments with one or more paid employees, excluding agricultural production, railroad, and household employment. We supplemented these private sector data with 1988 BLS Establishment Survey data on public sector employment in hospitals, education, transportation, public utilities, and the postal service. The industry-level U.S. data exclude self-employed individuals, but employment shares are calculated as the ratio of industry employment to total civilian employment including the self-employed.

[c]The log of the industry's U.S. employment share minus the log of the industry's Swedish employment share. The industries are ordered by ascending values of this quantity in the table.

[d]Industrial classifications are based on our concordance between the 1987 U.S. Standard Industrial Classification (SIC) system and the Swedish Standard Industrial Classification of All Economic Activities (SNI). The document on the Swedish SNI is dated 1985.

[e]The U.S. data do not include all public sector social service employees and, hence, understate the relative U.S. employment share in this category.

[f]Because the U.S. data do not include domestic household workers and the self-employed, they substantially understate the relative U.S. employment share in this category.

sion. For this reason, we lump all extractive industries into a single industry group. It turns out that the U.S.-Swedish employment share ratio is close to one for this industry group, even though it differs greatly from one for particular extractive industries.

We begin with the connection between employer size and the industrial distribution of employment. For fourteen broad nonmanufacturing industries and two broad manufacturing industries (durables and nondurables), we computed the establishment coworker mean—that is, the number of employees at the average worker's place of employment.[26]

Figure 9.6 illustrates the 1987 empirical relation between the Swedish establishment coworker mean and U.S.-Swedish differences in the industrial distribution of employment.[27] The figure conveys a clear message: relative to the United States, the Swedish industrial distribution of employment is tilted away from industries with relatively high fractions of employment in smaller establishments. This pattern holds for the sample of sixteen major industry groups, and it holds even more strongly in a fourteen-industry sample that excludes the manufacture of durables and nondurables.

Table 9.11 reports several bivariate regressions that relate U.S.-Swedish differences in the industrial distribution of nonmanufacturing employment to simple summary measures of the distribution of employees by employer size. Column 2 reports regression results corresponding to the dashed line in figure 9.6. Rather remarkably, the Swedish establishment coworker mean accounts for 47 percent of the variation in U.S.-Swedish differences in the industrial distribution of nonmanufacturing employment. The point estimate implies that the Swedish employment share is sixty-eight log points lower than the U.S. share for an industry group with a value of the coworker mean two standard deviations below its mean value.

The goodness of fit for the nonmanufacturing regression is unaffected when we replace the Swedish establishment coworker mean with the corresponding U.S. measure. In contrast, the Swedish firm coworker mean has much less explanatory power.[28] The inferior performance of the firm-based measure probably arises for several reasons: conceptual ambiguities in defining the scope of

26. The coworker mean equals the size-weighted mean of employer size; it is the first moment of the distribution of employees by employer size. Tables 9.14 and 9.15 below provide summary statistics for various measures of the coworker mean.

27. The log ratios plotted in fig. 9.7 below are constructed from Swedish data for 1987 and U.S. data for 1987 and 1988. The Swedish establishment coworker statistics plotted in fig. 9.6 are constructed from 1984 data, and the Swedish firm size statistics used below are constructed from 1987 data. The U.S. size distribution summary statistics draw on data for 1985 and 1987. For the U.S. manufacturing sector, the firm and establishment size distribution summary statistics are computed directly from the establishment-level and firm-level data described in Davis, Haltiwanger, and Schuh (1996). In all other cases, the size distribution summary statistics are estimated from data on the number of employees and establishments by employer size class using the algorithm described in Davis (1990).

28. The available data do not enable us to construct a measure of the U.S. firm coworker mean for several nonmanufacturing industries.

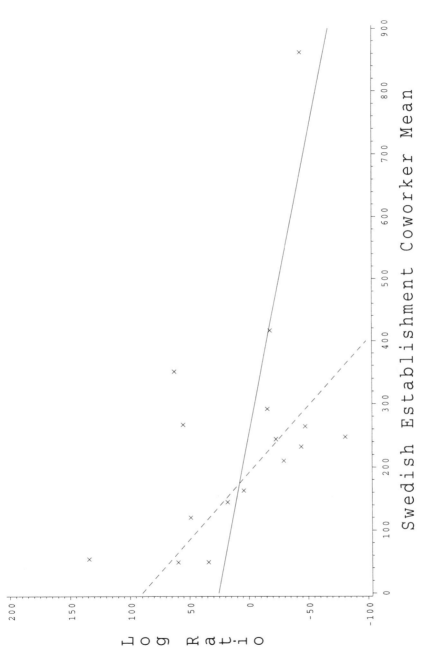

Fig. 9.6 Log(employment share ratio) vs. Swedish establishment coworker mean, sample of sixteen major industry groups

Note: The solid line shows the size-weighted regression line for the sixteen-industry sample, slope = −.102 (.046), R^2 = .263. The dashed line shows the size-weighted regression line for fourteen nonmanufacturing industries, slope = −.471 (.132), R^2 = .514. The log ratio equals 100 times the log of the ratio of industry share of U.S. employment to industry share of Swedish employment.

Table 9.11   **U.S.-Swedish Industry Employment Share[a] Ratio Regressions: Summary Statistics[b] and Regressions[c] for Nonmanufacturing Industries**

$$\text{dependent variable: } \log\left(\frac{\text{U.S. industry employment share}}{\text{Swedish industry employment share}}\right) \times 100,$$

$$\text{mean} = 3.07, \quad \text{SD} = 12.76$$

Regressor[c,d]	Mean (SD) (1)	Regression Slope Coefficients (SE)			
		(2)	(3)	(4)	(5)
Swedish establishment	199.2	−.471			−.267
coworker mean	(72.3)	(.132)			(.199)
Swedish firm	710.6		−.011		
coworker mean	(542.2)		(.029)		
U.S. establishment coworker	460.0			−.118	−.067
mean	(327.4)			(.033)	(.050)
Adjusted R^2		.473	−.072	.473	.506

[a]There are fourteen industry-level observations for each variable.

[b]All summary statistics are computed as employment-weighted quantities.

[c]All regressions include a constant and are weighted by the U.S.-Swedish average value of the industry employment share.

[d]The Swedish firm coworker mean and the U.S. establishment coworker mean are computed from private sector data only. The Swedish establishment coworker mean is computed from data that cover the public and private sectors.

a firm, practical difficulties in measuring firm size, and the exclusion of a large fraction of public sector employees in Sweden (relative to the United States) when measuring the firm size distribution.

While figure 9.6 and table 9.11 indicate that Swedish employment is tilted toward industries dominated by larger establishments, we found no evidence that Swedish employment is more concentrated in large establishments than U.S. employment. On the contrary, the U.S. establishment coworker mean exceeds twice the corresponding Swedish value, even though U.S. employment is more heavily concentrated in industries dominated by smaller production units. Perhaps this difference reflects smaller product market size in Sweden, but the same pattern holds in the manufacturing sector, which is presumably dominated by tradable goods. The difference may reflect different criteria in the two countries for defining the scope of an establishment, but we can offer no evidence on this score. In any case, the difficulty of interpreting comparisons of size distribution measures between countries argues in favor of the industry-based focus of our analysis.

We constructed a more disaggregated matched industry-level data set and a richer set of covariates for the manufacturing sector. The disaggregated manufacturing data also show higher shares of Swedish employment in industries dominated by larger employers, but the effect is weaker and less consistent than in the nonmanufacturing sector. Figure 9.7 shows a scatterplot of the log employment share ratio against the Swedish establishment coworker log.[29]

Table 9.12 reports bivariate regressions of the log employment share ratio on several alternative summary measures of the employer size distribution. Unlike for the nonmanufacturing sector, the results show little relation between the log employment share ratio and summary measures of the U.S. size distribution. For the full sample of manufacturing industries, the U.S. establishment coworker mean actually shows a positive relation to the log employment share ratio, contrary to the implications of our thesis. This anomalous result disappears when we exclude the aircraft and missiles industry, a major outlier in terms of both U.S.-based measures of employer size and the log employment share ratio.[30]

Table as a whole, we interpret the results in figure 9.7 and table 9.12 as supportive of the hypothesis that Sweden's distribution of employment is tilted toward industries with larger employers, as compared to the United States.[31] Our results for the nonmanufacturing sector in figure 9.6 and table 9.11 above strongly support this hypothesis. Thus, if one accepts our premise that the U.S. industrial distribution reflects a comparatively neutral set of policies and institutions, the evidence pushes one to the view that Swedish policies and institutions distorted employment and productive activity away from industries in which smaller businesses play a greater role. Although not speaking directly to the matter, the evidence also suggests that Swedish policies and institutions have distorted employment and productive activity away from smaller businesses within industries.

Table 9.12 also reports regressions of the log employment share ratio on industry-level measures of capital intensity, energy intensity, productivity growth, exposure to international trade, average production worker wages, and job reallocation intensity.[32] Figures 9.8 and 9.9 plot the log employment share ratio against the capital intensity and hourly wage measures, respectively.

29. The coworker log equals the size-weighted mean of log employer size. It equals the expectation of log employer size taken with respect to the distribution of workers by employer size.

30. The U.S. aircraft and missiles industry is dominated by large firms and plants that engage in much large-scale production for the U.S. military. There is no comparable source of demand for military aircraft and missile products in Sweden. In this respect, the aircraft and missiles industry is a special case, and we often report separate results for samples that exclude this industry. Our regression results are typically similar, but stronger and better fitting, when we exclude the aircraft and missiles industry.

31. This conclusion is not much affected if we exclude the six manufacturing industries in the wood and paper products sector from the regressions in table 9.12.

32. The import penetration ratio in table 9.12 equals the value of imports divided by imports plus domestic shipments. The export share equals the value of exports as a fraction of total domestic production. Excess job reallocation measures the extent of simultaneous plant-level job creation and destruction within an industry. It is measured as gross plant-level job creation plus gross job destruction minus the absolute value of the net industry employment change, all expressed as a percentage of industry employment. The wage and factor intensity variables that appear in table

These bivariate regressions and scatterplots for the manufacturing sector identify the following additional patterns of U.S.-Swedish differences in the industrial distribution of employment:

1. Sweden exhibits relatively high employment shares in capital intensive and energy-intensive industries. The point estimate in table 9.12 above implies that the Swedish employment share is sixty-six log points higher in an industry with a log capital per worker value two standard deviations above its mean.

2. Sweden exhibits relatively low employment shares in manufacturing industries that experienced rapid total factor productivity growth over the period 1973–88. The opposite effect holds with respect to labor productivity growth. For both productivity growth measures, the statistical relation is weak, and the point estimates imply small effects. These results provide no support for the view that Swedish industrial policy directed resources to high-productivity growth industries.

3. There is also weak evidence that Sweden's distribution of employment is tilted away from manufacturing industries that exhibit higher rates of excess job reallocation. This finding fits with the view that LAS employment security provisions penalize sectors characterized by less-stable establishment-level employment. The effects are moderate in size but imprecisely estimated. The point estimate implies that the Swedish employment share is thirty-two log points lower in an industry with an excess job reallocation rate two standard deviations above the mean.

4. Trade exposure, as measured by either U.S. import or export intensity, is unrelated to U.S.-Swedish differences in the distribution of employment.

5. Sweden exhibits higher employment shares in high-wage industries. The effects are fairly large and tightly estimated. For an industry with a mean hourly wage two standard deviations above the overall U.S. mean (4.92 in 1982 dollars), the point estimate implies that the Swedish employment share is seventy-two log points greater.

Statistically and quantitatively significant effects of capital intensity, energy intensity, employer size, and wages carry over to multivariate regression specifications as well (see table 9.13). The multivariate regression results differ from the bivariate results in two main respects. First, the sign of the coefficient on the capital intensity variable switches. That is, once we condition on the other regressors in table 9.13, Sweden's employment distribution is actually tilted away from capital intensive manufacturing industries.[33]

Second, the coefficient on the Swedish establishment coworker mean also switches sign. In this regard, note that the estimated effects on the Swedish

---

9.12 are averages of 1987 and 1988 industry-level values. The other variables are averages of annual industry-level values over the period 1973–88. Data on wages, factor intensity, productivity growth, and international trade are constructed from the NBER data files described in Abowd (1991). Job reallocation data are from Davis, Haltiwanger, and Schuh (1996).

33. No single covariate accounts for the reversal in the coefficient sign of the capital intensity variable.

Fig. 9.7 Log(employment share ratio) vs. Swedish establishment coworker log, sixty-seven manufacturing industries

Note: The solid line depicts the size-weighted least squares regression, excluding the aircraft and missiles industry.

Table 9.12   **U.S.-Swedish Industry Employment Share Ratio Regressions: Summary Statistics[a] and Bivariate Regressions[b] for Manufacturing Industries**

dependent variable: $\log\left(\dfrac{\text{U.S. industry employment share}}{\text{Swedish industry employment share}}\right) \times 100$

Regressor[c]	Mean	SD	Regr. Coeff.	SE	Sample Size[d]	Adj. R^2
Swed. est. coworker mean[e]	703.8	781.7	−.029	.01	66	.094
Swed. est. coworker log	5.25	1.064	−41.7	39.9	67	.046
Swed. est. coworker log[e]	5.22	1.041	−26.5	7.14	66	.165
Swed. firm coworker mean	1,338.4	1,255.5	−.025	.006	66	.21
Swed. firm coworker log	5.76	1.33	−16.9	6.03	67	.094
Swed. firm coworker log[e]	5.79	1.32	−22.4	5.54	66	.19
U.S. est. coworker mean	1,510.1	2,452.6	.0087	.0041	67	.05
U.S. est. coworker mean[e]	1,029.4	1,122.5	−.004	.007	66	−.012
U.S. firm coworker mean[e]	25,537	41,223	−.00029	.00017	66	.029
U.S. log(capital/worker)	2.96	.71	−46.8	10.4	65	.23
U.S. log(energy/worker)	.578	.864	−33.8	8.29	65	.196
U.S. excess realloc. rate	.141	.03	539.2	263.5	65	.048
U.S. labor prod. growth	.073	.011	−1,492	675	65	.057
U.S. TFP growth rate	.0018	.0091	2,078	900	65	.063
U.S. export share	.086	.077	12.7	117.2	65	−.016
U.S. import penetr. ratio	.075	.054	−67.4	165.5	65	−.013
U.S. PW hourly wage	10.5	2.63	−11.15	2.88	65	.18
U.S. PW hourly wage	10.26	2.46	−14.57	2.53	64	.338

Note: PW = production worker.

[a]All summary statistics are computed as employment-weighted quantities.

[b]All regressions include a constant and are weighted by the U.S.-Swedish average value of the industry employment share.

[c]The Swedish firm coworker mean and the U.S. establishment and firm coworker means are computed from private sector data only. The Swedish establishment mean is computed from data that covers the private and public sectors.

[d]The sample size varies because of missing observations on some variables.

[e]Excludes the aircraft and missiles industry.

firm and establishment coworker means are the same magnitude. Note, also from table 9.12, that the mean and standard deviation are roughly twice as large for the firm coworker mean as for the establishment coworker mean. Thus, the multivariate specifications also indicate that, on net, the Swedish distribution of employment is tilted away from industries in which smaller employers play a greater role.

Our multivariate regression analysis also reveals an interesting nonlinearity in the relation between the industry wage structure and U.S.-Swedish differences in the industrial distribution of employment. In particular, if we think in terms of low-wage, medium-wage, and high-wage industries, Sweden's distribution of manufacturing employment is sharply distorted away from low-wage industries and toward higher-wage and, especially, medium-wage industries. To state the point more precisely, consider three industries. Suppose that indus-

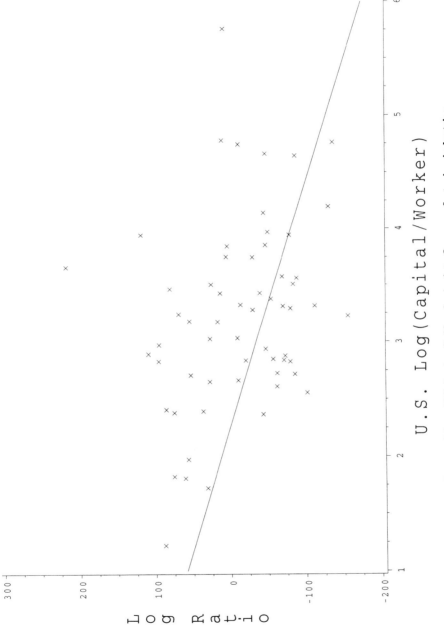

Fig. 9.8 Log(employment share ratio) vs. U.S. log(capital/worker), sixty-five manufacturing industries

Note: The solid line depicts the size-weighted least squares regression.

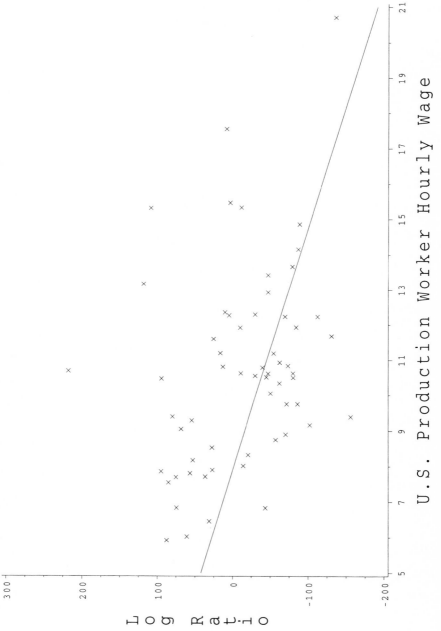

Fig. 9.9 Log(employment share ratio) vs. U.S. production worker hourly wage, sixty-five manufacturing industries

Note: The solid line depicts the size-weighted least squares regression, excluding the aircraft and missiles industry.

Table 9.13   **U.S.-Swedish Industry Employment Share Ratio Regressions: Multivariate Regressions for Manufacturing Industries**

dependent variable: $\log\left(\dfrac{\text{U.S. industry employment share}}{\text{Swedish industry employment share}}\right) \times 100$

	Regression Coefficients (Standard Errors)					
Regressor	(1)	(2)	(3)	(4)[a]	(5)	(6)[a]
U.S. establishment coworker mean	.0105					
	(.0083)					
U.S. firm coworker mean	−.0000					
	(.0002)					
Swedish establishment coworker mean		.0354	.0368	.0442	.0381	.0454
		(.0145)	.0141	(.0161)	(.0141)	(.0155)
Swedish firm coworker mean		−.0323	−.0398	−.0403	−.0418	−.0443
		(.0091)	(.0094)	(.0108)	(.0100)	(.0106)
U.S. log(capital/worker)	−2.18	53.14	70.08	52.36	62.7	40.9
	(21.96)	(22.49)	(23.15)	(26.16)	(23.87)	(25.85)
U.S. log(energy/worker)	−10.7	−34.66	−45.53	−50.69	−43.99	−46.8
	(15.0)	(12.72)	(13.31)	(15.21)	(13.32)	(14.83)
U.S. excess reallocation rate	−481	−646.8	−506.2	−632.6	−403	−409.2
	(347)	(312.6)	(309.7)	(353.9)	(320.4)	(357.2)
U.S. production worker hourly wage	−17.5	−22.55	−22.21	−17.28	−18.37	−10.59
	(5.5)	(5.21)	(5.05)	(5.65)	(5.96)	(6.25)
U.S. absolute deviation from mean wage[b]			9.94	12.15	8.37	8.7
			(4.58)	(5.23)	(4.75)	(5.3)
U.S. total factor productivity growth					1,021	2,000
					(853)	(908)
Observations	64	64	64	65	64	65
Adjusted R^2	.35	.451	.484	.395	.488	.433

Note: See also nn. b and c in table 9.12 above.

[a]Includes the aircraft and missiles industry. The other regressions reported in this table exclude aircraft and missiles.

[b]This variable equals the absolute deviation from the employment-weighted mean hourly wage for production workers in the U.S. manufacturing sector. It has a weighted mean value of 2.118 and a weighted standard deviation of 1.563.

try 1 pays a mean wage five dollars (about two standard deviations) below the overall mean manufacturing wage, industry 2 pays a mean wage equal to the overall mean, and industry 3 pays a mean wage five dollars above the overall mean. Then, the estimated wage effects in column 3 of table 9.12 imply that the U.S.-Swedish employment share ratio is 161 log points higher in industry 1 than in industry 2 (conditional on the other regressors). But the implied employment share ratio is only sixty-one log points higher in industry 2 than in industry 3. These are enormous effects, and the nonlinearity is a sharp one. Thus, the regression results confirm that the Swedish distribution of employment is tilted toward higher-wage industries, but this tilt primarily reflects small employment shares in low-wage industries and only secondarily reflects large employment shares in high-wage industries. For complementary evidence that Sweden's centralized wage-setting system tilted employment away from low-wage industries, see Edin and Topel (chap. 4 in this volume).

We examined the sensitivity of the regression results in tables 9.12 and 9.13 to the exclusion of the six manufacturing industries in the wood and paper products sector. Leamer and Lundborg (chap. 10 in this volume), for example, argue that relatively high Swedish employment shares in these industries reflect natural comparative advantage. Our results are not greatly affected by excluding these industries, except for results that pertain to the factor intensity measures. In both the bivariate and the multivariate specifications, the effects of the capital intensity and energy intensity variables are greatly attenuated when we exclude these industries. In many specifications, the factor intensity variables are statistically insignificant. The overall goodness of fit of the regressions deteriorates somewhat when we exclude the six industries. For the multivariate specifications in table 9.13, the adjusted R^2 values decline by 7–12 percentage points.

Finally, we investigated whether the industrial distribution of Swedish employment became more or less distorted (relative to the U.S. distribution) between 1984 and 1992. (see fig. 9.10). While changes in the Swedish distribution occurred over this period, they were unrelated to the U.S.-Swedish differences and (in unreported results) to any of the regressors in tables 9.12 and 9.13.

In summary, we uncovered systematic and quantitatively important U.S.-Swedish differences in the industrial distribution of employment. For the most part, the pattern of these differences fits well with the distortions we anticipated from our characterization of Swedish economic policies and institutions. In particular, Sweden's industrial distribution of employment is tilted sharply away from lower-wage industries and industries in which smaller employers play a greater role. In terms of a bivariate relation, Sweden's employment distribution is also sharply tilted away from less capital intensive manufacturing industries. The connection between capital intensity and U.S.-Swedish differences in the industrial distribution of employment reverses, however, when we condition on other variables that we considered.

On balance, we conclude that tax policy, credit policy, employment security provisions, and Sweden's system of centralized wage bargaining probably caused large distortions in the industrial distribution of Swedish employment. It stands to reason that these aspects of the Swedish system also seriously distorted the structure of employment within industries, although the limitations of our data preclude a direct assessment of this hypothesis. While we are not in a position to evaluate the overall productivity, employment, growth, and welfare consequences of these distortions, we think that our analysis lends cre-

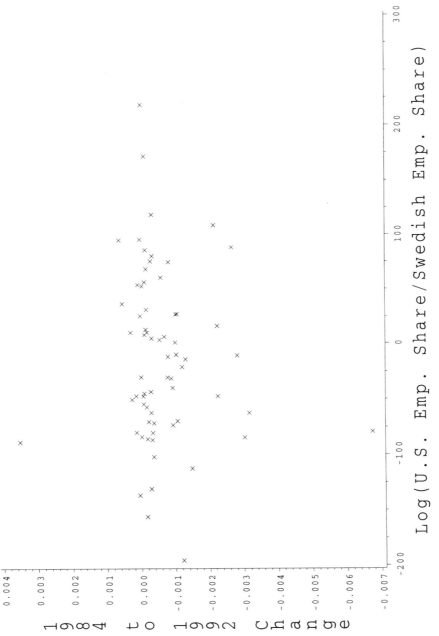

Fig. 9.10 1984–92 change in Swedish employment share vs. log(employment share ratio), sixty-seven manufacturing industries

dence to the proposition that the consequences were large and adverse. Further study of the costs of Swedish industrial policy seems highly warranted.

9.6   International Trends in Employment Structure

This section recounts three trends in the structure of employment common to many or all OECD countries in recent years. We mention these trends because they suggest the operation of exogenous economic forces that are likely to have amplified the costs of the distortions in the structure of Swedish employment induced by Swedish policies and institutions.

We have already remarked on the most important and widespread trend: the large, ongoing shift in employment from goods-producing to service-producing industries. This trend cuts sharply against those sectors of the economy that have traditionally been dominated by larger firms, larger production units, and more capital intensive production processes.

A second trend, less pronounced and consistent, is the movement away from employment in larger production units within industries. Loveman and Sengenberger (1991) examine changes in the distribution of employment by establishment and firm size in the six largest OECD countries. Only in the manufacturing sector are the available data adequate for drawing a clear picture. The data indicate that the secular trend away from employment in smaller manufacturing plants reversed or at least ended by the 1970s or 1980s in the countries under study.

Regarding a third and related trend, more open to measurement and interpretation problems, Loveman and Sengenberger also report evidence of a tendency toward employment in smaller firms in manufacturing and in the economy as a whole for the largest OECD economies.

These pieces of evidence suggest that the aspects of the Swedish system that disfavored smaller firms and establishments and less capital intensive production processes cut against some important changes in the economic environment that occurred during the 1970s and 1980s. Consequently, and aside from any endogenous dynamics in the evolution of the Swedish welfare state, it seems likely that the distortions induced by the Swedish model worsened over the course of the past two decades.

9.7   Concluding Remarks

This paper builds a plausible case for the thesis that Swedish economic policies and institutions seriously distorted the distribution of employment and output between and within industries and—as a consequence—reduced productivity, welfare, and economic progress.

If one accepts this thesis, then several recent economic policy reforms offer some grounds for optimism that Sweden will gravitate toward a less-distorted, more-efficient structure of employment with favorable consequences for productivity and growth.

The sharp reduction from 55 to 30 percent in statutory rates of corporate taxation mitigates several of the tax-induced distortions identified in section 9.2. On this point, OECD (1991) shows that estimated corporate tax wedges in Sweden became comparable in size to those in many other OECD countries after the 1991 tax reform. Termination of the investment fund system in 1991 removed another aspect of the tax system that favored established firms over entrants. Reductions in top marginal income tax rates facing individuals diminish the incentive to substitute socially inefficient forms of home production for goods and services that are more efficiently produced in the market sector. The introduction of a flat 30 percent rate of taxation on individual capital income greatly diminishes the harsh treatment of direct investment in businesses that prevailed under the old tax system. Moreover, since the late 1980s, Swedish credit markets have been substantially deregulated, eliminating another policy instrument that disfavored younger, smaller, and less capital intensive firms. And, finally, the demise of centralized wage bargaining has been associated with an uncompression of relative wages that, over time, is likely to contribute to a less-distorted distribution of employment between and within industries.

"The leveling of the playing field" for different types of owners and sources of finance was not complete following the 1991 tax reform (table 9.4 above). Further measures were taken in 1993–94, notably the abolishment of taxation of dividends at both the corporate and the investor level and the lowering of capital gains taxation to 12.5 percent. These measures strongly increased the relative attractiveness of direct household ownership of businesses, and they reduced the relative cost of equity financing. However, effective from 1995, these measures have to a large extent been undone through the reintroduction of double taxation of dividends and a doubling of the tax rate on capital gains. These changes reverse the previous movement toward a more neutral treatment of debt versus equity as sources of finance. The most recent changes also benefit foreign investors at the expense of domestic investors. In particular, it is noteworthy that the marginal effective tax rates for households buying a newly issued share almost doubled between 1994 and 1995 (McLure and Norrman, chap. 3 in this volume).

Thus, despite several favorable developments in the early 1990s, economic policy choices continue to generate incentives that seriously distort the structure of Swedish employment and business ownership. To a certain extent, tax-induced distortions in employment patterns are inevitable in an economy with such a large public sector. But, even given the size of the Swedish public sector, there is ample room for improving the design of the tax system in terms of the aspects discussed in this paper.

References

Abowd, J. M. 1991. Appendix: The NBER immigration, trade and labor market data files. In *Immigration, trade and the labor market,* ed. J. M. Abowd and R. B. Freeman. Chicago: University of Chicago Press.

Agell, J., and P. Lundborg. 1993. Theories of pay and unemployment: Survey evidence from Swedish manufacturing firms. IUI (Industrial Institute for Economic and Social Research) Working Paper no. 380. Stockholm.

Ashgarian, H. 1993. Inter-industry differences in capital structures. Department of Economics, University of Lund. Mimeo.

Baily, M. N., J. Haltiwanger, and C. Hulten. 1996. Downsizing and productivity growth: myth or reality? *Small Business Economics* 8, no. 4 (August): 259–78.

Bergström, V. 1982. Studies in Swedish post-war industrial investments. Ph.D. diss., Department of Economics, University of Uppsala.

Bertola, G. 1990. Job security, wages and employment. *European Economic Review* 34, no. 4:851–79.

Braunerhjelm, P., and B. Carlsson. 1993. Entreprenörskap, småföretag och industriell förnyelse, 1968–91. *Ekonomisk Debatt* 21, no. 4:317–28.

Brown, C., and J. Medoff. 1989. The employer size wage effect. *Journal of Political Economy* 97, no. 5:1027–59.

Commission of the European Communities. 1993. *Employment in Europe.* Luxembourg: Official Publications of the European Community.

Cragg, J. G., and B. G. Malkiel. 1968. The consensus and accuracy of some predictions of growth of corporate earnings. *Journal of Finance,* vol. 33.

Davidsson, P., L. Lindmark, and C. Olofsson. 1994. *Dynamiken i svenskt näringsliv.* Stockholm: Almqvist & Wiksell.

Davis, S. J. 1990. Size distribution statistics from county business patterns data. Typescript.

———. 1992. Cross-country patterns of change in relative wages. *NBER Macroeconomics Annual* 7:239–92.

Davis, S. J., and J. Haltiwanger. 1991. Wage dispersion between and within U.S. manufacturing plants. *Brookings Papers on Economic Activity: Microeconomics,* 115–80.

Davis, S. J., J. Haltiwanger, and S. Schuh. 1996. *Job creation and destruction.* Cambridge, Mass.: MIT Press.

Edin, P. A., and B. Holmlund. 1995. The Swedish wage structure: The rise and fall of solidarity policy? In *Differences and changes in wage structures,* ed. R. Freeman and L. Katz. Chicago: University of Chicago Press.

Familjeföretagens skatteberedning. 1988. Nyckeln till familjeföretagen. Mimeo.

———. 1989. Nyckeln till familjeföretagen. Mimeo.

Fukao, M., and M. Hanazaki. 1987. Internationalization of financial markets and the allocation of capital. *OECD Economic Studies,* 8:35–92.

Gandemo, B., and A. Lundström. 1991. *Medium-sized industrial firms: Financial performance—growth and change.* B 1991:3. Stockholm: NUTEK (Swedish National Board for Industrial and Technical Development).

Henrekson, M., L. Jonung, and S. Stymne. 1996. Economic growth and the Swedish model. In *Economic growth in post-1945 Europe,* ed. N. F. R. Crafts and G. Tonniolo. Cambridge: Cambridge University Press.

Hibbs, D. A., Jr. 1990. Wage compression under solidarity bargaining in Sweden. In *Generating equality in the welfare state: The Swedish experience,* ed. I. Persson-Tanimura. Oslo: Norwegian University Press.

Holmlund, B. 1978. Erfarenheter av åmanlagarna. *Ekonomisk Debatt* 6, no. 4:236–46.

———. 1986. A new look at vacancies and labor turnover in Swedish industry. Stockholm: Trade Union Institute for Economic Research, FIEF (Trade Union Institute for Economic Research). Mimeo.

Jensen, M. C. 1993. The modern industrial revolution, exit, and the failure of internal control systems. *Journal of Finance* 48, no. 3:831–80.

Jonung, L. 1993. Riksbankens politik, 1945–1990. In *Från räntereglering till inflationsnorm,* ed. L. Werin. Stockholm: SNS Press.

Kazamaki, E. 1991. Firm search, sectoral shifts, and unemployment. Ph.D. diss., University of Stockholm, Swedish Institute for Social Research.

Kazamaki Ottersten, E. 1994. Yrkeskompetens och rekryteringskrav. In *Om förlängd skolgång,* ed. G. Eliasson and E. Kazamaki Ottersten. Stockholm: Almqvist & Wiksell International.

King, M. A., and D. Fullerton, eds. 1984. *The taxation of income from capital: A comparative study of the United States, the United Kingdom, Sweden, and West Germany.* Chicago: University of Chicago Press.

Lindh, T. 1994. Privat sysselsättning under 50-talet. *Ekonomisk Debatt* 22, no. 5:557–61.

Little, I. M. D. 1962. Higgledy, Piggledy Growth. *Bulletin of the Oxford University Institute of Statistics,* vol. 24.

Loveman, G., and W. Sengenberger. 1991. The reemergence of small-scale production: An international comparison. *Small Business Economics* 3, no. 1:1–37.

Lundström, A., P. Davidssön, L. Lindmark, E. L. Löwstedt, P. Niederbach, and C. Oloffson. 1993. De nya och små företagens roll i svensk ekonomi. Report no. 18 to the Government Commission on Economic Policy. Statens Offentliga Utredningarsmå 1993:16. Stockholm: Allmänna.

Maddison, A. 1982. *Phases of capitalist development.* Oxford: Oxford University Press.

Morck, R., A. Shleifer, and R. W. Vishny. 1988. Management ownership and market valuation: An empirical analysis. *Journal of Financial Economics* 20, nos. 1–2:293–315.

Myhrman, J. 1994. *Hur Sverige blev rikt.* Stockholm: SNS Press.

Myrdal, G. 1994. Höga skatter och låga räntor. In *Studier i ekonomi och historia tillägnade Eli F. Heckscher.* Uppsala: Almqvist & Wicksell.

OECD. 1991. *Taxing profits in a global economy: Domestic and international issues.* Paris.

———. 1993. Long-term unemployment: Selected causes and remedies. *Employment Outlook,* July, 83–118.

Pontusson, J. 1992. *The limits of social democracy: Investment politics in Sweden.* Ithaca, N.Y.: Cornell University Press.

Rasmussen, P. -H. 1993. *Stillingsværn: Virkninger for ungdom.* SNF-rapport 79/93. Bewrgen: Stiftelsen for samfunns- och næringslivsforskning.

Silenstam, P. 1960. *Arbetskraftsutbudets utveckling i Sverige, 1870–1965.* Stockholm: Almqvist & Wicksell.

Södersten, J. 1984. Sweden. In *The taxation of income from capital: A comparative study of the United States, the United Kingdom, Sweden, and West Germany,* ed. M. A. King and D. Fullerton. Chicago: University of Chicago Press.

———. 1993. Sweden. In *Tax reform and the cost of capital: An international comparison,* ed. D. W. Jorgenson and R. Landau. Washington, D.C.: Brookings.

Statens Offentliga Utredningar (SOU). 1992. *Långtidsutredningen 1992.* SOU 1992:19. Stockholm: Allmänna.

Storrie, D. W. 1994. Regleringar av visstidsanställningar i kollektivavtal: Konsekvenser av 1994 års lagstiftning. Report no. 30 from EFA (Delegationen för Arbetsmarknadspolitisk), Arbetsmarknadsdepartementet. Stockholm.

10   A Heckscher-Ohlin View of Sweden Competing in the Global Marketplace

Edward E. Leamer and Per Lundborg

Besides the extensive welfare state, a salient feature of the Swedish economy is the substantial and long-standing degree of international interdependence. Imports as a share of GDP increased from 17 percent a few years after World War II to 45 percent in the early 1980s. This openness places Sweden in a group of countries that are vulnerable to changes in the international marketplace. In this group of small open economies are also the countries with the most extensive welfare states.

When Sweden started down the road to the welfare state, it was enjoying very positive growth figures and a favorable competitive situation in international trade. During the 1950s and 1960s, the growth in government went hand in hand with supporting trends in the basic economic indicators and with substantial increases in Swedish foreign trade. The extended period of economic slowdown that Sweden is experiencing has naturally stimulated a search for the cause and for appropriate remedies. One of the primary candidates is the size of the public sector and various features of the welfare state that tend to allocate workers to relatively unproductive tasks and that tend to discourage investments in physical and human capital. Another candidate is globalization. After all, the current Swedish economic malaise is unique for Sweden but

Edward E. Leamer is the Chauncey J. Medberry Professor of Management and professor of economics at the University of California, Los Angeles, and a research associate of the National Bureau of Economic Research. Per Lundborg is associate professor and a research fellow at the Trade Union Institute for Economic Research. The research was carried out when Lundborg was affiliated with the Industrial Institute for Economic and Social Research.

Partially supported by National Science Foundation grant SBR-9209845. The able research assistance of Torsten Dahlquist, Robert Murdock, and Christopher Thornberg is gratefully acknowledged. Pär Hansson has generously given the authors access to some of his data. The authors are grateful to anonymous referees and to Lars Lundberg, Mats Persson, and participants at the NBER-SNS conference in Stockholm, 2–4 December 1993, for comments.

comes at a time when all the major industrialized countries are experiencing difficulties. A high dependence on the international marketplace seems likely to expose Sweden particularly to external macroeconomic and microeconomic shocks.

In this chapter, we explore the hypothesis that the Swedish malaise comes from the interaction of the Swedish welfare state with changes in the global marketplace. The view that we offer here has a time frame that is long enough for underlying microeconomic forces to dominate the shorter-term macroeconomic disturbances. Among the events that have changed the nature and intensity of international competition and thus the viability of the Swedish welfare system are high rates of capital accumulation in Northern and more recently Southern Europe, the emergence of Asia, the formation of the European Economic Community, the recent liberalization of Eastern Europe, and the rise of the multinational corporation.

The micro theory of international economics offers three theoretical lenses through which one might view the Swedish economy. These are the Ricardian theory, the Heckscher-Ohlin (H-O) theory, and the Chamberlainian theory. The Ricardian model points to technological differences as the source of comparative advantage.[1] The Chamberlainian model refers to economies of scale and to product differentiation as the explanation of international trade.[2] An H-O model points to supplies of productive inputs as the source of comparative advantage. We present here an H-O view, which we think is clear and insightful. We leave the two other lenses on the shelf, not because they are not useful, but rather because the Heckscher-Ohlin lens offers a view that deserves to be lingered over.

The fundamental insight of a Heckscher-Ohlin model is that international trade in goods can turn a local Swedish labor market into a global labor market with wages selected to assure the international competitiveness of exporting and import-competing industries. There is one exception to this general statement. If the capital intensities of tradables produced in Sweden are all extreme, then the marginal demand for labor can come from the local nontraded goods sector, and Swedish wages can be set in Stockholm. But, if the capital intensities of Swedish tradables are more diverse, then the marginal demand for Swedish workers is external, and wages are set, not in Stockholm, but in Frankfurt,

---

1. If the Ricardian model were used as a guide, we might look to the spread of technological knowledge to Asia as a source of increased competition for Swedish products. It may be possible to characterize the Swedish economy in 1960 as enjoying a Ricardian cost advantage in capital intensive manufacturing, but, in the intervening years, technological knowledge has become footloose and is no longer a source of comparative advantage for Sweden or other industrialized countries.

2. An implication of this type of model is that competition focuses on product differentiation rather than on price cutting. One idea motivated by the Chamberlainian view is that Sweden in 1960 had managed successfully to differentiate its products (Volvo) but over time has had that advantage competed away by the introduction by other countries of close substitutes (Acura and Lexus).

or in Lisbon, or in Guandong, depending on the mix of Swedish products. If, to give an extreme example, Sweden had a product mix similar to the Chinese including an active apparel industry, then Swedish wages of unskilled workers could be forced by international competition to the level prevailing in China. Incidentally, it is the mere existence, not the size, of a tradable goods sector that matters since wages in a competitive setting are set on the margin. If the marginal Swedish worker is competing with the Chinese, all Swedish workers in the same skill group are subject to the pressure of Chinese competition, even the Swedish workers who are not making the same products as the Chinese worker.

High wages for unskilled workers and a reasonably low premium for skills can occur, according to the H-O model, if the Swedish product mix is sufficiently capital intensive. A capital intensive mix of products can occur only if Swedish capital inputs are in sufficient supply compared with Swedish competitors. This identifies our first hypothesis, the *Heckscher-Ohlin crowding hypothesis:* difficulties in Sweden's interactions with the international marketplace come from the reduced distinctiveness of its mix of factor supplies, with more competitors on all sides, some offering through international commerce to sell the services of the resources that have been an important traditional source of Swedish comparative advantage, namely, human, physical, and knowledge capital, and others offering to sell the services of unskilled labor at wage rates that are unconscionable from a Swedish standpoint.[3]

Although losing its distinctiveness in capital abundance, Sweden remains unusually well supplied with soft-wood forests. These forest resources can be a mixed blessing. Although contributing substantially to GDP, forest resources can also imply lower wages for unskilled workers and consequently greater income inequality. A country with abundant forest resources and also very abundant capital can produce capital intensive manufactures in addition to pulp and paper, but a country with more moderate supplies of capital can find most of its capital deployed in pulp and paper and end up with a mix of tradables that includes some relatively labor intensive products. This product mix may dictate relatively low wages for unskilled workers since the marginal unskilled worker may be employed in sectors that globally award low wages. This notion we call the *forest product capital starving hypothesis:* the forest product sector can starve other manufacturing of human and physical capital, forcing Swedish

---

3. Incidentally, the welfare implications of crowding are clear in an H-O model but not in a Chamberlainian model. Growth in Europe and Asia that crowds the markets for Swedish products causes a deterioration in the terms of trade and reduced Swedish welfare, according to the H-O model. But growth outside the borders of Sweden, according to a Chamberlainian model, allows worldwide production at more efficient scale and greater product variety, both of which can be welfare improving even for a country that is not keeping up with the rest of the world in capital accumulation. We repeat again for emphasis that we are offering a Heckscher-Ohlin view, not because it is necessarily correct, but rather because it is rich in insights and not altogether at variance with the facts. We will present measures of intraindustry trade, which increased for many commodities from 1970 to 1985, a fact that is difficult to square with an H-O framework.

manufacturing into relatively labor intensive activities. Incidentally, if capital is internationally mobile, the forest product sector can import its capital from abroad and need not starve the rest of manufacturing. While there is some international mobility of capital, Feldstein and Horioka (1980) have shown the remarkable degree of home bias in savings.

The public goods sector, on the other hand, absorbs relatively large numbers of unskilled workers, forcing Swedish manufacturing into activities that are relatively human and physical capital intensive. This notion we call the *public sector labor absorption hypothesis:* the withdrawal of unskilled labor from the manufacturing sector tends to yield a high wage to the unskilled.

Technology and tastes interact with factor supplies to determine the gains from trade in an H-O model. A country with an unfortunate mix of factor supplies may find its gains from trade disappearing over time because of changes in technology or tastes. For example, the value of comparative advantage in wood and paper will be reduced by shifts toward other building materials or toward the paperless office. The value of comparative advantage in computing equipment is reduced by "commoditization," which changes the technology of production from skill intensive to unskilled intensive. Technological change may lower the skill intensity of Sweden's traditional export products, and global demand may be shifting away from traditional Swedish exports.

The H-O model can allow mobility of one or more factors of production, in which case the source of comparative advantage rests on the immobile factors. If humans are the immobile factor, a failure to invest adequately in relevant human capital may make Sweden a loser in the worldwide competition for footloose financial/physical capital and footloose knowledge capital. For example, Swedish multinationals that successfully innovate may choose to deploy those intangible knowledge assets in foreign locations, possibly increasing foreign employment at the expense of Swedish employment. There is increased international mobility of factors of production, and Swedish investments in immobile human and physical assets (e.g., education and infrastructure) may not be enough to attract substantial amounts of internationally mobile physical and knowledge assets.

Crowding and increased fluidity would generally lead to reduced levels of trade dependence according to an H-O model, but over the last several decades there has been a great expansion of trade relative to GDP for all the OECD countries, including Sweden. The most obvious explanation is that decreased costs of transportation (especially air travel), technological revolution in the transmission of information, and successive rounds of trade liberalization are bringing Sweden closer to other countries, which opens Swedish markets to new competitors as well as creating new markets for products made in Sweden.[4]

4. The 1950s and the beginning of the 1960s were characterized by relatively high levels of tariff protection. The creation of the European Free Trade Association (EFTA) lowered tariffs, as

The Ricardian, Chamberlainian, and H-O models all allow a high-wage, high-growth, egalitarian equilibrium without government intervention in international commerce, even though there is increasing competition from low-wage Asian, South American, and Southern European suppliers. The Ricardian model points toward technological innovations in process and product as a means of assuring high wages. The Chamberlainian model points to product differentiation and investment in brand name capital. The H-O model relies on capital investment and choice of product mix. According to the H-O theory, high-wage countries have abundant capital, concentrate production on the most capital intensive products, and absorb unskilled labor into nontradables. But the viability of an H-O high-wage solution can be put in jeopardy by the effects discussed above, which may jointly be dictating a much higher return to skill than most European labor markets currently allow. This we will call the *discordant labor markets hypothesis:* the Swedish system of labor remuneration, which greatly compresses the distribution of wages, is becoming increasingly inconsistent with the international marketplace and therefore is increasingly costly to maintain.

The crowding hypothesis, the capital starving and labor-absorbing hypotheses, and the discordant labor markets hypothesis are all extensively discussed in this chapter. Some evidence is given regarding the inferior commodity hypothesis in section 10.2.5, where we show that Sweden's comparative advantage has generally been in low-growth sectors.

Both two-factor and three-factor models of H-O crowding are presented in section 10.1. This sets the stage for an examination in section 10.2 of a large amount of diverse data on the behavior of the Swedish economy in relation to other competitor countries. We present no formal econometric estimation or test of an H-O model because to do so would require more of a commitment to a specific model than we are prepared to make. It is better, we think, to be open to substantial amendments of the original model and to examine the data in ways that will stimulate a search for useful amendments. We thus view the examination of the data more as a puzzle-solving exercise than as an econometric estimation. The H-O model defines the rules by which the empirical

---

did the free trade agreement between the EFTA and the EC, in the beginning of the 1970s. The further tariff cuts of the Kennedy round drastically lowered the trade barriers. Needless to say, these tariff cuts were of importance in stimulating trade, in particular for a small trade-dependent country like Sweden.

While tariffs were being lowered, innovations in transportation and communication have greatly reduced the cost of international commerce. Since 1930, ocean transport cost have decreased by 55 percent, the cost of air travel by 80 percent, and the costs of an overseas telephone call by approximately 98 percent. However, some empirical estimates of gravity models (e.g., Leamer 1993) do not suggest that the effect of distance on trade patterns has diminished substantially. The greatly increased trade relative to GDP that most countries have experienced can be largely explained by increased dispersion geographically of GDP. Clearly, the least amount of international commerce would take place if all GDP originated in a single country. According to the gravity model, the most amount of trade would occur if world GDP were uniformly distributed across countries.

puzzle can be put together. We think that the parts fit together rather well. In particular, in section 10.2, we present substantial evidence in support of the H-O crowding hypothesis. This evidence takes the form of data on factor supplies of a variety of countries and also information on the competitiveness of the Swedish economy in the international marketplace.

One thing that comes across very clearly in this examination of the data is the long-standing and continuing comparative advantage in forest products. A forest product sector is explicitly introduced in section 10.3, where the starving hypothesis is first discussed.

While experiencing crowding and starving, Sweden is attempting to maintain a large public sector and a very low level of income inequality. The role of a public sector and institutional wage setting in maintaining high wages for unskilled workers is discussed in section 10.4. Our calculations suggest that employment in the public sector has helped maintain Swedish wage rates by allowing a relatively capital intensive mix of traded products. Our discussion of institutional wage setting is strictly theoretical. We argue that the economic liberalizations sweeping the globe have left the world's labor markets saturated with human beings willing to do mundane tasks for extremely low wages. It is not surprising that these international markets are dictating higher compensation for skills, especially in labor-abundant countries.[5] If Sweden does not have adequate investments in human and physical capital, Sweden will end up producing an increasingly labor intensive mix of tradables, and Swedish wages will be set in Frankfurt, or in Rome, or in Beijing, not in Stockholm. Labor market institutions that are designed to resist this trend will prove very costly.

The Heckscher-Ohlin model suggests only one remedy for these problems: Sweden needs much higher rates of physical and human capital formation. With more capital will come naturally higher wages for low-skilled workers. This of course will be helpful, but technological change and globalization together are dictating a much higher degree of income inequality, regardless of the capital abundance of the country. Countries that seek both efficiency and income equality may need to find creative new ways to reward and thereby encourage effort and investment, without at the same time creating unacceptable inequality.

10.1   A Heckscher-Ohlin Theoretical Economic History of Modern Sweden

According to the H-O model of international comparative advantage, the economic health of a country is determined by its supplies of internationally immobile factors of production, including natural resources, workers, knowledge capital, and physical capital. The greatest gains from international trade

---

5. It should be expected that the real return to physical capital will rise as well, although the current worldwide slowdown has so lowered the demand for capital that the real interest rates on financial capital are now quite low.

accrue to countries that have relative factor supplies that are very different from the rest of the world. These unusual countries enjoy very favorable terms of trade, exporting products that are dear and importing products that are cheap.

The H-O model suggests that changes in the economic health of a country, both absolutely and in comparison with other countries, come from (1) rapid or slow factor accumulation (e.g., a relatively high investment rate); (2) technological change, which affects some sectors and some factors more than others (e.g., the computer revolution); (3) shifts in demand (e.g., a building boom affecting the market for lumber); (4) altered mobility of factors (e.g., increased labor migration associated with EU membership or increased physical and knowledge capital mobility brought about partly by the increased importance of multinational corporations); and (5) changes in internal institutions (e.g., an increase in the minimum wage) that affect international competitiveness. In this chapter, we focus on the first and last items on this list: capital accumulation and labor market institutions, using them to interpret Sweden's modern economic history beginning after World War II.

It would not be surprising to find Sweden facing increasingly tough competition in the markets for its manufactured products. World War II left Japan and much of Europe with badly damaged capital stocks but relatively undamaged human capital. Countries like the United States and Sweden that emerged from the war relatively intact enjoyed the enormous economic benefits of being able to produce capital intensive products with virtually no competitors. Although trade immediately after the war was limited, European reconstruction, supported by the Marshall plan and foreign investments, was surprisingly rapid, and only a few years after the war exports of most goods were back to their prewar levels. Sweden's geographic proximity to this region of high growth was an important source of its economic success.

This initial Swedish advantage was rapidly eliminated by the high rates of capital accumulation in Europe and later in Japan. As the rate of human and physical capital accumulation in Sweden continues to lag behind the other European countries, Sweden may find its gains from trade further eroded.

10.1.1   A Two-Factor Heckscher-Ohlin Model

- The first response by a very capital abundant country to rapid capital accumulation in labor abundant regions of the world is an upgrading of the product mix toward more capital intensive products. With this product upgrading comes increased imports of labor intensive manufactures and improved terms of trade.

- When the opportunities for product upgrading are exhausted, a previously uniquely capital abundant country finds itself in direct competition with foreign suppliers. This competition causes a deterioration in the terms of trade.

A two-factor H-O model with capital and labor as inputs is presented in this section. This model is a good starting point, but it has limitations. First, the

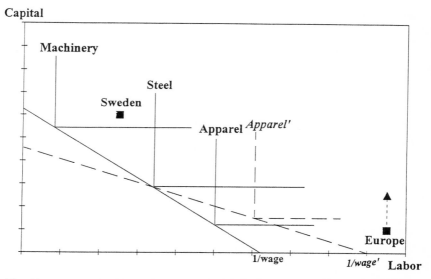

Fig. 10.1   **Unit-value isoquants and isocosts: Hypothetical initial postwar period**

model fails to distinguish human from physical capital, which is important because the war presumably had a relatively great effect on physical capital. The distinction is also very important for recent history because the international marketplace may be dictating a higher return to human capital compared with raw labor. A second deficiency of this two-factor model is that it makes no reference to natural resources. Sweden enjoys a long-standing comparative advantage in forest products, and no model of Swedish international interactions can be considered adequate without explicit consideration of the forest product sector.

A hypothetical postwar equilibrium of an H-O model is illustrated in a Lerner-Pearce diagram, figure 10.1, on which is drawn the initial unit-cost line and the initial unit-value isoquants for the three sectors ordered by increasing capital intensity: apparel, steel, and machinery. These unit-value isoquants are all tangent to the same unit-cost line indicating that the zero profit condition is satisfied for all three products even though the capital abundant countries have factor endowments that are more suited to the capital intensive products.

The capital scarce countries initially concentrate production on the labor intensive product, apparel, which is shipped to Sweden in exchange for steel and machinery. The initial levels of shipments are not enough to displace production in Sweden, but over time, as capital accumulates in the capital scarce countries, Sweden surrenders the apparel sector and concentrates its product mix on steel and machinery. Except for adjustment costs, this is an entirely beneficial transition as the wage rate and the return to capital are unchanged and the price of apparel falls, making both labor and capital in Sweden better

Capital

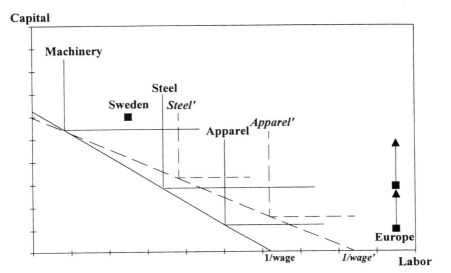

Fig. 10.2   Unit-value isoquants and isocosts: With large European capital increases

off. This fall in the price of apparel is evidenced by an improved terms of trade, apparel being the imported good.

Further capital accumulation in the capital scarce countries in Europe and Asia induces changes that are not so pleasant for Sweden. As capital accumulates in the emerging capital scarce countries, they shift away from apparel production in favor of steel, a shift that will be accompanied by a decline in the price of steel, illustrated in figure 10.2 by the shifting of the unit-value isoquant away from the origin. This price decline lowers the wage rate in Sweden, but it raises the return to capital. Overall, the GDP declines in terms of purchasing power of machinery or apparel, but it increases in terms of steel. If Sweden is so capital abundant that production is heavily concentrated on machinery, then steel will be an import item, and the price decline would be evidenced by an improving terms of trade. Otherwise, the terms of trade declines. This process can go full circle if increases in the supply of machinery in the reemerging nations lower the machinery price and bring all relative prices back to their initial level. Then the comparative advantage that came from having an undamaged capital stock would be completely eliminated.

In summary, then, a simple H-O model suggests that the postwar period can be characterized by four phases: *declining isolation:* increasing imports and less production of the labor intensive goods, no change in product prices or factor prices; *initial distinctiveness:* complete displacement of the labor intensive production, decline in the price of labor intensive products but no change in factor earnings, improved terms of trade, increased real per capita GDP;

eroding distinctiveness: capital intensive product mix, relative decline in the prices of moderately capital intensive goods, decline in the wage rate and increase in the return to capital, terms of trade deterioration for moderately capital abundant countries and fall in real per capita GDP, further terms of trade improvements for the most capital abundant countries and corresponding increase in real per capita GDP; and *head-to-head competition:* capital intensive product mix, relative decline of the prices of the most capital intensive goods, increasing wage rate, terms of trade and real GDP changing in either direction.

This economic drama has been written without parts for Eastern Europe, Latin America, and China. The liberalizations that have swept over the globe in the last several years have enormously increased the unskilled labor that is available for economic interaction with Swedish workers. An optimistic scenario would take Sweden back to the period of initial distinctiveness as a result of export opportunities in these emerging regions, particularly Eastern and Southern Europe.

10.1.2 A Three-Factor Heckscher-Ohlin Model

- The internal labor market premium for human skills is dictated by competition in the international product markets.
- Global capital accumulation can either increase or decrease the skill premium depending especially on where the accumulation takes place.

A three-factor H-O model offers improved understanding of postwar European economic history and is also richer in implications with regard to the relative compensation of skilled and unskilled labor. The three-factor model illustrated in figure 10.3 has one commodity that uses human capital as an input (chemicals), three commodities that use only capital and labor (apparel, textiles, and machinery), and one commodity that uses only labor (handicrafts). The initial equilibrium that is depicted here occurs in what is termed above the period of initial distinctiveness, namely, after the price of apparel has fallen because of increases in global supply. With this relatively low price of apparel, Sweden finds itself in the cone suited to the production of textiles, chemicals, and machinery. Germany and Japan are in the moderate-wage cone, producing apparel, textiles, and chemicals. Asia (other than Japan) is very poorly endowed in capital and finds itself in the low-wage cone, producing mostly apparel and handicrafts. Sweden has a strong comparative advantage in machinery but imports chemicals from Germany, apparel and textiles from Japan, and apparel from Asia (and Southern Europe).

The arrows emanating from the points with the country labels depict hypothetical changes in factor supplies. Although enjoying an initial advantage from the uniqueness of its endowment mix, Sweden finds itself over time crowded on the one side by Japan and on the other by Germany. In the meantime, capital accumulation takes Asia into the moderate-wage cone. These changes in factor supplies of Swedish competitors change the worldwide pro-

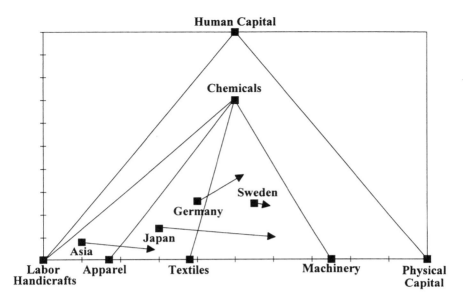

Fig. 10.3   Cones of diversification: Physical capital, human capital, and labor

duction levels of the five products, which in turn induces compensating price adjustments. These price adjustments alter the Swedish terms of trade and also force changes in the Swedish factor prices including the returns to skill. The terms of trade effect depends on which goods are Swedish export goods and which are import goods. For this discussion, we assume that Sweden is exporting only machinery and importing all the other products, although price reductions in machinery can force Sweden to export either chemicals or textiles, even if there is no change in Swedish production levels.

The effects of product price reductions on Swedish factor prices are summarized in table 10.1.[6] The message from this table is that, although reductions in

6. The effects of a reduction in the textiles price on the factor earnings in Sweden can be computed in the following way (more fully explained in Leamer [1987b]). Extend the line connecting the chemicals point and the machinery point. If a factor input (say labor) is on the same side of this line as the textile point, then the factor and the commodities are "friends" (Ethier's [1984] terminology): a reduction in the price of textiles will lower the return to the factor. The opposite is true for factors with vertices on the other side of the line. As the figure is drawn, in the Swedish cone, textiles are a friend of labor but an enemy of both human and physical capital. Thus, a reduction in the price of textiles causes a fall in the wage of raw labor and an increase in the return to both physical and human capital. For the Asian cone, the results are quite different: textiles is an "enemy" commodity for labor and human capital but a friend of physical capital. If the technological inputs are changed, some of these conclusions can be substantially altered. For example, if the machinery point is swung to the left, selecting a capital/labor ratio less than chemicals, then human capital and textiles become friends for the capital abundant countries.

Incidentally, a similar phenomenon applies as a country accumulates enough capital to move between the cones: the rate of return to human capital is higher in the Swedish cone than in the Asian cone. This is the case even though Sweden has an abundance of human capital and exports

Table 10.1   Effects of Price Reductions on Swedish Terms of Trade, Real Factor Earnings, and Skill Premium

Reduction in Price of:	Terms of Trade	Raw Labor	Human Capital	Physical Capital	Skill Premia
Machinery	−	+	+	−	?
Chemicals	+	0	−	0	−
Textiles	+	−	+	+	+
Apparel	+	+	+	+	

the price of textiles and the price of chemicals may both improve the Swedish terms of trade, the reduction in the price of textiles forces Sweden to adopt a higher return to skill in the sense that the wage of raw labor must fall and the return to human capital must rise. Also, a reduction in the price of machinery causes a deterioration in the Swedish terms of trade and may also increase the skill premium.

The effects of factor accumulation on the output levels in each of the three cones of diversification are indicated in table 10.2. From this table, we can find the kinds of factor accumulation that lead to increased supplies of each of the products. The most difficult effects for Sweden to deal with come from increases in the worldwide supply of machinery, which is the result of physical capital accumulation in the Swedish cone, precisely, the final parts of the paths taken hypothetically by Germany and Japan. This final factor accumulation reduces the supply of textiles, but this is likely to be more than offset by the concomitant capital accumulation in Asia, a change that, although beneficial from a terms of trade standpoint, increases the skill premium and puts pressure on the Swedish commitment to wage compression.

The expansion of textile production in the tail of the Asia path is a repeat of early Japanese and German history, which according to the figure both begin after the war in the "Japanese cone" selecting the output mix of apparel, textiles, and chemicals. Germany, which is relatively well endowed in human capital, has a relatively great supply of chemicals and moves completely out of the production of textiles at relatively low levels of capital per worker.

10.1.3   Summary

It is now time to test these ideas with actual data. The Heckscher-Ohlin theory suggests a careful examination of (a) relative rates of factor accumulation in Sweden and in other comparison countries, (b) changes in the Swedish terms of trade, (c) changes in Swedish trade dependence ratios, and (d) skill premia in the global marketplace. We are looking particularly for evidence of

the human capital intensive product (chemicals) to Asia. The reason for this result is that the movement from the Asian cone to the Swedish cone comes about from the accumulation of physical capital, not human capital. The complementarity between human skills and physical capital means that the physical capital abundant countries have a higher return to skill. For a discussion of the skill premium for a number of countries, see Davis (1992).

Table 10.2   **Effects of Factor Accumulation on Output Levels in Figure 10.3**

	Handicrafts	Apparel	Textiles	Machinery	Chemicals
Sweden cone:					
Capital			−	+	
Human capital			−	−	+
Labor			+	−	
Japan cone:					
Capital		−	+		
Human capital		+	−		+
Labor		+	−		
Asia cone:					
Capital	−	+			
Human capital	+	−			+
Labor	+				

the *Heckscher-Ohlin crowding hypothesis.* This is the hypothesis that Sweden is being squeezed from three directions. In one direction are the low-wage labor-abundant countries offering to sell labor intensive goods such as apparel at low prices. In another direction are countries like Japan that are accumulating physical capital rapidly and offering to sell capital intensive products such as machinery at low prices. In the third direction are human capital abundant countries like Germany that dominate the skill intensive sectors such as chemicals.

10.2   Evidence

10.2.1   Productivity and Capital Accumulation

Symptom: Swedish Labor Productivity

- Swedish labor productivity, properly measured, is slipping badly.

As discussed in the introduction to this book, Swedish real output per worker has not been growing as rapidly as in many other European countries but has nonetheless been among the highest. However, this fairly optimistic assessment does not hold up if the data are adjusted for variations of the exchange rate from its purchasing power parity (PPP) value.[7]

Symptom: Declining Swedish Shares of OECD Value Added

- The Swedish share of OECD value added in manufacturing is lagging behind.

The Swedish share of OECD manufacturing valued added declined substantially from 1.53 percent to 0.94 percent over the period 1975–83, at which

---

7. OECD PPP estimates indicate that the Swedish krona was overvalued by as much as 30 percent in the late 1960s.

point a modest recovery set in, lifting the share to 1.15 percent in 1990.[8] Japan had a very expanded market share. But the situation looks even worse if the data include only European countries. Here Sweden drops from a 3.16 percent share to a 2.60 percent share. This puts Sweden with Norway and Italy as the only countries to lose market share over the period.

Disease: Inadequate Physical Capital Accumulation

- Sweden is not keeping pace in the accumulation of physical capital.
- The slow rate of capital accumulation comes from a low ratio of investment to GDP, high prices of investment goods, and low labor productivity.

One reason why Swedish labor productivity is growing slowly may be inadequate capital accumulation. Capital accumulation per worker can be expressed as the product of the investment to GDP ratio, times the relative price of GDP to investment goods, times labor productivity:

INV/WORKER = (INV/GDP)(PGDP/PGDI)[(GDP/PGDP)/WORKER].

All three of these factors contribute negatively to the capital accumulation per worker in Sweden. We have already pointed out that Swedish labor productivity growth has been slow. In addition, the Swedish investment share of GDP is low, and the price of investment goods relatively to GDP is high.[9]

The investment share of GDP is significantly lower than in comparison countries, with the exception of the United Kingdom. When in the 1980s the Swedish investment share was around 18 percent, Germany had about a 22 percent share. The rate had been as high as 24 percent in the early 1960s, and the decline in the investment share in the 1980s is likely to have a continuing negative effect on Swedish capital per worker well into the twentieth century.

In addition to this low investment ratio, Sweden suffers from a high price of investment goods relative to GDP compared with other countries. This price ratio is found by dividing the PPP adjustment factor for investment by the PPP adjustment factor for GDP. Dividing the nominal investment ratio by this price ratio produces the real investment shares depicted in figure 10.4. The fall in this investment ratio since the 1960s is dramatic and seems certain to have contributed to the performance of the Swedish economy in the 1980s and 1990s.

The decline in the Swedish investment rate after 1968 that was evident in

8. It should be mentioned that the 1975 base year exaggerates the fall in Sweden's relative position since, that year, value added in Sweden was large compared to that in the OECD area. Most base years would yield a fall in Sweden's position, but few as large as 1975 does.

9. The three factors should not be looked on as independent determinants. For instance, while the above text implies that labor productivity affects capital formation, Hjalmarsson and Walfridsson (1992) provide evidence that investment in Swedish manufacturing is a major determinant of labor productivity. Still, it is convenient and useful for descriptive purposes to divide capital accumulation into these three factors.

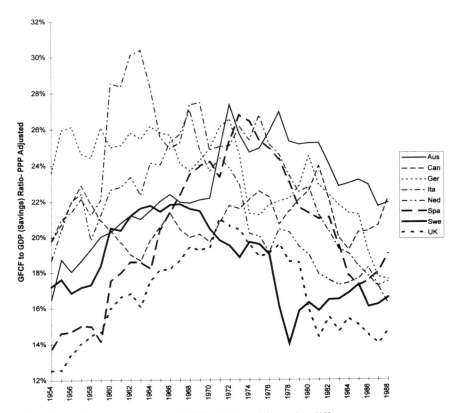

Fig. 10.4   Investment share of GDP: Adjusted for price differences

figure 10.4 translates into a very sluggish series on capital per worker (see Leamer and Lundborg 1995). Until 1974, Sweden had virtually the highest ratio of capital per worker. But the complete lack of growth in capital per worker from 1977 to 1985 left the Swedish advantage in capital completely eroded, especially in comparison with Spain, Canada, and Austria.

Human Capital Accumulation

- For a long time, Sweden did not keep the pace in the accumulation of human capital.

- The share of GDP going to education is high but not growing like competitors.

- A large fraction of educational expenditures pays for primary and preprimary education. Tertiary enrollment rates were very low for many years.

Productivity is influenced by human capital accumulation as well as physical capital accumulation. Simple measures based on expenditures on education make it appear that Sweden has been and remains one of the most human capital abundant countries, although European competitors are hot on the Swedish heels. But a different picture emerges if one adjusts for the fact that a large share of Swedish expenditure pays for preprimary and primary education and relatively little is spent on tertiary education, an allocation that is a reflection of the egalitarian ambitions of the Swedish welfare state. Those ambitions seem increasingly in conflict with global trends in international trade and in technology, which are concentrating productivity gains from educational investments on tertiary expenditures.

Swedish educational expenditures as a share of GDP are very high in international comparisons (see Leamer and Lundborg 1995, graph 3.4). Although Swedish expenditures on education seem lavish, a relatively small share goes to tertiary schooling, and a particularly large share goes to preprimary education. This seems especially troubling as changes in technology and in the international marketplace may be dictating higher returns to skill and thus concentrating the returns to schooling at higher levels.[10]

The neglect of higher education may show up most clearly in the enrollment rates in tertiary education in figure 10.5. The jump in the middle of this graph comes from a change in the definition of tertiary education to include nonuniversity higher education and adult nighttime schooling. In your mind, you should be linking these series either by adjusting upward the pre-1977 data or adjusting downward the post-1976 data. In either case, Sweden is not keeping pace with the increase in investment in higher education in competitor countries. The difference is whether Sweden is at the very bottom or only near the bottom.[11]

There are several possible reasons for the Swedish lag in tertiary education. First, the overall number of students admitted to higher education was regulated starting in 1979. This supply constraint clearly affected the number of students during the 1980s. The university premium is slightly lower in Sweden compared to other countries. As in most other countries, the premium fell from the 1960s but increased again in the latter half of the 1980s. This fall, to some extent caused by an increasing supply of university educated relative to high school graduates up to the mid-1980s, partly explains the fall in demand for higher education (see Edin and Holmlund 1993). Furthermore, during decades of high unemployment rates in Europe, Sweden was one of the few countries

10. Wolff and Gittleman (1993) have shown that, among the industrial market economies and upper-middle-income countries, the university enrollment rate is the only variable yielding a significant effect on growth of per capita income. However, this conclusion applies only to the earlier part of the postwar period, and none of their educational variables are significant in the latter part of the period. Primary and secondary school enrollment exert positive growth effects in lower-middle-income and low-income countries.

11. International human capital comparisons are notoriously difficult to make. Definitions and periods of measurement differ across countries. Moreover, the structure of education and differences in quality are aspects of human capital that are difficult to consider.

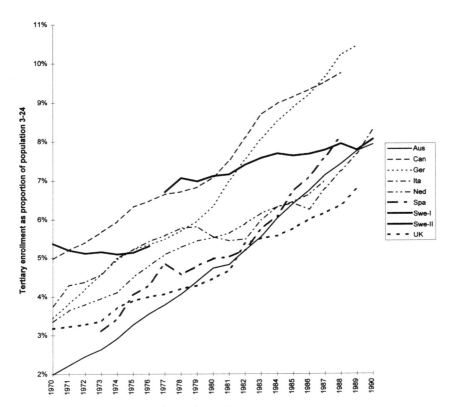

Fig. 10.5   Enrollment rates in tertiary education

enjoying full employment, thus raising the opportunity cost of higher education.

That higher unemployment among the young may stimulate university education is also consistent with the most recent enrollment data. While the absolute number of enrolled remained around 150,000 for the period 1977–88, it has increased markedly ever since and in the fall of 1992 reached 209,300 (see Statistics Sweden, Statistiska Meddelanden 1992). In particular, enrollment in the universities of technology has increased (from 19,900 in 1977 to 47,100 in 1992), and a large part of this increase took place during the last five years.

Factor Supplies in 1965 and 1988

- In 1965, Sweden had a unique number of people in professional positions and physical capital. The special Swedish position was substantially eroded by 1988.

Changes in human capital and real capital formation may partly be reflected in a data set compiled by Song (1993) and Leamer (1984) covering the number

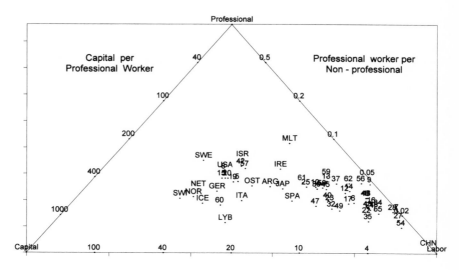

Fig. 10.6   1965 factor supplies

of professionals, nonprofessionals, and real capital. Figures 10.6 and 10.7 display the relative supplies of physical capital, skilled labor (professional and technical), and unskilled labor in the years 1965 and 1988, respectively. With a combination of physical capital and a large number of professionals, Sweden stands away from the pack of other countries in 1965. By 1988, Sweden is closely and hotly pursued by a large number of competitors. The United States, which was on the edge of the pack in 1965, is surrounded by competitors in 1988. Japan, in contrast, was way back in the pack in 1965 but is rushing toward the physical capital vertex as a result of its high investment rate.

Growth and Capital Accumulation

- Growth rates of labor productivity are closely linked with growth rates of physical and human capital.

Capital accumulation and growth have been linked in a large number of theoretical and empirical papers, including the early theoretical contribution of Solow (1956, 1957) and the more recent empirical work of Barro (1991) and Mankiw, Romer, and Weil (1992). The regressions reported in table 10.3 compare the growth rates of real GDP per worker for a small sample of countries over three six-year intervals with (*a*) growth rates of real physical capital per worker, (*b*) growth rates of real human capital per capita, (*c*) growth rates of real human capital per worker, and (*d*) growth rates of total capital per worker. These simple regressions do indicate a link between growth in per capita GDP and physical capital accumulation, but the association of growth with human capital accumulation is hidden if it is there at all. The association

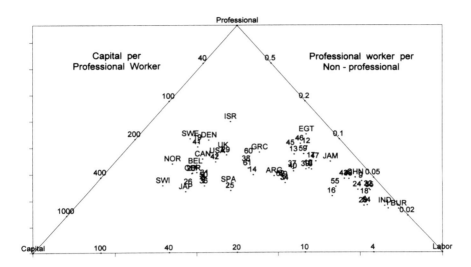

Fig. 10.7   1988 factor supplies

Table 10.3   **Regressions of Growth in GDP per Worker on Growth in Capital per Worker**

Intercept	Physical Capital (1)	Human Capital (2)	Human Capital (3)	Total Capital (4)	R^2
.0514 (3.68)	.547 (7.01)				.69
.091 (2.68)		.13 (.89)			.04
.0663 (2.56)			.305 (2.54)		.23
.0226 (1.02)				.629 (5.07)	.54

Note: *t*-values are given in parentheses. Definitions of variables: (1) physical capital per nongovernment worker; (2) human capital per capita; (3) human capital per worker; and (4) human + physical capital per worker. Database: Three six-year time periods (1970–76, 1976–82, 1982–88) and eight countries (Canada, Italy, Germany, the Netherlands, Austria, Spain, Switzerland, the United Kingdom). Exchange rate treatment: GDP: local deflators, 1985 PPP-adjusted exchange rate; human capital: locally accumulated, local deflators, separate current and capital stocks, 1985 PPP-adjusted exchange rate; physical capital: locally accumulated, local deflators, 1985 PPP-adjusted exchange rate.

seems somewhat better if the measure of abundance is human capital per worker, not per capita, but the increase in the R^2 from .04 to .227 may seem big numerically but is hardly evident in the scatter. (The per capita figure is theoretically preferred if educational expenditures are spread evenly across the population. The per worker figure is theoretically preferred if the educational expenditures are concentrated on the workforce.)[12] Although the R^2 of the last regression with total capital per worker is inferior to the first with physical capital per worker, the last regression seems preferred because the association is broadly supported by the data set whereas the first association appears to be sensitive to the exclusion of one of several observations.[13]

From these simple regressions, one should not jump to firm conclusions about the relation between capital accumulation and growth. There is obviously some causal force in the opposite direction from growth to capital accumulation; the number of observations is limited; the measurements of capital are imperfect. But it is hard to escape the conclusion that a major reason for poor Swedish growth rates is the problems of factor accumulation.

10.2.2   Net Exports per Worker: Ten Trade Aggregates

- Sweden has a very significant comparative advantage in forest products. Sweden trades forest products and machinery for labor intensive manufactures and petroleum.

- The Swedish trade pattern at the level of ten aggegrates has been very stable and does not offer dramatic evidence of problems with the Swedish economy. There has been an increase in the net exports of "capital intensive" manufactures, an aggregate that includes textiles and iron and steel. This represents a half step backward on the ladder of development.

If the H-O model is accurate, the factor accumulation patterns ought to be evident in trade patterns, to which we now turn. We use a list of ten aggregates formed from two-digit SITC commodity groups as in Leamer (1987a) to characterize the international patterns of net exports (exports minus imports). These commodity aggregates were formed from observed correlations across countries of the net export levels. For example, countries that tend to export a large amount of cork and wood also export pulp and paper. These accordingly are combined into a forest products aggregate.

The ten aggregates include two natural resource groups (petroleum products [PETRO] and raw materials [MAT]), four crops (forest products [FOR], tropical agricultural products [TROP], animal products [ANL], and cereals [CER]), and four manufacturers (labor intensive [LAB], capital intensive [CAP], machinery [MACH], and chemicals [CHEM]). In terms of input intensities, these four manufactured aggregates are ordered by physical capital intensities, but chemicals is generally much more intensive in human capital than is machin-

---

12. Keep in mind that the depreciation rate for human capital has been set to 8 percent while the depreciation rate for physical capital is set to 15 percent. This makes the human capital stock much larger and much more sluggish.

13. The coefficient on the capital stock in the regressions reported in table 10.3 can be interpreted as the capital share, and the intercept is the growth in total factor productivity over the six-year period. The two successful regressions have this growth rate of TFP at about 1 percent per year.

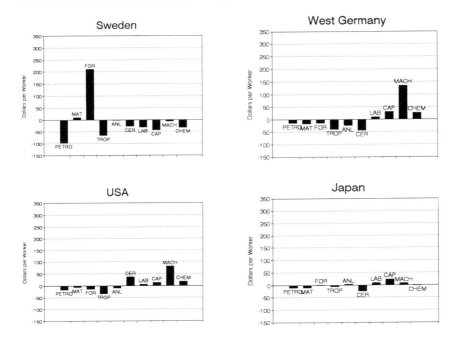

Fig. 10.8   Net exports per worker: 1958

ery. These four manufactured products form a ladder of development that many countries seem to follow, beginning with exports of apparel (LAB), then moving on to textiles and iron and steel (CAP), and finally to machinery (MACH) and chemicals (CHEM).

Net exports per worker of these ten aggregates in 1958, 1965, 1974, and 1988 for Sweden, Germany, the United States, and Japan are illustrated in figures 10.8–10.11.[14] The scales are the same in 1958 and 1965, but they are larger in 1974 and larger still in 1988. These data conform rather well with the three-factor H-O history described in section 9.1. In 1958, the United States is not particularly trade dependent and is exporting the full range of manufactured products, especially machinery. Germany has already escaped the ravages of the war, exporting the full range of manufactured products, and importing all the crops and raw materials. Japan is hardly participating in international trade, presumably because of the incompleteness of recovery, but has a comparative advantage in manufactures concentrated lower on the development ladder (LAB and CAP).

The Swedish trade pattern in 1958 is particularly interesting since net exports are completely concentrated on forest products. About U.S.$200 per worker of forest products net exports paid for a mixed bag of imports including

14. Data assembled by Song (1993) and in Leamer (1987a).

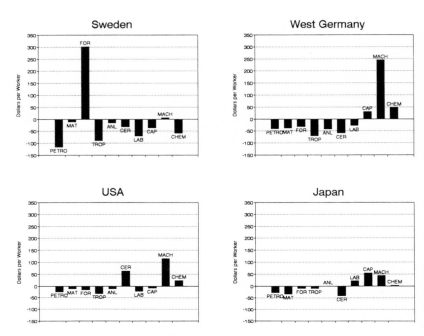

Fig. 10.9   Net exports per worker: 1965

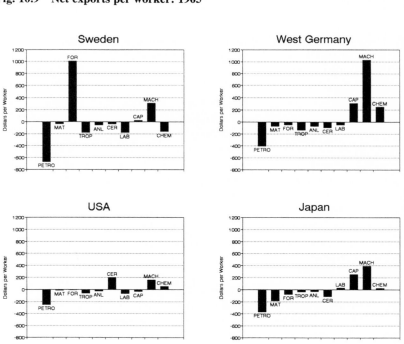

Fig. 10.10   Net exports per worker: 1974

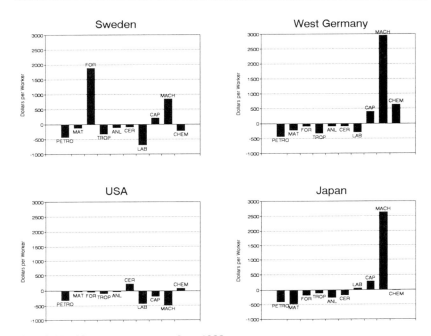

Fig. 10.11   Net exports per worker, 1988

especially petroleum, tropical agricultural products, labor intensive manufactures, and chemicals. This Swedish trade pattern is in conflict with the three-factor H-O theory, which led us to expect at least a temporary comparative advantage in capital intensive manufactures. The defect of that theory is that it excludes natural resources as an input. What seemed to be happening in Sweden during this period is that the large export earnings from forest products were supporting the imports of everything else, including the full range of manufactures. Incidentally, the United States has an analogous comparative advantage in cereals. Among the manufactures, Sweden was least dependent on machinery, which emerges as an export item in the next figure. In the next figures, you can see this machinery sector emerge.

From 1958 to 1965, there was a substantial increase in the amount of trade. Both Germany and the United States "climbed the ladder of development" in the sense that they became net importers of labor intensive manufactures. The United States became a net importer of capital intensive manufactures as well. By 1965, Japan is emerging as a major global competitor in manufactures, concentrating low on the ladder of development by exporting labor intensive manufactures but not chemicals. For Sweden, forest products exports per worker increased from U.S.$200 to U.S.$300, and the machinery sector is just beginning to emerge by 1965 with positive net exports. By 1974, the emergence of the machinery sector in Swedish net exports is very pronounced. The big increase in the price of petroleum is evident in all four countries with

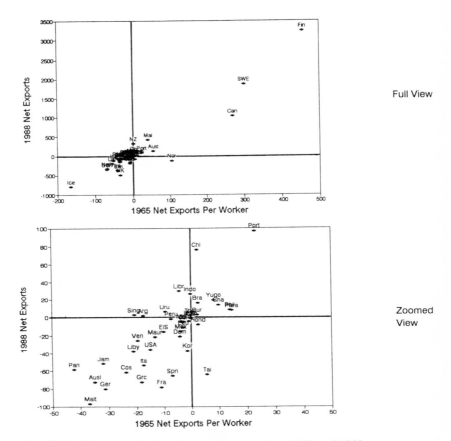

Full View

Zoomed View

Fig. 10.12   Forest products net exports per worker, 1965 and 1988

greatly increased petroleum imports. In Sweden, this petroleum bill was paid with greatly increased exports of forest products and also machinery. Otherwise, the 1974 picture is very similar to the 1965 picture, although you can see Japan in 1974 starting to give up on labor intensive manufactures.

From 1974 to 1988, both German and Japanese exports of machinery increased enormously, apparently pushing Sweden a half step backward into great reliance on CAP (principally iron and steel) net exports. The United States is basically knocked on the mat by this competition and ends up looking like an agrarian society with also enough human capital to support a very modestly successful chemicals sector. Unless the trade deficit apparent in this graph is offset by receipts for services, the 1988 U.S. pattern seems unsustainable, and we should be expecting a correction, probably in the machinery category.

The U.S. pattern in 1965 is rather similar to the Swedish pattern in 1988. Both have one crop that is a substantial source of export receipts. For Sweden,

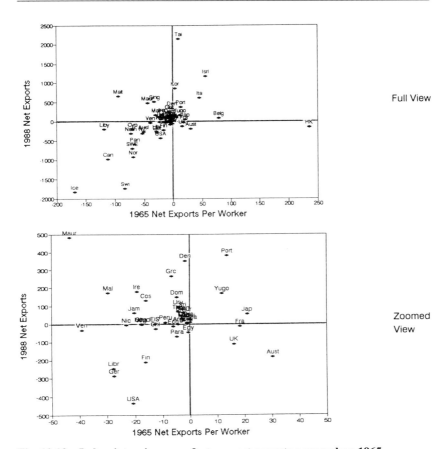

Fig. 10.13   Labor intensive manufactures net exports per worker, 1965 and 1988

it is forest products; for the United States, it is cereals. Both countries export a capital intensive mix of manufactures in addition to the crop. The United States goes through a dramatic change, switching from being a net exporter to being a net importer of machinery.

Figures 10.12–10.16 report these net export data for a large number of countries, comparing 1965 with 1988 with both an overall view and a zoomed view of the countries with smaller trade dependence levels. Take a look first at forest products, figure 10.12. If there were no change in comparative advantage from 1965 to 1988, these data would all lie on a straight line. If you flip through these figures, you will discover that forest products have a very permanent comparative advantage in the sense that the points are most close to forming a straight line. The big exporters of forest products in both years were Finland, Sweden, and Canada. Iceland was a big importer. The smaller traders generally

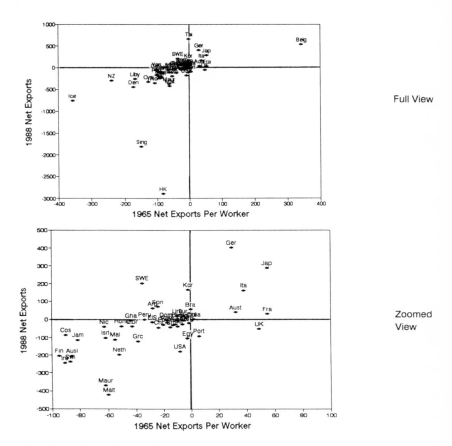

Fig. 10.14   Capital intensive manufactures net exports per worker, 1965 and 1988

did not change the sign of their net exports. Norway experienced the most substantial change, switching from being a large net exporter to a large net importer.

Contrasting clearly with the apparent permanence of the pattern of forest products trade, the data on the trade in labor intensive manufactures in figure 10.13 do reveal major changes in the international division of labor, with many countries switching from importing to exporting and four switching the other way. Sweden seems relatively unaffected by this turmoil, sitting in a pack of similar countries that were fairly significant importers in both periods, probably enjoying the favorable price trends caused by increased worldwide supply. This long-standing comparative disadvantage in labor intensive manufactures suggests that Swedish workers are not competing with the Chinese or even the Southern Europeans.

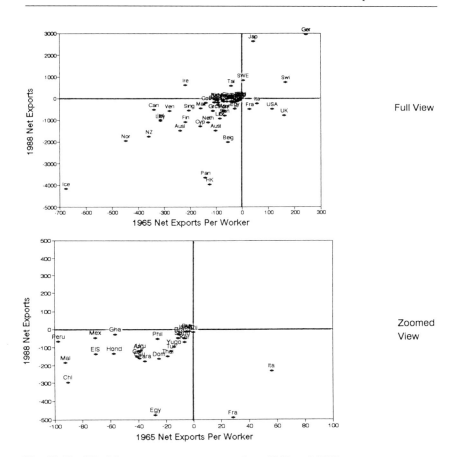

Fig. 10.15   Machinery net exports per worker, 1965 and 1988

The Swedish experience with capital intensive trade illustrated in figure 10.14 does indicate a major change in comparative advantage since Sweden switched from being a significant importer to being a significant exporter. The major commodities in this group are textiles and iron and steel. In this aggregate appear, together with Sweden, traditional competitors like Belgium, Japan, and Germany but also emerging exporters like Taiwan, Korea, Argentina, Spain, and Brazil.

The machinery aggregate depicted in figure 10.15 is characterized by large expansions of exports by Sweden, Japan, and Germany and the emergence of Taiwan and Ireland at a time when France, Italy, the United Kingdom, and the United States are being forced out of the category. In sharp contrast with the two previous figures, here there are only two emerging competitors in the machinery category: Taiwan and Ireland.

Figure 10.16 indicates that Sweden continues to be a major net importer of

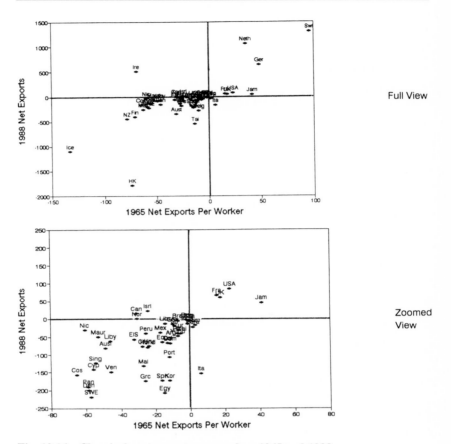

Fig. 10.16   Chemicals net exports per worker, 1965 and 1988

chemicals, which is the most physical/human capital intensive aggregate and exported by the most advanced countries, including Switzerland, Netherlands, Germany, the United States, France, and the United Kingdom. The Swedish experience with chemicals contrasts with the performance of Ireland, Israel, Canada, and Norway, which emerged as net exporters of chemicals. The experience with chemicals of the major forest product exporters is interestingly diverse. Canada emerged as an exporter of chemicals while retaining a comparative advantage in forest products. Norway surrendered its traditional comparative advantage in forest products over this period in favor of chemicals. But Sweden and Finland are stuck with forest products.

In summary, the Swedish trade dependence on exports of capital intensive manufactures and the absence of exports of chemicals suggests that Swedish wage setting is drifting south, not to China or to other low-wage Asian countries since Sweden is not at all dependent on labor intensive manufactures. But, in capital intensive manufactures, Sweden finds itself together with low-wage exporters including Taiwan, Korea, Argentina, Spain, and Brazil.

10.2.3   Manufacturing Trade Dependence Ratios, Four-Digit Detail

- Globalization is very evident in Swedish manufacturing as the trade dependence ratios went from 30 percent on average to 48 percent between 1970 and 1989.

- Gains in initial comparative advantage came in some resource intensive sectors (pulp and paper) and a moderately capital intensive sector (iron and steel).

- Comparative advantage emerged in some human capital intensive sectors (drugs and medicine, professional and scientific equipment, chemicals not elsewhere classified [nec]). A very capital intensive sector (petroleum refineries) almost emerged with a positive trade balance.

- Increases in initial comparative *disadvantage* come in wearing apparel, footwear, knitting mills, tires, and tubes.

- Comparative *disadvantage* emerged in office and computing equipment.

Table 10.4 reports data at five different points in time on Swedish exports, imports, and net exports of manufactured goods all relative to Swedish apparent consumption. Commodities are subclassified depending on the behavior of these trade ratios. The globalizing sectors have increasing ratios of both exports and imports to consumption. The localizing sectors have reductions in both ratios. The Swedish winners have increases in the ratio of exports to consumption and reductions in the ratio of imports to consumption. The Swedish losers have decreasing export/consumption ratios and increasing import/consumption ratios. Within each of these categories, the data are sorted by the change in the trade balance relative to consumption.

The same data are displayed in table 10.5 but without dividing by the consumption levels. Here, the data are sorted within category by the change in the net export levels. This makes the economically larger sectors stand out, whereas the data scaled by consumption put every sector on an equal footing.

The news here is globalization. In the vast majority of sectors, both the import ratio and the export ratio increased from 1970 to 1989. Among the globalizing sectors, the average ratio of exports to consumption increased over this period from 25 percent to 48 percent, and the average import ratio increased from 34 percent to 54 percent.

Most Improving Swedish Performance in the Globalizing Industries

Sectors that are at the top of both lists have added substantially to Swedish export earnings and have experienced a much larger change in exports relative to consumption compared with imports relative to consumption. These are es-

Table 10.4   **External Performance of Swedish Industry Relative to Swedish Consumption (%)**

ISIC Commodity	Exports/Consumption					Imports/Consumption					(Exports − Imports)/Consumption					1970–89 Change		
	1970	1975	1980	1985	1989	1970	1975	1980	1985	1989	1970	1975	1980	1985	1989	X/C	M/C	(X − M)/C
	Globalizing Sectors (Increased Relative Exports and Relative Imports): Improving Relative Trade Balance																	
3419 Pulp, paper nec	80.2	106.4	115.0	148.3	209.2	51.7	58.5	58.7	61.0	75.6	28.5	47.9	56.3	87.3	133.6	129.0	23.9	105.1
3319 Wood, cork nec	21.4	24.5	36.5	68.8	117.5	12.3	15.8	20.8	22.2	43.2	9.1	8.8	15.6	46.6	74.3	96.2	31.0	65.2
3522 Drugs & medicines	21.1	27.0	45.1	55.0	95.9	43.9	48.3	48.0	49.1	57.1	−22.8	−21.3	−2.9	5.8	38.8	74.8	13.2	61.6
3851 Prof. & scientific	41.4	55.6	86.9	100.6	88.3	78.0	81.1	101.1	101.7	79.3	−36.6	−25.6	−14.1	−1.1	9.0	46.9	1.3	45.6
3529 Chemicals nec	24.9	42.1	48.3	54.5	73.7	51.0	59.5	50.4	55.0	62.3	−26.1	−17.4	−2.1	−.5	11.4	48.7	11.3	37.4
3823 Metal, woodworking	78.5	71.9	87.7	125.7	165.0	72.8	70.0	63.9	91.4	123.5	5.7	1.9	23.8	34.3	41.5	86.6	50.7	35.9
3231 Tanneries	57.6	68.4	100.4	146.7	92.0	67.1	66.4	92.0	93.1	77.9	−9.5	2.0	8.4	53.6	14.1	34.5	10.8	23.6
3513 Synthetic resins	24.9	30.9	40.7	47.5	50.2	62.4	59.2	64.0	69.1	68.4	−37.4	−28.3	−23.3	−21.7	−18.3	25.2	6.1	19.2
3720 Nonferrous metals	21.0	22.8	38.7	43.3	43.3	43.5	43.4	45.7	46.3	52.5	−22.5	−20.5	−7.1	−3.0	−9.2	22.3	9.0	13.3
3829 Machinery nec	44.8	52.5	82.5	83.8	83.1	33.2	41.4	55.7	55.3	58.9	11.7	11.1	26.8	28.5	24.3	38.3	25.7	12.6
3560 Plastics nec	11.9	17.6	21.1	28.1	30.1	30.7	31.1	35.8	38.9	37.6	−18.7	−13.5	−14.7	−10.7	−7.6	18.1	7.0	11.2
3119 Chocolate, sugar conf.	6.6	12.4	16.4	22.7	27.2	20.2	23.1	28.2	29.5	30.5	−13.5	−10.7	−11.9	−6.9	−3.3	20.6	10.3	10.2

Table 10.5   External Performance of Swedish Industry (thousand kronor)

ISIC Commodity	1970 Values				1989 Values				Change in X − M	Annual Rate of Change (%)		
	X	M	C	X − M	X	M	C	X − M		X	M	C
	Globalizing Sectors (Increased Relative Exports and Relative Imports)											
3411 Pulp, paper	5,660	138	2,786	5,522	42,480	2,142	20,743	40,337	34,815	11	15	11
3843 Motor vehicles	3,205	2,277	5,411	928	47,448	34,262	63,444	13,186	12,257	14	15	14
3829 Machinery nec	2,628	1,944	5,860	683	24,191	17,130	29,094	7,061	6,378	12	11	9
3419 Pulp, paper nec	282	182	351	100	5,807	2,098	2,776	3,709	3,609	16	13	11
3522 Drugs & medicines	167	346	788	−179	6,399	3,810	6,672	2,589	2,768	20	13	12
3832 TV, communication	1,354	1,232	2,379	122	18,502	16,385	20,674	2,117	1,996	14	14	12
3823 Metal, woodworking	593	550	756	43	6,804	5,091	4,123	1,712	1,670	13	12	9
3529 Chemicals nec	280	572	1,122	−293	5,639	4,770	7,654	869	1,162	16	11	11
3851 Prof. & scientific	352	662	849	−311	8,096	7,271	9,165	825	1,136	17	13	13
3320 Furniture	190	175	1,299	14	4,043	3,413	6,498	630	615	17	16	9
3319 Wood, cork nec	58	33	271	25	892	328	759	564	539	15	12	6
3813 Structural metal	224	150	1,829	75	2,012	1,654	13,402	359	284	12	13	11
3412 Containers	84	37	835	47	715	392	5,055	323	276	11	13	10
3117 Bakery products	58	49	1,472	9	700	433	7,718	266	257	13	12	9
3812 Metal furniture	47	33	392	14	715	518	2,343	197	183	15	15	10
3231 Tanneries	117	137	204	−19	418	354	454	64	83	7	5	4
3849 Transport nec	27	10	70	17	216	188	472	28	11	11	16	11
3312 Wooden containers	6	8	87	−2	85	85	417	0	2	14	12	9
3833 Elec. appliances	114	132	442	−18	1,850	1,873	2,674	−22	−4	15	14	10

(continued)

Table 10.5   (continued)

ISIC Commodity	1970 Values				1989 Values				Change in X − M	Annual Rate of Change (%)		
	X	M	C	X − M	X	M	C	X − M		X	M	C
	Globalizing Sectors (Increased Relative Exports and Relative Imports)											
3119 Chocolate, sugar conf.	35	105	522	−71	931	1,045	3,424	−113	−43	18	12	10
3134 Soft drinks	2	10	173	−8	49	108	446	−59	−51	16	12	5
3521 Paints, varnishes	57	100	599	−43	950	1,055	3,627	−104	−62	15	13	10
3215 Cordage, rope	3	17	46	−13	19	105	161	−86	−73	9	10	7
3692 Cement, lime	1	10	382	−8	63	147	979	−84	−75	21	14	5
3902 Musical instr.	8	43	67	−36	49	272	247	−223	−188	10	10	7
3903 Sporting, athletic	63	68	110	−6	415	616	523	−201	−196	10	12	9
3219 Textiles nec	96	245	492	−149	920	1,269	1,493	−349	−200	12	9	6
3116 Grain mill	14	56	709	−41	101	373	2,297	−272	−231	10	10	6
3140 Tobacco	16	72	398	−56	125	438	2,198	−313	−257	11	9	9
	Globalizing Sectors (Increased Relative Exports and Relative Imports)											
3620 Glass	108	230	566	−122	1,707	2,135	3,401	−428	−307	15	12	10
3691 Structural clay	42	128	313	−87	169	635	1,106	−467	−380	7	8	7
3560 Plastics nec	124	318	1,036	−194	2,699	3,381	8,983	−681	−487	17	13	12
3610 Pottery, china	75	84	261	−9	442	967	1,519	−525	−516	9	13	10
3212 Made-up textiles	45	129	415	−84	464	1,092	2,311	−628	−544	12	11	9

3822 Agricultural mach.	324	271	892	54	1,700	2,206	2,266	−506	−559	9	11	5
3720 Nonferrous metals	849	1,758	4,045	−909	7,025	8,511	16,218	−1,486	−578	11	8	8
3699 Nonmetal minerals	119	209	2,249	−90	1,192	1,935	11,079	−744	−654	12	12	9
3233 Leather	26	60	176	−34	149	866	975	−717	−683	9	14	9
3214 Carpets, rugs	21	203	329	−182	204	1,097	1,014	−892	−710	12	9	6
3211 Spinning, weaving	291	875	1,870	−584	2,035	3,360	4,415	−1,325	−741	10	7	5
3559 Rubber nec	123	203	700	−79	1,589	2,424	4,207	−835	−756	14	13	10
3841 Shipbuilding	1,599	451	1,960	1,148	2,726	2,414	2,560	312	−836	3	9	1
3121 Food nec	39	205	1,345	−166	533	1,561	5,404	−1,028	−863	14	11	8
3523 Soap, cosmetics	49	140	559	−91	863	1,872	2,498	−1,009	−917	15	14	8
3831 Elec. ind. mach.	470	546	1,172	−76	4,592	5,675	6,879	−1,084	−1,008	12	12	10
3845 Aircraft	149	359	1,566	−210	4,042	5,385	9,849	−1,343	−1,133	18	15	10
3113 Fruit, veg. canning	38	273	1,192	−235	507	2,066	7,095	−1,559	−1,324	14	11	10
3420 Printing, publishing	138	234	3,867	−96	1,733	3,156	30,406	−1,423	−1,328	13	14	11
3114 Fish canning	31	341	617	−310	454	2,100	3,630	−1,645	−1,335	14	10	10
3909 Manf. ind. nec	94	297	446	−203	861	2,527	2,511	−1,666	−1,463	12	11	10
3852 Photo, optical	93	296	299	−203	876	2,858	2,774	−1,982	−1,779	12	12	12
3240 Footwear	68	290	518	−223	332	2,474	2,501	−2,142	−1,919	8	11	9
3839 Elec. apparatus nec	298	813	2,406	−515	3,604	6,089	14,134	−2,485	−1,970	13	11	10
3513 Synthesis resins	481	1,203	1,929	−722	7,709	10,517	15,367	−2,809	−2,087	15	11	12
3819 Fab. metal nec	979	1,487	4,850	−509	9,844	12,750	29,199	−2,906	−2,397	12	11	10
3511 Industrial chemicals	613	1,293	2,168	−680	6,360	9,969	16,435	−3,609	−2,929	12	11	11
3220 Wearing apparel	262	765	2,487	−504	1,199	8,412	9,668	−7,213	−6,709	8	13	7

(*continued*)

Table 10.5 (continued)

ISIC Commodity	1970 Values				1989 Values					Annual Rate of Change (%)		
	X	M	C	X − M	X	M	C	X − M	Change in X − M	X	M	C
Swedish Winners (Increased Relative Exports, Decreased Relative Imports)												
3710 Iron & steel	2,929	1,905	6,532	1,024	19,236	8,438	30,306	10,798	9,774	10	8	8
3530 Pet. refineries	200	2,196	3,359	−1,996	7,279	7,965	20,559	−685	1,311	20	7	10
3112 Dairy products	28	77	2,974	−50	469	422	16,909	47	97	15	9	10
3118 Sugar factories	13	70	506	−57	170	141	2,475	29	86	14	4	9
3115 Veg., animal oils	60	364	1,075	−304	453	952	4,120	−499	−196	11	5	7
3131 Distilling spirits	2	99	191	−97	250	575	2,589	−325	−228	29	9	15
3540 Misc. pet & coal	72	358	717	−286	787	1,460	3,812	−673	−387	13	7	9
3122 Animal feeds	3	125	899	−121	105	813	6,019	−708	−587	19	10	11
Swedish Losers (Decreased Relative Exports, Increased Relative Imports)												
3311 Sawmills, planing	1,974	296	4,331	1,677	12,724	2,736	29,710	9,988	8,311	10	12	11
3824 Special ind. mach	1,700	982	1,353	719	16,017	10,448	13,320	5,569	4,851	12	13	13
3842 Railroad equip.	77	42	524	36	330	358	3,500	−28	−64	8	11	11
3844 Motorcycles	30	106	194	−76	169	683	1,144	−514	−438	9	10	10
3901 Jewelry	15	33	95	−19	32	579	928	−546	−527	4	15	13
3551 Tires and tube	164	213	620	−49	582	2,239	2,739	−1,657	−1,608	7	12	8
3213 Knitting mills	240	755	1,114	−515	1,050	5,122	5,489	−4,072	−3,557	8	10	9
3825 Office, computing	875	716	839	159	9,186	15,071	14,352	−5,884	−6,043	12	16	16
Localizing Sectors (Decreasing Relative Exports and Relative Imports)												
3811 Cutlery, hardware	474	166	435	307	2,223	1,480	5,430	743	436	8	12	14
3133 Malt liquors	5	75	673	−69	29	199	5,126	−170	−101	9	5	11
3111 Meat slaughtering	325	388	5,811	−63	950	1,401	26,828	−452	−389	6	7	8

Note: M = imports; X = exports; C = production + imports − exports.

pecially drugs and medicine, pulp and paper, nec, professional and scientific equipment, and chemicals, nec.

Pulp and paper (3411) and motor vehicles and machinery, nec, have added substantially to Swedish export earnings (table 10.5) but have mixed performance indices reported in table 10.4 above. In both cases, the level of imports has grown rapidly, although from a very low base in the case of pulp and paper.

Most Deteriorating Swedish Performance in the Globalizing Industries

Wearing apparel and footwear are the only major sectors that are clearly moving out of Sweden. The import to consumption ratio in apparel increased from 31 percent to 87 percent, while the export ratio held pretty constant at around 10 percent, and consumption was unchanged. The import to consumption ratio in footwear increased from 56 percent to 99 percent.

Industrial chemicals, fabricated metal, nec, synthetic resins, and electrical apparatus nec all had substantial increases in an unfavorable trade balance, but they have mixed revealed comparative advantage measures because exports grew at least as fast as imports, although from a smaller base.

Shipbuilding was one of the major export items in 1970 but had imports and exports about in balance in 1980.

Swedish Winners

Iron and steel and petroleum refineries are clear Swedish winners, with substantial improvement in the trade balance and with exports growing much faster than consumption, which in turn grew more rapidly than imports. Animal feeds is one of those mixed sectors. It is a winner in the sense of having export growth exceeding import growth, but, nevertheless, the net trade balance deteriorates.

Swedish Losers

The big losers are office and computing equipment, knitting mills, and tires and tubes. Sawmills and special industrial machinery are mixed sectors, with imports growing more rapidly than exports but with an improvement in the trade balance.

10.2.4   Swedish Sectoral Shares of OECD Production

- The increased international division of labor from 1970 to 1990 is evident in a more extreme sectoral distribution of Swedish output with much more wood and paper compared with other OECD countries and with much less output of labor intensive consumer goods.

- The gain in relative market share of the moderately capital intensive sector, iron and steel, is very substantial.

- Offsetting that gain in iron and steel are losses in machinery and in industrial chemicals.

Table 10.6   **Swedish Revealed Comparative Advantage
(relative share of OECD output)**

Commodity	ISIC	1970[a]	1975[a]	1980[a]	1985[a]	1990[b]	Ratio 1990/1970
				1970 Comparative Advantage			
Wood	331	2.64	2.77	3.10	3.03	3.58	1.36
Paper	341	2.42	2.79	2.68	2.66	3.15	1.30
Fabricated metal	381	1.04	1.12	1.19	1.13	1.31	1.26
Misc. petro.	354	1.10	.95	1.06	1.16	1.25	1.13
Food	311	1.23	.93	1.02	.98	1.05	.85
Machinery	382	1.25	1.35	1.22	1.15	.99	.79
Ind. chemicals	351	1.05	1.08	.64	.63	.83	.79
Other nonmetal	369	1.04	.84	.84	.74	.82	.78
Furniture	332	1.23	1.20	1.12	1.27	.90	.73
Printing	342	1.32	1.26	1.33	1.38	.94	.71
Total manufactures	3	1.00	1.00	1.00	1.00	1.00	1.00
				1970 Comparative Disadvantage			
Petroleum	353	.35	.39	.70	.91	.65	1.84
Iron & steel	371	.86	.80	.94	1.02	1.46	1.70
Beverage	313	.38	.38	.46	.48	.61	1.62
Prof. & scien.	385	.55	.62	.58	.61	.77	1.39
Other chemicals	352	.65	.62	.80	.77	.83	1.28
Other food	312	.85	.73	.98	1.00	1.05	1.23
Nonferrous metal	372	.97	.80	.92	.89	1.09	1.12
Transport equip.	384	.90	1.11	1.03	1.07	1.00	1.11
Plastics	356	.44	.47	.53	.46	.46	1.03
Tobacco	314	.26	.24	.25	.26	.27	1.01
Elec. machinery	383	.72	.94	.82	.80	.69	.96
Rubber	355	.82	.74	.73	.67	.62	.76
Glass	362	.89	.77	.96	.85	.65	.73
Pottery, china	361	.91	.84	.68	.82	.64	.70
Textiles	321	.62	.55	.48	.41	.31	.51
Leather	323	.89	.71	.55	.56	.36	.41
Other manufactures	390	.54	.55	.54	.53	.21	.39
Footwear	324	.41	.41	.36	.22	.14	.35
Wearing apparel	322	.68	.53	.44	.26	.20	.30

[a]Excludes production of Iceland and Switzerland.

[b]Excludes production of Australia, Belgium, and Ireland.

The composition of output in Sweden in comparison with other OECD countries is reported in table 10.6. The data reported here are the Swedish sectoral share divided by the Swedish overall share, which will be called the revealed comparative advantage multiple (RCAM). An RCAM exceeding one indicates a sector in which Sweden has a revealed comparative advantage in the sense that the Swedish share of that sector is above the Swedish average.

In this table, sectors are first divided into those with 1970 numbers exceeding and falling short of one. Then they are sorted by the ratio of 1990 share to 1970 share, which is reported in the last column. At the top of each subcategory are those sectors that had the greatest gains in comparative advantage. At the bottom of each subcategory are the sectors with the biggest deterioration. If there were merely an increase in trade dependence from a shrinking globe with no substantial change in comparative advantage, then the ratios in the last column would all exceed one for the commodities with a 1970 comparative advantage and all fall short of one for the commodities with a 1970 comparative *disadvantage*. As a matter of fact, there seems to be quite a bit of shuffling of comparative advantage, with several sectors switching from one side of one to the other.

The sectors that conform to the simple shrinking-globe hypothesis fall at the top and the bottom of the list in table 10.6. Wood and paper head the list with a substantial RCAM in 1970 and with an amplification of that comparative advantage in 1980. At the bottom of this list are the other kind of products that began with a very weak Swedish comparative advantage, which deteriorated even further. These include wearing apparel, footwear, leather products, textiles, pottery, and glass.

The Swedish 1970 comparative advantage in several products dissipated by 1990. Furniture and printing are examples, as are machinery and industrial chemicals.

Offsetting these losses are gains in sectors that did not enjoy a comparative advantage in 1970. Most noticeable is the behavior of iron and steel, which went from a 0.86 ratio to a 1.46 ratio. Other food and nonferrous metal also managed to switch from a position of comparative disadvantage to a position of comparative advantage.

10.2.5   OECD Product Mix

- Sweden's comparative advantage is generally in low-growth sectors. Where there was initial comparative advantage in high-growth sectors, Sweden did not participate in the growth.
- The trends in OECD product mix and in Swedish revealed comparative advantage are very consistent with the Heckscher-Ohlin crowding model, with Sweden squeezed on the one side by low-wage labor abundant countries and on the other by high-growth capital abundant countries.

While Sweden was undergoing changes in product mix compared with other OECD countries, the product mix of OECD output was also changing substantially. Table 10.7 indicates the ratio of 1990 OECD share of value added to 1975 share of value added for two-digit ISIC categories. The OECD was shifting value added into plastics, nec, other chemicals, printing and publishing,

Table 10.7   OECD Manufacturing Value Added Shares (%)

	1976	1977	1978	1979	1980	1981	1982	1983	1984	1985	1986	1987	1988	1989	1990	Ratio of 1990/1975
Plastics nec	1.76	1.90	2.11	2.14	2.04	2.12	2.24	2.32	2.46	2.54	2.68	2.87	2.83	2.88	2.97	1.69
Other chemicals	3.25	4.16	4.27	4.12	4.14	4.36	4.69	4.84	4.75	4.88	5.00	5.14	5.11	5.20	5.47	1.68
Printing, publishing	4.52	4.46	4.64	4.63	4.77	5.05	5.42	5.51	5.57	5.85	5.85	5.89	5.50	5.85	5.99	1.32
Elec. machinery	8.80	9.08	9.62	9.53	9.96	10.20	10.79	10.92	11.70	11.50	11.56	10.83	11.05	11.03	11.11	1.26
Professional equip.	2.52	2.48	2.35	2.21	2.31	2.46	2.63	2.51	2.60	2.59	2.35	3.06	2.97	3.02	3.10	1.23
Nonmetal minerals	2.22	2.27	2.69	2.72	2.57	2.48	2.34	2.43	2.35	2.30	2.42	2.45	2.50	2.49	2.41	1.08
Machinery	11.71	11.81	11.98	11.94	12.20	12.53	12.30	11.39	11.77	11.82	11.56	11.53	11.82	12.10	12.46	1.06
Pottery, china	.22	.20	.27	.25	.25	.24	.23	.25	.24	.23	.24	.25	.25	.31	.24	1.06
Food manf.	7.76	7.60	7.97	7.84	7.97	8.18	8.55	8.65	8.34	8.53	8.63	8.38	8.12	8.02	8.19	1.06
Tobacco	1.20	1.14	1.00	1.02	1.04	.97	1.15	1.17	1.11	1.18	1.16	1.18	1.17	1.17	1.26	1.05
Total manf.	100.00	100.00	100.00	100.00	100.00	100.00	100.00	100.00	100.00	100.00	100.00	100.00	100.00	100.00	100.00	1.00
Transport	11.06	11.30	11.18	10.86	10.06	10.35	10.52	11.03	11.18	11.55	11.11	11.04	10.74	11.04	11.04	1.00
Glass	.87	.92	.93	.85	.89	.87	.84	.86	.83	.84	.86	.90	.86	.88	.84	.97
Furniture	1.36	1.46	1.47	1.45	1.49	1.44	1.39	1.42	1.34	1.34	1.37	1.36	1.34	1.32	1.31	.96
Paper	3.48	3.23	3.15	3.29	3.33	3.38	3.42	3.40	3.58	3.46	3.51	3.33	3.37	3.44	3.34	.96
Other manf.	1.40	1.48	1.37	1.40	1.35	1.38	1.41	1.34	1.33	1.28	1.26	1.27	1.27	1.29	1.34	.96
Fabricated metal	6.51	6.78	6.90	6.69	6.69	6.63	6.54	6.31	6.09	6.18	6.14	6.02	6.12	6.07	6.18	.95
Beverages	1.97	1.90	2.00	2.00	1.98	1.96	2.10	2.08	1.91	1.88	1.93	1.88	1.82	1.70	1.73	.88
Industrial chemicals	6.32	5.96	5.48	5.75	5.51	5.26	4.94	5.16	5.33	5.09	5.29	5.67	6.03	5.77	5.47	.86
Nonferrous metals	1.62	1.63	1.62	1.82	1.78	1.63	1.33	1.47	1.48	1.35	1.34	1.31	1.49	1.46	1.39	.85
Wood	1.76	1.86	2.10	2.13	1.88	1.70	1.54	1.77	1.64	1.60	1.67	1.64	1.57	1.52	1.50	.85
Rubber	1.38	1.41	1.29	1.25	1.26	1.25	1.23	1.26	1.21	1.22	1.23	1.24	1.21	1.16	1.16	.84
Misc. pet. & coal	.25	.22	.26	.24	.23	.24	.24	.26	.24	.24	.27	.24	.24	.24	.21	.83
Petroleum refineries	2.54	3.00	2.54	3.67	3.26	3.00	2.64	2.53	2.05	2.08	2.17	1.94	1.99	1.93	1.98	.78
Textiles	3.91	3.80	3.90	3.76	3.61	3.48	3.38	3.55	3.41	3.29	3.36	3.41	3.19	3.06	2.73	.70
Iron and steel	5.24	4.82	5.36	5.55	4.93	4.63	3.94	3.61	3.78	3.63	3.44	3.47	3.91	3.86	3.53	.67
Wearing apparel	2.51	2.56	2.32	2.23	2.23	2.23	2.26	2.22	2.10	2.02	1.98	1.95	1.82	1.74	1.67	.66
Leather	.34	.34	.33	.31	.31	.30	.27	.28	.25	.24	.24	.26	.24	.23	.20	.58
Footwear	.51	.52	.45	.46	.48	.46	.44	.44	.40	.37	.36	.34	.31	.28	.23	.46

electrical machinery, and professional equipment. The OECD was shifting value added out of footwear, leather, wearing apparel, iron and steel, textiles, and petroleum refineries.

These changes in value added shares can come from three sources: (*a*) shifts in demand, associated with things like increases in per capita incomes or changing demographics; (*b*) technological change such as the computer revolution; or (*c*) changes in the division of labor between OECD and non-OECD countries. It is impossible from an examination of this table alone to determine which of these forces predominates, but it is possible nonetheless to speculate. The increases in the importance of electrical machinery presumably reflects the computer revolution. The loss in "industrial chemicals" is more than offset by again in "other chemicals," which seems like a classification phenomenon. Wearing apparel, leather products, footwear, textiles and iron and steel are probably being outsourced.

Swedish comparative advantage in 1970 was generally concentrated in sectors that experienced sluggish growth of OECD value added. An important exception is printing and publishing, which grew from an OECD share of value added in 1970 of 4.52 percent to 5.99 percent in 1990. However, Sweden did not participate in this growth and failed to maintain its comparative advantage, slipping from a RCAM of 1.32 (reported in table 10.6 above) to 0.94 in 1990. Another exception is machinery, which grew from an OECD share of 11.71 percent to an OECD share of 12.46 percent. But again Sweden fell behind, with an RCAM falling from 1.25 in 1970 to 0.99 in 1990.

The other high-growth sectors in table 10.7 are all sectors in which Sweden had an early comparative *disadvantage* as measured by the Swedish share of production compared with the OECD share overall, numbers that are reported in table 10.6. Plastics had a steady RCAM equal to 0.44 in 1970 and 0.46 in 1990. Electrical machinery had a deteriorating RCAM equal to 0.72 in 1970 and 0.69 in 1990. The RCAM for other chemicals that began low did improve, but this was offset by an opposite movement in industrial chemicals.

The two sectors in which Sweden had a substantial relative comparative advantage in 1970 did not do so well. The paper sector held pretty steady at around 3.4 percent of OECD value added. Wood declined from a 1.76 percent share to 1.5. percent.

The big Swedish winner, iron and steel, which went from an RCAM of 0.86 to an RCAM of 1.46, was a sector of greatly declining importance in the OECD, dropping from a 5.24 percent share to a 3.53 percent share.

From these data, one gets the impression of an economy that is sitting on the sidelines watching the growth of printing and publishing and electrical machinery but holding on to iron and steel even as it declines in importance in the OECD. The dynamism of the Swedish economy is evident only in one negative way. Sweden is letting go of the labor intensive sectors (footwear, leather products, and wearing apparel) even more rapidly than the OECD generally. These trends are very compatible with the H-O model, with Sweden being squeezed on the one side by low-wage non-OECD (Asia and Northern Africa) producers offering labor intensive goods at low prices and on the other side by the industrialized world, which is generally making physical and human capital investments at rates much in excess of Sweden. These competitive pressures force Sweden out of the markets for the most labor intensive products and also out of the markets for the most capital intensive products, leaving Sweden in the middle, producing moderately capital intensive goods like iron and steel in addition to the forest-related products.

10.2.6   Terms of Trade

- The overall Swedish terms of trade is driven more by the relative price of forest products to oil than by the relative price of capital intensive to labor intensive manufactures.
- Other than the price behavior of petroleum and the forest product sectors, the external changes in relative prices are generally consistent with the H-O crowding hypothesis: lower prices for imported labor intensive products (apparel), lower prices for exports of the most capital intensive products (chemicals and machinery), and improved prices for moderately capital intensive goods (iron and steel, transportation equipment, and professional equipment).

According to the H-O model, the effects of nationally uneven rates of growth of factors are transmitted internationally by product price changes and only product price changes. Relative price variability is thus a key component of the Heckscher-Ohlin crowding hypothesis, and, if we cannot find the right kind of price changes, all the supportive evidence discussed so far is put in doubt.

The theory and evidence heretofore presented do not leave a very clear picture of what should be expected regarding Sweden's overall terms of trade. A simple H-O model with several goods but only two factors—capital and labor—would lead us to expect a period of improving terms of trade following the war, after which there would be a period of terms of trade deterioration as the markets for Swedish capital intensive manufactured goods get crowded with competitors. In fact, because of the substantial comparative advantage in forest products, Sweden did not have positive net exports of any of the four manufactures aggregates displayed in figures 10.8–10.13 above. For that reason, the early performance of the terms of trade is greatly influenced by the price of forest-related products. Later, the wild swings in petroleum prices (a major import item) greatly affect the terms of trade. Changes in the relative prices of the manufactured goods, which are a critical feature of the Heckscher-Ohlin crowding hypothesis, are thus not likely to show up clearly in the overall terms of trade. With these caveats in mind, we briefly examine the overall terms of trade and then discuss the more relevant disaggregated data.

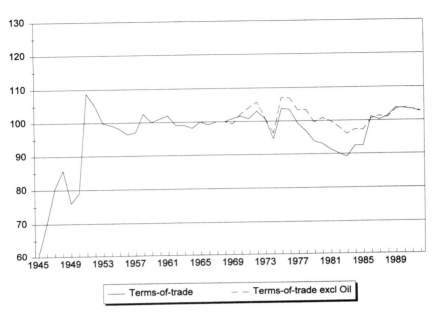

Fig. 10.17   Swedish terms of trade

Immediately after the war, when demand for the destitute countries was targeted at Sweden and a few other capital abundant countries, Sweden's terms of
trade improved dramatically (fig. 10.17), largely because of higher prices for
Swedish forest products. Thereafter, the terms of trade has hovered around a
constant level, although with dips in 1951–56, 1973,and 1976–82, the first dip
due to price reductions for forest products and the latter two dips associated
with increases in the price of imported petroleum. After the phase of reconstruction in Europe, and during the increased competition in capital intensive
goods, we might expected Sweden to experience a decline in its terms of trade.
The terms of trade did fall from 1951 to 1956, but the change is by no means
dramatic, possibly because of lower prices for imported labor intensive
products.[15]

The terms of trade excluding oil is indicated by the broken line in figure
10.17. This adjustment of course does not account for the indirect effects of
oil price hikes, for example, those implying higher relative prices of oil intensive goods are not accounted for. Still, adjusting only for these direct effects
by disregarding oil in the terms of trade calculations gives rise to a generally
less volatile terms of trade. In particular, the drop in terms of trade after 1979

15. Incidentally, these relative prices have to be interpreted with care. High prices for exports
are desirable if substantial sales are occurring at these prices, but exchange rate appreciations can
temporarily drive up the relative price of exports and give a misleading impression of improved
economic health.

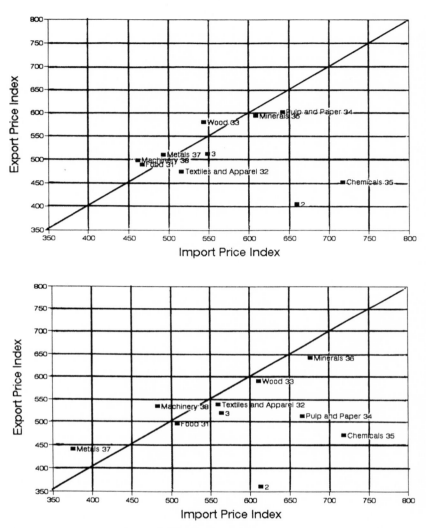

Fig. 10.18   1989 (top) and 1992 (botom) import and export price indexes, 1968 = 100

is not as pronounced, and, in the early 1990s, oil prices do not have much effect on the terms of trade.

Clearly, the evidence in favor of the Heckscher-Ohlin crowding hypothesis is slight in the overall terms of trade, but understandably so since the overall relative price of exports to imports is driven by the prices of forest products exports relative to the price of petroleum imports. Greater detail on the behavior of import and export prices is revealed in figures 10.18 and 10.19, the first applying to two-digit aggregates and the second to three-digit components of

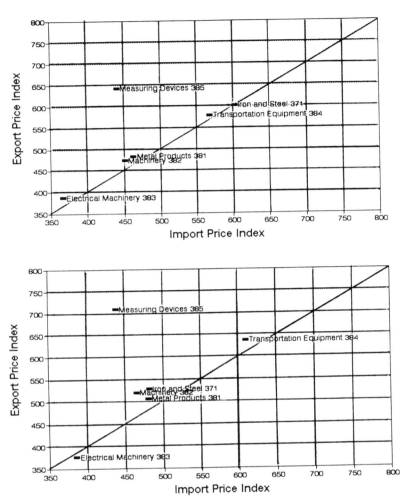

Fig. 10.19   1989 (top) and 1992 (bottom) import and export price indexes, 1968 = 100 (detail)

ISIC 38 (machinery) and ISIC 37 (metals). In each of these figures, the import price index (1968 = 100) is on the horizontal axis and the export price index on the vertical axis. The upper panel has the prerecession 1989 data and the lower panel the 1992 data. There are two aspects of these graphs that should attract your attention. First is the amount of spread along the forty-five degree, line and second is the identity of the points lying off the forty-five degree line. If products were homogeneous, then import and export prices would be identical, and all these points would lie on the forty-five degree line. The points to the upper right would then indicate commodities that had relative price increases and the points to the lower left commodities with relative price reductions. If the import and export aggregates are very different in composition, then the points in the graph can lie substantially off the forty-five degree line.

Thus, from the upper panel of figure 10.18 can be seen the increase in the relative price of pulp and paper and the reduction in the relative price of food products and textiles and apparel. The point representing textiles and apparel is substantially off the forty-five degree line, with import prices keeping up much better than export prices. Chemicals is quite extreme in that regard, with the very largest increase in import prices and the very lowest increase in export prices. In words, Sweden is exporting increasingly low-priced chemicals and importing increasingly high-priced chemicals.

A comparison of the upper and the lower panels of figure 10.18 shows how much the recession affected relative prices, with metals prices falling by about 10 percent and prices of pulp and paper exports falling by about 20 percent.

The three-digit detail for metals and machinery is provided in figure 10.19. From 1968 to 1989, there was a substantial relative price decline of electrical machinery and a substantial relative price increase in iron and steel and in transportation equipment. The relative export price of measuring devices rose substantially, while relative import prices were relatively constant. As in figure 10.18, the contrast between the upper and the lower panels indicates the effect of the recession, with iron and steel prices plummeting.

In summary, the external changes in relative prices partly confirm the Heckscher-Ohlin crowding hypothesis: lower prices for imported labor intensive products (textiles and apparel), lower prices for exports of the most capital intensive products (like chemicals and basic metal industries), and improved prices for moderately capital intensive goods (like transportation equipment).

An exception to a general fall in the export prices of the capital intensive goods is pulp and paper. Here, the Japanese and German buildups of real and human capital stocks has had no price-pressing effect since these countries lack the natural resources to support large-scale forest industries. Obviously, it has been profitable for Swedish firms to expand further the forest-based industries.

10.2.7   Intraindustry Trade

The H-O model is commonly criticized for its failure to account for intraindustry trade: exports offsetting imports for finely defined categories of commodities. In this section we report sectoral details regarding Swedish intraindustry trade as a form of criticism of our H-O view.

A standard measure of intraindustry trade in industry i is

$$\text{IIT}_i = 1 - |\text{exports}_i - \text{imports}_i|/(\text{exports}_i + \text{imports}_i),$$

which takes on a value between zero and one: zero if either exports or imports are zero, and one if exports and imports exactly balance.

In table 10.8, we report the proportion of H-O trade, defined as $1 - \text{IIT}$. Commodities in this table are sorted by their 1985 levels of H-O trade. At the

Table 10.8   **Heckscher-Ohlin Trade as a Percentage of Total Trade:**
|Exports − Imports|/(Exports + Imports).

ISIC Commodity	1970	1975	1980	1985	1989	Change 1970–89
Average	30.5	23.2	17.2	13.2	18.3	− 12.2
3411 Pulp, paper	95.2	95.6	94.6	91.8	90.4	−4.8
3122 Animal feeds	94.9	87.7	95.9	85.6	77.2	− 17.7
3118 Sugar factories	68.0	99.9	19.4	84.1	9.4	− 58.6
3311 Sawmills, planing	73.9	73.5	66.7	76.9	64.6	−9.3
3240 Footwear	62.2	57.9	65.4	76.6	76.3	14.1
3901 Jewelry	39.5	74.3	57.7	66.5	89.4	49.9
3113 Fruit, veg. canning	75.8	77.2	75.1	66.0	60.6	− 15.2
3114 Fish canning	83.3	77.9	74.3	64.4	64.4	− 18.9
3220 Wearing apparel	49.1	54.0	65.2	64.3	75.0	26.0
3213 Knitting mills	51.8	40.8	55.2	60.7	66.0	14.2
3233 Leather	39.7	65.1	68.0	60.5	70.7	31.0
3131 Distilling spirits	96.8	97.7	95.5	60.3	39.4	− 57.4
3849 Transport nec	47.1	58.3	53.4	55.6	6.9	− 40.1
3902 Musical instr.	69.4	70.3	64.1	54.4	69.4	.0
3214 Carpets, rugs	81.1	76.2	64.8	53.6	68.6	− 12.5
3412 Containers	39.2	50.9	53.3	52.5	29.2	− 10.0
3319 Wood, cork nec	27.1	21.7	27.3	51.2	46.2	19.1
3551 Tires and tube	12.9	44.8	43.4	50.8	58.7	45.8
3133 Malt liquors	86.9	74.5	40.3	48.5	74.6	− 12.3
3852 Photo, optical	52.2	61.2	53.4	48.4	53.1	.9
3116 Grain mill	59.0	37.8	41.7	48.3	57.3	− 1.7
3842 Railroad equip.	30.0	4.7	29.3	47.2	4.1	− 25.9
3710 Iron & steel	21.2	14.9	33.4	47.0	39.0	17.8
3811 Cutlery, hardware	48.1	45.5	42.1	45.0	20.1	− 28.0
3121 Food nec	67.8	48.5	56.5	44.9	49.1	− 18.7
3134 Soft drinks	63.7	46.9	37.7	42.4	37.8	− 25.8
3419 Pulp, paper nec	21.6	29.0	32.4	41.7	46.9	25.3
3844 Motorcycles	56.3	41.4	64.6	37.8	60.4	4.0
3523 Soap, cosmetics	48.5	52.6	46.8	37.7	36.9	− 11.6
3320 Furniture	3.9	18.2	24.0	37.4	8.4	4.5
3211 Spinning, weaving	50.1	45.0	41.0	36.1	24.6	− 25.6
3813 Structural metal	19.9	31.9	25.0	35.9	9.8	− 10.2
3691 Structural clay	51.0	56.5	39.0	35.0	58.0	7.0
3843 Motor vehicles	16.9	19.1	28.7	33.8	16.1	−.8
3909 Manf. ind. nec	52.1	38.5	35.7	33.1	49.2	−2.9
3115 Veg., animal oils	71.7	56.0	49.6	32.0	35.5	− 36.1
3540 Misc. pet. & coal	66.4	70.4	42.4	29.1	29.9	− 36.5
3140 Tobacco	63.2	26.1	31.3	28.9	55.7	−7.6

(continued)

Table 10.8 (continued)

ISIC Commodity	Heckscher-Ohlin Trade					Change 1970–89
	1970	1975	1980	1985	1989	
3111 Meat slaughtering	8.8	22.5	2.7	27.9	19.2	10.4
3839 Elec. apparatus nec	46.4	29.4	24.7	26.9	25.6	−20.7
3511 Industrial chemicals	35.7	35.4	34.6	26.0	22.1	−13.6
3824 Special ind. mach.	26.8	31.1	27.2	25.4	21.0	−5.8
3312 Wooden containers	14.1	11.5	7.3	23.8	.1	−13.9
3812 Metal furniture	17.3	14.6	3.7	23.4	16.0	−1.3
3530 Pet. refineries	83.3	80.3	47.9	22.9	4.5	−78.8
3231 Tanneries	7.6	1.5	4.4	22.4	8.3	.7
3822 Agricultural mach.	9.0	4.6	.8	22.1	12.9	3.9
3829 Machinery nec	14.9	11.9	19.4	20.5	17.1	2.1
3610 Pottery, china	5.6	23.5	33.1	19.3	37.2	31.6
3513 Synthetic resins	42.9	31.4	22.2	18.6	15.4	−27.5
3560 Plastics nec	44.0	27.7	25.8	16.0	11.2	−32.8
3692 Cement, lime	75.2	39.9	14.7	16.0	40.0	−35.1
3823 Metal, woodworking	3.8	1.3	15.7	15.8	14.4	10.6
3420 Printing, publishing	25.7	6.5	18.1	13.3	29.1	3.4
3212 Made-up textiles	48.0	46.4	31.5	13.2	40.4	−7.6
3119 Chocolate, sugar conf.	50.5	30.2	26.6	13.1	5.7	−44.7
3117 Bakery products	8.7	7.9	12.4	13.1	23.5	14.8
3112 Dairy products	47.2	19.4	13.8	12.1	5.3	−41.9
3825 Office, computing	10.0	6.1	3.9	10.9	24.3	14.2
3521 Paints, varnishes	27.2	7.3	13.2	8.9	5.2	−22.0
3833 Elec. appliances	7.4	10.4	12.0	8.5	.6	−6.8
3903 Sporting, athletic	4.3	2.0	22.1	7.7	19.5	15.2
3832 TV, communication	4.7	18.0	12.9	7.6	6.1	1.4
3699 Nonmetal minerals	27.6	22.3	16.1	7.6	23.8	−3.8
3819 Fab. metal nec	20.6	17.8	16.6	7.2	12.9	−7.8
3845 Aircraft	41.4	50.7	54.3	7.1	14.2	−27.1
3559 Rubber nec	24.3	12.0	10.4	5.6	20.8	−3.5
3522 Drugs & medicines	35.0	28.4	3.2	5.6	25.4	−9.6
3620 Glass	36.1	24.3	2.3	5.3	11.2	−25.0
3841 Shipbuilding	56.0	36.3	46.5	4.1	6.1	−49.9
3219 Textiles nec	43.8	22.1	17.7	3.6	15.9	−27.8

Table 10.8   (continued)

ISIC Commodity	Heckscher-Ohlin Trade					Change 1970–89
	1970	1975	1980	1985	1989	
3720 Nonferrous metals	34.8	31.0	8.4	3.4	9.6	−25.3
3831 Elec. ind. mach.	7.5	8.6	1.8	.8	10.6	3.1
3851 Prof. & scientific	30.6	18.7	7.5	.6	5.4	−25.3
3215 Cordage, rope	66.9	68.3	2.2	.6	69.6	2.7
3529 Chemicals nec	34.4	17.1	2.2	.5	8.4	−26.0

top of the list is pulp and paper, with such a small level of imports compared with exports that 92 percent of trade in 1985 was Heckscher-Ohlin trade. Next on the list with mostly H-O trade are agricultural products, other forest products, and labor intensive manufactures. At the other end of the list are commodities with imports and exports almost exactly offsetting each other. Chemicals, nec, cordage and rope, professional and scientific, and electrical industrial machinery all had H-O trade less than 1 percent in 1985.

A quick glance at this table might seem very troubling for our H-O view since, according to these numbers, three-fourths of these commodity aggregates had more intraindustry trade than H-O trade. But keep in mind that, at the highest level of aggregation, the trade balance condition, exports = imports, implies an H-O share of zero. The higher the level of aggregation, the more likely are the aggregates to include some products that are H-O exports and some products that are H-O imports. Thus, measured H-O trade will necessarily decline with aggregation. The numbers in table 10.8 should therefore be viewed with alarm only if the commodities are finely enough defined, a condition that must be subjectively assessed. Textiles, for example, is a notoriously broad class, with some crude cloth made by very labor intensive methods and other highly specialized fabrics made with great amounts of human and physical capital. Many of these other aggregates are capable of the same interpretation.

What is not so cavalierly dismissed is the general increase over time in intraindustry trade and the reduction in H-O trade. The average level of H-O trade declined from 30.5 percent in 1970 to 13.2 percent in 1985 but recovered to 18.3 percent in 1989. Although the big increase in world trade relative to GDP over the last several decades is a quite understandable consequence of the lowering of natural and manmade barriers to trade regardless of the theory of trade, an H-O model would not lead us to expect an increase in intraindustry trade unless there were something perverse about the commodity categories. We are inclined to make the sweeping conclusion from this table that scale economies and product differentiation were an important aspect of the expansion of trade into the 1980s but that perhaps the increase in H-O trade from

1985 to 1989 signals a reversion to H-O trade as North-South trade between developed and developing countries is displacing East-West trade among developed countries.

10.3 Swedish Forest Resources

10.3.1 Forest Resources in a Heckscher-Ohlin Model

- Capital that is used in the Swedish forest product sector is unavailable for the rest of manufacturing. The use of capital in the Swedish forest products sector can starve manufacturing of capital that would otherwise be used to upgrade the product mix and thereby support higher wages.

- The extraction of labor and capital into the forest products sector lowers the capital intensity of resources available to manufacturing by 21 percent from SKr 170,000 per worker to SKr 135,000 per worker.

- Earnings from forest resources generate demand for importables that contributes to the Swedish dependence on imports of other manufactured goods.

The H-O model in section 10.1 has labor, physical capital, and human capital as inputs. The heavy dependence of Sweden on exports of wood, paper, and pulp suggests that forest resources need to be explicitly included when the model is applied to Sweden. A multicone model that is inspired by the graphs of net exports of the ten aggregates is illustrated in figure 10.20. The inputs are labor (human and physical), capital, and forests. A labor intensive forest product (lumber) and a capital intensive forest product (paper) are included. Along the horizontal are the four manufactures: apparel, textiles, machinery, and chemicals. By the way, if pulp were costlessly transportable, then forest resources would not be a source of comparative advantage in paper production, and, in this diagram, it would be appropriate to locate the paper point along the horizontal with the other manufactures that use only labor and capital as inputs. Paper, pulp, and lumber historically have had a strong locational interconnection, although, according to Leamer (1987a, 74), paper became more footloose by 1978, the end of the period he studied.[16]

Figure 10.20 has Sweden in 1945 positioned in the cone that selects as outputs both forest products and the moderately capital intensive manufacture textiles. With Swedish capital accumulation comes a shift in the mix of forest products toward paper and a shift in the mix of manufactures from textiles to machinery. Although Sweden then produces textiles and machinery, the output levels may leave Sweden an importer of these manufactured products. Indeed,

---

16. As an exercise, the reader may wish to trace out the implications of the model in which forests are not a source of comparative advantage in paper production.

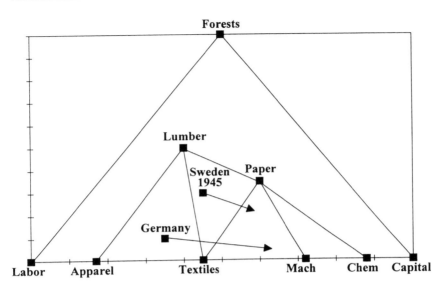

Fig. 10.20   Cones of diversification: Forests, capital, and labor

this is what the data indicate, with positive net exports of machinery not emerging until the early 1960s. Another way of saying this is that earnings from exports of forest products may generate so much demand for other manufactured importables that Sweden imports them all, even though Sweden has a relatively high capital/labor ratio in manufactures.

In this figure, Germany is much more poorly endowed in forest products and concentrates production on the set of manufactures that have capital intensities suited to the German capital abundance. Expansion of Germany and Japan into machinery causes a terms of trade deterioration for Sweden as a net exporter of machinery. Expansion of Asia and Southern Europe into apparel and textiles causes a terms of trade improvement.

In this model, the existence of forest products causes Swedish deindustrialization in the sense that an increase in forest resources reduces absolutely the outputs of the manufactured products (the Rybczynski theorem) other than paper. Indeed, the greater is the abundance of forest resources, the more likely it is that Sweden remains in the relatively low-wage cone, including lumber. In contrast, Germany flows quickly through this cone and moves early on into the production of machinery.

10.3.2   The Swedish Forest Product Sector: The Starving Hypothesis

Figure 10.20 fits the facts well, although we have not yet provided much evidence on the product upgrading in the forest product sector that should come with capital accumulation in Sweden. The forest industries may be classified into labor and capital intensive ones (see Ohlsson and Vinell 1987). Labor intensive forest industries include production in sawmills and planing and some manufacturing of wooden fiber tiles. Capital intensive forest industries include industries for mechanical and semichemical pulp and paper and carton industries. Over time, value added and employment has increased much faster in the capital intensive sectors than in the labor intensive ones.

One of the central hypotheses of this chapter is that demand for capital in the forest product sectors can starve other manufacturing of capital and can force Sweden into a more labor intensive mix of outputs. Table 10.9 offers some idea of the effect of the forest product sectors on the availability of capital and labor for the other manufacturing sectors.[17] In 1988, the capital per employee in Swedish manufacturing was SKr 170,000 per worker. The paper products sector employed 26 percent of the capital but only 7 percent of the workers. After extracting the capital and labor used in paper and in wood, the capital intensity drops from SKr 170,000 per worker to SKr 135,000 per worker. This makes it difficult to support a pharmaceuticals sector or a chemicals sector, which have capital intensities of 302 and 284, respectively.[18] The major sectors with capital intensity below 135 are transport equipment (122), nonelectrical machinery (108), and electrical machinery (89).

10.4   Nontraded Goods and Labor Market Distortions

- High wages can be supported by high demand for labor intensive nontradables. This demand can come from the government or from net foreign earnings from natural resource products.

- The cost of a minimum wage as a means to redistribute income has been raised by the low rates of physical and human capital accumulation in Sweden and also by increased competition in the markets for Sweden's relatively labor intensive products.

The preceding discussion has abstracted from two important features of the Swedish economy. The first is nontraded goods, particularly the huge share of the workforce that is employed in the government sector. For instance, in 1960, the Swedish nontradable sector employed 44 percent of the total labor force,

---

17. In comparison with other sectors, the productivity increase in the wood industry has been lower than in most other industries; the only sector that during 1964–89 has had a lower total factor productivity increase than the wood industry is food processing. The productivity increase in pulp and paper is average and comparable with that in most other sectors.

18. This discussion follows the theory that takes as given the capital and labor allocated to manufacturing. Given K and L, the allocation of employment across sectors must satisfy two conditions. The overall capital/labor ratio is an employment-weighted average of the sector capital/labor ratios $K/L = \Sigma\, L_i(K/L)_i/\Sigma\, L_i$, and the labor allocated to each sector must exhaust the labor supply $L = \Sigma\, L_i$. Thus, if a substantial amount of labor is allocated to a capital intensive sector, an offsetting amount must be allocated to a labor intensive sector to maintain the first condition. These conditions in practice are not that confining, but the more important constraint theoretically comes from the choice of factor and goods prices that tends to force a concentration of manufacturing on a small band in the capital per worker spectrum.

Table 10.9   Allocation of Capital and Labor in Manufacturing

Commodity	Capital/Employee	Employees 1988	Total Fixed Capital
Petroleum refineries	1,214	1,600	1,942,305
Paper products	634	53,700	34,046,959
Food products nec	361	6,330	2,287,834
Drugs and medicines	302	8,100	2,443,078
Industrial chemicals	284	18,600	5,289,620
Beverage ind.	261	5,100	1,329,975
Iron and steel	230	33,300	7,642,665
Cement, nonmetallic mineral	210	14,900	3,129,154
Office, computing, and accounting	206	9,300	1,914,837
Food manf.	163	56,970	9,288,233
Wood and wood products	147	44,200	6,508,467
Fabricated metal products	129	73,900	9,496,652
Nonferrous metal basic industries	126	11,300	1,421,193
Transport equipment	122	112,600	13,771,537
Other chemical products minus drugs	117	16,600	1,942,154
Plastic products nec	109	14,300	1,563,229
Machinery except electrical	108	102,200	11,037,047
Printing and publishing	108	42,700	4,591,917
Glass and glass products	99	4,300	425,011
Rubber products	96	8,900	853,180
Electrical machinery	89	67,600	6,002,803
Textiles	87	14,700	1,280,765
Other manufacturing industries	85	3,800	321,382
Misc. products of pet. & coal	83	1,700	141,307
Pottery, china, and earthenware	66	2,500	164,438
Furniture	57	12,200	700,407
Professional and scientific equip.	51	13,400	686,079
Footwear	46	900	41,658
Leather	33	1,400	46,058
Wearing apparel	23	9,000	209,349
Total manufacturing	170	766,100	130,519,291
Minus wood and paper manf.	414	97,900	40,555,425
Equals residual	135	668,200	89,963,866

and, in 1990, 75 percent were employed in sectors protected from international trade. The second neglected feature is institutional wage compression, which acts like a high minimum wage. This minimum wage makes it more difficult for Sweden to produce labor intensive tradables and forces workers who might otherwise find jobs in these sectors to look for work in nontradables or to opt for unemployment.

Institutional wage compression would be a nonissue if Sweden had no reason to produce labor intensive tradables. Distinctive abundance in physical and human capital once conveyed on Sweden a strong international comparative advantage in capital intensive tradables. This, together with a high demand for unskilled workers in nontradables, made wage compression a natural competitive outcome, not something that had to be imposed. Over the last several decades, Sweden failed to maintain its lead in human and physical capital, thus allowing the capital intensity of Swedish international comparative advantage to drift downward and thereby exposing Swedish unskilled workers to competition from lower-wage foreigners. This has raised the economic costs of wage compression. It is an irony, by the way, that increased investments in human and physical capital that in the long run would lead naturally to income equality probably in the short run will only occur if the inequality is worse, that is, if there is adequate incentive to make the investments.

10.4.1 Nontraded Goods

- A high demand for labor intensive nontraded goods can support a high-wage solution. This demand keeps the price of nontradables high and shifts resources from tradables to nontradables. On the assumption that nontradables are labor intensive, this shift tends to leave tradables with relatively little labor compared with capital. This higher capital intensity supports a higher wage.

- The government is one important source of demand for nontraded goods. Some simple calculations suggest that government employment has played an important role in maintaining Swedish wages.

- Net external earnings from natural resources also generate demand for nontradables. Swedish earnings from forest products were partially offset by expenditures on imported petroleum, making the forest resources less capable of supporting a high-wage equilibrium immediately after the oil price shock, but reduced petroleum expenditures have restored the very favorable Swedish trade balance in natural resource products.

A nontraded sector is added to the H-O framework in this section. According to the multicone H-O model, Sweden will be able to sustain high wages if the supply of factors to the traded goods sector is suited to the most capital intensive mix of products. If too much labor is supplied relative to capital, then some of the labor has to be absorbed into the production of labor intensive commodities like apparel and some forms of textiles. Workers in these sectors necessarily compete head to head with low-paid workers in Southern Europe, Northern Africa, and Asia. These labor intensive sectors can survive international competition only if wages fall to the low levels paid by these foreign producers. If a scarcity of human and physical capital forces Sweden to compete directly against low-wage suppliers, then Swedish wages will be set in the labor markets of Lisbon and Beijing, not in Stockholm.

Communities and countries with enough capital can have high wages for unskilled workers if they concentrate on capital intensive tradables and absorb unskilled workers partly in these skill intensive sectors and partly in nontradables. Figure 10.21 illustrates this possibility with two traded goods, machinery

Capital

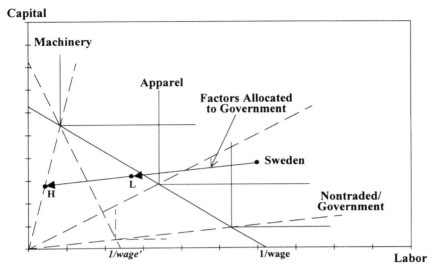

Fig. 10.21   High-wage and low-wage equilibria: Use of factors in government

and apparel, and one nontraded good, government. Two possible equilibria are depicted, one with low wages and apparel production, the other with high wages and no apparel production. The low-wage equilibrium is associated with the solid-line isocost through the vertices of the machinery and apparel unit-value isoquants. This equilibrium occurs when some, but not enough, of the factor supplies are used in the government sector, leaving, for example, the amount L for the traded goods sector. If the government absorbs more resources, leaving the amount H for the traded goods sector, then not enough labor is available to support apparel production, and only machinery is produced. Then the high-wage equilibrium indicated by the dotted unit-cost line will occur.

Incidentally, figure 10.21 is prejudiced in one very serious way. It is drawn on the assumption that extraction of resources into the government sector leaves the remainder more suited to the production of the capital intensive mix of commodities. In fact, the workforce in government is quite highly educated, and government employment may be starving manufacturing of needed human capital. This could be depicted in figure 10.21 if the government sector were more capital intensive than the machinery sector, in which case allocating resources to government shifts manufacturing toward apparel, not toward machinery. This can force Sweden into a low-wage equilibrium. Another possibility is that government is intermediate in capital intensity, lying between apparel and machinery. Then government does not fundamentally alter the mix of resources available to the traded goods sector.

Another source of demand for nontradables is the earnings from the sale of

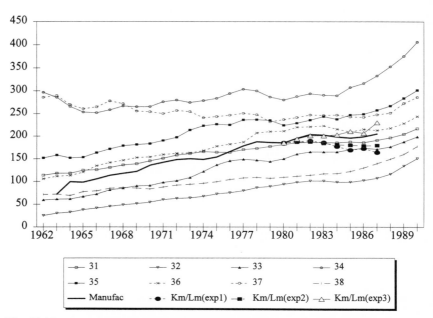

Fig. 10.22   **Capital-labor ratios in manufacturing sectors, 1962–90, and experiments 1–3**

natural resource products. If these earnings are high enough, Sweden can afford to import the labor intensive manufactures and avoid direct competition with the low-wage emerging countries around the globe. The increased bill for petroleum in 1974 that is very evident in figure 10.10 above offsets earnings from forest products, thereby reducing the demand for nontradables and making high wages more difficult to sustain. But the lowered demand for petroleum in 1988 evident in figure 10.11 above restores the very favorable balance on natural resource trade, which makes it again a source of support for high wages.

The model depicted in figure 10.21 suggests some simple accounting to determine the effect of the resource demands in the nontraded goods and natural resource sectors on Swedish wages. Let K_m and L_m denote capital and labor used in manufacturing and K_n and L_n the corresponding factors used in non-traded sectors. If K_f and L_f are inputs into natural resource sectors like forestry, agriculture, mining, and quarrying and K and L are the Swedish totals, then the capital intensity of factors supplied to manufacturing is $K_m/L_m = (K - K_f - K_n)/(L - L_f - L_n)$. The higher is this ratio, the more capital intensive will be the mix of Swedish manufacturing products, and the higher is the sustainable level of wages.

By varying the levels of capital and labor in the nontraded goods sectors under different assumptions regarding the behavior of government, this simple

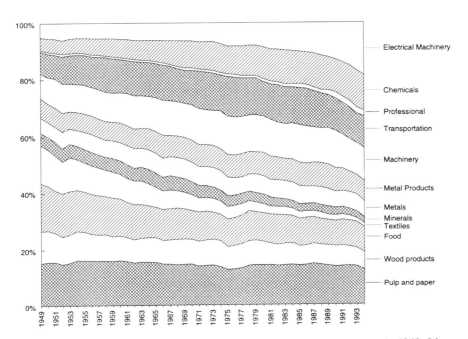

Fig. 10.23   Manufacturing production by sector (in percentage shares), 1949–94

formula allows us to compute the capital/labor ratio of the factors remaining for manufacturing.

Swedish capital labor ratios in ISIC sectors 31–39 from 1962 through 1990 are illustrated in figure 10.22 together with the overall ratio. Figure 10.23 shows the relative shares of value added of the industries from 1949 to 1994. Food, textiles, minerals, and wood products have lowered their shares of overall manufacturing production, pulp and paper is relatively unchanged, and chemicals and manufacturing of metal products have increased. This is broadly what the H-O model predicts.

The capital/labor ratios depicted in figure 10.22 have three noticeable features: (*a*) a general upward trend, (*b*) a relative slide in ISIC 37, metals, from the most capital intensive sector to a more moderate level (this is the Swedish winning sector!), and (*c*) a slow slide upward, relatively speaking, of the overall ratio in manufacturing until 1978, when the Swedish mix of output stopped increasing in capital intensity.

Into this figure we have inserted hypothetical values for the capital/labor ratio in manufacturing for three different scenarios differing in the role of the public goods sector as an absorber of labor.

Experiment 1: No Growth in Employment in the Nontrade Sector after 1980. In the first calculation, we fix employment in the nontraded sector and allocate the increase in total labor supply after 1980 totally to manufacturing. Capital allocation is unaffected. This is the extreme "starving" scenario in the sense of reducing the capital/labor ratio in manufacturing by the largest amount.

Experiment 2: Fixed Employment Levels in the Nontraded Sector, Fixed Total Employment. Next, we fix the employment level in the nontraded sector and also total employment at 1980 levels to reflect the extreme, but not altogether unrealistic, assumption that, absent the expansion of the public sector, these government employees would have opted out of the labor force. (It is often argued that a reason why Sweden is able to keep a leading position in terms of female labor market participation is because of the extended government sector.)

Experiment 3: All Additions to Capital Allocated to Manufacturing. In this experiment, we fix also the capital stock of the nontraded sector at the 1980 level and assume that increases in the capital stock are absorbed in the manufacturing sector. The assumptions under experiment 2 continue to hold.

Under experiment 1 depicted in figure 10.22, the overall capital/labor ratio drops precipitously, falling below the capital intensity in ISIC 33, wood products, and moving in the direction of ISIC 38, metal products, and ISIC 32, apparel and textiles. The implication of this first calculation is that government employment has been a key reason for high wages in Sweden since, absent that employment, the traded goods manufacturing sector would have had to absorb labor by shifting into labor intensive sectors that, because of international competition, cannot pay high wages. This product downgrading effect is less severe but still noticeable under the second experiment, which holds the employment levels fixed. The capital/labor ratio in manufacturing noticeably improves if all additions to capital are allocated to manufacturing, experiment 3.[19]

10.4.2   Labor Market Distortion: Wage Compression from Above

- Labor market institutions that attempt artificially to lower wages of high-skilled workers put out of business the labor intensive tradables sectors, thus shifting the output mix of manufacturing toward products that use physical capital (but not skills) intensively.
- The reduction in the rate of return to skills causes an even larger reduction in the rate of return to physical capital, provided that the total capital requirements in the skill intensive sector are higher than any other sectors.
- Some of the workers released from the labor intensive tradables sector find jobs, but others are unemployed. The level of unemployment is a decreasing function of the supplies of human and physical capital. Sup-

---

19. The assumptions in this experiment imply, however, that the size of the Swedish labor force would fall by 350,000 people.

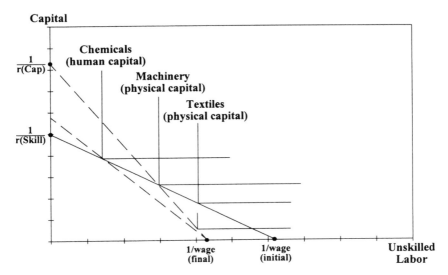

Fig. 10.24   Effects of wage compression

plies of physical capital are choked off because the return to human capital is relatively high. Additional supplies of human capital are also choked off since the return to skills is lower by design.

Income inequality can be fought from below with minimum wages or from above with maximum wages. In this subsection, we consider the effects of a maximum wage, which we take to be a limit on the rate of return to human capital. The differences between the effects of a minimum and a maximum wage are minor.

Figure 10.24 has the unit-value isoquants for three traded goods: chemicals, machinery, and textiles. The vertical axis refers to both human and physical capital, which we assume initially to have the same rates of return. For the sake of argument, we assume also that the chemicals sector uses only human capital and that machinery and textiles use only physical capital.

Now suppose that centralized age bargaining attempts to eliminate inequality by lowering the return on human skill to the level r(skill) in the figure. This lowered price for human capital makes the chemicals sector highly profitable, and it attempts to expand by employing both skilled and unskilled workers. Since all the skills are already employed in the chemicals sector, there is no possibility for expansion. The higher profits in the chemicals sector are eliminated only if the wage rate for unskilled workers is bid up to the level indicated by wage(final). This higher wage for raw labor must be offset by cheaper physical capital costs if the physical capital is to be employed. The return on physical capital must accordingly fall to the level r(cap), low enough to keep the machinery sector in operation. This reduction in the return to physical capital exceeds the forced reduction in the rate of return to human capital.

Operation of only the chemicals sector and the machinery sector can employ all the physical and human capital but cannot generate enough demand for unskilled workers to keep them all employed. A transfer of capital from textiles to machinery does allow an expansion of employment there, but not enough to offset the loss of textiles jobs. The exact amount of unemployment depends on the supplies of physical and human capital. If $(H/L)_{chem}$ is the human capital per worker in the chemicals sector, and if H is the total amount of human capital, then the labor used in the chemicals sector is $L_{chem} = H/(H/L)_{chem}$. If $(K/L)_{mach}$ is the physical capital per worker in machinery and K is the total physical capital, then the labor used in the machinery sector is $L_{mach} = K/(K/L)_{mach}$. Thus, the level of unemployment is $U = L - H/(H/L)_{chem} - K/(K/L)_{mach}$, and the unemployment rate is $U/L = 1 - (H/L)/(H/L)_{chem} - (K/L)/(K/L)_{mach}$. This unemployment rate can be lowered only by investments in human and physical capital. But investments in physical capital are entirely choked off because of its inferior return, and investments in human capital are discouraged by the forced reduction in its rate of return.

Economic Costs of a Minimum Wage

This figure does not allow a precise statement regarding the economic costs of wage compression since that would depend in fairly complicated ways on supply and demand elasticities that would determine the allocation of factors among the tradable sectors, the nontradable sectors, and unemployment. What can be said generally is that, the greater the distortion, the greater the cost. The distortion is partly a function of the difference between the undistorted and the distorted compensation levels and partly a function of the intersectoral resource transfer that are necessary to support the distorted equilibrium. These are fundamentally driven by three phenomena: technology, international competition (price determination), and Swedish physical and human capital accumulation.[20]

10.5   Final Remarks: A Heckscher-Ohlin Forecast for Sweden

We have presented substantial evidence of Heckscher-Ohlin crowding (closer competitors for Sweden) and Heckscher-Ohlin starving/enriching (for-

20. Until the first half of the 1980s, wage bargaining took place at the centralized level between LO and SAF. The wage compression that is a natural outcome of centralized bargaining operates essentially like a minimum wage, trading increases in returns for unskilled labor for reduced returns for human capital. This institution was abandoned during the first half of the 1980s and, since then, wage differences have increased. If this theory is correct, with this reversal will come initially a shift in resources out of the nontraded goods sector and into relatively labor intensive manufacturing, say, textiles. Over time, the increased incentive for human capital accumulation can be expected to produce a shift in the manufacturing product mix in favor of the more skill intensive and capital intensive sectors, machinery and chemicals.

est products and the public sector affecting the physical and human capital available for tradable manufactures). We have employed a conceptual framework in which Swedish wages and Swedish compensation for skills are determined in the global product markets. According to this theory, both crowding and starving can have serious consequences, lowering wages for unskilled workers and raising the premium for skills. The effects of crowding and starving on the wages of the unskilled can be offset by public sector employment and by high rates of capital formation, particularly, in our view, investments in human capital.

This framework can be used for some speculative remarks concerning other aspects of Sweden's future economic development. Internationally, Sweden today faces two major changes. One is further globalization that would come from membership in the European Union. These steps toward integration hopefully will not be offset by the erection of new tariff and nontariff barriers elsewhere. The second is the challenge of the previously centrally planned economies (PCPEs) entering the global marketplace. The emergence of such large countries in the proximity of Sweden could over time fundamentally alter Sweden's external economic opportunities.

Concerning globalization, Sweden may have little to fear as the Swedish economy for a long time has been free-trade oriented. The removal of the remaining trade barriers is not likely to expose Sweden to any major changes in the manufacturing sectors. Swedish manufacturing firms are to a large extent multinationals or, if national, have a long-standing experience of foreign competition in domestic markets. But more important changes might occur in other parts of the economy. Service sectors, such as legal and financial services, that today face mostly local competition may find themselves increasingly exposed to international competition. This might imply a great deal of structural change in the Swedish economy as, today, a large share of the workforce produces services in the nontradable sector.

The second change, the challenge of the PCPEs like Russia, the Baltic states, Poland, and other countries, is likely to have more of an effect on Swedish industries. This challenge can be captured in figure 10.3 above, which has been used to depict increased competition from three sides: from Germany, in sectors intensive in human capital; from Japan, in sectors intensive in physical capital; and from Asia, in labor intensive sectors. The emergence of the PCPEs in the world market can be added to figure 10.3. Where they are placed initially depends on the extent to which these physical capital poor countries can put their human capital to productive work.

Two possibilities are depicted in figure 10.25, differing in terms of the initial level of PCPE human capital. The abundant human capital point, PCPE1, and the associated path of capital accumulation, has the PCPEs relatively little involved in either apparel or textile production. This path is likely to be associated with downward price pressures on the human capital intensive products, which in turn raises the real wage of raw labor and lowers the skill premium.

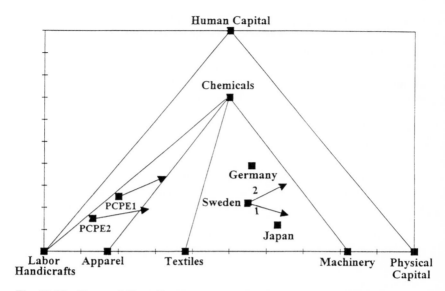

Fig. 10.25   Cones of diversification: Labor, human capital, and physical capital

In response to these factor price changes, it is appropriate for Sweden to shift its investment mix away from human capital and toward physical capital, which we depict as path 1 emanating from the Swedish point in figure 10.25.

In the second case, represented by the initial point PCPE2, it is assumed that those educated in the planned economies cannot be used efficiently in the market economies. The initial product mix is more labor intensive, and the growth path takes the PCPEs through apparel and textiles, never including much of the human capital intensive chemicals production. In this case, it is even more urgent that Sweden quickly abandon her most labor intensive sectors, and the falling prices of these goods will encourage Swedish producers to do so. The falling price of apparel will mean mostly an improved terms of trade since apparel is hardly at all produced in Sweden. But, with further capital accumulation, the PCPEs will enter into markets that are more important for Swedish manufacturers, products that are labeled *textiles* in figure 10.25 that use more physical capital but little human capital. Declining prices for these goods will lower the wage rate of raw labor and increase the skill premium, encouraging a shift in the Swedish investment composition in favor of human capital, denoted by arrow 2 in figure 10.25.

In both cases, Sweden is likely initially to enjoy terms of trade improvements, but more so in the second case than in the first. As these countries have a long way to go in terms of catching up in real capital formation, these terms of trade improvements might be considerable and taper off sometime in the future when the PCPEs enter the chemicals-machinery-textiles cone.

Although both paths offer initial terms of trade improvements, the paths have very different implications for the optimal investment mix and the effects of wage compression. The first path, with human capital abundant PCPEs, is compatible with Swedish low rates of investment in human capital and a low premium for skills. On the other hand, if the PCPEs are scarce in human skills, the international marketplace will dictate a higher skill premium, thus creating an opportunity that should be seized by much higher rates of investments in human capital.

The major benefits from the emergence of the PCPEs will accrue to those countries with capital in place when the process hits full stride. Now is the time to make the investment decisions in preparation for these market opportunities. We conjecture that the effective PCPE human capital stock is small and that the PCPE2 path is the more likely. This could be remedied by an increase in the Swedish investment rates in human capital, in education, and in training.

Data Sources

Euromonitor. 1993. *European marketing data and statistics.* London.

Food and Agricultural Organization of the United Nations. 1992. *FAO yearbook production, 1991.* Rome.

Heston, A., and H. Summers. 1988. A new set of international comparisons of real product and prices for 130 countries, 1950–1985. *Review of Income and Wealth,* Ser. 34, no. 1 (March): 335–55.

———. n.d. Penn world data [supplementary data on Heston and Summers (1988)]. Accessed at http://nber.harvard.edu/pwt56.html.

Hulten, C. R., and Wykoff, F. C. 1981. The measurement of economic depreciation. In *Depreciation, inflation, and the taxation of income from capital,* ed. C. R. Hulten. Washington, D.C.: Urban Institute Press.

International Labour Office. Various years. *Year book of labour statistics.* Geneva.

International Monetary Fund. 1992. *International financial statistics yearbook.* Washington, D.C.

Office of Business Analysis. 1992. *National trade data bank* (CD rom). Washington, D.C.: U.S. Department of Commerce.

OECD. 1989. *Education in OECD countries, 1988.* Paris.

———. 1992. *Public educational expenditures, costs and financing: An analysis of trends, 1970–1988.* Paris.

Statistics Directorate. 1966. *National accounts statistics, 1956–1965.* Paris: OECD.

———. 1968. *Labour force statistics, 1956–1966.* Paris: OECD.

———. 1978. *National accounts of OECD countries, 1961–1978.* Paris: OECD.

———. 1986. *Historical statistics, 1960–1984.* Paris: OECD.

———. 1991. *Labour force statistics, 1969–1989.* Paris: OECD.

———. 1992a. *Historical statistics, 1960–1990.* Paris: OECD.

———. 1992b. *National accounts detailed tables. 1978–1990.* Paris: OECD.

———. 1992c. *National accounts main aggregates, 1960–1991.* Paris: OECD.

———. 1993. *National accounts detailed tables, 1979–1991.* Paris: OECD.

Statistics Sweden. Various volumes. *Industri.* Stockholm.

Statistics Sweden. Statistiska Meddelanden. 1992. *Högskolan: Grundutbildning registrerade studerande höstterminerna, 1977–1992.* U 20 SM 9303.

————. 1993. *Prisindex i producent- och importled under 1992.* P 10 SM 9302.
Unesco. Various years. *Statistical yearbook.* Paris.

References

Barro, Robert. 1991. Economic growth in a cross section of countries. *Quarterly Journal of Economics* 106:407–43.
Davis, Stephen J. 1992. Cross-country patterns of change in relative wages. *NBER Macroeconomics Annual* 7:239–92.
Edin, Per-Anders, and Bertil Holmlund. 1993. Avkastning och efterfrågan på högre utbildning. *Ekonomisk debatt* 21, no. 1:31–45.
Ethier, Wilfred. 1984. Higher dimensional issues in trade theory. In *Handbook of international economics,* vol. 1, ed. Ronald Jones and Peter B. Kenen. Amsterdam: North-Holland.
Feldstein, Martin, and C. Horioka. 1980. Domestic savings and international capital flows. *Economic Journal* 90:314–29.
Hjalmarsson, Lennart, and Bo Walfridsson. 1992. Den fysiska kapitalbildningens betydelse för produktiviteten i svensk tillverkningsindustri. *Ekonomisk debatt* 20, no. 1:15–26.
Leamer, Edward E. 1984. *Sources of international comparative advantage: Theory and evidence.* Cambridge, Mass.: MIT Press.
————. 1987a. Cross section estimation of the effects of trade barriers. In *Empirical methods for international trade,* ed. Robert Feenstra. Cambridge, Mass.: MIT Press.
————. 1987b. Paths of development in the three-factor n-good general equilibrium model. *Journal of Political Economy* 95:961–99.
————. 1993. U.S. manufacturing and an emerging Mexico. *North American Journal of Economics and Finance* 4, no. 1(Spring): 51–89.
Leamer, Edward E., and Per Lundborg. 1995. A Heckscher-Ohlin view of Sweden competing in the global marketplace. Working Paper no. 5114. Cambridge, Mass.: National Bureau of Economic Research.
Mankiw, N. G., D. Romer, and D. N. Weil. 1992. A contribution to the empirics of economic growth. *Quarterly Journal of Economics* 107:407–37.
Ohlsson, Lennart, and Lars Vinell. 1987. *Tillväxtens drivkrafter: En studie av industriers framtidsvillkor.* Stockholm: Industriförbundets.
Solow, Robert. 1956. A contribution to the theory of economic growth. *Quarterly Journal of Economics* 70:65–94.
————. 1957. Technical change and the aggregate production function. *Review of Economics and Statistics* 39:312–20.
Song, Ligang. 1993. Sources of international comparative advantage: Further evidence. Ph.D. diss., Australian National University.
Wolff, Edward N., and Maury Gittleman. 1993. The role of education in productivity convergence: Does higher education matter? In *Explaining economic growth,* ed. Adam Szirmai, Bart van Ark, and Dirk Pilat. Amsterdam: Elsevier Science.

Contributors

Thomas Aronsson
Department of Economics
Umeå Universitet
S-901 87 Umeå, Sweden

Anders Björklund
Swedish Institute for Social Research
    (SOFI)
S-106 91 Stockholm, Sweden

Steven J. Davis
Graduate School of Business
University of Chicago
1101 East 58th Street
Chicago, IL 60637

Per-Anders Edin
Department of Economics
Uppsala Universitet
Box 315
751 20 Uppsala, Sweden

Stefan Fölster
Industrial Institute for Economic and
    Social Research (IUI)
Box 5501
S-114 85 Stockholm, Sweden

Anders Forslund
Department of Economics
Uppsala Universitet
Box 513
S-751 20 Uppsala, Sweden

Richard B. Freeman
National Bureau of Economic Research
1050 Massachusetts Avenue
Cambridge, MA 02138

Magnus Henrekson
Industrial Institute for Economic and
    Social Research (IUI)
Box 5501
S-114 85 Stockholm, Sweden

Alan B. Krueger
Woodrow Wilson School
Princeton University
Princeton, NJ 08544

Edward E. Leamer
Anderson Graduate School of
    Management
University of California
110 Westwood Plaza
Los Angeles, CA 90095

Lars Ljungqvist
Research Department
Federal Reserve Bank of Chicago
Chicago, IL 60690

Per Lundborg
Trade Union Institute for Economic
    Research (FIEF)
Wallingatan 38
S-111 24 Stockholm, Sweden

Charles E. McLure
Hoover Institution
Stanford University
Stanford, CA 94305

Erik Norrman
Department of Economics
Lunds Universitet
Box 7082
S-220 07 Lund, Sweden

Sam Peltzman
Graduate School of Business
University of Chicago
1101 East 58th Street
Chicago, IL 60637

Sherwin Rosen
Department of Economics
University of Chicago
1126 East 59th Street
Chicago, IL 60637

Thomas J. Sargent
Hoover Institution
HHMB-Room 243
Stanford University
Stanford, CA 94305

Birgitta Swedenborg
Center for Business and Policy Studies
 (SNS)
Box 5629
S-11486 Stockholm, Sweden

Robert Topel
Graduate School of Business
University of Chicago
1101 East 58th Street
Chicago, IL 60637

James R. Walker
Department of Economics
University of Wisconsin
Social Science Building
1180 Observatory Drive
Madison, WI 53706

Author Index

Subject Index

Antitrust policy, 19, 321. *See also* Cartel agreements; Cartels; Concentration; Firms, large
AP (Allmänna Pensionsfondend) fund, 373
ATP (Allmän Tilläggs) pension system, 373

Beveridge curve (unemployment-vacancy relation), 284–87
Budget deficit: actual reduction, 28; reduction proposals, 27
Budget set, 260

Capital: accumulation, formation, and growth in Sweden, 415–18; allocation in Swedish forest products industry, 452–53; tax treatment, 149. *See also* Human capital
Cartel agreements: changes at time of output and price changes, 334–38; legality of, 315–16; products under, 329–30; register of, 328
Cartels: as barriers to competition, 19; effect on manufacturing performance, 348–51. *See also* Firms, large
Child allowances: effect of reduction, 72; effect on income distribution, 46–49, 91; eligibility and amounts, 220; families with children, 56
Child care: facilities and spending for, 13, 221; higher fees for, 72; policy influence on women's labor force participation, 89–90; subsidies for, 13–14, 80, 91, 92t, 100–101; work incentives in policy for, 47. *See also* Day-care system

Collective bargaining, centralized: decentralizing, 33, 41, 195–97; development of and shifts in, 158–60; effect of, 20, 28–29; employers' rejection of (1983), 193; as private sector initiative, 158–61; in Swedish model of labor market, 155; wage compression with (1968–91), 30, 156, 169
Comparative advantage: forest products, 21, 418; of immobile factors of production in H-O model, 402, 404–5; in low-growth sectors, 403, 454; revealed, 438; sectors of, 439
Comparative disadvantage: 1970–90, 438; in labor intensive manufactures, 421–24, 427
Competition: changes in international, 400; constraints on, 315–16; EC rules influencing, 316, 318; effect of weak, 19; factors in changes in terms of trade, 405; with industrial concentration, 321. *See also* Heckscher-Ohlin crowding hypothesis
Concentration: of cartels by industry, 329–30; Herfindahl index measurement of, 321, 333; policies influencing large firm, 364–77; relation to profits, 322–23; Swedish multinational firms, 320–21
Consumption tax model, 116–17
Credit market: debt financing of firms, 367–68, 373–74; pension fund lending in, 373–74; regulation, 19, 372–73